A HISTORY OF CHELSEA

ON THE PITCH & OFF THE DRAWING BOARD

Art by
PAUL TREVILLION
"The Master of Movement"

Foreword by
KEN BATES
Legendary Chelsea Chairman

Words by
HARRY HARRIS
Multi Award-Winning Journalist

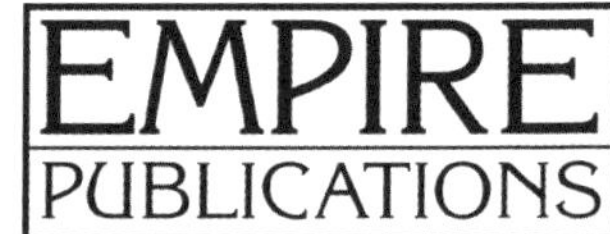

EMPIRE PUBLICATIONS
1 Newton St., Manchester M1 1HW

Printed and Bound by: Ozlem Print, Türkiye

ISBN: 9781915616159

Dedication

I dedicate this book to my youngest son John, a third year student at UCFB Wembley, the University Campus of Football Business. He is also a walking, talking authority on Chelsea both on and off the field. Known because of his initials JT, he decided to hang up his boots when, unlike JT the Chelsea legend, he took the man more often than he took the ball! In John's words "LONDON IS BLUE!"

Acknowledgements

To my wife Lorraine 'thank you' for your constant support and assistance in researching and collating the Trevillion Chelsea art for the book. To my team-mate and striking partner Harry 'the legend' Harris – I defy ANYONE to pick up an article by Harry and not put it down until the finish. Harry's THE BEST. To Peter Willis, my personal manager and friend of 60 years who has followed Chelsea all his lifetime and is also the best proofreader in the business. Finally, last but by no means least, Ashley Shaw of Empire Publications who has worked 24/7 tirelessly and devotedly over the weeks, but always with a smile on his face.

PT

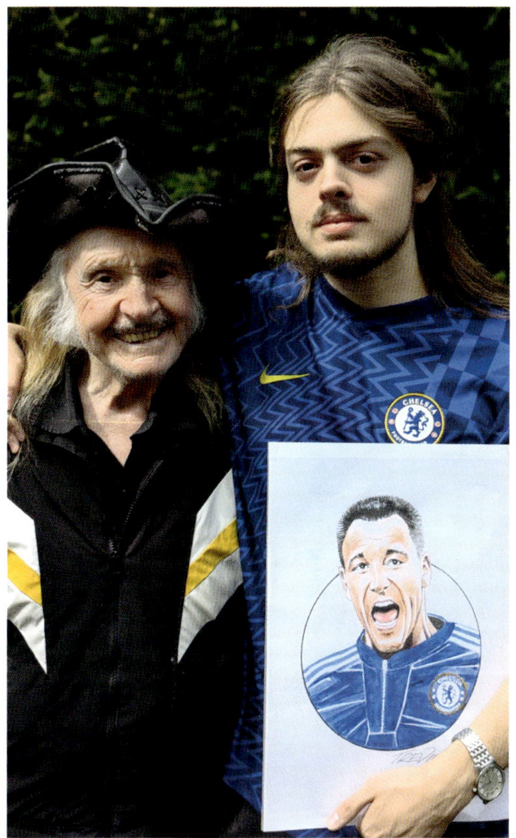

Dedication

To my late father-in-law Ken Udall, a Chelsea season ticket holder for decades who is still sadly missed.

Acknowledgements

My thanks to Ken Bates for his illuminating and as always fascinating foreword and for a different introduction thanks to Linda Udall (aka Linda Harris) as we incorporate, quite rightly, the Chelsea women's team's incredible achievements. Thanks also to designer Ashley Shaw, editorial assistant Simon and Empire Publications proprietor John for having the faith to invest in the books that are proving to be iconic histories of the clubs.

As co-author I'd like to personally thank Paul Trevillion for his 300 works of art in this book, which I am sure will make it worth many times its current cover price - especially if anyone is lucky enough to get it signed!

Special thanks to Lorraine, Paul's wife, for having the patience to sort out all of Paul's massive amount of art work for this book.

HH

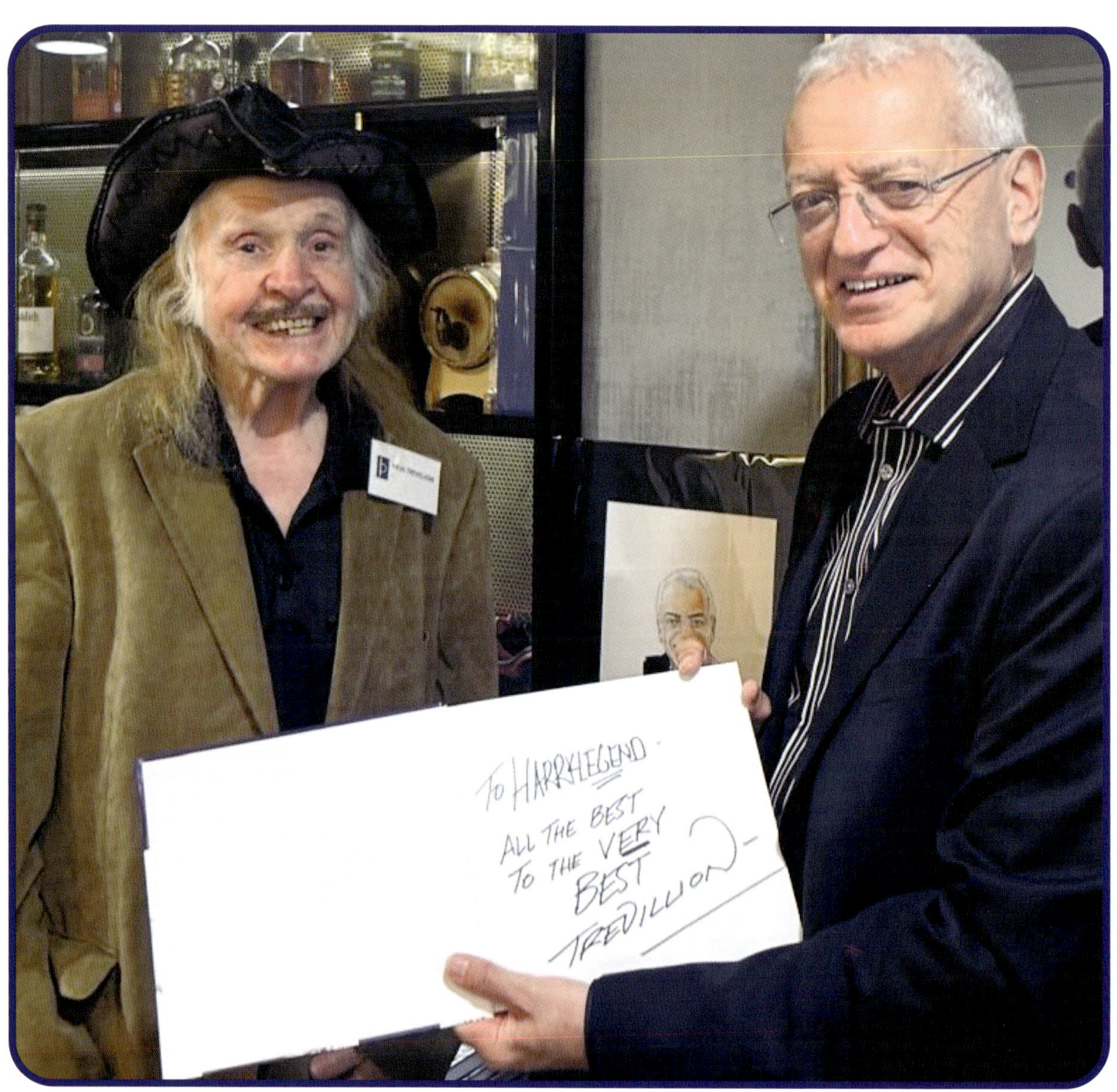
To HARRY LEGEND -
ALL THE BEST
TO THE VERY
BEST
TREVILLION -

About the Author

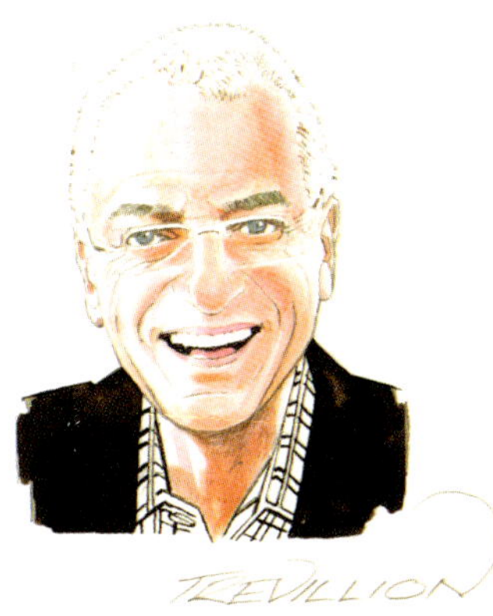

Harry Harris has written about 20 books on Chelsea, including FOUR tomes on José Mourinho, THREE on Ruud Gullit, plus biographies of Franco Zola, Luca Vialli, Antonio Conte, and an autobiography of Kerry Dixon. He took part in a documentary about "Battle of the Bridge" behind the scenes conflict between Ken Bates and Matthew Harding which he turned into a best selling book. In fact Harry has written a record 90 football books in his distinguished career.

As a young journalist at the London *Evening News* Harry ghosted a column for Chelsea manager Danny Blanchflower and was close to many of the Chelsea players. Harry went on to become a double winner of the British Sports Journalist of the Year award and was presented with the British Variety Club of Great Britain Silver Heart for 'Contribution to Sports Journalism' and is the only journalist ever to win the Sports Story of the Year accolade twice. Harry has a total of 24 industry awards.

One of the most influential football columnists for three decades, Harry is one of the most acclaimed investigative journalists and news gatherers of his generation. He is currently Sports Development Director for SmartFrame Technologies.

About the Artist

PAUL TREVILLION has devised and drawn thousands of sporting features since the early 1950's and, over his eight decades in sport, has become known as the 'Master of Movement' for his unique ability to convey dynamic movement in a static image and bring the personality of a subject to life.

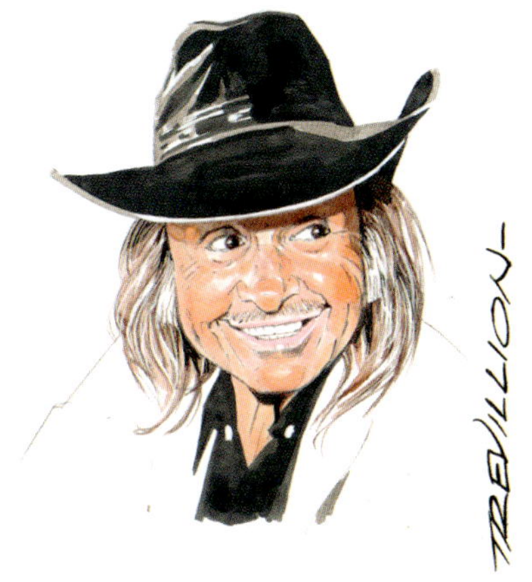

His extraordinary artistic talent was discovered at a very young age and he was drawing for *Eagle*, *Tiger* and the Spurs supporters magazine, *The Lilywhite*, while still a school boy. In 1952, he met and sketched HRH the Duke of Edinburgh at an awards ceremony at Mansion House, which resulted in a letter from His Royal Highness in praise of the young artist being published in the national press, launching his career in sporting art. In 1955 he met Sir Winston Churchill who signed a smiling portrait painting of the great war leader, which is still today the only signed smiling portrait of Churchill in existence.

Paul then created the iconic refereeing feature 'You Are The Ref' which began in 1957 as 'Hey Ref!' in the *Sunday People*, and went on to appear in *Shoot!* magazine in the 1970's and 1980's and from 2006 in *The Observer*. In 1963 he revolutionised *Roy of the Rovers* with his 'Comic Art Realism' style and within weeks children were writing in for Roy Race's autograph convinced he was real! Thanks to 'Comic Art Realism' – Roy Race, a footballer who never existed, lived FOREVER!

An acclaimed sports artist, author, inventor and motivator he has worked with the likes of Pelé, George Best, Paul Gascoigne, Gary Player, Lee Trevino and Sugar Ray Robinson… to name just a few. His work has appeared in major London exhibitions and at the FIFA Museum and the National Football Museum. A lifelong Spurs fan, one of Paul's first memories is being taken to see a cup tie between Spurs and Everton and in the process developing a childhood obsession with Dixie Dean.

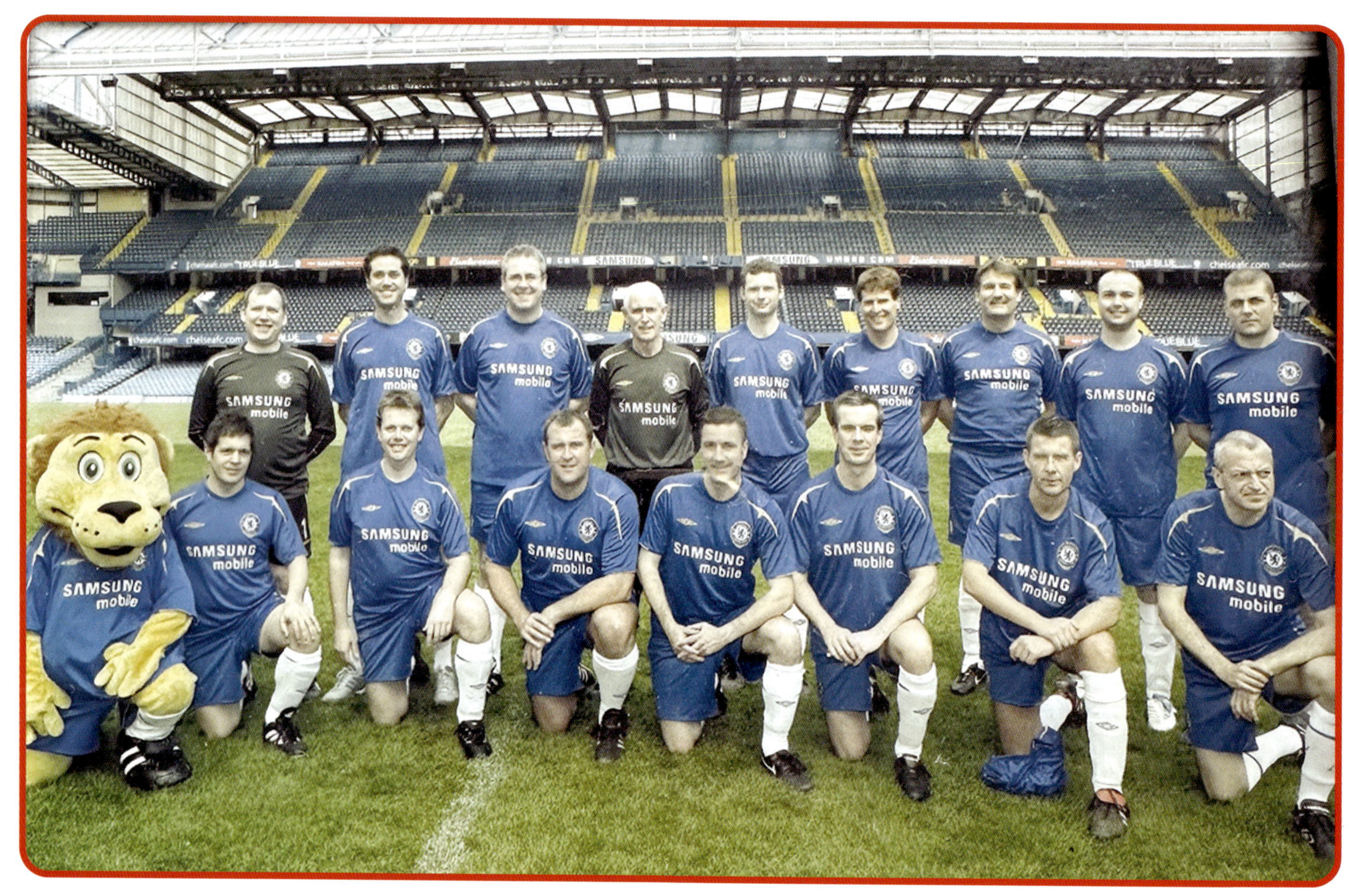

Spurs fan turned Chelsea player for a day Harry Harris (bottom right).

Introduction

Being born and bred in the World's End, SW10, to a family of football fanatics, there was really only one club that would be in my blood. As a very young girl I would watch my Dad, Uncle, cousin and their friends set off down the King's Road to the Bridge every other Saturday and wish I could join them, but my mum insisted that I was too little. My Dad, Ken, now no longer with us, had seen the Blues win their first League title in the 1954/55 season and followed them religiously throughout the years so we are certainly not a 'Johnny Come Lately' family of Chelsea fans.

One of my earliest memories of the club is of six year-old me sitting on my Dad's shoulders watching the team bus parading the FA Cup down the King's Road in 1970. In among that throng of fans I was hooked. From the following season my mum let me go to the games with 'the boys'. We used to stand in the Shed End to the right of the White Wall. We'd to try to get into the ground as early as possible so that we could nab a crash barrier

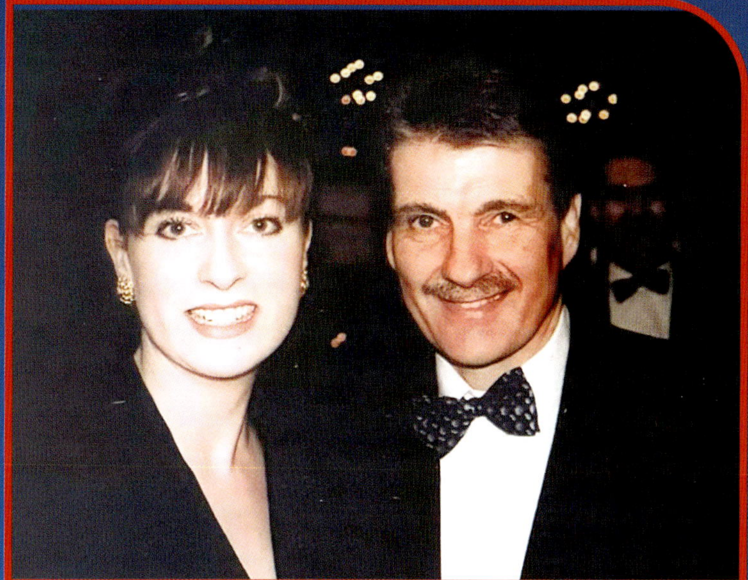

OUR LINDA

OK GIRLS, IT'S YOUR SHOUT

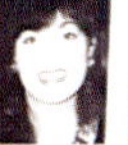

Linda Udall, lifelong Chelsea fan and assistant features editor of *The People*, introduces her new monthly column especially for women...

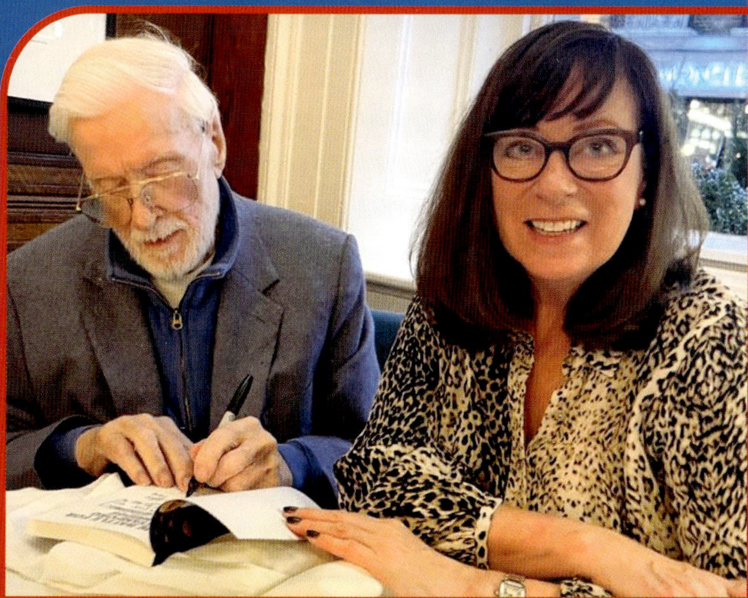

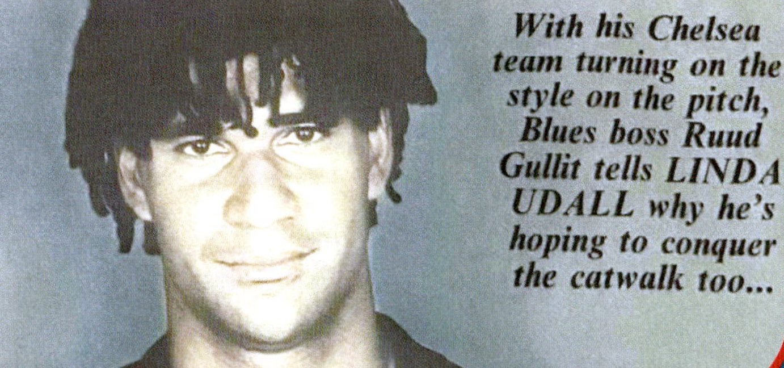

With his Chelsea team turning on the style on the pitch, Blues boss Ruud Gullit tells LINDA UDALL why he's hoping to conquer the catwalk too...

for me to sit on. My cousin, who was older and taller than me, took a little wooden step to stand on to get a bit of extra height!

Over the years the Shed End became a little 'boisterous' so finally we opted for the East Stand from where I watched the Blues from the age of 16 onwards.

As a very special treat for my Dad's 70th birthday my mum bought us Director's Box tickets for a season. By May of that year I was heavily pregnant and the Chairman, Ken Bates, suggested we have the St John's Ambulance on standby for when we scored!

Following Chelsea has been a pleasure, a privilege and, at times, a pain! But I wouldn't have had it any other way. Watching them win the Champions League was a highlight, but I'll still remember the really old days, standing in the Shed End the day after having had two wisdom teeth removed, with a swollen face, wadding in my mouth and celebrating as we won promotion back into the old Division One! Special days, special club.

Linda Udall

A former Fleet Street journalist, Linda is the wife of Harry Harris. and a Chelsea fan for over 50 years.

PREVIOUS PAGE: Here I am with Chelsea legend Charlie Cooke; Dinner with Ken Bates; My column in the Chelsea magazine and an interview with Ruud Gullit in the *Sunday People* which was a real career highlight for me.

BELOW: With the FA Cup won by Ruud in 1997; and Tore Andre Flo. Finally a quote from the late, great Jimmy Greaves which sums up my feelings for Chelsea FC.

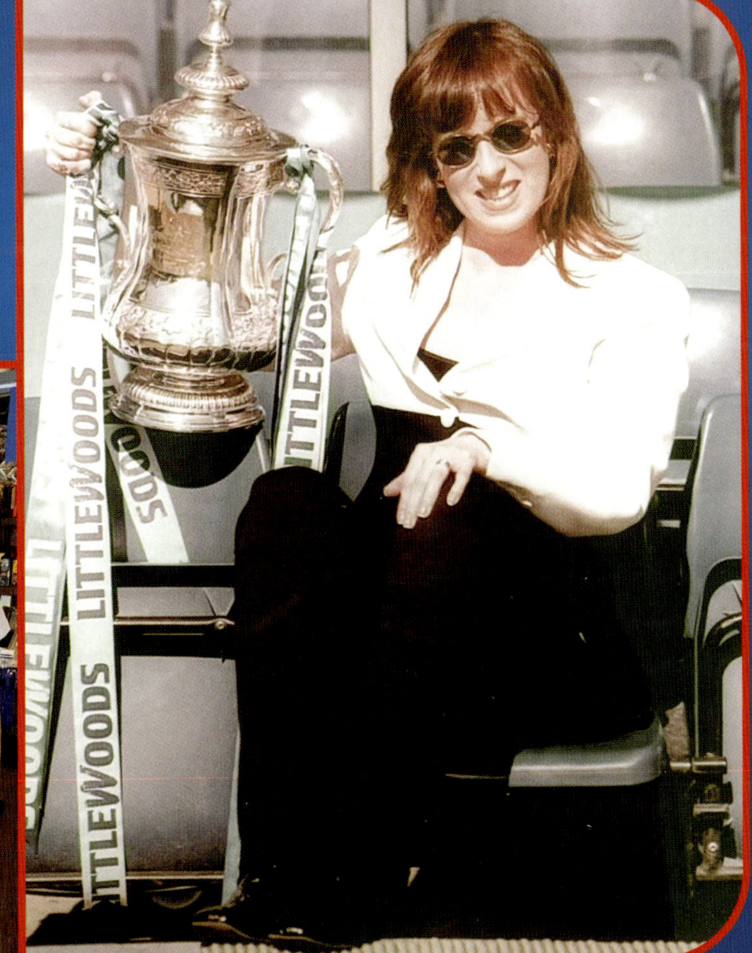

IT'S PROBABLY THE GREATEST NAME IN THE WORLD:
CHELSEA
YOU THINK ABOUT IT.
IT CONJURES UP THE BEST PART OF THE BIGGEST CITY IN THE WORLD.
CHELSEA
IT'S MAGICAL.

Jimmy Greaves
Chelsea 1957–1961

Foreword

Chelsea's history can be best summed up by the club's founding family who went from rags to riches to rags in three generations. Joe Mears founded Chelsea in 1905 and took it from rags to riches then his grandson took the club back to rags and by the early 80s the club was on the brink of collapse. It's a Lancashire saying that if you give your children everything from the best education to all that they need, they just take it all for granted, and don't live in the real world. That's what happened to Chelsea when Joe handed it Chelsea to his son, and his son handed it to his grandchild. It ended up with Brian Mears and the club was 72 hours from going bust in 1982 when I came along to rescue the club.

I am very proud, very pleased, that I saved Chelsea FC. You know you have done a good job when somebody else gets the credit… Roman Abramovich, but I was there for 21 years from 1982 until 2003.

My proudest moment on the field was when we were officially welcomed by UEFA as part of the European elite. It was in 1998 at Monaco's stadium: Chelsea 1, Real Madrid 0 - the European Cup winners had been beaten by the holders of the European Cup Winners' Cup in the annual Super Cup. After that famous victory for this club, the President of UEFA wrote a personal letter to me in which he said: "Congratulations on becoming the Champions Of Europe and we welcome you now as a member of the European elite".

I'm often asked about my favourite Chelsea players, and I was recently asked that very same question in front of 400 fans in a Q & A session at a supporters' club dinner with players such as Speedie, Nevin, Bumstead and Kerry Dixon present. I responded, "What a stupid question! If I answer it and give you a name then I am going to make eight enemies in this room!" But I gave them an answer… "my wife Suzannah…and she was a free transfer!" the whole place erupted!

It has often been said I didn't like the boys of the sixties and seventies, the old King's Road set, but that wasn't true. It was true

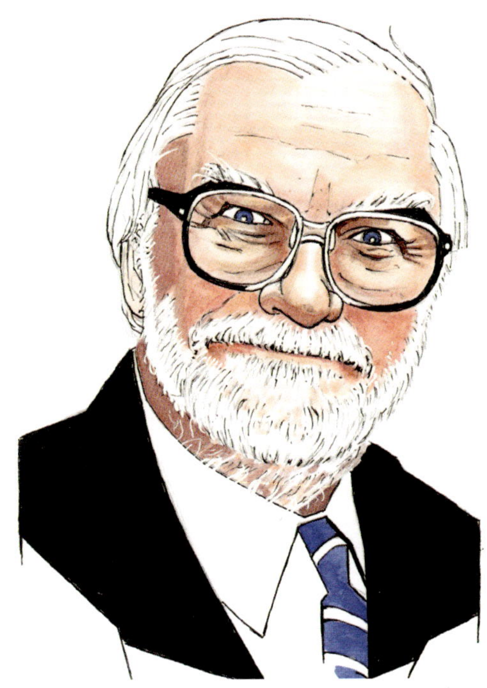

that I fell out with a few of them, but with good reason. When I took over Leeds United the legends of the club never had a bad word to say about the current players, or the team or the club no matter how badly they were doing. Aside from Gary Sprake when he had a go in his book, they were all very respectful. I didn't find the same at Chelsea. Some ex-players such as Peter Osgood slagged off the club. When we faced a relegation fight, Osgood was sitting in his bar in Windsor being interviewed and said that he couldn't see the team avoiding relegation, that they were so bad they would be relegated all the way to the Conference. This was one of our former players who felt they were entitled to 20 tickets for every home game. When our club secretary Sheila Marston told Peter that he could have two tickets, not 20, he got so angry with her he stormed out saying he hoped she would catch Syphilis! I didn't like his attitude or that of other former players such as Alan Hudson and Ron Harris, who only seemed interested in free tickets. When I took over the first thing I did was to end the hand-outs that the freeloaders had come to expect.

When I bought the club for £1 it was because the board could no longer afford to pay the players. I came in with a cheque

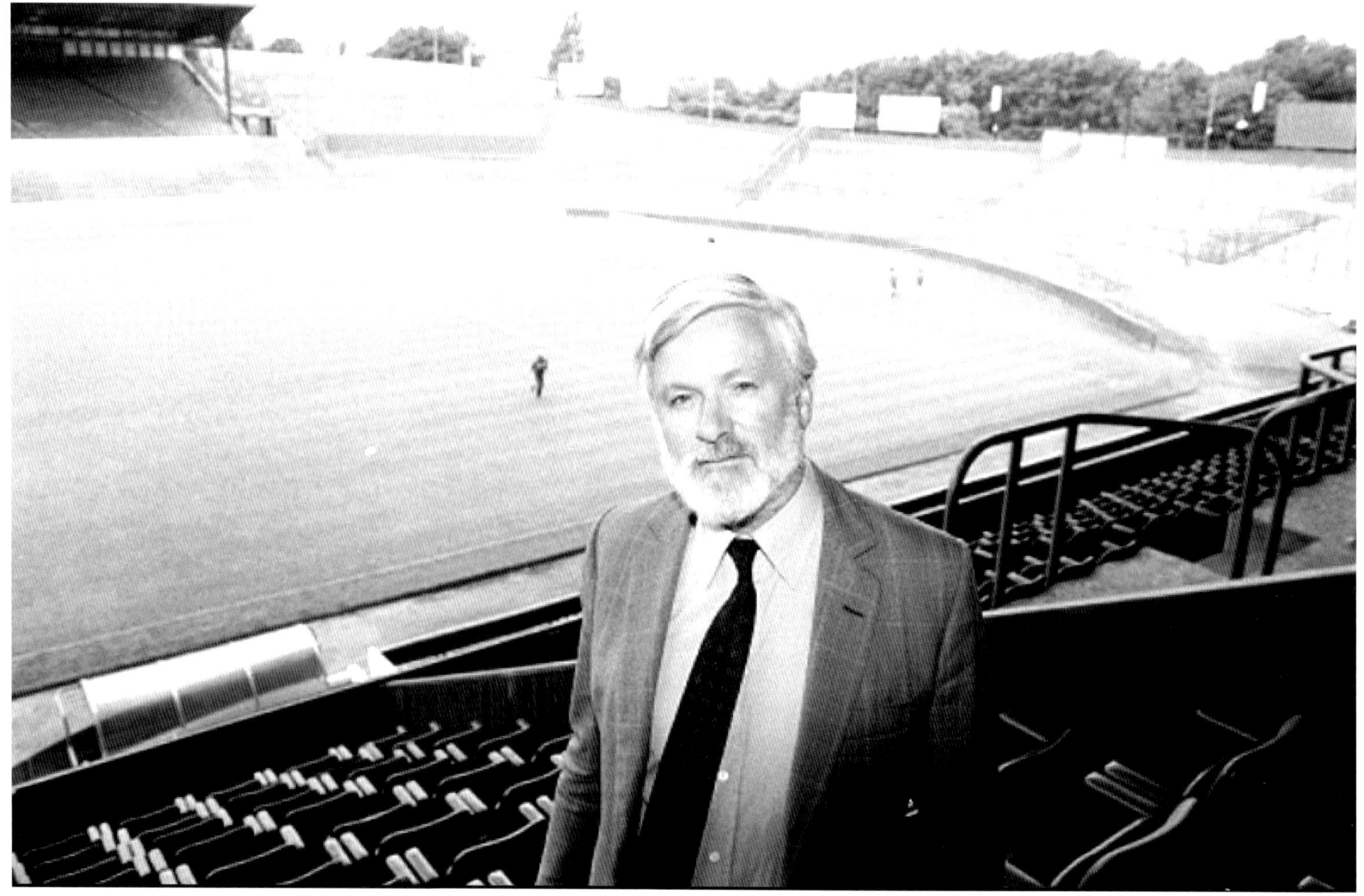

Ken Bates on his first day in charge at Chelsea FC following his purchase of the club for £1

to cover the wages and handed over a crisp pound not to take control. Viscount Lord Chelsea was at the meeting and he turned to me and said, "You must be my guest at the next home game". I thought to myself, "I've just bought the club and he is inviting me when I should be inviting him!". However I knew my place, as one of the working-classes when addressing a Lord, so I dutifully accepted his very kind invitation!

The next day, I discovered that there were 36 in the board room for home games all enjoying luxurious hospitality with Chelsea picking up the tab. And it was some hospitality. You couldn't have got any better at The Ritz. A lavish five-course meal finished off with the cheese board, the finest ports and Havana cigars. And yet the club couldn't afford to pay the players. You could see why.

On that first Monday as the new owner I turned up at the Bridge early, around 8am, to see who was coming in. You can tell by the way they walk and the look on their faces whether they were of any use. At 9am I asked to see the club chauffeur as I discovered he had been ferrying all the directors of the club on all sorts of non-Chelsea business all over London. At 9.20 the chauffeur turned up and asked me where I wanted to go. I told him where to go… through that door, turn left and then turn right, collect your cards on the way out.

Next I discovered at that every home game the club gave away 700 tickets to hangers-on - I cancelled the lot. On day one I had immediately made 700 enemies! But it was easy to see that the club was being run down toward bankruptcy and it needed someone to be ruthless to save it.

Yes I am proud I saved Chelsea when it was 72 hours from the knacker's yard, but I am most proud of the fact that in all that time I never took a penny out of the club, not a penny out of the game. I did it for the love of the game, because I loved football. Am I saying others took money out of the club? No, but I am saying I am proud that I didn't take a penny from the club in all my time there.

That being said, I don't love the game anymore, so I'm not interested in what is happening currently with the Chelsea club and its team. It's really sad to say this but football is not the game that got into my blood. That was back in the old days when I loved the game. Football began as an inter village rivalry: 100-a-side played on the village green and has evolved into what it is today. The game sprang from honest working class roots and Victorian values, but today's game isn't English football as I knew it.

I am most proud of the fact that in all that time I never took a penny out of the club, not a penny out of the game. I did it for the love of the game, because I loved football.

Back then we would show our contempt for European football. We loved our game, it was a man's game, played by proper men with a proper attitude, a proper working-man's sport, and we sneered at those Continentals who indulged in the dark arts of ankle tapping, deliberate blocking, spitting, feigning injury, and time-wasting. Now we have acquired all those traits in our game here in England. Worse still, back in the day, a team wanted to go forward, attack, score, entertain, but today it is a game of ping pong in your own penalty area - what we used to call 'keep ball' - it's so bloody boring!

I loved the game when with 10 minutes to go in a cup semi-final the players would run themselves into the ground in search of a winner, but now both teams are happy enough to play it out to go into extra time and penalties, they would prefer the ping pong in their penalty area of playing it back to the goalkeeper whenever they are fed up playing the ball across their back line, when they should be getting the ball into the opponent's penalty area not playing it out in their own penalty area. I'm sorry but that doesn't interest me as a sport.

I am not sceptical about the billionaires who now rush to own football clubs, but in reality it is nothing more than a play thing for them. If it isn't billionaires then clubs are falling into the hands of asset wealth managers. With so many American funds and investor consortiums buying up Premier League clubs it won't be long until it eventually follows the American sporting model. In the States there are five major national sports and in each of their leagues there is no promotion or relegation, they are all owned by wealth management companies and investment trusts and they will not allow one of their assets to be demoted and have its value affected. Now we have so many big clubs like Arsenal, Liverpool, Manchester United, Newcastle that are either state owned via their investment funds or American wealth management. To them, the fans are necessary evils, the investors are interested in big money sponsorships. When the new American owners at Chelsea arrived on the scene they thought a North v South international challenge would be a great idea, but it's nothing more than a money-making scheme and an unnecessary addition to an already ridiculously over-burdened schedule that is eventually going to catch up on the players. This new band of owners won't stop until they have Premier League games abroad, in the States or Saudi Arabia, and own a new European Super League.

Another of my proud moments was stopping the first attempt of a Super League with owners such as David Dein at the heart of it when he was deeply in league with ITV who were desperate to sign up to a TV deal. We all argued about it at league meetings and I made it plain that if they went ahead with a European Super League we would ensure that the league fixtures were released on the same day as any Super League fixtures, so needless to say their plans collapsed. Then Robert Maxwell came along with his

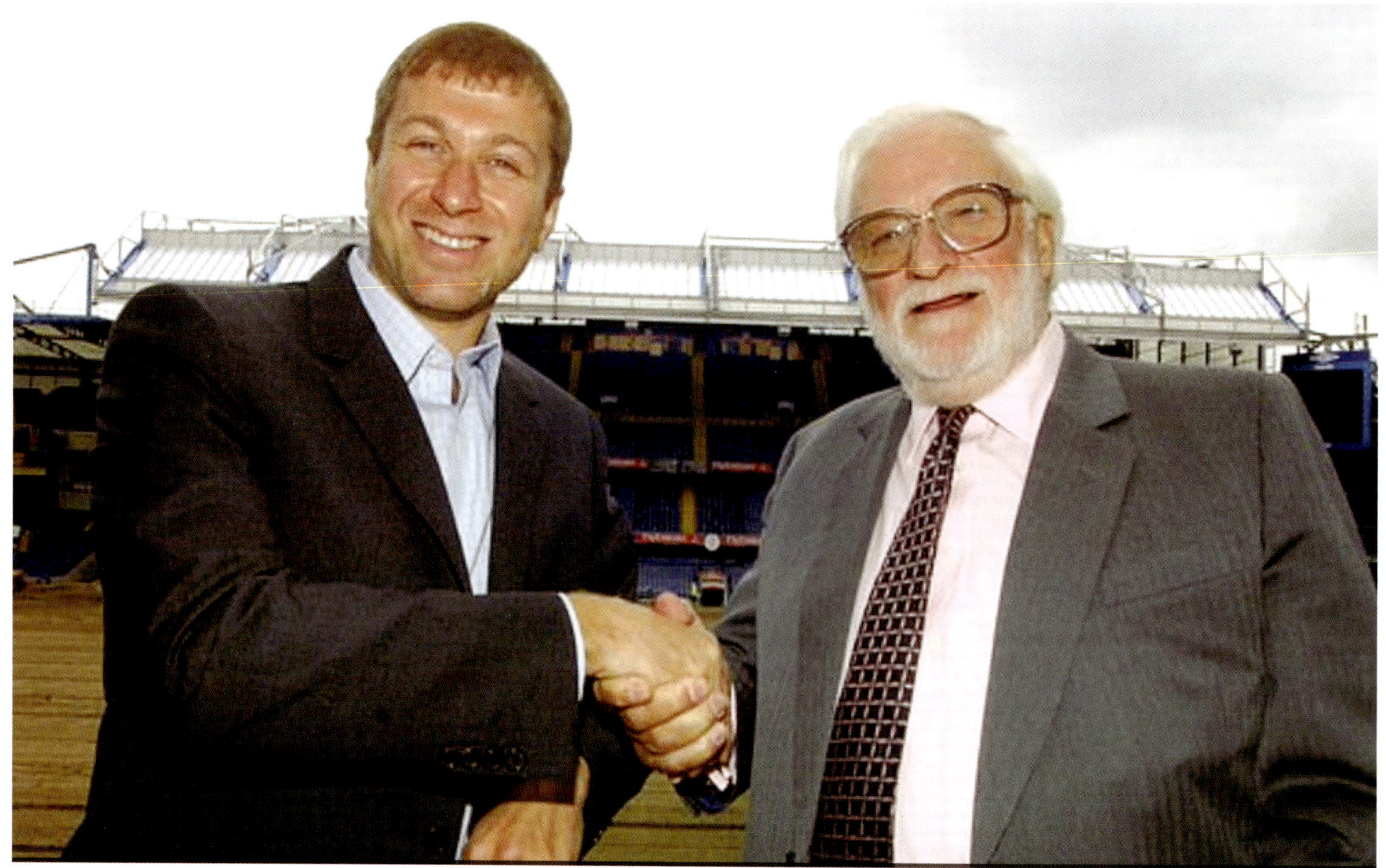

Ken welcomes Roman Abramovich following the Russian's £60m takeover in June 2003

ideas on the real value of TV rights. He was not the total rogue he was made out to be, or people said he was. He took on the TV cartel that kept a tight reign on the value of football's TV rights. Maxwell took football's case to the Attorney General and claimed that the BBC and ITV were acting as a monopoly to artificially suppress the value of the rights at a time when they would get together and pay just £2m a year for all the rights between them. As soon as Maxwell broke the cartel, ITV were quick off the mark to offer £3m a year for exclusive rights ahead of the BBC. I also met Rupert Murdoch behind the scenes when Sky came onto the scene. I was invited to his penthouse overlooking St James' Palace, and, along with Spurs chairman Irving Scholar and Alan Sugar, I was very much involved in agreeing a deal with Sky. Sam Chisholm was a big tough Aussie who was present when I met Murdoch and he was keen to ensure the price was right for his boss, but I told him it was £50m for a four-year contract, and that there would be no negotiations, that was the price.

When Sky got the deal it really pissed off ITV and David Dein. Dein tried to talk up ITV in a subsequent league meeting but I told him, "You've lost David, sit down and shut up!" and the rest is history.

Ken Bates - Aged 91½

Introduction

Founded in 1905 to fill Stamford Bridge stadium after Fulham FC turned down the option to take up a lease, Chelsea FC were an instant hit with the public. Although trophies were thin on the ground, the Bridge was soon redeveloped into a 100,000 capacity stadium making it the second biggest ground in England after Crystal Palace, as a result it hosted the last three FA Cup Finals before the showpiece was moved to Wembley in 1923.

The club itself were a bit of a musical hall joke for not winning trophies before the Second World War but came to prominence in the post-war years, winning the First Division title in 1955, followed by various cup competitions between 1965 and 1971 during their first glory years.

The Roman Abramovich era heralded unparalleled sustained success. Abramovich took over in 2003 and hired and fired numerous managers during his ownership. José Mourinho has been the most successful manager in the club's history, winning the Premier League three times with Chelsea, plus three League Cups and the FA Cup. Although the holy grail for Abramovich was the Champions League, the tournament that first lured him to football, and while it proved elusive for Mourinho, the club have since won it twice and also been crowned World Club champions.

I've known most of the Chelsea managers, and can speak from personal experience, sharing fascinating anecdotes about them. From Danny Blanchflower, Geoff Hurst, Bobby Gould, Bobby Campbell and John Hollins through to Ray Wilkins, Ruud Gullit, Roberto di Matteo, Glenn Hoddle and Frank Lampard. I've met them all and had some fascinating conversations to get to know them as well as anyone in the football industry.

I've written five books on José Mourinho, three on Ruud Gullit, two with Glenn Hoddle, and one on Luca Vialli and Gianfranco Zola. I've also written books on Abramovich about the Chelsea takeover and Roman Conquest which concerned the winning of the Champions League, and one on Antonio Conte's first highly successful season. I have written more books about Chelsea than any other.

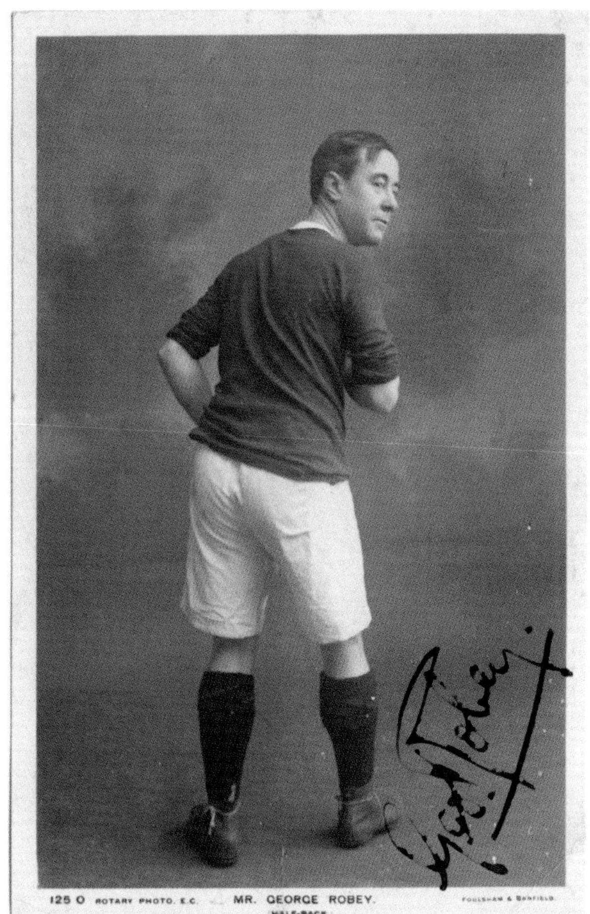

Edwardian Music Hall star George Robey was once on Chelsea's books

If you find this odd coming from a Spurs fan, then blame her indoors! My wife, Linda, is a big Chelsea fan and insisted that I stopped writing about Tottenham all the time, and focused instead on West London. That I did with several books on the club's most prolific trophy gatherer, Mourinho, and before him their record silverware hoarder Vialli, and before him, the manager who won a trophy for the first time in a quarter of a century, Ruud Gullit.

But my association with the Blues goes back before that, all the way to Tommy Docherty, although I only got to know him more closely later in life. But I knew many Chelsea managers under ubiquitous chairman Ken Bates, starting with John Neal, but going back even further, having known dear old well-meaning Chelsea loving chairman Brian Mears for some time, and his appointments such as Danny Blanchflower, Geoff Hurst and Bobby Gould, all of whom I had long associations with before and after their stints at the helm of the ship being steered by Old Grey Beard himself.

Because of that close association with so many managers, chairman, and players during several generations it is fascinating to pen a history of the club, especially in this unique format alongside the world's No. 1 sport artist Paul Trevillion for a book that will entertain as well as inform.

I've also met many famous celebrities who gravitated to the Bridge. One such genuine Blues supporter is an old mate, Ivor Baddiel, brother of the slightly more famous David. Given the club's notorious past, it is unusual to find many Jewish Chelsea fans, certainly few that go as far back as Ivor. Not many will know but Ivor is the writer behind many of TV's top shows, including X-Factor. Ivor tells me: "Chelsea first impinged on my consciousness at the age of seven. Sadly, in terms of making me as old as a tin of Heinz Beans – they're always 57. How come they don't age? That was in 1970. Gloriously though, it was a time when Chelsea were cool, classy and playing some of the best football around. It was the era of Osgood, Cooke, Hutchinson, Chopper and Bonetti. We won the Cup, we won the Cup Winners' Cup, we nearly won the League Cup. It was also the era of Dave Sexton. Now, I'd love to say that he loomed large in my life then, but he was in his forties and I was seven for goodness sake. At that age I was only vaguely aware that teams had managers, let alone what they actually did. I probably thought he was the players' dad. That said, somehow he must have seeped in to my mind and lodged himself there because, to me, he is the Chelsea manager, the rock on whom all the others sit.

"Of course I know there were managers before Sexton, but they exist only as ghosts to me. He was there at my birth as a Chelsea fan, so as far as I'm concerned, he is the daddy. (For any psychotherapists out there, yes, I know I'm clearly searching for a father substitute, but if that is the case, Dave Sexton fits the bill well, so I'll take him.) As a rock though, Dave must, initially at least, have been quite slippery, because the next eleven managers came and went without ever really making their mark on me. Or possibly for the rest of us. I was at the Bridge a lot in the late seventies and sighties and I don't remember many chants of,'Ken Shellito's Blue and White army,' or 'Super, super Ian, super Ian Porterfield.' (The exception was John Neal, who I do remember us chanting about.) Of course that was because the team were pretty rubbish in those days and a lot of the fans were too busy fighting, but then along came Mr. Hoddle, and everything changed. Or at least began to change.

"I've been lucky enough to meet Glenn and quite a few of the subsequent managers, but I'm not going to pretend I really know what they were like as managers. That would be like gauging someone's personality by the way they are on telly 'oh, that Jimmy Saville seems like such a nice bloke,' fraught with assumptions and inaccuracies. Instead, here are my encounters with them and how they seemed to me. It might give some indication as to how they were as managers, it might not.

"With Glenn in the room, I once made a joke at his expense. Could have gone badly wrong (for me), but after a short pause, he laughed. He was astute, level-headed and considerate, whilst also letting others know he was the boss."

I've dedicated this book to my late father-in-law Ken Udall. For generations the Udall family held strong Chelsea connections and also had season tickets for decades. Come the end of one very depressing poor performing season Ken had had enough of all the disappointment and shocked the entire family by giving up his long standing season tickets from himself and Linda. Then, come the pre-season, Ken had the football itch once again and changed his mind. He contacted the club to renew his season tickets, only to be told they had been sold, in fact season tickets for that season were sold out, and the best they could do was offer him a place on the waiting list for the following season. In desperation I contacted Ken Bates. I didn't want to ask for a favour, as a working journalist that was always a touch tricky but on this

Ken still divides opinion among fans but it is indisputable that, despite all the rhetoric and bluster, he was the man who saved Stamford Bridge from being turned into a housing estate.

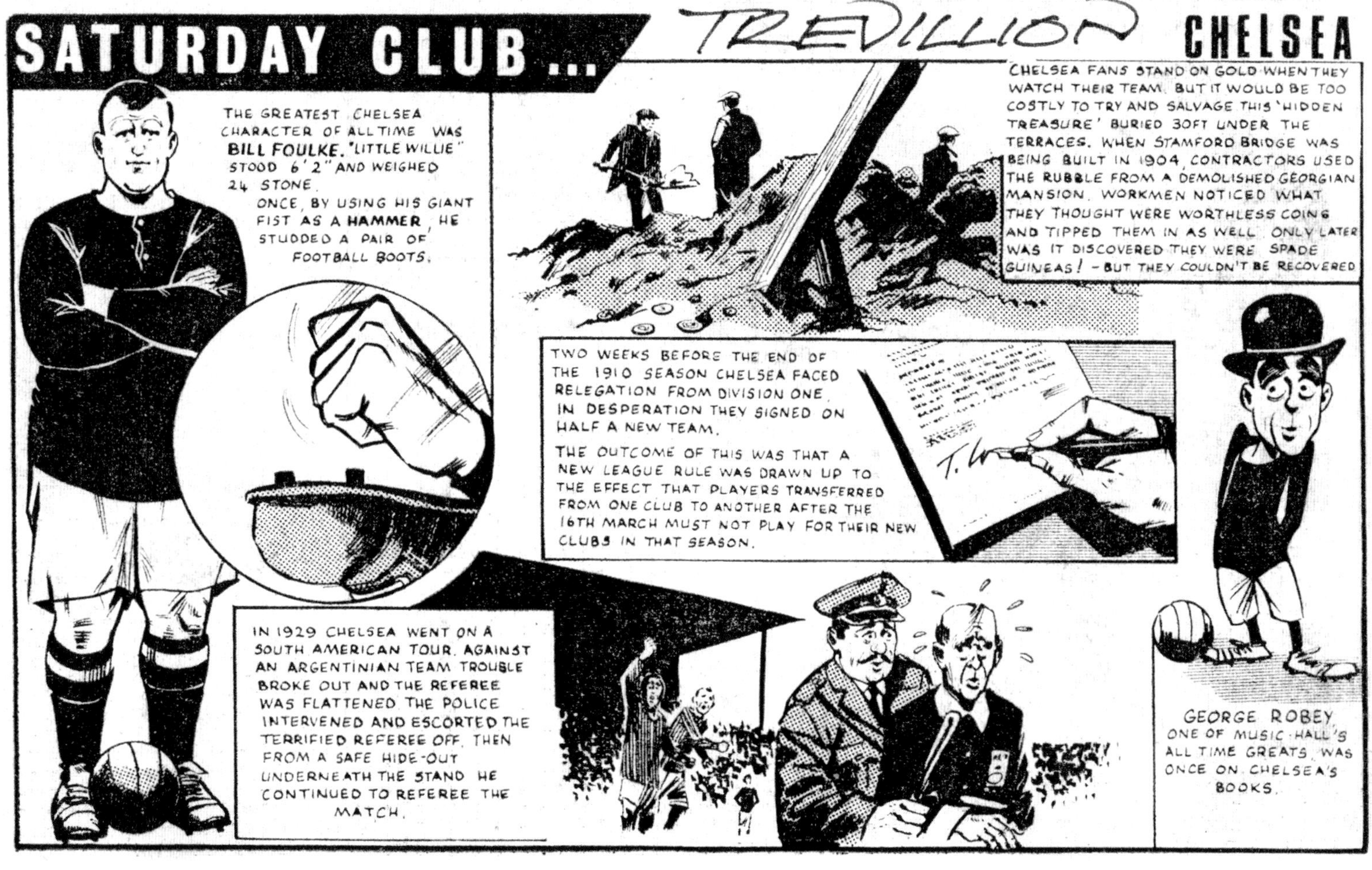

occasion I wanted to help out my father-in-law. Bates was brilliant. "No trouble," he told me, "Ken and Linda will be welcome in the Directors' Box" and he told me he would be dispatching them two Directors' Box season tickets. I told Ken and he said, "well it just goes to show you, Ken isn't as bad as he's made out to be!" Within days, the two Directors Box season tickets arrived... accompanied by an invoice!

I'm sure Mr Bates thought that, as I was then the chief football writer on the *Daily Mirror*, and the highest paid sports journalist of my generation at the time, I could afford them. He might have been right and I duly did pay for them to treat Ken and Linda. "Don't worry", I said, "you will be royally looked after in the Directors' Box as there will be the usual lavish three course meal before the game, and drinks and the works at half-time and at the end, you will want for nothing, it will be a great experience".

I couldn't wait to hear all their stories after their first game in there. Well, I wasn't to be disappointed. While Ken and his directors, and the visiting directors enjoyed a lavish lunch and all the works, the paying Directors' Box season ticket holder went in a different direction - there was nothing before the game, tea and biscuits at half-time, nothing at the end of the game!

While we all ended up having a laugh about it all, it did remind

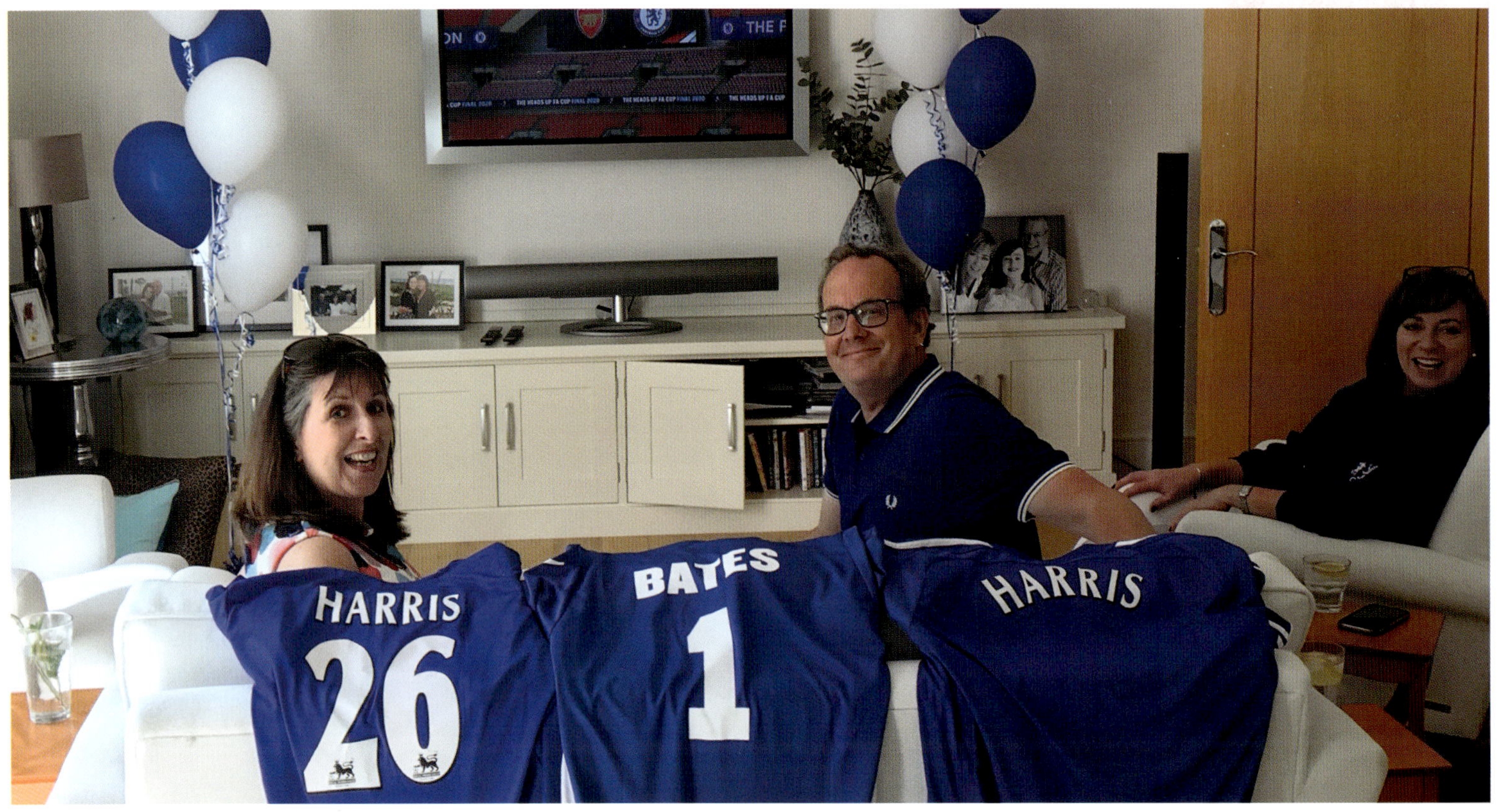

Former OK magazine and Sunday Express Editor Martin Townsend and his wife Jane O'Gorman, the Daily Star's long-standing agony aunt and her best friend, my wife Linda, enjoying a Chelsea match, at our home aptly named Bridge House.

me how Bates had told me not long after he walked through the door as the new Chelsea owner to take over from the Mears family, that one of his first tasks was to shed all the hangers-on within the Directors' Lounge. I knew Brian Mears when he was chairman and he would be a lavish and generous host, even to us journalists, and the chief football writers were welcome guests in the Directors' Lounge, with all the usual goodies on offer. That changed under Bates because the Mears' regime had nearly bankrupted the club (although not because they gave the media free sandwiches and drinks), while cuddly Ken ran a very tight ship and got the club financially ship shape.

More recently Ken invited myself and Linda to a lunch at the swish Chelsea restaurant Charlie's to celebrate his 90th birthday where he could take me to task on one of my latest Chelsea books *The Battle for Stamford Bridge* which depicted the boardroom machinations between himself and Matthew Harding which featured in a BT Sport documentary called *Poundland*, named after the price Ken paid for the club way back in 1982 – a quid.

Ken arrived looking frail with the need of a walking stick, but his mind was as active as ever and those piercing eyes just as probing as ever. He still divides opinion among fans but it is indisputable that, despite all the rhetoric and bluster, he was the man who saved Stamford Bridge from being turned into a housing estate and to many he remains a legend, especially after he sold the club to Roman Abramovich whose vast wealth took the club into the European elite.

So this is Chelsea – London's most successful football club of the past three decades and a club I have a lot of affection for, and not just because every win makes my wife happy!

HH

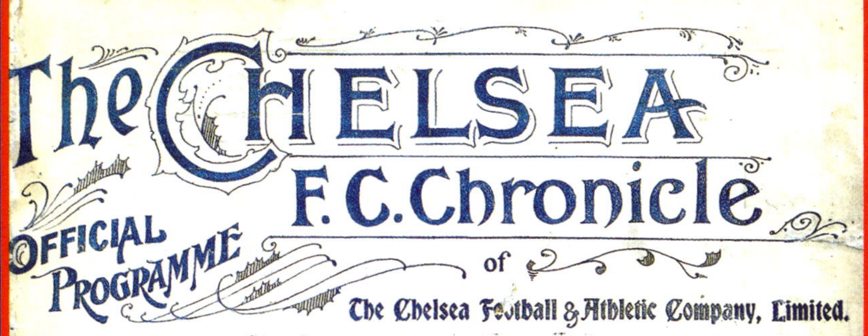

The Chelsea F.C. Chronicle

OFFICIAL PROGRAMME of

The Chelsea Football & Athletic Company, Limited.

President: The Right Hon. The EARL of CADOGAN, K.G.

Vice Presidents:
C. A. Whitmore, Esq., M.P.
Colonel Leslie Powell, J.P.
C. B. Fry, Esq.
W. Hayes Fisher, Esq., M.P.
Major W. F. Woods, J.P.
H. Venn, Esq.

Directors:
W. Claude Kirby, Esq., *Chairman.*
H. A. Mears, Esq.
A. F. Janes, Esq.
G. Thomas, Esq.
J. T. Mears, Esq.
H. Boyer, Esq.
T. L. Kinton, Esq.

Manager: Mr. John T. Robertson. *Hon. Financial Sec.* F. W. Parker, Esq. *Secretary:* Mr. William Lewis.

Colors: Light Blue and White.

Vol. i. No. 1.] MONDAY, SEPTEMBER 4TH, 1905. [One Penny.

DAISY CUTTERS.

"They're Off!"

* * *

Racing men talk of "the saddling bell at Lincoln" in March.

* * *

Bah! It's at the "bottom of the League" compared with the first trill of the Ref's whistle in September.

* * *

Well, now what do you think of our Ground—and the stand—and the terracing? Good enough for SECOND Division Football, is it not?

* * *

And it is only a baby as yet. Wait until it is full grown, and then—well, we shall see what we Chel-sea.

* * *

Don't be over sanguine and expect *too* much of the teams at the first start. We don't expect to "stroll" into the First Division, but we *shall* get there in time.

* * *

One thing, we have a team of genuine triers, who are on the best of terms with themselves and with one another. If they cannot always command success, they will do their level best to deserve it.

* * *

Hearty congratulations to our friendly opponents to-day upon their elevation to the "Upper House."

* * *

And may we follow in their footsteps!

* * *

True, "We've got a long way to go," but we are good stayers, and one of our mottoes is "Excelsior."

Yes, that is one of our mottoes. We have another one, which we owe to (and is typical of) the Father of the Chelsea F.C.—Mr. "Gus" Mears. It is "Don't Worry."

* * *

When the baby-Club, a fine healthy child from the first, was scarcely opening its eyes upon the world, it found—like all good children in the fairy tales—an evil genius, which took the form of a Dakoit, seeking an opportunity to destroy it. Good word, Dakoit, look it up in Nuttall's. We had some anxious moments, but the "happy father" merely smiled good humouredly and said "Don't Worry!"

* * *

Then we had some more anxious moments. There were many and vexatious delays caused by various formalities with the constructional work, and doubts were freely expressed as to the completion of the Stands, &c., in time for the season. Again the same cheery optimism and emphatic "Don't Worry!"

* * *

And so the expression has become our watchword, and you will hear it twenty times a day at Stamford Bridge.

* * *

Bye-the-way, one of our most enthusiastic followers is "Count" Schomberg, who states that we can "count" on him to follow the first team wherever they go. We cannot have too many of this class of sportsmen!

* * *

Next Saturday we have our longest journey of the League Season—to Breezy Blackpool. We hope and expect to draw the full two points after a tough fight.

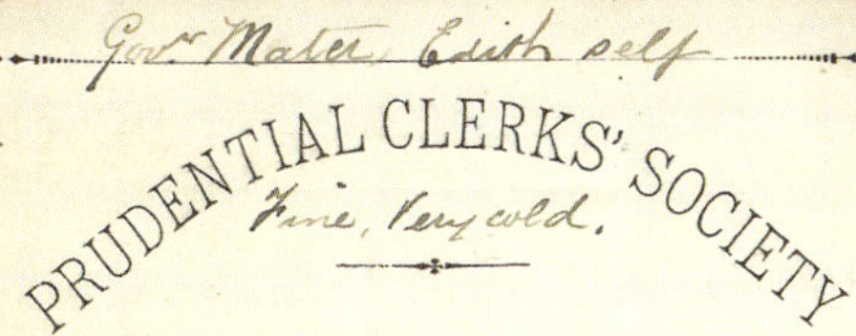

Govr. Mater Edith self

PRUDENTIAL CLERKS' SOCIETY

Fine, very cold.

President—H. HARBEN, Esq.

Vice-Presidents.
T. C. DEWEY, Esq. W. HUGHES, Esq. W. J. LANCASTER, Esq.

Committee, 1883.
W. A. F. BOULGER, S. DAWS, F. FISHER, J. D. LIDBURY, C. S. MARSHALL, T. H. RICHARDSON, F. SCHOOLING, A. C. THOMPSON, J. YARDLEY, G. YOUNG

IBIS ATHLETIC SPORTS,

SATURDAY, MAY 5, 1883,

STAMFORD BRIDGE GROUNDS,

FULHAM ROAD, S.W.

THE SPORTS WILL COMMENCE AT 3.15 O'CLOCK PRECISELY.

The Starting, Judging, and general arrangements will be managed by those Members of the Committee who are not competing.

The Prizes will be presented by EDGAR HORNE, Esq., Chairman of the Prudential Assurance Company, Limited, immediately after the last race.

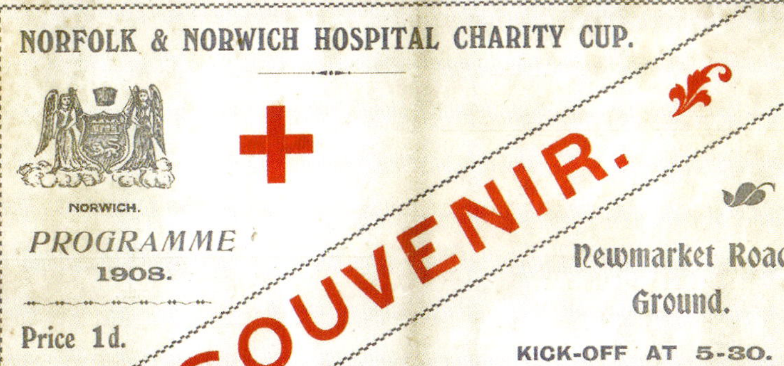

NORFOLK & NORWICH HOSPITAL CHARITY CUP.

NORWICH.

PROGRAMME 1908.

Price 1d.

SOUVENIR.

Newmarket Road Ground.

KICK-OFF AT 5-30.

Thursday, April 30th.

Norwich City v. Chelsea.

GIBBS & WALLER, PRINTERS, COLEGATE STREET, NORWICH.

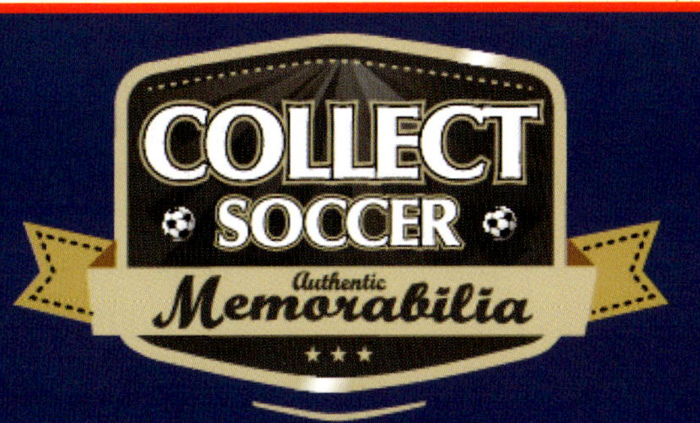

Stephen Cleeve

As a youngster we spent some time in north London, everyone supported one of the two big north London teams. My friend, who lived opposite, supported Chelsea and it was not long before I did too. In 1977 I persuaded my father to take me to watch my first Chelsea game - a 1-1 draw with Wolves at the Bridge. I remember it as if it was yesterday. I have been a blue ever since.

These are a few of the sought-after items I have acquired over the years - many of these items have never been published before. You can see more on my website - www.collectsoccer.com. I buy and sell Chelsea memorabilia and I can create libraries/collections of very rare material for those wishing to collect. I am happy to purchase the collections of ex-Chelsea players or staff discreetly. Give me a call on 07787 518007 or email: s.cleeve@btinternet.com.

PREVIOUS PAGE
Athletics meeting held at Stamford Bridge - Super early programme that pre-dates Chelsea - it is the oldest that I have seen.

Chelsea v Liverpool 1905 (Volume 1 Number 1) - this is Chelsea's first ever programme.

Norwich v Chelsea Hospital Cup 30/4/1908 - only known copy (at Newmarket Rd - pre-dates Carrow Rd) - Chelsea's 3rd season.

THIS PAGE
1955 Championship Season Itinerary for Juniors to visit Amsterdam on tour.

1955 Championship season Itinerary for Chelsea playing a Dutch XI and then watching France v England in Paris.

1955 Celebration Banquet - 50 year Jubilee (there was a large photo album produced of the event which I also have).

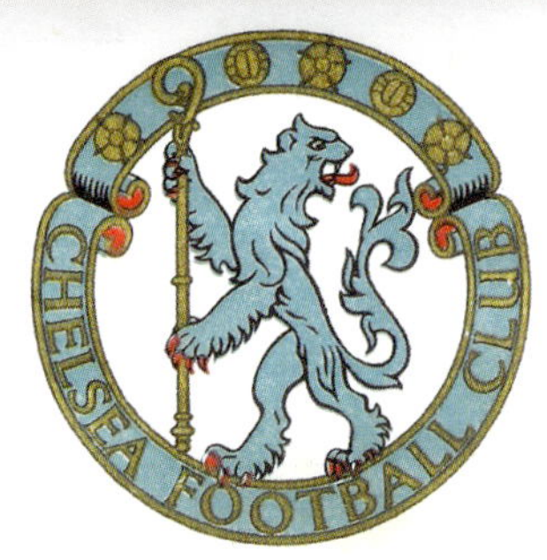

CONTINENTAL TOUR

MAY 1955

ITINERARY

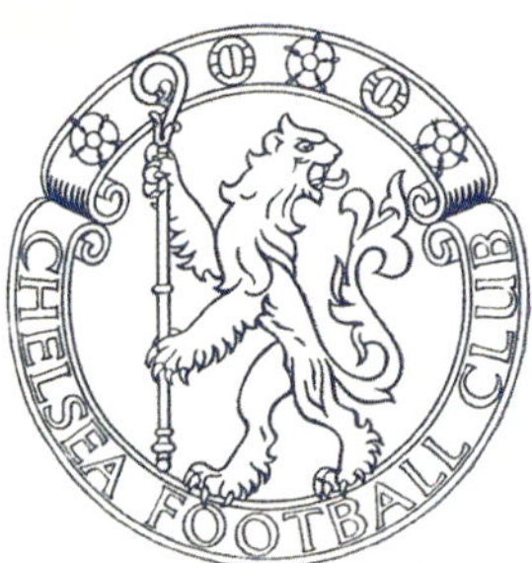

JUNIORS TOUR OF

AMSTERDAM HOLLAND

EASTER · 1955

ITINERARY

CHELSEA FOOTBALL CLUB 1905–1955

JUBILEE CELEBRATION BANQUET

WEDNESDAY, 14th SEPTEMBER, 1955

CHAMPIONS

Football League, Division I.
Football Combination, Division I.
Metropolitan Football League.
South East Counties League.

WINNERS

Metropolitan Football League Challenge Cup.
Metropolitan Football League Professional Challenge Cup
London Minor F.A. Challenge Cup.
Horace Alaway Memorial Bowl.
Z.S.G.O. Trophy Amsterdam.

THE DORCHESTER, LONDON

The Blues Are Born

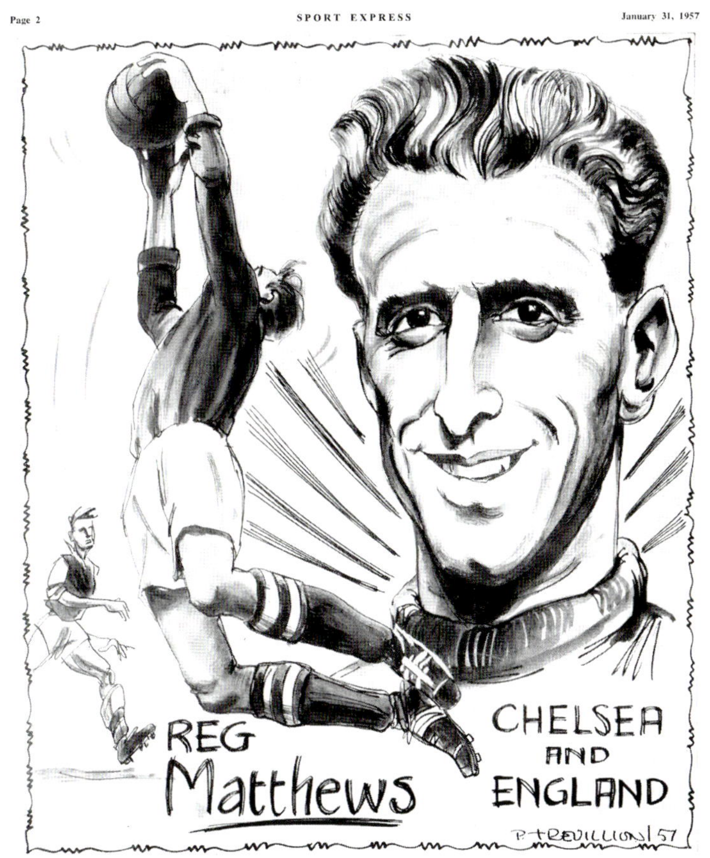

NEXT WEEK: Albert Quixall, Sheffield Wednesday and England

Former Arsenal and England centre-forward Ted Drake arrived at the Bridge from Reading on 30 April 1952 and transformed Chelsea from a music-hall joke into league champions. He ditched the 'Pensioners' nickname and crest, replacing it with the Lion Rampant Regardant crest and 'The Blues' nickname.

Before Drake arrived Chelsea had never won a thing, and were the butt of jokes from football supporters all over London and an irrelevance to supporters elsewhere. Drake reigned from 1952 until 1961 and he totally transformed the club from no-hopers into a club to be respected.

He immediately brought a new professionalism to the West London club. First of all he put the players on an intensified fitness regime. A dapper figure in a pin-striped suit he would, on occasions, join training, ending up with mud all over his suit to get his point across. He introduced tougher training based on ball work, a rare practice in English football at the time, and gambled on young or amateur players, as he also introduced scouting reports to recruit the best young talent.

He rid the club of its amateurish outlook, and that reliance on fresh new talent attracted the tag 'Drakes Ducklings', with the emergence of stars such as Jimmy Greaves, Peter Brabrook and Bobby Tambling, following in the footsteps of Matt Busby, then bringing through his legendary Busby Babes at Manchester United.

Despite a less than impressive start, within three seasons he had steered his 'Blues' to the club's first league title in 1954/55, during the club's golden anniversary season – just as he had predicted on his arrival. In doing so he became the first to win the league title both as player and manager having played a crucial part in Arsenal's dominance of 1930s football.

The final table shows a tight but low-scoring battle for supremacy, Chelsea pipping Wolves by just four points. Yet the Blues lost 10 games during the season and their final points total of 52 is the equivalent to just 72 points today in an era of three points for a win and 42 games in a season. The top flight was much more competitive back then!

Unsurprisingly, perhaps, Chelsea failed to follow-up this success and with only this isolated success Chelsea were once again the butt of the jokes, this time that the club would never win the FA Cup.

A demerit mark on the club's history came when Chelsea bowed to pressure from the Football League and turned down UEFA's invitation to compete in the inaugural European Champions' Cup. It was a decision the far-sighted Matt Busby would reverse the following season, a move that turned Manchester United into a worldwide household name and an opportunity spurned by Chelsea, particularly as they had a history of playing European

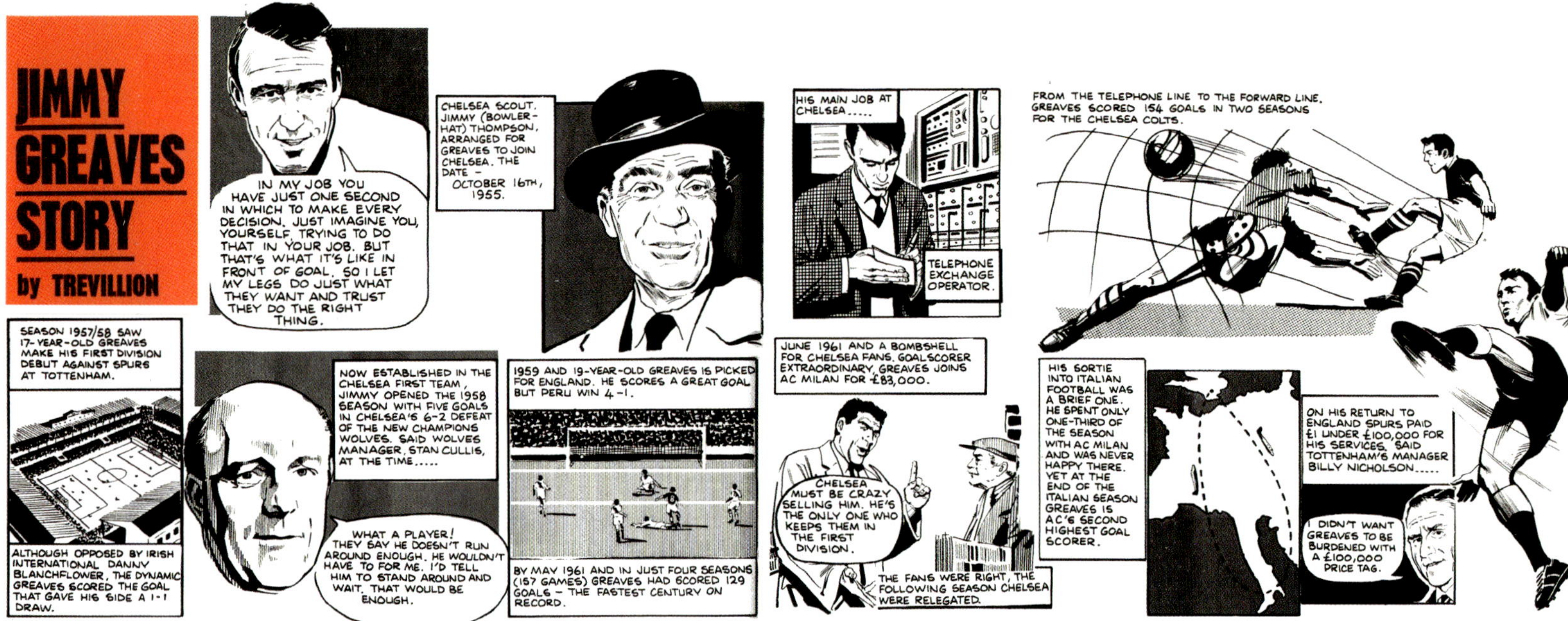

teams, especially the famous game against Dynamo Moscow in November 1945 before a crowd estimated at 100,000.

Jimmy Greaves later described Ted Drake as an 'all the best' type of manager: he gave the team plenty of dressing-room motivation but none of the tactical ethos that would soon enter the game. Greaves was one of the brilliant home-produced stars of the 'Drake's Ducklings' eras, but for all of the innovations the manager brought to the Bridge, he was soon to be overtaken by a new wave of tactical thinking.

Greaves, of course, became a Spurs legend, but prior to his eventual move across London, he was already one of the games great goalscorers with Chelsea. Jimmy broke into the first-team in 1957 after scoring 114 goals for the youth team in his final season at junior level. He scored 132 goals in 169 games for Chelsea including a goal for them on his League debut against Spurs at the Lane in August 1957. After leaving Chelsea in 1961 he then spent an unhappy six months at AC Milan, where he scored on his debut, before returning to London to join Spurs in December 1961, scoring a hat-trick on his debut in a 5-2 win over Blackpool at the Lane.

After nine years at Tottenham he moved across the capital to West Ham, scoring on his debut for them in a match at Maine Road, before quitting Upton Park at the age of 31 and seeing out his career lower down the leagues following a battle with alcoholism. After retiring, Greaves co-hosted the popular Saturday lunchtime football show *Saint and Greavsie* alongside former Liverpool forward Ian St John and was later inducted into the Spurs Hall of Fame.

The record books show Harry Kane to be the greatest all-time England goalscorer, but Harry Redknapp picked Greaves as his personal favourite in a Three Lions shirt, saying, "It's a tough one but I have to go with Greaves. I'm one of his biggest fans and he's the best striker I've played against. When he had the ball in the opposition area the world would stop. He'd have a defender come in and he'd feint one way then go the other, then the keeper would rush out towards him and he'd fake to shoot in one corner sending the keeper that way only to put it in the other corner. He was such an incredible finisher. I remember when he scored five at the age of 17 for Chelsea against a Wolves side that basically had the England back three. He was a special talent."

On the opening day of the 1957/58 campaign Greaves scored the first of record 357 top flight goals in a 1-1 draw at Tottenham at the age of 17. Over the next four years he kept on scoring; 22 in that first season, 37 the next, then 30, and finally 43. In all

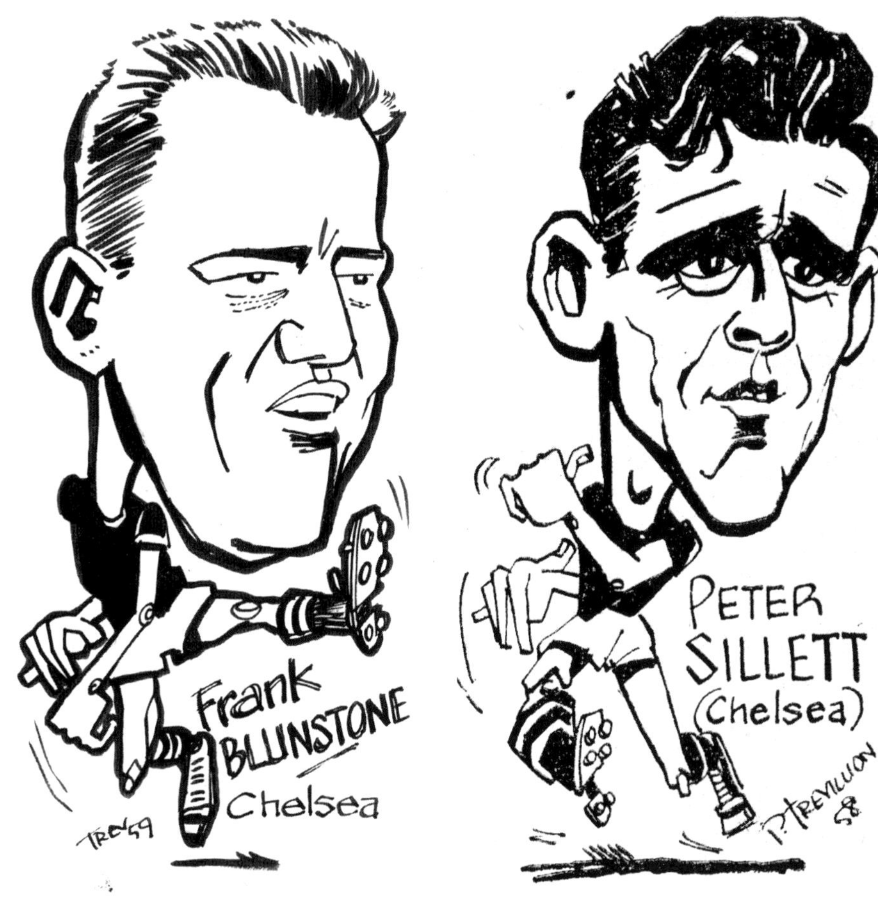

war and instead Jimmy signed for Tottenham where he continued to break records for club and country. He scored 44 goals in 57 games for England and was a member of the 1966 World Cup-winning squad, with one of his biggest regrets in life failing to be named in the team for the Final. He holds the record for most goals in the English top flight with 357, and scored 266 in 379 matches for Tottenham. Greaves' 41 goals in 1960-61 remains a record in a season for Chelsea, and he also holds the Spurs record with 37 in 1962-63.

Sadly, Jimmy suffered a life-threatening stroke and became wheelchair-bound in his final years, he passed away at the age of 81.Then Prime Minister at the time Boris Johnson tweeted: "Sad to hear the news about Jimmy Greaves. He will be remembered as a goalscoring legend and one of the greats of English football." England captain Harry Kane said he was a "true legend". Gary Lineker described Greaves as a "giant of the sport". He tweeted: "Quite possibly the greatest striker this country has ever produced. A truly magnificent footballer who was at home both in the box and on the box. A charismatic, knowledgeable, witty and warm man."

Chelsea said they "mourn the loss of a truly remarkable player and one of our own". Gareth Southgate's team paid tribute before a game against Hungary at Wembley. "Jimmy Greaves was someone who was admired by all who love football, regardless of club allegiances," said the England manager, "Jimmy certainly deserves inclusion in any list of England's best players, given his status as one of our greatest goalscorers and his part in our 1966 World Cup success."

After 10 years in charge, and his team heading for relegation, Ted Drake made way for Tommy Docherty, who had originally been brought in to freshen up the coaching staff. The board fired him citing 'a general lack of success' and Drake later enjoyed a spell as assistant to manager Vic Buckingham at Fulham and Barcelona, becoming scout and then life President at Craven Cottage. He died on 30 May 1995 aged 82, his family attending Chelsea's centenary events a decade later as honoured guests.

Jimmy scored 13 hat-tricks for Chelsea, including five in a game on three occasions and four another three times. His hat-trick against Manchester City in November 1960 included his 100th league goal. He was just 20 years and 290 days old. This remains a league record. During this time however Chelsea did not win a trophy and the board decided to cash in on their prize asset. They arranged a transfer to Milan against the player's wishes and Greaves' last game for Chelsea was the final game of the 1960/61 season. He was made captain for the day and inevitably stole the show scoring all Chelsea's goals in a 4-3 win.

After an unhappy six months in Italy, Greaves wanted to return to Chelsea but the board did not want to get into a bidding

Bobby Tambling

A Sixties Goalscoring Sensation

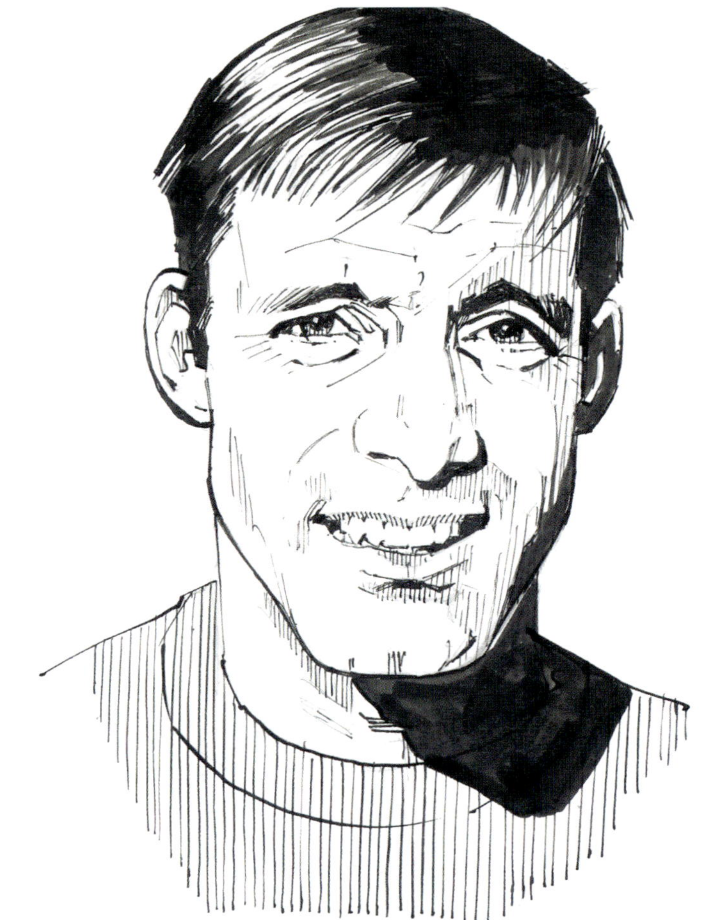

Signed as a schoolboy aged just 15 in 1957, Bobby Tambling spent the next 12 years of his career in West London. He made his debut as a 17-year-old in a 3-2 win over London rivals West Ham United in 1959. Following the departure of Jimmy Greaves in 1961 to AC Milan, he was made the main striker. He got the club promoted immediately after the relegation in 1962 following the addition of quality players in Terry Venables and Peter Bonetti to the team. He was part of the squad that lifted the 1965 League Cup beating Leicester City 3-2 and Chelsea's top scorer in five seasons in the 1960s.

He lost his place to younger strikers like Peter Osgood and Ian Hutchinson. He only played a few games in his last season (1969-70) and was not selected in Chelsea's FA Cup final success. Joined Crystal Palace in January 1970 and wound down his career in the Irish league for Cork Celtic, Waterford, Shamrock Rovers and Cork Alberts, before managing Cork Celtic, Cork City and AFC Crosshaven

Tambling was named in the centenary XI that was made to mark Chelsea's 100-year history.

When Lampard overtook his 47-year-old record as the club's top scorer, he quipped: "I thought we had a typical West Ham poser in our midfield. Boy, has he proved me wrong." His admiration for Lampard grew as it took time for him to realise just how good he would become. "I have never said this in public, but when I first saw Frank in the blue shirt of Chelsea he was a very different player to what he is today," he told BBC Sport. "Frank is a fantastic player, but he is also a gentleman off the field. He plays in midfield like a striker and that is why he joined my club - the 200 club - and has now overtaken me. You can see that in the way he moves, the way he anticipates. His anticipation makes him special. Frank will always anticipate the goalkeeper is not going to make a clean catch so he is a yard or two in front of everyone. He is probably the best player Chelsea have ever had."

Tambling was making his comments on the day Lampard signed a one year contract extension at £120,000-a-week, compared to the sixties goalscoring legends whose wage packet was £10 a week, and down to £8 a week in the close season! Tambling used to catch the train and then the Tube to matches, mixing with the fans before and after games.

"I have a photo of me on the train on the way to a game, 'strap handing' they used to call it. That was how we travelled and we weren't upset about it - that was our life. The most embarrassing times would be when someone would spot you and send over their young lad to ask for your autograph. Then you would spend the rest of the journey with people looking at you thinking, 'Who is that?' But I can honestly say, certainly of the Chelsea lads, we would have played for nothing. We were doing what we loved doing, and then on top of that getting paid."

He was back in SW6 to reflect on and remember a career which saw him play alongside Greaves and Osgood during the Swinging Sixties. "Can I just make one thing clear - I don't talk about Frank Lampard any more! As the games ticked on this season I thought I might yet be able to keep my record for the summer, but I can honestly say I am pleased. When you have a record for 47 years you grow accustomed to having it, but to lose it to a guy like him, a player like him - you couldn't ask for better, really."

Tambling describes the moment Lampard scored twice against Villa to claim the record. "I was in a quiet room in a pub in Ireland [where he lives]. There were a good few friends around the table, it was a great afternoon." Tambling began to hear the groups on the tables around him discussing Lampard's pursuit of the record, not knowing the man who had held it for six decades was sitting only a few feet away. "When Frank got the first goal against Villa, there wasn't a big yell because I think everyone around our table felt for me. When he scored the second one it was even quieter. But I have been prepared for this day for a long while now - five or six years ago, I thought he would be the man to break it."

Lampard also had the advantage in silverware as well as golden goals as Tambling acknowledged: "If he put his trophies on one end of a table and I put mine on the other, I think the table would lean his way."

Tambling and Lampard became good friends. Throughout Tambling's battle with pneumonia and then a painful and debilitating leg condition, Lampard was in touch on the phone and in person.

But having been unable to leave his hospital bed in Cork for three months earlier this year, he is growing stronger by the day and can now walk again, with the aid of crutches. I asked about his friendship with Lampard. "We have grown close over the last few years because I think we both realised this was a day that was going to come," he said. "We always have a joke with each other, I say 'come on Frank, rush along.' My partner would always say 'come on Frank, don't take any more penalties'. Before the Swansea game we saw Frank and John Terry and she said 'Frank, will you do something special for me today?' He said 'Of course.' She said 'Don't take any more penalties'. Frank turned to John and said 'If we get any more penalties, you take them'. John turned round and said 'Not after the last one.' It has been that sort of friendship and we have got closer and closer. I am not in England that often but whenever we can chat, we do."

"When Frank got the first goal against Villa, there wasn't a big yell because I think everyone around our table felt for me. When he scored the second one it was even quieter. But I have been prepared for this day for a long while now - five or six years ago, I thought he would be the man to break it."

Tambling took centre stage at Stamford Bridge during half-time at Chelsea's 2-0 victory over Swansea. "It was very emotional," he said. "I have been out on the pitch two or three times - I call it walking the walk. But the Swansea game was something very, very different. I had not been out of hospital long, my partner Valerie and her brother were both there with me and we all got very emotional, because the applause seemed to go on forever. We were very close to one end of the ground, the stand was still very full and you could see the warmth they had for you and that made it even more emotional. The three of us had tears in our eyes and when we got home we told people about it and they said 'Don't worry, we were in bits here'. It was a tonic for me, a special tonic. The first week I was out of hospital and back where I love being."

Tambling enjoys the quiet life at his home in the picturesque fishing village of Crosshaven in the Republic of Ireland. "I always remember walking through the old Stamford Bridge gates when I first joined, thinking 'This is a proper club'," he added. "I used to bring over young lads from Ireland and walk them in from Fulham Broadway. We would turn the corner by the West Stand and their faces would just be filled with astonishment and excitement. That is how I still feel."

He received a text from Lampard's fiancee at the time, Christine Bleakley, in the moments immediately after the record had passed from one Chelsea hero to another, a message arrived saying, "Bobby is still a legend - always will be."

The Doc

One Of The Funniest Men In Football and a Brilliant Coach

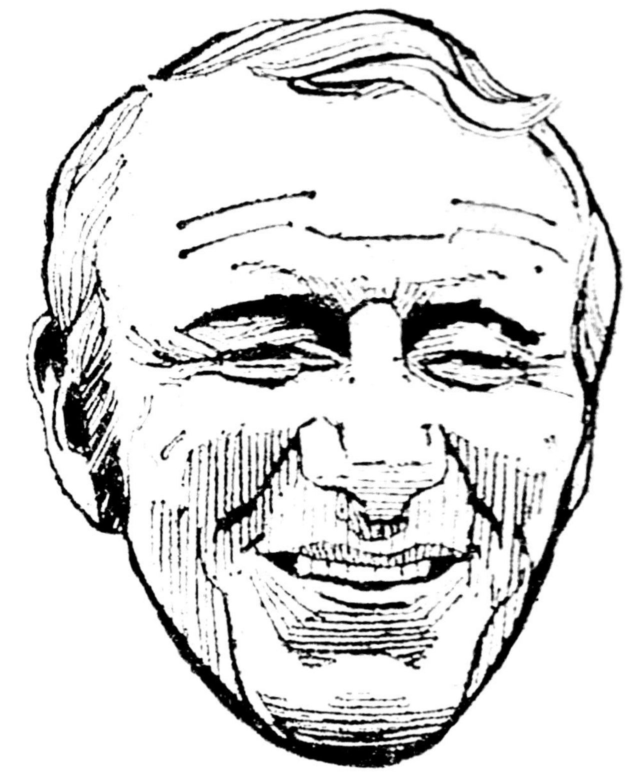

Tommy Docherty had one-liners for every day of the week, well, make that for every time he opened his mouth! But as a manager he was abrasive, charismatic, and determined to be a winner.

On 26 September 1961 the combative Scottish international midfielder succeeded the only Chelsea manager ever to win a trophy, Ted Drake, who was just four years into a 10-year contract — the longest ever handed to a manager at the time — but the Board felt it was time for a major change in direction. Most would have felt reservations about filling the shoes of the club's first title-winning manager but not "The Doc", never a man short of self-confidence, self-belief, or self-assurance.

Chelsea's new manager was sharp-witted and unorthodox. He introduced training and tactical innovations from Europe's top clubs. Docherty also introduced the iconic blue-blue-white Chelsea strip. Just four appearances into his role of player-coach, the maverick Scot was tasked with succeeding where his predecessor had failed in making the most of arguably the most talented group of youngsters in the club's history.

'Doc's Diamonds' were a swashbuckling side who captured the imagination of the supporters, but only won a solitary League Cup, scant reward for The Doc's thrilling reign in West London that brought the club to the forefront of the capital's football conversation and threw off the club's music hall joke reputation and replaced it with a slick and stylish image suited to the sixties West End and London's resurgence as a cultural epicentre for fashion and music.

Alan Hudson recalls, "When Peter Osgood was showing great potential Tommy Docherty, against the boos of the Chelsea crowd, told the press, 'I'm playing young Osgood for a dozen games no matter how he plays because I believe in his outstanding talent and potential.'" It was the Doc's belief in the talent of his youngsters which transformed the fortunes of the club.

Yet some players found The Doc's unpredictability difficult to handle and, in turn, the manager resented the influence of young skipper Terry Venables. Club secretary John Battersby relates a story from a European trip of an air stewardess coming to the back of the plane to ask if someone in authority might stop the high-jinks of the players at the front, who were disturbing other passengers. Battersby obliged and found the source of the uproar to be Docherty himself! However The Doc's relationship with chairman Joe Mears was such that it spared the manager from any rebuke, at least in public. Mears indulged Docherty because the manager had produced the most exciting Chelsea team for decades, attracting thousands more on the gate, without breaking the bank.

After relegation in the first few months of his management, his team bounced back with promotion in 1963 and the following season 'Docherty's Diamonds' challenged for the domestic treble, ending up with London's first-ever League Cup success. Yet while there was silverware to celebrate, it didn't seem sufficient reward for their brilliant football. The reason The Doc fell short of winning the League title in 1965 was chiefly due to what became known as the 'Blackpool Incident' an away trip that has gone down in Chelsea football lore.

By the spring of 1965 Chelsea were in a three-way race for the title with upstarts Leeds United, renowned for their hard, but not so fair, play under rugged Yorkshireman Don Revie and a regal Manchester United containing Denis Law, Bobby Charlton and teenage sensation George Best. But staying over in Blackpool before a crucial fixture at nearby Burnley, eight Chelsea players broke curfew and were immediately sent home; they went on to lose 2-6 at Turf Moor. It was a knee-jerk decision that The Doc came to regret as Chelsea faded from contention and finished third. "Possibly I'm too impulsive," he later admitted. "Possibly I could be more understanding." Chelsea had also lost in the semi-finals of the FA Cup, so going close but not quite getting over the line was becoming something of a hallmark during The Doc's Chelsea reign.

The following season the Blues enjoyed a fantastic Inter-Cities Fairs Cup campaign, falling to Barcelona in the semi-finals only after a replay. That same year though Mears died suddenly of a heart attack and, with him gone, the Doc's tempestuous side would no longer be tolerated. After the huge disappointment of losing the first 'Cockney Cup Final' to Spurs at Wembley in 1967, Docherty abused a local official on a Caribbean tour and was handed a lengthy ban from the game. Chelsea swiftly sacked him and one of the Scot's coaches, Dave Sexton, inherited a much-admired squad.

The end of such a rollercoaster era was widely lamented. One supporter paid for a death notice in *The Times*: 'In Memoriam, Chelsea Football Club, which died Oct. 6 1967, after five proud and glorious years.'

During his time as Chelsea boss Docherty had spent £615,750 but recouped £776,000 in sales — a surplus of £160,250 — and he turned Chelsea into one of the biggest names in English football. Few Chelsea managers can boast the same success while actually making a profit in the transfer market.

Alan Hudson was one of the most famous members of the King's Road set of the seventies. Now he has turned his hand to writing, hence he has penned this of his early career.

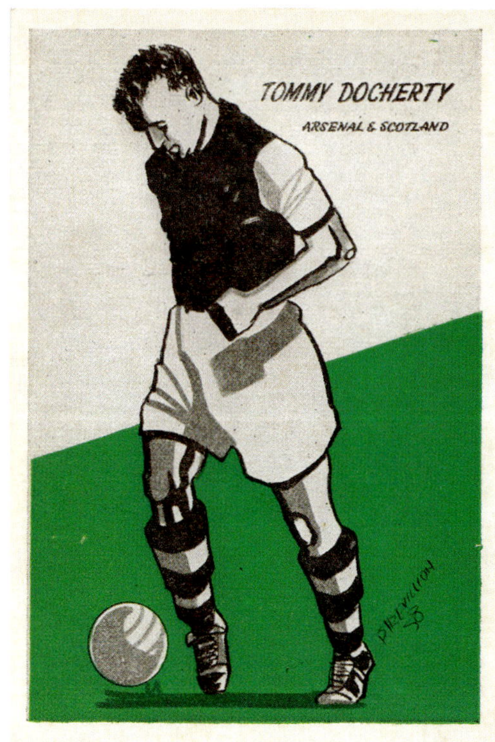

"Although I wanted to follow Johnny Haynes at Fulham, after they turned me away for being 'too small', my father, Bill, took me to the Bridge where Tommy Docherty took a liking to me immediately. Tommy always said he saw me as a replacement for Terry Venables at that time, even picking me in a squad as a 15-year-old at Morton in the old Inter Cities Fairs Cup, I think it was. Anyhow, Tommy signed me as an apprentice and I played in the Youth Team with his son Michael and we made a good pairing in midfield before Tommy sent Michael to Burnley. When I was diagnosed with Osgood-Schlatter Disease (a knee injury) in 1967, Tommy very wisely put me on regular dressing-room duty because I was unable to touch a ball or even run (jog) while my knee was fusing. The doctor said it "might take up til you're 21!" which was a terrible blow because I would have been finished before I started. Luckily it took about eight to nine months but what it did was get me close to all the players on a daily basis, therefore when I finally broke into the team they all looked after Young Hudson and the new signings thought I was just a boot-boy. Brilliant management by the Doc!

"Tommy, or 'The Tyke' as the lads called him, was a prankster, a joker, a piss-taker of the highest order, everything seemed like a joke to him, but the one thing you had to give him was his running of the club with regards to scouts and his Scottish connections. Of course Tommy could be ruthless and underhand. He promised to sign my brother John as a professional and reneged on it and my father chased him round his office and threatened to take me away. Tommy said 'If you do I'll see he never kicks another ball anywhere'. As for the sending home of the chaps from Blackpool, well, they reckon it was because they went out without inviting him, which I can believe! Tommy was sacked while I was fulfilling my dressing-room duties... enter Dave Sexton, who had never seen me play, so had to go by Frank Blunstone and the 'great' Tommy Harmer, who were my Youth Team coaches, for an update on my progress - playing that is. I truly believe Chelsea missed the greatest opportunity when sacking Docherty. They should have kept him and brought Dave Sexton back to coach, and they'd have made the perfect combination, like Clough and Taylor or Mercer and Allison.

"The team before I got into it was going to take on Liverpool. Docherty's Diamonds went to Anfield, then as now a fortress, and knocked them out of the FA Cup with Oz in full flight. 'The Catch Us If You Can' (The Dave Clark Five) team they called them. We were all at a great age and it was no coincidence that Venables and Graham, not forgetting Eddie [McCreadie] for a year at the Bridge, became top, top managers. They learned a lot from Docherty - not all good by the way, but the Good, Bad and the Ugly part of management. The Doc had some lovely sayings and some which were unprintable - that was Tommy the Tyke and he taught Ron Harris how to hurt opponents, that's a fact!"

George Graham was a disciplinarian as Arsenal manager but back in his playing days he was known as Gorgeous George, a bit of a lady's man, and a rebel. Graham recalls: "I was playing for Aston Villa and still only 18. I also played for Scotland Youth, when there was a youth World Cup tournament being played around England, with some really top talent who would go onto to make it big in English football. Tommy Docherty came to see

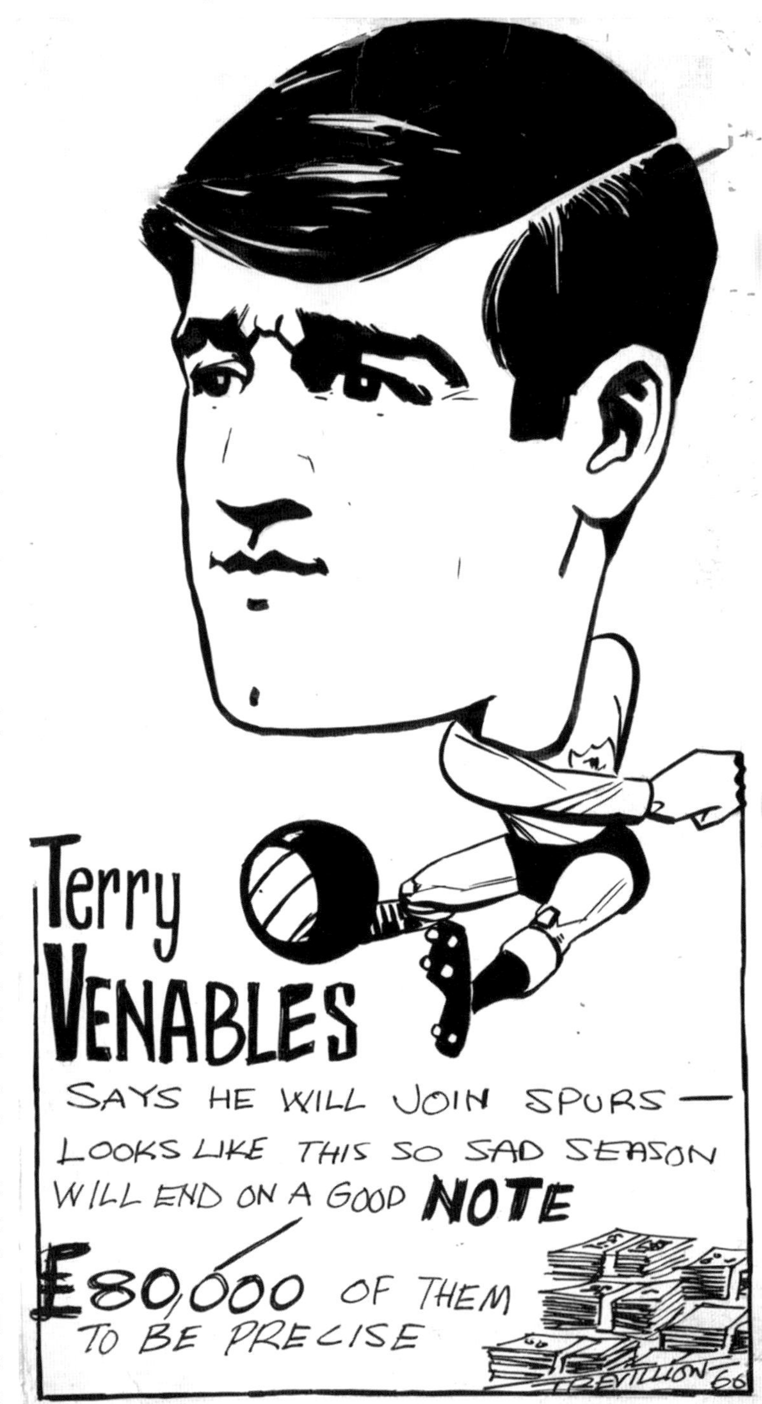

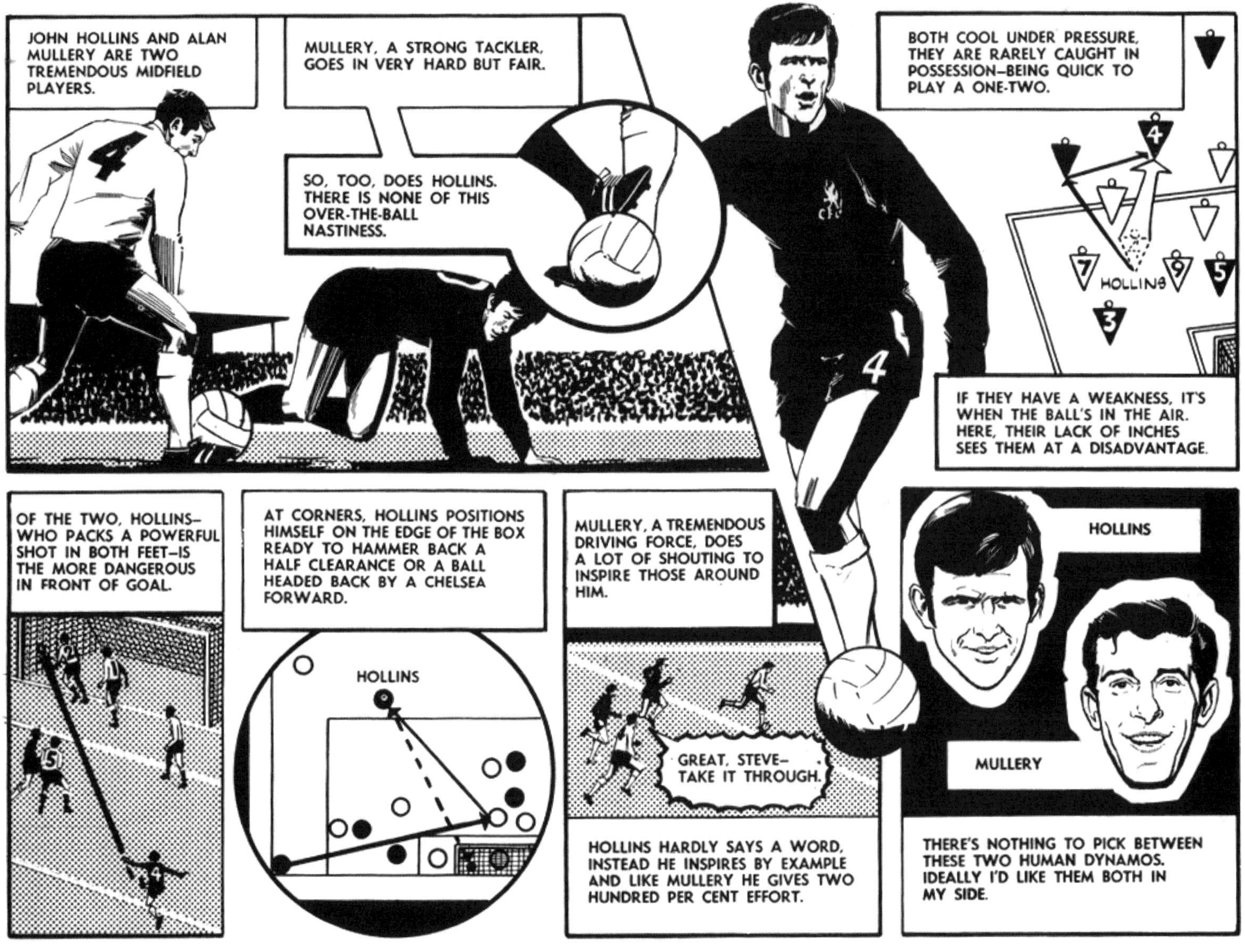

me. He bid £5,000 to Villa to bring me to Chelsea. I was on holiday close to Poole visiting my brother when The Doc rang up out of the blue. I was going to sign for Southampton at the time as that would have suited me as it would have been close to where my brother lived. I told Tommy that I had been offered the princely sum of £27-a-week by the Saints and I was going there - quick as a flash The Doc said, "I'll give you £30-a-week".

"So I joined Chelsea where there was an outstanding young team with the likes of John Hollins, the Harris brothers, Terry Venables was captain, Peter Brabrook and Eddie McCreadie. As soon as I arrived top scorer Bobby Tambling was injured in pre-season and I went straight into the team, and in my first season

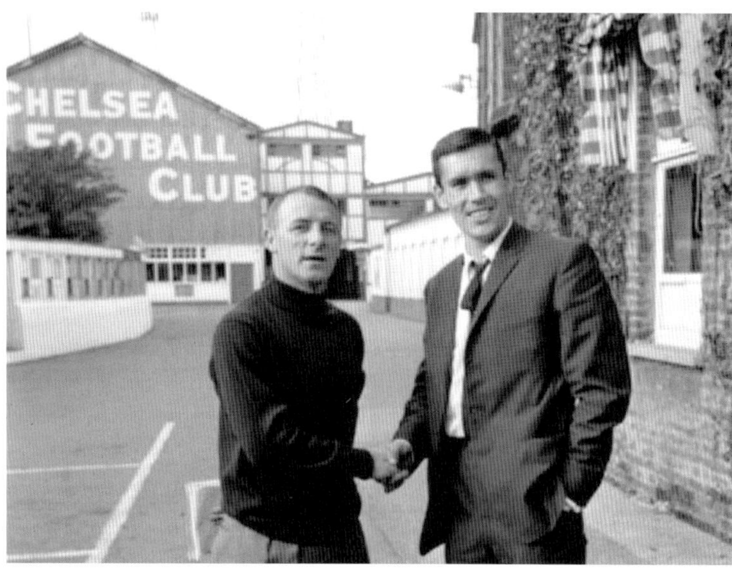

The Doc and new signing Tony Hateley, 1966

I finished top scorer. Fair dos, The Doc appreciated how well I was doing scoring so many goals, and he more than doubled my wages in that same season. Dave Sexton was the coach, he was absolutely brilliant, the best I worked under in my entire career along with the likes of Don Howe and Terry Venables.

"I am still not quite sure how I got the nickname of 'Stroller'. I thought it was when I went to Arsenal, but I think it was starting while I was still at Chelsea. The reason was simple enough, I was never the quickest! Quick thinking, yes, but I didn't move very quickly over the ground. I did not get into the team because of my pace, that's for sure, and I would not get into any team in this modern game which is all about pace. Perhaps I got the name because I was also young, single, it was the King's Road and I was the new boy on the block scoring all the goals and the new up and coming star. Who knows? All I do know for sure is that I had a very enjoyable couple of years at Chelsea, I loved every minute of it.

"Of course I had a fall out as I was one of those sent home from Blackpool for staying out too late and having some fun before the game. He never summoned us to his room, never saw us as a group, never said a word to us in fact. We all just got a letter pushed under the door saying here's your train ticket, you are on the next train back to London. It made huge headline news at the time, it was quite some shock, as we were going for the title. Although as players we didn't make much of it, we lost our momentum after that incident and finished second or third, I think. I couldn't tell if it was true or not that The Doc was upset because we didn't invite him on our night out! That's the first I've heard of that one but it signalled the break-up of such a great young team. The heart of the team was ripped out when Terry Venables was sold to Tottenham, I was sold to Arsenal and Peter Brabrook also went on his way. Such a shame. It was such a blossoming team we could have gone on to even greater heights. That was The Doc for you though; he was amazing, life could be fabulous or horrific. One week you were Gunter Netzer, the world class brilliant German midfield player, the next you were nothing if you had a bad game. He was up and down like a yo-yo.

"But The Doc had the best one-liners in the game. You couldn't take him on in any verbal banter, he was the master. There was no point trying to be clever with him. When he finished in the game he became an entertainer, one of the best after dinner speakers, a great comedian, and he remained so until the end of his days."

I knew "The Doc" to a degree as manager of Manchester United, where he suffered another controversial end to his career at Old Trafford due to his private life, but it was when he was out of football, and known more for his after dinner speaking, that I contacted him to 'appoint' him manager again of Chelsea. Well, Chelsea Legends, but an elite selection for an elite legends London Cup event for a new form of football, Football 30, 15 minutes each half so the old boys could still produce their best but over a short period, and there would be a four team tournament, at Craven Cottage; Fulham, Spurs, Arsenal and Chelsea. The Doc was delighted and he was a bag of laughs from the moment he turned up at Craven Cottage, and I would imagine he didn't stop while in the dug out.

Tommy Docherty sadly passed away on 31st December 2020 at the grand old age of 91. After leaving Chelsea his managerial career took in clubs all over the world and included a spell as Scotland boss. His name was still being sung by Manchester United fans in the 1980s as a possible replacement for Alex Ferguson during the early years of the Scot's reign at Old Trafford.

Dave Sexton

A Student of the Game

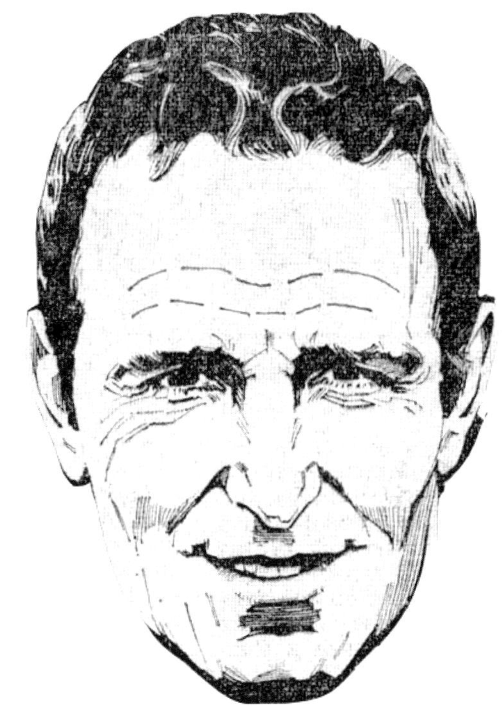

Dave Sexton is best remembered for leading Chelsea to FA Cup glory against Leeds United in 1970, following it up by securing the European Cup Winners' Cup against Real Madrid the following season. His acumen and wisdom was utilised by the FA and a succession of England managers in his later years, leading the Under-21 team to back-to-back European titles in 1982 and 1984. He coached the England Under-21 team between 1977-90, and again from 1994-96. He was an assistant to Ron Greenwood and Bobby Robson, and worked with Terry Venables, Glenn Hoddle and Kevin Keegan. He wrote a book on coaching called *Tackle Soccer* in 1977. In his seventies, he was still at the forefront of modern coaching techniques and when Sven-Göran Eriksson was appointed England manager in 2001, he turned to Sexton to run a team of scouts who would compile a database and video library of opposition players, a strategy Sexton had pioneered three decades previously.

He was one of the great elder statesmen of English football – both an innovator as a coach and a success as a manager. He died in November 2012 aged 82.

A quiet, modest man who was regarded as one of English football's great thinkers, Sexton had a love of art and poetry and completed an Open University degree in the humanities. He was made an OBE in 2005.

Sexton eventually left Chelsea for QPR in 1974 and led the West London team to their best league finish of second in the 1975-76 season, one point behind champions Liverpool when he came close to arguably his greatest triumph.

In 1977 he succeeded Tommy Docherty yet again at Manchester United but was sacked in April 1981 after four years without winning a major trophy at Old Trafford - although he did win his final seven games in charge and he took Manchester United to the FA Cup Final in 1979, where they lost to Arsenal and took them closer to the league title than any other manager before the appointment of Alex Ferguson in 1986, finishing runners-up to Liverpool in 1979-80.

Sexton was the polar opposite of Docherty; an introverted football thinker whose personality proved a perfect foil for the wide array of larger-than-life characters coming through the ranks at Stamford Bridge.

Chelsea held a minute's applause in tribute to Sexton before their Premier League match against Manchester City at Stamford Bridge back in November 2012. "It is a sad day for English football," said then FA director of football development, Sir Trevor Brooking, "anyone who was ever coached by Dave would be able to tell you what a good man he was, but not only that, what a great coach in particular he was. In the last 30-40 years Dave's name was up there with any of the top coaches we have produced in England - the likes of Terry Venables, Don Howe and Ron Greenwood. His coaching was revered."

Chelsea released a statement saying they "would like to express our

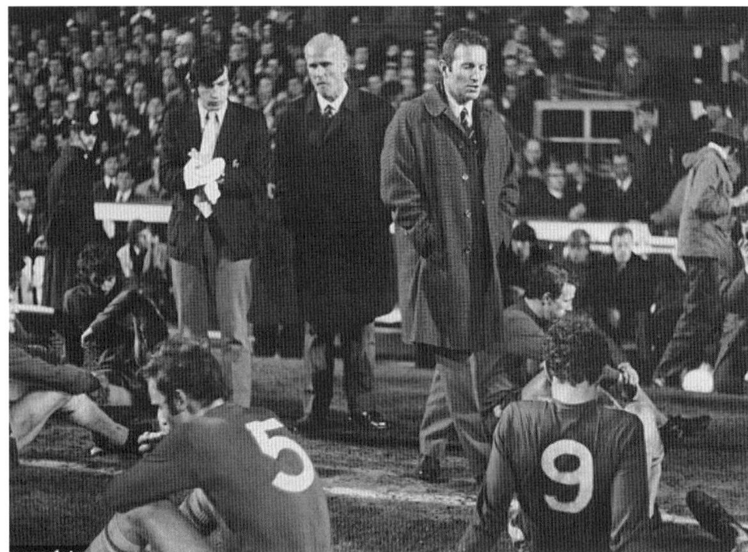

enormous sadness and send our deepest condolences to the family and friends of Dave Sexton. Sexton is without doubt one of the greatest managers in Chelsea history".

He began his managerial career at Leyton Orient in 1965 but it was during that seven-year spell with Chelsea that he made his name. Sexton succeeded Tommy Docherty, who had given him his first coaching job at the club four years earlier.

Sexton was the polar opposite of Docherty; an introverted football thinker whose personality proved a perfect foil for the wide array of larger-than-life characters coming through the ranks at Stamford Bridge. Having led Chelsea to sixth and fifth in his first two seasons, he finally won the club's first FA Cup with a 2-1 replay victory over Leeds at Old Trafford after the first match had ended in a 2-2 draw at Wembley - David Webb scored the winner in extra time after Peter Osgood's late equaliser had cancelled out Mick Jones' effort for United. Chelsea finished third in the league but won that epic, engrossing. ill-tempered FA Cup final after a replay at Old Trafford which was watched by 28 million people on television.

A year later Sexton's the Blues lifted the European Cup Winners' Cup - Real Madrid were the opposition and Ignacio Zoco's last-minute goal cancelled out Osgood's opener, leading to another replay. Chelsea triumphed 2-1 with Osgood and John

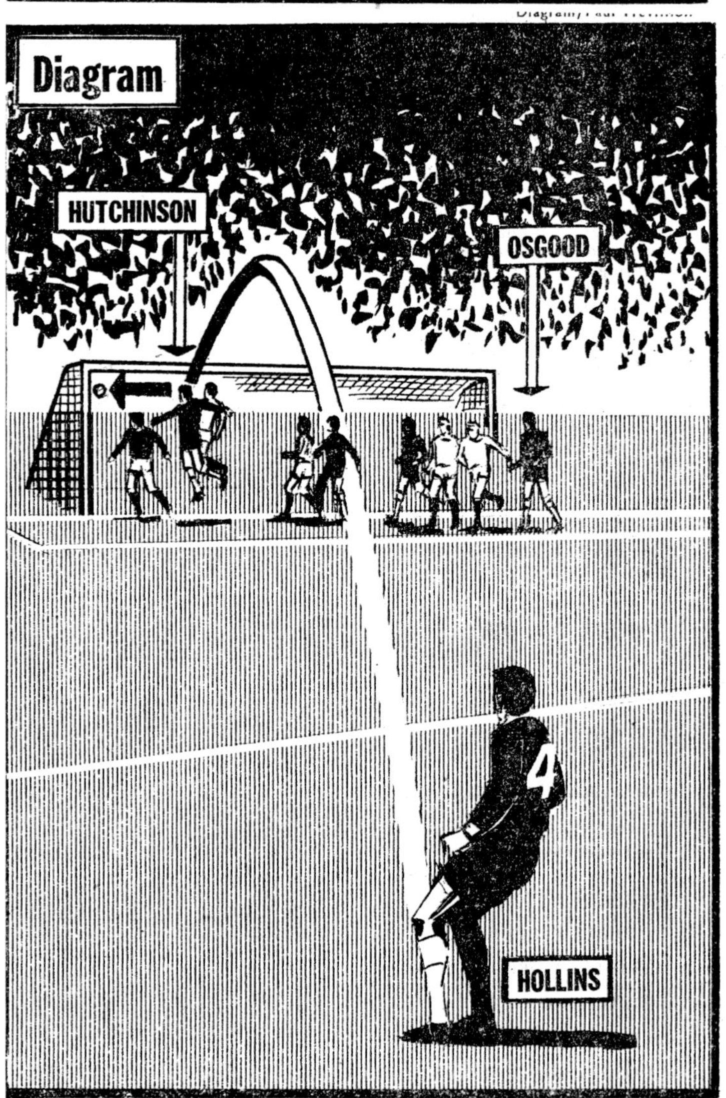

Chelsea (1) 2 Leeds United (1) 2

Houseman, Hutchinson Charlton, Jones

After extra time—score 90 mins. 2-2. Att. 100,000. Rec. £128,000.

(Replay at Old Trafford, April 29)

Osgood draws the Leeds defence to the far post to allow Hutchinson space to sneak in and head Chelsea's equaliser

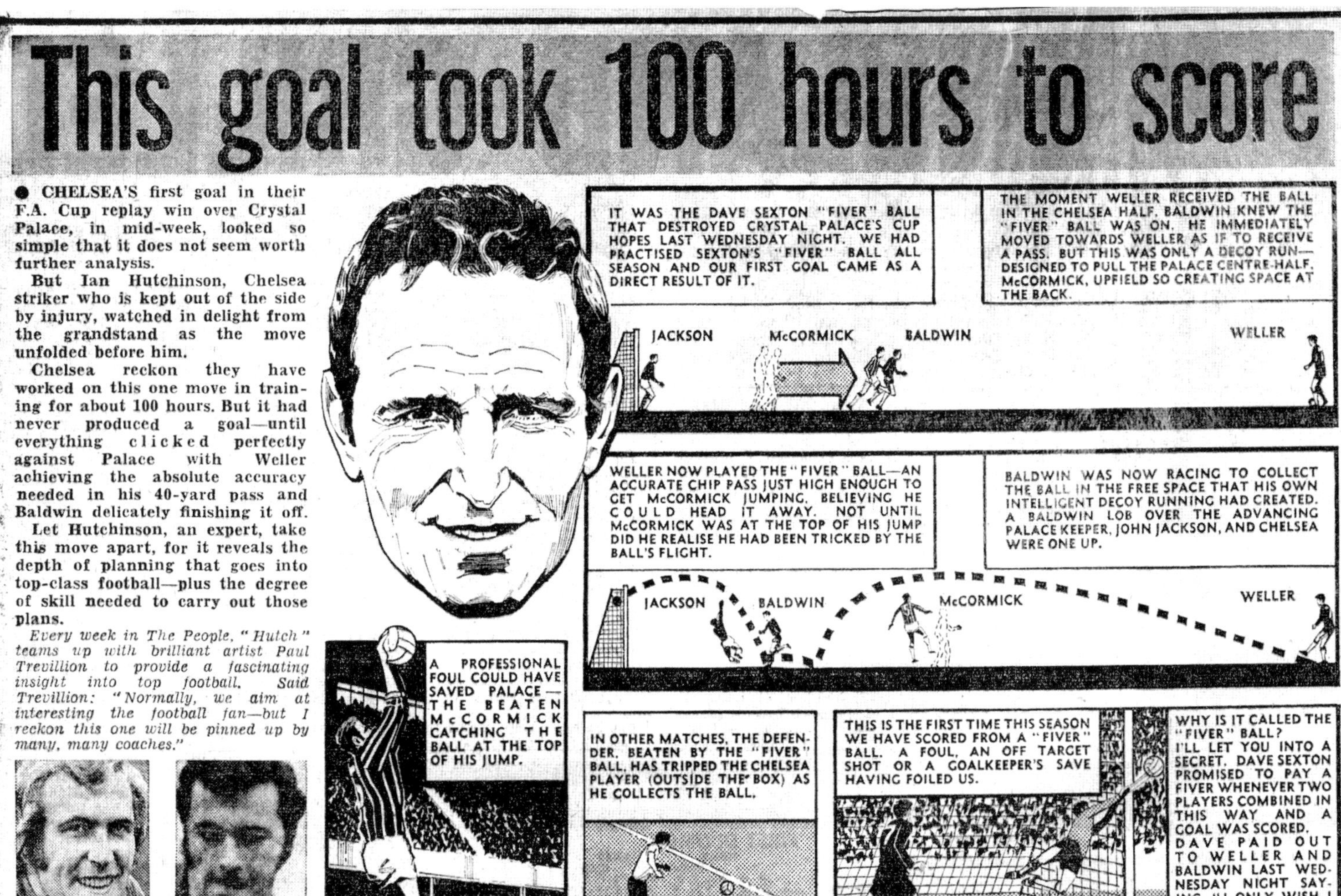

This goal took 100 hours to score

● **CHELSEA'S first goal in their F.A. Cup replay win over Crystal Palace, in mid-week, looked so simple that it does not seem worth further analysis.**

But Ian Hutchinson, Chelsea striker who is kept out of the side by injury, watched in delight from the grandstand as the move unfolded before him.

Chelsea reckon they have worked on this one move in training for about 100 hours. But it had never produced a goal—until everything clicked perfectly against Palace with Weller achieving the absolute accuracy needed in his 40-yard pass and Baldwin delicately finishing it off.

Let Hutchinson, an expert, take this move apart, for it reveals the depth of planning that goes into top-class football—plus the degree of skill needed to carry out those plans.

Every week in The People, "Hutch" teams up with brilliant artist Paul Trevillion to provide a fascinating insight into top football. Said Trevillion: "Normally, we aim at interesting the football fan—but I reckon this one will be pinned up by many, many coaches."

● BALDWIN . . . decoy run.

● WELLER . . . "fiver" ball.

Dempsey scoring before half-time.

The team reached another final, the League Cup, in 1972, losing 2-1 to Stoke City, before Sexton's relationship with the board soured. The club overspent on a new stand, which put the manager under financial pressure, and he fell out with Osgood and Hudson, two star players who were sold to the dismay of supporters, to Southampton and Stoke respectively. Sexton was sacked in 1974 and moved to QPR.

A student of Rinus Michels and Dutch 'Total Football', a fluid and highly technical system in which all 10 of a team's outfield players were able to switch positions quickly to maximise space on the field, Sexton would sometimes fly to Holland at his own expense to watch games. At QPR he inherited a talented group of players, including Gerry Francis, Stan Bowles and Frank McLintock, and also signed Don Masson. He instilled in the side a discipline and aesthetic that was ahead of its time, emphasising the importance of diet and fitness, and video analysis using footage that he had painstakingly edited himself. The brand of

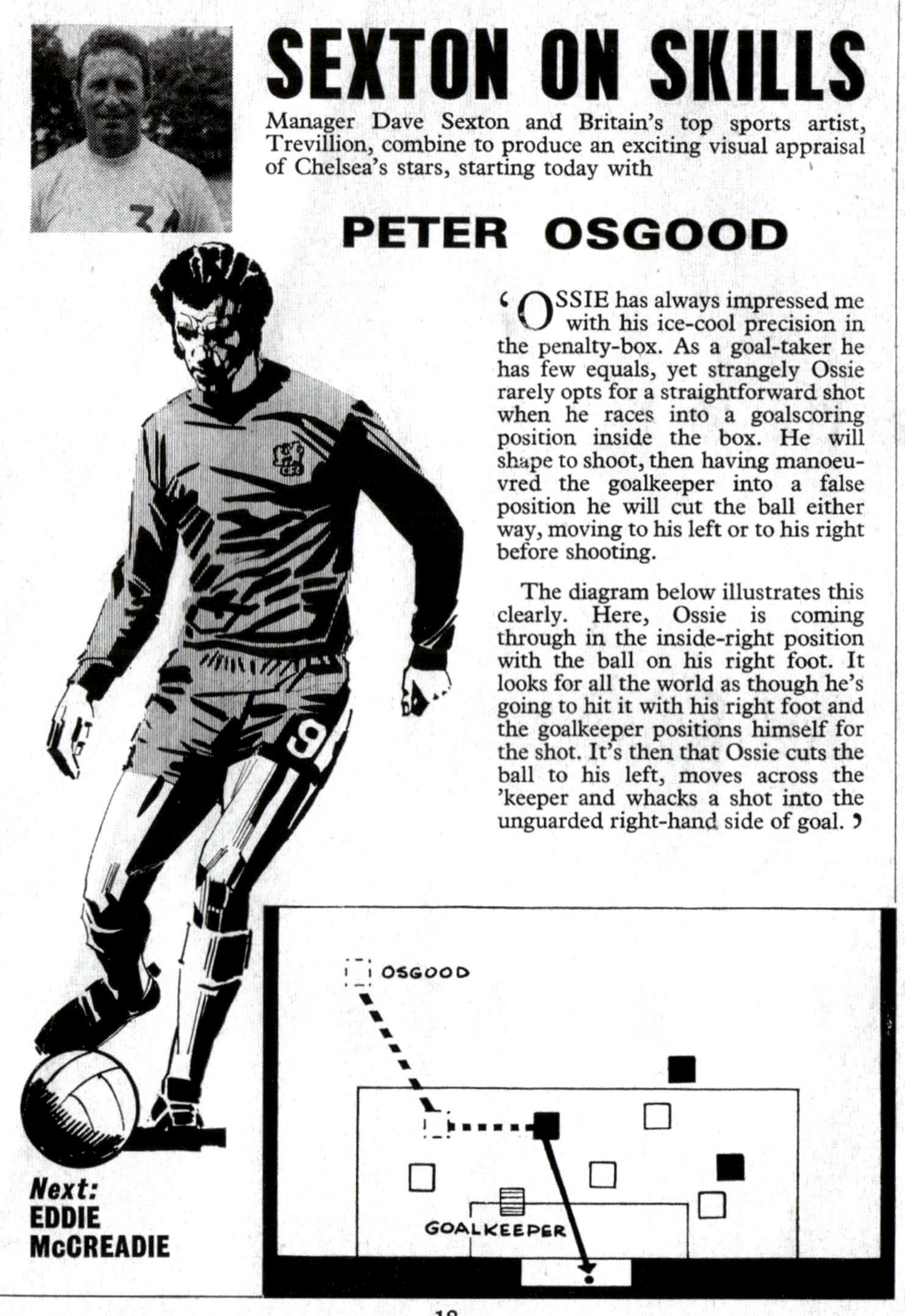

SEXTON ON SKILLS

Manager Dave Sexton and Britain's top sports artist, Trevillion, combine to produce an exciting visual appraisal of Chelsea's stars, starting today with

PETER OSGOOD

'OSSIE has always impressed me with his ice-cool precision in the penalty-box. As a goal-taker he has few equals, yet strangely Ossie rarely opts for a straightforward shot when he races into a goalscoring position inside the box. He will shape to shoot, then having manoeuvred the goalkeeper into a false position he will cut the ball either way, moving to his left or to his right before shooting.

The diagram below illustrates this clearly. Here, Ossie is coming through in the inside-right position with the ball on his right foot. It looks for all the world as though he's going to hit it with his right foot and the goalkeeper positions himself for the shot. It's then that Ossie cuts the ball to his left, moves across the 'keeper and whacks a shot into the unguarded right-hand side of goal.'

Next: EDDIE McCREADIE

18

football took the league by surprise; the R's did not lose a game at home and beat the reigning champions, Derby, 5-1 away, with Bowles scoring a hat-trick. They were only pipped to the title by Liverpool on the last day of the season. The following year, QPR reached the quarter-finals of the UEFA Cup but could only manage 14th in the league.

Sexton attracted the interest of bigger clubs and arrived at United in the summer of 1977, after being expected to join Arsenal. He again replaced Docherty, who had been sacked. Sexton was seen as a safe option by the United board to replace the brash Docherty, whose affair with the wife of the club's physiotherapist had been made public.

He ended his full-time managerial career at Coventry in 1983 but continued coaching the England Under-21s in a part-time capacity.

ALAN HUDSON

"Just before my 17th birthday Dave Sexton gave me a run-out in a testimonial at QPR for Mike Keen at Loftus Road on a very muddy pitch. I hadn't played for so long but I knew QPR well as I'd watched them all through their League Cup run of 1967. It was the end of May I think. I must have shown Dave enough and he signed me on my 17th birthday, the longest day of the year, 21 June 1968 - and a few days later I was in Mozambique with the likes of Osgood, Cooke, Tambling, Bonetti, Hinton, Baldwin, Dempsey (who I made my Chelsea debut with). Bobby 'Jumbo' Tambling wore Jimmy Greaves' Number

8, but I took that from him and years later Frank Lampard wore it. It's a very special shirt at Chelsea.

Dave Sexton, as I was to find out, should have stuck to coaching, because like Don Howe, he was no good in the manager's office, that's where all the trouble began at Chelsea… I liked Dave but he didn't drink and therefore didn't like our socialising, which was where we got our great team spirit from. Unlike Tony Waddington at Stoke City, Dave was more concerned about what we did from Monday to Friday than on a Saturday, whereas TW didn't give a hoot about midweek, it was all about Saturdays – a little like the Elton John song 'Saturday Night's Alright for Fighting'!

It was the Dave Sexton/Peter Osgood Show most of the time as they often fell out, even offering one another out behind the North Stand, a fight I stopped after returning from a Cup Winners' Cup match on the plane where the offer was made!

I took Oz to the Imperial to calm him down. I often wondered who would have won that fight as Osgood fancied himself as a fighter and he was a former hod carrier from Windsor while Dave, as you know, was the son of Archie Sexton and looked like he could handle himself. Can you imagine the headlines today back then with Harry's mates in Fleet Street and a 'THE BATTLE OF THE NORTH STAND' headline!

This was what led to Dave's demise, as he sold both me and Osgood – Peter went on to win the FA Cup with Southampton, while I took Stoke into the UEFA Cup (they were fourth bottom when I signed) and the

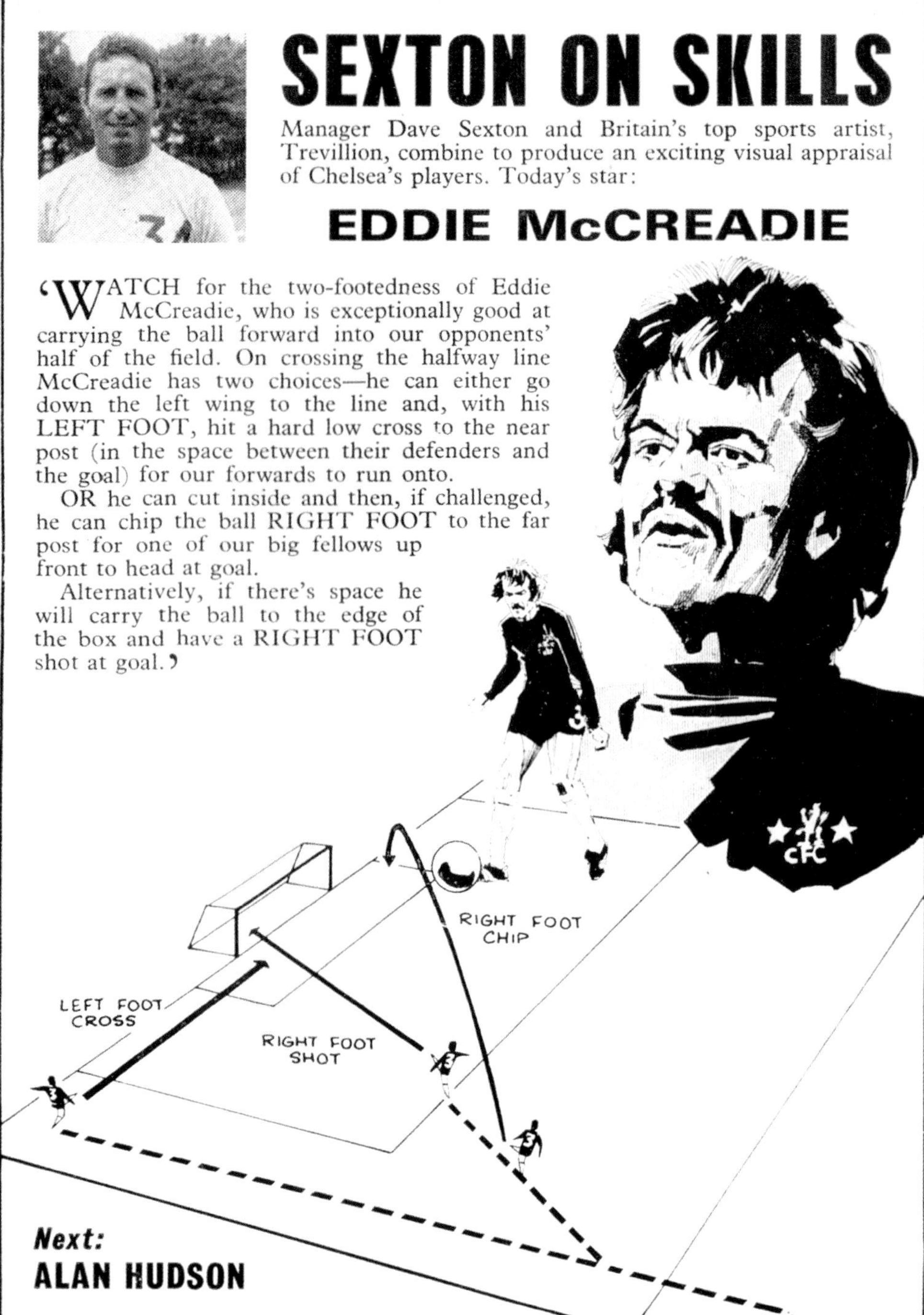

SEXTON ON SKILLS

Manager Dave Sexton and Britain's top sports artist, Trevillion, combine to produce an exciting visual appraisal of Chelsea's players. Today's star:

EDDIE McCREADIE

'WATCH for the two-footedness of Eddie McCreadie, who is exceptionally good at carrying the ball forward into our opponents' half of the field. On crossing the halfway line McCreadie has two choices—he can either go down the left wing to the line and, with his LEFT FOOT, hit a hard low cross to the near post (in the space between their defenders and the goal) for our forwards to run onto.

OR he can cut inside and then, if challenged, he can chip the ball RIGHT FOOT to the far post for one of our big fellows up front to head at goal.

Alternatively, if there's space he will carry the ball to the edge of the box and have a RIGHT FOOT shot at goal.'

Next:
ALAN HUDSON

following season Chelsea were relegated. It was poor leadership from the directors which I told Brian Mears after coming out of my coma years later.

Those days were my early experiences of management but as I was going into a definite decline, Tony Waddington saved me and took me to Stoke. Under Dave, I missed the FA Cup Final and the Mexico World Cup after my injury had been neglected by the club and I was drinking for all the wrong reasons and went into a deep depression which led to my loss of form and that started me to fall out with Dave. Bad management!

It seemed that whenever Chelsea had a blip it was all down to Osgood and Hudson and with that stand being unfinished through lack of finance they saw us two as their saviour: selling me for a record £240,000 to Stoke and Ossie for another record £325,000 to Saints.

I went on to play the best football of my career at Stoke and, although Osgood won the FA Cup, he could quite never live up to the tag he'd had at Chelsea 'King of Stamford Bridge'; at The Dell. At the Bridge I was more the 'Local Boy Made Good' so it annoys me even more the way the club and supporters treated me, through no fault of my own. The Chelsea fans turned on me following a campaign by the club to justify our sale. I try to tell them to this day; Oz and I were made scapegoats. This was the reason we were ignored when four players were on the field to celebrate 50 years of winning the FA Cup while I was sitting in a pub a mile away. I got phone calls where friends even called me 'out of order' for not turning up, and I told them "I knew nothing about it" which was the honest truth. I would have loved to have gone on the pitch with my old mates Marvin, Johnny Dempsey and Sponge. Nobody ever mentions how much damage building that awful stand caused and I always say instead of selling me to Stoke they should have brought Waddington to Chelsea and we would have won the League, because all the in-house fighting would have stopped immediately. Osgood would have stayed, Tony would have broken the bank and bought George Best who wanted to sign, whereas had Dave signed George he would have been found hanging from Chelsea Bridge within a month! Dave couldn't handle Osgood, Cooke, Baldwin, Boyle and Hudson let alone the Belfast Boy!

Mind you, had Tony Waddington come down and pulled off the 'Signing of the Century', Chelsea most certainly would have needed a bigger stadium.

30 THE SUN, Friday, December 15, 1972

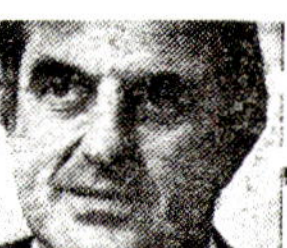

THE FRANK NICKLIN COLUMN

A turkey trot for Ossie!

ONE of football's big faults today is that it has lost its sense of humour. It is grim, sordid, sour and violent and you cannot blame the once-happy fan for telling them to stick it.

But Paul Trevillion, my scatty young artist friend with the Milligan wit and a million ideas to resell soccer, is doing just that.

Having given Leeds their gimmicks, he has now moved in, predictably, on dear old Chelsea. And I must warn their fans about his Christmas stunt for the home match with Everton tomorrow week.

Parade

He is planning to have "Ossie" parade round the ground on a wire rope held by Buster, a 20-stone Chelsea fan who works at Smithfield market.

And to one lucky programme holder, "Ossie" will be handed over to take home after the match—trussed, naked and well stuffed.

I should explain that "Ossie" lives in Buster's back garden. He is moving rapidly towards the 80lb mark, and for safety reasons is heavily guarded in a nearby Stalag.

"A frightening beast," says Trevillion. "Half the players won't go within a hundred yards of him."

"Ossie" is a king among turkeys. You can actually hear him when he walks.

"We call him 'Ossie' because he looks more like a bloody ostrich,'" says one horrified defender whose moral fibre has never before been questioned.

David Webb tried to put his sock on "Ossie's' leg. The sock was too small.

Flashed

They placed the ball on the penalty spot to see if he could kick. But he flashed his beak and burst it first bite.

So have fun on the 23rd, you Chelsea fellows, because that's what the game is all about.

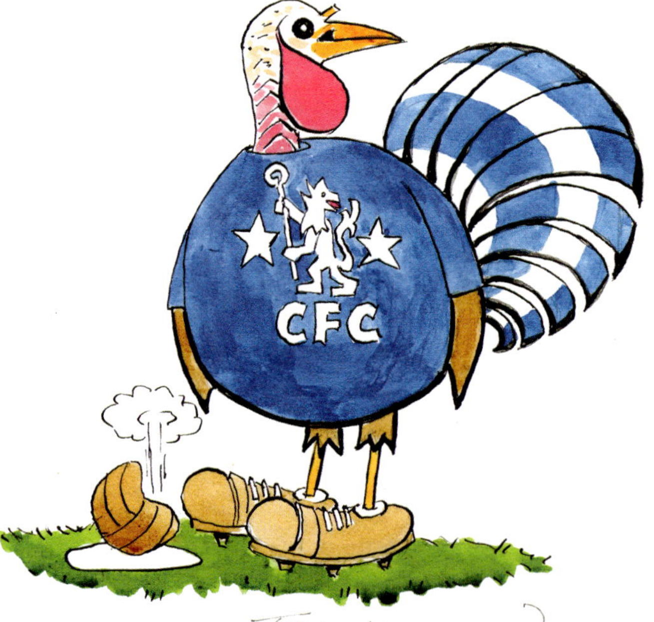

The King of Stamford Bridge

Peter Osgood, the Epitomy of West End Cool

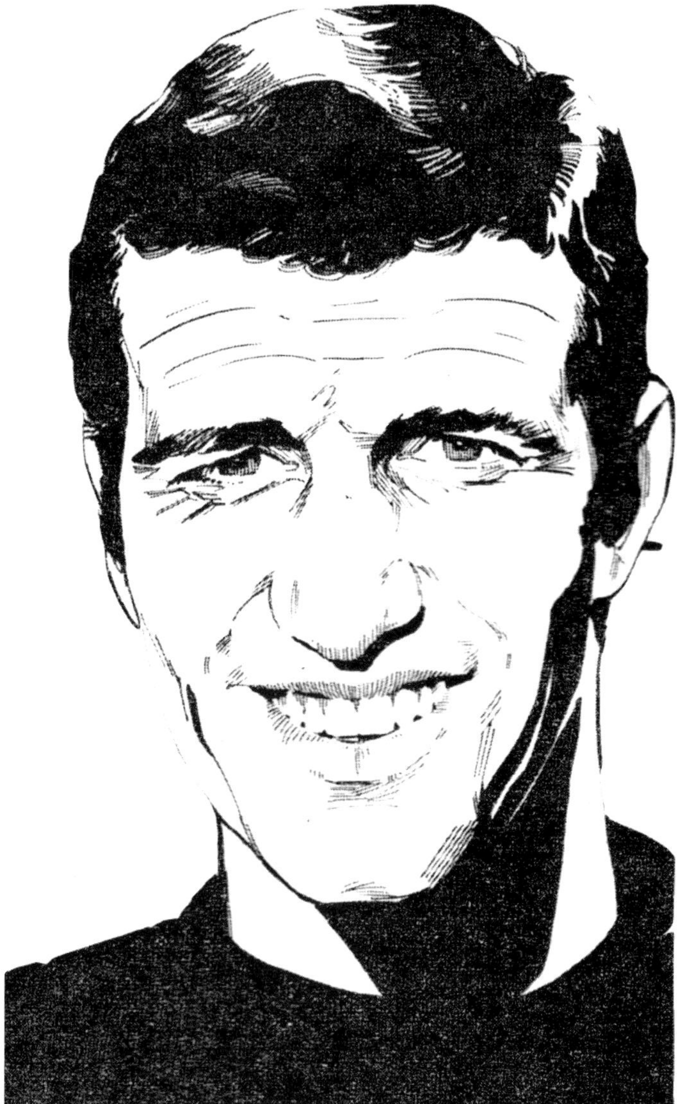

Peter Osgood visited me twice for lunches at Cafe Blue in Virginia Water, where I lived at the time, to talk about book projects. He brought along a signed limited edition photograph of himself for my late father-in-law Ken Udall, it was a treasured item for him. Ossie also put his name to a Foreword to my book *Chelsea Century* published by Blake Books.

During our chats the one-time darling of the Chelsea faithful who once stood on the notorious Shed End and adored this big, bold and aggressive centre-forward with the long side burns leading them to glory at home and abroad, made no secret of his views about the modern day club.

His love affair with Chelsea remained as strong as ever with the arrival of Russian oligarch Roman Abramovich. Ossie told me, "It is a fantastic time to be a Chelsea fan, to be a Chelsea player, and generally to have any connection with the club… while someone like Roman Abramovich owns the club and José Mourinho manages the team, it won't only be True Blue fans fascinated by events at the Bridge. As long as Abramovich is there, the future is just fantastic, mind boggling. Chelsea have a fabulous team already and with Abramovich they can go out and buy even more great players and be a force to be reckoned with for years to come. What Mourinho has achieved in such a short space of time as the coach is equally unbelievable. Mourinho is cocky, arrogant, and confident, but all in a nice way, a positive way. The players think the world of him and there is a remarkable camaraderie among them and with that kind of atmosphere and the quality of their players, Chelsea can be a force to be reckoned with."

Of course, every word came to pass, and more so, as Ossie went on, "I've met José a couple of times and introduced my son Darren to him, and he came across as one of the game's absolute gentleman. I was welcome at Stamford Bridge any time, which is more than I used to get when Ken Bates was in control of the club! But the supporters are only really interested in the players, the results and the performances, and under Mourinho the club have an awesome team that can only get better and better and is guaranteed to fill the stadium all the time."

Despite his deep and unflinching affection for the club he played for with such pride and goalscoring prowess, he failed to persuade those running the club on behalf of the owner, that he should be given access to write a book I had suggested, to help him through his period of financial stress. We talked a great deal of a book entitled *The Bridge*, Inside Out, and he was enthused

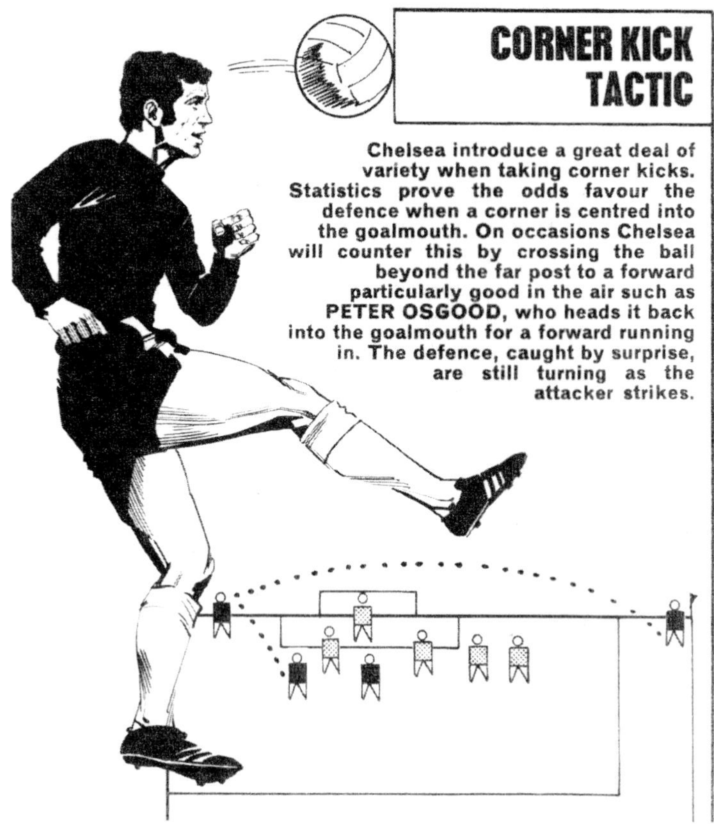

about the idea and keen to pursue it. The plan was for Ossie to interview all the component parts that make up a football club from the inside so the fans on the outside would finally get a real view of what goes on inside their club. I told him the only way it would work was that a publisher would offer a good advance and would gain the approval of the club to make it sort of official. We spoke to Mark Mitchinson, who ran Samsung back then, and he was eager to help out any way he could, but Ossie couldn't gain the authorisation he asked for, as the club had their own contract to promote authorised books sold in their Megastore. It was something I felt they could make an exception for, or worked with their official publisher.

It was a shock to Ossie when he was rejected and it was a terrible shock to me and the footballing world when the news broke of Ossie's premature death just a few months later!

While Ossie felt forgotten by the powers that be at his beloved Chelsea, no-one will ever forget his contribution on the pitch. Fewer than 8,000 people saw a 17 year-old Osgood make his first team debut in the last eight of the League Cup on December 16, 1964. He netted both goals in this League Cup 2-0 replay win against Workington Town, the first coming in the 82nd minute having already netted around 30 goals in 1964-65 in youth and reserve team football.

One of Ossie's earliest heroics occurred in the FA Cup against Liverpool on January 22, 1966. Chelsea stunned the FA Cup holders at Anfield, coming from a goal down in the third round. Roger Hunt had given the hosts a first minute lead, but six minutes later Osgood headed home after Barry Bridges and George Graham had combined to send the ball into the area. Osgood played in a deep-lying centre-forward role which caused Liverpool problems. Seven days later Chelsea prepared for an epic European tie against AS Roma who had suggested in the media that they would make a bid for Osgood and Blackpool's Alan Ball. It came to nothing, but highlighted the impact Ossie was having. Against Burnley at Turf Moor, Ossie scored twice, but it was the winner after 54 minutes that made headlines, a run from the halfway line that saw him beat three before shooting past Adam Blacklaw.

Osgood was destined to be capped by England but then on a chilly night at Bloomfield Road, Emlyn Hughes tackled the 19 year-old breaking his right leg. Ossie signalled for a stretcher, "It was no-one's fault," said Osgood, "ee were both going for the ball. He got it first and his boot was blocking the ball as I connected." The League Cup tie ended one apiece on October 5, 1966. Osgood took time to regain his confidence after his broken leg but got his first under-23 cap at Swansea. He scored, latching onto a John Hollins free-kick and shooting left-footed into the top corner. Dave Sexton shifted Osgood into midfield at Leicester, an unexpected switch that brought a 4-1 win at Filbert Street. Wearing the unfamiliar number 4, he showed he had not lost any of his talent. Two goals confirmed he was on the way back to being at his best as Sir Alf Ramsey watched on. Ossie was desperate to play for England. The crowd continued to chant, "Ossie for England".

Dave Sexton stumbled across an ideal partner for Osgood

in Ian Hutchinson, a short-lived but quite spectacular front-line pairing. Ossie's most prolific spell came in 1969 as the turned into unexpected title contenders. Ossie felt sorry for Crystal Palace after a 5-1 win at Selhurst Park saying, "By the time the fourth goal went in, I was feeling a bit embarrassed."

Title rivals Leeds won 5-2 at the Bridge but Chelsea bounced back by winning through to the fifth round of the FA Cup in 1970, comfortably disposing of relegation-bound Sunderland. Osgood's hat-trick helped cement his place in the England squad for the forthcoming game with Belgium. One report described Osgood as being "as swift as a cobra".

Before the infamous cup tie with Leeds, Osgood made his England debut in Brussels on February 25, 1970 against a side that had already qualified for the World Cup in Mexico. He was involved in England's first goal, scored by Alan Ball, and Sir Alf was delighted: "Osgood had a great first match for England," pronounced the England boss.

For all his flair, skill on the ground, power in the air and some formidable goals, Peter will be best remembered for his part in the most brutal game of all time, the 1970 FA Cup final replay. Osgood had been having an ongoing battle with Jack Charlton, where several headbutts were thrown, knees smashed into sides and some colourful language used for good measure. As the game wore on and the light faded above Old Trafford, the violence taking place on its pitch only increased. Osgood fouled Charlton, who immediately leapt to his feet and barged the striker to the turf - an immediate act of retribution from the Leeds centre-back. It was another attempted act of revenge from Charlton that cost Leeds their lead with the defender leaving Osgood unmarked to score as he went off in search of a Chelsea player who had whacked his thigh moments earlier. Osgood's iconic flying header for the equaliser took the game into extra time. Chelsea went on to win the cup with David Webb scoring the winner in the 104th minute.

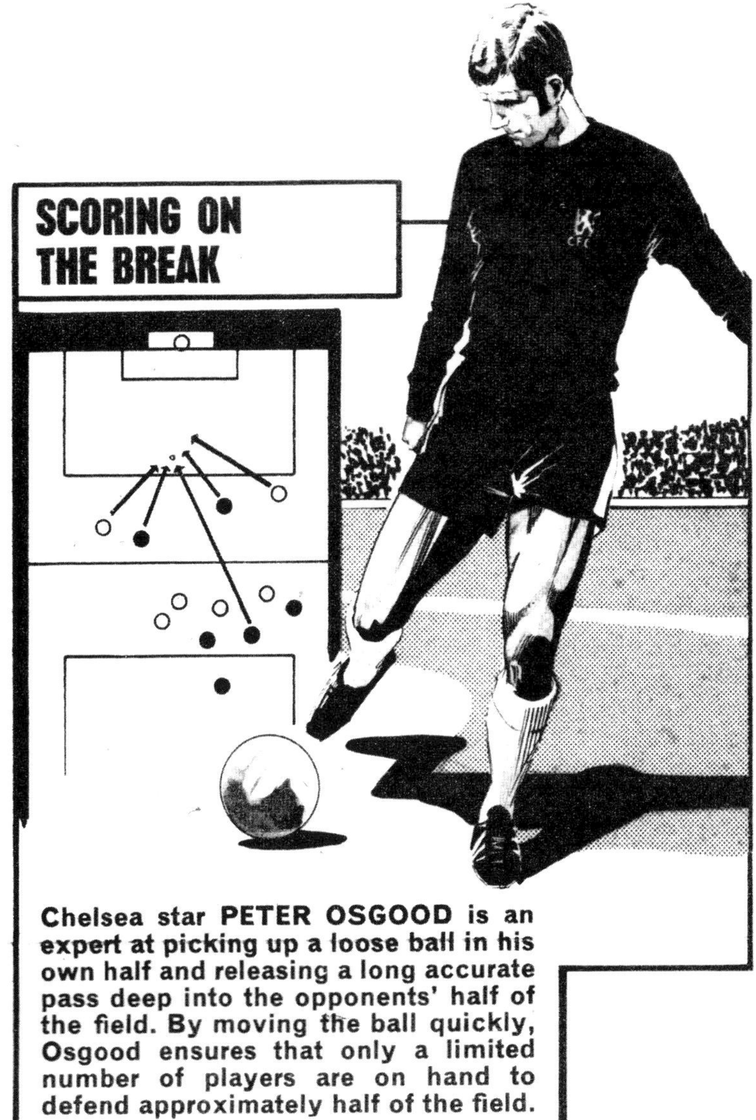

Chelsea star PETER OSGOOD is an expert at picking up a loose ball in his own half and releasing a long accurate pass deep into the opponents' half of the field. By moving the ball quickly, Osgood ensures that only a limited number of players are on hand to defend approximately half of the field.

Osgood's 78th minute diving header from Charlie Cooke's cross is part of Chelsea folklore. Osgood scored in every round up to the final but wasn't on the scoresheet at Wembley in the 2-2 classic. At Old Trafford, he became one of the few players to have found the net in every round. He scored eight in the competition, including a hat-trick at Loftus Road as Chelsea beat QPR 4-2 in round six.

Osgood had a habit of getting booked in the late sixties and early seventies, often for dissent. The FA disciplinary committee made an example of him, banning him for 10 games. By the time he returned Chelsea's season had run out of steam and by late March they were on the brink of elimination in the European Cup-Winners' Cup after losing 2-0 in the first leg of the quarter-final to Bruges. Osgood was thrown into the second leg, scoring twice in an incredible night at Stamford Bridge. The tie went to extra time and Chelsea added two goals to win 4-0 and go through to meet Manchester City in the semi-finals.

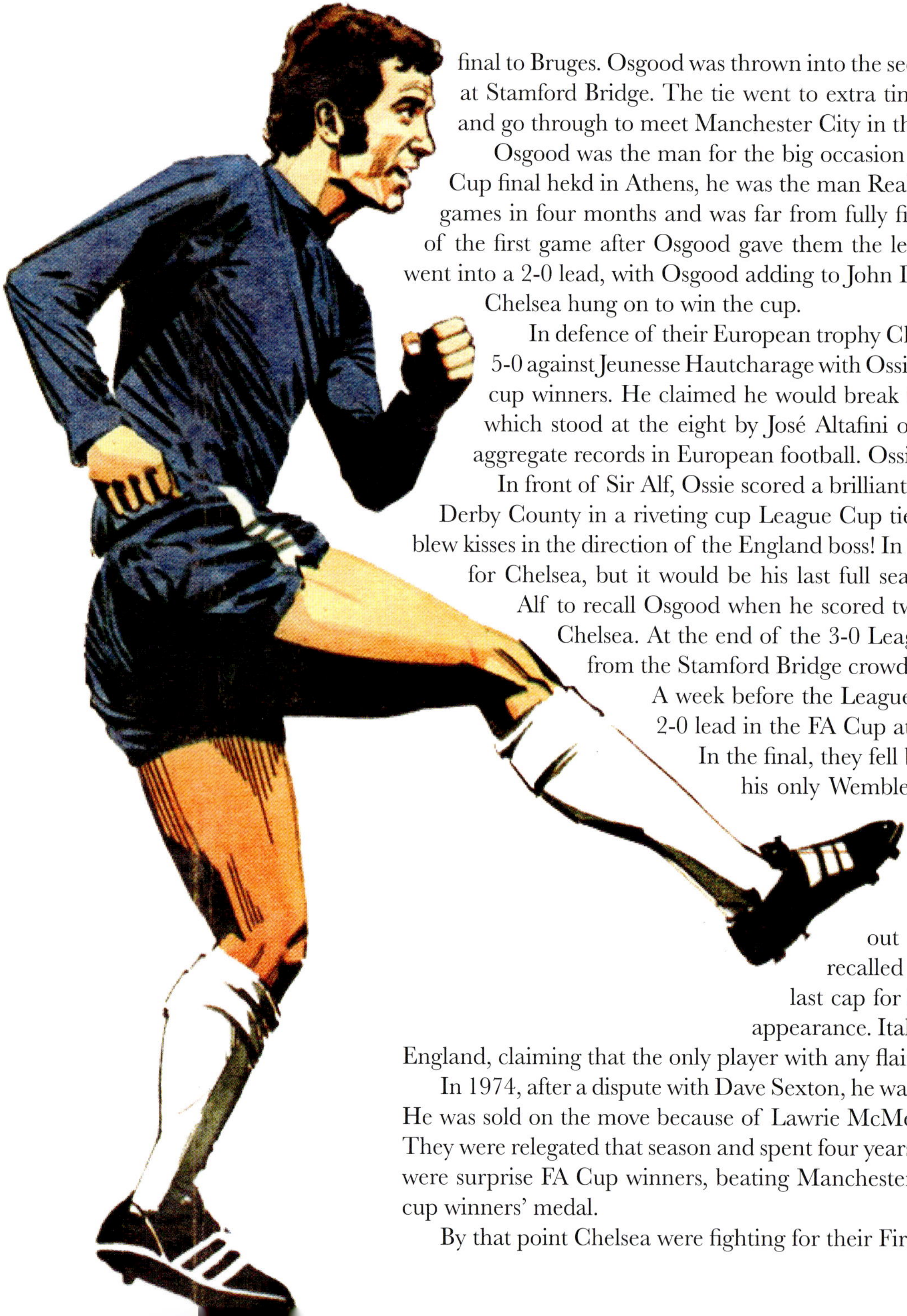

Osgood was the man for the big occasion and in the two games in the Cup-Winners' Cup final hekd in Athens, he was the man Real Madrid feared. Ossie had only played four games in four months and was far from fully fit. Chelsea were denied in the final seconds of the first game after Osgood gave them the lead after 56 minutes, but in the replay they went into a 2-0 lead, with Osgood adding to John Dempsey's opener. Real pulled one back but Chelsea hung on to win the cup.

In defence of their European trophy Chelsea won the first leg of their first round tie 5-0 against Jeunesse Hautcharage with Ossie scoring a hat-trick against the Luxembourg cup winners. He claimed he would break the individual scoring record over two legs, which stood at the eight by José Altafini of AC Milan. Chelsea won 13-0 to beat all aggregate records in European football. Ossie scored five, equalling Altafini's haul.

In front of Sir Alf, Ossie scored a brilliant volleyed goal to clinch a 3-2 victory against Derby County in a riveting cup League Cup tie. When he scored, he ran to the stand and blew kisses in the direction of the England boss! In 1972-73, he played some of his best football for Chelsea, but it would be his last full season for the club. The media pressured Sir Alf to recall Osgood when he scored twice to secure his 100th and 101st goals for Chelsea. At the end of the 3-0 League Cup tie, he received a personal ovation from the Stamford Bridge crowd.

A week before the League Cup Final in 1972, Chelsea threw away a 2-0 lead in the FA Cup at Orient and were victims of a giant-killing. In the final, they fell behind to an early goal but Ossie equalised, his only Wembley goal. Stoke won 2-1 as Chelsea failed to win their third trophy in as many seasons. It was arguably the beginning of the end of the club's most charismatic team.

Just a month after England were knock-out of the World Cup by Poland, England recalled Osgood to lead the line against Italy; his last cap for his country. It was also Bobby Moore's last appearance. Italy's coach, Franco Valcareggi, was critical of England, claiming that the only player with any flair was Osgood.

In 1974, after a dispute with Dave Sexton, he was transferred to Southampton for £275,000. He was sold on the move because of Lawrie McMenemy and linking up with Mick Channon. They were relegated that season and spent four years in the Second Division. In 1976, the Saints were surprise FA Cup winners, beating Manchester United 1-0 as Ossie picked up his second cup winners' medal.

By that point Chelsea were fighting for their First Division lives and re-signed Osgood after

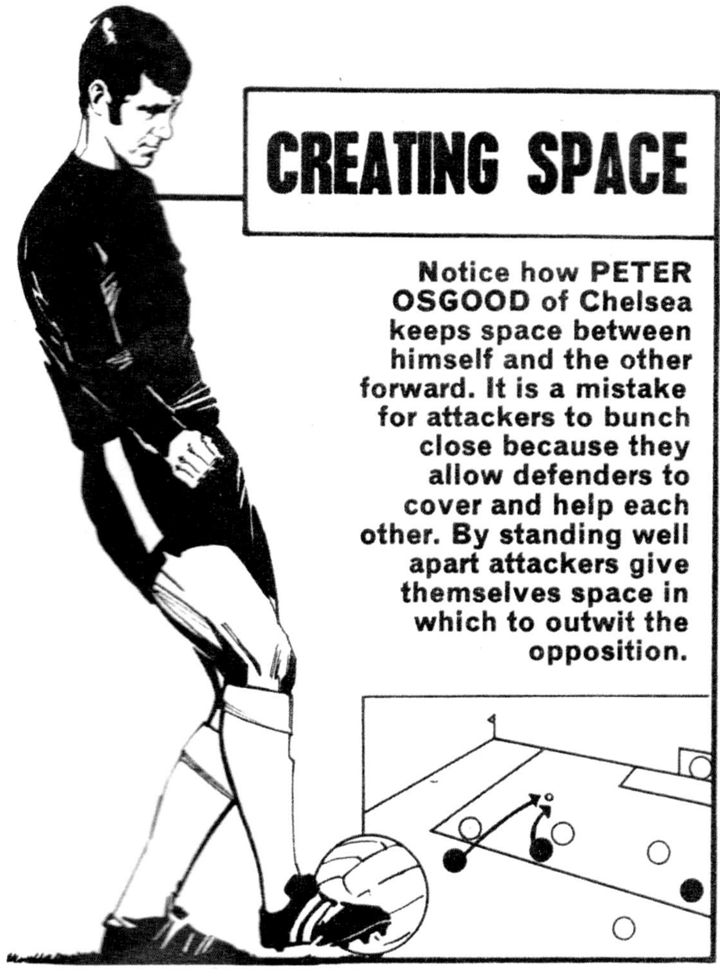

he had endured an injury-stricken period in the US. While the crowd were overjoyed at their hero's return, he was unable to perform a miracle. In his first game he headed Chelsea in front at Middlesbrough, but by the final whistle, the extent of the club's problems was made clear as the Blues had crashed 7-2 at Ayresome Park. Peter left the club in September 1979.

Ossie passed away on March 1 2006. Tributes were paid at the following two games and that same year a memorial service was held at Stamford Bridge during which Peter's ashes were interred under the penalty spot at the Shed end of the pitch. Family, friends, former team-mates and many fans were in attendance. The first anniversary of his passing saw a more permanent memorial announced. Now, upon entering via the Britannia Entrance, there is a statue of Peter Osgood. It is the only statue at Stamford Bridge. Initially it was to be life-sized bust, located in the East Stand executive club reception, but after correspondence with supporters, a more public position outside the stadium was confirmed. Peter's widow Lynn was involved in the process, including choosing the right design which grew from the original idea for a bust into a full statue. The sculptor, Philip Jackson, had created the statues of Sir Bobby Moore and Sir Alf Ramsey at Wembley Stadium, Sir Matt Busby and Sir Alex Ferguson at Old Trafford and away from football, the Queen Mother's memorial on The Mall in central London, the Queen's equestrian sculpture at Windsor and Mahatma Gandhi's in Parliament Square in Westminster.

"I put Ossie in [the team] straight away and he was a revelation. He was great in the air, he had two great feet, he was quick, skilful, brave. He didn't have a lot after that," joked Tommy Docherty at the unveiling. Docherty was the manager when the teenage player broke through and is now sadly deceased too, as is Peter Bonetti who also addressed the gathering added,. "Once you met him [Osgood] you never forgot him and that is why the fans really idolised him because he used to get along with them," he said. "Without a doubt he should be the one with a statue here."

Two days later, when Chelsea beat Arsenal, supporters had their chance to view the new addition to the Stamford Bridge landscape. There is a time capsule buried underneath the statue which contains a copy of the 1970 FA Cup final replay programme, a replica 1970 team shirt and a poem, selected by Lynn Osgood from many entries to a competition on chelseafc.com. "It's amazing," she said, speaking to the same website having seen the statue in all its glory. "You talk about it for a long time when it is a work in progress but it is completely overwhelming seeing it full size. I was a nervous wreck before that moment because you have in your mind's eye what it is going to look like, but having seen it, it's a thousand times better than I imagined. It depicts him perfectly. It's definitely got his character and personality - The King of Stamford Bridge."

So what made Ossie stand out? He wasn't a prolific goalscorer

OSSIE'S ON HIS OWN

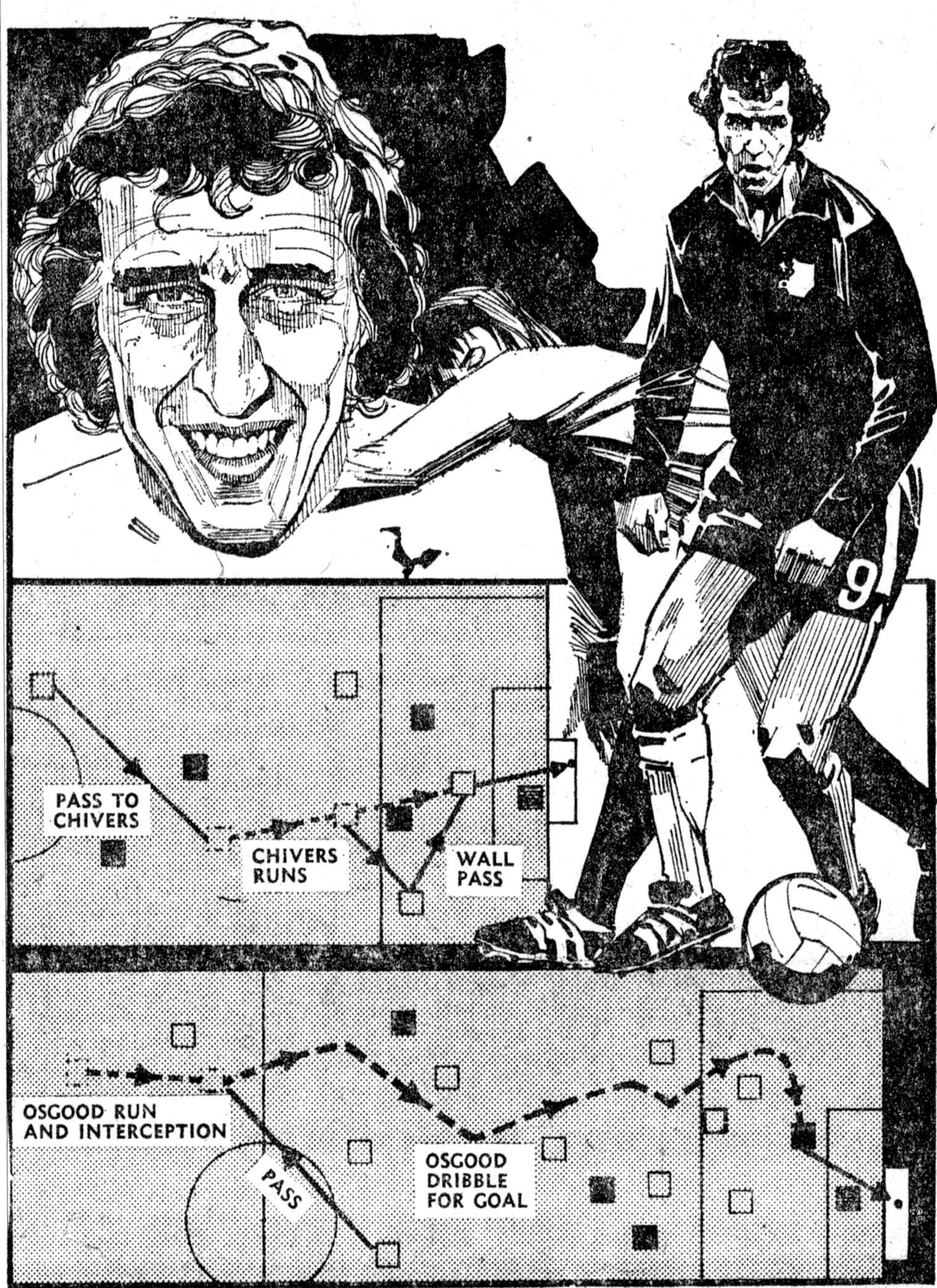

At one time Martin Chivers threatened to be the world's no.1 striker - but that threat has long since died. A truly world-class player can do it on his own but Chivers, in common with 98 per cent of strikers, can't.

They need players around them to make them perform well, players to win the ball for them and to act as walls when beating opponents.

Peter Osgood stands alone as the best all-round striker in the Football League. Osgood is a world class footballer. He doesn't need other players to make him play.

Agreed, he's not the greatest at winning the ball for himself but what he lacks physically he more than makes up for mentally.

He reads the game so brilliantly. He's always getting into positions to intercept passes and then set up an attack - or when it's on, to go it alone - and there's nobody cooler than Osgood when it comes to knocking in chances inside the box.

If there's any justice in football not only will Osgood play for England against Italy this week, he will also collect the many caps he has been denied.

WILLIE MORGAN
Manchester United

compared to some of the other legendary strikers who have graced this football club, while others could certainly claim to be more skilful or have led the club to the highest honours in the game. None, however, connected with the supporters quite like Ossie. A Chelsea career which produced 150 goals across 380 appearances was accompanied by many more tales away from the football field. Plenty of those stories have been told time and time again. Instead, we're focusing on the lesser told tales from the beginning of this Chelsea legend's career and how those early experiences, particularly under Docherty, shaped a career and a life which touched so many Blues supporters along the way.

Osgood always seemed destined for a career at the top level of sport. He was an all-rounder as a kid, representing Dedworth Secondary Modern at football, cricket, basketball and tennis. But when he left school at 15 to work in an office in Slough, soon to become a bricklayer working alongside his father, his football dream seemed to be slipping away. Though he was excelling for local sides Spital Old Boys and Windsor Corinthians – turning out for one on the Saturday and the other the following morning – and trial opportunities arose with Reading and Arsenal, the side he had followed as a boy, it wasn't until his uncle Bob wrote to Chelsea that he gave himself a chance. With the words of Bob ringing in his ears – 'Come on now, you can't let me down' – he grasped it with both hands.

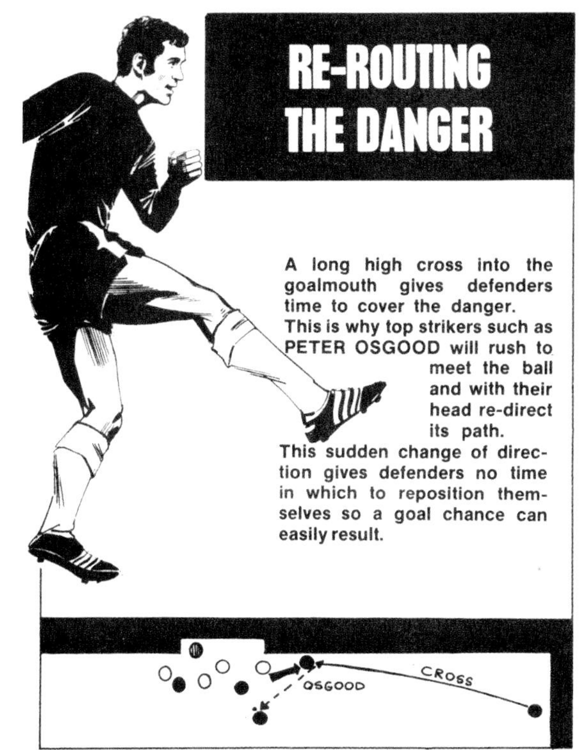

Dickie Foss, the former Blues half-back and the man running what was already being talked about in football circles as one of the finest youth set-ups in the land, took all of 30 minutes to make his mind up. 'You had natural ability,' he told Osgood. 'You moved well, hit the ball with both feet instinctively. It was the way you played the ball rather than what you did it with it that impressed me.' Funnily enough, his early performances in the youth and reserve sides were also met with approval by a man whose Chelsea goal tally he would later go on to equal: Roy Bentley. 'His father was working at Buckingham Palace,' recalled the man who captained Chelsea to the club's first championship in 1955, 'and I was talking to him about this up and coming footballer, not knowing he was Peter's father. I used to go and watch the youngsters and you didn't need to know much to see he had something, and I knew he was going to be great.'

Only 10 months later The Man From Uncle – as his new team-mates wryly dubbed him – had stepped up into the first team, just the latest diamond to shine under Docherty's infectiously enthusiastic management. "I've always been a great believer that if you're good enough, you're old enough," said the Doc, years later, when evaluating Osgood. "People said to me, 'He's a good player but he's got no experience.' You can't just say to a player here's five years' experience, though. He's got to go and play; good and bad, have setbacks and so on. We had a wealth of talent, and I thought, 'What are they playing in the youth team for? They're too good for the youth team.' So, I started bringing them into the first team." Doc was repaid by Ossie netting twice on his debut in a League Cup tie against Workington. The next morning the 17-year-old bought a copy of each newspaper to begin his first scrapbook. Although he had to wait for another chance, with the Blues going for glory in all three domestic competitions right up until the final weeks of the 1964/65 season, England came calling and handed him a call-up for a youth tournament dubbed 'the little World Cup'. Ossie was named as the best player in the competition, despite England losing the final to East Germany. Without his young charge having so much as graced the turf in a First Division match, Docherty was already tipping him for the top. "I'd like to bet you fellows a year's wages that my centre-forward Peter Osgood could, if he tried a little harder, be England's centre-forward for the 1966 World Cup," he told the assembled hacks ahead of the new season. His big chance to impress Alf Ramsey came in a practice match for the Three Lions – against his Chelsea team-mates! Looking for a tune up ahead of their match against Wales, but without the services of centre-forward Alan Peacock, Ossie was 'loaned' to England. He duly found the back of the net not once, but twice, and clearly enjoyed getting one over on his mate Peter Bonetti between the sticks for the Blues. "Pick that one out, Catty," he exclaimed after netting his second.

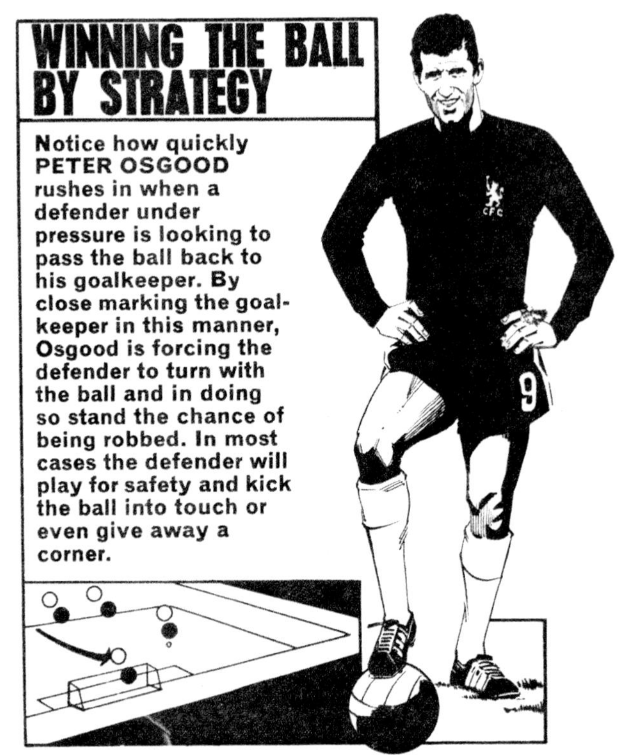

It wasn't long before he was given an extended run in Chelsea's starting line-up at the expense of crowd favourite Barry Bridges, who had been involved in the infamous Blackpool incident the previous season and was soon to be heading for the exit door. Docherty, famously, had told Osgood not to panic if things didn't start off according to plan – no matter what, he would be given a 10-game run to show his worth. After a slow start he scored a wonder goal in the snow at Villa Park, beating four men and hammering home from a tight angle. Others were beginning to stand up and take notice. With the Blues enjoying an extended run in Europe for the first time, seeing off Italian giants Roma and AC Milan, envious glances were being cast from Serie A. Milan manager Nils Liedolhm, one of the all-time greats, predicted that Osgood would be 'the star of England's national side'. Soon, the club were in receipt of, as Ossie put it, a 'gigantic offer' from an Italian club. He had grown up idolising Jimmy Greaves and, perhaps wary of following his hero's ill-fated decision to leave Chelsea to chase the lira, the idea wasn't even entertained. Besides, the club had just helped him celebrate his 19th birthday by giving him a house near Twickenham.

Before his teenage years were out, however, fate was to deal Osgood a cruel hand. In the space of 18 months he had gone from being paid £10 as a bricklayer to being rated as one of English football's brightest talents, but his career soon lay in tatters. A broken leg, suffered in a challenge with Blackpool's Emlyn Hughes, was to rule him out of the game for a year. As well as the physical scars left by such an injury, the manner of the break affected him mentally.

Watching footage of Osgood pre- and post-injury is akin to comparing two different players. In one clip from a game at Anfield, the speed and grace with which this gangly centre-forward bursts through banks of midfielders and defenders is startling; after his comeback, he had lost not one, but maybe even two yards of pace, noticeably filling himself out in order to deal with the bruising centre-halves he faced on a weekly basis. As any great player should, he adapted. After a spell in midfield during the 1968/69 season, his now legendary strike partnership with Ian Hutchinson was struck up in the following campaign. For every yard of pace he had lost on the ground, he regained it in his head, aided by a velcro-like first touch and preying on the apprehension of defenders who perhaps began to think twice about giving a clump to a bloke who was now well versed in the dark arts of the game. FA Cup glory, of course, was to follow and Osgood was a scorer in every round – a feat which hasn't been achieved since – before he led Chelsea to European silverware in the Cup Winners' Cup. Nobody could touch him as the King of Stamford Bridge.

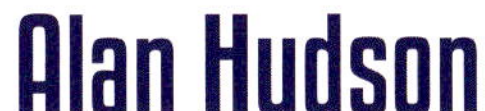

Alan Hudson

Alan Hudson and I often bumped into each other in the Chelsea 'Big Easy' sipping a beer by the bar when I lived not far from Stamford Bridge just off the King's Road. Alan was also my guest at a number of Chelsea related events, and I was invited to his book launch in one of his favourite King's Road pubs when George Best came in late, spotted me, and sat down and asked me to write his book - which turned out to be his last.

Alan was one of football's midfield mavericks who was never quite trusted by the rigid 4-4-2 managers that dominated the game in the seventies, and so he never won as many caps as his talents deserved, but the guy from the wrong side of the Chelsea tracks refused to compromise his beliefs.

Born and brought up near the King's Road, Alan was initially rejected by his boyhood club Fulham before signing schoolboy forms with Chelsea and made his debut for the Blues in 1969 in a 5-0 defeat to Southampton, but it was a season later, together with the combined talents of Peter Osgood and Charlie Cooke, that Alan came to national attention in a flamboyant team that re-defined Chelsea in the minds of the general public and led to the club finishing third in the First Division. Yet, having played in every round of the 1970 cup run, Alan was brought down by injury and missed the infamous final and replay.

Nevertheless he did play a key role in Chelsea winning the Cup Winners' Cup the following season with a superb performance in the replayed final against Real Madrid in Athens. Alan helped Chelsea to another cup final in 1972 when Chelsea lost 2-1 to Stoke City in the League Cup but both he and Peter Osgood were transfer listed in 1974 after falling out with manager Dave Sexton and Alan moved on to Stoke City.

In later life misfortune dogged Alan; he has been made homeless on more than one occasion, was run over and spent 59 days in a coma and then lost all his injury compensation in a fraudulent property deal. Yet he wrote one of the most well-received football biographies about life in the game in the 1970s as well as several other books and a novel.

Alan would often send me his thoughts, and they were always long, detailed and provocative. Here are some of his thoughts about the player he considered the best he had ever seen.

THE BEST

When I was young and dreaming of becoming a player, us kids would watch *Match of the Day*, which I think was on at around 5.30 in those days, and after watching our heroes we would go into our 'Cage' and try to emulate them or *be* them playing street football. Law, Best and Charlton were the biggest ticket in town – then as now Manchester United would fill every ground wherever they went. Law was the very first complete 'Showman' although Derek Dougan did not do a bad job at Wolves, but Denis was 'The Lawman', the scorer of 46 goals in 1963-64 including seven hat-tricks! Soon the young George Best took over and sent shivers down the spine of defenders, blondes and brunettes all over the planet. I was fifteen when Bobby Moore carried off the World Cup, but it was the Belfast Boy who was the 'Best on the Planet' and that was his downfall, purely and simply because he could never show his incredible talent on the biggest stage every four years because of his Irish heritage, where only he and Pat Jennings, arguably the best goalkeeper around at that time, were world class. I was very fortunate to have played with and against both of them. Even more important I went on to be good friends with them both. I first played against George when I was eighteen after he had tortured the likes of Benfica with that unforgettable goal at Wembley when he walked it into the net. He was hailed as The Fifth Beatle and in some respects was an even bigger figure than John, Paul, George and Ringo because you could still pay to see him perform in your town years after The Beatles had stopped touring. He was football's first 'Pop Star' and although he did not make music he weaved his magic to the sound of my book title *The Working Man's Ballet.*

I had wonderful times in his clubs in both London and Manchester and was allowed in to see him on his first day in The Cromwell Hospital to give him not only mine, but the best wishes of all of those who lived around him in Chelsea. We were never what you might call bosom buddies but there was a great respect between us and I remember him sending me a letter from his club Oscar's in Manchester after my three-year England ban, taking time out to tell me in a few words that I was by far the best player in the country and go and show those who gave me such a harsh sentence on the field. The pitch was where Best did his talking; he used it as a stage to show your opponents on and off the field just who was who and who wasn't 'The Best', which he certainly was.

As with Bobby Moore, I cherished his friendship and out of everything good and bad in playing the game we were born to play, I can hold that closest to my heart, because having watched such people perform and then being on the same field was something to behold at such close quarters. To have the ball at my feet at Old Trafford in front of sixty thousand people knowing they wanted George to have it was my greatest triumph and I did this on many occasions, actually getting possession with only one thing in my mind, 'Keep it away from George Best' and by doing that we had so much more of a chance of coming away with the points, which we did so often. I still watch him on YouTube and as I sip my V&O I still keep him here in my room with me and I really should have a chilled bottle of Bubbly in my fridge just in case he turns up, because that was what he did. George did things that others could not do and that is why he was...

The Best On The Planet!

CHELSEA v LEEDS

Everyone knows the thuggery that existed when Chelsea confronted Leeds United in both games of the 1970 FA Cup Final, but there was generally an edge to all of their contests. Here are some thoughts that Alan sent me:

My early career at Chelsea had been curtailed after being diagnosed with Osgood-Schlatters Disease, a knee joint problem through wear and tear of playing in the streets in and around Upcerne Road, just off Lots Road. Strange how three years on I went down that hole in the Hawthorns which led to my not being able to perform on hard surfaces, through an injury far worse than any break - a ligament injury can be horrendous.

Many a youngster would have been told "unlucky son" and turned away but Tommy Docherty saw enough in me to give me a job cleaning anything that moved in and around the Stamford Bridge Dressing Room to keep me in and around the squad. On top of that he gave me the great opportunity to travel with the first team which I learned years later to help other young players, the experience was invaluable, however, there was one game that put a seed of doubt about becoming a player, and it wasn't my debut when we got beat 5-0 at the Dell! Southampton's team that day contained three players who I would come across later in life; Jimmy Gabriel, who signed me for Seattle Sounders, Ron Davies, who joined us there, and Mick Channon, who I played with in both the Under 23's and full international team and against

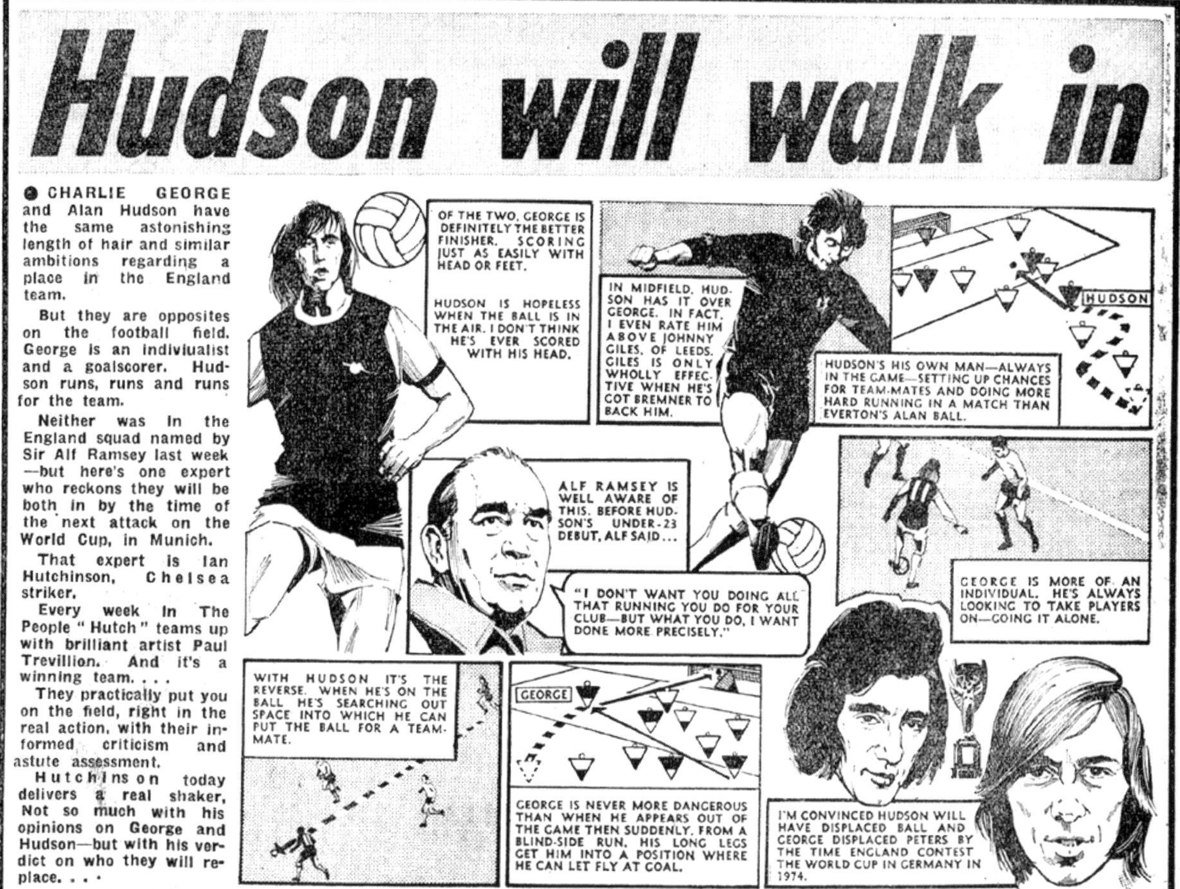

Hudson will walk in

● CHARLIE GEORGE and Alan Hudson have the same astonishing length of hair and similar ambitions regarding a place in the England team.

But they are opposites on the football field. George is an indiviualist and a goalscorer. Hudson runs, runs and runs for the team.

Neither was in the England squad named by Sir Alf Ramsey last week—but here's one expert who reckons they will be both in by the time of the next attack on the World Cup, in Munich.

That expert is Ian Hutchinson, Chelsea striker.

Every week in The People "Hutch" teams up with brilliant artist Paul Trevillion. And it's a winning team. . . .

They practically put you on the field, right in the real action, with their informed criticism and astute assessment.

Hutchinson today delivers a real shaker. Not so much with his opinions on George and Hudson—but with his verdict on who they will replace. . . .

OF THE TWO, GEORGE IS DEFINITELY THE BETTER FINISHER. SCORING JUST AS EASILY WITH HEAD OR FEET.

HUDSON IS HOPELESS WHEN THE BALL IS IN THE AIR. I DON'T THINK HE'S EVER SCORED WITH HIS HEAD.

IN MIDFIELD, HUDSON HAS IT OVER GEORGE. IN FACT, I EVEN RATE HIM ABOVE JOHNNY GILES, OF LEEDS. GILES IS ONLY WHOLLY EFFECTIVE WHEN HE'S GOT BREMNER TO BACK HIM.

HUDSON

HUDSON'S HIS OWN MAN—ALWAYS IN THE GAME—SETTING UP CHANCES FOR TEAM-MATES AND DOING MORE HARD RUNNING IN A MATCH THAN EVERTON'S ALAN BALL.

ALF RAMSEY IS WELL AWARE OF THIS. BEFORE HUDSON'S UNDER-23 DEBUT, ALF SAID . . .

"I DON'T WANT YOU DOING ALL THAT RUNNING YOU DO FOR YOUR CLUB—BUT WHAT YOU DO, I WANT DONE MORE PRECISELY."

GEORGE IS MORE OF AN INDIVIDUAL. HE'S ALWAYS LOOKING TO TAKE PLAYERS ON—GOING IT ALONE.

WITH HUDSON IT'S THE REVERSE. WHEN HE'S ON THE BALL HE'S SEARCHING OUT SPACE INTO WHICH HE CAN PUT THE BALL FOR A TEAM-MATE.

GEORGE

GEORGE IS NEVER MORE DANGEROUS THAN WHEN HE APPEARS OUT OF THE GAME THEN SUDDENLY, FROM A BLIND-SIDE RUN, HIS LONG LEGS GET HIM INTO A POSITION WHERE HE CAN LET FLY AT GOAL.

I'M CONVINCED HUDSON WILL HAVE DISPLACED BALL AND GEORGE DISPLACED PETERS BY THE TIME ENGLAND CONTEST THE WORLD CUP IN GERMANY IN 1974.

World Champions West Germany at Wembley.

As bad as my debut against Southampton was, it was nowhere near as damaging as this match at Elland Road and you might remember them beating up the Saints pretty badly some time later and scoring a goal with a record number of passes that was featured on *Match Of The Day* with the commentator saying they were toying with the opposition. On Saturday, 7 October 1967 this Leeds United team were in full cry, they should have been glorious to watch but as always there is a downside – in my opinion Leeds' downside was Don Revie. It has to be said that by 1967 this Leeds team were useful, but you'll notice they were missing a vital link - a player to replace Bobby Collins. His replacement was a player who I have heard called many a different name from 'The Poison Dwarf' to 'The Silent Assassin' but whatever he was, Johnny Giles was a magnificent inside-forward and he and Bremner, a man of similar build (who said you're too small?) started the real Leeds United Revolution, a revolution of hatred perhaps. Make no mistake, if you weren't in the right frame of mind they'd tear you limb from limb with their immaculate passing and deceitful challenges.

In this day and age we watch the "new" face of football which is leap years behind the way Leeds United played not only the game but went about winning it, they made the gangsters in two of the greatest movies ever produced, *The Godfather* and *The Irishman*, look like baby-sitters. No pulling shirts. No diving. No time for shirking. They were simply a football club who stood alone and whilst watching them let seven goals into their net in Manchester a few days ago my mind couldn't help but rush back to this match.

If that game is remembered fondly in Leeds, there are two matches that are never discussed in that part of Yorkshire, firstly the FA Cup final replay of 1970 when Blue Fire met White Fire. Yet even better for me was when they led 2-0 at the Old Vic in the Potteries having swaggered on their way to surpassing their record 29 match unbeaten run when it all went pear-shaped with Stoke winning 3-2 and I scored my first goal for the Potters. The red and white striped 1974/75 Stoke City team also had fire. The reason I write about these matches is because had they won in both these matches it would have been the main talking point in pubs around Elland Road for years - we silenced that talk.

To sit on the touchline that horrific day in 1967 as a 16-year-old apprentice watching your team get smashed 7-0 was frightening knowing that one day you'd be on the same field adding to the fun. Another thought is that among the seven different scorers was Jimmy Greenhoff, a player who was kicked out of Elland Road and ignored by Revie eight years later as England manager, yet was one of the finest players I have ever had the pleasure to have been involved with on the same football field. Within a few months that Leeds team had changed, as youll see from the team sheet there was no Johnny Giles or Allan Clarke, two players who added guile and goals along with brutality. I watched Clarke as a Fulham supporter before he left for Leicester City and onto Leeds United. Another man I will only remember for one thing and that is walking into George Best's Night Club in Manchester standing in the corner on our entrance and one of Revie's squad of players commenting, "The Don won't be happy with you lot" and he wasn't, especially with Geoff Salmons who got in the same elevator as him at 3am when the curfew was 11pm! It was Sammy's fault as I called him several times about our mini-cab being there and his face was a picture as he came into our room to explain, "That's my international career over, old love," as indeed it was, that really was the end for Sammy, who himself was a Yorkshireman, from Mexborough in fact, but Don never forgot those two matches and one in particular when Sammy played a big part in stopping them break that record.

Look at this, ouch!

LEEDS UNITED 7 CHELSEA 0 (40,460)

Scorers: Johanneson, Greenhoff, Charlton, Lorimer, Gray, Hinton (og), Bremner.

Leeds United: Sprake; Reaney, Madeley; Bremner, Charlton, Hunter; Greenhoff, Lorimer, Jones (Hibbitt), Gray, Johanesson.

Chelsea: Bonetti; Thomson, Hinton; Harris, Butler, Hollins; Boyle, Cooke, Osgood, Baldwin, McCreadie.

Referee: K.Dagnall (Bolton).

On the eve of Chelsea's Division One game at Elland Road, manager Tommy Docherty quit for 'personal reasons' within hours of being suspended by the FA over incidents on the club's tour of Bermuda.

HUDSON COULD TAKE OVER, SAYS SEXTON

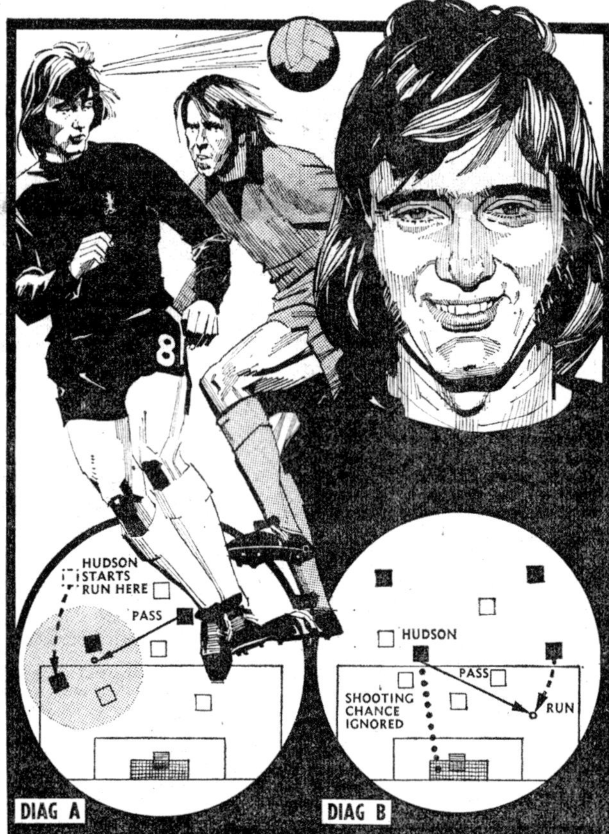

TEXT AND DRAWINGS BY TREVILLION

'ALAN HUDSON is magic at his best — a world-class player. Unfortunately he's lost a little of his appetite for the game.

His work-rate can be as high as Alan Ball's. When he's playing like that he's always in the game — either dropping back to make a 2-against-1 situation with one of our defenders, or racing upfield to make it 2-against-1 when one of our attackers receives a pass. (Diagram A.)

Change of pace is his outstanding attribute — he'll pick up a ball around his own penalty area and suddenly go past three players before they realise he's going for goal.

At the moment he's fighting a psychological block outside the box. He's become a reluctant shooter, preferring to pass. Why he should mistrust his shooting baffles me, he can bang the ball harder than Osgood (Diagram B).

Hudson's also a lot better in the air than he thinks. When he wants, he can really hammer the ball.

His best game this season was against Sheffield Wednesday in the Cup. If he could maintain that level over a season he could fill the gap Bobby Charlton is going to leave.'

DAVE SEXTON, Chelsea manager.

Ron Suart, who had joined Chelsea as assistant manager after many years at Blackpool, took charge of the still shaken Chelsea players. Now the time was ripe for Leeds to take quick revenge against a shocked Chelsea team for that controversial FA Cup semi-final defeat five months earlier, but few could have envisaged such a one-sided rampage, as United scored seven without reply. Although the wisecracking Docherty had hit the headlines, it was another Scot under impending suspension, Billy Bremner, who overshadowed events on the pitch. The fiery Leeds skipper was making his last appearance for United before starting a twenty-eight day ban for being sent-off against Fulham in September and he was at his impish best as Leeds turned on a superb attacking display. Eric Stanger of the *Yorkshire Post* reported, "Bremner teased and tormented them with his astonishing dexterity of foot and his remarkable sense of balance so that he could turn and twist on the proverbial sixpence". It was Bremner's spectacular Brazilian-style bicycle-kick eight minutes from time which crowned a five-star Leeds performance.

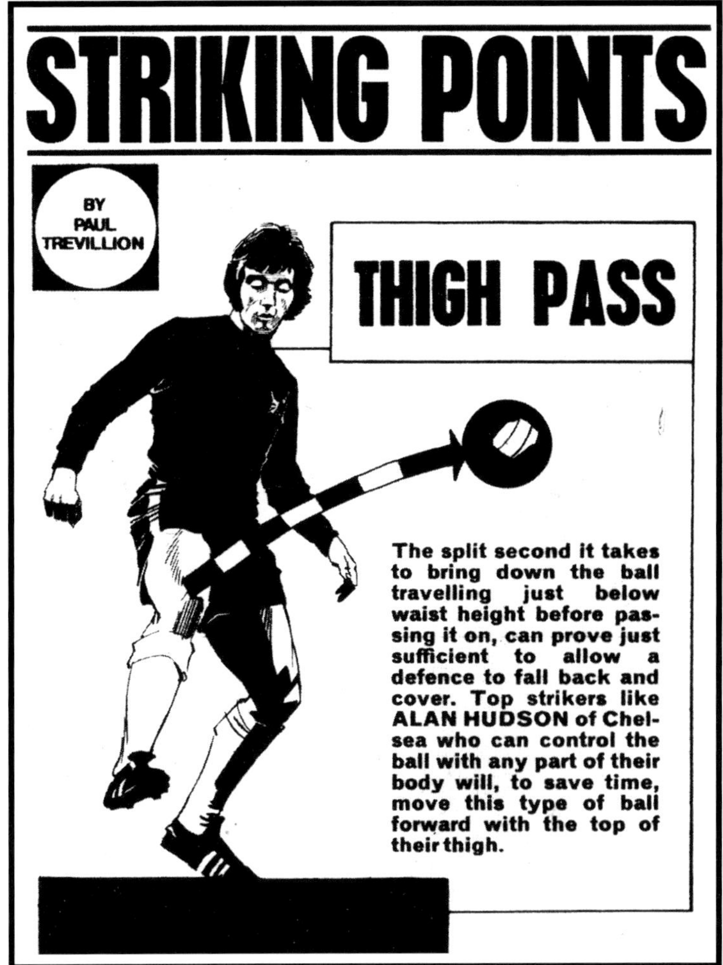

Chelsea were short of England forward Bobby Tambling, who was injured, and one of Suart's choices for the clash saw twenty-year old Geoff Butler, a £60,000 full-back signing from Middlesbrough just two weeks previous, replace ex-Bury central defender Colin Waldron, who was made substitute. United were hampered by injuries. Neither Johnny Giles nor Mike O'Grady were fit but Gary Sprake and Jimmy Greenhoff both passed late tests to play in a game which saw United race to a three goal lead. The first strike came after just five minutes as Billy Bremner released Paul Reaney with a reverse pass and the full-back unleashed a good centre for speedy winger Albert Johanneson, who had been recalled to the side, to produce a rarity by heading the ball home. Peter Lorimer laid on a goal for Jimmy Greenhoff in the eleventh minute and three minutes later Jack Charlton headed in from close range, after Peter Bonetti missed his grab for an in-swinging corner from Eddie Gray. United went into a 4-0 lead seven minutes from half-time when Peter Lorimer rounded off a splendid round of passing with a roaring angled shot that left Bonetti helpless. Eddie Gray got the fifth on the hour with a nineteen yard shot after good work by Jimmy Greenhoff, who had cut inside from the right.

United's biggest crowd of the season, 40,460, saw Chelsea hand United their sixth goal, in the eightieth minute, Marvin Hinton heading into his own net following a Peter Lorimer corner. It was left to the ubiquitous Bremner to round off the scoring two minutes later and, apart from the quality of Bremner's spectacular overhead kick, the goal earned a place in the record books as it was the goal which made it the first time in the Football League in which seven different players had scored for one side.

One name missing from the scorers was centre-forward Mick Jones, a recent £100,000 buy from Sheffield United. He left the pitch injured midway through the game and was replaced by substitute Terry Hibbitt."

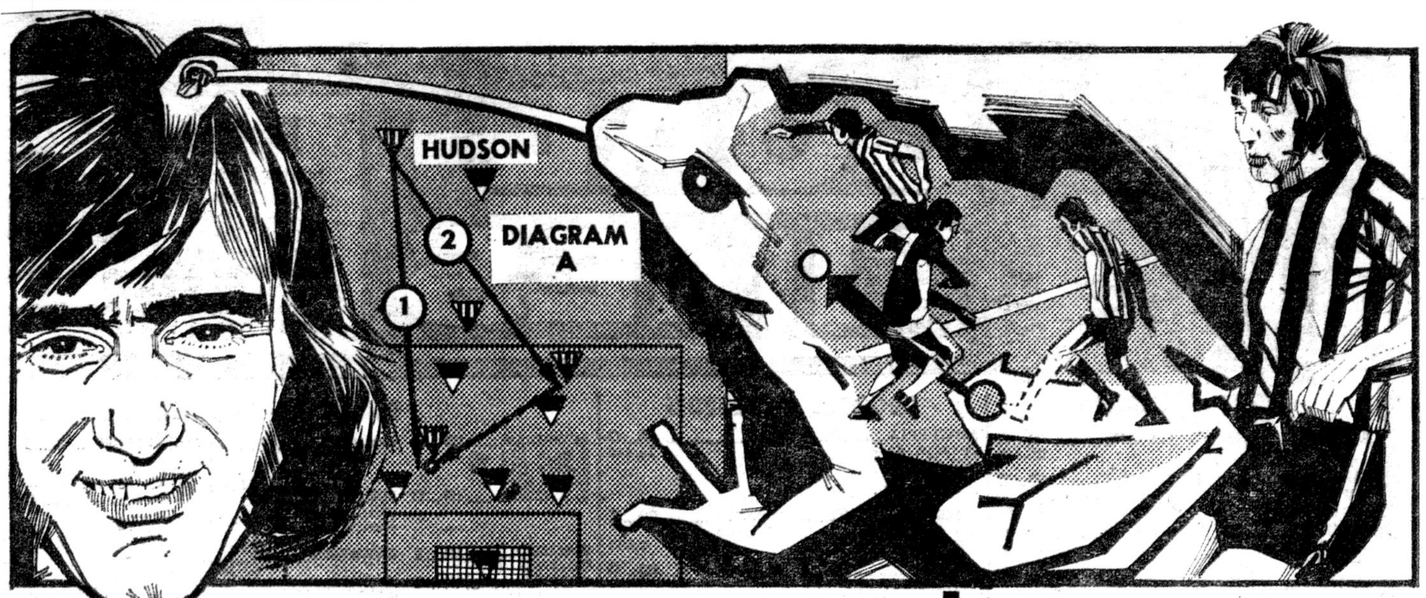

George Eastham, assistant manager of Stoke, talks about Alan Hudson, one of the club's super-stars: "The thing I admire most about Hudson is his ability to rob an opponent and pass the ball in one movement. He jockeys the man in possession then flicks out a leg and knocks off the ball to a team-mate. Sometimes it's too quick to see. You've seen the way a frog's tongue darts out to catch a fly - well Hudson is that quick.

"The criticism aimed at Alan is that he doesn't score more goals. He has a powerful shot and it's argued he should be trying shots from 40 to 30 yards.

"My answer is that he would be out of order shooting from that range because only one in 50 attempts from such distances hit the target.

"When Hudson picks up a ball in midfield his first priority is to find a player near enough to get inside the six-yard box and have a go - or alternatively find a team-mate in a better position to set up a similar goal chance" (diagram A)

Not too long ago Alan demanded that the FA delete his playing records with England, the first ever to make such a request. In his letters to the FA, Hudson accuses them of failing to support him in a long struggle against devastating permanent injuries inflicted by a hit-and-run driver in 1997. Hudson wrote: 'My dream of a long international career was ruined and has led to long-term depression, anxiety and panic for which I still have counselling. It will be a great relief to be removed from my links with the history of England football." The FA's response was that they held him in 'high esteem', as 'a great player who had a distinguished football career'.

Hudson said: 'I don't want anything to remain in the FA statistics to remind me of the demoralising and very depressing way I was passed over for all but two England matches.' The last straw was watching Jack Grealish marginalised in the Euros by Gareth Southgate, arguing it was similar to how highly-gifted players such as himself were ignored by previous managers of the national team. He claimed Sir Alf imposed an arbitrary three-year England suspension on him for failing to answer an Under-23 call-up when he was suffering from an ankle injury. That exile was ended by two caps from Don Revie, of whom Hudson says: 'He only did that under pressure from the media and then discarded me, even though we won both those games and I was man of the match against West Germany in one of them.'

Chopper

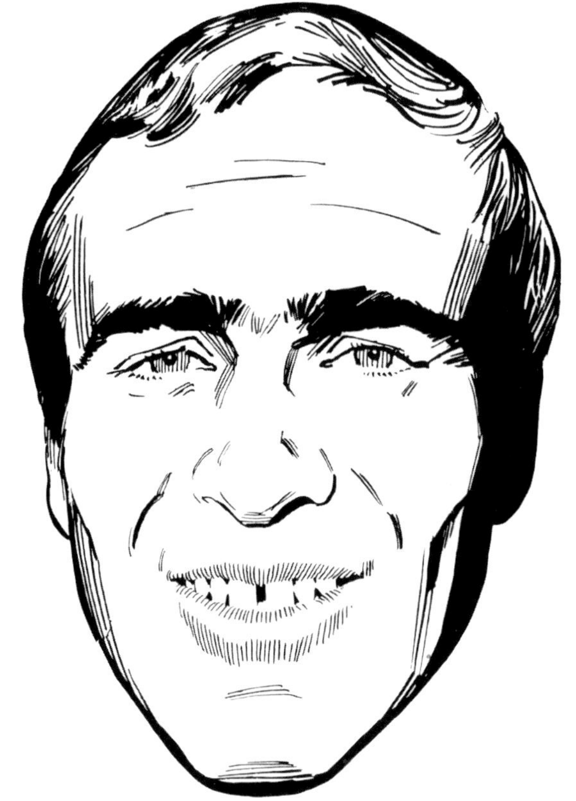

Ron 'Chopper' Harris could be cutting with his comments, his opinions often as savage as his tackles used to be, and I have received a Chopper rebuke in my time, in fact two or three! Fortunately, even though I have played at the Bridge in charity games, I have avoided him on the pitch, thank goodness.

'Chopper' rang me to respond to an article that appeared in the Express when I was chief football writer on the paper for eight years, quoting chairman Ken Bates talking about some of the club's players in the seventies. Bates was fed up with the fans and the media harking back to past glories and was none too pleased about some biting comments attributed to 'Chopper' about how everything had improved with the arrival of Roman Abramovich. Bates' remarks published with an equally provocative headline, prompting the call from the club's former midfield enforcer Ron Harris who launched into a right old rant. Chopper was particularly upset as Bates' comments came on the day after the death of one of his seventies team-mates, which ignited abject fury in one of the most notorious hit men of his generation. Ron was eager for his response to be published and, of course, I duly obliged. Now it was Bates' turn to vent his anger, but he didn't take it out on me, as he could see I was lapping up these two heavyweights of Chelsea past having a good old go at each other. No, it was "Chopper" he had in his sights, and with Bates still lingering at the club in the short period after the Russian's takeover, "Chopper" duly got the chop, as it was never going to end well for him. I reported soon afterward that Ron had been sacked by the club.

On another occasion Ron caught up with me when I was a guest of Samsung Mobile in a challenge match at Stamford Bridge, where I was lined up at left-back, and Chopper was hired as guest speaker. He popped into a meet-and-greet Samsung Executive box when I was a guest of the director at that time, Mark Mitchinson. Wherever and whenever we bump into each other he still remained indignant as though the articles were written yesterday. We also met up in bizarre circumstances at the Gatwick Hilton hotel for a dinner function, and he still could not get the Bates issues off his chest quickly enough! "Look", he glared at me menacingly, "I have never been sacked by Chelsea, but I lost my £5,000-a-night job as an after dinner speaker down at the Bridge as a result of your articles, and let me tell you, I never apologised in writing for that article about Bates despite what he said at the time." To give "Chopper" his due, even though he believed I was at fault, when I approached him about helping me launch a Chelsea book at the King's Road branch of Waterstones, he was more than happy to be involved.

Of course, this all stirs memories of the most brutal game in English football history, the notorious FA Cup final between Chelsea and Leeds United, and how "Chopper" left his mark on one of Leeds' most dangerous players that ultimately had such a bearing on the result. Eddie Gray had been sensational in the Wembley final and Chelsea had been fortunate to scrape a draw, so when the Scot collected the ball in the centre circle and immediately sets his sights on Peter Bonetti's goal the Chelsea team reacted accordingly. First David Webb, fuelled by fresh memories of his roasting at the hands of the Leeds winger a few days prior, hit him, both feet off the ground, in the first two minutes of the 1970 Old Trafford replay. Both games were not for the faint-hearted, the final that has gone down in football folklore as a meeting of pure malice between a Leeds United side renowned for having the muscle to match their magnificence and a victorious Chelsea team with flashiness and ferocity in equal measure who had learned that to beat Revie's men, they would have to fight fire with fire.

With tackling from behind a regular and accepted part of a game played by men for men, the leniency afforded to the hatchet men was part of the spectacle. Crunching, full-blooded tackles were applauded not frowned upon, with no protection for the gifted individual, instead the referee appeared to give defenders a licence to maim the skilful attackers. It was pure and simple brutality.

The game is so notorious that it has since been re-refereed by leading officials according to modern interpretations of the rules. In 1997 David Elleray concluded he would have shown six red cards, while in 2020 Michael Oliver went for 11. On the night, referee Eric Jennings cautioned just one player!

"The rivalry was there because Leeds had a name, a reputation as being dirty," said Bonetti, "I'd call them physical because dirty doesn't sound a very nice word. We matched them in the physical side of things because we had our own players who were physical and that was probably why we were such big rivals. We weren't unalike in the way we played." In his autobiography, Leeds midfielder Johnny Giles attests to "a special sort of animosity" between the teams. "I had that bit of 'previous' with Eddie McCreadie," adds the Irishman, "John Hollins, who would usually mark me, could do a bit. And Ron 'Chopper' Harris had made a name for himself." Chelsea striker Ian Hutchinson put it more simply: "We hated them and they hated us."

Leeds had carried the vendetta from their 1967 FA Cup semi-final defeat by the 'softies' from the south, in which they felt they had a perfectly good Peter Lorimer free-kick ruled out. In the 1969-70 season they faced each other six times, with Leeds winning both league games, including a 5-2 win at Stamford Bridge, and the Blues coming out on top over two games in a League Cup third-round tie.

By the final game that season there were numerous individual scores to settle, with one of the freshest wounds being between Webb and Gray. Leeds' Scottish winger had given the Chelsea full-back an absolute chasing in the drawn final at Wembley that prompted the replay. Leeds dominated but failed to win on a national stadium surface buried under a mountain of sand, in an attempt to make it playable following poor weather. Webb was switched to centre-back for the replay to get him away from Gray and give Harris the task of keeping the winger quiet, but fate drew the two back together almost immediately and gave the Chelsea man a chance to make his mark. This he did, about halfway up Gray's left shin.

"I did a corporate golf day with Eddie [Gray] and in the clubhouse afterwards, he announced he wanted to make a special presentation to an old friend. He reached into his pocket, handed me one of those metal screw-in studs and said, 'Chopper, you left this in my kneecap at the cup final – I thought you'd like it back'."

"Chopper" finished the job on Gray in the first half, catching the winger on the back of his left knee, leaving him with an injury that restricted him for the remainder of the game and crucially robbed Leeds of arguably their most talented attacking player. "Chopper" attempted to do the same to Gray's left-wing colleague Terry Cooper in the second half but only tore right through his shorts.

It has been said that while teams of that era had a couple of hard men, Leeds boasted a team of them. It's difficult to pick out their nastiest, although the man at the heart of the Leeds defence, Norman Hunter, who attracted an infamous banner that read 'Norman Bites Yer Legs' held aloft by Leeds fans at the 1972 FA Cup final, was the most notorious. His first touch in the 1970 replay - a throw-in - attracted boos from the Chelsea fans, while his second meaningful involvement, after relinquishing possession

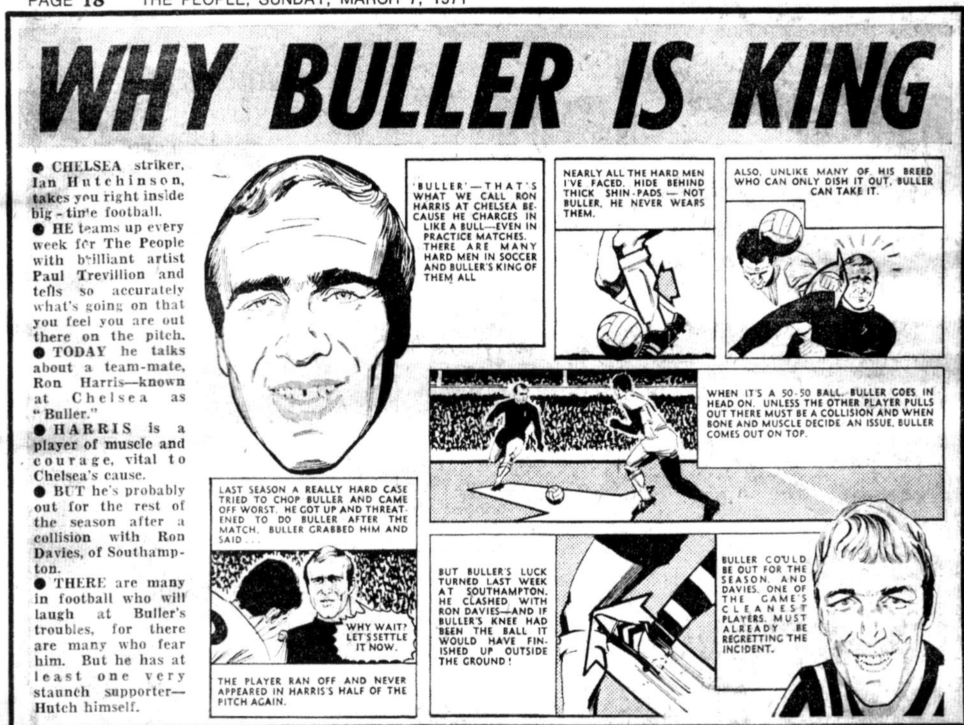

PAGE 18 THE PEOPLE, SUNDAY, MARCH 7, 1971

WHY BULLER IS KING

● CHELSEA striker, Ian Hutchinson, takes you right inside big-time football.

● HE teams up every week for The People with brilliant artist Paul Trevillion and tells so accurately what's going on that you feel you are out there on the pitch.

● TODAY he talks about a team-mate, Ron Harris—known at Chelsea as "Buller."

● HARRIS is a player of muscle and courage, vital to Chelsea's cause.

● BUT he's probably out for the rest of the season after a collision with Ron Davies, of Southampton.

● THERE are many in football who will laugh at Buller's troubles, for there are many who fear him. But he has at least one very staunch supporter—Hutch himself.

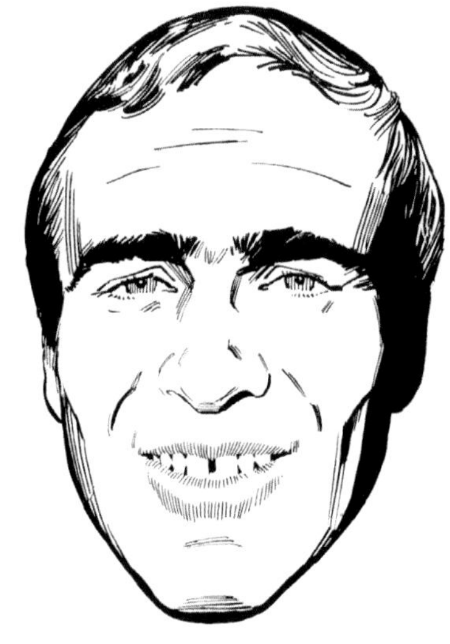

Being First

'I usually consider the games in which I hardly make a tackle as being my best' says RON HARRIS, Chelsea.

'For this is the proof,' smiles Harris, 'that I was always first to the ball played up to my opponent. I also made the required interception when necessary and I kept so tight to my man, his team-mate usually considered it too big a risk to pass to him.'

following a forward run, saw Hunter and McCreadie come together in midfield, leading to a brief flurry of post-challenge blows. Later in the game the Leeds defender is seen after another heavy challenge, fists clenched and ready for battle. Off the pitch, Norman was a warm, generous and beloved figure. His death on 17 April 2020 was deeply felt. "I worked with him on the after-dinner circuit," "Chopper" recalled. "On the field he was an animal, but away from the football you won't meet a nicer fella, a gentleman."

Five days prior to Hunter's death, Chelsea also lost one of their all-time legends in Peter Bonetti, whose influence over the 240 minutes of the 1970 final is perhaps greater than any other. His heroics at Wembley was one of the main reasons for the replay. Then, in the 31st minute of the replay, he suffered a painful knee injury in a fiercely contested aerial duel with Leeds' bruising centre-forward Mick Jones - one that required lengthy treatment and prompted BBC commentator Kenneth Wolstenholme to comment: "This almost deserves an X-certificate". He emerged after half-time heavily strapped and unable to take goal-kicks. Jones would take advantage almost immediately after the injury by giving Leeds the lead, but Bonetti lived up to his reputation as 'The Cat' by launching off his one good leg to make a string of important saves. Fittingly, Bonetti collected the base of the trophy at its presentation.

As the game wore on and the light faded at Old Trafford, the violence increased. Peter Osgood fouled Jack Charlton, who immediately leapt to his feet and barged the striker to the turf. Then Big Jack left Osgood unmarked to score as he went off in search of a Chelsea player who had whacked his thigh moments earlier. The most brutal moment came in the 85th minute. Billy Bremner was shoved by Hutchinson, which earned the game's only booking, but it sparked a running battle for the remainder of the game that saw late tackles and retaliatory kicks. The clash between Ossie and Big Jack bordered on GBH, while McCreadie, leaping high into the air in the box, missed the bouncing ball and struck a karate kick to the head that "almost cut Bremner in

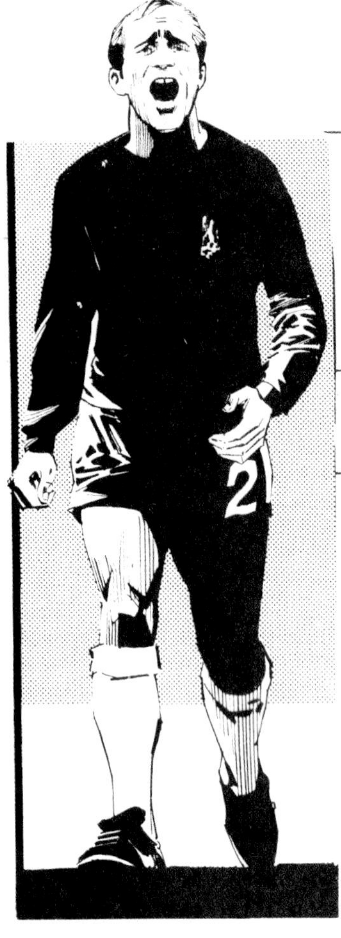

STAND OFF

Top defenders like RON HARRIS of Chelsea mark tight, even so they always keep a yard between themselves and their opponent. Says Harris: "I never get too close to a forward when he has his back to me because if he turns you the wrong way with a feint he's got you off balance with no room to recover so you either foul him or let him go. By holding off a yard I'm always able to move when he moves, re-adjust when necessary and at all times keep with him."

half" according to John Dempsey. Jennings, in his final game as a professional referee, waved play on. Nowadays it'd be a six-match ban!

Hutchinson and Webb would ultimately win the war in extra time, with Hutchinson's booming long throw making its way to the back post off the head of Charlton for Webb to nod in the winner for Chelsea's historic first FA Cup triumph.

Years later, Gray was enjoying himself at a black-tie dinner when Harris tapped him on the shoulder, put his hand out and, with a grin, asked: "Can I have my studs back?" Gray has told that joke many times, but he also told me that when he turned round and saw "Chopper" he was petrified!

Ron recalls, "I did a corporate golf day with Eddie and in the clubhouse afterwards, he announced he wanted to make a special presentation to an old friend. He reached into his pocket, handed me one of those metal screw-in studs and said, 'Chopper, you left this in my kneecap at the cup final – I thought you'd like it back.' We played the game differently 50 years ago. Nobody complained if they thought a challenge was a bit rough. You got up, walked away and thought, 'I'll get you back later on.' Eddie had given David Webb a hard time in the first game so I swapped flanks in the replay and I was told to follow him wherever he went. If I could rattle him, that was my job – and without patting myself on the back too much, I did that quite successfully. In fairness, it took me eight minutes to catch up with Eddie on the night, which was about seven minutes later than I would have liked. I've never liked being late for appointments, or to catch a train. The only things I've ever been late for are tackles."

"Chopper" remains the club's record appearance maker donning the Chelsea shirt in 795 games. "The thing I remember most about 1970 is that the pitch at Wembley was a disgrace. Whoever decided to stage the Horse of the Year show a few days before the FA Cup final needs locking up. We didn't play on bowling greens every week in those days, but you also didn't expect to play a major final among potholes and craters left by horses jumping fences. And the other thing that stands out now is the tackles that went on. In the replay at Old Trafford, Eddie McCreadie caught Billy Bremner on the back of his neck with a high tackle. If he did that today, he would have been banned for six months. Both teams dished it out, but both teams took it. There was no rolling around, squealing and feigning injury, like you see these days. I can't stand all that play-acting. I think there was only one player booked over the two games. If I was still playing now, I'd be lucky to get through the warm-up without a red card. But football wasn't a non-contact sport in 1970. We were allowed to get on with it, so we got stuck in. Over the two games, I would admit Leeds were the better team. But you have to give us credit – three times we were behind against a great side, and three times we fought back. We didn't roll over. I've been up to Leeds on many occasions since then, and I always take my medal along with me – to show them what a winner's medal from 1970 looks like!"

HH

Ian Hutchinson

Long Throw Expert and Brave Centre-Forward

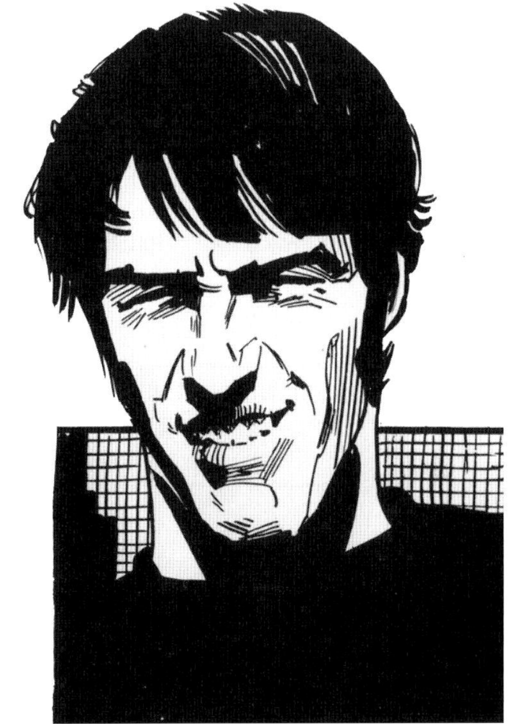

Ian Hutchinson was an integral member of the great 1970 FA Cup-winning side that defeated Leeds United in a replay at Old Trafford following a 2-2 draw at Wembley, but he will always be remembered as the man with the game's longest-ever throw, reminiscent of the pre-war Chelsea left-half Sam Weaver, a renowned specialist.

Chelsea captain Ron Harris recalls, "If you got a ball down the line, he was so brave. He used to go where other players feared to go. He was a 110 per cent player."

Hutch combined fearsome heading ability with a devastating long throw as he wound up his arms to launch the ball into the opponent's box to devastating effect as he did in that defining final that brought glory to the West London.

In the first game, on a muddy Wembley pitch, though a notable finisher, Hutchinson was well capable of figuring in the leading-up play, and it was after a neat exchange of passes with midfielder John Hollins that, on 38 minutes, Hollins crossed, Osgood shot, and Jackie Charlton desperately cleared from the Leeds goalmouth. Soon after that Chelsea scored a much more fortuitous goal, in which Hutchinson was again involved. He headed on Eddie McCreadie's high cross, Peter Houseman shot and the erratic Welsh keeper Gary Sprake let the ball squeeze away from him and into the goal. Leeds were, however, 2-1 ahead when, on 86 minutes, Hollins, receiving a free-kick from Harris, curled in a cross from the left and Hutchinson, typically brave, plunged for a diving header wide of Sprake and into the near corner for 2-2. He had outshone Osgood himself.

In the replay at Old Trafford, with the game locked at 1-1 in extra time, a huge Hutchinson throw wreaked havoc in the Leeds box and David Webb scored from close range - Chelsea had won the FA Cup for the very first time in their history.

In the FA Charity Shield at Goodison Park the following August he had a memorable first half in which he was described as "a kind of one-man Panzer division". Inevitably perhaps, he faded in the second half, yet came to life again to score Chelsea's spectacular goal in a 1-1 draw. Keith Weller crossed high from the right; it looked certain that Everton's goalkeeper Gordon West would clutch the ball, but, with a stupendous jump, Hutchinson beat him to it and back-headed the ball into the net.

But it was in the two FA Cup finals where Hutchinson made his mark in a tournament where Chelsea had suffered disappointment down the years. Having lost their first cup final, known for the preponderance of soldiers present as the Khaki Final, at Old Trafford against Sheffield United, 3-0, in 1915, they had to wait until 1967 to reach their second, when London rivals Spurs beat them 2-1 at Wembley. In 1970, it proved to be a case of third time lucky, although they seemed certain to lose to bookies' favourites, Leeds. A 1930s song, by the comedian Norman Long, was even exhumed: "On the day that Chelsea won the final, the universe went off the wheel." Ian Hutchinson had other ideas.

Born in Derby, standing half an inch over 6ft and weighing a couple of pounds short of 13st, 'Hutch' was playing non-league

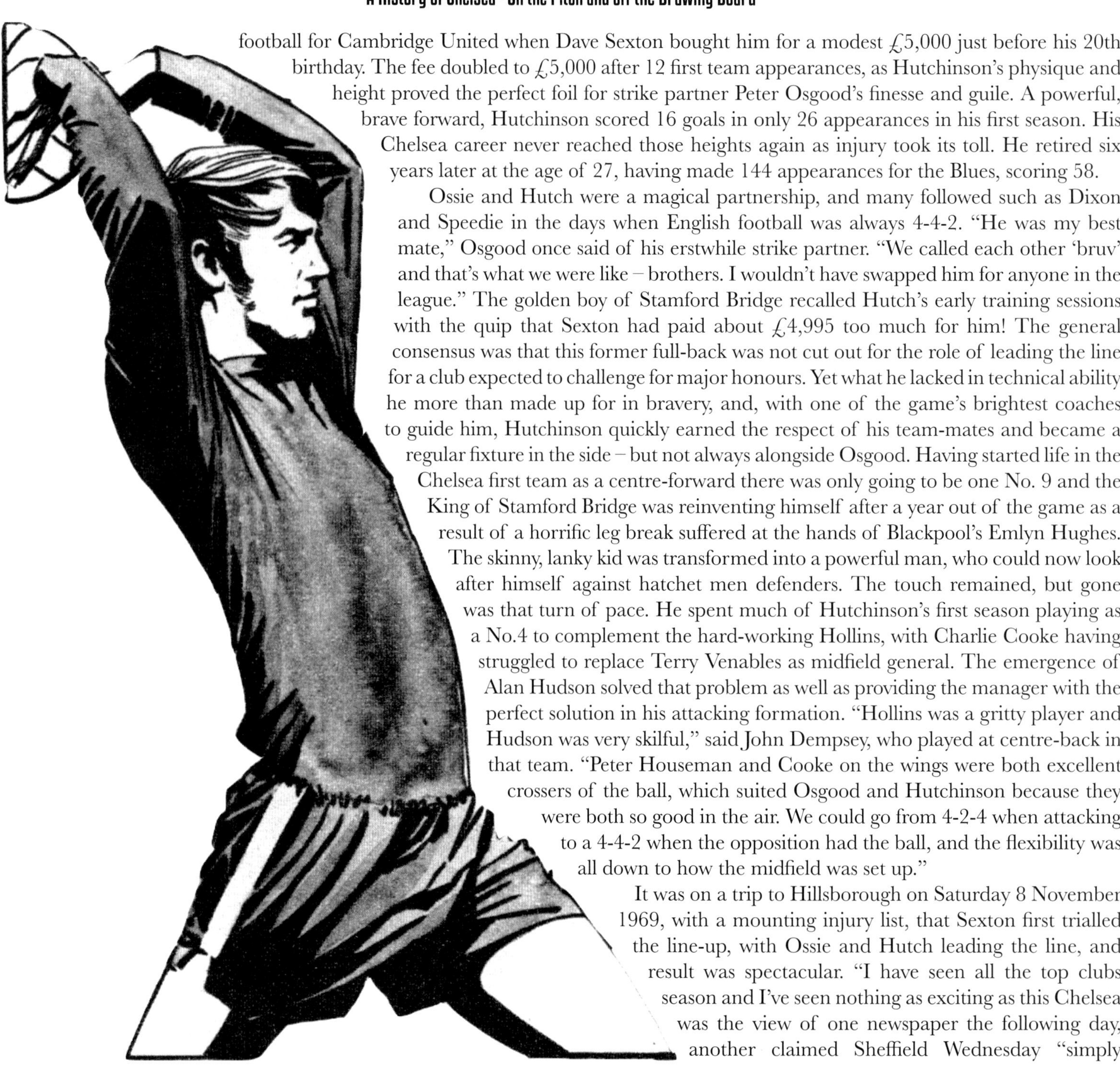

football for Cambridge United when Dave Sexton bought him for a modest £5,000 just before his 20th birthday. The fee doubled to £5,000 after 12 first team appearances, as Hutchinson's physique and height proved the perfect foil for strike partner Peter Osgood's finesse and guile. A powerful, brave forward, Hutchinson scored 16 goals in only 26 appearances in his first season. His Chelsea career never reached those heights again as injury took its toll. He retired six years later at the age of 27, having made 144 appearances for the Blues, scoring 58.

Ossie and Hutch were a magical partnership, and many followed such as Dixon and Speedie in the days when English football was always 4-4-2. "He was my best mate," Osgood once said of his erstwhile strike partner. "We called each other 'bruv' and that's what we were like – brothers. I wouldn't have swapped him for anyone in the league." The golden boy of Stamford Bridge recalled Hutch's early training sessions with the quip that Sexton had paid about £4,995 too much for him! The general consensus was that this former full-back was not cut out for the role of leading the line for a club expected to challenge for major honours. Yet what he lacked in technical ability he more than made up for in bravery, and, with one of the game's brightest coaches to guide him, Hutchinson quickly earned the respect of his team-mates and became a regular fixture in the side – but not always alongside Osgood. Having started life in the Chelsea first team as a centre-forward there was only going to be one No. 9 and the King of Stamford Bridge was reinventing himself after a year out of the game as a result of a horrific leg break suffered at the hands of Blackpool's Emlyn Hughes. The skinny, lanky kid was transformed into a powerful man, who could now look after himself against hatchet men defenders. The touch remained, but gone was that turn of pace. He spent much of Hutchinson's first season playing as a No.4 to complement the hard-working Hollins, with Charlie Cooke having struggled to replace Terry Venables as midfield general. The emergence of Alan Hudson solved that problem as well as providing the manager with the perfect solution in his attacking formation. "Hollins was a gritty player and Hudson was very skilful," said John Dempsey, who played at centre-back in that team. "Peter Houseman and Cooke on the wings were both excellent crossers of the ball, which suited Osgood and Hutchinson because they were both so good in the air. We could go from 4-2-4 when attacking to a 4-4-2 when the opposition had the ball, and the flexibility was all down to how the midfield was set up."

It was on a trip to Hillsborough on Saturday 8 November 1969, with a mounting injury list, that Sexton first trialled the line-up, with Ossie and Hutch leading the line, and result was spectacular. "I have seen all the top clubs season and I've seen nothing as exciting as this Chelsea was the view of one newspaper the following day, another claimed Sheffield Wednesday "simply

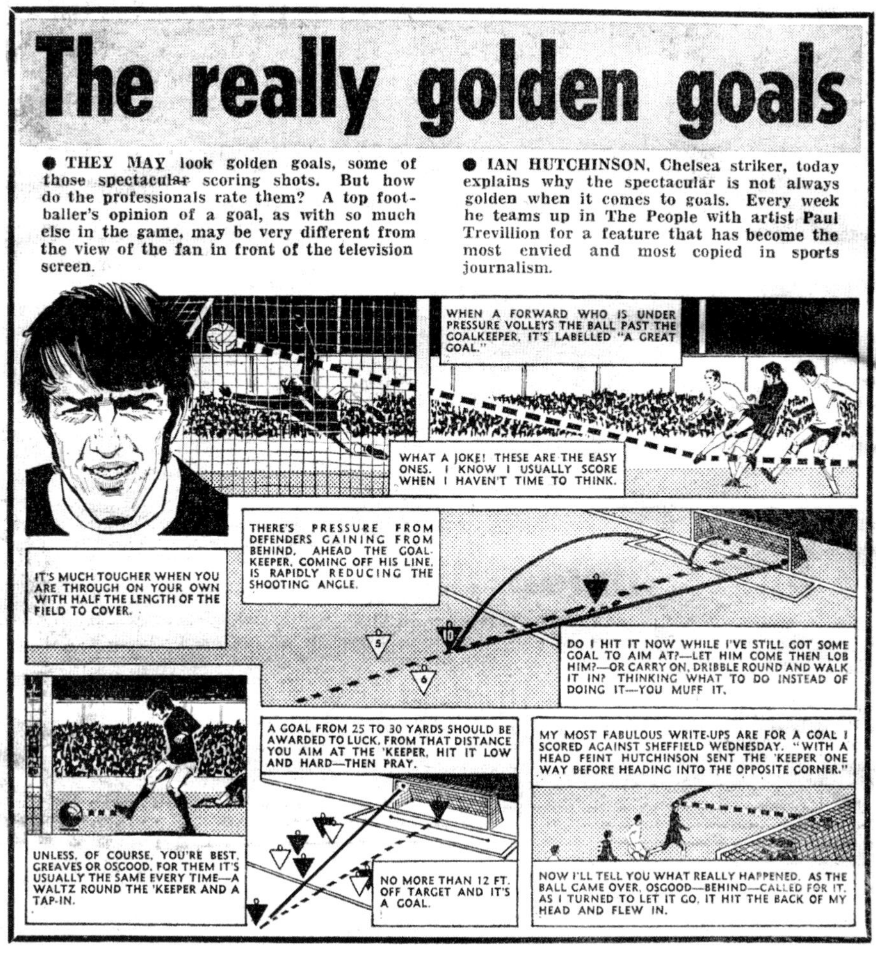

The really golden goals

● THEY MAY look golden goals, some of those spectacular scoring shots. But how do the professionals rate them? A top footballer's opinion of a goal, as with so much else in the game, may be very different from the view of the fan in front of the television screen.

● IAN HUTCHINSON, Chelsea striker, today explains why the spectacular is not always golden when it comes to goals. Every week he teams up in The People with artist Paul Trevillion for a feature that has become the most envied and most copied in sports journalism.

could not contain Osgood and Hutchinson". Both were on target in a 3-1 victory, Hutch with a brace, and so began a partnership. As Osgood noted, the dynamics of the duo suited him; he had previously played his best football at Chelsea while operating just off the main frontman, George Graham. Now he was back as the secondary target behind the main focal point, although this time it was a centre-forward who was the bravest of the lot, capable of taking punishment from bruising defenders. "I wouldn't have swapped him for anybody – he was awesome," noted Osgood. "He came here at 22 and packed up at 27, breaking every bone in his body! To play up front with him, and with Charlie, Huddy and Houseman knocking the balls in, they couldn't stop us." Osgood and Hutchinson went on to score regularly throughout that campaign. A few weeks later, Desmond Hackett described Hutch as 'the soccer find of 1969' after he scored twice in a 3-1 win over Southampton, as Chelsea surged up the table. Birmingham City were beaten 3-0 in the third round of the FA Cup with Hutch scoring two and Ossie the other, and a goal apiece bookended a 4-1 victory over Crystal Palace in round five, although Eagles boss Bert Head felt both men were guilty of foul play. That, however, was a big part of their partnership – the dark arts and their ability to mix it. The devastating duo were both on target in the semi-finals, and by this stage Osgood had found the back of the net in every round as Chelsea prepared to meet Leeds United at Wembley Stadium as underdogs. Though he failed to add to his goal tally at Wembley, the Blues lived to see a replay thanks to a late equaliser from Hutchinson, the big centre-forward putting his head in where it hurt to meet a cross and place a perfect header past Sprake, earning Chelsea a 2-2 draw that Chelsea scarcely deserved. "Most people probably wouldn't have thrown themselves at it, they'd have been a bit dubious about spoiling their looks," said Ron Harris. "Hutch didn't have to worry about that, though!"

"If you look back over that season, I must have scored eight to 10 similar goals," said Hutch. "Houseman or Hollins knew it was their job to deliver the ball either to the near or far post. Ossie tended to go far as he didn't like the studs up his arse! We scored a hell of a lot of goals that way and it was just short of programmed into us from the training ground, really." In the replay at Old Trafford, both men were protagonists in the game's big moments, but there was one which summed up their partnership better than any other. After Billy Bremner had left one on Osgood and got up for some afters, Hutchinson was straight on the scene to send the Scot flying with a shove. What sticks in the mind though is Ossie's beautiful diving header, with Hutch involved in the build-up dragging a

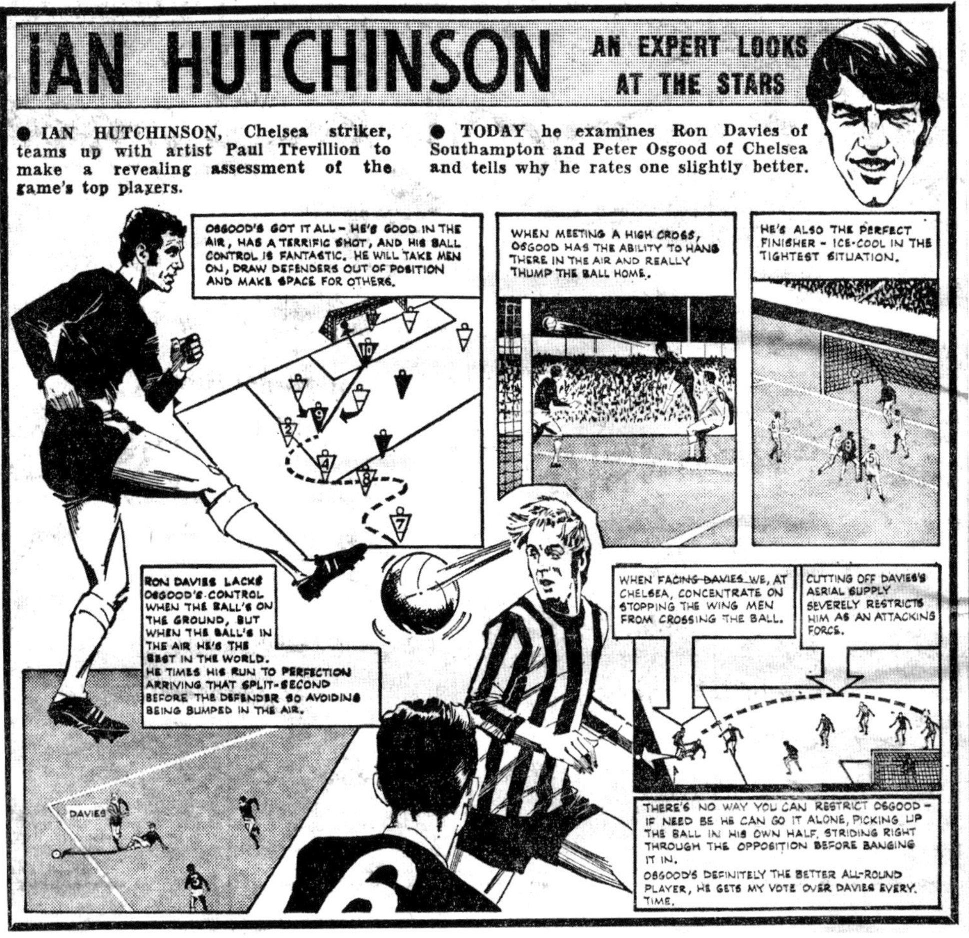

defender out of position to leave the space for his strike partner, and the huge long throw from Hutchinson, his trademark move which led to David Webb heading home the winning goal in extra time. Chelsea, finally, had won the FA Cup. Osgood scored 31 goals across all competitions that season, along with 22 from Hutchinson.

It should have been the catalyst for a title challenge, but that was as good as it got for them. Ossie moved on in 1974, his deteriorating relationship with Sexton beyond repair, with Hutchinson remaining at Chelsea for a further two years before his litany of injuries finally ended his brave football career, yet their friendship endured. They were back in unison in retirement as they partnered up in a surrounding equally as comfortable to them as a football pitch: the pub. The Union Inn in Windsor launched Ossie and Hutch MkII and the roles remained the same, as Osgood took on the glamorous position behind the bar while Hutchinson put his culinary skills to good use in the kitchen. Hutch was even best man at all three of Osgood's weddings, and he began a relationship with Elaine Thatcher, the best friend of his mate's third wife, Lynn!

Ian Hutchinson died in September 2002 aged just 54 following a long illness.

Peter Bonetti

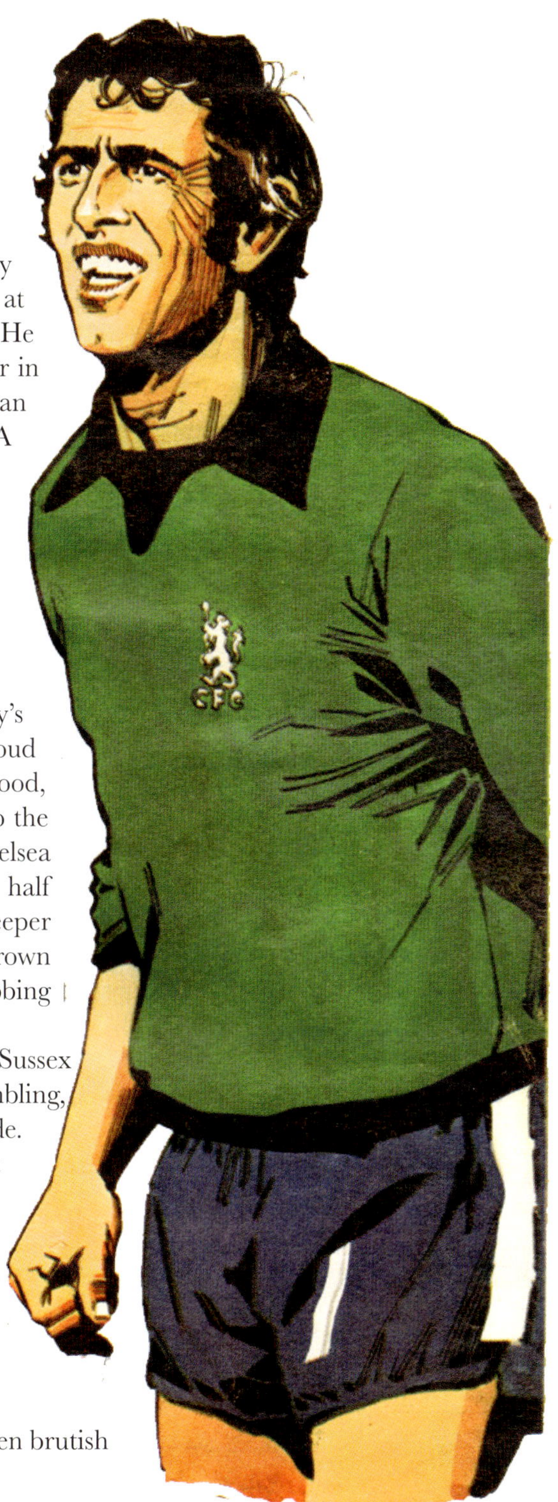

Peter Bonetti is one of the truly legendary figures at Stamford Bridge. It was my privilege to have known him and also to have played in the same team with him at Stamford Bridge. 'The Cat' possessed astonishing reflexes and graceful agility. He played 729 times for the club, which makes him the second-highest appearance maker in Chelsea's history. Peter made his debut in March 1960 at the age of 18 keeping a clean sheet, the first of 208 for the club. Four months later he helped Chelsea win the FA Youth Cup. The Cat was a key figure in all of the successes of the sixties and seventies. His brilliant last-minute save gave Chelsea a vital win at Sunderland in the promotion season of '63, he was inspired in the goalless draw at Leicester that won the '65 League Cup and his greatest moment came in the '70 FA Cup final win over Leeds United. An early foul left him limping heavily in the replay but he defied the injury to put in an outstanding display. A year later he again saved one of his best performances for a final, the Cup Winners' Cup replay win over Real Madrid.

Bonetti was one of the keystones of the side that emerged under Tommy Docherty's management but was polished by Dave Sexton. Most of that team, Chelsea fans were proud to say, emerged from the club's youth scheme. Like his future team-mate Peter Osgood, Bonetti was recommended to the club for a trial by a member of his family writing to the club, in his case his mother. For two decades, a succession of young aspirants to the Chelsea keeper's shirt were seen off by a familiar figure with his green sleeves tugged up to half mast. Most of the records Bonetti set for clean sheets and trophies won by a Chelsea keeper were only surpassed in the past few years. He remains the club's most successful homegrown goalkeeper. His nickname 'the Cat' was coined by early team-mate Ron Tindall, ad-libbing mock TV commentary during a game of billiards in the old players' lounge.

Born in nearby Putney, Peter grew up learning football outside of London on the Sussex coast. Following his successful Chelsea trial, he started on the same day as Bobby Tambling, Terry Venables and others who would establish themselves in the Swinging Sixties side. After a year in the juniors and a brief spell in the reserves, he made his debut against Manchester City in April 1960. The Blues had lost their previous three matches, conceding 10, but won 3-0. Still eligible for the Juniors, he helped them win the FA Youth Cup that season – another Chelsea first. Chelsea won only their second every senior trophy in 1965, the League Cup. Having edged a tight first leg at home, the return at Filbert Street saw Bonetti make a succession of stops as opponents Leicester sought parity in the tie. The second leg ended goalless and Bonetti did most to land the club's first League Cup.

Despite standing under six foot tall, he pioneered coming off his line, braving an often brutish melée and catching any high ball in his area. He broke the mould by rolling or throwing the ball out rather than hoofing it upfield. He was first to recognise a role for gardening gloves in handling slippery winter balls, leading to his Peter Bonetti-branded specialist gloves which were a first and so successful they were sported not only by kids, but by many of his contemporaries at the top level of the game. Forward-thinking Peter later became the club's first goalkeeping coach.

In 1966 Bonetti was Chelsea's sole representative in the England squad at the World Cup, but with Gordon Banks the first choice and injury-free throughout, he remained unused by Alf Ramsey. Only the 11 players on the pitch at the end of the final against West Germany were eligible to receive medals. However, thanks to an FA-led campaign many years later that persuaded FIFA to reward every squad member and Bonetti was presented with a medal by Gordon Brown, the Prime Minister, at Downing Street in 2009. But for the rich crop of goalkeepers at the time, and especially the durability of Banks, Peter would have played many more times for his country. In his first six internationals he conceded one goal. Game seven for England was a World Cup quarter-final in 1970 with Banks incapacitated by food poisoning. Though Bonetti acknowledged being at fault for the first goal conceded as West Germany recovered from two goals down to win, he shouldered an unfair proportion of the national blame for the defeat when the game had changed after Ramsey's controversial substitutions of Bobby Charlton and Martin Peters. He deserved a much better legacy on the international stage. Pelé, who watched Bonetti in his prime, said 'The three greatest goalkeepers I have ever seen are Gordon Banks, Lev Yashin and Peter Bonetti.'

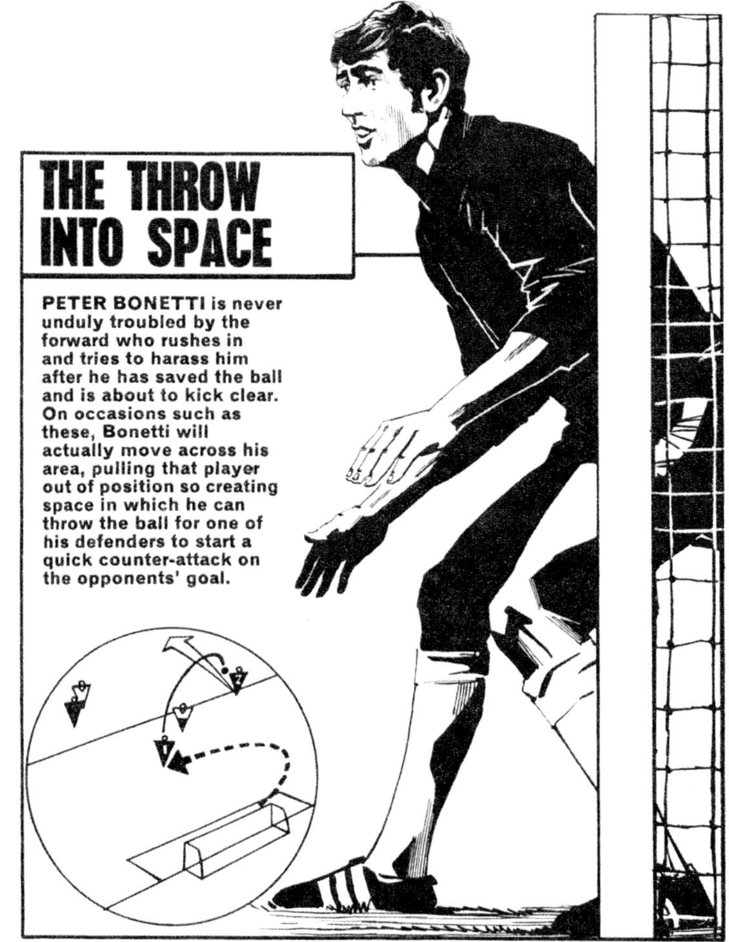

Chelsea fans knew ribbing from opposition supporters was unjust but it emphasised Bonetti's strength that it never affected his confidence, and he quickly followed that World Cup by winning his second trophy with Chelsea. Bonetti had been in goal at Wembley in 1967 for Chelsea's first FA Cup final at the national stadium. That was lost but when Chelsea returned, managed by Sexton, to face Leeds United in 1970, on a surface far from conducive to good goalkeeping, Bonetti was important in keeping the country's most physically dominant side at bay with the game locked at 2-2 and into extra-time. At Old Trafford in the replay, he produced one of the most memorable goalkeeping performances in FA Cup final history. Early in the match he suffered an injury to his left knee when clattered by centre-forward Mick Jones. An awkward landing left him struggling to even walk properly and this was a time before substitute goalkeepers. He would have to finish the half virtually on one leg. When Jones scored to give Leeds the advantage shortly afterwards the Blues were up against it. The Leeds forwards targeted Bonetti at every opportunity. There was an agonising wait for Blues supporters, most of whom were packed into the Stretford End, after the outfielders returned from the changing room for the second half with Bonetti delayed inside for a pain-killing injection. After he emerged he defied the

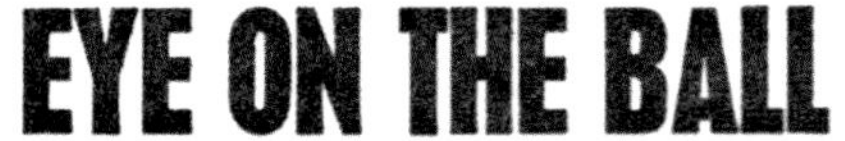

EYE ON THE BALL

PETER BONETTI of Chelsea and England —the scourge of all strikers—is never afraid to leave his line when danger threatens. Goalkeepers are fortunate in as much as they have only to keep their eye on the ball, unlike the rest of the defence who have to keep their eye on the ball and the man they are marking. Therefore Bonetti is never caught unprepared by the through-ball which can, on occasions, pierce his defence. Bonetti, acting as an extra full back, will race out of his goal, if necessary beyond the penalty area, and kick clear.

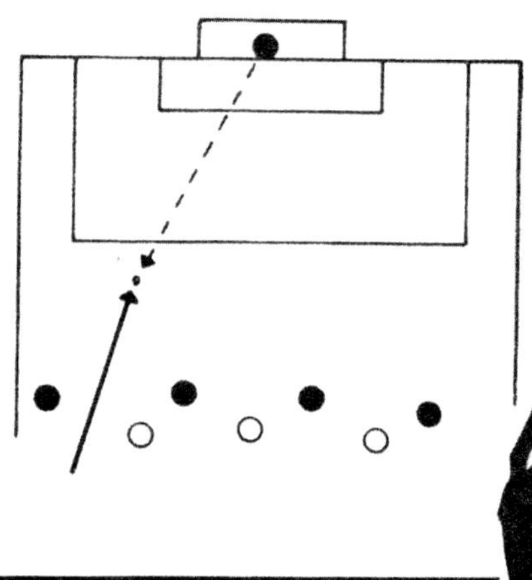

odds to make save after save with Osgood equalising and David Webb bundling in his famous extra-time winner. Bonetti played the full 120 minutes of the breath-taking and bruising contest.

'The Cat' was voted runner-up in the Footballer of the Year award for 1969/70 for the consistently high standard of his displays over the whole season. He had been the winner of Chelsea's first Player of the Year award in 1967 and was voted the club's greatest in a fans' poll two years later. The European Cup Winners' Cup followed the FA Cup win, with Bonetti overcoming pneumonia to play Real Madrid in Chelsea's first European final. Again it took two games to win the trophy and though not as busy as against Leeds, he repeated his feat at Sunderland almost a decade earlier when he pulled off an outstanding late save to maintain a decisive single-goal lead. A team which had won two trophies in as many years also finished third and sixth respectively in the league.

Few older players would survive the rebuilding, but Bonetti again proved himself indispensable. By 1975 the club was in low water financially and in terms of form. Bonetti had begun playing more for the reserves than the first team, so he spent the summer in America at the St Louis Stars. He returned to the Bridge anticipating a free transfer but with his replacement floundering, he was quickly restored to the starting eleven, the source of experience in

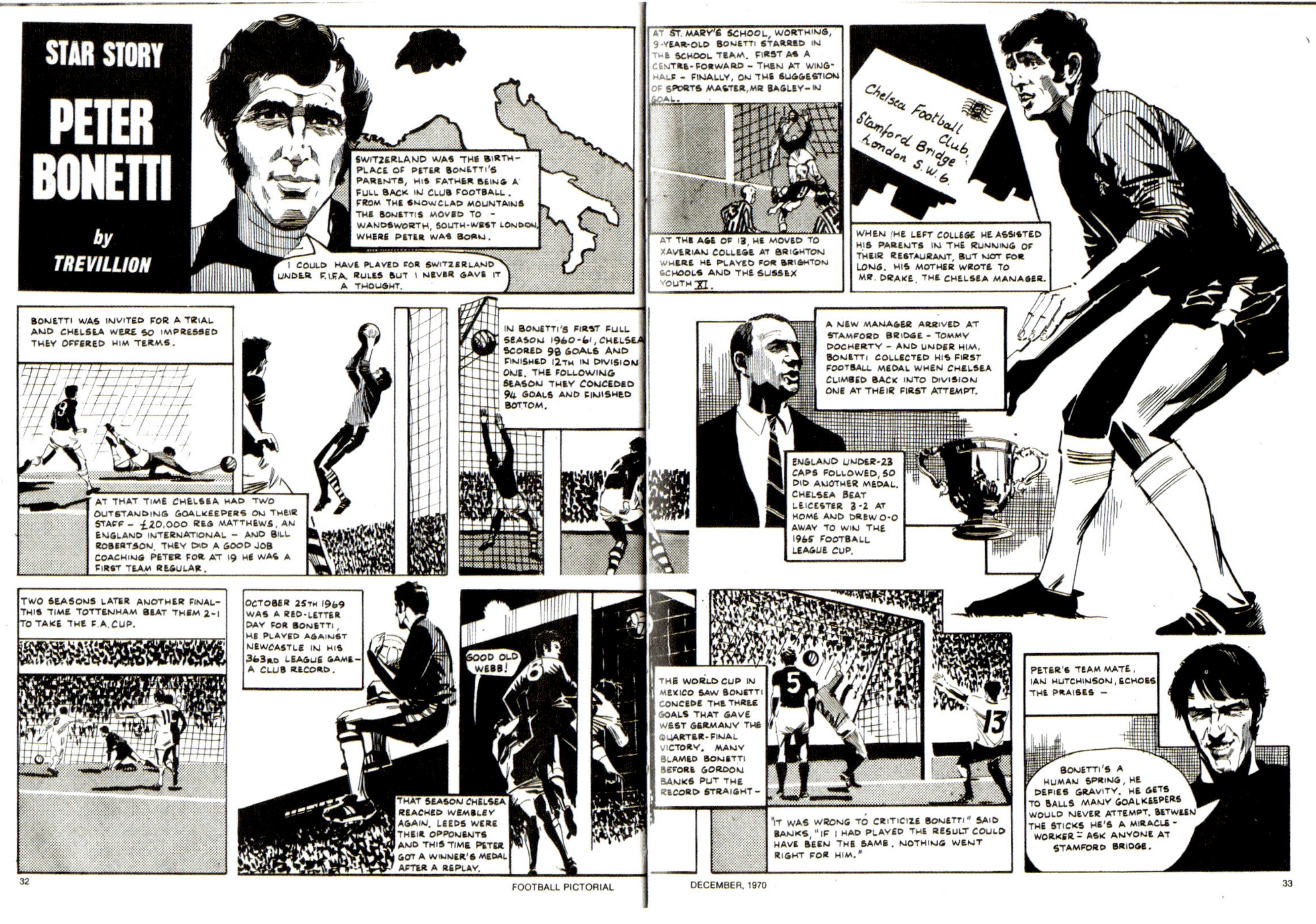

a largely youthful and homegrown Chelsea side which secured promotion back to the top flight in 1977. Two years later Bonetti announced his retirement, although a brief spell with Dundee followed but he could not be kept from his beloved Fulham Road for long. Even when he was still playing for the club he had begun to coach the younger goalkeepers in an era when there were no such specialist coaches. In 1983 he rejoined as the club's first dedicated goalkeeper coach, and how the Shed enjoyed chanting his name again and receiving a response when he came out to warm-up Eddie Niedzwiecki before each game, a ritual 'The Cat' and his fans had started way back in the 1960s. There was always a strong connection between Bonetti and the Chelsea support. He continued in the role into the 1990s and also worked with the England national team including at Italia '90, before coaching at other clubs.

For many years he continued his long association with Chelsea as a well respected and knowledgeable matchday host in the hospitality areas at the stadium, one of which carries his name. As fit as any outfielder during his playing days, he appeared in goal for the Chelsea Old Boys team well into his sixties. Peter passed away in April 2020 after suffering from long-term illness.

He's the prince of players

● Pele is the greatest footballer in the world — and when Chelsea ran up against him recently they had that proved to them all over again.

Ian Hutchinson was in that Chelsea team— and came home dazzled by what he had seen.

Today he tells why Pele is the prince.

● Every week "Hutch" teams up in The People with brilliant artist Paul Trevillion for a close-up expert look at football.

● It's the feature that fascinates fans and coaches — because it takes you on the pitch and puts you in the boots of a top player.

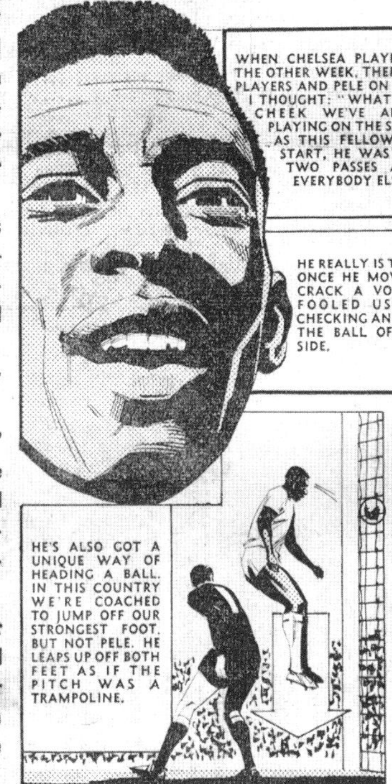

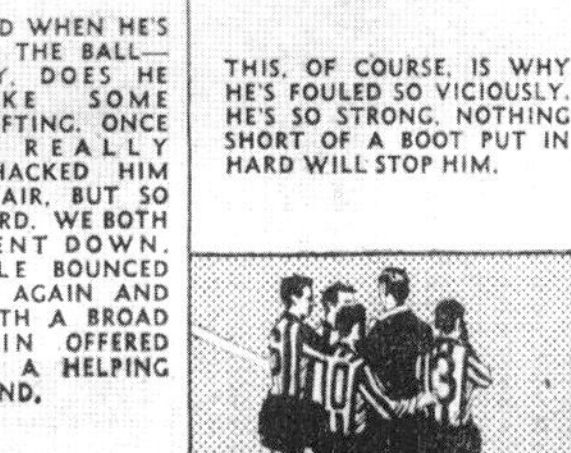

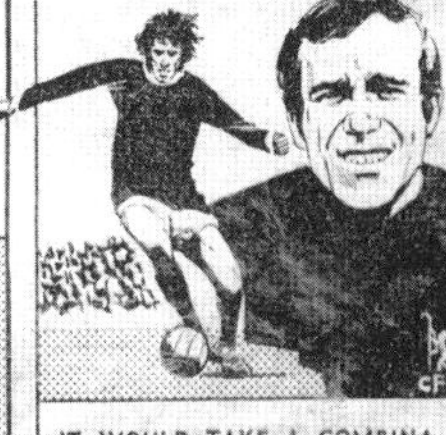

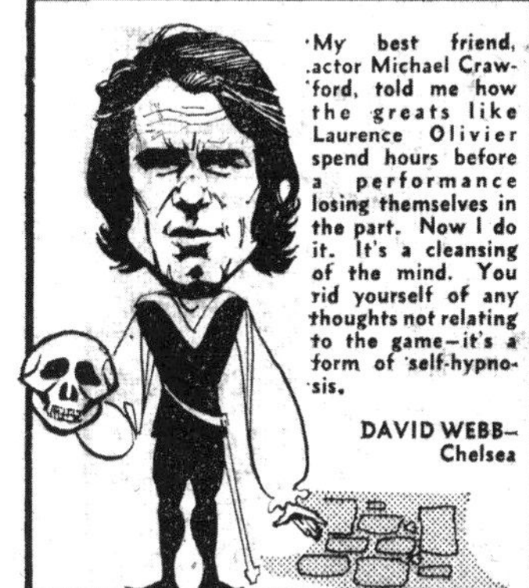

'My best friend, actor Michael Crawford, told me how the greats like Laurence Olivier spend hours before a performance losing themselves in the part. Now I do it. It's a cleansing of the mind. You rid yourself of any thoughts not relating to the game—it's a form of self-hypnosis.

DAVID WEBB—Chelsea

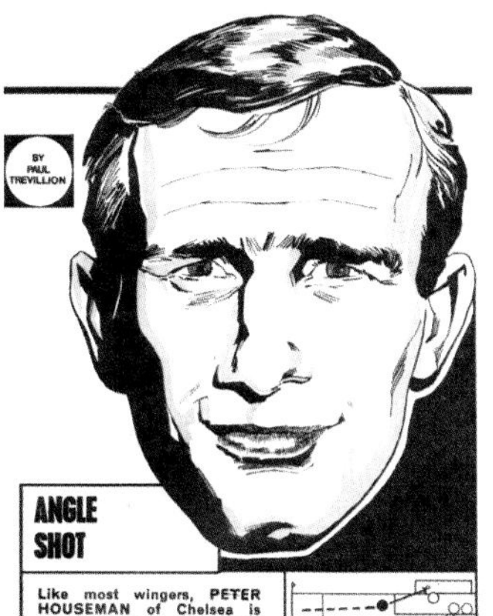

ANGLE SHOT

Like most wingers, PETER HOUSEMAN of Chelsea is highly skilled at cutting into goal at an oblique angle. In these situations the goalkeeper has to move slightly off his line as he prepares to cut out a possible centre. On occasions such as this a shot aimed at the near post behind the goalie can often catch him unprepared.

CROSSFIELD PASS

When a full back such as DAVID WEBB finds the only spare player is a team-mate standing free on the opposite side of the park he will, if he decides to pass to him, employ a lob.

A lob is the only safe way of passing across field when you are positioned close to your own penalty box—the reason being a cross-field pass along the ground can be intercepted leaving the way to goal open.

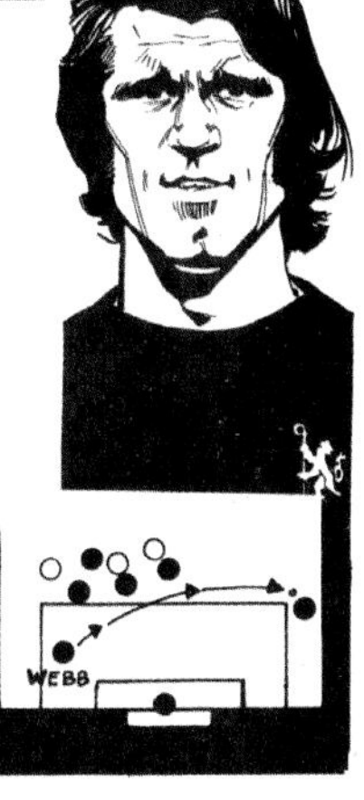

THE LONG THROW

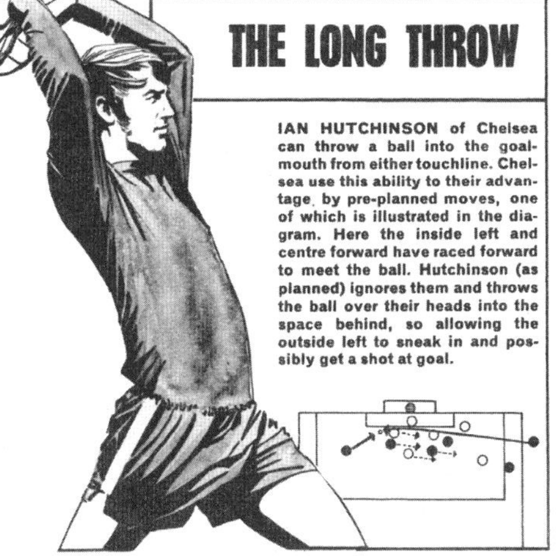

IAN HUTCHINSON of Chelsea can throw a ball into the goalmouth from either touchline. Chelsea use this ability to their advantage by pre-planned moves, one of which is illustrated in the diagram. Here the inside left and centre forward have raced forward to meet the ball. Hutchinson (as planned) ignores them and throws the ball over their heads into the space behind, so allowing the outside left to sneak in and possibly get a shot at goal.

SHOCK ABSORBER

Notice how Chelsea goalkeeper PETER BONETTI jumps and catches a head high ball in his chest. The goalkeeper who stands with his feet on the ground and catches this type of shot in front of his face is taking an unnecessary risk for there is the possibility he will not be able to hold a fiercely hit shot. Bonetti's method of taking it in his chest is far better for the body acts as a shock absorber, rather like a cushion.

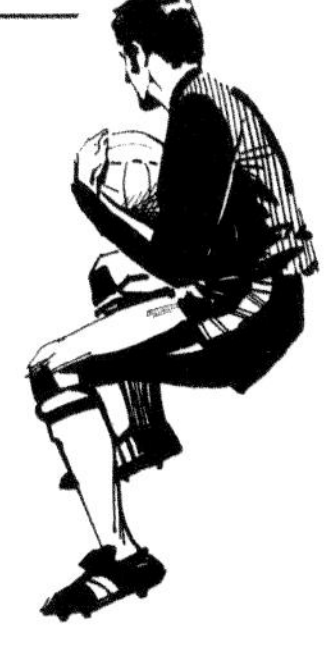

The Chelsea Razzle-Dazzle

In 1972 the eighteen-strong First Team squad of Chelsea players had a two-day stay at Bisham Abbey in Buckinghamshire going through special training routines in an attempt to erase a 3-1 defeat at Southampton. All this was in readiness for their League Cup quarter-final against Notts County. By this time I had gained a reputation at Leeds United for pre-match entertainment, so I was welcomed at Chelsea when I told Dave Sexton I had a plan of action which would heavily swing the match in their favour.

The idea came to me because Stamford Bridge was undergoing redevelopment. When I first outlined my idea to the Chelsea lads and manager, telling Dave Sexton that he should not leave the field for the dressing rooms at half-time but stay on the pitch, it was greeted with howls of laughter, but I continued: mentioning the handy pitch-side shed which would have two buckets inside for any players who were caught short, explaining that Dave could give his half-time pep talk at the side of the pitch. The gales of laughter from the Chelsea players continued but then, having given it a little thought, to a man they all agreed it would definitely leave Notts County perplexed. After a short talk among the players with Sexton joining in, it was unanimously agreed to do it, but there was more... I suggested that before the game the Chelsea players should show their appreciation to the fans by saluting the Shed by waving blue and white scarves which would then be thrown to the fans to keep as souvenirs. With a big smile

The Chelsea set... and their new look razzle-dazzle

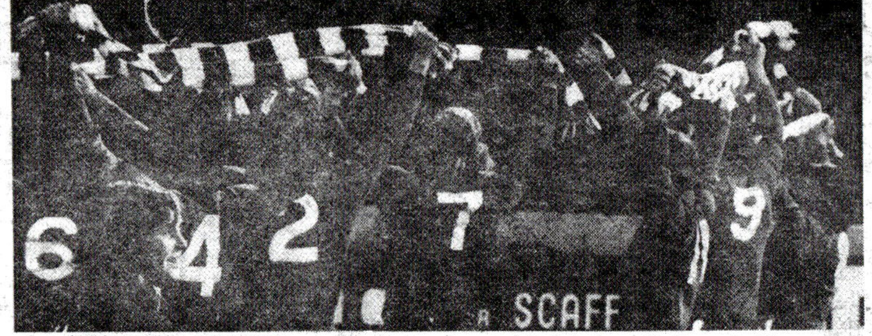

YOU ARE THE CHAMPIONS . . . The Chelsea players salute their fans with blue and white scarves.

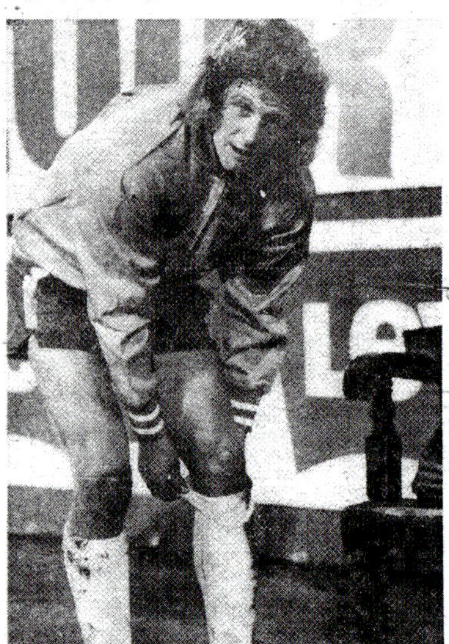

CHELSEA'S Cup hero, Chris Garland, takes a half-time breather.

THE FANS went home happy—a 3—1 win and a North Bank-style salute from their heroes, writes Michael Hart.

Before dumping Notts County out of the League Cup, the Chelsea players showed their appreciation to the supporters at Stamford Bridge last night.

Brandishing blue and white scarves, they first saluted the Shed end, then the main stand and finally threw their scarves to the crowd as souvenirs.

Sucking oranges, changing shirts and going over problems with manager Dave Sexton . . . it was a bit like a Sunday morning soccer scene on the local park pitch.

● Pictures by Michael Fresco.

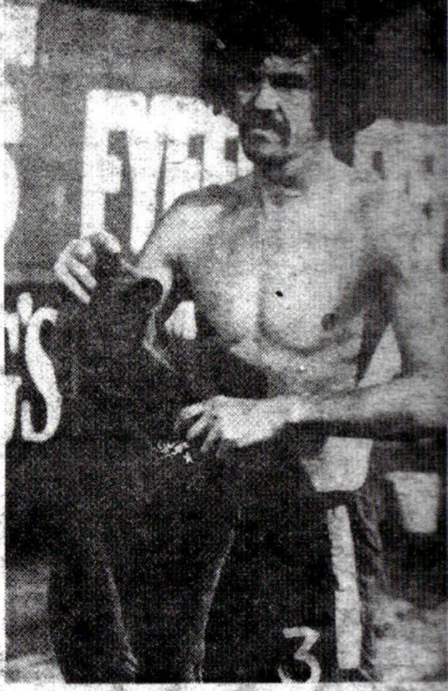

STRIPPING OFF . . . Skipper Eddie McCreadie quick change at half-time.

Dave Sexton nodded his approval at my every word.

Notts County had enjoyed an enviable League Cup that season, beating York, Southend, Southampton and Stoke, while scoring twelve goals and conceding just five, so they were no pushovers.

The pre-match plan worked perfectly, even better than we had all imagined. Then at half-time as Notts County players and their manager, Jimmy Sirrel, started to leave the field, they stopped when they saw the Chelsea players had decided to stay on. John Phillips went back in goal for Hollins and Osgood to fire in a few shots. Other players on the pitch started passing the ball about. The County players watched as Sirrel raced back on the pitch. The Referee caught up with him and simply shrugged his shoulders advising him it was the Chelsea players' choice, and left. The Notts County players decided to stop watching and finally trouped off for the few minutes remaining in their dressing-room. THE RESULT WAS A 3-1 WIN FOR CHELSEA. The fans went home happy and there are still those who remember that game and when I mention it to the Chelsea fans they always add a couple of goals to the scoreline... A 5-1 WIN FOR CHELSEA!

PT

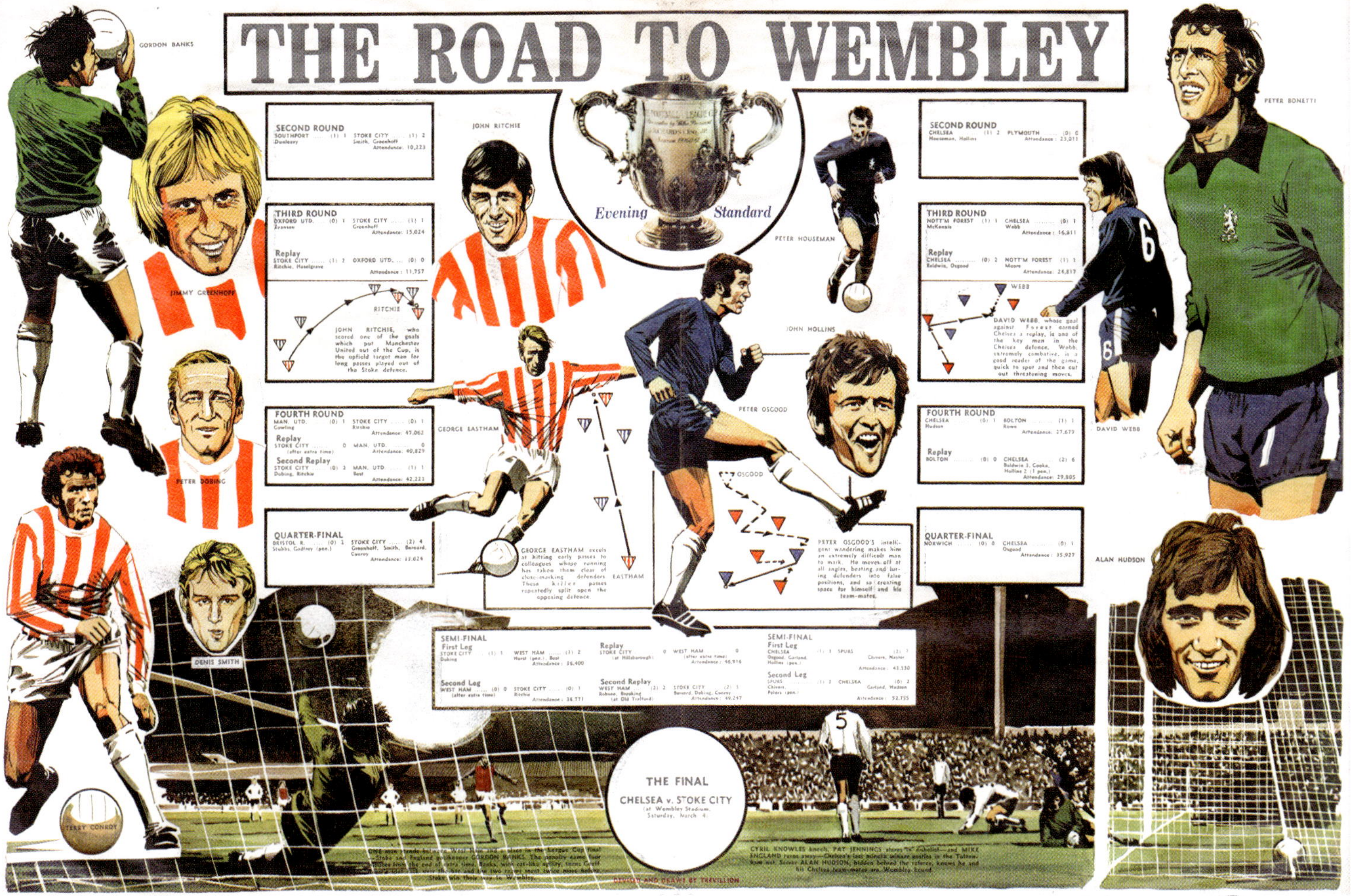

THE ROAD TO WEMBLEY

Evening Standard

GORDON BANKS · JIMMY GREENHOFF · JOHN RITCHIE · PETER DOBING · GEORGE EASTHAM · DENIS SMITH · TERRY CONROY · PETER HOUSEMAN · JOHN HOLLINS · PETER OSGOOD · PETER BONETTI · DAVID WEBB · ALAN HUDSON

SECOND ROUND
SOUTHPORT ...... (1) 1 — STOKE CITY ...... (1) 2
Dunleavy — Smith, Greenhoff
Attendance: 10,223

THIRD ROUND
OXFORD UTD. ...... (0) 1 — STOKE CITY ...... (1) 1
Evanson — Greenhoff
Attendance: 15,024

Replay
STOKE CITY ...... (1) 2 — OXFORD UTD. ...... (0) 0
Ritchie, Haselgrave
Attendance: 11,757

RITCHIE

JOHN RITCHIE, who scored one of the goals which put Manchester United out of the Cup, is the upfield target man for long passes played out of the Stoke defence.

FOURTH ROUND
MAN. UTD. ...... (0) 1 — STOKE CITY ...... (0) 1
Cowling — Ritchie
Attendance: 47,062

Replay
STOKE CITY ...... 0 — MAN. UTD. 0
(after extra time)
Attendance: 40,829

Second Replay
STOKE CITY ...... (0) 2 — MAN. UTD. ...... (1) 1
Dobing, Ritchie — Best
Attendance: 42,223

QUARTER-FINAL
BRISTOL R. ...... (0) 2 — STOKE CITY ...... (2) 4
Stubbs, Godfrey (pen.) — Greenhoff, Smith, Bernard, Conroy
Attendance: 33,624

EASTHAM

GEORGE EASTHAM excels at hitting early passes to colleagues whose running has taken them clear of close-marking defenders. These killer passes repeatedly split open the opposing defence.

OSGOOD

PETER OSGOOD'S intelligent wandering makes him an extremely difficult man to mark. He moves off at all angles, beating and luring defenders into false positions, and so creating space for himself and his team-mates.

SECOND ROUND
CHELSEA ...... (1) 2 — PLYMOUTH ...... (0) 0
Houseman, Hollins
Attendance: 23,011

THIRD ROUND
NOTT'M FOREST (1) 1 — CHELSEA ...... (0) 1
McKenzie — Webb
Attendance: 16,811

Replay
CHELSEA ...... (0) 2 — NOTT'M FOREST (1) 1
Baldwin, Osgood — Moore
Attendance: 24,817

WEBB

DAVID WEBB, whose goal against Forest earned Chelsea a replay, is one of the key men in the Chelsea defence. Webb, extremely combative, is a good reader of the game, quick to spot and then cut out threatening moves.

FOURTH ROUND
CHELSEA ...... (0) 1 — BOLTON ...... (1) 1
Hudson — Rowe
Attendance: 27,679

Replay
BOLTON ...... (0) 0 — CHELSEA ...... (2) 6
Baldwin 3, Cooke, Hollins 2 (1 pen.)
Attendance: 29,805

QUARTER-FINAL
NORWICH ...... (0) 0 — CHELSEA ...... (0) 1
Osgood
Attendance: 35,927

SEMI-FINAL

First Leg
STOKE CITY ...... (1) 1 — WEST HAM ...... (1) 2
Dobing — Hurst (pen.), Best
Attendance: 36,400

Second Leg
WEST HAM ...... (0) 0 — STOKE CITY ...... (0) 1
(after extra time) — Ritchie
Attendance: 38,771

Replay
STOKE CITY ...... 0 — WEST HAM 0
(at Hillsborough) — (after extra time)
Attendance: 46,916

Second Replay
WEST HAM ...... (2) 2 — STOKE CITY ...... (2) 3
Robson, Brooking — Bernard, Dobing, Conroy
(at Old Trafford)
Attendance: 49,247

SEMI-FINAL

First Leg
CHELSEA ...... (1) 3 — SPURS ...... (2) 2
Osgood, Garland, Hollins (pen.) — Chivers, Naylor
Attendance: 43,330

Second Leg
SPURS ...... (1) 2 — CHELSEA ...... (0) 2
Chivers, Peters (pen.) — Garland, Hudson
Attendance: 52,755

THE FINAL
CHELSEA v. STOKE CITY
(at Wembley Stadium, Saturday, March 4)

ONE man stands between West Ham and a place in the League Cup final—Stoke and England goalkeeper GORDON BANKS. The penalty came four minutes from the end of extra time. Banks, with cat-like agility, turns Geoff Hurst's shot over the bar and the two rivals meet twice more before Stoke win their way to Wembley.

CYRIL KNOWLES kneels, PAT JENNINGS stares in disbelief—and MIKE ENGLAND turns away—Chelsea's last minute winner nestles in the Tottenham net. Scorer ALAN HUDSON, hidden behind the referee, knows he and his Chelsea team-mates are Wembley bound.

DEVISED AND DRAWN BY TREVILLION

NO SUCKER NOW, says Chelsea's Dave Webb

I'M going to kiss the Wembley turf when I step out for the League Cup Final, for it was here, in the Cup Final against Leeds, my days at right back ended. Eddie Gray gave me a terrible roasting — I kept diving in . . . then nothing!

In the Final replay, Harris went to back and I played in the middle. I've been there ever since.

Gray spelt out something that, deep down, I already knew. I was the sucker who dived in and sold himself. Through playing in the middle I've been forced to exercise restraint. Sell yourself too quickly and it's a down payment on a goal — for the other side.

This season I've gone a long way to proving I'm a lot better than kick-and-rush. I put this down to all the positions I've played—goal, right and left-back, centre-half, striker.

I've found out, shoulder-to-shoulder, how Chivers shields a ball, Hurst kills an awkward pass, Davies heads, Best beats a man. And most important—how Bobby Moore cools it when the heat's on.

I realised how well I read a game when I played in goal. I played like a deep centre-half—with hands!

During Chelsea's great run I've seen off Dougan, Macdonald, Channon, Clarke, Jones, Ritchie. It's a fair old record, and at 25 I feel I'm young enough to fancy my chances of getting a cap.

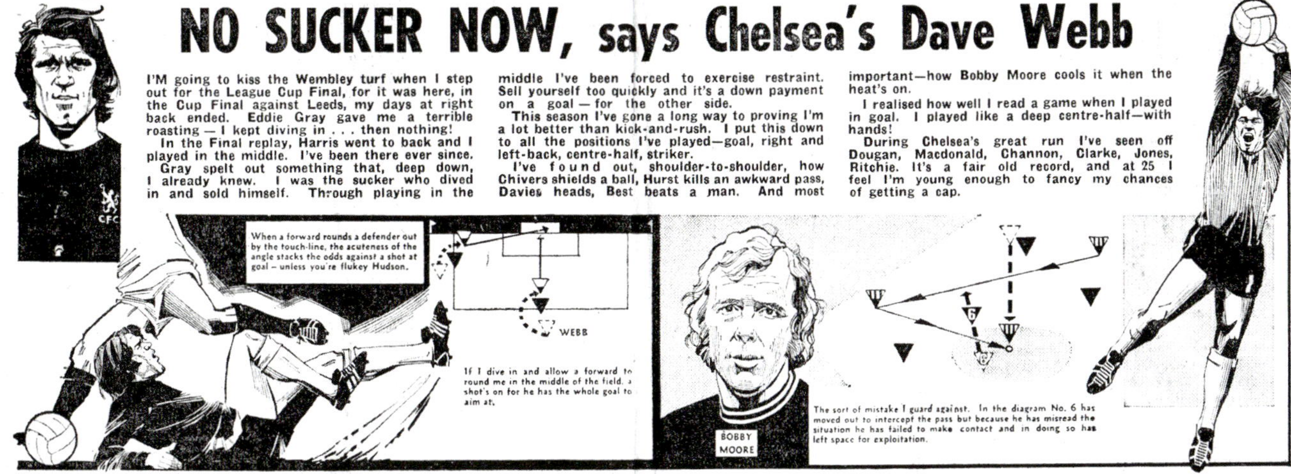

DEVISED AND DRAWN BY TREVILLION

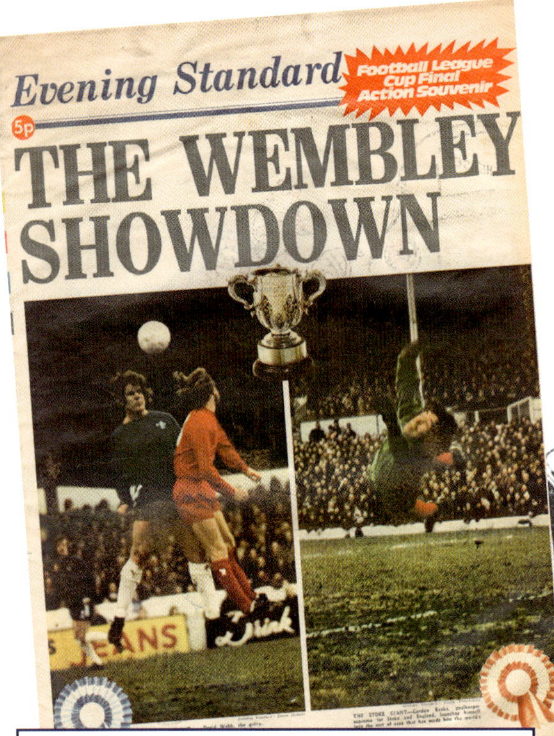

Stoke City 2 Chelsea 1

Chelsea were overwhelming favourites to win their third trophy in three seasons while Stoke were playing for their first major honour.

Terry Conroy gave Stoke a shock lead after just 5 minutes, heading home following a goalmouth scramble. Chelsea upped the pressure approaching half-time and Peter Osgood slid home an equaliser a minute before the break. As the second half grew tense it was the underdogs who forced a winner when 36 year-old George Eastham converted from close range. A member of the 1966 World Cup squad, his transfer from Newcastle to Arsenal was the subject of a test case that ended the 'retain-and-transfer' system that tied players to one club for life.

STEVE PERRYMAN (Spurs) and Geoff Hurst (West Ham) — defeated semi-finalists in the Football League Cup—have this to say on the teams that beat them. . . .

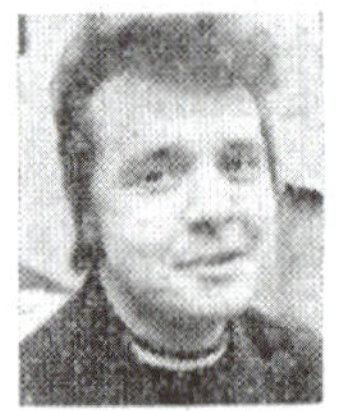

ARTIST PAUL TREVILLION'S TIP— STOKE

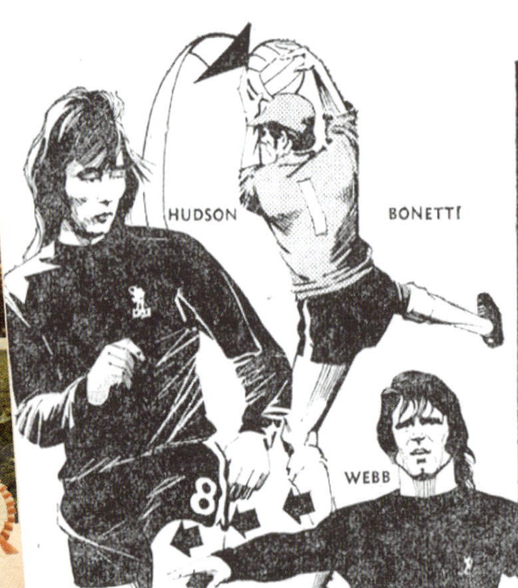

PERRYMAN WEIGHS UP CHELSEA'S KEY PLAYERS

BONETTI—Playing with great authority—grabbing everything around his six-yard box.

WEBB—The best centre-half in the country. Reading the game well—dominant in the air—bubbling with enthusiasm.

HUDSON—Will dominate midfield-collecting, carrying and turning the Stoke defence with long and short passes.

HOUSEMAN—One of the best orthodox wingers in football. Nobody's better at hitting inch-accurate centres when moving at speed.

OSGOOD—The moment of magic that turns a match is always on with Ossie.

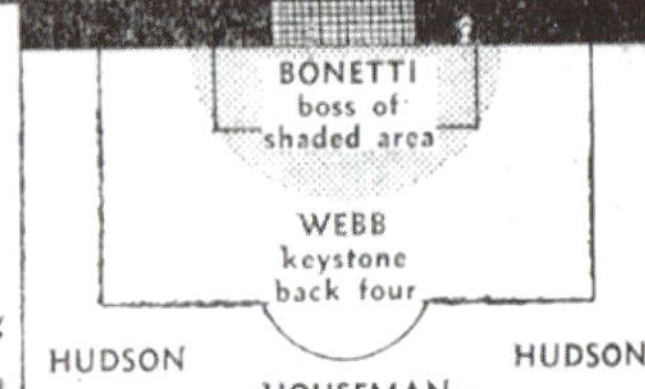

VERDICT
Chelsea are a great all-round team—I believe they have too much class for Stoke—They'll win.

HURST WEIGHS UP STOKE'S KEY PLAYERS

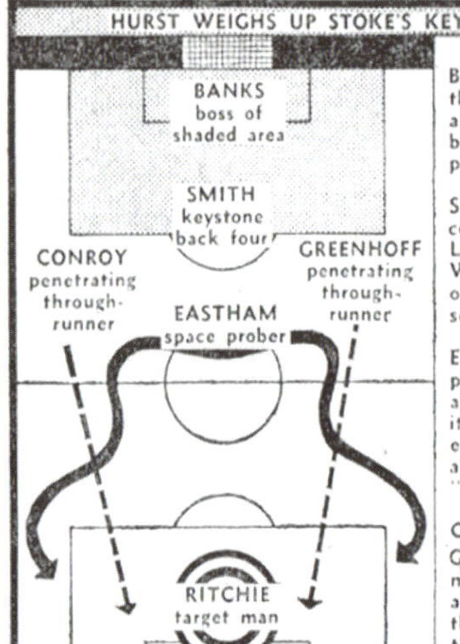

VERDICT
Chelsea to win! In our four games against Stoke we created enough chances to beat them. But I'm not writing Stoke off completely—they're a very good side.

BANKS—Commands the whole penalty area. He's not bad at saving penalties, either!

SMITH—Very combative centre-half. Like Chelsea's Webb, has the knack of scoring from set-pieces.

EASTHAM—Always probing for space and when he spots it, ruthlessly exploits it with an accurate "killer" pass.

CONROY, GREENHOFF—Quick movers, these two—and never more so than when sprinting through from the deep on to Eastham's defence-splitters.

RITCHIE—His height will cause Chelsea problems in the air. Extremely effective target man—and a good finisher.

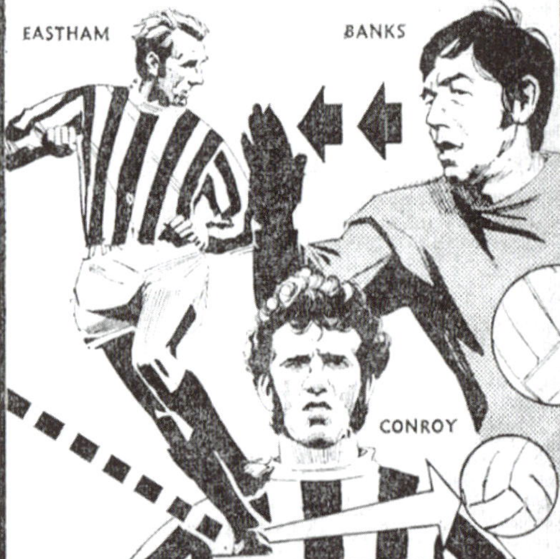

Charlie Cooke

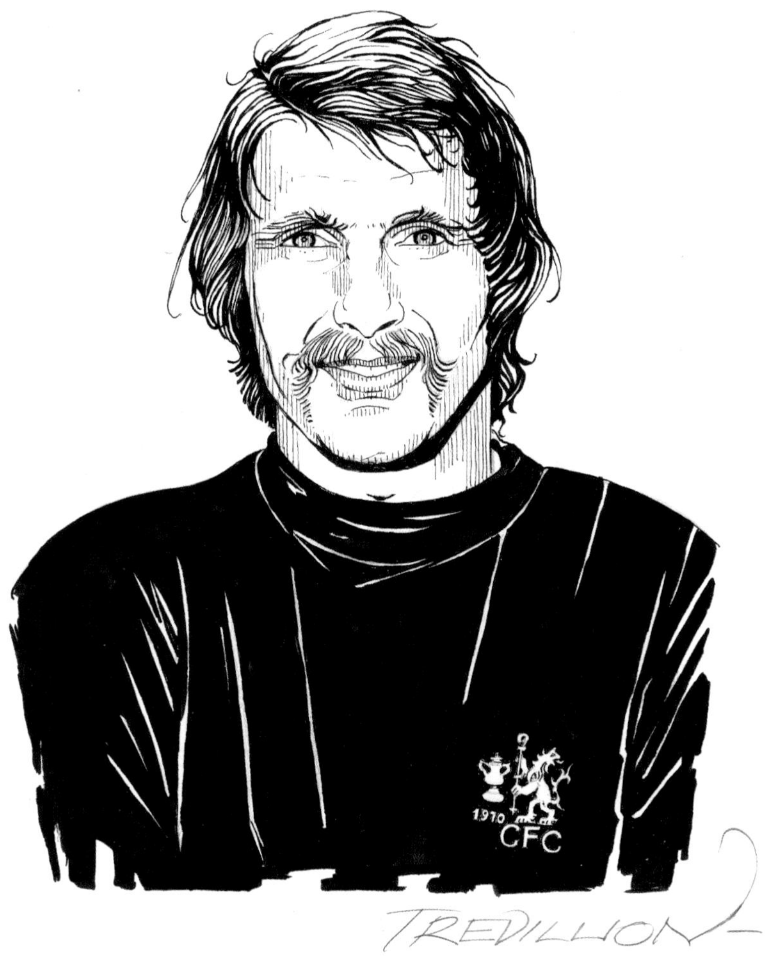

There is a lovely picture of Charlie and my wife Linda after she had come up with the idea of a Chelsea magazine and interviewed the likes of contemporary greats such as Ruud Gullit and legends like Charlie (see page 7). There is an even better story of a little Linda being taken by her dad Ken after school in West London to watch the Friday afternoon training session on the rock hard concrete at the entrance to the Bridge at a time when the players had a unique connection with the fans. Spotting little Linda watching the guys go through their paces - and there is a picture of Ron 'Chopper' Harris looking as though he meant business irrespective of the surface – Charlie found some flowers and presented them to her. To this day Linda never fails to tell the story of those flowers from Charlie. Such a lovely touch, and far removed from some of the over paid mega stars who walk past their own ball boys/girls, although there are some notable exceptions.

Charlie was one of the idols of the King's Road set during the sixties and seventies when Chelsea were short on success but long on characters. He was one the most skilful and best-loved players at a time when the national sport was still predominantly working class, as were the players. A generation before the superstars would sometimes catch a bus to the ground, in the days of the Swinging sixties they were able to afford cars, but not the million pound versions some of todays players can afford.

Signed from Dundee in 1966, Cookie made his debut in the Fairs Cup semi-final against Barcelona. He had to wait until August to make his league debut when he embarrassed England's World Cup winning captain Bobby Moore scoring the winner against West Ham. Over the next six seasons, Charlie entertained the Chelsea faithful with his extravagant skills and he was a crucial part of the 1970 and 1971 cup-winning teams. His dribble and cross to set up Peter Osgood's late equaliser in the FA Cup final replay will forever remain part of Chelsea folklore.

Charlie now lives in America: "I always wanted to be in the States, I married an American girl and I loved Westerns and American detective series and the blue skies of America always seems to be a place I wanted to try." He returned to Stamford Bridge during the Roman Abramovich era: "One of the wonderful things about the takeover at Chelsea is that they invite all the old farts back who had been thrown out the door before. I have no gripe about Ken Bates, that's what he wanted, but it's wonderful that they invite us back now, it's lovely for me and all the guys really appreciate it. You feel the love fans still have for you and it's fantastic."

Charlie was a genius of the dribble, a brilliant Scottish midfielder who replaced Terry Venables in the heart of the

Chelsea side and rivalled Peter Osgood for the affections of The Shed. He was phenomenally gifted, an extraordinary dribbler and visionary passer, but coupled with a prodigious work ethic, he was named Chelsea's player of the year three times – a record shared with Franco Zola.

Despite being part of a team full of captivating and maverick talents, he only won two major trophies in his two spells at Stamford Bridge. "We were underachievers, and that was our own fault," says Cooke, "we underachieved on the big occasions – we were dreadful in the FA Cup final against Spurs in 1967, and we lost to Stoke in the League Cup final in 1972. We were out of control, wild and crazy, we egged each other on with the drinking culture. I have regrets. From this perspective, it was a lot of nonsense. At the time, you're having fun, or you think you are, but I'm not one to say that if I had it all to live over I'd do it exactly the same. I'd be a bit smarter, more self-controlled, not so willing."

The Chelsea of Peter Osgood, Alan Hudson, Peter Bonetti, Ron 'Chopper' Harris, Ian Hutchison, David Webb and Cooke won the 1970 FA Cup after a replay, with Cooke finding an angle in the middle of the bare brown pitch to lift the ball over Leeds' Jack Charlton for Ossie's diving header. The following season he lifted the European Cup Winners' Cup in Athens again after a replay. The trophy was almost theirs in the first game – Cooke watched it being brought to a table at the side of the pitch – but Real Madrid equalised in the last minute. With 48 hours to kill, what did Cooke and his best drinking buddy, Tommy 'The Sponge' Baldwin do? "Get hammered!" replies the Scot. Thankfully the "diabolical" hangover had subsided sufficiently for Charlie to be crucial to the victory.

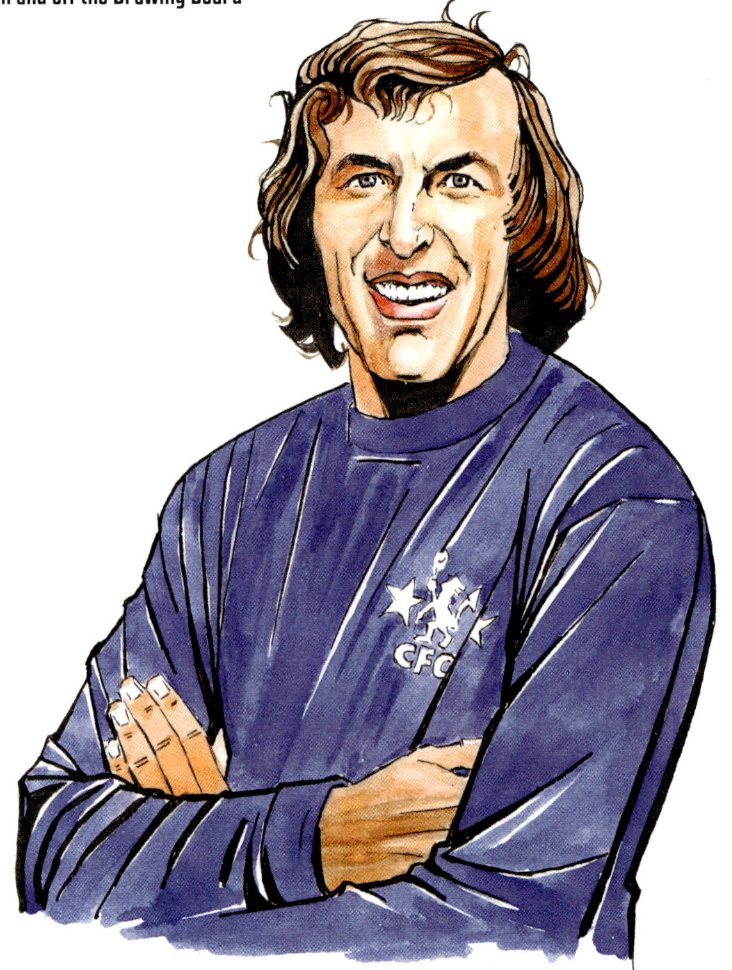

Tommy 'The Sponge' Baldwin

Cooke rivalled George Best as a sixties heart throb, as the Shed sang "Oh, Charlie Charlie … " to the tune of Chicory Tip's chart-topper 'Son of my Father'. The Swinging Sixties in the King's Road attracted celeb royalty with everyone from Raquel Welch to Steve McQueen turning up at the Bridge. Welch's rumoured romance with Osgood was, according to Cooke, "just a publicity stunt for her" – although he still laughs at the memory of *The Great Escape* star McQueen taking out a cigarette in the Chelsea dressing-room and fellow Scot Eddie McCreadie "jumping up to light it for him like he was a flippin' butler!".

Cooke's autobiography *The Bonnie Prince*, touches on the drinking culture and his drinking partner, Tommy Baldwin, nicknamed 'The Sponge' for his ability to soak up booze. But however much they drank in West London, it was more professional drinking north of the border. His Scotland days, too, were notable for promise unfulfilled. Although unbeaten against Brazil and England and having been part of a team scoring thirteen goals in two games against Cyprus and nine in two against Wales, he was involved in five qualifying campaigns, all ending in failure. "Looking back, I see how dilettantish I was. There was a crazy social scene at Chelsea: it was stupid, uncontrolled childishness. And I know folk like to remember Jimmy Johnstone getting stranded in his wee sailing boat but to me all these colourful stories are a bit pathetic. Don't get me wrong, I was part of that rubbish. And I know that in my career I didn't achieve one iota of what I should have done."

Does he think it's been over-romanticised? "Yes I do. I played some trash, I know that. But no matter what I did off the field I never cut corners as regards my fitness. I don't think I got enough respect for my graft and I was over-praised for the fanciness. Don't laugh, but I wanted to be a Di Stefano who could do it all ways. If the team needed someone to go over the top and break a leg, this guy would do it. If they needed craft he'd do it and if they needed goals, he'd score them. But here's the really inane thing about me: I thought goalscorers were morons. There was one season at Aberdeen where I scored a lot, but after that hardly any. I got carried away with being called the playmaker, the midfield general. Scoring goals was easy, I thought – the real art was in making them. What utter horseshit…"

Charlie was surprisingly allowed to join Crystal Palace in 1972 but returned 18 months later. He was unable to help prevent relegation in 1975 but two years later played a part in supporting a young team win promotion. He made a handful of appearances over the next two seasons, playing his 373rd and final Chelsea game in a memorable FA Cup win over Liverpool. In the summer of 1978 Cooke moved to the United States where he played for several clubs before retiring and opening a soccer school in Ohio.

Charlie finally hung up his boots at 40 with California Surf then helped form Coerver Coaching, based for a long time in Cincinnati before a move to his second wife Diane's native California. Cooke's career took him from Greenock High School to California Surf, via Aberdeen, Dundee, Chelsea and Crystal Palace. "I took it as an opportunity to retrace a lot of my life and find out things I'd forgotten," he said, "one of the strange things was that my sister had been doing some genealogy and the interesting thing to me – although it may be of no interest to anybody else – is that we, the Cookes, came from a long line of circus people. My umpteen great grandfather was the first person to take a big top to America. Another Cooke would ride round the ring on a horse taking off costumes of different Shakespearean characters. I come from a long line of hairy-chested women, Romanian jugglers and fat men. Entertainers, sure, but I'm not sure it's a rich lineage – maybe a tacky one."

Cooke scored barely 20 goals in nearly 300 league games for Chelsea, admitting, "I allowed the headlines about my being the team schemer and midfield general to get into my head, with the result that I ignored finishing."

Biggest Win in Chelsea History

Chelsea in 1971/72 were the holders of the Cup Winners' Cup after beating Real Madrid in the final the previous May having just finished sixth in the league. It was still very much the 'Kings of the King's Road' side with Osgood, Cooke, Hudson, Bonetti et al, although the successful spell under manager Dave Sexton was coming to an end. Jeunesse Hautcharage had been surprise winners of the Luxembourg Cup the previous season; a club from a village with 704 inhabitants, they were in Luxembourg's Third Division when they stunned the country by winning the cup final 4-1 after extra-time against Jeunesse Esch, one of the country's biggest clubs, although they also won promotion to the Second Division by the end of the season as well. In the club's 52-year history they had only played in the top flight for one season and their previous best run in the cup had taken them to the quarter-finals. The local brewery celebrated the 1971 cup win by offering free beer to the village for three days and three nights but everyone had sobered up by the time Chelsea arrived in mid-September for the first European match in Hautcharage's history. "I must admit that we didn't know much about them before we played," Bonetti admitted when he recalled the tie, "but it soon became clear it would be an easy game. We were obviously in a different class from them and it was their first time in Europe and we had a bit of experience of playing in Europe."

Player/coach Romain Schoder was one of Hautcharage team members who had played at a higher level in Luxembourg but that was as a goalkeeper. Now he was his team's sweeper. They only trained two nights a week and for their home game against Chelsea, some made the journey to the ground by bicycle, directly from work. Joseph Thill was the club chairman and Guy Thill was their youngest and most promising player, despite only having one arm. Only 1,500 could have attended the first leg had it not been moved to Luxembourg's national stadium where a 13,000 crowd watched. Before the game, a Jeunesse official admitted, "We have no hope! If we lose 7-1 we'll be happy." After two minutes Osgood scored, Peter Houseman hit a second and Ossie headed another to make it 3-0 inside half-an-hour and completed his hat-trick before half-time with Houseman, again, plus Tommy Baldwin and John Hollins, with a 25-yarder, added to the scoresheet before the interval. Baldwin and David Webb scored in the second half to complete the 8-0 win. Five goals were headers, Osgood (twice) and Baldwin also struck the woodwork.

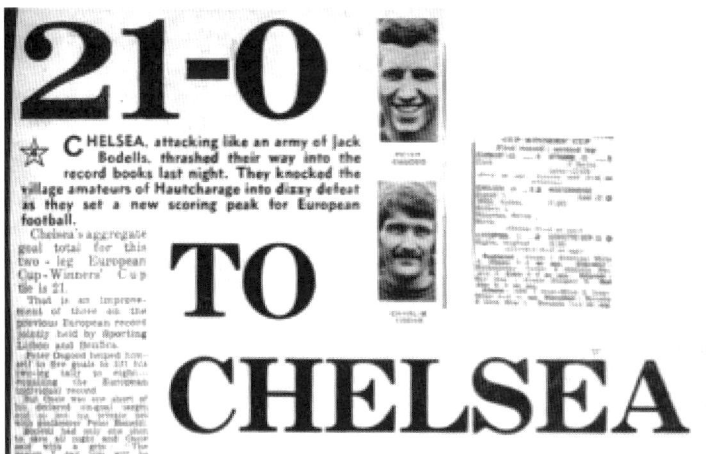

21-0 TO CHELSEA

CHELSEA, attacking like an army of Jack Bodells, thrashed their way into the record books last night. They knocked the village amateurs of Hautcharage into dizzy defeat as they set a new scoring peak for European football.

Chelsea's aggregate goal total for this two-leg European Cup-Winners' Cup tie is 21.

That is an improvement of three on the previous European record jointly held by Sporting Lisbon and Benfica.

[illegible]

In an attempt to maintain some interest, the Chelsea match programme for the return game carried words on the need to 'put on a show' for the 27,621 supporters, although it did speculate that that rarest of scorers, Ron Harris, could find the net on the night, and on the possibility that Bonetti would play in attack at some stage with David Webb going in goal. The programme also made everyone aware of records that might be set. Chelsea had not hit double figures in a single game before, and the previous best aggregate scoring by any club in a European tie was 18 with the best score by a British club 16-0. "Records were something I didn't even think about before the game," said Bonetti. "it was only when we had finished I thought blimey, we might have scored a record amount here but I couldn't have told you what the record score in Europe was anyway. It certainly didn't cross my mind for a minute going into that second leg. And I was never going to play elsewhere in the team. We weren't going to muck around. It was a serious game and to start changing positions wouldn't have been very professional. When you are playing a side like that who might not be as experienced as we were you can't let them off the leash, you have to go out and play your best because you have a duty to yourself and your team and to the fans. I don't think we took the mickey at all, we played our stuff and got the goals and were very professional about the whole situation."

All four Welschers brother were in the Hautcharage team at the Bridge; there were also two Thills in the side and one of the visiting team wore glasses during the match. Osgood declared before the game that he would score six goals, which would have set a new best for a player in Europe, but was positively sluggish at the start compared with the first leg, taking four minutes to open the scoring although he had two goals by the sixth minute when keeper Lucien Fusilier dropped a cross. Hollins's successful penalty put Blues 4-0 up after 13 minutes and, as in the first leg, the half-time score was 6-0. As speculated in the programme, the sixth was scored by Harris who ended a 20-minute 'goal drought'.

The eighth gave Osgood his second hat-trick of the tie and Houseman struck the historic 10th in the 77th minute, taking Chelsea beyond the nine-goal hauls put past both Glossop and Worksop back in the first three seasons of the club's existence. When Osgood made it 11-0 Chelsea had set a new European record. He headed goal number twelve from a corner for a personal haul of five on the night. Baldwin completed his second-half hat-trick with the last kick of the game as Chelsea won 13-0, from 54 goal attempts, five of which hit the post or crossbar. Eight-goal Osgood fell short in 'only' scoring five in the second leg; he had equalled rather than surpassed the eight-goal record for individual scoring in any European tie and had also lost a bet with team-mate Bonetti. "Ossie had said to me in the dressing-room before we went out that he was going to get six having got three in the first leg, and I was winding him up by saying I bet you don't. In the end I said I'll bet you a fiver. After the game he told people that when we got the penalty, I came up to him and said you can't take that because John Hollins is our penalty-taker but I don't remember that at all! Fair enough though, he came into the dressing-room and gave me the fiver straight away."

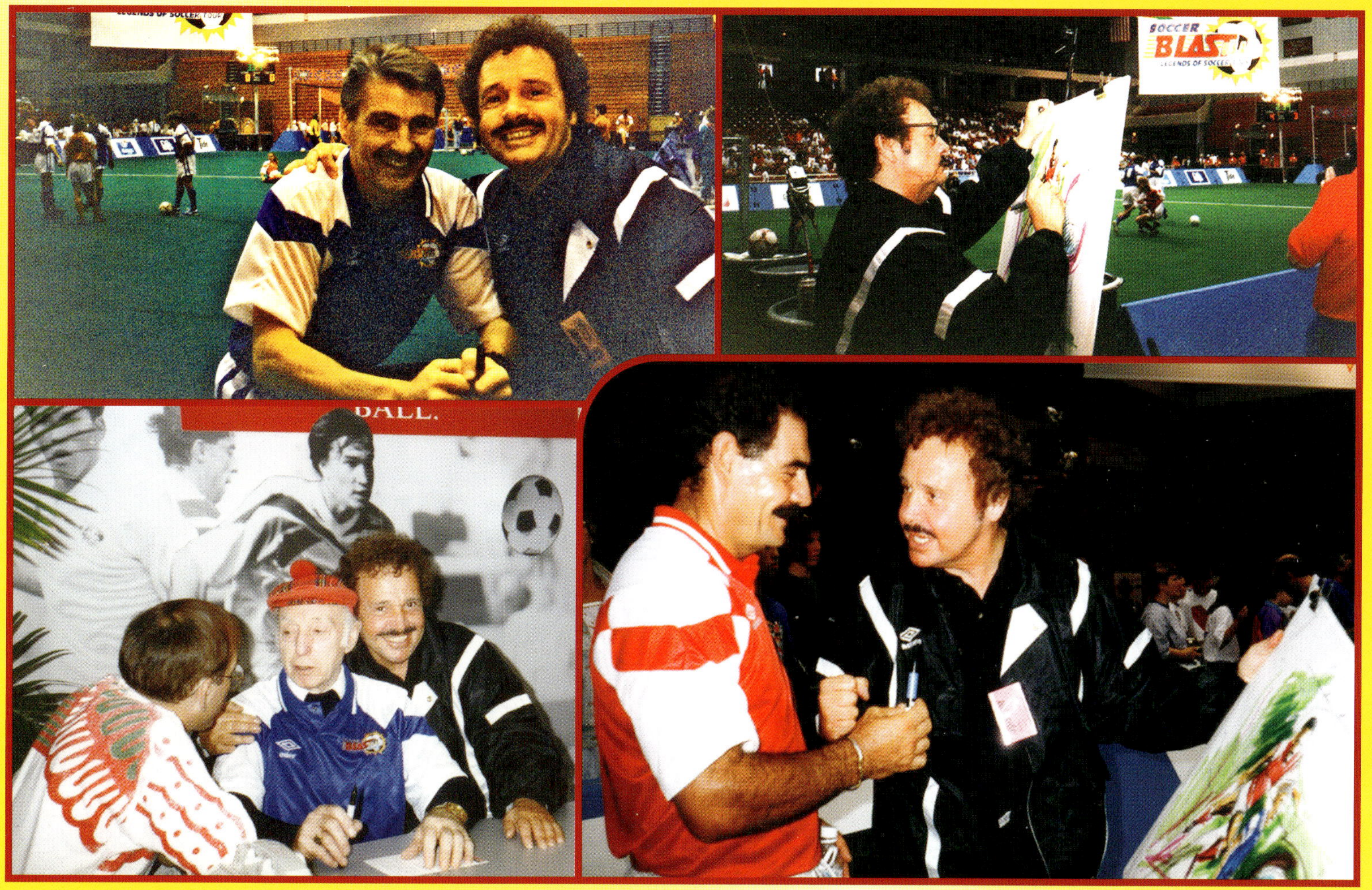

I knew Charlie Cooke from my days in the 1970's working with Ian Hutchinson for the *Sunday People*. The next time I met him was 20 years later and we were not at the Bridge, we were in America for the World Cup in 1994. I was working for Umbro on the 'Soccerblast' Legends Tour and Charlie was coaching with various US Soccer clubs. The first words I said to Charlie as we shook hands was "Great to meet a true Soccer ARTIST, one who crossed the 'white line' and played for Chelsea." Charlie laughed "In those days, in a one on one situation, I would always take the defender on and 9 out of 10 times beat him! I was never one to pass on my responsibility. Truth is, I always fancied myself in a 2 on 1 and I usually, but not always, pulled it off. Of course once I was through, it was a shot at goal or a shout from Ossie to give him the ball and as always the big man banged it into the net. Great days and great unforgettable memories."

Also appearing was Sir Stanley Matthews (bottom left), Gordon Banks and Roberto Rivellino, who made the cross in 1970 from which Pelé headed Brazil's 100th goal in the World Cup. It was my job 'pitchside' to draw the goals as they went in. Rivellino asked me how quickly I could draw? I replied "as quick as you can score!" Rivellino scored a hat-trick in four minutes and then ran off the field to see if I had captured the hat-trick goal. He was so pleased with the result that he grabbed the pen from my hand and signed his drawing - which is captured in the photograph!

PT

Trevillion's Troupes

I was sitting in the Soho Square office of Les Reed who *The Guinness Book of Hit Singles* called 'The Eighth Wonder of the Pop World'. Reed was the mastermind behind most of Tom Jones' and Engelbert Humperdinck's greatest hits, but I received a definite "NO" to my latest idea. "Sorry Paul", said Reed, "I appreciate you convinced me to get behind the Leeds football anthem 'Marching on Together' but I'm not into football. But I know a man at MAM (Management Agency & Music) who works alongside Jones and Humperdinck, who is a football nut! His name is Sydney Rose."

Thanks to Les's tip off, I convinced Sydney Rose to get involved with my idea of players who were approaching the autumn of their playing days drawing huge crowds and making big money in a worldwide 7-a-side competition. Names such as BEST, OSGOOD and MOORE would sell out stadiums all over the world, especially America, and I had already sounded them out and they were all up for it. Rose jumped at this football opportunity and with his knowledge of rubbing shoulders with showbiz superstars thanks to MAM, he immediately put the wheels in motion.

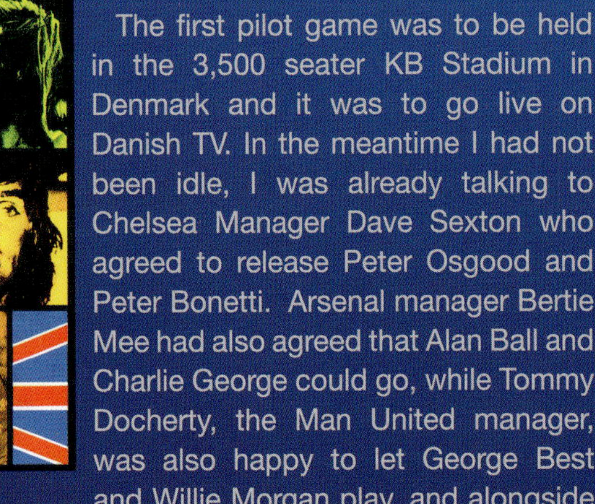

The first pilot game was to be held in the 3,500 seater KB Stadium in Denmark and it was to go live on Danish TV. In the meantime I had not been idle, I was already talking to Chelsea Manager Dave Sexton who agreed to release Peter Osgood and Peter Bonetti. Arsenal manager Bertie Mee had also agreed that Alan Ball and Charlie George could go, while Tommy Docherty, the Man United manager, was also happy to let George Best and Willie Morgan play, and alongside England '66 World Cup Captain Bobby Moore in the side it was, in Sydney Rose's term, 'LIFT OFF!"

The tickets for the game sold out in less than two hours and were immediately re-selling for four times the ticket price. The programme was printed with every other page an advert. It was a runaway financial success. The players would make double the promised fee.

Ball for Trevillion's troupe

ARSENAL manager Bertie Mee has given Alan Ball and Charlie George permission to play in the £500-a-man seven-a-side tournament in Copenhagen on December 16.

Chelsea have refused to release Peter Bonetti and Peter Osgood, but Mee is willing to take the risk provided the insurance details are right. The organisers expect Ball and George to be joined by George Best and Willie Morgan of Manchester United.

Paul Trevillion, whose idea it is, says he will announce the names of the other three members of his team later in the week.

If the Copenhagen tournament, played in front of 3,500 fans in an indoor stadium, is successful Trevillion intends to take a tennis-style circus of footballers in 18 months' time playing exhibition matches around the world.

'We are off the ground,' he said. 'This scheme will work and quite a few players will make fortunes.'

He is aiming to offer the players £100,000 three-year contracts.

Players like former England captain Bobby Moore and Alan Ball, their World Cup ambitions now ended, would be very interested.

But a phone call from Dave Sexton opened with the words, "Sorry Paul, I've had the press on and from what they've told me, I am refusing Osgood and Bonetti permission to go. At Chelsea we are always sympathetic for opportunities for our players to make money on a one-off basis, but not for a series of matches. So please count Osgood and Bonetti out, and I mean OUT!"

Who let the cat out of the bag? I still don't know. But when the press carried the story on the back pages they made it quite clear it was not just a pilot game. "The TREVILLION TROUPES envisaged a series of 12 Sunday matches in European cities this winter…". Reading those newspaper headlines I realised the game in Denmark was OFF. Rose had also read the papers and was quickly on the phone. "Not to worry Paul. I'll sort it, and when the dust settles next year we'll go again and this time to the US."

Both Rose and I did try to go again, but this time the players had been scared off. There was no interest and no takers except for one. Surprisingly the Australian TV media magnate Kerry Packer had made his presence felt. Rose arranged a meeting with Packer who told us in no uncertain terms that we had screwed up big time. Our 7-a-side football competition was now DEAD IN THE WATER. Packer made it very clear he wanted to take our idea into cricket. We both listened but it was not for us, but as it proved it Packer followed through with his plans and just three years later changed cricket forever: floodlit day/night matches, colourful cricket kits, white balls and all with Packer owning the TV rights along with the signings of Viv Richards, Imran Khan, Dennis Lillee, Alan Knott, Clive Lloyd, Michael Holding, John Snow et al.

Both Sydney Rose and myself agreed that had Packer been into football, the game as we know it would have changed, but ask yourself – would it have changed for the BETTER?

PT

Daily Mail, Saturday, November 10, 1973

Rebel Stars Inc.

BOBBY MOORE and George Best are involved in plans which could take a group of major stars out of the English First Division and into a rebel circus of touring footballers.

Massive cash incentives are tempting the biggest crowd-pullers in the League to join a Soccer version of the international professional tennis troupes.

Moore, Osgood in move to set up world tour circus

JEFF POWELL EXCLUSIVE

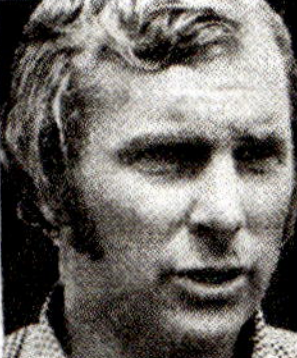
BOBBY MOORE

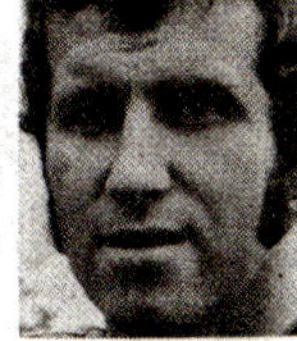
PETER OSGOOD

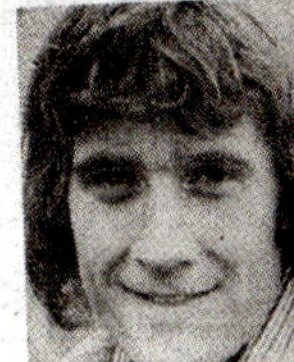
RODNEY MARSH

Former England captain Moore, controversial Manchester United Irishman Best, Arsenal's Alan Ball and Charlie George, Manchester City's Rodney Marsh and Chelsea's Peter Osgood are among top names who have been approached to play in a pilot seven-a-side exhibition match in Copenhagen on either the first or second Sunday in December.

£500-a-man

Like the tennis stars, they would form a group drawing a huge percentage of the gate-money . . . and this weekend they are studying contracts worth £500-a-man for that one match.

The flying visit to Denmark threatens to be the start of as big a political battle in Soccer as the one fought so bitterly in tennis since the first group turned professional under Jack Kramer.

The top clubs are certain to instruct their stars not to go globtrotting for profit in between League matches.

Chelsea manager Dave Sexton has, I understand, already told his former England goalkeeper Peter Bonetti that he will not be released to play in Copenhagen.

The touring soccer troupe is the brainchild of Paul Trevillion, artist, TV personality and fledgling recording star.

Live wire Trevillion and Sidney Rose, his showbiz-connected partner in this latest enterprise, have been secretly meeting leading players most recently on Thursday night in London.

Trevillion has been interested in the project since returning from the United States where he made something of a success in a series of television appearances.

Approached

Among others he has approached so far has been West Ham striker Pop Robson, Manchester United's Willie Morgan, Southampton's England forward Mike Channon, Chelsea's Alan Hudson and Spurs pair Steve Perryman and Mike England.

Trevillion's group are known to want to work in co-operation with the clubs if possible. But I believe details have been worked out under which the game's leading players could break away from their clubs to join a full-time circus if those clubs refused to release players for a limited programme of matches.

The pro tennis organisers have long since proved the viability of taking all the gate money and paying their stars the bulk of the cash.

Some of the players would probably support such a scheme.

Moore and Ball, for example, probably came near the end of their international careers when England failed to beat Poland at Wembley and so went out of the World Cup. There would be a strong temptation for men who have accumulated a host of honours to finish their playing days with a financial killing from exhibition matches round the world.

Best years

Some of the younger players with the best years of their straightforward careers ahead of them—Channon and Perryman for example—have already rejected the bait without prompting from their clubs.

SIDE 15

Peter Bonetti Chelsea

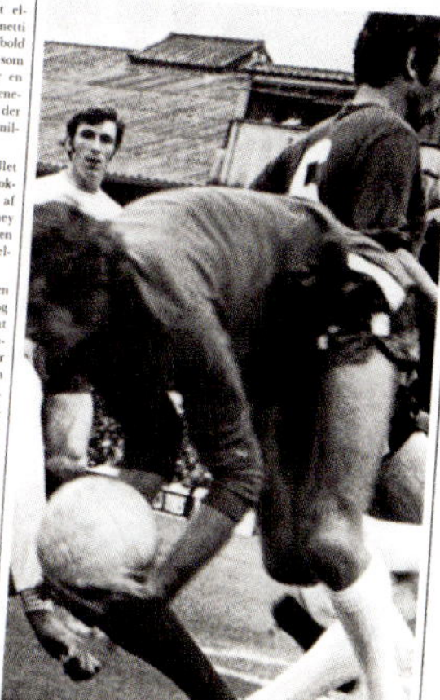

Folk stormede til Stamford Bridge, da Chelsea lod sin højt elskede målmand Peter Bonetti spille, det man i engelsk fodbold kalder „afskedskamp", men som mere er en „æreskamp", for en spiller der for lang trofast tjeneste får kampens indtægter – der ofte løber op mod en halv million kroner.

Peter Bonetti har aldrig spillet for andet end Chelsea. Han voksede bogstaveligt op i skyggen af klubbens bane i kvarteret Putney Bridge – og der skulle kun en prøvekamp til, så var han Chelsea-spiller.

I mange år stod han i skyggen af fænomenet Gordon Banks, og det er blevet Bonettis skæbne, at det folk husker ham for, er kampen under VM i Mexico, hvor han afløste Banks, og hvor han var lidt med i de vesttyske mål.

Det tog Bonetti næsten et år ...t komme over dette – der for ...am selv var en enorm skuffelse. ... dag er han atter tilbage på ...ppen, og lever helt og aldeles ... til det kælenavn, han er ble...t kendt og elsket under Peter "...he Cat" Bonetti.

Bonetti har søde minder fra ...øbenhavn. Her havde han i ...66 sin landsholdsdebut for ...gland, som vandt 2-0. I dag ... han spillet over 600 kampe ... Chelsea, han har været med ...t vinde Europa-cup'en i 1971 ... den engelske pokalfinale i ...

... hjemmefronten klarer Peter ...tti sig også. Han ...

DANMARK

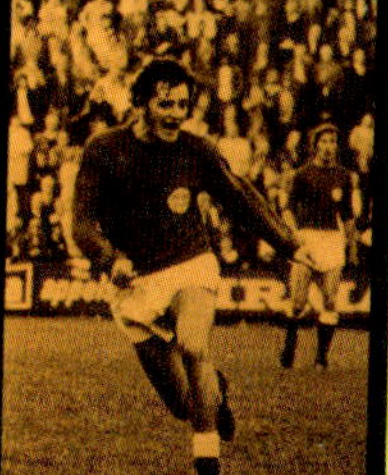

Jørgen Henriksen
Utrecht, Holland
Kresten Bjerre
Racing White, Belgien
Ole Bjørnmose
Hamburger SV, Tyskland
Per Røntved
Werder Bremen, Tyskland
Jørgen Kristensen
Feyenoord, Holland
Hans Aabech
F.C. Brügge, Belgien
Flemming Lund
Royal Antwerpen, Belgien

BRITANIA

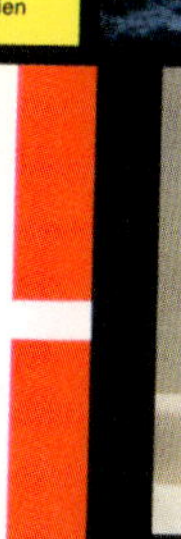

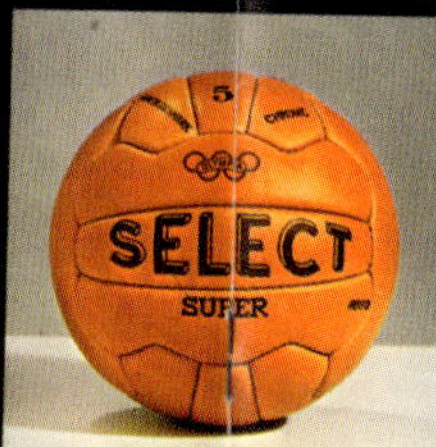

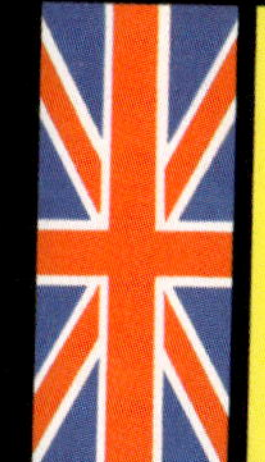

George Best
Manchester United
Willie Morgan
Manchester United
Peter Osgood
Chelsea
Peter Bonetti
Chelsea
Alan Ball
Arsenal
Charlie George
Arsenal
Bobby Moore
West Ham

Ekstra Bladet

Ekstra Bladet lige på og sport

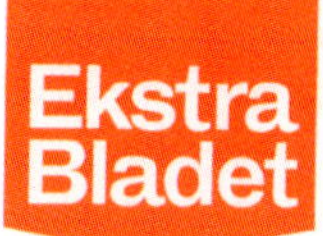

SIDE 12

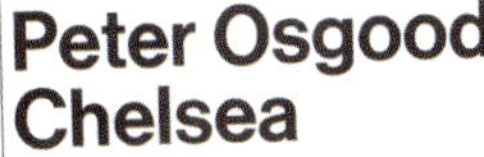

Peter Osgood Chelsea

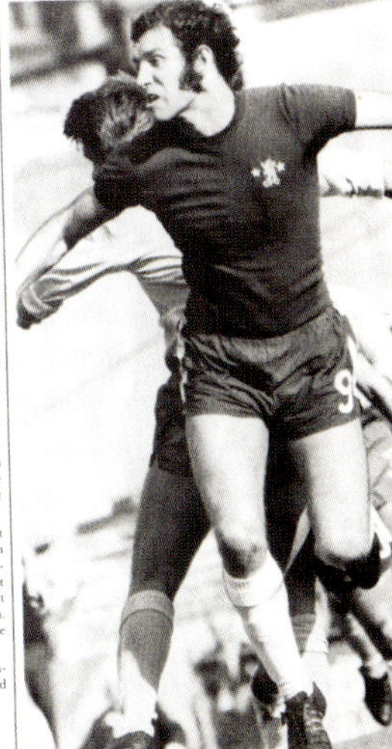

Det var slet ikke meningen, at Peter Osgood skulle have fodboldspillet som levevej. Han var en god og anerkendt mand udi murerfaget i byen Windsor i Londons omegn. Men om søndagen tordnede han bolden i nettet, og så fik Chelsea øje på ham – gav ham en kontrakt. Han har aldrig spillet for andre.

Det, der først og fremmest kendetegner den høje slanke Osgood, er, at han mere ligner en italiensk fodboldspiller på banen end en engelsk. Han styrter ikke afsted i ét væk, som en række engelske spillere gør.

Osgood er først og fremmest boldspilleren. Den kælne tekniker med den dejlige boldbehandling og det eminente hovedspil, der kan se en aflevering – før han spiller bolden. – Jeg spiller ligeså gerne en spiller fri, som scorer selv, siger han.

Han har ikke været Sir Alf Ramseys mest udprægede kæledægge, men på det sidste er han atter kommet med, og mange mener, at han burde have været det hele tiden.

Peter Osgood kunne have haft endnu flere landskampe, hvis han havde kunnet styre sit temperament. Det har knebet gevaldigt et par gange. Peter har været henvist til karantæne-bænken. Men er altid kommet strålende igen.

Nu lader han mere temperamentet gå ud over bolden end over modspillerne.

Eddie McCreadie

Dropped The Stars and Picked The Kids

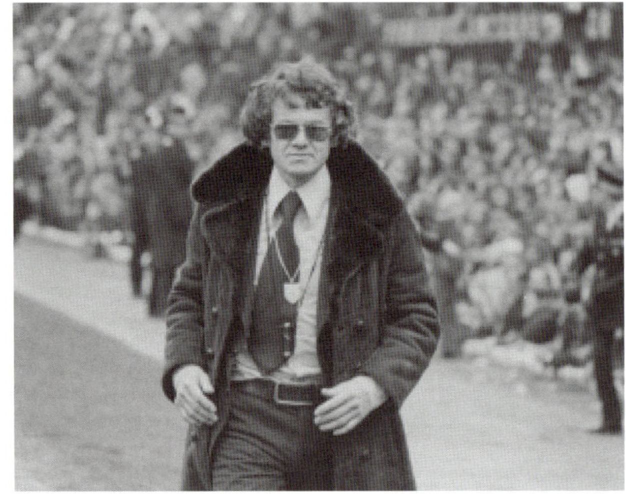

On October 1974, with the Blues 20th in the First Division, Ron Suart took over as caretaker manager once more following the sacking of Dave Sexton whom he had succeeded in the assistant role seven years earlier. Suart's first act was to promote Eddie McCreadie, whose reserve side topped the Football Combination, to first team coach (Sexton's assistant Dario Gradi went in the other direction).

Chelsea's desire to appoint a permanent boss was evident in the unsuccessful pursuit of legendary player Frank Blunstone, who elected to remain a youth team coach at Old Trafford.

On 16 April, Suart stepped upstairs to become general manager, with retired left-back Eddie McCreadie handling day-to-day team duties.

Chelsea were relegated for the first time in 12 years, Suart finishing with the second-lowest win rate of all Blues managers albeit in very difficult circumstances. Out of 34 games, Suart's Chelsea side won just eight, drew 12, lost 14, scoring just 38, conceded 62. Suart's win percentage was a dreadfully low 16%. To be fair, he took over when they were struggling near the bottom of the league.

In his 16 years with Chelsea, Suart served as general manager, chief scout, and then later worked as a scout for Wimbledon. He took charge of first-team affairs from October 1974 until April 1975. Ron passed away in March 2015 aged 94. In his various roles, he was assistant to Dave Sexton when Chelsea won the FA Cup and European Cup Winners' Cup in 1970 and 1971. John Hollins played in both of those finals, against Leeds United and Real Madrid, and praised Suart's impact by way of a tribute. "In the Leeds game he gave a talk at half-time, then a different type of talk at full-time before extra-time," Hollins told the official Chelsea website."He told us to make sure if we lost the ball we won it back as quickly as possible, it was simple advice but just what we needed at the time. I've got great memories of Ron, he was what we call a solid man in football. Ron was an assistant to Dave but to the players he was a fatherly figure. He'd come around and tell us if we weren't looking after ourselves properly. He had a very strong northern accent and was a lovely man. Ron and Dave made a brilliant pair because they were both football men through and through. He'd give you a little tap on the shoulder before a game and offer little bits of encouragement. He was always there on time, never late.We'd always ask him what time he got up in the morning, but he could give a joke as well as take one. He had time for everyone, he was never too busy for you.You simply couldn't dislike the man, even if he dropped you he did it in the right way. He did a hell of a lot for me in many ways and I'll always be grateful."

Tommy Langley had his first taste of regular first team football under Suart's guidance: "He was a really lovely, old-school type of character and he had a nice manner. He would have a go at you and be very forceful, but there would always be a bit of a glint in his eye and a wink at the same time.He was very strong in terms of discipline but we were all young kids and we needed that. Ron brought all of the young boys up into first team training and coached us all the way through. He was a proper Chelsea man and a proper football man. He certainly helped me in my career, for sure, and there are a lot of people who will say the same."

Clive Walker was another young player who benefited from coming through the ranks while Suart was at the club. "I was a young man that obviously needed some guidance, and Ron was an authoritative figure within the camp at the time, which is what all youngsters need. We looked up to him and appreciated the kind of guy he was and the work he put in. Ron was a real gentleman and I have very fond memories of that time, growing up and coming through the youth team. He had the full respect of all the players, especially the youngsters. He was always hugely involved in terms of coaching and training, and always there if you needed somebody to talk to. It was a pleasure to have him around the camp. He was a great guy, really good to be around."

Eddie McCreadie was the manager who would take the team to the next level, once again returning to youth. Just 72 hours into the job, Chelsea's brilliant former left-back axed his former team-mates Marvin Hinton, John Hollins, Peter Houseman and Steve Kember and drafted in fledglings John Sparrow (17), Ray Wilkins and Teddy Maybank (both 18), and Ian Britton (19) for a crunch relegation six-pointer at White Hart Lane in April 1975. It was the kind of bold move that set the tone for a short but exhilarating managerial reign that lives long in the affections of Chelsea fans.

Eddie could do nothing to prevent relegation but soon forged a vibrant team full of youngsters blending with seniors. He was persuasive enough to have all the players accept a salary cut as financial strife threatened the club's very existence. The poetry-writing, tinted glasses and fur coat-wearing young boss was something else!

Ray Wilkins epitomised the new generation; promoted to skipper in the first team he became the flag bearer for the new generation at the Bridge, yet with Peter Bonetti still in goal, Ray Lewington the water carrier, and Kenny Swain adding the style and Steve 'Jock' Finnieston the fearless finisher, the 1976/77 promotion campaign became one of the most memorable for years, the young Blues finishing second with a huge away following.

Top-flight status was regained in flamboyant fashion with a 4-0 triumph over Hull City in May. Yet by July 1977 Eddie was out of the door and preparing for a new life in the USA, where he still lives. The move mystified supporters who had been looking forward to seeing his bright young side captained by teenager Wilkins take on the elite teams in the First Division. It quickly emerged that Eddie had walked out after chairman Brian Mears rejected his request for a company car! Mears quickly relented and offered him the car but McCreadie's pride prevented a reconciliation and he left England for roles in America, first with Memphis Rogues and then Cleveland Force. He finally retired from football in 1985.

"I'm not going to tell you what I was offered, but it wasn't very much at all," Eddie recalls. "I couldn't believe it. I'd saved them from bankruptcy and this was how they valued me.What made it worse was they made it perfectly clear there was to be no negotiating. It was a case of take it or leave it." Eddie didn't return to the Bridge for many years, his prolonged absence an indication of the bitterness of his sudden and shock departure."It broke my heart," he said, "I had to get as far away as possible."

Eddie headed to the United States, coaching in the North American Soccer League before retiring to Tennessee, where he lives on the family farm of his wife Linda. After battling alcoholism and depression, he found God and contentment.Yet, despite his iconic status in West London, it was 40 years before he returned. In May 2017 he was at the launch of his life story. *Eddie Mac Eddie Mac: The Life and Times at Chelsea under Eddie McCreadie* is about his two-year spell managing the club and, unusually, has five authors in Mark Meehan, Mark Worrall, Kelvin Barker, David Johnstone and Neil Smith.

The book describes how McCreadie brought success back to West London against a gloomy backdrop of economic recession, trouble on the terraces and the club on the verge of bankruptcy after Chelsea's huge investment in a new stand. Chelsea fans often sing, even to this day, to the tune of the old Martha Reeves song, "Eddie Mac, when are you coming back!" and in 2017 they finally welcomed him back! Eddie visited the Cobham training ground where the then manager Antonio Conte gave him a guided tour."Mr Conte was so hospitable, what a gentleman," he says. "I kinda felt I'd left a footprint at the club. I never realised quite how big it was until I went back after 40 years. It was the biggest compliment I have ever been paid in my life."

McCreadie added:"I watch all the games in the United States. I'm absolutely thrilled with the success they've had. I've come back here and the stadium, the facilities, it's a remarkable change."

He recalled the day when he caused such a shock by elevating the kids led by his new skipper 'Butch' Wilkins: "Butch was a player I wanted to rebuild the team around. I remember when I told him he was to be my captain, him saying to me: 'You think

I can do it?' I never had a moment's doubt. We were going into the Second Division, which was a tough league. I knew he wasn't going to win many tackles for me, but I knew he had the skill to unlock any defence.So I formed the midfield around his strengths. I played him just behind the front two, at the head of a diamond formation.Though nobody called it that at the time."

McCreadie confronted head on a dressing-room full of uncompromising characters such as Ron Harris and John Hollins. He summoned the most uncompromising into his office, the giant centre-back Mickey Droy (right). "I told Mickey that, while Butch was to be the captain on the field, I was making him club captain. And I told him it was his responsibility to watch Butch's back out there."

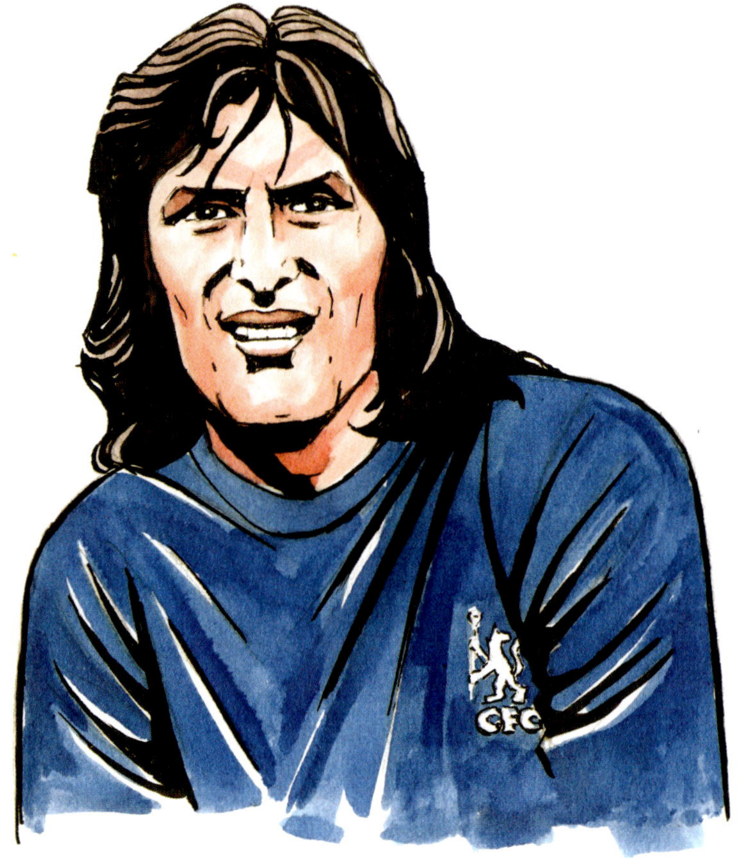

A tough-tackling and uncompromising full-back, McCreadie had made 410 appearances for the Blues between 1963 and 1972, before that two-year managerial spell beloved of supporters. Capped 23 times by Scotland, he scored in the 1965 League Cup Final and won the FA Cup in 1970.

McCreadie recalled the notorious 1970 FA Cup final against Leeds United."People have called that a battle, it wasn't a battle, it was a war. Leeds were the dirtiest team in the history of football. They tried to break your legs. And there were people in our side who weren't going to stand for it, especially me and Chopper Harris. I read that a ref reviewed the game 30 years on and said that, if it had taken place in modern football, there would have been six red cards. I reckon that's an underestimate. It should have been 10!"

Wilkins came from a West London football family, his father had played for Brentford and Nottingham Forest, and his three brothers all played professionally. Ray joined Chelsea as an apprentice and it was apparent that with his talents he would soon break through into the first team. This he did in October 1973 aged 17. While a new era dawned, the old one went out with a degree of sadness. The break-up of a famous cup-winning team was tough to take for some and experienced players left, as Wilkins was made the club's youngest ever captain, just 18, but he could do little to prevent relegation. Two years later, Ray led a young team to promotion. He was the outstanding player, his range and accuracy of passing was so creative but he also contributed seven goals, many of them spectacular long-range efforts. He quickly graduated to the England team, first called up while still a Second Division player. He was becoming a celebrity away from the pitch and was undoubtedly the star of the team. Even Ray's talents could not help a team that was being crippled by a lack of investment. He suffered his second relegation with the club in 1979 and was immediately transferred to Manchester United for £825,000.

From Old Trafford to Milan, Paris Saint-Germain and Rangers, he was respected everywhere he played from the mid-1970s to the end of the eighties. He left Old Trafford in 1984 as the supporters' player of the season in a team who also included Bryan Robson and Arnold Muhren, and is warmly remembered at San Siro, where he spent three years during a difficult era for the Rossoneri and made his exit only when a new owner, Silvio

Berlusconi, reshaped the squad around a group of Dutch masters at a time when only two foreign players were allowed. His stay at PSG was brief but at Ibrox he won the Scottish league title and wept with the fans when saying his farewell.

Of his 84 caps, 10 were as captain. He played under Don Revie, Ron Greenwood and Bobby Robson in a midfield where Bryan Robson, Glenn Hoddle and Peter Reid were vying for places. Ron Atkinson nicknamed him 'The Crab', for his supposed habit of passing sideways, but that was a simplistic view and far from the truth.

He was happy to slide down the scale, from Queens Park Rangers and Hibernian to fleeting spells at Wycombe Wanderers, Millwall and Leyton Orient, where he hung up his boots after three games in 1997, aged 40. He had made just under 700 league appearances for his 11 clubs in England, Italy, France and Scotland, scoring 49 goals.

By that time he had already spent two years as player-manager at QPR, taking them to eighth in the Premier League in his first season but to relegation in his second. He spent a year as Fulham's head coach, taking them to the play-offs in the Second Division (as the third tier was then known) before being removed by Mohamed Al-Fayed, who installed Kevin Keegan, previously the club's chief operating officer, as manager.

Wilkins moved into coaching and twice was assistant manager at Chelsea, under Gianluca Vialli from 1999 to 2000, and from September 2008 to November 2010, under Luiz Felipe Scolari, Guus Hiddink and Carlo Ancelotti. It was a role and an environment that suited Wilkins, particularly after the arrival of his friend 'Carletto', a fellow ex-Milanista. Together in 2009-10 they won the first League and Cup double in the club's history and Wilkins's first trophies in his long and intimate association with the club. "Ray is one of those select few, always present, noble in spirit, a real blue-blood," Ancelotti wrote in his autobiography. "Chelsea flows in his veins."

But one day at the training centre at Cobham, a few weeks into the following season, he was fired, the reason never made public, although it was suspected that he may have said something out of turn in the presence of the owner, Roman Abramovich. After being handed a four-year driving ban Ray admitted to problems with alcohol. He also suffered from ulcerative colitis and underwent a double heart bypass operation. He passed away in 2018.

I had met up with Ray at a hotel in central London not long before he died to discuss the possibility of making a documentary film of his life, as I had done with Kerry Dixon, and a few other football legends. He said he would think about it, but we both knew he felt better to keep his own counsel to protect others.

That was Ray, one of football's gentlemen.

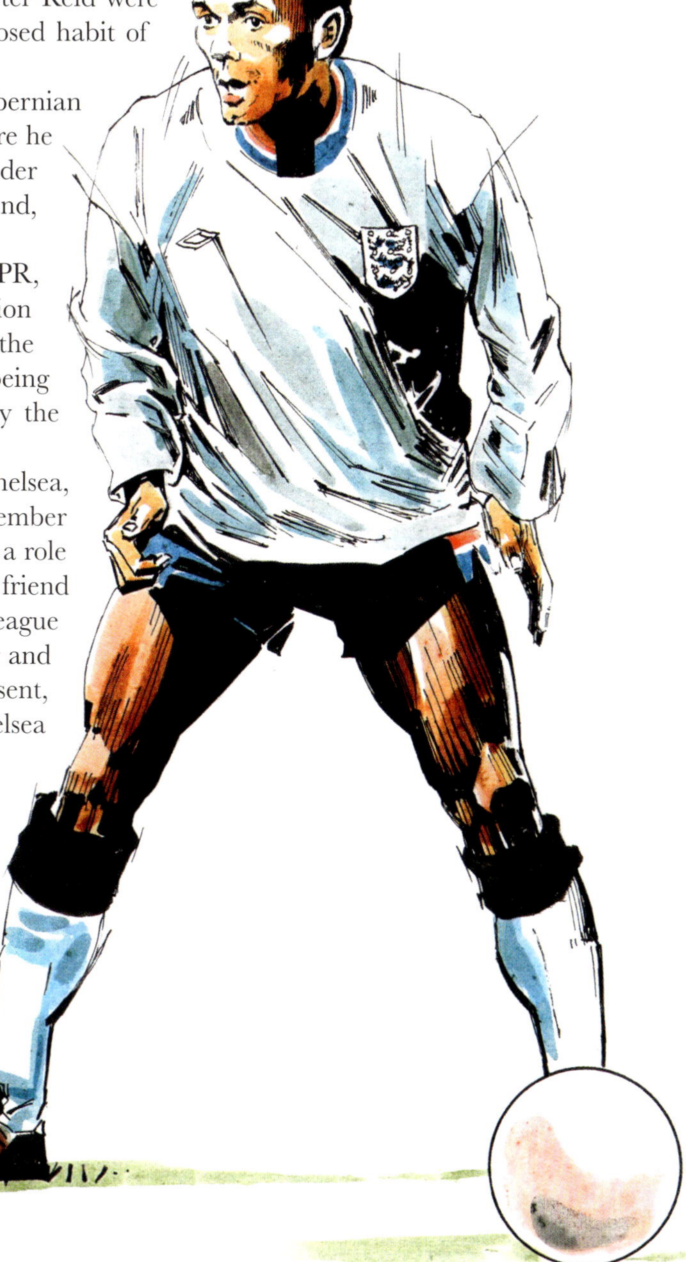

Ken Shellito

When Ken Shellito passed away at the age of 78 in October 2018, he was remembered as one of Chelsea's favourite sons. The full-back spent his entire career at Stamford Bridge, making 123 appearances and scoring two goals. He won a single England cap in 1963. After suffering a serious knee injury he quit playing in 1965 and had a spell as a boss from 1977-78.

Born in East Ham, Ken signed for Chelsea as a 14-year-old on the same day as Jimmy Greaves in 1955, and was part of the team which were runners up in the FA Youth Cup in 1958, the club's first appearance in the final of that prestigious competition.

Unlike the goalscoring prodigy, he was not fast-tracked into the senior ranks, and had to wait until April 1959 for his debut against Nottingham Forest, with a handful of appearances following in subsequent years, but following the appointment of Tommy Docherty as manager in 1962, his career really began to move forward, having spent most of the previous two seasons refining his game in the reserves.

Chelsea had just been relegated and Docherty planned for a quick return - a major part of his strategy was influenced by the football he had been studying in Spain – attacking full-backs. The Doc chose two young athletic defenders – Shellito on the right and McCreadie on the left. "We came in for pre-season in 1962 and the training was completely different, a hell of a lot better," Shellito recalled, "Tommy Doc came to us and said, 'this is how we are going to play'. I'd always been a good passer of the ball and wanted to get more involved but it was always a case of 'don't go any further up the pitch'. But Tom and Dave Sexton opened up the game and it all stemmed from there. Eddie and I started it and other clubs in England followed."

Chelsea were unstoppable before the 'Big Freeze' of 1962-63 which stopped all football for almost 3 months. Afterwards it took some time to recapture their form, but a 7-0 win over Portsmouth in the final game ensured second place and promotion. Eight days later Ken lined up alongside Moore, Greaves, Gordon Banks and Bobby Charlton for England in Bratislava as part of one of new England manager Alf Ramsey's earliest teams.

For two young east Londoners it was a landmark occasion. Bobby Moore, then just 22, became England's youngest-ever captain, while at right-back, 23-year-old Shellito won the first of what appeared certain to be many caps. Yet while Moore went on to lead England to World Cup glory three years later and represent his country 108 times, Shellito later suffered a lung infection and kidney disorder, otherwise he might well have joined him as one of the boys of '66 but instead became a one-cap wonder after injury and illness ravaged his career. To make matters worse Ken's career was all but ended in October 1963 in a game against Sheffield Wednesday at the Bridge when, with no-one nearby, he turned and his studs caught in the turf and he suffered a serious knee injury. He had been due to play for England against the Rest of the World the following Wednesday as part of the FA's centenary celebrations.

Regular England captain, Jimmy Armfield, was also a right-back. The Blackpool man had sat out the 4-2 win in Bratislava due to injury but re-called in his autobiography: "Ken really looked the part. I remember thinking 'I could struggle to get back in here'." Manager Alf Ramsey restored Armfield against East Germany four days later while Ken's injury woes opened the door for George Cohen and, as Shellito recalled: "Every time I see George Cohen, he says 'thank you Kenny!' It hurts but he does appreciate it. He always says he would not have got in and that is your luck in football. But you can't feel sorry for yourself too much."

After several operations Shellito regained his Chelsea place and was even recalled to the England squad before the knee broke down again. His 123rd and final appearance for the Blues came against Wiener SC of Austria in an Inter-Cities Fairs Cup tussle in December 1965, although he did not officially retire for a further three years.

After 123 appearances and two goals (scored in a 4-3 win at Birmingham in March 1964 and a 3-1 win over Sunderland at the Bridge in August 1964) he worked with the youth team, helping bring through Ray Wilkins and Clive Walker among others, who helped the Blues to promotion in 1977.

When McCreadie walked out during the close season, the club

turned to Shellito. Relegation from the top flight was narrowly avoided during his first season and sixteenth place was regarded as a success. His reign also included a stirring FA Cup victory over European champions Liverpool, but with the team floundering again the following year, Shellito departed in December 1978 with the club bottom of the league and the Chelsea board publicly flirting with a Yugoslav coach, a humiliation which led Shellito to resign after 17 months.

Ken went on to coach Queens Park Rangers, Crystal Palace, Preston and Wolves before managing Cambridge United in 1985 but spent his later life in Sabah in Malaysia with his Malaysian wife, Jeany. He coached young players there and worked with the Chelsea Foundation to establish a grass-roots football programme in the region. He served as Selangor's coaching director and also worked for the Asian Football Confederation as a match analyst. He had also setup the Ken Shellito Football Academy in Penampang.

"Football is my life. And I am glad that I am still at it at my ripe age," he said in 2014. "The game has certainly given me a great deal and it is only fair that I continue to give the game back as long as I can."

TEDDY MAYBANK

It was really sad so few people attended Ken Shellito's funeral. It made it such a harrowing day for many of us there, for many reasons but it was disappointing not more people were there. Steve Finneston, Gary Stanley, Ray Lewington, Trevor Aylott, Tommy Langley and Derek Richardson were there and Bobby Tambling and I did the eulogies.

I first trained at our home ground aged 10 and was one of a number of players to come through our youth system in the mid-1970s. Loads of the lads; Ray Wilkins, Ray Lewington and Clive Walker trained at the Bridge on Tuesdays and Thursdays. We did that from when we were about 10 or 11.

I ended up playing for South London where lots of scouts would be watching, but I didn't sign any schoolboy forms. When I was 15, I had a bad injury and needed a cartilage operation. I was at QPR, but Chelsea called me in and operated on me on Christmas Day! Ian Hutchinson was having a steel plate put in on his leg, and the same surgeon operated on me. I hadn't signed for anybody but I had a few clubs after me, including Man United, Arsenal and Tottenham but I thought because Chelsea did that without me even being on their books I would sign for them. When I was 10, we used to train in the car park at the front of the ground! There were boards we would use as goals, and we would train on the asphalt. Then we trained upstairs where the snooker tables were! There were loads of pillars we had to duck in and out of.

Once we signed as apprentices we went down to Mitcham and that was a lovely training ground.

I played 32 times for Chelsea, scoring six goals, during an injury-interrupted three years as a first team squad member, before moving on to Fulham and later Brighton and PSV Eindhoven. Unfortunately, a chronic knee injury brought a premature end to my playing days at the age of just 24.

Of the squad that came through together in 1976 when we won promotion, eight or nine were from the youth team. We came through with the right attitude. We had enthusiasm and we played for the manager. The crowd really appreciated that squad coming through and getting Chelsea back into the First Division in 1976/77. We had such a close-knit unit. I went to school with Ray Lewington from the age of 11 at Stockwell Manor. We were in the same class. I sat next to him until we were 14 or 15. We played in the same Sunday teams. We were like brothers. Then there was John Sparrow and Tommy Langley. We were all so close. We grew up together, we mowed the pitches, painted the dressing rooms, swept the terraces, cleaned the boots, the sort of chores the youth players did in those days. That creates a bond. We would die for each other. We would fight and fight and fight, and if anyone let someone else down, boy would they know about it! That was what we had at Chelsea. It was the greatest squad I was ever in.

Ken Shellito was our youth team coach and I would have to say he had the biggest influence on me. He was like a second dad to me, and all the boys there. He was always there for you, Ron Suart as well. He was the most important manager I played under because in your youth you are like a sponge you take it all in and with Ken it was the right way of playing, he gave you good information and he got a unity in the team that had never been seen, but most importantly he taught us the game, about tactics, and I gained more knowledge from his advice than from anyone else.

Ken Shellito was such a legend. He would have been an England player for years if it wasn't for injury. He was the best full-back in the country, and would have made the 1966 World Cup squad, but for his knee. He would take the micky out of us in training in five-a-side games, he'd stand on the ball on the goal line and beckon us to get it off him before he tapped it in, but he would wait until we were just a yard away and then score off our legs, as it would make him happy to see us score an own goal! He was a great man and a great coach. We enjoyed enormous success even though there were some in that generation who were outstanding but a few who shouldn't have even been there, yet Ken instilled the sort of mentality and developed such a good playing unit even though we were up against teams like Arsenal that had Liam Brady and Graham Rix. Ken made training so enjoyable that we all looked forward to it.

Eddie McCreadie was fantastic as well. When I made my debut in 1975 in front of 65,000, it was in the middle of a relegation battle. I was on £40-a-week, but also on £210 appearance money, while the superstars like Peter Osgood were on £210-a-week and £40 appearance, which mean we were all paid the same when we played, it made for a great team spirit. In my debut against Tottenham, whoever lost was relegated. They had to delay the game by half-an-hour because of crowd violence. It was a hell of a debut to make. We lost and were relegated!

Eddie sent me out on loan to Fulham because Steve Finneston was scoring so many goals, he told me that I was a better player than Jock but he scored more. At Fulham I scored about five in four, and was playing with George Best, Rodney Marsh, Peter Storey, Bobby Moore. When I went back to Chelsea I was straight back in the reserves and I asked to leave. I was sold to Fulham where Bobby Campbell was manager. It was a great time playing with those players. I was only there for a little while before going to Brighton. Alan Mullery was the Brighton manager and they paid £230,000 for me which helped pay for what is now the Riverside Stand at Craven Cottage!

Clive Walker

A Brilliant Winger in a Terrible Team

In his time Clive Walker was the fans' hero, a terrace favourite, but as the club grew into a global super brand, wingers of supreme talent came and went with such regularity that his wing wizardry became long forgotten by the majority - but not by those of a certain vintage! Clive was pacy and exciting and on his day he terrorised the best defenders of his generation. Yet while he was one of the club's best players of any era, he was unfortunately playing in some of the worst teams in Chelsea history.

Clive made his debut at the tail end of the 1976/77 promotion season and broke into the first team the following year. He hit the headlines when he scored two on his debut against Wolves at Molineux. He soon became a huge fan favourite, a fast winger who had the knack of scoring stunning goals. He made a name for himself by scoring spectacular goals, in particular a brilliant effort in an FA Cup win over Liverpool. Walker, then 19, was playing in a struggling side, but with his blond hair flowing, he embarrassed Ray Clemence with a 20-yard drive which sent the then European and English champions crashing to a shock FA Cup third-round defeat at Stamford Bridge.

Having knocked out champions Liverpool in '78, Clive cemented his standing among Blues fans with a remarkable performance against newly-promoted Bolton Wanderers. On the morning of Saturday 14th October 1978, Chelsea sat in 21st place in the top flight having won just one of their nine matches. Bolton, newly promoted back to the First Division, were hoping to become the fifth side in a row to thump the Blues at the Bridge and contained a youthful Peter Reid in midfield and two veteran former Manchester United stalwarts in the shape of Willie Morgan and Tony Dunne in their side. In a sign of the desperation surrounding the club, earlier that week the Blues had failed to persuade Johan Cruyff to come out of retirement. Three times during that first half the Chelsea faithful were forced to watch Bob Iles, signed for £10,000 from non-League Weymouth, retrieve the ball from the back of his net. Alan Gowling's 18th and 41st-minute goals arrived either side of a penalty converted after 35 minutes by Frank Worthington. As referee Eric Read blew for half-time not even the most ardent fan believed that Chelsea, captained by teenager Ray 'Butch' Wilkins and managed by Ken Shellito, could turn this around. Shellito threw on Clive Walker to replace Garry Stanley and in desperation The Shed sang: "Clive Walker on the wing", more in hope than anything. Walker tormented right-back Paul Jones in the second half, "Jones seemed to stand still," Walker said afterwards, but it took until the 75th minute for Chelsea to get one back: Walker cutting past Jones and his low centre was stabbed home by Tommy Langley: 1-3. In the 82nd minute the ball sat up for Kenny Swain in the box, but he was surrounded by Mike Walsh, Sam Allardyce, Roy Greaves and keeper Jim McDonagh - Swain slipped but scuffed the ball into Bolton's net: 2-3. In the 87th minute a Wanderers attack broke down on the edge of the Chelsea box, Ray Lewington hit a great pass, a long, high, raking effort that fell into Walker's path on Chelsea's left wing. Clive reached the edge of the box at an acute angle and struck a left foot belter of a low cross-cum-shot, past McDonagh. Then, in the dying minutes of the game, Walker beat Jones again and drove in a cross that Bolton defender Sam Allardyce, retreating desperately, could only slice into his own net. From 0-3 to 4-3. Cue pandemonium at the Bridge for the majority of the 19,879 present as Read blew the final whistle. Yet far from helping to turn Chelsea's season around, this would prove to be one of only five wins during a campaign that saw Chelsea end the season rock bottom with just 20 points.

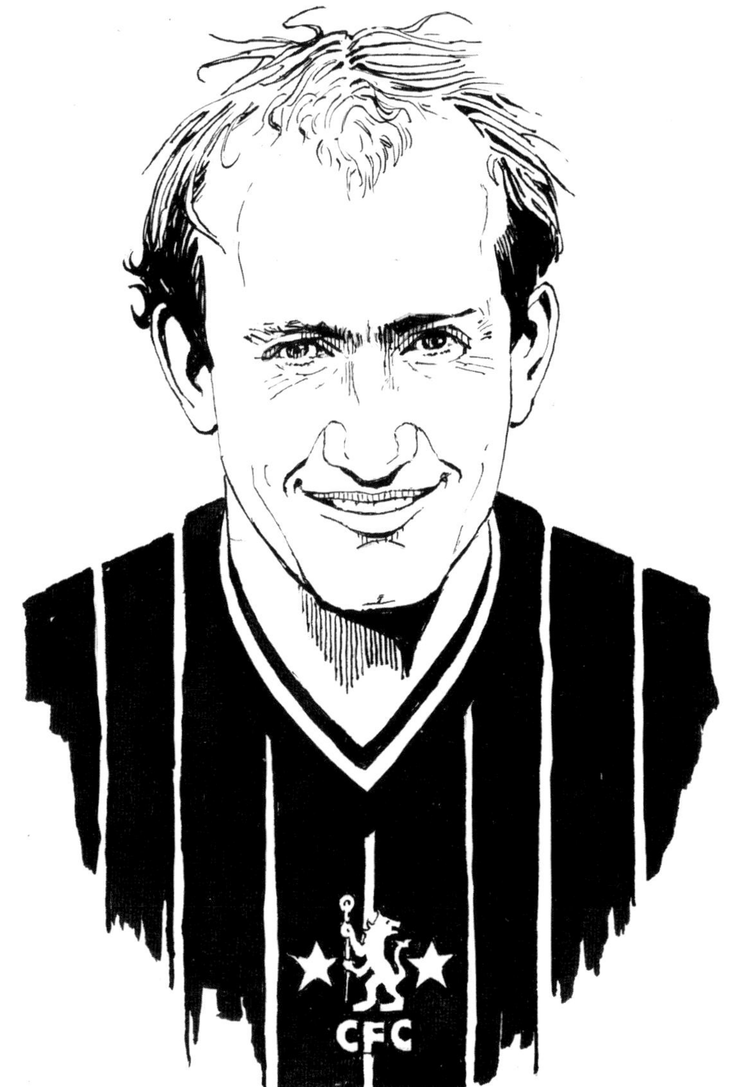

Clive's best season came in 1981-82 when he netted 17 times. Although he continued to impress he could do nothing to stave off relegation. As the team stagnated in the Second Division he was often the best talent on show. It was in the penultimate game of 1982-83 that Clive scored arguably the most important goal in the club's history, notching the only goal of the game against Bolton, when defeat would surely have led to the Third Division.

At the start of the following season Walker was playing some of the best football of his time at Chelsea when he was injured, and with the team playing so well in his absence, he failed to regain his place. The emergence of Pat Nevin and a contract dispute saw him sold to Sunderland in May 1984 for £75,000. He returned to haunt the Blues when he denied them a place in the Milk Cup Final. He went on to play over 1,000 games in a career that lasted until he was 40. Walker ending his career as he began it, by scoring crucial FA Cup goals, this time for non-League Woking. He hit the winner against Millwall and an opener against Cambridge United. Clive later worked for an auction house in Buckinghamshire, and ran a company with fellow Chelsea old boy Jason Cundy. He is now an analyst for BBC Radio London and appears regularly on Chelsea TV.

Danny Blanchflower

A One-Off Manager

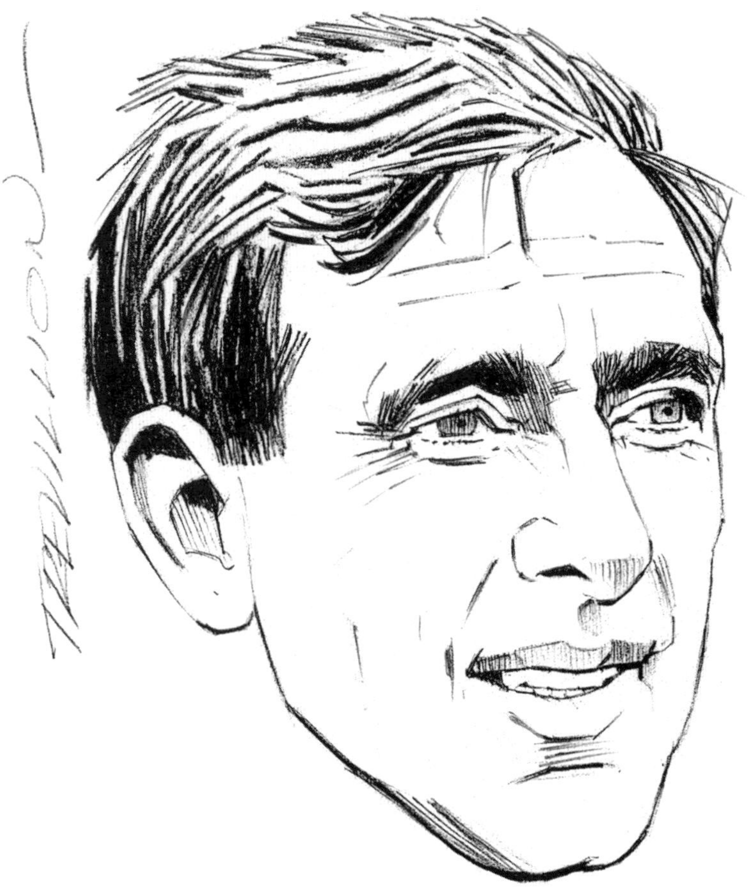

Danny Blanchflower replaced Ken Shellito in 1978; he was one of the first managers that I came to know really well after I joined the London *Evening News* at the very outset of my breakthrough into Fleet Street. The appointment was unexpected as Blanchflower had worked as a journalist since his retirement from playing in 1964 and his only managerial experience had been a short stint with Northern Ireland.

While not many people "got" Danny, particularly the players, media and the fans, I found him absolutely enthralling, absorbing, and far from the clichéd football type; he was hugely intelligent and a deep thinker on the game. His thinking was often convoluted, but genuine, honest and his philosophy on the game was absolutely absorbing. Perhaps that proved to be his biggest drawback. While I understood him implicitly, he failed to communicate on the same level that he'd achieved as a journalist, with his players, fans and the popular press.

Regrettably, Danny's reign at the Bridge was a very short one, one of the shortest in the club's history, and the club won only five games under him during the season, which eventually led to relegation and he left the job after only nine months. It was particularly upsetting at the time that Danny was kicked out before he'd had any chance to establish his new-age philosophy inside the club. He had enormous insight and wisdom, the only trouble was that you need to be on the same wavelength as the players to get your ideas across. Danny had been a world class performer in his prime while the squad he inherited weren't in that class at all. The mix didn't work, and I am sure Danny realised it.

Apart from getting to grips with his players, Danny also had to put up with me! Somehow, he did put up with my intolerable enthusiasm, ambition, and relentless search for stories at the start of my Fleet Street adventure. I've no idea why he put up with this young whippersnapper of a journalist? One of my particular irritating traits was to pester managers like Danny at the crack of dawn. In those days the old *Evening News*, long since defunct, ran seven editions a day, the first was mostly a racing paper with ridiculously early deadlines of 7am, meaning 6am would be the time to deliver copy to the desk for that first edition.

If one of the big dailies appeared with an important story about Chelsea, that would no doubt involve the manager as it would be about a player or about the club's financial difficulties reflecting on the manager's ability to buy players and so on, it was the manager in those days who would take the call from the journalist.These days there are a profusion of communications executives doing all that for the club and manager. Not back then, there was nothing in the way of a media department, just the guy who wrote the programme who had probably been with the club from school!

I think Danny's wife must have complained about my regular 6am calls to check out stories, or to try to break my own for the first edition, because he picked me up on it quite early into his managerial stint at the Bridge. He told me that he had actually installed a plaque positioned above the bed which said, "Don't take any calls from Harry before 7am". I didn't believe him, and thought it was his typical sense of humour. Then again, with Danny you just didn't know!

He did not manage any team after Chelsea, but continued to report on football with the *Sunday Express* until 1988.

Statistically he ranks as the worst Chelsea manager of all time: from 32 games he won just five, drew eight and lost 19 for an unremarkable win rate of 16%. Chelsea scored 34, conceded 68, again disastrous stats!

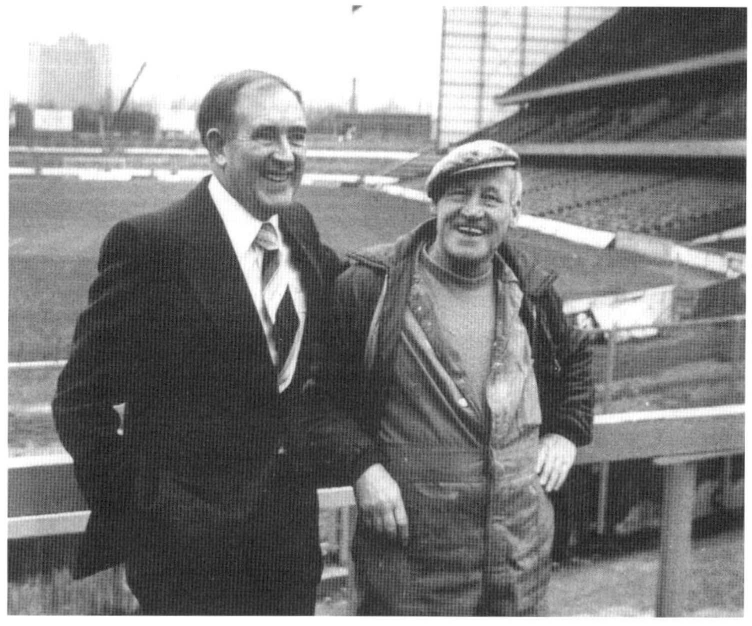

As a player Blanchflower had been one of the greatest and most influential in Spurs history. In 1954 he was bought for a snip at £30,000, and during his ten years at the Lane made 337 League appearances, 382 in total, scoring 21 goals. The highlight of his career was captaining Spurs to the first League and Cup double of the 20th century in 1960-61. Spurs won their first 11 games that season, a record for English football and eventually won the league by eight points.They then beat Leicester City in the FA Cup final to achieve sporting immortality. No one had achieved the double since Aston Villa in 1897 and many believed it was impossible.

In 1962 he again captained the Spurs team to victory in the FA Cup Final against Burnley, scoring a penalty and the club narrowly missed completing a second double finishing a close third behind Ipswich Town and Burnley, and lost narrowly to Benfica in the semi-final of the European Cup. In 1963 Danny captained the side to victory over Atletico Madrid in the final of the European Cup Winners' Cup, the first British team to win a major European trophy. During his time with Spurs, Danny also had a short spell with Toronto City, alongside Stanley Matthews and Johnny Haynes. Between 1949 and 1963, he earned 56 caps for Northern Ireland alongside brother Jackie until the younger Blanchflower's playing career was cut short by the Munich Air Disaster, and in 1958 he captained his country when they reached the quarter-finals of the World Cup, arguably his most brilliant individual campaign. Deservedly, he was named Footballer of the Year that year (an accolade repeated in 1961).

On 4 December 1957 he captained the Northern Ireland team against Italy in Belfast, in a bad tempered game that came to be known as the "Battle of Belfast"; Blanchflower attempted to keep the peace as the game turned nasty, which was typical of the man. Blanchflower was a subtle, all-pervasive influence from his position of right-half, a term that long since went out of fashion, re-placed by a profusion of descriptive midfield specialities. In his prime, between 1957 and 1962, he was one of the most creative players in the game, capable of dictating the tempo of a match like few others.

The players simply didn't buy into his regal philosophy of the game, and relegation by a huge margin of 11 points was taken in Blanchflower's usual cheery manner.

He announced his retirement as a player on the 5 April 1964 at the age of 38, having played nearly 400 games in all competitions for Spurs and captained them to four major trophies. Following his retirement, Blanchflower coached at Spurs, and double-winning manager Bill

Nicholson intended for him to be his long-term successor. When Nicholson resigned from the club in 1974 however, Blanchflower was passed over in favour of Terry Neill and subsequently left the club.

"I came to Chelsea because of my friendship with [chairman] Brian Mears," said Danny Blanchflower of his surprise arrival at the Bridge,"and my regard for the history and the meaning of the football club. There is so much about Chelsea that is wrapped up in the romance of the game; Chelsea is much more than a football club, it is a state of mind and that is worth fighting for."

Nevertheless Blanchflower was an unusual choice as boss for the near-bankrupt London club. His ideological romanticism, love for the spirit of the beautiful game, fell on deaf ears in a hardened dressing-room filled with the pragmatism of survival and growing commercialism.

His first task was to explain away the following results; a 2-7 defeat at Middlesbrough, a 1-5 hammering at Ipswich, 0-6 at Nottingham Forest and 2-5 at Arsenal. The players simply didn't buy into his regal philosophy of the game, and relegation by a huge margin of 11 points was taken in Blanchflower's usual cheery manner. He still insisted that that things would improve once the players understood what he was talking about. However Danny confided in me at one stage that the players didn't have a clue what he was talking about, their eyes glazing over when he delved into the deeper meaning of the game, and he even told me that he sometimes didn't even understand it himself!

Following relegation the jewel in Chelsea's crown of their blossoming youth scheme, Ray Wilkins, was soon sold to Manchester United. That summer, the ambitious Geoff Hurst came in to provide a more robust interpretation of Blanchflower's kindly, fatherly manner. The World Cup hero was brought in to be Danny's assistant but it seemed inevitable that a few poor results would lead to him being offered the job. Sure enough after a poor start and a home defeat by Birmingham, Hurst replaced the Northern Irishman.

Perhaps Danny had been absent from day-to-day involvement in football for too long for it to ever work and undoubtedly the results were awful. In any case, he professed himself disillusioned with values in the modern game. He was dogmatic in those beliefs and annoyed by the intrusions of modern life; he once dismissed Eamonn Andrews by refusing, on live television, to take part in the *This is Your Life* programme. He gained notoriety as the first man to refuse Eamonn Andrews' invitation. As a result the show was never again filmed live... Blanchflower made a mark wherever he went!

He once said:"The great fallacy is that the game is first and last about winning. It's nothing of the kind. The game is about glory. It is about doing things in style, with a flourish, about going out and beating the other lot, not waiting for them to die of boredom."

Sadly, Danny passed away from Alzheimer's disease on 9th December 1993.

Geoff Hurst

World Cup Hat-Trick Hero Turned Chelsea Boss

The first man to score a World Cup Final hat-trick, a legend as one of the Boys of '66, a local hero at West Ham United, Geoff was a surprise appointment as Chelsea manager. How much of a surprise can only be gauged by the fact he arrived at such a difficult club with so little experience, just a couple of seasons with non-League Telford United.

Sir Geoff enjoyed a unique place in English football history for the momentous achievement that justifiably earned him a knighthood, and that was, arguably, the main reason behind his recruitment at the Bridge.

The King's Road club needed a big name and there were few bigger at the time than Geoff Hurst. He was initially recruited as first team coach to aid Danny Blanchflower's failing managerial reign in May 1979.

My relationship as journalist with the new Chelsea manager was sound, despite such turbulent times at the Bridge. Geoff always seemed to be cool, calm and in control off the pitch, even if matters didn't go his way on it. There were times when, after the main media debriefing after a game, Geoff would get the press steward to summon me to a private area, a small room with hot water pipes overhead, for a private word and invariably I would

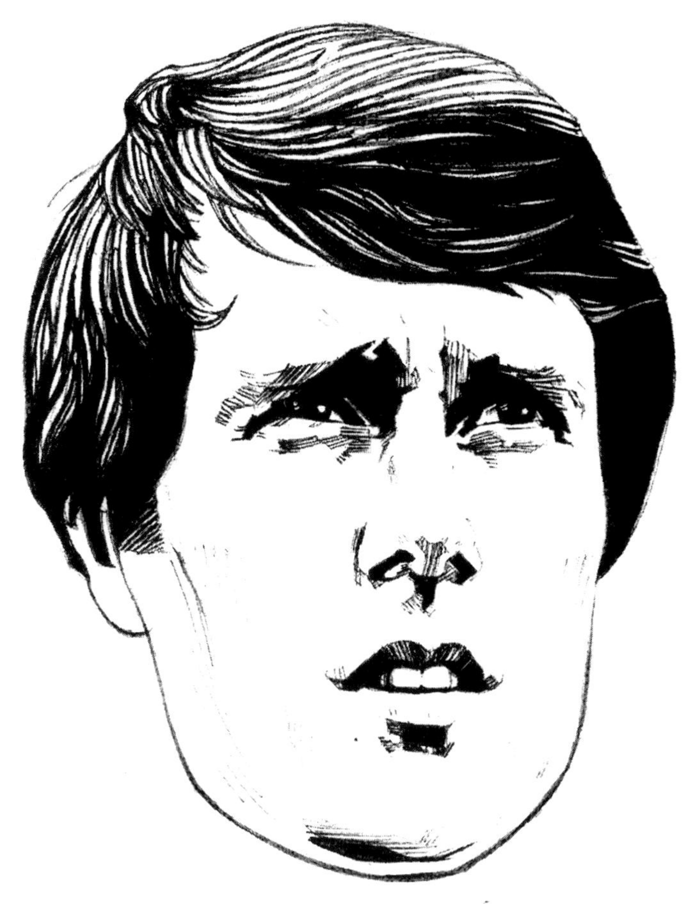

emerge with a good enough story for the back pages. Geoff trusted my judgement and integrity not to let slip inside information, and I never let him down.

Hurst was allowed to buy and sell with the hope of reviving the club's fortunes, but there were already rumblings of mutual mistrust between him and some players. He recruited experienced full-back Dennis Rofe from fellow top-three contenders Leicester City to bolster his defence. At Filbert Street, Rolfe had been club captain and Hurst was hoping his experience of over 500 senior appearances, would help get a Chelsea side that blend of youth and experience into the top tier. By way of coincidence, I had actually played alongside Rofe in my youth! I was a year younger than the full-back who played in the senior school team for Davenant Foundation, which began life in Whitechapel High Street, next to the Salvation Army before moving out to the sticks, to Debden in Essex. It was quite a long trek when I opted to stay in their Sixth Form. I used to have a kick about on the concrete outside our block of flats with Barry Silkman, who went on to play on the wing for clubs from Crystal Palace to Manchester City and still turned out when he turned 70! The only piece of grass was in an area near where the Krays were brought up and I recall kicking the ball into their front garden and having to knock on their door to ask their mum if I could have our ball back! Having applied for a trial with Spurs, at least my mother had, scouts turned up to watch my disastrous goalscoring performance as our team lost 5-1, even though I did save a penalty. You've guessed it, they wanted to sign Dennis, and our midfield star Terry Brisley, both of them ended up starting their careers at Orient.

Anyway, back to the 1979-80 season, which saw a dramatic conclusion as Rolfe's former side Leicester won the Second Division title and Sunderland defeated West Ham nine days after Chelsea's final fixture (and two days after the Hammers had won the FA Cup) to leapfrog both the Blues and Birmingham City. Chelsea missed out to the side from the Midlands on goal difference.

Rofe, a powerful left-back adept with either foot, was made club captain by Hurst before the new season, 1980-81. Expectations were high after the previous season's near-miss, and the early signs were promising. At the beginning of December, Chelsea were second. Unfortunately, very little went right from then on in. Chelsea scored in just four of their remaining 23 league fixtures – winning just three – consigning the club to mid-table mediocrity by season's end.

Hurst was sacked in April, the same month Rofe's impressive run of consecutive appearances came to an end. The Blues' failure to score in 19 of their last 22 games even become a novelty 'and finally' item on national news. For the last of those, a 0-2 defeat by Notts County, Hurst's place had been taken by John Neal. Disillusioned, Hurst moved out of football and into insurance, apart from a brief spell in Kuwait.

Ken Bates

He Bought Chelsea for a Quid

Ken Bates was Oldham Athletic chairman for five years in the sixties, and in the eighties became co-owner and vice chairman of Wigan Athletic with his old business associate Freddie Pye. He provided bank guarantees that enabled manager Larry Lloyd to sign players, including Eamonn O'Keefe from Everton for £65,000 and Wigan gained promotion to the Third Division in May 1982. Bates become a sponsor of Chelsea in 1981. The following year, Chelsea went bust with debts of £2m. Eyeing the potential of owning a large chunk of real estate in fashionable Chelsea, Bates bought the club from the Mears family. Bates said at the time: "You can go from rags to riches to rags in three generations. They were the third generation!" Bates purchased Chelsea for £1 on April 2, 1982 taking over a sizeable £1.5m debt with the club struggling lying 12th in the old Second Division, their joint-lowest position at the time since being founded in 1905.

Gus Mears founded Chelsea in 1905. After his death in 1912, Mears' relatives retained ownership until 1982 when Bates purchased it from Mears' great-nephew Brian Mears. Bates looks back on the final act for the Mears family and Lord Cadogan. Bates tells me: "When I took over the club were bankrupt, otherwise they would never have sold it to me, but it had reached such a bad state that they could no longer afford to pay the wages. We got together to finally thrash out the deal, there was The Lord Cadogan, Brian Mears, and his son David. They realised they couldn't go on a day longer as they were up to their eyes in debt and the Bank had had enough of bailing them out, as they had by now exceeded their overdraft. My offer was to pay £1 and take over the massive debts and pay the £300,000 needed immediately to head off bankruptcy. I said I had two signed cheques, one for £300,000 to pay the wages, and another to pay the FA, as back then you had to pay a third to the away side, and a third to the FA of your gate receipts, and the club hadn't been able to pay the FA, and with Brian Mears on the FA committees it was a huge embarrassment if he had to own up that Chelsea couldn't even afford the the money they owed the FA. But I was only, at this stage, going to pay the wages or the FA. So I asked them which one of these cheques should bounce. Brian Mears said he would prefer to bounce the wages and sort them out next week! But I told them we would need to sign the club to me before I handed over an unsecured loan of £300,000 'to a company run by people like you, or you lot are bigger c*nts than I thought you were!'"

The Cadogan family's wealth is based on landholdings in Chelsea including much of Sloane Street. Charles Gerald John Cadogan is one of the richest people in the United Kingdom, the second richest peer behind the Duke of Westminster, owning 93 acres of Kensington and Chelsea, his worth is estimated at £7 billion. At the time he was Chelsea chairman the value of his estates was £400m. From 1963 to 1982 Lord Cadogan was actively involved first as a director and latterly as chairman of Chelsea FC and chairman and now life-President of the Cadogan Estate. Lord Cadogan, the 8th Earl of Cadogan, the first cousin of the Aga Khan IV, British billionaire and landowner, known as Viscount Chelsea before inheriting the title of Earl Cadogan on the death of his father on 4 July 1997, was educated at Ludgrove School and Eton College, and was Chelsea Chairman in 1982. As Bates recalls, the chairman quickly accepted his offer, "He said 'I'll sign', and he did and then pushed the document to Brian Mears who signed, and he passed it onto David Mears, who also signed, and then I handed over the cheque and we all shook hands. Then Lord Cadogan said, 'Ken, I would like you to be my guest at the next home game, join me for lunch.' Well, I had just bought the club, so Chelsea was now mine, and yet Lord Cadogan was inviting me to my own place as *his* guest. I nearly told him what I thought, but I knew my place before The Lord Cadogan and didn't say anything other than, 'it would be an honour Charlie!'"

Bates would strip away the privileged classes he felt were a drain on the club's finances. The new down to earth owner detested the freeloaders. Now in his nineties, Bates recall remains as sharp and as biting as ever: "A huge part of a football club's operation occurs on non match days, much of which the supporters don't understand as it's something they don't see, so don't appreciate. But for match days the biggest curse is free tickets, and that was

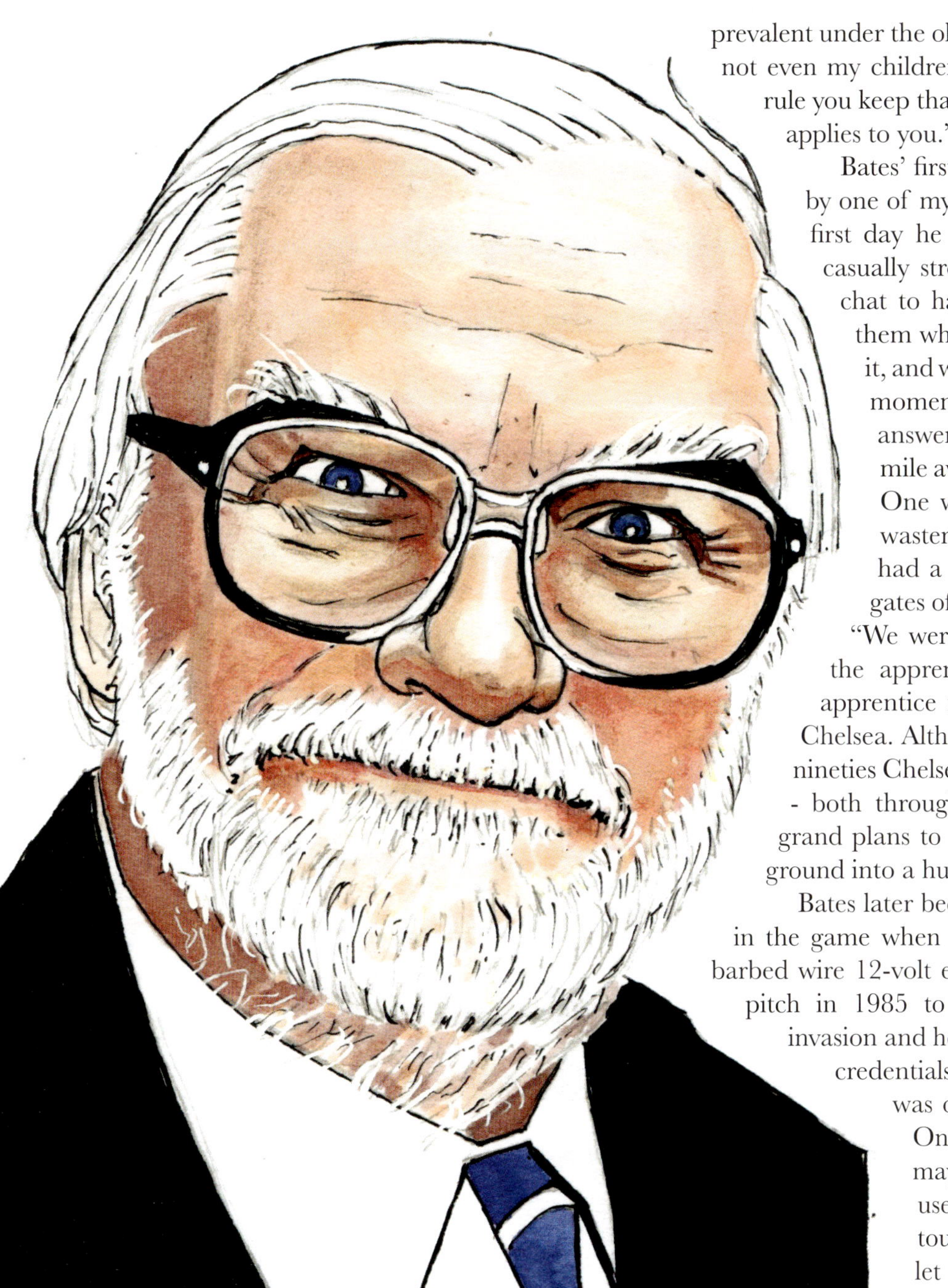

prevalent under the old regime at Chelsea. I stopped free tickets, not even my children were allowed freebie:, as if you make a rule you keep that rule and lead by example as that rule also applies to you."

Bates' first mission was cost cut cutting as evidenced by one of my first stories for the *Daily Mirror*. On Bates first day he gave no prior notice of his arrival. He casually strolled through the main gates, stopping to chat to half a dozen people along the way, asking them what they did, how long they had been doing it, and what exactly where they doing at that precise moment. A number didn't provide the right answers! For Bates, he could spot a malingerer a mile away. A few of those workers he met on Day One were summarily dismissed for being time-wasters. But it didn't stop at the workers. "We had a guest list, free tickets for 700 people with gates of 14,000. That soon stopped." He went on, "We were also paying people to clean boots while the apprentices stood around and watched." The apprentice footballers would now clean the boots at Chelsea. Although costs were cut, toward the end of the nineties Chelsea began to accumulate a mountain of debt - both through ambitious transfer dealings and Bates' grand plans to redevelop the run down Stamford Bridge ground into a huge hotel and leisure complex.

Bates later became one of the most controversial figures in the game when he proposed the installation of a 12-foot barbed wire 12-volt electric fence around the Stamford Bridge pitch in 1985 to deal with the rising problem of pitch invasion and hooliganism. Bates emphasised his hard-line credentials, attracting support from some clubs but was overwhelmingly condemned in the media. On announcing his plan Bates said: "People may howl at it being dangerous but it's been used in farming for a long time. Any fan touching the fence will immediately have to let go and fall 15 feet." Opponents included Sports Minister Neil Macfarlane, who labelled the fence 'one step too far'. Bates rebuffed

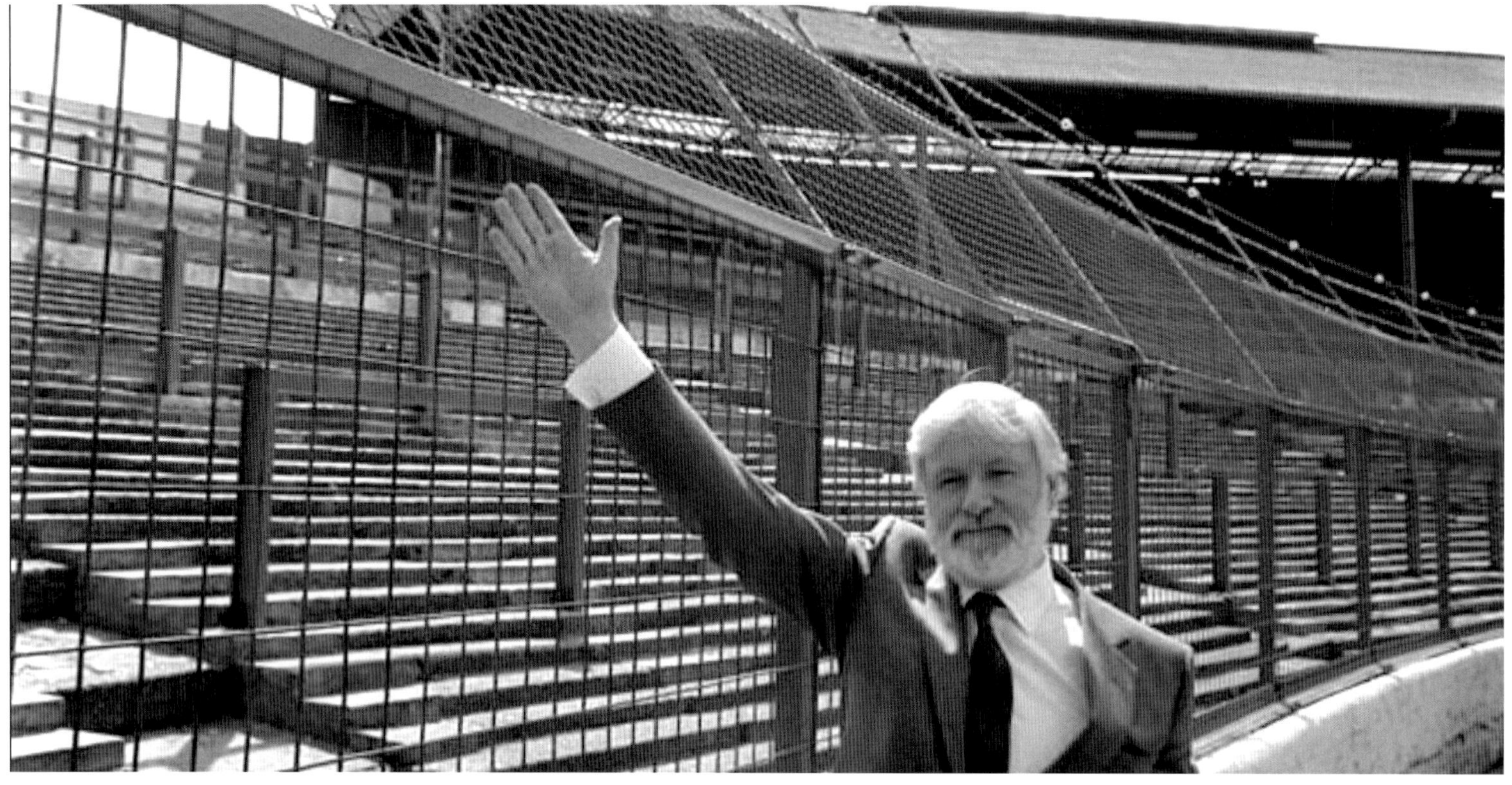

Macfarlane calling on him to resign and 'get stuffed'. The fence was to be switched on for a home fixture against Tottenham on April 27, 1985, but Greater London Council stepped in and threatened legal action, refusing to grant permission. Bates continued his case but eventually removed it in October 1985. It was never turned on.

Bates' brain child was to set-up Chelsea Pitch Owners in 1993 where shares were sold to ordinary fans in a bid to have a legal enforcement of the right not to develop the Stamford Bridge pitch. The club lent them money to buy the freehold from the club so that CPO owned both the freehold of Stamford Bridge and the club's naming rights. The future of the club's home turf was then effectively in the hands of fans. The CPO then leased the freehold back to the club on a 199-year term from 1997. CPO is independent of the club and if Chelsea want to relocate without its permission they would have to surrender the club's name. This was the case in 2011 when, within Roman Abramovich's expansive new stadium plans, the club offered to buy the freehold back and CPO rejected the offer. CPO is still active and fans can buy shares from £110 - over 13,000 shareholders own 23,000 shares. With today's calls for increased fan involvement and the fan-led review chaired by Conservative MP Tracey Crouch, Bates was ahead of his time. A spokeswoman from CPO said: "The playing surface at Stamford Bridge looks a lot like every other pitch in the country but for Chelsea fans it has a more powerful resonance as it is the only pitch in English football owned by fans. The fact that this happened at all is due to Ken Bates when he decided to protect the legacy and set up CPO. This has particular relevance this year during the current situation at the club and every Chelsea fan has Ken to thank for that."

Bates is much loved by the fans for seeing off the developers, saving the club from extinction, developing Stamford Bridge into an all-seater stadium, and setting up the CPO. By 2001 the ground was refurbished and modernised to a capacity of over 42,000 with the old running track that surrounded the ground removed. Bates also tried to improve the fan experience as he diversified the club's income with an expansion into hotels, retail, flats, a travel agency and a sports club. While these were not as successful as he had hoped, Abramovich built on this and expanded the Chelsea brand.

Bates was never afraid to tackle the fans head on. He was in charge of Chelsea for 21 years, in which time he would criticise the fans if he needed to and in 2002, he described members of the Chelsea Supporters Association as "parasites". The outburst led to him being taken to court as the supporters club took legal action against him. Chelsea supporter David Johnstone spearheaded the libel action but Bates settled out of court without accepting liability.

When Bates took over in 1982, Chelsea were averaging crowds of 13,000 and languishing in the Second Division. His willingness to spend big on new players ensured on-pitch success was regular throughout his tenure, but he earned the nickname of 'Bluster Bates' in the media and detested it. He kept his hugely expensive libel lawyers Carter Ruck busy. Because of the 'bluster" tag Bates actually spoke very quietly - unless he was roused, and then there was plenty of industrial language to accompany the sudden rise in volume!

One notorious incident came in the wake of Chelsea's defeat to Middlesbrough in a relegation/promotion play-off that saw the Blues drop back into Division Two and was marred by fan violence and a pitch invasion. Despite a disastrous afternoon on and off the pitch, Ken still sat down to talk with journalists for two hours. Tired and emotional, Bates ended the media get together saying, "I'm knackered, and I'm going off to my 500 acre farm and you can all bugger off to your council houses!" Everyone laughed. However, the humour of the situation got lost when his remark was reported out of context by a member of the press who was present in the next day's papers.

It was a moment typical of a figure who was loved and hated in equal measure by the fans and press. He saved the Stamford Bridge ground and the future of the club but was all too ready and willing to threaten a minority of them with either legal proceedings or electrocution!

John Neal

Brought Chelsea Back from the Brink

John Neal had been appointed successor to Geoff Hurst by Bates' predecessor, Brian Mears; Chelsea exchanging the glamour of a World Cup hat-trick hero for no-nonsense true Geordie grit. Yet Neal demonstrated his managerial brilliance by halting the club's slide into the Third Division before guiding them to the Second Division title in 1984.

Kerry Dixon became Chelsea's top goalscorer, a status he held until surpassed by Frank Lampard. I had the pleasure of writing Kerry's life story in his autobiography *Up Front*, in which he talks warmly about working under Neal. Kerry said of his first manager at the Bridge, "John Neal was a quiet, deep-thinking character, proud of his no-nonsense Geordie origins. He didn't say too much at our first meeting and would answer me with a 'champion' or that's canny, aye'. With time I would realise that John was Batsey's Mr Fix-It, his go-to man, the great Chelsea survivor."

When Ken Bates took over as chairman he took control of everything from the number of toilet rolls purchased to the price of new signings. Ken had bought Chelsea for £1 following a boardroom coup which ousted Brian Mears with the club on the brink of total collapse. Bates took over promising to put the club back on a sound financial footing but it didn't stop him from driving prospective new signing Kerry Dixon to the pre-season training camp in Wales to meet his new manager in his Rolls Royce. En route the chairman discussed the terms, when at that time it was still the prerogative of the manager.

Neal had inherited a team with a soft centre so Neal brought in Tony McAndrew, a battle-hardened central midfielder who had played alongside Graeme Souness at Middlesbrough under him. He seemed like just the man to add a bit of steel and personality to the dressing-room. Pat Nevin recalls: "McAndrew wasn't the flashiest of players, but the work he did was the type that allowed the more flamboyant players such as myself to express ourselves.

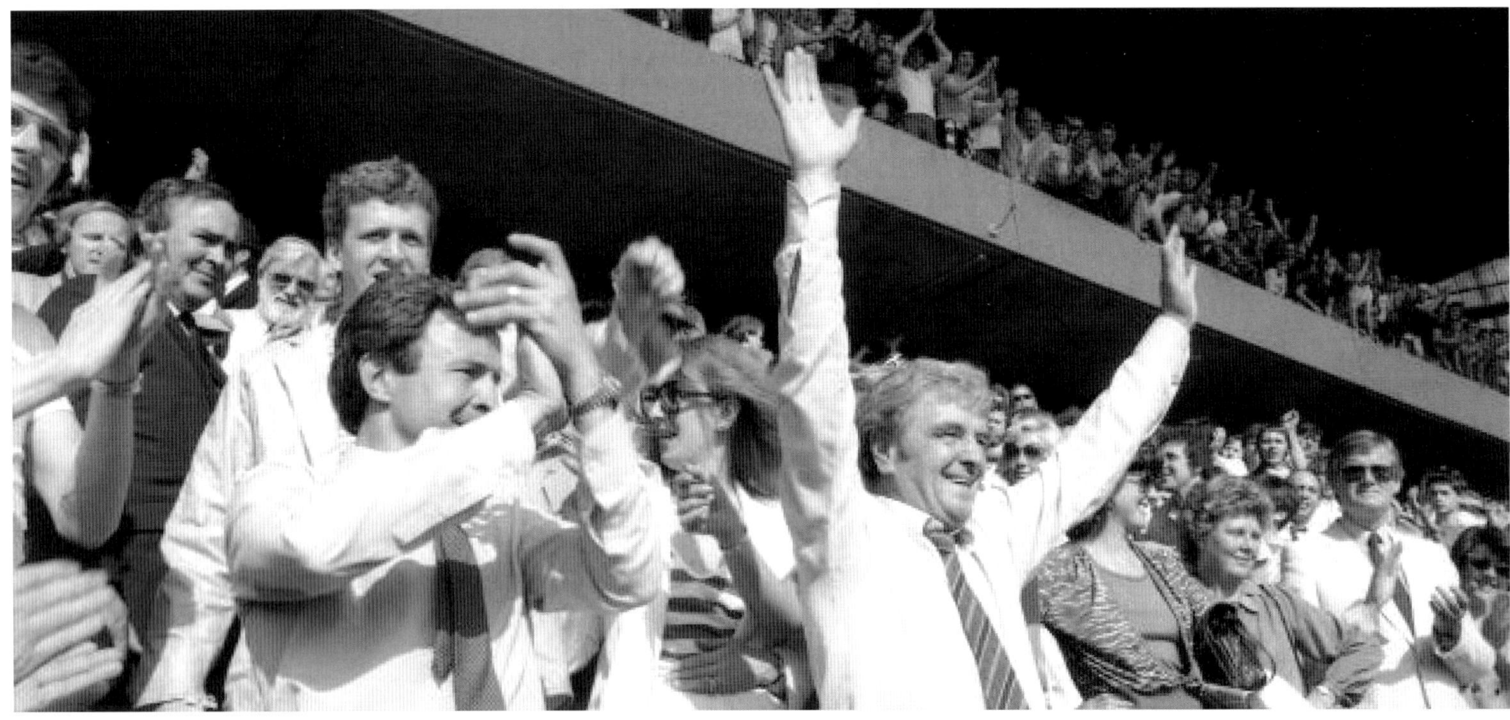

More importantly than that was the effect he had on the ethos of the side. John Neal had made him skipper because he understood the respect he had from the rest of the squad and also for the fact that he always had the most supportive attitude. In the end many of the fans never really did take to Tony but when he left Chelsea the team lost a fine leader and one or two of the less positive role models took his place and the team suffered accordingly."

Bates needed the wisdom and calmness of Neal at a time of huge transition within the club, on and off the field. Inside the dressing-room there were difficult times to start with as Dixon pin-pointed in his autobiography with the old guard making way for a new generation led by him and strike partner David Speedie. The fractured dressing-room would be sorted out by the manager, as Neal told Dixon it would, "Speedo and I were to discover that John Neal was a man who lived up to his promises."

Quiet and unassuming, Neal's impact at Stamford Bridge was profound. A resourceful and exceptionally shrewd operator, he did much to transform the playing fortunes during the first half of the 1980s, providing a welcome interlude of stability and improvement in turbulent times before standing down in 1985 following heart surgery and being appointed to the club's board. He never managed again, but the supporters of that generation will always fondly remember his efforts.

Neal took over Chelsea at a time when financial problems were crippling, but the manager's eye for a bargain – notably the small-fee signings of Dixon and Nevin - helped get the club back on track. Club historian Rick Glanvill wrote, "A succession of novices had found turning round London's cash-strapped former giant beyond them before Neal arrived in 1981. After a dismal two seasons, his proper old-school football nous would produce two years of unforgettable drama and togetherness in the middle of a troubled decade and a half. Had his reign not been cruelly curtailed by illness, silverware looked highly possible."

A pacy, intelligent, sharp-tackling full-back, Neal started his career at second-tier Hull City after impressing at local team Silksworth Colliery, as a teenager in 1949, but over the next half-decade, despite being versatile enough to occupy either defensive flank, he struggled to make an impact and in July 1956 he left the recently demoted Tigers for King's Lynn. He returned to the Football League with Swindon Town in July 1957, captaining the Wiltshire side and soon being feted as the best full-back in the lower divisions. After two seasons at the County Ground he was snapped up by Aston Villa, newly relegated from the First Division, and flourished under Joe Mercer as the Midlanders were crowned Second Division champions in 1959-60 before lifting the inaugural League Cup in 1961 beating Rotherham United in a two-legged final. Star attackers Gerry Hitchens and Peter McParland were the headline acts but Neal was widely praised for his smart defending. In November 1962, having entered his thirties, Neal returned to the Third Division with Southend United, with whom he remained until 1966, latterly as a coach under Alvan Williams. When Williams became Wrexham manager in 1967, Neal joined him as trainer then moved into the managerial seat when the Welshman resigned in September 1968. Proving a natural in the role, he led them to promotion from the Fourth Division as runners-up to Chesterfield in 1970, and laid huge emphasis on a youth system which produced the eminent likes of Mickey Thomas (later of Manchester United), Joey Jones (Liverpool), David Smallman (Everton) as well as numerous others.

Neal made a huge impression at Wrexham; he twice took them into the European Cup Winners' Cup owing to their Welsh Cup successes, with brave defeats to Hajduk Split and Anderlecht ending their runs. He spent four years with Middlesbrough after replacing Jack Charlton in 1977, before the start of his Blues spell. He could hardly reject the massive fees offered for Graeme Souness and David Mills, and left Ayresome Park in May 1981 following disagreement with the board over the sale of Craig Johnston to Liverpool.

Unlike Hurst and his immediate predecessors Blanchflower, Shellito and McCreadie, Neal had previous managerial experience and, after a traumatic brush with demotion to the Third Division in 1982-83 – they escaped by three points – Neal turned them around with expertise and commonsense.

Backed by a voraciously ambitious new chairman in Ken Bates, he rebuilt the team, bringing in a wave of excellent new players including strikers Dixon and Speedie, winger Nevin and goalkeeper Eddie Niedzwiecki, achieving an entertaining blend of flair, industry and determination which earned them the divisional title in 1983-84. That summer Neal underwent heart surgery, but he recovered to guide Chelsea to a rousing sixth place in the 1984-85 championship race and the semi-finals of the League Cup, only to be replaced by coach John Hollins at season's end, moving "upstairs" to become a director, an arrangement that didn't last long before Neal was lost to the game, an unfittingly downbeat exit for a man who had done enough to suggest that, but for his health problems, he might have taken his place in the very front rank of football managers.

Chelsea paid tribute to John when he died in November 2014, aged 82, and recognised him as the man who helped keep the club afloat. "Chelsea Football Club is deeply saddened by the passing of John Neal, one of the most significant and loved managers in our history," the club said in their statement at the time of his death.

Pat Nevin told me: "It's only in retrospect that it becomes much clearer when you are comparing managers and reviewing their influence at Chelsea and from this distance I'd have to say that John Neal was one of the best Chelsea managers for a number of reasons.The problem is that when players, or former players, talk about their managers, they usually do so from a very bias perspective; if the manager liked you and picked you, you would tend to like the manager, and vice versa.

"So, I have to confess that John Neal was the manager who brought me to the club and to whom I had much to thank for my career, maybe that is the reason I would speak so highly of him. Of course, the other reason is that he was a damn good manager and together with his assistant Ian McNeil you not only had to admire their methods but also respect their sincere love of the game, their attitude toward the game; they loved the excitement the game can create with stylish, attacking, attractive football. Equally, they didn't like bullshitters!

"John Neal had an intelligence about the way he understood people and could see things in people that he would be able to use to get the best out of them, but always by treating players differently because each player is different, and Jock Stein was a genius at this, but John Neal had that too.

"Along with Ian McNeill, he knew how to get the best out of me, and did so in some very surprising ways.They didn't shout,

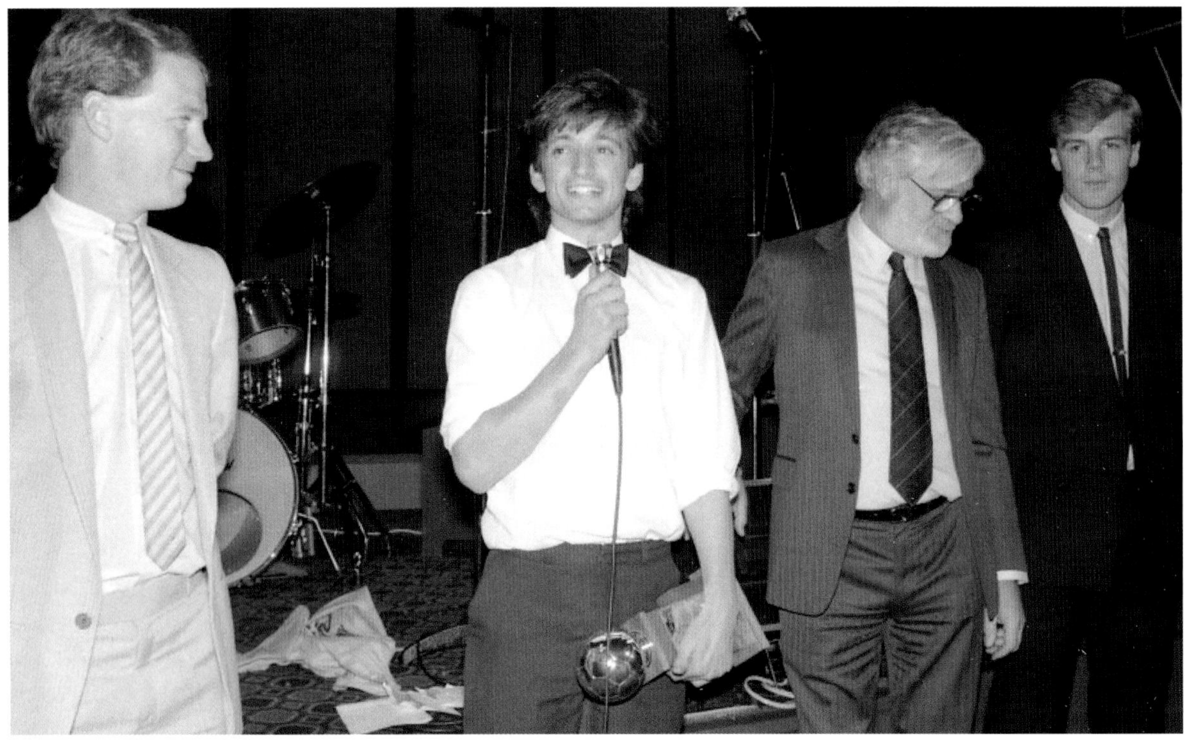

rant or bully, that was not how they conducted themselves, and it was not the kind of treatment that someone like myself would respond to in any case. I'd had a lot of that up in Scotland and I tended to ignore it and think you were an idiot going on like that, so it would have failed to get the message across. Instead John Neal would use some weird and wonderful methods. For example, during a team talk he would just say 'give it to Pat', and that took me aback. Here I was; a young kid, among all these seasoned professionals, and he had singled me out as the most creative player. He knew it would shock me, a quiet kid sitting in the corner, but who had confidence once he got onto the pitch. He also knew that it wouldn't antagonise the other players and he could see that they thought I could do it and that I had a good relationship with the rest of the team.

"He also tricked me into believing he knew how my mind worked, what I was thinking and how I would react best. What I didn't know was that he would talk to my dad every week to find out exactly what I *was* thinking to work out the best way to handle me. Whenever he did something with me I would think 'God, he really understands me' because he almost seemed to knew what I was thinking and how to get the best out of me. That's what I call good management, backing up his methods with real knowledge about the individual player and knowing how people are, what makes them tick. I watched him do it with other players and in retrospect I can appreciate what he was trying to achieve, although it didn't always make much sense at the time. For example, he made a player [Tony McAndrew] skipper, when that player hardly, if at all, ever got into the team!

"He did it with McAndrew because he was the butt of the boo-boys, but also because he was one of the strongest characters in the club and he could cope with it, and he had the sort of attitude that would rub off on the other players. It showed that the manager had an ethical approach, and I loved working with him, and that's not to say he didn't tell you if you got something wrong, but he would tell you to your face. He was straight talking and he was a straight guy. He was strong, would tell you what he thought, he had the balls to tell you something that meant something, whereas today's managers often turn to phrases that mean nothing. They 'ghost' you in modern parlance. But John was different, he told you to your face and people reacted positively to that kind of honesty."

Paul Canoville

"I didn't want to come out on the pitch. I would warm up inside the changing room and go out just before. I hated being a sub. When I warmed up it was 'sit down, you nigger'. At the old Stamford Bridge I used to stay behind the goal. It was a long way to the crowd at the old ground."

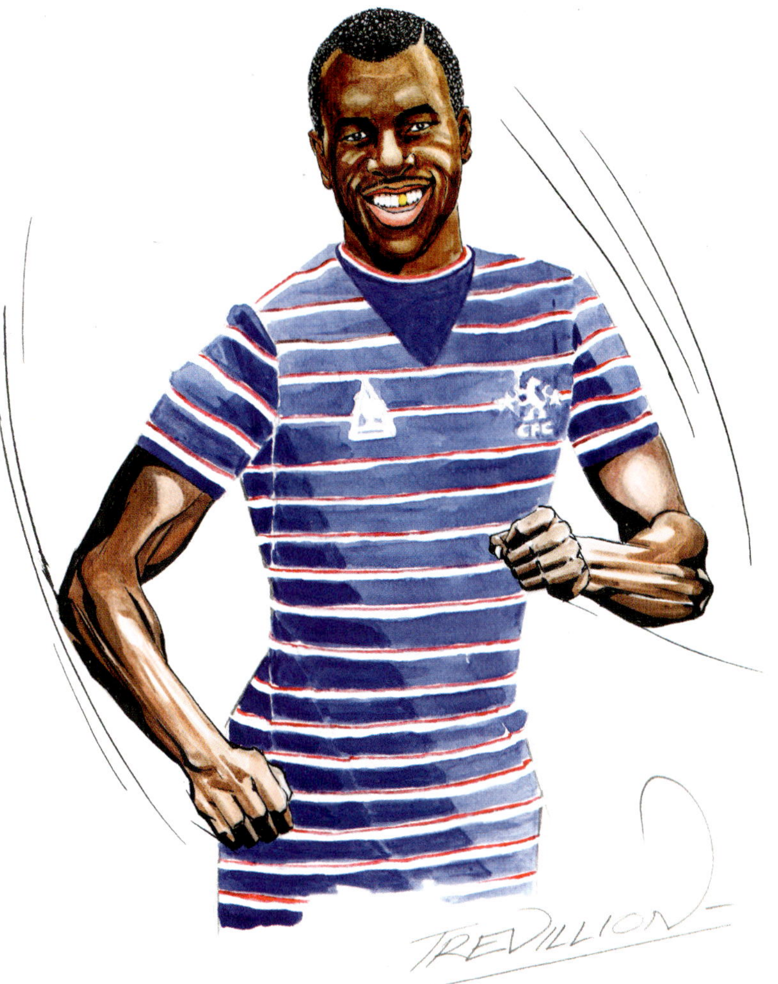

Paul Canoville, was Chelsea FC's first black footballer and took the brunt of the abuse from his own fans during a period when the club was closely associated with the worst excesses of extreme race hatred. In an exclusive interview for my research into race hate in English football, Paul told me that it should have been an honour and privilege to have been Chelsea's first black player but instead it became a stigma and a curse, from which he set an example of tolerance and became a flag bearer for the fight against bigotry in the game.

The winger, who played 103 games for the Blues scoring 15 goals, told me: "Yes, being the first player for Chelsea should be something to savour, and in a way it was then, and remains so now." However, it came at a price. A very heavy price; Paul was subject to vile racist abuse when he made the breakthrough in the early eighties. Much of that abuse from the club's own "supporters". Paul went on: "Dealing with such adversity has become second nature."

Paul has battled drug addiction, successfully fought cancer on three occasions, seen his baby son die in his arms and coped with a "seriously complicated" personal life that has seen him father 11 children with 10 women.

"Let's start with the good things" he says today, "winning the Division Two title in 1983-84 was amazing. We had a good, good team. Personally, there are three highlights. Scoring a goal against Fulham that got us a draw and played a big part in helping avoid relegation when we were in a mess in 1983. Also scoring a hat-trick against Swansea. But the one that everyone loves to talk about is the Milk Cup game against Sheffield Wednesday [4-4 in quarter-final replay in 1984] when I scored about 10 seconds after coming on as a sub and then got another in an amazing game."

These highpoints sat side-by-side with utterly reprehensible acts: being subject to monkey chants, having bananas hurled at him and being threatened with physical violence.

A pacy, powerful winger who played for the Blues for five years from 1981, he told BBC Sport at the time of the publication of his chilling, award-winning autobiography: "I remember scoring a goal and hearing that some fans wouldn't count it because a black player scored. It didn't count, so they said we had lost and not drawn. How do you live like that? I had to control my anger so many times so outsiders couldn't see. I had to see the bigger picture."

Canoville's mother dealt with racism after arriving in England from the Caribbean. He credits her with giving him the strength to deal with the excessive abuse and now uses his experiences positively, working part-time for Educate Through Football for his former club Chelsea. He also runs his own business, the Motivate To Change Foundation, where he visits primary schools around the country and abroad and has recently started a new project called Motivation4Change. "It's brilliant doing what I do," Paul says today, "I go into schools, telling them how important education is, as well as telling them what I went through - the racism, bullying, the problems, following your dreams and the good times - everything. My new venture is working with ex-offenders and youngsters with behaviour problems, giving them the life skills to get back into the community. I share my story."

Born in Hillingdon on 4 March 1962, Canoville was plucked from his hometown non-league club Hillingdon Borough in December 1981, in an era where there were few black players. 'Canners' was booed and had all sorts of racist abuse hurled at him by Chelsea fans as he warmed up before his debut in an away game against Crystal Palace on 12 April 1982. "I didn't want to come out on the pitch. I would warm up inside the changing room and go out just before. I hated being a sub. When I warmed up it was 'sit down you nigger'. At the old Stamford Bridge I used to stay behind the goal as it was a long way from the crowd at the old ground.

"John Neal signed me on a seven month contract to give me my big chance, a chance I was not going to waste. The manager told me I had to prove myself, and after four months I had gained his trust to the point where he gave me my debut. It was a difficult period for the club, they were third from bottom of the table in the Second Division, and in danger of dropping down to the Third, there was talk of the club folding. Clive Walker was on the left wing, the darling of the fans, and when I came on at Selhurst Park for the final 13 minutes and the manager hauled Clive off, I got my first introduction to playing in the big time, a dream come true, but as I stepped onto that pitch I also got the shock of my life, a barrage of racial abuse from our own fans. Our own fans! It was a welcome from our fans that I did not expect, it was some shock.You could sense they were saying 'how can you take off Clive Walker and put him on', I could tell it didn't go down well, but the way they expressed themselves was something else, something I most definitely wasn't expecting. They were calling me all sorts.

"My cousins and friends had come to Crystal Palace in the hope of seeing me come on. I was in awe of the occasion, so excited that I might come on and with 13 minutes remaining that the governor told me to warm up. But when I stepped onto the pitch I heard and then felt the racial words that came pouring out. It was a minority of our fans, but still, it was our fans giving me racial abuse. I thought how can they do that? How can they see a player in the colours, in their shirt, and do this to one of their own? I didn't understand it but I was a black lad now scared.

"It was determination that got me through it, because it was my dream to play at this level, and I knew I'd had so many ups and down to get there. Ever since I had come out of borstal, playing non-league football, having a few trials without success, when finally Ron Stuart, the scout at Chelsea, invited me for trials, then after the first week, when nothing was said, I got invited back for a second week and signed at the end of that week. At that moment, with all the abuse flying at me I had to fight myself, hold back because I didn't want to be kicked out of the club, so I didn't say anything, I suffered in silence, and did so well that, at the end of that season, the manager gave me another three-year contract. We won promotion to the First Division and I will never forget my first game in the top flight at Arsenal when we drew 1-1 - the team grew from there. It was a good team that improved and progressed."

In the same fixture two seasons later on 14 April 1984, the abuse was just as bad. His then team-mate, now respected pundit, Pat Nevin scored the only goal of the game and came out in support of Canoville afterwards, calling the abuse disgusting. "I respected Pat and was honoured when he came out and said what he said. I was getting hardcore abuse. But he scored, and he made that statement and boy did people take notice. It eased things for me. I had family members saying 'why are you playing for them?' But that helped massively."

It is to his credit that during the worst season in the club's history, 1982-83, Paul made a significant contribution to the

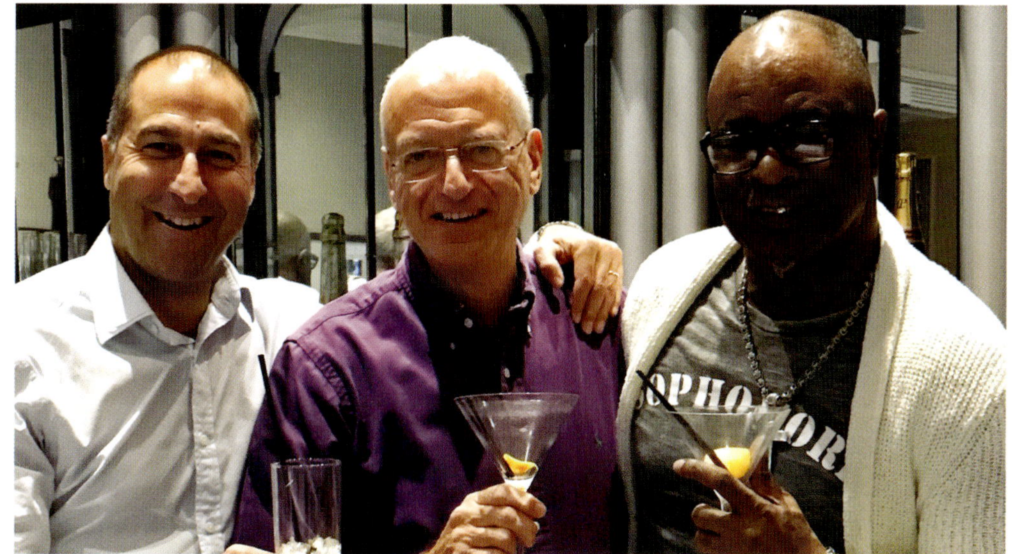

young black player aspiring to play for a big club, but the verbal abuse and chanting at the black players was scary. Paul acted with such dignity. He never responded, and proved people wrong with his ability. He just took it on the chin and how he dealt with it was fantastic. He undoubtedly paved the way for black players."

Paul acknowledges the changes that the game has undergone over the past four decades. "Kick It Out not only acknowledge racism that goes on within football, but have worked hard to be recognised as the official 'body' to go to; be it a fan or a footballer experiencing racism - on or off the pitch," he says, "something I wish could have been there when I was playing. But given my experience and other black players back then, I am delighted that Kick It Out is there. It shows the players of today that you don't have to 'shoulder' it alone as Kick It Out will take it seriously, look into the matter - take on the clubs/management, which in itself is not an easy task. But most importantly give support. Something that was so much needed when I was going through it.

"My one criticism, if any, would be the lack of punishment that can be meted out against players or fans once convicted, which might not be so lenient if the governing football bodies were more heavily committed to stamping out racism in football. Whilst statically incidents being reported are increasing, it also shows the success of 'Kick It Out' being viewed in the eyes of the new generation of fans and footballers, as a recognised anti-racism body; and that these incidents are being reported, rather than being kept under the radar. In my day, these incidents weren't even aired, much less recognised, it was just deemed an acceptable part of football culture, which it is not. Kick It Out are there to ensure this."

Paul has been involved with the work of the Chelsea FC Foundation and runs his own foundation which supports young people facing adversity and helps them reach their full potential. What was previously the Centenary Hall in the Shed End at Stamford Bridge now bears his name.

ultimately successful fight against relegation to Division Three. He was a vital member of the squad that won promotion in 1984, while his greatest moment as a Chelsea player came in a League Cup quarter-final in 1985. Trailing Sheffield Wednesday 3-0 at half-time Paul came on as substitute and scored within 11 seconds. He later added another in a 4-4 draw.

He left Chelsea for Reading in 1986, but his time at Stamford Bridge - which saw him help the club win the old Second Division title in 1983-84 - was the peak of his career. A knee injury forced him to retire within two years aged just 24, and so began a downward spiral, trying to be a father to 11 children and fighting drug addiction. He cradled his baby son Tye as he died in his arms from a heart defect in 1995 and he was diagnosed with cancer for the first time in 1996. When Chelsea became the first team to win the FA Cup with a black manager in charge in 1997, 'Canners' watched Ruud Gullit's team beat Middlesbrough from his hospital bed.

Frank Sinclair commented: "My first memory of going as a nine-year-old was the racist abuse the players suffered. It was so intimidating and being in the minority and seeing the abuse players like Paul got was terrible. I was a Chelsea fan and then I joined as schoolboy and was also a ballboy. It was really difficult. I got to the point thinking maybe I didn't want to stay. I was a

Pat Nevin

An Old-Fashioned Winger Loved By Fans

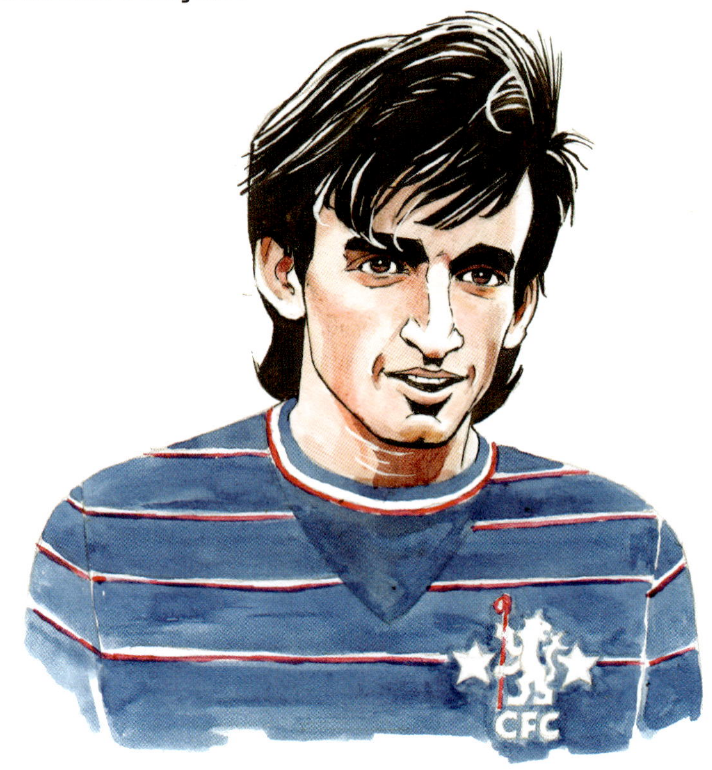

Pat won the Chelsea Player Of The Year award twice in four years but he has never been your archetypal footballer. He saw himself as a student, music critic and activist before be became a footballer. During his eighties heyday, he was the game's great outsider, regularly appearing in the *NME*, and after his illustrious playing career he didn't opt to be just your regular pundit, he became a writer-cum-pundit, renown for his expert analysis and rare tactical understanding. He remains a supporter and contributes to the club's website, matchday magazine and TV channel. I'm in regular touch with him and when he's is down south he comes to my events. He starred in the victorious Chelsea Elite Legends team that myself and Glenn Hoddle put together in the London Challenge Cup at Craven Cottage. Interestingly, in the vote for this book about the legend's favourite team and all time greatest player, there was one vote for Pat Nevin. He was a fan's favourite for sure, and such a wonderful character, a real fan himself.

Pat was the least well-known of the clutch of summer signings in 1983 as manager John Neal rebuilt a team that had nearly been relegated to the Third Division the season before. Signed from Scottish minnows Clyde for just £95,000, Nevin had to wait until the sixth game of the season to make his debut but then made an immediate impact. 'Wee Pat' scored 14 and made many more, as Chelsea stormed to winning the Second Division championship, the trickery of his wing play made him popular with supporters, so much so that he was voted Player of the Year in his debut season.

The sparkle in his first two seasons slowly waned after Neal was forced to retire and successive managers preferred a more rigid style. Even so, Nevin was frequently the most-exciting talent and again won the Player of the Year award in 1987. As the team was broken up, Nevin joined Everton when his contract expired in the summer of '88 but he was devastated when his final Chelsea game resulted in relegation to the Second Division.

There was a recent reunion of the class of 1983/84 as Pat recalls, "It turned out to be a brilliant night at Stamford Bridge, well Under the Bridge below the East Stand. I was part of that team who won the league in the second tier, scoring loads of goals, getting to the top flight, and then quickly becoming a team who were battling for the top places in the top league. Nearly 400 fans crammed into the room for what was an unforgettable trip down memory lane. I couldn't even begin to tell you all the special moments that happened but suffice to say, Chelsea fans who were there had a joyous end to the season, they deserved that. I got the job of MC, and as usual I didn't prepare a word. These players have plenty to say and usually a very funny way of saying it, so filling the time wasn't going to be a problem. Mickey Thomas made us laugh effortlessly while Colin Pates and John Bumstead carried on with the surreal humour that I loved every day in the home dressing-room all those years ago. Rather wonderfully, the larger-than-life former owner of the club Ken

Bates was there as the special guest. Ken, never short of a sharp word and harsh criticism when he thought it was due, was on top form. Considering he is in his 92nd year he was little short of a phenomenon. I will admit that as I interviewed him I was initially ready to whip that microphone away from him if he strayed into dangerous territory. I needn't have worried. The only territory he had to steel himself for was his rarely seen over-emotional side. My memories of Ken are almost all good, but this memory of him will live long in the mind. Once again, thank you Mr Chairman for saving the club when you did.

"I decided to get Kerry Dixon and David Speedie on stage at the same time," Pat says, "as a partnership up front that season 40 years ago, they were dynamite together. They didn't disappoint and even if they hadn't answered a single question I asked, it would have been worth it just for the picture opportunity of them both together again. I admit I was happy to be in the frame too – well, I did add a few goals myself during that campaign! Between the three of us we scored over 60…not bad for a trio thrown together at the start of the season. I got that picture of us from my Twitter feed and now it is downloaded, I will make sure I never lose it. Even so it wasn't the most poignant moment of the night and there were many of those. We remembered our old manager John Neal, his assistant Ian McNeil and everyone individually who helped at the club back then, including Theresa and Jane who still work for us! There was however a truly glorious moment when a feud that had lasted almost four decades was finally put to bed. Our legendary winger Paul Canoville and David Speedie finally made up their differences. There was forgiveness and bravery with the honest apologies that were needed being made, man to man, beforehand. Getting those two together finally was without doubt the best moment of the night. It was unforgettable…as was that team for those who witnessed it."

Looking back on his personal feelings during his career at the Bridge, Pat says: "My favourite has nothing got to do with playing. My first season at Chelsea I was Player Of The Year, and after one of the games I was quite pleased with myself having played well, walked out of the stadium, and an old guy came and walked with me. He said, 'do you know what, I came out to see you today,' adding, 'I enjoyed it, you entertained me,' and I went to chat to him, and he walked away. That's my highlight, now that's weird isn't it? The reason why it's my highlight is because it reminded me that we never meet all the fans, and you do things that sometimes make people happy and make fans happy. The time, the effort, the money: be it a fan who's there every week, be it a fan who visits from a far or a fan who comes once a year, it's not important. What's important is that you can give something back, and it changed me, and it made me somebody who always recognised every time I played I had to give everything for the fans."

Eddie Niedzwiecki

'Steady' Eddie Niedzwiecki celebrated promotion to the top flight with the Blues in 1984 but little was known about this Welsh keeper outside of Wrexham when he signed for Chelsea in the summer of 1983. Soon fans were singing his praises as he formed part of a new-look side which led the club to promotion under beloved John Neal, sealing the deal with an historic 5-0 win over Leeds. "It was a great day," the Welshman recalls, "one thing that stands out is Peter Lorimer playing for Leeds. He was a very experienced player, renowned for the power of his shooting, and I fielded one of his shots. It really was an incredible season and when I look back it makes me smile. All the characters, everything we had at that time. Just special."

Niedzwiecki had previously worked under Neal in North Wales and went on to play every fixture in his first season, conceding less than a goal a game, as Chelsea claimed the Division Two title during a period in history where even small gains felt huge: "There were six of us who came in at the start of that season and we gelled straight away, both on and off the field. We beat Derby, who were promotion favourites, on the opening day and just grew from there – the snowball got bigger and bigger and bigger. The fans, as they kindly remind me from time to time, were so excited that season. It was like that for all of us. John signed me for Wrexham as a 14-year-old schoolboy, so he obviously saw something. When you've got someone who shows great confidence in you, you want to give that back to the manager. And he did a wonderful job at Chelsea. He was a quiet man, but when he spoke, you listened. He was very astute, very canny. He'd come down the corridor signing 'Ee Aye Addio'! He thought a great deal about the game and he loved his players, and we all loved him back. He signed Joey Jones, Mickey Thomas and me as schoolboys when he was at Wrexham. We were all from the same area, within a five-mile radius. They were four or five years older than me and very much the beacons of light in our area to get a career in professional football. Beacons of light to you, but a pair of lunatics as far as everyone else was concerned! They're brilliant. We still speak, we keep in touch, more so with Joey, but I always look forward to seeing them. They're special guys. Those of us from North Wales who managed to get a career in the game – people like Neville Southall, Kevin Ratcliffe, Ian Rush, Gary Speed – would say it was because Joey and Mickey were the guys who came through. More and more scouts starting coming to watch kids in the North Wales area, which meant more of us came through and the quality of football improved."

Eddie would have won more than two caps for Wales but for Neville Southall, then considered the greatest goalkeeper in the world. He suffered serious knee ligament damage in 1986 while at his peak and shortly before winning the club's Player of the Year award. Numerous operations in an attempt to come back were to no avail. His tally of 55 clean sheets and 175 appearances would have both been far greater, otherwise. It happened against QPR, "It was obviously a very sad night for me. Someone landed awkwardly on my knee and when you do your anterior cruciate ligament, you get excruciating pain for a couple of minutes and then the nerve endings in your ligament go numb and you feel nothing. So I continued and shortly after I took a free-kick and, as I planted my knee, it just collapsed. After the initial injury, the fear of everything comes racing into your mind. It wasn't a very nice experience and obviously it was one that cost me dearly in the end." Eddie picked up his Player of the Year award on crutches! "Unfortunately the injury was 10 days before the Full Members Cup final, so I missed out on Wembley. I've been lucky enough to go there as a coach but that dream never came true for me as a player. But I can still remember that reception when I walked on the pitch at Wembley on my crutches, and it was tremendous."

I suggest that maybe the outcome of that final would have been vastly different than conceding four! "That's a bit unkind to Steve Francis! What pushed me to great heights was Steve being so good behind me. He was a quality goalkeeper in his own right, with a great pair of hands. And we were very lucky we were coached by one of the Chelsea greats, Peter Bonetti. We both benefited greatly from his expertise. That's the biggest regret – that I wasn't able to go on. I played my last game at the age of 27 and goalkeepers typically reach their prime between 28 and into their thirties."

Chelsea legend Bonetti was one of the first goalkeeper coaches. "Bob Wilson was the very first and then it took a few years before it became common," Eddie says, "Peter would come in part-time on a Tuesday and Thursday, and then on a Saturday when we were playing, unless it was a long away trip. It was always great to have him there. One of the great things about Peter wasn't just his enthusiasm and his knowledge of the position, but even if you'd had very little to do in the game, we used to call it being hypercritical, so you'd pick up on the minute details. It just helped to improve us as goalkeepers. And he's a wonderful man."

Peter's example inspired Eddie to follow in his footsteps. "When I knew I was going to have to hang up my gloves, the club were very good to me. Whenever I could, I would go with the team – I was one of those who had to be there, I missed matchdays so much. Whether it was to give support, or just help in any way, it's what I did. That was just me – I couldn't stand being home on a Saturday with no match. The club were very good and they offered me a three-month trial period to see how I'd get on coaching. It fell into place and that summer they offered me the youth team job. I'd lost one career, but luckily for me I was able to start another one quite quickly. But coaching or whatever will never substitute being a professional player. Never, ever. I always thought I'd play until I was 40, at least. But one incident changed that, and it's something that can happen to anybody."

Eddie had no regrets about what he achieved at Chelsea, and how the club has mushroomed in importance, influence and acquiring silverware, "It was all about the club winning trophies again. Once we won one, we won loads. There was the FA Cup, then a special night in the Cup Winners' Cup, when Gianfranco came on in Stockholm to score the winner. And playing at the San Siro in the Champions League, when Dennis scored his famous goal that the fans sing about. I still remember the reception Marcel Desailly got from the Milan fans that night, it was absolutely incredible. "

Kerry Dixon

The Eighties Golden Boy Who Ended Up Behind Bars

Kerry Dixon was the golden boy of Chelsea until the shine wore thin and he ended up in prison. With 193 goals for Chelsea, the big No 9 was on his way to breaking Bobby Tamblings record when he was shifted off to Southampton, more in exasperation by Ken Bates due to his star striker's continued quest for more money due to his gambling debts.

Dixon retains a grudge that he was never able to become the top scorer of all time which he expressed in his autobiography which I ghost wrote for him when he came out of jail, as much to aid his non-existent finances as anything.

Dixon signed for Chelsea in Summer 1983 when the club had only just escaped relegation to the Third Division. Under manager John Neal, Chelsea was undergoing a radical change, with Dixon and Pat Nevin at the core of this new Chelsea side. Dixon had an immediate impact, scoring twice on his debut against Derby and then went on to score 32 more as Chelsea were promoted as Second Division champions. Nevin, Dixon and David Speedie together scored 200 goals over the next three years as they formed one of the most lethal front three in Europe.

Drawing the attention of Arsenal, he nearly left the club but stayed to become integral the following season in the First Division, as he finished joint top scorer, with Gary Lineker, on 24. Dixon was loved at Chelsea not only because he got the club up to the First Division and then cemented their promotion with a top half finish, but also because he never left despite a lot of offers. Seeing his form and his ability, he could have easily left for greener pastures and could have won several titles. However, he stuck with Chelsea and got them promoted again when things were starting to fall apart. Chelsea were relegated in 1988 following clashes between key players, but the Blues got back up straight away with Dixon scoring 25. Kerry is 9th in the all-time appearances list yet he only won two Second Division champion medals.

His hat-trick of Golden Boots, sharing the trophy with Lineker, a pre-Mexico 86 World Cup acclimatisation trip, scoring twice on his full debut in a 3-0 win against West Germany were other career highlights. "As a debut it was one of the great days of my life," said Dixon. "Playing for England was every kid's dream. In the Panini album [for the 1986 World Cup] it was Kerry Dixon, Chelsea and England. To score two against the Germans and beat them was just incredible." Breaking into Bobby Robson's starting line-up was huge. Dixon rattles off a long list of names who won England caps when he was at his peak. "I played in an era where there was Paul Mariner, Tony Woodcock, Garry Birtles, Ian Wright, Mick Harford, Brian Stein, Paul Walsh, Clive Allen, Tony Cottee, Gary Lineker, Peter Beardsley, Mark Hateley, Steve Bull, John Fashanu and Trevor Francis. But I scored so many goals during that time that he couldn't ignore me. Now there is a serious dearth of strikers. There's Harry Kane and Jamie Vardy, then you are looking at Danny Welbeck, Marcus Rashford and Daniel Sturridge. And Wayne Rooney, but is he a striker now? The competition is not so great."

Dixon only played six minutes at the World Cup, appearing as a substitute against Poland. "As a player, everyone had their thing when they finished training - drinking, going to the golf course, the snooker hall or whatever," said Dixon. "I went to the betting shop. It's what I loved and what I did. It got totally out of control. Betting accounts and shouting numbers down the phone - it was crazy. You can have a game of pool for £1 but I was ending up betting a grand or more on the dogs and horses. I ended up in trouble, thinking, 'What am I doing?'"

Kerry was eventually sold to the Saints when he became a sinner in the eyes of Bates, and then was carted off to prison after he was found guilty of GBH. He left Chelsea in 1992 reluctantly because he was closing in on the club's all-time leading goalscorer at the time, Bobby Tambling. But he was told he would be playing in the reserves and he desperately needed the money to pay off more debts. "One of my biggest regrets is not getting the record," he said. "I could have put that record out of sight so Frank Lampard couldn't have beaten it. But I didn't want to play in the reserves - that's just not me. And I had obligations - and debts - and the bonuses would have dropped off." After a miserable time at Southampton came a rewarding near three-year spell at Luton Town - which included facing Chelsea in an

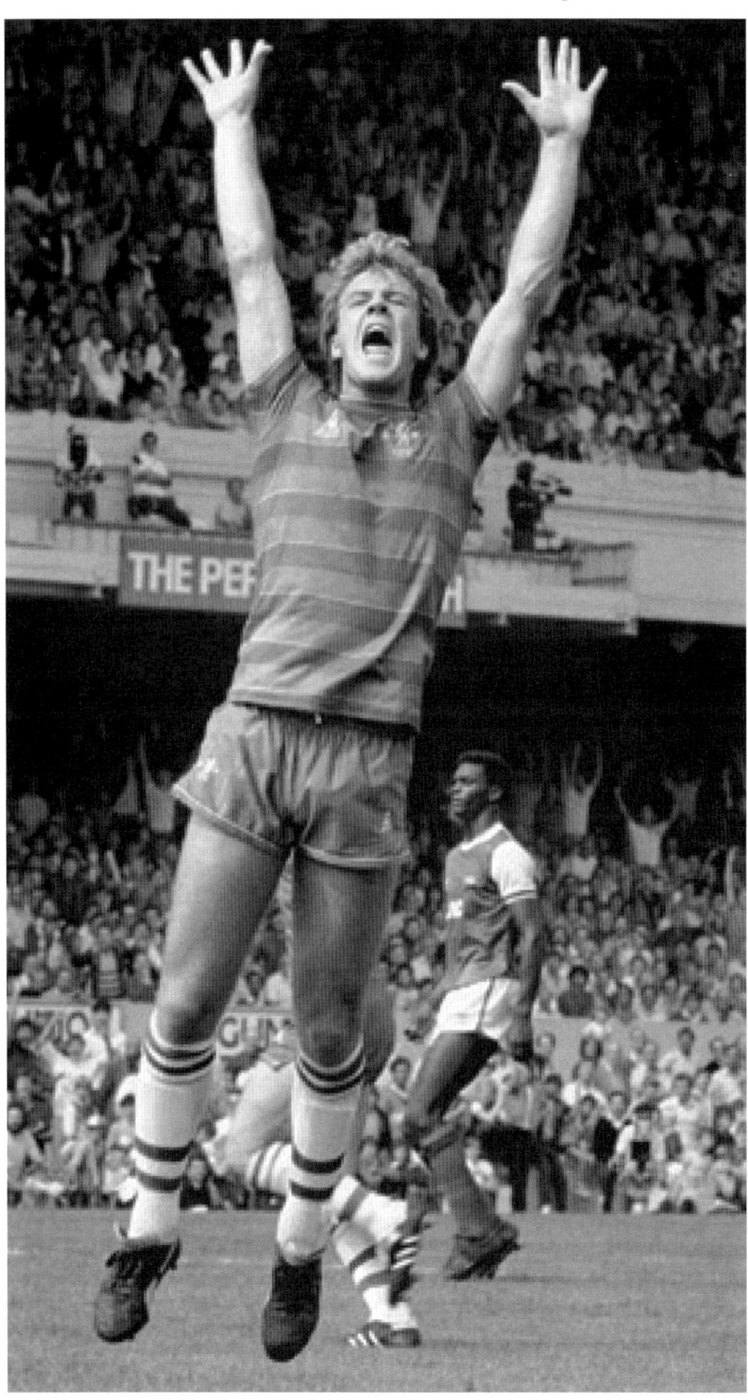

FA Cup semi-final at Wembley. "That was one of the greatest days of my life in football," recalled Dixon. "We lost 2-0, but afterwards it seemed the whole ground was singing my name." He also played for Millwall, Watford and Doncaster Rovers as a player-manager, before eventually retiring in his mid-40s. Again, partly because of financial necessity, but partly because he simply loved playing.

The book *Up Front* was a best seller but the publishers were generous to Kerry affording him several advances ahead of the schedules contract to his pleas of poverty and the need for funds. The blurb says: "Kerry's life in recent years has been bedevilled by problems with gambling, drugs and, worst of all, a prison sentence in 2015, after he was convicted of grievous bodily harm following a fight in a pub. At that point, one of football's golden boys finally hit rock bottom. This book is the honest, unflinching account of his rise and fall, and of the new life he is now slowly and patiently building. His memories of playing in a more robust era of the game, before the days of multi-million-pound salaries and all the rest of the modern football circus, will appeal to plenty of nostalgic football fans, as well as to all those who remember him as one of the game's all-time greats. Equally, his unflinching recollections of his darkest days, culminating in his time in prison, are about as far from the Beautiful Game as anyone can imagine. The world is all too familiar with tales of once-famous footballers falling from grace. *Up Front*, however, is unique for its flashes of humour in adversity, its clear-eyed reflections on a different age of football, when leading players could all too easily be treated as disposable, and finally for its humility. For Kerry Dixon, as this often moving autobiography shows, the only way is up."

In the book, Kerry was honest about how he squandered his wages: "At one point in my Chelsea career, I was £135,000 down when I was earning £130,000-a-year at my peak. I urgently needed bailing out and went to the manager, Bobby Campbell, for help. I'm guessing he went to the chairman and, whatever they decided to do, they sorted out some sort of deal. The bookies settled for £25,000 as a one-off payment and the club insisted that all my betting accounts were closed down. But it was probably only a matter of weeks before the debts began mounting up again. I was out of control. This was when the bookies began to send threatening messages. They were plain in saying they would soon be dispatching the heavies."

He said Bates sent him to an addiction centre, but he only went three times. He added: "I never wanted to leave Chelsea, but when Southampton came in with an offer in 1992 I had no option but to take it. My accumulated debts were to be paid out of my new contract, so it was a problem solved overnight."

A brief spell as manager of Doncaster Rovers, where Dixon's office doubled as the physio's room, did not work out and a bright media career also eventually tailed off due to ongoing problems with gambling, alcohol and depression.

Dixon was convicted of drink-driving in 2000 and given a caution for common assault when he pushed a former team-mate against the wall in 2002. Dixon was sentenced to nine months in jail after being found guilty of assaulting a man in a pub. Judge Barbara Mensah said that the violence used was "disproportionate, unnecessary and completely over the top" at his sentencing at Luton Crown Court. Dixon denied attacking another man in the Nag's Head Pub in Dunstable, Bedfordshire, who had been sitting on a bar stool. CCTV revealed that the victim Ben Scoble had been punched off the stool in the early hours of 15 May 2014, and then been subjected to a flurry of blows when on the floor. The judge said the shocking footage showed how Dixon launched an attack "out of the blue", which had drawn "a gasp" from jurors when first played to the court during his trial. "You were not just striking him, knocking him off his bar stool, but continuing to strike him when he was on the ground," she said. "Then you continued to pummel him on the ground." Dixon pleaded not guilty to assault occasioning actual bodily harm. He alleged he had acted in self-defence, however, Dixon was convicted by a jury after a five-day hearing.

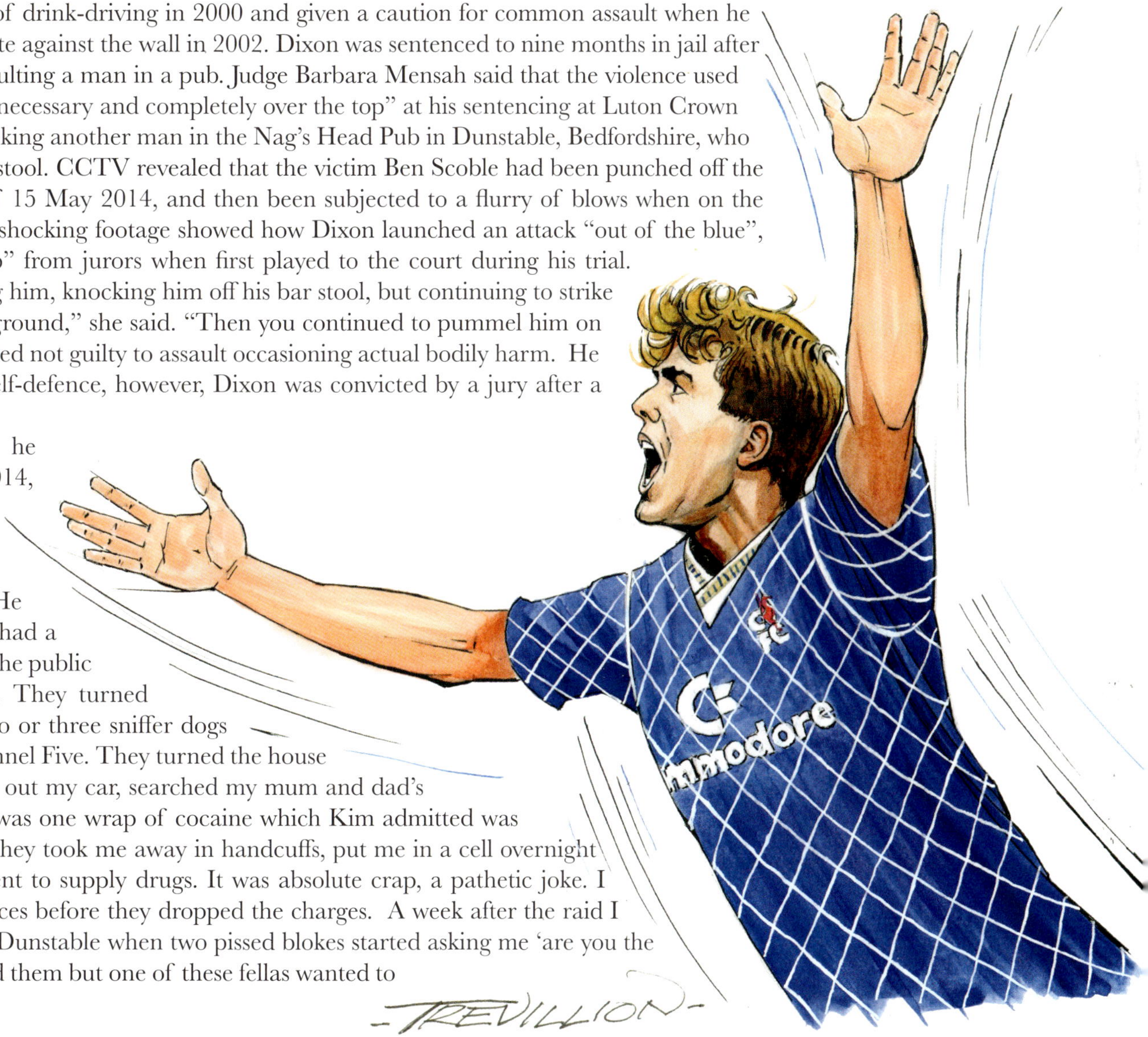

In his autobiography he revealed how in May 2014, the police raided his home, an event which spiralled into the attack that sent him to prison. He claimed: "They said they had a tip-off from a member of the public that I was dealing drugs. They turned up with 20 policemen, two or three sniffer dogs and a film crew from Channel Five. They turned the house upside down, were in and out my car, searched my mum and dad's house and all they found was one wrap of cocaine which Kim admitted was for her personal use. But they took me away in handcuffs, put me in a cell overnight and charged me with intent to supply drugs. It was absolute crap, a pathetic joke. I made two court appearances before they dropped the charges. A week after the raid I was in the Nag's Head in Dunstable when two pissed blokes started asking me 'are you the drug dealer?' I just ignored them but one of these fellas wanted to take it a stage further and a couple of hours later he sat in my seat at the bar. I asked him to move, he just looked at me and said 'f*** off, fatso'. I was aware he was holding a pint glass. I still had the scars from when someone stuck a glass in my face ten years earlier and I didn't want the same thing happening again. So I whacked him in the face. And then I hit him a few more times to make sure he stayed down. Then me and Kim walked out of the pub and this builder and his mate chased after us with a glass in his hand. He'd lost a few teeth and there was a lot of blood but he wasn't so badly injured he couldn't chase me."

The intervention of a doorman and some pub regulars prevented any further damage but he was arrested and charged with actual bodily harm. He added: "The judge refused to allow CCTV footage of the two blokes chasing me with a glass to be admitted into the trial. The jury decided I had broken the law and, in the cold light of day, I agree with their decision. Someone got injured and I regret it. I wish this chapter wasn't in my book. I wish it was all just the fairytale of my football career, scoring goals for Chelsea and for England. But that's not the way things happened and I want to be honest. The phone calls and the work have dried up since I came out of prison so now I'm working as a heating engineer's mate, laying pipes and installing air conditioning. It barely pays the bills but I'm grateful for the work and I'm certainly not complaining. I'm just looking for a second chance."

"Gambling was my downfall but I have done that all my life," he told BBC Sport. "It's been an addiction and I don't think it can ever be completely controlled or contained. I believe it's in my DNA. It is something in me I would argue that maybe made me the footballer I was. It was the drive, the will to win, the need to score goals. When I gamble, it's wanting to win because of the buzz I get from it." Gambling brought nothing but misery, bankruptcy, the loss of three houses, a breakdown in his marriage, a journey into drugs as the lowest point.

Chelsea stopped using him on their club's television channel in 2014 after he was charged with possession of cocaine even though the case was later dropped. I facilitated a reconciliation with Chelsea who had refused him access to return to his part time job as an ambassador on match days, but Kerry was still never far from a new low of financial issues due to his problems which he never quite got to grips with. He hoped the release of his autobiography would be a cathartic process and help him draw a line under the bad times, and get him back working in football. A year after leaving prison Dixon is "still very much on the floor". "But the only way is up and it's going to be up," he quickly adds when reflecting on his new life. His punditry work dried up, so he paid the bills by working as a heating engineer's assistant - pipe fitting, boiler work and "various other bits and bobs". "However you describe it, I am an assistant," he explains.

The Chelsea fans were "magnificent" and he has been told the door is not shut on him resuming his match-day hospitality work at Chelsea at some point. The Professional Footballers' Association were a huge help, but it was an ongoing battle. Bobby Barnes, the PFA's deputy chief executive, told BBC Sport: "Kerry is an object lesson in how a player can fall from grace. But he has also displayed tremendous strength of character because the hardest thing sometimes is to take that step and admit you need help and you have a problem. It took a little while, but Kerry has very much embraced what we have been trying to do to help. We have done as much as we possibly can, and continue to do as much as we can, to support him. I'm in regular contact with Kerry and Chelsea have been very supportive, in particular chairman Bruce Buck. Bruce and I are in regular dialogue to see what we can do to assist."

But time did not prove a healer and Kerry's fall from grace has not proved to be the catalyst that ended his addictions once he dropped out of the limelight. "I did the crime and paid the penalty," said Dixon. "I am sad it happened but I am not one to live in the past - I will move on and am determined not to let it happen again. I haven't become a new person but it has given me a new idea on what can happen and where life can take you. Jail is a very lonely place; it gives you a lot of time to reflect on everything, how you will be remembered, how many years you have left and what you will do with them. I have kids, a mother and father and I have responsibility to them. It's there on my CV and I cannot change that and I am not proud of it - I want people to remember me for being a good bloke, not an ex-footballer who has gone off the rails and gone to prison."

Dixon suffered panic attacks while sharing a tiny cell with an armed robber in Bedford Prison. "You hear stories of people

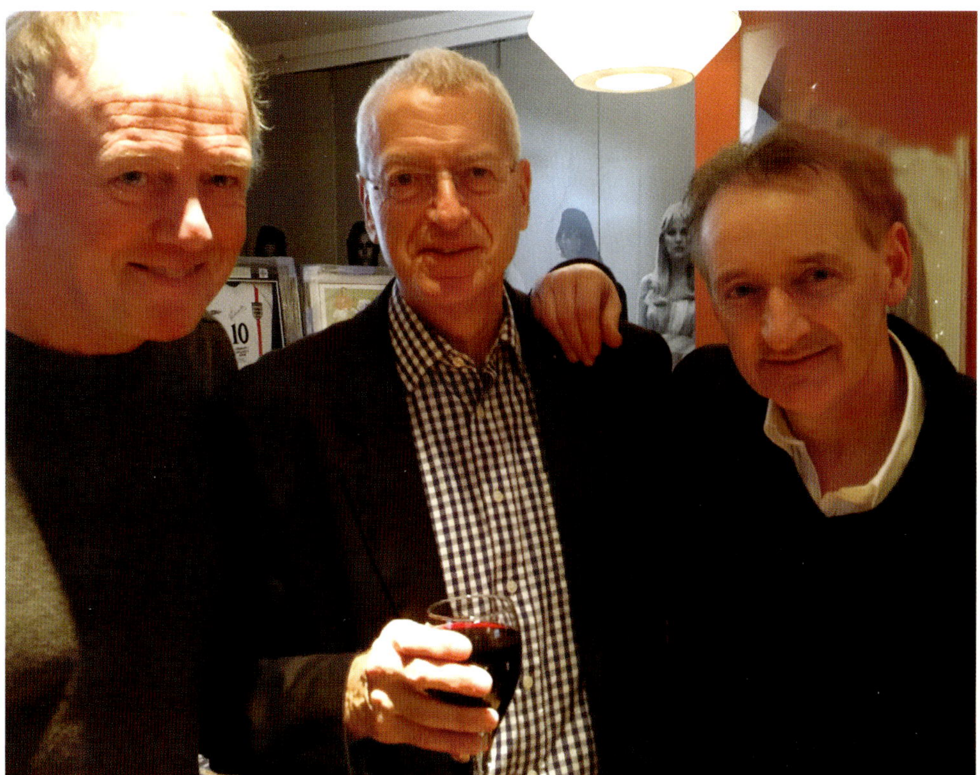

having it easy in prison, having a laugh. But it's not easy. It's lonely, it's scary, it's boring and it's harrowing. I didn't realise I was claustrophobic until they put me in the security van to take me from the court to prison. They call it the sweat box but it was more like a metal coffin. You can just about sit down but your knees touch the front wall, your shoulders touch the sides and the roof is about six inches above your head. There's a tiny darkened window but as soon as they slammed the door I had a panic attack and was screaming 'let me out, let me out'. The journey lasted 45 minutes and was the worst thing I'd ever experienced. It borders on inhumane, a heart attack waiting to happen. I had a few more panic attacks in prison as a result of that. It was sweltering hot in the cell and the window only opened a couple of inches. There were nights when I'd have my mouth pressed up against the window, desperately trying to suck in some air. It was an awfully lonely place. One inmate hanged himself while I was there. When something like that happened they put the entire prison in lock-down, but word quickly got round."

Dixon also discovered an intimidating cell-mate who would later be sentenced to 13 years for a string of armed post office raids. "As soon as I got out of that prison van I was taken to my cell, where this very large and very muscular bloke made it clear that he didn't want me in there with him. He was waiting to be sentenced and was obviously agitated about sharing a cell. And he wasn't the sort of bloke to pick an argument with. I wasn't scared, but I was apprehensive. You hear all sorts of stories. He used to lie in his bed watching *Jeremy Kyle* and *Storage Hunters* on TV. I'd lie on the top bunk, staring at pigeons and the same bit of concrete. Was I depressed? I don't really know. It could be argued that I've been in a depression for 20 years since the slide started."

He added: "I was still involved in non-League football when I started taking cocaine at the age of 39. I was running a pub to pay off my debts and was working so hard that there were a couple of times I simply flaked out. One of the regulars suggested if I had a sniff of cocaine I'd be able to stay up longer. I'd always been fiercely anti-drugs but I was so tired that I gave it a go and it eventually had the desired effect. Suddenly I could stay up until three or four in the morning. It wasn't something that happened on a regular basis. Maybe on a Saturday night over an 18-month period before it sort of filtered away."

I devised a series of *Legends Lives* documentaries of which Kerry was the first, which raised considerable sums from a live auction as well as tickets for the film premiere at the Sanctum Soho Hotel. Owner Mark Fuller is a big Chelsea fan and so facilitated the event with the hotel boasting a state of the art cinema in the basement as well as a fab roof top bar. The chef created a special Chelsea cake (see p.252) in Kerry's honour and there was a big turn out to help with his finances.

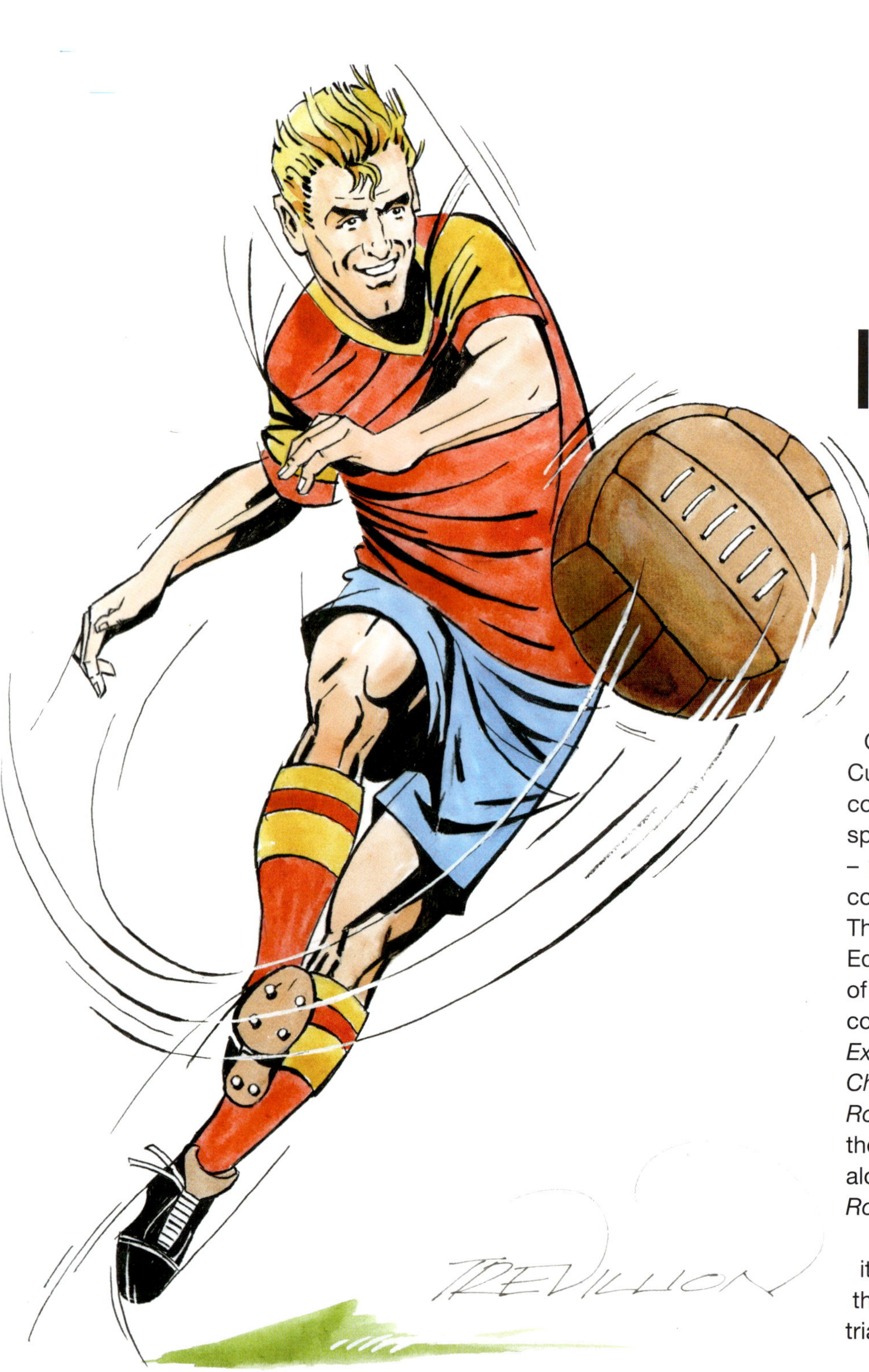

When Kerry Dixon Was *Roy of the Rovers*

Chelsea Ace was Real Life Roy Race

In 1963 I was approached by Steve Wallace, editorial director of Fleetway, to draw Roy of the Rovers. Joe Colquhoun had been drawing Roy from the start, he was a brilliant comic artist but I was not a comic artist as such, I was a 'REALISM ARTIST'. I was working in Scotland for the *Sunday Mail*, The *Evening Citizen* and Scottish *Daily Express* among others, drawing realistic football strips which featured names such as Bill Shankly, Denis Law and Dave Mackay. These had proved so successful I was asked to draw a special front page for the *Evening Citizen* prior to the Glasgow Rangers v Tottenham Hotspur European Cup Winners' Cup match in December 1962. I completed the front, back and inside double page spread, but unfortunately the game was fogged off – yet surprisingly the paper still sold over 10,000 copies even though the match was cancelled! This prompted the *Evening Citizen* editor, Robert Edwards, to write to Kennedy Aitken, Strip Editor of the London *Express*. When I completed my contractual deals in Scotland I was off to the *Daily Express* in London and lined up to draw *Bobby Charlton's Life Story*. So I suggested to *Roy of the Rovers* editor Steve Wallace we treat Roy Race the same – draw him as though he was playing alongside Bobby Charlton and bring *Roy of the Rovers* to LIFE.

Wallace wasn't sure, but he was willing to give it a try for two months, check on the reaction and then make a decision. For the first six weeks of the trial period Wallace was not a happy man, but then

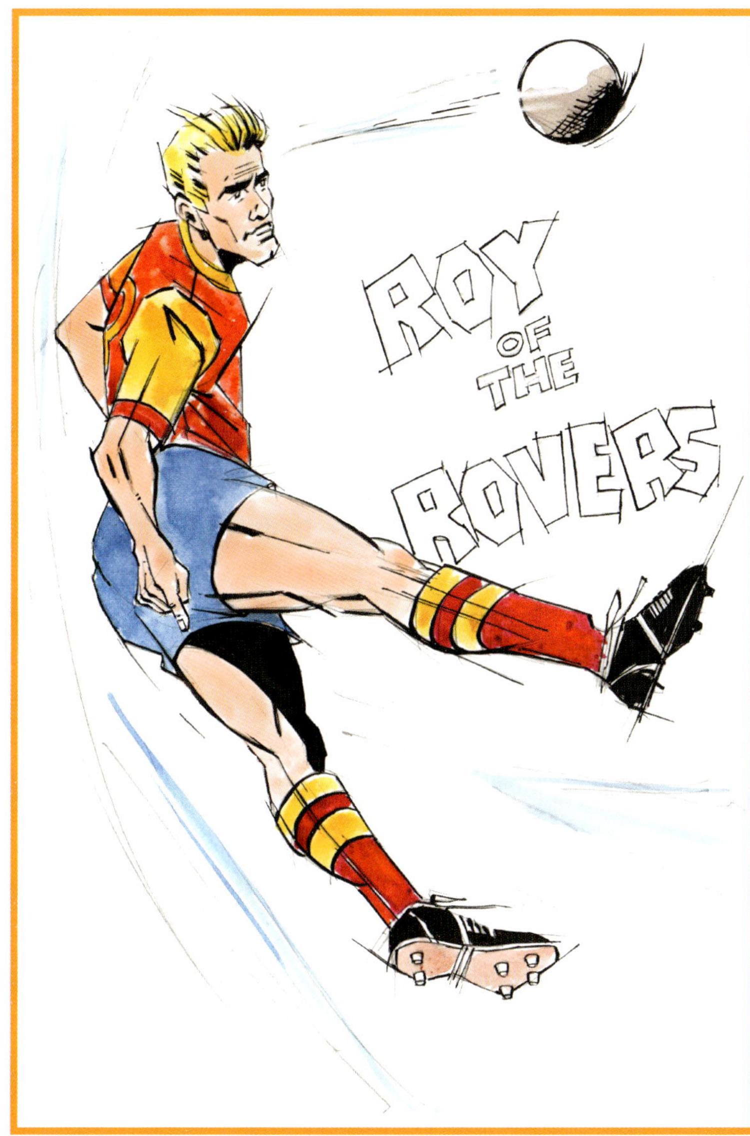

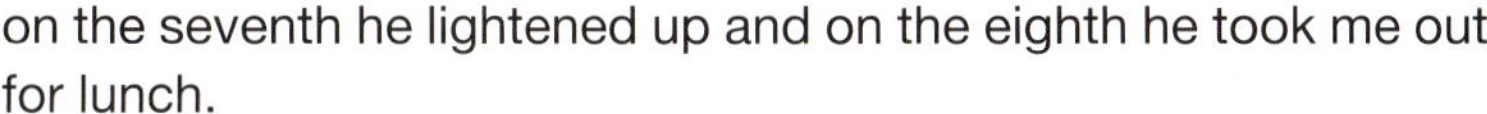

on the seventh he lightened up and on the eighth he took me out for lunch.

"Congratulations Dr Henry Frankenstein," said Wallace, "Frankenstein now has a playmate! ROY RACE IS REAL! Children have been writing in for his autograph, inviting him to their schools, even their birthday parties and Roy amazingly got mentioned a couple of times on radio."

So how REAL was Roy? Just ask Kerry Dixon.

Born in Luton in 1961 Kerry had just *one* ambition – to be a professional footballer, but his dream hit a brick wall when he

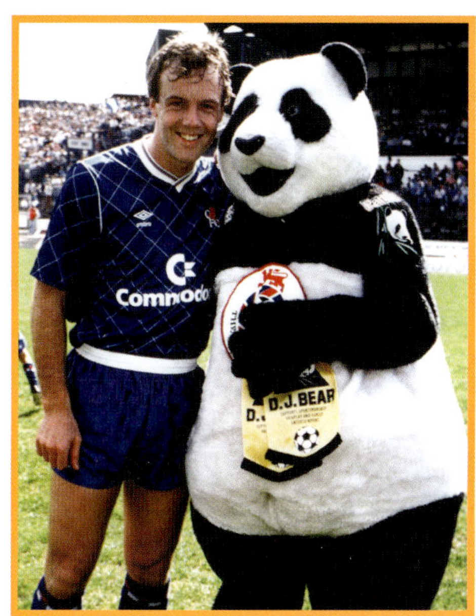

was turned down by his home town Luton and then Tottenham. It meant non-league football for Kerry with Dunstable. There his goal-scoring feats meant that after just one season he was signed by Third Division Reading. The goals kept coming for Kerry and he won the Golden Boot that season and the Reading fans were now calling him 'Roy Of The Rovers'. It all came about when a story about the goal-scoring ace 'Roy Race' appeared in the Reading matchday programme alongside a photograph of the other goal-scoring ace, Kerry Dixon. Immediately the Reading fans started calling Kerry their goal machine - Roy Of The Rovers. Even when he was walking through the streets people would shout out "Quick look, that's Roy Of The Rovers!"

Like Roy, the goals kept coming and in 1983 Kerry was transferred to Second Division Chelsea and at the Bridge there was no stopping Kerry from hitting the back of the net. The Chelsea fans were delighted when they gained promotion to the First Division and Kerry picked up another 'Golden Boot'. With Chelsea, Kerry was in pure Roy Race mode and picked up another Golden Boot to become the only player in football history to win the golden boot in the Third, Second and First Divisions in consecutive seasons! Then, when Kerry was selected for England, and with the Three Lions on his shirt, he scored four goals in his first three Internationals. It was net-busting story-telling, straight off the pages of *Tiger*! PT

Evening Citizen
Limited

ALBION STREET, GLASGOW, C.1

TELEPHONE
BELL 3550

December 6th, 1962.

Kennedy Aitken, Esq.,
Strip Editor,
Strip Dept.,
Beaverbrook Newspapers Ltd.,
Fleet St.,
LONDON, E.C.4.

Dear Kennedy,

I thought you would like to know that we sold over 10,000 copies of your Rangers v. Spurs Cartoon Souvenir, even though the match was cancelled.

This was a most remarkable achievement. It equals the highest figures we've achieved even when the match was being played and all the crowd has turned up.

We salute your enterprising department.

Yours sincerely,

Bob

Robert Edwards
EDITOR

DIRECTORS :— Hon. Max. Aitken, T. Blackburn, A. H. Bruce, F. C. Dench, J. M. Paterson, A. C. Trotter.

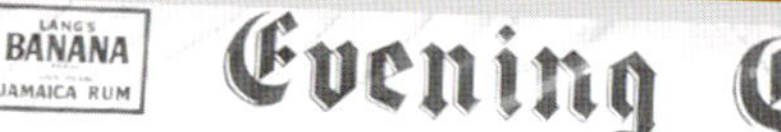

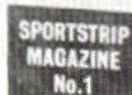

Pola-Cola
PURE DELIGHT!
Oh so COOL and Refreshing

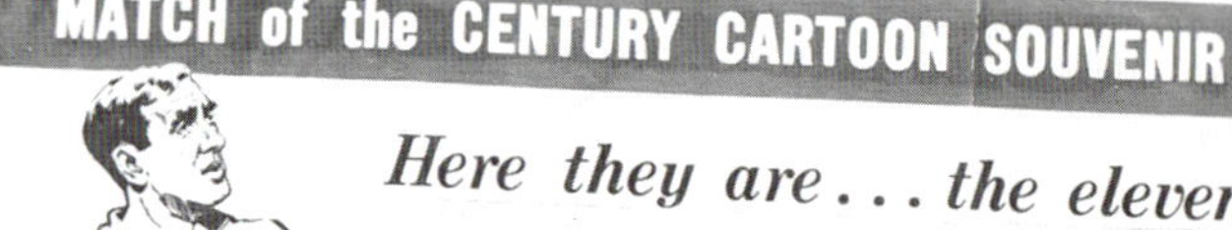

Featuring

MEET THE SUPER SPURS

MEET THE MIGHTY RANGERS

THE FABULOUS JIMMY GREAVES

Here they are . . . the eleven idols of England's £350,000 wonder team

SUPER SPURS

F.A. CUP WINNERS 1901, 1921, 1961 AND 1962. FIRST DIVISION CHAMPIONS 1951 AND 1961. SECOND DIVISION CHAMPIONS 1920 AND 1950. MOST NOTABLE ACHIEVEMENT—"THE DOUBLE."

TOTTENHAM HOTSPUR BECAME THE FIRST CLUB TO WIN THE CHAMPIONSHIP OF THE LEAGUE AND THE F.A. CUP IN THE SAME SEASON SINCE 1897 WHEN ASTON VILLA LAST PERFORMED THIS FEAT.

BLANCHFLOWER

AT 37, DANNY BLANCHFLOWER IS THE OLDEST PLAYER IN THE SPURS TEAM. HE WAS TWICE VOTED "FOOTBALLER OF THE YEAR"—A RECORD HE SHARES WITH TOM FINNEY. BORN IN BELFAST, THIS SLIGHTLY BUILT RIGHT HALF RECEIVED ALL HIS EARLY FOOTBALL TRAINING FROM HIS MOTHER.

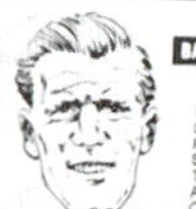

BAKER **HENRY**

FULL-BACKS PETER BAKER AND RON HENRY NEVER COST SPURS A PENNY. BAKER MODELS HIMSELF ON FORMER SPURS PLAYER ALF RAMSEY—YES, THE SAME ALF RAMSEY WHO IS NOW ENGLAND'S NEW TEAM MANAGER. HENRY STARTED HIS CAREER AS AN OUTSIDE-LEFT. HE BREEDS PRIZE-WINNING CANARIES IN HIS SPARE TIME.

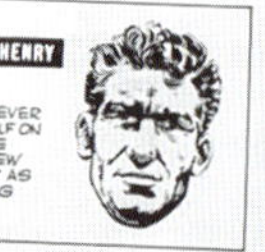

WHITE

OF INSIDE-LEFT JOHN WHITE, FORMER ENGLAND WINGER REG SMITH, WHO WAS WHITE'S MANAGER AT FALKIRK, SAID: "HE IS THE MOST COMPLETE FOOTBALLER I HAVE EVER SEEN." KNOWN THROUGHOUT FOOTBALL AS THE "GHOST", WHITE SNIFFS AMMONIA CAPSULES BEFORE EVERY MATCH TO START HIS BLOOD RACING.

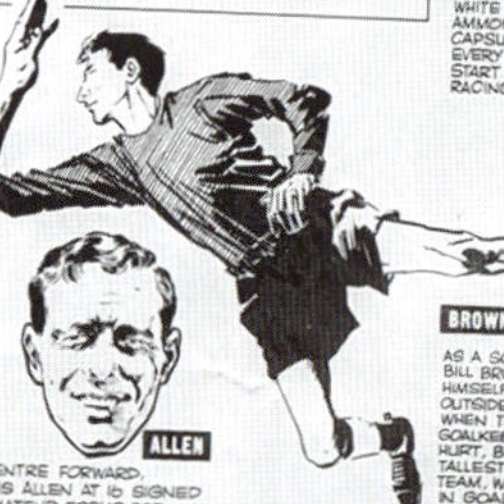

ALLEN

CENTRE FORWARD, LES ALLEN AT 16 SIGNED AMATEUR FORMS FOR SPURS. BUT SPURS LOST INTEREST—SO ALLEN BECAME A CHELSEA PLAYER. FOUR YEARS LATER, SPURS, REGRETTING THEIR MISTAKE, SWOPPED THEIR ENGLAND INTERNATIONAL JOHNNY BROOKS FOR HIM. A QUIET DETERMINED PLAYER WHO LIKES BREAKFAST IN BED.

BROWN

AS A SCHOOLBOY, BILL BROWN FANCIED HIMSELF AS AN OUTSIDE-LEFT. BUT WHEN THE SCHOOL GOALKEEPER GOT HURT, BROWN, THE TALLEST BOY IN THE TEAM, WAS POPPED IN GOAL—AND THATS WHERE HE STAYED.

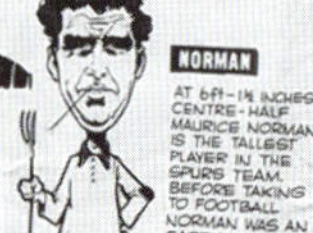

NORMAN

AT 6FT-1½ INCHES, CENTRE-HALF MAURICE NORMAN IS THE TALLEST PLAYER IN THE SPURS TEAM. BEFORE TAKING TO FOOTBALL NORMAN WAS AN EAST ANGLIAN FARMER.

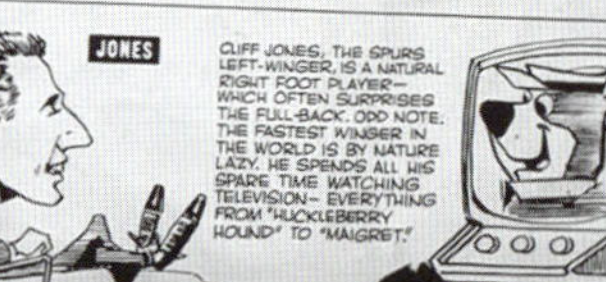

JONES

CLIFF JONES, THE SPURS LEFT-WINGER, IS A NATURAL RIGHT FOOT PLAYER—WHICH OFTEN SURPRISES THE FULL-BACK. ODD NOTE: THE FASTEST WINGER IN THE WORLD IS BY NATURE LAZY. HE SPENDS ALL HIS SPARE TIME WATCHING TELEVISION—EVERYTHING FROM "HUCKLEBERRY HOUND" TO "MAIGRET."

MACKAY

LEFT-HALF DAVE MACKAY STARTED LIFE AS A JOINER AND SIGNED PROFESSIONAL FORMS FOR HEARTS ON A TENEMENT STAIRCASE IN EDINBURGH. JOINED SPURS IN 1959 AND IS ACKNOWLEDGED BY ALL AS THE STRONG MAN OF THE SIDE.

WELSH INTERNATIONAL TERRY MEDWIN HAS BEEN WITH SPURS SIX YEARS. A FORMER SWANSEA PLAYER, TERRY IS A FAMILY MAN WITH SIX CHILDREN. STRANGE NOTE: TERRY WAS BORN IN GAOL. THE ONLY BOY AMONG A BEVY OF SISTERS, TERRY CAME INTO THE WORLD IN THE WARDERS' QUARTERS AT SWANSEA PRISON, WHERE HIS FATHER WAS AN OFFICER.

INSIDE: DOUBLE-PAGE RANGERS CARTOON

From Bobby Charlton to Roy of the Rovers

Paul Trevillion's 60th Anniversary of Drawing Roy of the Rovers 1963-2023

In 1963, I received an SOS call from Fleetway Publications, who were desperately in need of a Roy of the Rovers artist.

Unfortunately, I was busy drawing Manchester United and England wonder boy Bobby Charlton, nicknamed 'Bobby Dazzler', for the Daily Express.

Sir Matt Busby claimed: "From 30, even 40 yards, for Bobby it's a tap-in. Nobody in football has hit the ball harder."

The SOS calls from Fleetway kept coming and I finally agreed.

"Sorry, your drawings are not 'comic' enough - we can't publish them," was the reaction of the Fleetway editorial staff.

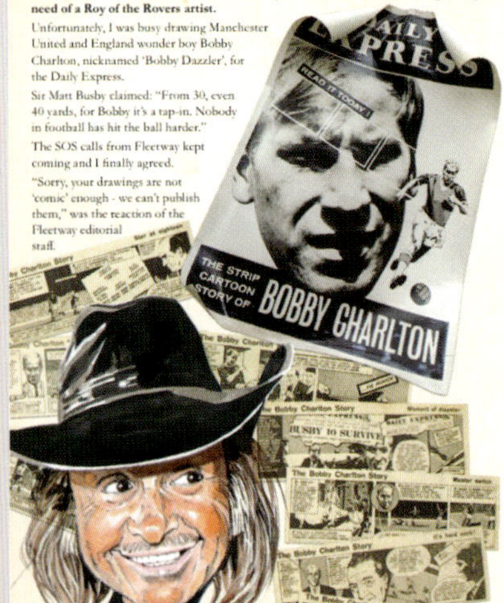

I replied: "This is comic art realism – no place for bandy legs and busted noses."

Believing this was the end, I left. However, Fleetway were chasing a deadline and had no option but to go with me.

By adding more hair and making the chin squarer, Bobby Charlton from the Daily Express strip became Roy Race in the Tiger comic.

I was drawing the final strips when I heard children had written in for Roy's autograph, believing he was real.

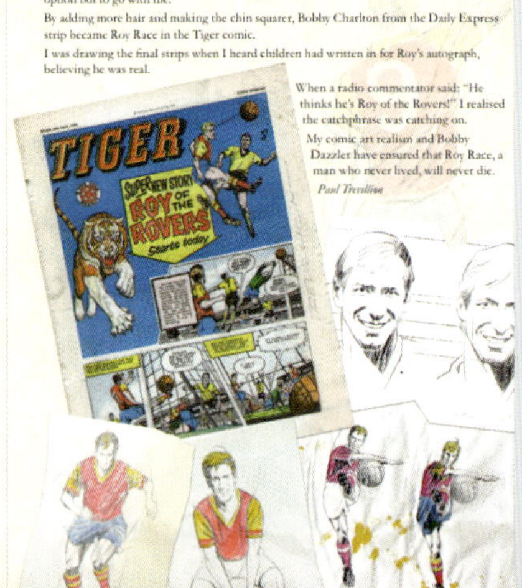

When a radio commentator said: "He thinks he's Roy of the Rovers!" I realised the catchphrase was catching on.

My comic art realism and Bobby Dazzler have ensured that Roy Race, a man who never lived, will never die.

Paul Trevillion

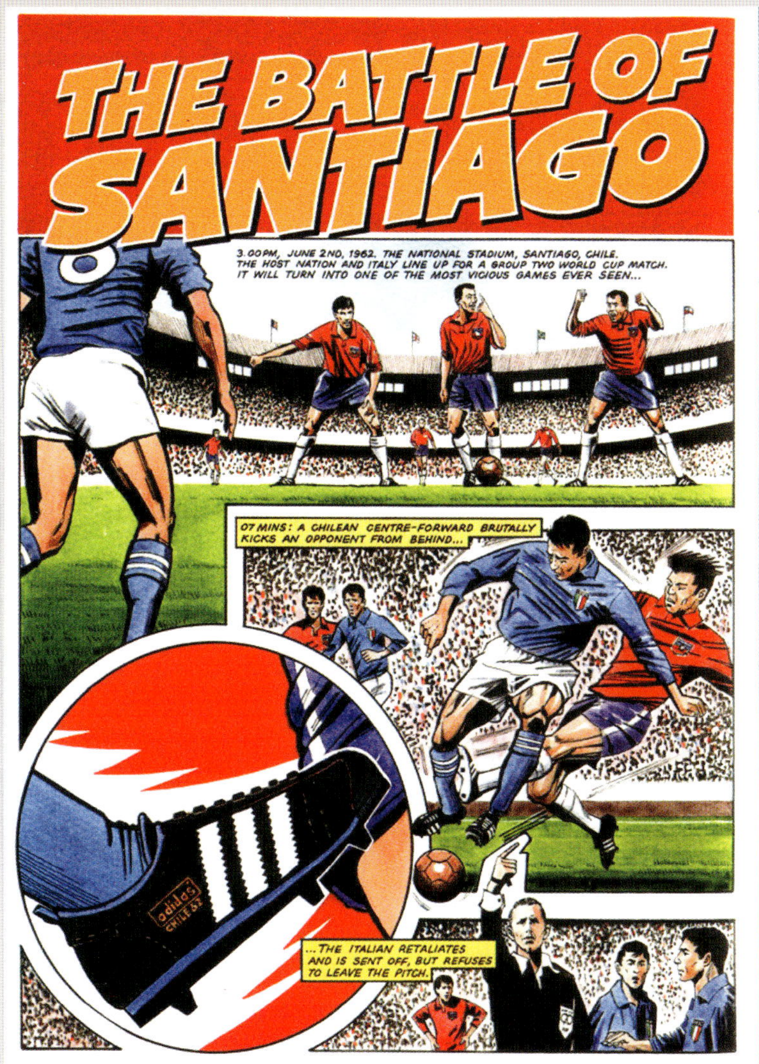

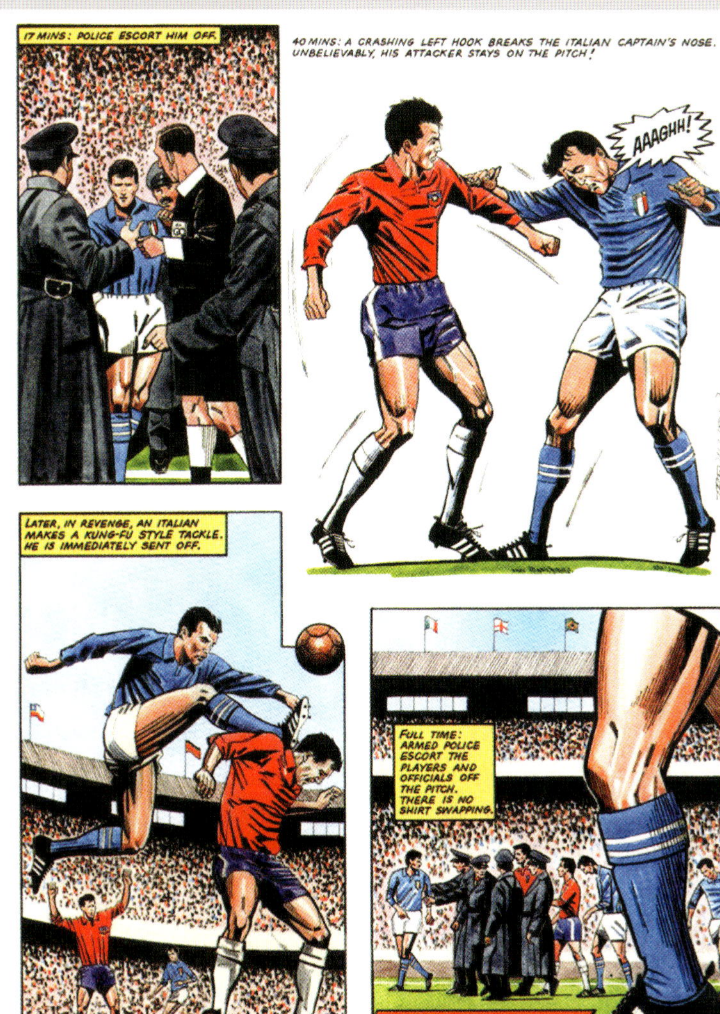

Almost forty years to the day since I first drew Roy, I was approached by Adidas who were re-introducing their retro 'THREE STRIPE' boots used in the 1962 World Cup Finals in Chile. They wanted their advertising booklet drawn in the style of *Roy Of The Rovers* in the early sixties and the game they picked from the 1962 finals for their front cover was the 'Battle of Santiago' – Chile v Italy.

I was amazed - this is known as the blackest day in World Cup history – it was the most brutal game ever seen. Players were given their marching orders and referee Ken Aston said later, "The match was uncontrollable. I had considered abandoning it, but feared for my own and the players safety."

My artwork entitled 'The Battle of Santiago' shows the three striped boots kicking lumps out of players. Thankfully, it never got associated with ROY RACE of *Roy Of The Rovers* or either BOBBY CHARLTON nor KERRY DIXON who never raised a boot in their football lives.

PT

John Hollins

Legendary Player, If Not Legendary Manager

Chelsea supporters prefer to remember John Hollins for his effervescent displays in the middle of the park during a golden era for the club in the sixties and seventies, a spell which brought major honours and two Player of the Year awards for a midfielder rated one of the best in the game, rather than his spell in the Chelsea hot seat.

I grew to know John extremely well as a manager more so than a player, and thoroughly enjoyed his company over many lunches and meetings after he left the Bridge. I also got to know his son, Chris, who went onto to become a TV sports presenter and win *Strictly Come Dancing*.

A product of the club's outstanding youth system of the early sixties, John Hollins made his professional debut at the age of 17 and immediately established himself as one of Chelsea's mainstays of the team that won the FA Cup, Cup Winners' Cup and League Cup in the space of a few seasons. Hollins was a superb distributor of the ball, covered vast areas of ground and contributed 64 goals in 592 appearances during his two spells at Stamford Bridge between 1963 and 1984. Hollins is fifth on Chelsea's all-time appearances list behind John Terry, Frank Lampard, Ron Harris and Peter Bonetti.

Hollins' son Chris, a former BBC presenter, tweeted at the time of his father's death: "My hero, best friend and dad left us today. He was so modest but I will say it: He was a great player, brilliant team-mate and one hell of a person. My Mum, sister and all his grandchildren will miss him so much." John Terry tweeted condolences to the friends and family of Hollins, who was described as a "smashing guy" by former Wales international John Hartson. David Speedie, who played alongside and under Hollins at Chelsea, said: "Long before the days of big money, social media and billionaire owners, John cemented his place as an all time Chelsea FC legend. He'll be missed by everyone who knew him."

"He was a hero to the fans of this club, and very much that to me," Chelsea board member Daniel Finkelstein added, "he was at the heart of one of Chelsea's greatest teams and, as well as contributing to its trophy success, he expressed its spirit. He lifted up the team with his play and lit up the Bridge with his smile. He gave a life of service to this club, as a player, as a manager and as a match-day ambassador. He was greatly loved and will be much missed."

Hollins won one England cap at the age of 20 in 1967, starting in a friendly win over Spain. He lifted the FA Cup, Cup Winners' Cup and League Cup during his first period at the club, before leaving in 1975 and returning eight years later to help them earn promotion from the second tier.

Remarkably consistent, he led by example, transforming defence into attack with well-timed tackles, clever positioning and outstanding vision. The club's legendary midfielder returned following spells at QPR and Arsenal to take up a playing and coaching role at his boyhood club in summer 1983 under John Neal, with his training sessions earning rave reviews as Chelsea earned promotion. "He was out of work and we thought it would be nice to bring an old boy back to the club," said John Neal a year later, "we didn't expect him to stay long." When Neal's time in the dugout was cruelly cut short because of ill-health, Hollins took full charge in 1985 and initially carried on in the same vein as his predecessor, matching his fifth-place finish but his appointment was not welcomed by everyone within the dressing-room. He was Chelsea manager for three years, and he later went on to manage Swansea City, with whom he won the fourth-tier title in 2000, Rochdale, Raith, Stockport, Crawley and Weymouth.

Players have vastly different life experiences with managers. On the big managerial influences in his career Graham Le Saux told me, "John Hollins obviously deserves a huge amount of credit but I didn't get to work with him for too long, I think he got sacked on the strength of signing me! He was fantastic as a person, I didn't really know what he was like as a coach but clearly things weren't going well. He was someone I looked up to and kept in touch with throughout my career. He was always a good pair of ears and had a lot of experience."

In Kerry Dixon's autobiography he said of Hollins: "I was committed to Chelsea, I even signed a new four-year contract

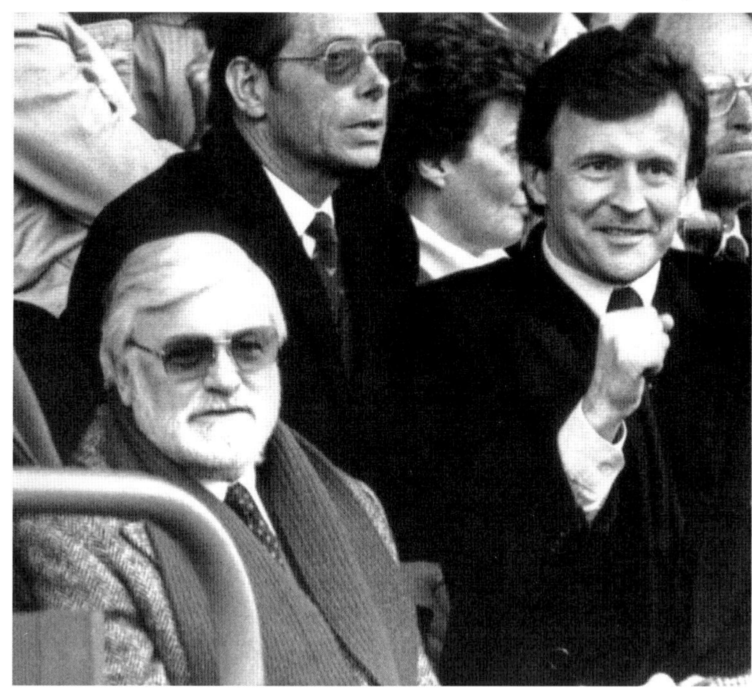

when I still had a year to go on the old one. And then came so much upheaval before the season began in 1985 that it seemed nothing was certain any longer. I thought I was in it for the long term at Chelsea as I trusted the manager, liked the chairman, and believed in the vision that the club was going places, but then I heard that John Neal was to be moved to an advisory role and was being replaced as manager by John Hollins, who brought in Ernie Walley as his coach. Walley had, for a brief period, been Crystal Palace manager and was to make an immediate impact with this strict training regime. We soon had a nickname for him - 'Sergeant Major'.

"I was deeply disappointed by the change, as John Neal commanded my special respect for having taken such a big chance with me. I owed him, big time. The new manager telephoned me at home and congratulated me warmly for the success I had achieved with England during the summer tour, and then business with Chelsea continued as usual."

In March 1986, Hollins delivered longed-for silverware to supporters, albeit if only in the poorly-regarded Full-Members Cup, after a 5-4 Wembley thriller against Manchester City.

Hollins was the consummate professional; hard-running, wholehearted, clean-living. He was frustrated by the failure of the modern footballer to show similar traits, and when his team developed a lack of consistency, he began to chop and change in a bid to discover the right formula, and inevitably that led to dressing-room unrest. Hollins' reign became plagued by the reluctance of flair players to do more weight-training in a very physical league, some of his buys were questioned, and the training methods of his coach, Ernie Walley were unpopular. Dixon, with 10 league goals, was the only player to reach double figures that season to emphasise the loss of momentum.

Hollins' final season, 1987-88, was undermined by a series of behind the scenes events. To his surprise, Walley was sacked as coach and replaced by Bobby Campbell but with results continuing to send the club towards relegation, the manager's position became untenable under ruthless chairman Ken Bates. Hollins was sacked in March 1988 with the club in the midst of a four-month run without a league win which would see the season end in relegation in the first ever two-leg relegation/promotion play-offs against Middlesbrough. Campbell was brought in as interim manager with eight games to go, but couldn't avert the slide toward relegation.

Hollins, though, continued to be an iconic figure in the game. He was awarded the MBE for services to football in 1981, and also made a memorable anti-smoking commercial for television in the same year as part of a Government campaign entitled 'Look After Yourself '. I always enjoyed my working relationship with him. He was always one of football's gentleman, held in high regard within the industry. "See you at the far post" was John's charming catchphrase, ever since I've know him, and he didn't change much, and really you wouldn't want to change him!

It was because of John's issues at the Bridge, after Bates sent him a letter notifying him that his contract would not be renewed at the end of the season, that I first came into contact with John's lawyer Mel Goldberg, an Arsenal fan who specialises in sports law, and as a consequence of researching the story which I broke in the *Daily Mirror* at the time, I became very close friends with Mel as well as John.

It was refreshing for me to talk to John and Mel at this time because it was proving hard to get a straight answer from managers and chairman, who had a natural distrust of the media, and didn't have the buffer of the super agents who have such a profound influence on the game both on and off the field today. John was working under intolerable conditions as the letter effectively terminated his position in advance of his contract expiring – a quite unusual occurrence. Certainly when I reported the big news story of the goings on inside the club, there was no confirmation from the club, and the fans were left to draw their own conclusions, as indeed did the players and it was surely no surprise that results continued to deteriorate in such stressful conditions.

Within the dressing-room, there was total confusion as Dixon pointed out in his autobiography, when he thought he was being moved on to Arsenal, but couldn't be sure and still really doesn't know whether it was his chairman or his manager who wanted him out, "Players didn't know for sure the relationship between John Hollins and Ken Bates and when and how the chairman had decided he wanted to change the manger. Bobby Campbell had been brought in to assist Hollins, but now he was appointed interim manager, effectively until the end of the season and we had eight games to go. But Campbell couldn't prevent us from going down as the damage had been done by then and there was little he could do to remedy it in such a short space of time."

Nigel Spackman

Another eye-witness to the dressing-room unrest was midfielder Nigel Spackman: "When I was scouted by Chelsea John Neal was the manager, Ian McNeil his assistant and they came to Wigan along with chairman Ken Bates to watch a Wigan player that the chairman wanted Chelsea to buy. Ken Bates still had some interest in Wigan, and was selling shares in the club because, having taken over at Chelsea, he was unable to own two clubs under Football League rules. It just so happened on that day Bournemouth were the visitors, and I was in the Cherries team. John Neal told me this story that Ken Bates was going on about how much he liked the Wigan number eight, and kept tapping John Neal on the shoulder every time the player did something good. John Neal was always a quiet, thoughtful sort of fellow, and so said very little. The game was getting to half-time and Ken Bates continued going on about 'the number eight'. Then in the second-half Ken asked John if he liked anyone and John replied 'Yes, I do, I like the number four'. Bates responded, 'Well we don't want him at Chelsea he's far too old he's 31 or 32, we don't want to sign players of his age.'

"'No' said John Neal, 'the number four of Bournemouth!'

"I actually signed on the same day as Pat Nevin, as John Neal began his rebuilding job with the club close to relegation the previous season; he came in, we managed to stay up and Ken was ready to spend a wee bit. Bates brought in Kerry Dixon, they wanted to mix it up and they did, it worked as we ended up winning the old Second Division championship, an amazing feat under the circumstances but we had some decent players in Colin Pates, John Bumpstead, Joey Jones and Paul Canoville whom John Neal gave his debut. The manager was old school, didn't do much, if any, coaching and left that to his coaches. He picked the team and sorted the tactics, which was very much go out and play but John and Ian could spot a player. John was a good guy, a gentleman, and got it together, taking us to the old First Division. In the first game back we played Arsenal at Highbury on the opening day of the season, with our fans there in their thousands for an 11.30 kick-off. You felt 'we've made it'. We drew 1-1 with Kerry getting the goal.

"Unfortunately John smoked 40 fags a day and eventually had a triple heart by-pass and John Hollins became the coach and a very good coach indeed. But invariably in this game a good coach doesn't always make a good manager and this was the case with Hollins. There was a fall out and he sold me off to Liverpool. He was entertaining as a coach; lively, informative, someone you admired after what he achieved as a player. The problems began when he took over as manager. The decision to appoint him was a major mistake. Maybe he thought I was too strong a voice in the dressing-room, I don't actually know, but there was a fall out for some reason, and perhaps he viewed me as too strong a personality within the dressing-room. I was surprised when he left me out of the team, and maybe that was one of the reasons the team didn't do too well. When he brought me back in and the results picked up but the improvement with me back in the team didn't seem to matter too much as it seemed he couldn't wait to get me out of the door. I didn't want to leave Chelsea, but when Liverpool came knocking on the door it turned out to be a dream move."

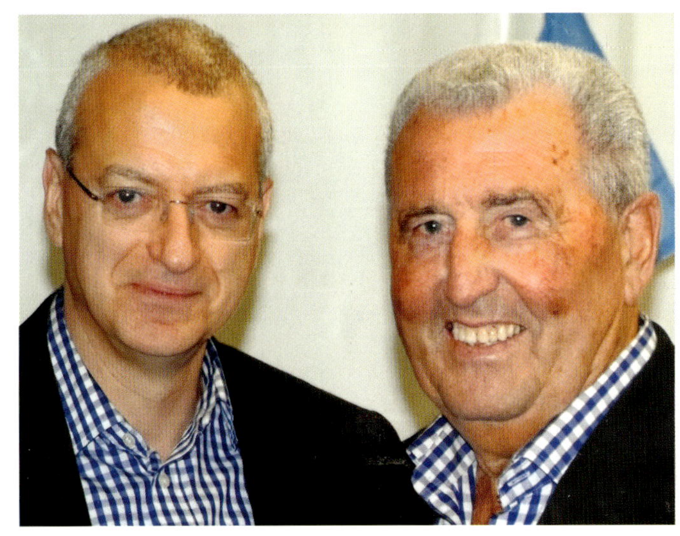

Bobby Campbell

Bobby Campbell led Chelsea back to the top flight and to a fifth place in the old First Division, the club's highest finish in 19 years, during his time as manager from 1988 to 1991. Appointed on 9 May 1988, initially for a two-year 'caretaker' period, Campbell was the right man for a difficult moment in the club's history. Campbell had originally been brought in to replace Assistant Manager Ernie Walley, who was unpopular in the dressing-room, three months earlier. Bates previously announced he would not hand his friend and confidant the management job, but squabbles on and off the pitch and poor results under Hollins and Walley eventually forced the chairman's hand. Campbell was installed for the final eight games, but a talented yet demoralised squad fell foul of the play-off system and Campbell's first task was to face a queue of relegated players wanting to leave. As star striker Kerry Dixon pointed out, Campbell operated in intolerable conditions, "There was little money to spare and Campbell had to use a hotel near the training ground as his office."

Renowned for his physically and mentally demanding approach, Campbell's first act was to recruit the powerful central defender and former Spurs captain Graham Roberts. His side played fast, direct football, with a focus on set-plays, and they soared straight out of the second tier with a then record points haul of 99. With 15 goals, a dozen of them penalties, Roberts was second top scorer to a revived Kerry Dixon who described the shift in atmosphere that season, "With Bobby Campbell in charge, the dressing-room changed. There had been a degree of confusion before, with Hollins walking around saying one thing and Bobby Campbell saying another. I really didn't know who to listen to and I was never quite sure who had the final say on team selection.I wondered if the chairman was pulling the strings? I could ignore it for the most part as a player, but I guess it made a difference for John Hollins, particularly if he suspected he was for the chop. Now at least there was just one voice, although I'd still say that overall I had the best times at the Bridge when John Neal was the manager."

Campbell's pragmatic football had only marginally less impact in the First Division, the Blues storming to fifth in 1989/90, their best finishing position since 1970. Chelsea's second success in the Full Members Cup (rebranded the Zenith Data Systems Cup) final came the same season as Dixon said in *Up Front*, "To go from the Second Division to fifth in the First Division in the space of a year had been a remarkable effort. Campbell had shown himself to be adaptable, continuing to make room for the three forwards as well as playing a sweeper."

"They are a decent bunch of lads, there is no doubt about it.They really are good people with Chelsea's best intentions at heart. I can't tell you much more about my relationship with Roman, other than to say if I did, I would have to kill you!"

However cracks began to appear the following season, highlighted by a 0-7 thrashing at Nottingham Forest and a disappointing League Cup semi-final defeat by Sheffield Wednesday. Still, the manager was bringing through youngsters such as Jason Cundy and Graham Stuart plus signing Ken Monkou from the Netherlands and Norwegian Erland Johnsen, alongside British stars such as Dennis Wise and Andy Townsend.

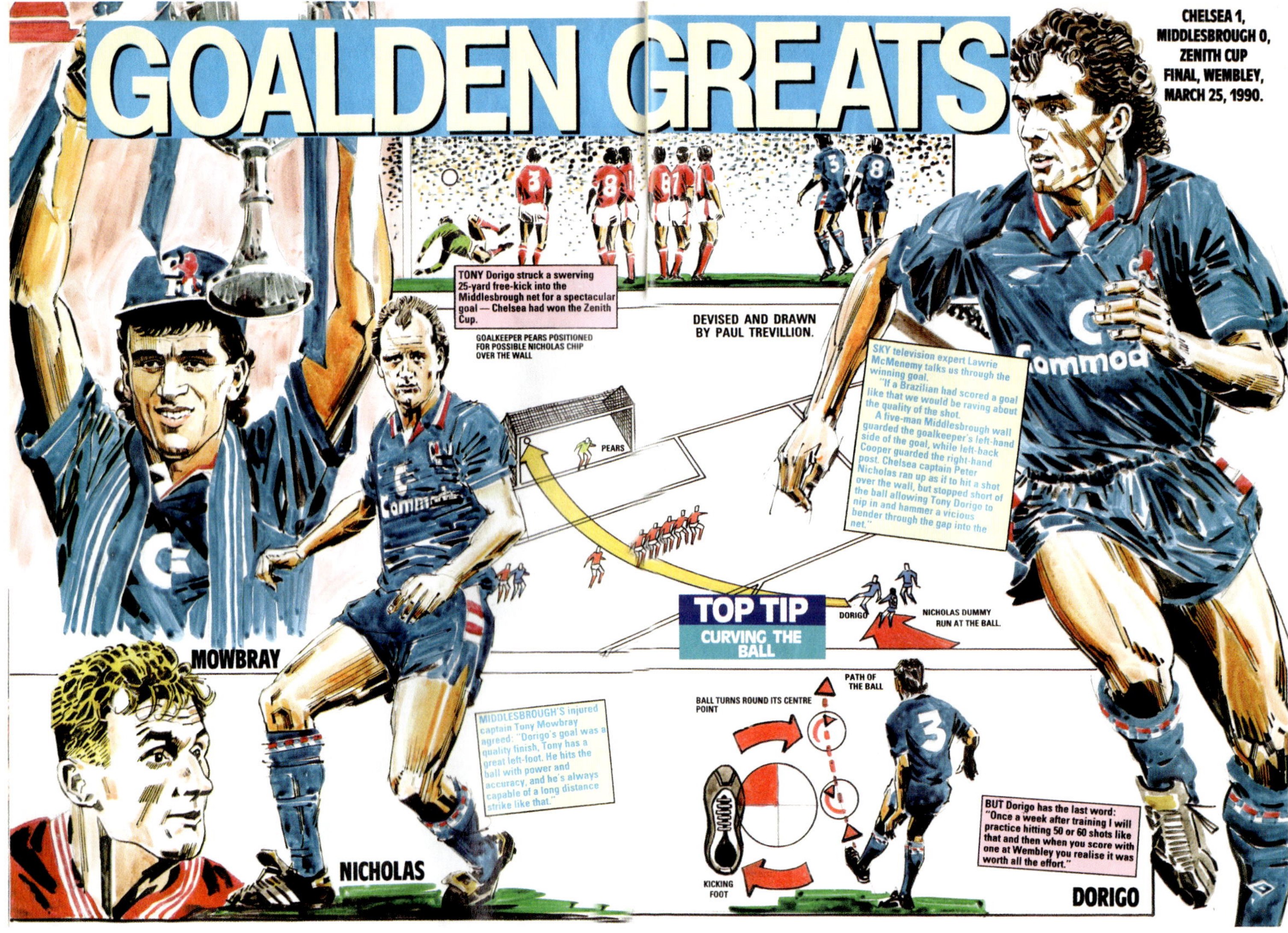

Moments of glory, such as ending Arsenal's 23-match unbeaten run in February 1991, were rare. That summer Campbell moved 'upstairs' and Ian Porterfield, who had been a coach under him a few years earlier, was promoted to the number one slot. Campbell was such a trusted member of staff that when he was sacked as manager he was appointed as personal assistant to owner Ken Bates in 1991. Bates trusted Campbell, but much later it was Bates successor who came to trust Campbell even more.

Bobby Campbell became more than just an ex-manager at Stamford Bridge, he became part of owner Roman Abramovich inner circle for over a decade until his death from cancer. Campbell might well have advised rather than influenced the owner's decision making over the years, but it was clear that Abramovich trusted his counsel. Despite playing for Liverpool and Portsmouth as well as managing Fulham, it was Chelsea that was closest to Campbell's heart, and he could often be spotted sitting next to

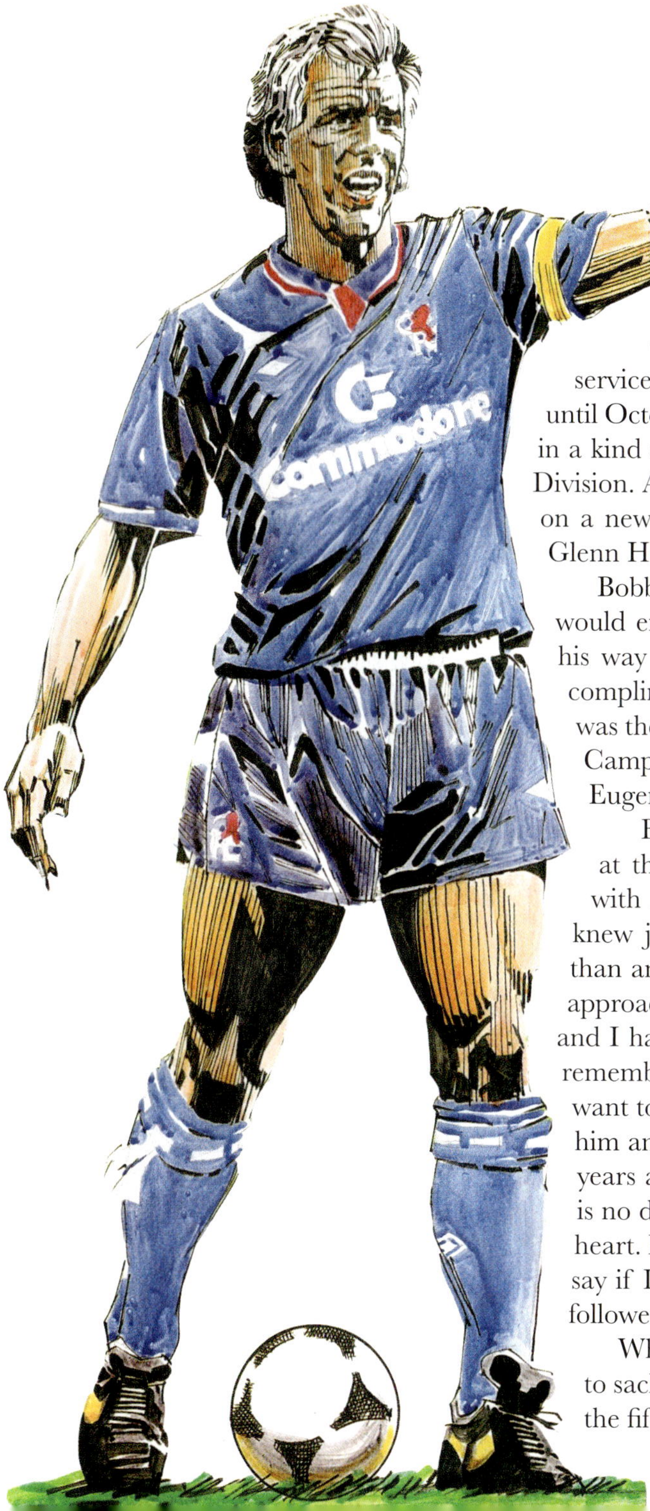

Abramovich at home games in the owners box at Stamford Bridge.

I got to know the tough-looking manager in his days as Fulham boss, but once he drifted out of the game, I caught up with him purely by chance outside a Virginia Water estate agents, and he told me his family home was in Sunningdale, not far from where I lived. It was a pleasure to spend time in Bobby's company en route to Belfast for George Best's memorial service and I travelled back with him. As manager at Craven Cottage from 1976 until October 1980, he had worked alongside Best, Rodney Marsh and Bobby Moore in a kind of supergroup of star footballers which packed grounds in the old Second Division. After that we met up a few times and then grew very close, working together on a new legends football tournament called 'The Football 30 project' along with Glenn Hoddle.

Bobby moved out of Sunningdale and returned to a flat in Chelsea, where he would enjoy hopping on the bus from his home on the King's Road and making his way to the luxurious health club at Stamford Bridge, where he was granted complimentary membership thanks to his close association with Abramovich. It was there, as legend has it, they got to know each other while on the treadmill after Campbell was introduced to Abramovich through the owner's right-hand man Eugene Tenenbaum.

Bobby spent most days there, working out and spending time talking to staff at the fitness suite as part of his daily routine. On matchdays he spent time with Abramovich and his close associates. Bobby rarely gave interviews as he knew journalists wanted to know the secrets of the owner's inner circle rather than anything about his former career as manager, so he was very cautious when approached by reporters. But in one interview he said: "Roman is a wonderful man and I have a very good relationship with him. He is a good man, but you have to remember he is Russian and there is a big cultural difference which people don't want to accept in this country. I accept him because I know the man and I respect him and like him. I have been invited to watch games with him for seven or eight years and I have learned a lot from him.They are a decent bunch of lads, there is no doubt about it.They really are good people with Chelsea's best intentions at heart. I can't tell you much more about my relationship with Roman, other than to say if I did, I would have to kill you!" That was one of Bobby's favourite sayings, followed by one of his genuine broad smiles.

When asked if he was part of the decision-making process behind the decision to sack Roberto Di Matteo and hire Rafael Benitez, Campbell said: "I'd best take the fifth amendment on that." Bobby died, aged 78, in November 2015.

Ian Porterfield

As a player, he will always be remembered for the sensational goal with which Second Division Sunderland won the 1973 FA Cup against overwhelming favourites Leeds United, yet his reign as Chelsea manager is probably best forgotten! Ian was Chelsea's first ever Premiership manager but an unremarkable record of Won 29, Drawn 27 and Lost 29 meant he wasn't to be one of Chelsea's longest serving. A 12-game run without a win, including three defeats in a week and a particularly painful League Cup exit against Tranmere Rovers, prompted chairman Ken Bates to finally lose patience and show Ian the door, making him the first Premier League manager to be sacked.

Ian's claim to everlasting fame came with his goal after 31 minutes from a Billy Hughes corner at Wembley in 1973. The ball fell to Porterfield, known as a strictly left-footed midfield player, but it was with his right foot that he drove the ball past Leeds keeper David Harvey for the only goal of a dramatic cup final, producing one of the biggest shocks in FA Cup history.

Born in Dunfermline, Scotland, Porterfield was signed by Sunderland from Raith Rovers in December 1967 for what was then the substantial fee of £45,000. Yet by September 1974, having been omitted by Sunderland from pre-season games, he was granted a transfer, but returned to the team before a car crash that December left him with a fractured skull. The injury kept him out until September 1975, and he announced his retirement in August 1976.

BEING FIRST

The quick through-ball which can suddenly pierce the defence, never catches England's Tony Dorigo by surprise! The reason Dorigo is so quick to cut out the danger in situations like this, is because he keeps on his toes, never allowing himself to relax and be caught off guard. The only time you see Dorigo flat-footed with his heels on the ground is when there is no chance of a quick counter-attack on his goal.

Porterfield initially agreed to manage Hartlepool United, but changed his mind and decided to go on playing, moving on loan from Sunderland to Reading, then in the Third Division. "The sole reason I quit," he explained, "was because I was sick of hearing about insurance claims and medical reports." He finally left the north-east for Sheffield Wednesday in July 1977 for £20,000, as player-coach, having scored 19 goals in 266 appearances for the Wearside club.

His first managerial post came in 1979 at Rotherham United, earning them promotion in the 1980-81 season but in July 1981 he moved to Sheffield United, then in the Fourth Division, and in just three seasons he had taken them up to the Second Division while seeing crowds rise to more than 20,000. In March 1986, however, with results by then dismal, he was sacked with five years still on his contract, with £100,000 compensation, and the following

November was made manager of Aberdeen as successor to Alex Ferguson, who was off to Manchester United after remarkable achievements at Pittodrie. Porterfield later claimed Ferguson had left behind him a team in decline.

In March 1987, his wife Isa, who married Porterfield when she was 19, left him for a wealthy meat trader. In May 1988, when results were bleak and just two weeks after the club directors had given him the vote of confidence, he resigned. In July 1988, he married Elaine Allister - an event marred by a brawl involving his brother Billy and his father, Jack, both of whom were ejected from the wedding reception. A month after that Chelsea made him their assistant manager under Bobby Campbell and his methods proved highly popular with the players, helping Chelsea to gain promotion back to the top flight, but in November 1989 he was off again, to manage Reading. That lasted until April 1991, when he was sacked, only to be made full-time manager of Chelsea two months later. His demise at Reading coincided with a four-year ban for drink-driving, followed in later years by an eight-year ban. He was paraded as Bobby Campbell's successor on 11 June 1991 and announced, "We should be a top-six side". The club splashed out on central defender Paul Elliott and midfielder Vinnie Jones, but no replacement was bought for departing striker Gordon Durie. Porterfield also had the foresight to try winger Graeme Le Saux at full-back – a position the Channel Islander initially rejected.

"He was an exceptional footballer, blessed with a lot of natural talent. He may have been a football man all his life, but I know him best as a wonderful human being who was liked by everyone he came in contact with."
Sir Alex Ferguson on Ian Porterfield

After six matches of the 1991/92 season, Chelsea were second in the First Division but that was as good as it got. With Kerry Dixon off form, a lack of goals brought inconsistency. There were a few bright moments such as a 3-1 win away to Spurs and a first away win in 56 years at Anfield when the Blues stunned Liverpool 2-1 in February 1992, the goalscorers, Dennis Wise and Jones, were both midfielders. They and others were big personalities, a challenge to any manager, let alone an inexperienced one. But, according to Dixon, he was a popular figure within the dressing-room, which he also described as a "pretty lively place" with the likes of Jones, Wise and Andy Townsend around. Jones was "big and intimidating", while Wise was "just as fearsome" despite his height, according to Dixon.

After Dave Beasant's errors contributed to Norwich coming from 0-2 down to win 3-2 at the Bridge in September 1992, the manager told reporters the goalie had played his last game for the club, it was the kind of public outburst that can alienate a dressing-room and by the following February the Blues were marooned in mid-table without a win in 12 games. Porterfield had to deal with "confrontation, arguments, and internal strife" as Dixon put it.

Graeme Le Saux recalls how intimidating it was for life as a young player at the Bridge, and the great relationship he enjoyed with the fans until the Boxing Day fixture when he was substituted and he ripped his shirt off and threw it to the ground in disgust. He recalled "It was a vacuous, enormous and dated stadium. It was quite intimidating as well because it was huge. The problem was that with the track around it you were slightly disconnected from the fans, so going away from home was a different feeling than it was at Stamford Bridge, where the noise seemed to go out and up rather than on to the pitch. But I very quickly built a relationship with the fans. They appreciated hard work and I think they saw that effort and endeavour in me, and I put in some good performances early on which helped me get a bit of a following, particularly from the Benches in the West Stand, they were always really good to me. All the fans were until that infamous day with Ian Porterfield where I was misunderstood. It wasn't intended as an insult to the club and fans. It was a cry for help and due to frustration. Certainly all the fans I speak to now say they know it was a reaction to the situation rather than anything disrespectful to the club."

Porterfield spent £6m on players at Chelsea, but also sold Kerry Dixon to Southampton, which baffled fans at the time. As Kerry explained in his autobiography, the move was motivated by his desperate need to cash in and pay off gambling debts. One Chelsea fanzine led with a front page photo of the manager stood up at the dugout, pointing to the field and the words "He's Good! Let's Sell Him!" His better purchases, however, included Andy Townsend and in particular, Dennis Wise. But the truth of Dixon's exit still remains something of a mystery to the player himself. He wanted to stay, as he was only a handful of goals shy of breaking Bobby Tambling's record, but it seemed that the chairman was bringing in a new striker and wanted to cash in. But Dixon had only recently signed a new long term contract: "I went to see Ian Porterfield and he told me that he didn't want to get rid of me! That only added to the intrigue. You would think that the chairman would have discussed such an important matter with his manager. If the manager wanted me to stay, I reasoned, that it must be the chairman who reached the decision about my future. A week later Porterfield told me that Southampton had made an approach." To clear all his gambling debts Dixon reluctantly accepted the move to the south coast.

Few managers lasted long under the impatient and autocratic Ken Bates, who dismissed Porterfield in February 1993 and turned to David Webb, a famous name from the days when Chelsea last had a trophy-winning team. On 15 February 1993 Porterfield became the first managerial casualty of the Premier League era. Ten weeks earlier Chelsea had been fourth in the table, threatening to challenge Manchester United and Aston Villa. They say a week in football is a long time, well it was a life time for Porterfield at the Bridge. Ian couldn't halt a dramatic decline which, in a catastrophic eight-day spell, saw them removed from both the Coca-Cola Cup and the FA Cup.

Successful in securing the club's future at the Bridge off the field, Bates could afford to spend more time on team matters and, he decided defeat by Aston Villa, the 12th game they had failed to win in a miserable sequence, was one loss too far. "We have reviewed the results and the fact is we lost as many as we have won over the last two seasons," Bates said at the time. "That's not in keeping with our aspirations." Unaware of developments, Porterfield took the usual morning training session before learning he would be the first Premier League manager to lose his job. "We have parted on amicable terms and wished each other all the best," Bates added. "We were looking at the situation all the time and I decided over the weekend that it was time to make a change. We have been plagued with injuries and we have not had the rub of the green. By making changes at this time it gives us a chance to get things straight for next season. David Webb was very successful at Southend and is Chelsea through and through."

When the former Wimbledon and Chelsea striker John Fashanu returned from the funeral of the 18 Zambian players who perished in an air crash in 1991, he approached Porterfield to take over the national team. This he did successfully, but he was on the move again in July 1994, signing a lucrative deal to coach a Saudi Arabian club. That lasted till January 1996, when he returned to England as assistant manager to Colin Todd, once a team-mate at Sunderland, at Bolton Wanderers. He moved again the following May to coach the Zimbabwe team, but resigned in 1997, citing "too much unwarranted criticism". June 2000 found him coaching Trinidad and Tobago, where in a further instance of bad driving, he ran over and killed a pedestrian.

Then in August 2006 Ian signed a contract to coach the Armenian national team. Though he had been suffering from cancer, he steered Armenia to a surprising 1-1 draw against Portugal in a European championship qualifier in Yerevan.

He died on September 11, 2007 at the age of 61. He had two sons and two daughters with his first wife, two children with his second, and is survived by his third wife Glenda, whom he married in 2002.

Sir Alex Ferguson said at the time: "His death so young is a tragedy for his family and for football. It isn't long ago when he was coaching in Korea that I spoke with him with the intention of getting a few young players over to United. I played against him when he was with Raith Rovers. He was an exceptional footballer, blessed with a lot of natural talent. He may have been a football man all his life, but I know him best as a wonderful human being who was liked by everyone he came in contact with. Just over two weeks ago, we flew to Armenia for the Portugal game and I'll always remember what happened at the open training session at the stadium on the day before the game. The stadium was packed to see all the Portuguese stars like Ronaldo, Deco and the rest, but when Ian walked out, they all stood up and shouted his name. It was very moving."

David Webb

The Cup-Winning Hero Who Steadied The Ship

David Webb, whose headed goal won the FA Cup for Chelsea in 1970, was welcomed 'home' with a three-month contract and told to show he was worthy of a long-term arrangement by the Chelsea chairman Ken Bates, who, in characteristic, unorthodox style, announced his managerial change to surprised callers on the club's telephone information service.

FA Cup winner Webb replaced FA Cup winner Ian Porterfield and it was hoped that while his predecessor's magic cup dust hadn't worked at the Bridge, Webb's would. Yet few at the time believed it would, apart from the man who hired him. Over six years Webb had made 299 Chelsea appearances, scoring an impressive 33 times despite playing largely as a defender, in one of the club's most celebrated sides. He played in the League Cup Final in 1972 against Stoke (Chelsea lost 2-1) and the European Cup Winners' Cup Final against Real Madrid in 1971. The match was a tie, but Chelsea won the replay.

He will be best remembered by the Chelsea faithful for clinching the FA Cup in 1970. Chelsea drew with Leeds at Wembley and were still tied at 1-1 after 90 minutes of the replay at Old Trafford so the game went into extra time. In the 104th minute Dave, wearing the number six shirt, rose to head the goal that saw Chelsea lift the trophy. It was even more special because in the first game at Wembley, Webb had been tormented by Leeds winger Eddie Gray.

A cornerstone of Dave Sexton's team, he was twice voted Player of the Year, in 1969 and 1972, he wore every shirt possible except for the number eleven, even playing one game in goal against Ipswich Town (and kept a clean sheet). After 230 League appearances for the Blues, he was sold in July 1974 after six years at the club for £100,000 when he grew unsettled following the departures of Alan Hudson and Peter Osgood. Webb moved on to Queens Park Rangers, Leicester and Derby. As a manager he guided Bournemouth to promotion from the Fourth Division and, after a spell with Torquay, led Southend to successive promotions before falling out with the chairman, Vic Jobson.

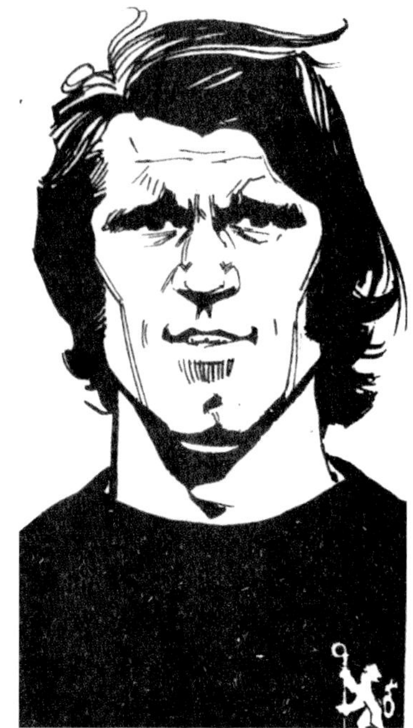

Of his new challenge, Webb said: "Chelsea and their supporters haven't had a great deal to cheer about in the last 20 years and it is up to me to do my best and give them back some success. Ian Porterfield is a good friend of mine and I'm sorry to see him go in such circumstances, but the door to success is the same distance away as the door to failure."

Webb was instantly installed as Porterfield's three-month caretaker replacement on 15 February 1993. He was seen as a unifying figure after turmoil at the end of Porterfield's regime, returning to the Bridge as a self-professed 'Red Adair' – referencing the Texan famous for putting out oil well fires. A 1-0 win at home to George Graham's Arsenal was the club's first victory over their north London rivals in 14 attempts, so that was a great start, and he revived the fortunes of Erland Johnsen and Steve Clarke. He was not happy about the departure of Graeme Le Saux.

Eleventh when he took over, Chelsea were eleventh when he left in May, nevertheless they were in better shape for Webb's short spell. After the 13 game run with Chelsea, he went straight to Brentford where he stayed for over four years from May 1993 to August 1997 before managing Torquay, Bournemouth, Southend, Yeovil and Brentford. David currently divides his time between the New Forest and Portugal where he has property interests.

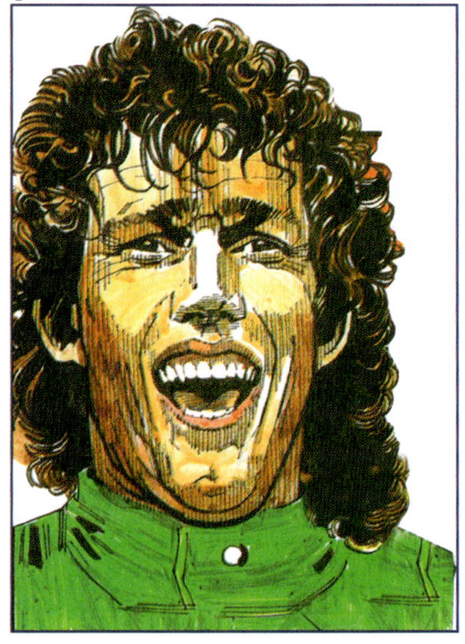

Dave Beasant

"Bobby Campbell signed me, Ian Porterfield caused me enormous mental stress, David Webb gave us a laugh in training, and Glenn Hoddle had to cope with my salad cream moment!

"Bobby was a lovely guy, a Liverpudlian who sweet-talked me into signing for the club after Chelsea had been relegated, saying 'I think we will get promotion,' then adding, 'if you sign I guarantee we will get promotion'. Bobby had the gift of the gab alright and true to his word we went on a 23-game unbeaten run heading for promotion. It all came to an abrupt end at Leicester where we lost 2-1, and knowing how Bobby could blow hot and cold, this time we were sure it would be red hot back in the dressing-room. But he didn't go mad as we expected, instead it was a very sombre Bobby Campbell. Unbeknown to us the Hillsborough tragedy was unfolding while we were playing and, being a Liverpudlian, it hit him hard. He had a reputation for being a hard man, but he was quite an emotional guy, and on that day it hit us all, but more so Bobby and it rendered our result insignificant.

"It's so sad that Bobby is no longer with us, but my overriding memory of him was that he would bring one of his friends into our dressing-room, totally unexpectedly, and minutes before we were due to actually play a game. Jimmy Tarbuck was one brought into our dressing-room and he introduced him to us just as we were about to run out. Bobby was all smiles as he said "I would like to introduce to you an old pal of mine, Tarby". Tarby came in, said hello, and out we went to play the game!

"When Bobby was sacked Ian Porterfield took over having been Bobby's assistant. Ian was a good number two, he liked a laugh and a joke with the lads and was always supportive as number twos tend to be, saying that he would disapprove of the manager's approach and do something different, just to cheer you up if you were down. It's a different scenario when you are then promoted to manager. I didn't think he was up to it. He was too influenced by the players and what they had to say for themselves. He would still act like a number two in many ways, joining the players for a beer on the bus journey home from away games and if he grabbed you for a beer, it would last an hour! Then I had a difficult period and made a couple of mistakes, but it was the way he handled it that really upset me and caused me nothing but grief. It hit me hard when I was told by a couple of journalists I knew very well that the manager had come out in the after match press conference and announced that I would never play for the club again after those errors. Clearly, he felt he was hedged into a corner, but what he said hit me hard. We lost a game 3-2 at home to Norwich and a couple of the goals were down to me, that's right to say, but the manager knew that I wasn't well and should never have played in the game. I was suffering from an inner ear infection which affected my balance and coordination, I couldn't focus. I couldn't concentrate, but I was the only senior goalkeeper available and the manager virtually begged me to play. At half-time we were winning 2-1 and I told the manager that I couldn't focus and couldn't concentrate and instead of putting the sub keeper on, I was told to rub more Vicks on my shirt and keep sniffing in it, and I would be alright. I wasn't alright and a couple of mistakes cost us the game.

The next day I asked for a face-to-face with the manager, and he said "No, I didn't say that", but I still ended up training with the youth and reserve teams, no longer with the first team, so it seemed he was sticking to his guns.

In the modern game mental health issues have been highlighted, but they didn't exist back then. Now I know I was suffering mental health issues. A number of clubs wanted me on loan, but I couldn't face it. I couldn't face going out of the house. I was scared to walk down the streets in London, I just felt that because of my size that people could see me from Tottenham Court Road to Hyde Park Corner. Of course it was illogical, but that is how mental health issues attack you. Although I refused to go out on loan, after a period of time you do get over it, and Alan Buckley rang me and asked if I would help out his struggling Grimsby team. Grimsby Town? Really? You would think that's the last place you want to go to recuperate, but when I looked at their fixtures - Newcastle away, home to West Ham, away to Portsmouth - I thought, these were the sort of games I ought to be playing in. They were 18th in the table when I agreed to sign for a month and we won five out of six, drew the other, and after that month we went from 18th to 6th in the table!

They wanted me to stay on, but I said, 'no'. I had shown the Chelsea manager and the Grimsby manager what I could do, it was enough for me at that time. I was through it. I went back to Chelsea, and straight back to training with the kids, and soon went out on loan to Wolves.

Then Ken Bates sacked Ian Porterfield and brought in David Webb with the task of keeping us in the league, and in his first game he put me on the bench at Blackburn, but in the next game at Arsenal I was back in the team and we won 1-0. I carried on in the team and played every game for the rest of the season.

Whatever you might think about David Webb's appointment as manager of Chelsea, he had played for Chelsea and his heart was in the club. He would talk to you. His training sessions were old school, but fun. One day it was pouring down and the pitch was not fit for proper training, knee deep in puddles. So he decided we were going to do a tackling session, and even had me doing it! He placed balls 12 yards apart and we had to run at the ball and slide into a tackle. If anyone had seen David Webb play, he would launch himself into a tackle four feet away from an opponent and hopefully land somewhere near the ball! He had us all launching into David Webb style tackles as the session progressed, as it was it was so much fun. But there was a method to his madness as we were running so much, it turned out to be disguised running. Because of the conditions there wasn't much else he could have done, but he made the entire session so much fun.

David stayed until the end of the season and then Glenn Hoddle came in and I thought this would be brilliant but my first chat with Glenn was from my hospital bed in Wexham Park Hospital, the famous case of the salad cream! I tried to grab some tea bags lurking at the back of the cupboard but knocked over a jar of salad cream. As a keeper my natural reaction was to go for it, so as it was heading for the ground I stopped it with my foot, it hit my big toe and cut it severing the tendon! The surgeon had to reattach the tendon with a four-inch metal pin, I was out for three months so would miss pre-season. Glenn had no other choice but to find a new keeper and he signed Dimitri Kharine, although 'Hitchi' (Kevin Hitchcock) deserved to have had more games. When I was fit I was pushing Glenn to return to the side, but eventually Southampton came in for me and I took up that option.

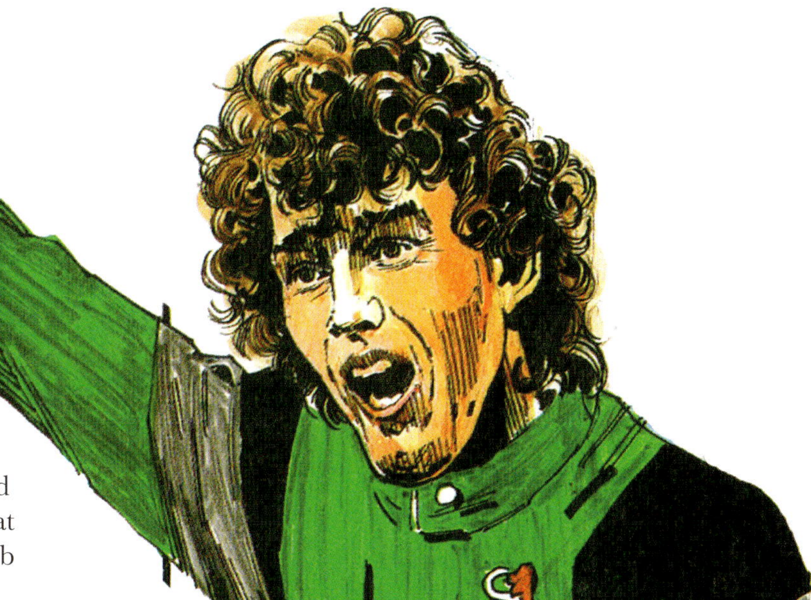

Dennis Wise

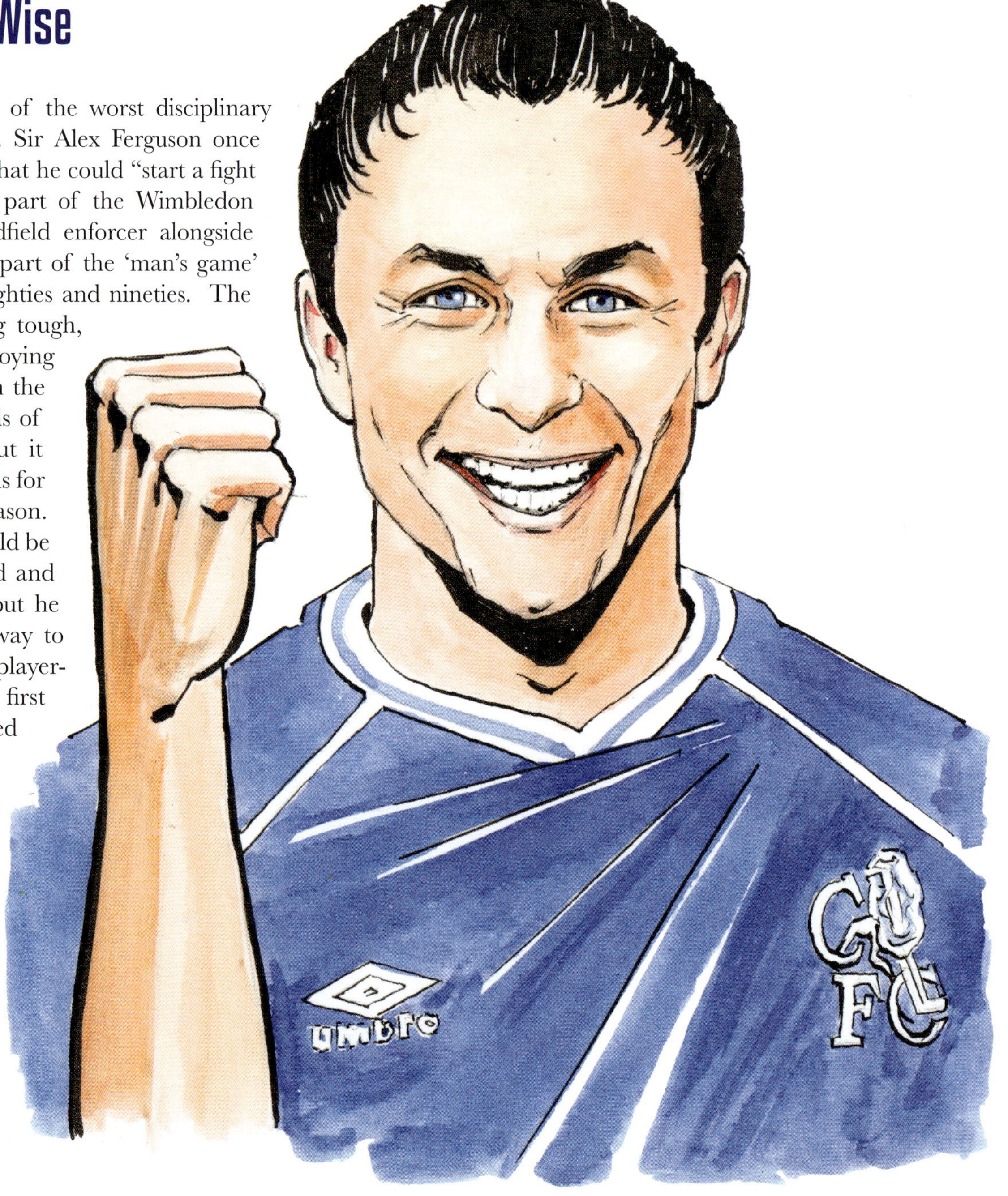

'Little' Dennis Wise had one of the worst disciplinary records in Chelsea's history. Sir Alex Ferguson once said that Wise was so fiery that he could "start a fight in an empty house." An influential part of the Wimbledon 'Crazy Gang', Wise played the midfield enforcer alongside Vinnie Jones, which became a huge part of the 'man's game' attitude of English football in the eighties and nineties. The 'Crazy Gang' were known for being tough, even border-line with the rules and enjoying their finest hour beating Liverpool in the 1988 FA Cup final. Yet their methods of achieving success proved divisive, but it was at Chelsea that Wise broke records for the number of red cards in a single season.

A charismatic character, Wise could be tempestuous but he was also talented and enjoyed a hugely successful career, but he was always deep in trouble all the way to the very end when he was sent off as player-manager for Millwall in 2003, in his first match in the role. Wise accumulated 11 red cards, one fewer than Vinnie, and of course couldn't compete with Jones' booking after just three seconds after flying into Sheffield United's Dane Whitehouse.

'Dennis the Menace', though, holds the record for the most red cards earned in a season, when he was given his marching orders four times in the 1998-99 season. Having been dismissed in a pre-season match against Atletico Madrid, he saw competitive reds against Everton, Aston Villa, and

Oxford and was also accused of biting Mallorca's Marcelino in a Cup Winners' Cup match, though he was later cleared of any wrongdoing by UEFA. Fans responded by unveiling a banner saying "Dennis Wise: Cannibal".

Originally signed from Wimbledon as a wide man, Wise was soon converted to a central midfielder. He took over the captaincy in 1993 and within a year was leading his team out in an FA Cup final. His leadership qualities were most apparent with the influx of foreign players in the late nineties as he was the man who made sure that there were no divisions within the dressing-room. On the pitch Wise flourished, his game improving as the quality of his team-mates did. He was a central figure as he lifted six trophies in four seasons.

His dismissal in an FA Cup match against Oxford United prompted one of his own team-mates to express their dismay. "I could not believe Dennis did it," former Chelsea defender Dan Petrescu recalled, "Even if the ball was going in it didn't really matter as we were already 4-1 up with 15 minutes to go. All the lads were disappointed afterwards even though we had won the game."

Dennis played alongside Vinnie Jones in the centre of midfield in the 1991-92 season and was the Blues' top scorer with 14 goals. Wise was also an enforcer in the dressing-room. John Terry wasn't always Chelsea's captain, leader, legend. During his early days, Dennis taught him a harsh lesson about his lavish lifestyle. Terry appeared on *The Footballer's Guide to Football* podcast with Carlton Cole and Marlon Harewood in 2020 when he told a story about the time he bought an expensive car at the age of 19 after securing a Champions League bonus. He drove the car into training, where he was confronted by his furious teammate. Wise grabbed Terry by the throat in front of everyone and said, "Who do you think you are? Go and take the car back." JT returned the car and later thanked Wise for trying to keep him grounded.

At Chelsea, Wise briefly wore the number seven before switching to eleven – the same number he had at Wimbledon. The famous number eleven shirt was later worn at Chelsea by Didier Drogba. Wise also played with the number 11 on his back at Leicester, but he had to resort to wearing 19 at Millwall and 25 at Coventry.

On October 26, 1999, Wise cemented his status as a Chelsea legend by scoring an important equaliser against AC Milan at the San Siro. Roberto Di Matteo launched a long pass over the Milan defence, which contained Paolo Maldini, and Wise was there to control with his right foot and finish with his left. The goal led to the birth of this Chelsea song: "Oh Dennis Wise, he scored a f*****g great goal, in the San Siro, with 10 minutes to go…" There were actually 13 minutes to go plus stoppage time! The match finished 1-1 and Chelsea ended up winning the group ahead of Hertha Berlin, Galatasaray and Milan.

Altogether Dennis made 445 Chelsea appearances and scored 76 goals, the most famous of which was in the San Siro. Wise would probably have broken the 500 game barrier if disciplinary problems had not caused him to miss so many matches. In 1998/99 he missed no fewer than 15 games through suspension. Wise finally left the club in June 2001 as new manager Claudio Ranieri looked to lower the average age of the squad. His Premier League record actually reflects a player with skill as well as tenacity; appearances: 278. Goals: 34. Assists: 39. Not too bad for someone whose career is best remembered for him crunching opposition players in half. He represented seven clubs as a player between 1985 and 2006: Grebbestads IP (loan), Leicester City, Millwall, Southampton and Coventry as well as Wimbledon and Chelsea. Swindon Town was another destination, but he never put himself on the pitch during his five-month stint as player-manager.

Wise's England career couldn't have got off to a better start. In 1991, he scored the only goal of the game on his debut as the Three Lions beat Turkey in a Euro 1992 qualifier. Wise won 21 caps between 1991 and 2000, and never scored again for his country. His last match was a goalless draw against Finland during qualification for the 2002 World Cup, having became an England regular under Kevin Keegan at Euro 2000, where he featured in all three group games.

Between 2003 and 2008, Wise managed Millwall, Swindon and Leeds. His biggest managerial achievement came in 2004 when he led The Lions to the FA Cup final, where they were beaten 3-0 by Manchester United.

Wise now works as the CEO of Como 1907. The Italian club rose from Serie D to Serie B in three years under Wise. In 2022, they snapped up their biggest marquee signing, Cesc Fabregas, on

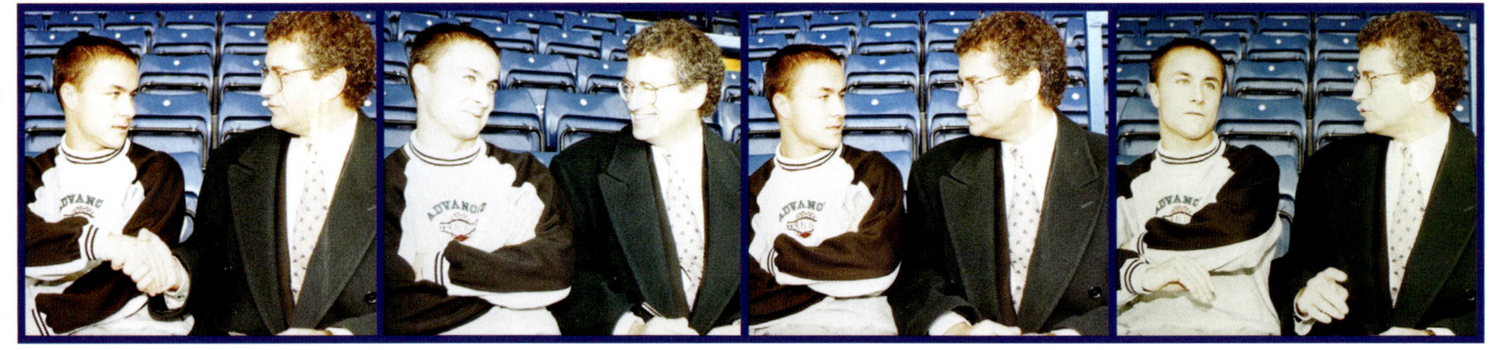
An uneasy interview with the Chelsea captain

a two-year deal. Another Premier League legend, Thierry Henry, is also involved with Como 1907 as a board member.

Dennis appeared on hit ITV show *I'm a Celebrity…Get Me Out of Here!* in 2017. *Made in Chelsea*'s Georgia Toffolo, aka Toff, was crowned Queen of the Jungle that year, Wise lasted 19 days in the jungle finishing sixth. He was joined in the Aussie outback by 11 other celebs, including boxer Amir Khan and Jamie Vardy's wife Rebekah. Co-host Declan Donnelly mocked Wise's height every night, often referring to him as "teeny tiny little Dennis" and "a very small man". The segments were genuinely hilarious and all in good fun. At 5ft 6in, Wise is only three inches shorter than the average man in the UK. But that fact didn't stop Dec, who is also 5ft 6in, from cracking dozens of jokes at the Chelsea great's expense. Wise seemed to take the mocking well. He went on to appear on another ITV show, *Ant and Dec's Saturday Night Takeaway*, a few months later.

I've known Dennis since his Wimbledon days as part of the 'Crazy Gang' that caused one of the biggest FA Cup shocks of all time beating Liverpool in the Final at Wembley. But it was in West London that his reputation grew to such heights that he was picked for his country, something he is ultra proud of. He was a Rotweiller on the field, but off it he could be charming, but equally quite aggressive if the mood took him, particularly if you've ever rubbed him up the wrong way. He doesn't do 'forgive and forget' very easily, if at all.

It was my misfortune to receive a very angry and intimidating call from the little midfielder with the big heart on the field, and an enormous presence off it. After playing a blinder for England, the *Daily Mirror*' gave him a derisory four marks out of ten! He was livid, and didn't he let me know how livid, with a volley of abuse. I tried to calm him down and explain to him that as the match reporter I would concentrate on the match, in this case the marks had been done by one of the sports desk team working in the office and watching on TV, which is never ideal. The sub editor or journalist in the office can often be distracted by answering the telephone, or talking about the night's work load or just going off for ten minutes for a cup of tea and a sandwich in the canteen on the floor below; all of which would mean not focusing totally on a player's performance - they aren't really the best judges. I told him that had I been deciding on the marks, I would have given him an eight out of ten, maybe even a nine but unfortunately I don't think he accepted my explanation, as we didn't end the call on good terms, and nor did I think he would ever forgive me.

Nonetheless, as a close friend of the Chelsea chairman at this time (we fell out as often as we fell in), Ken Bates agreed to try to be peacemaker and interceded on my behalf, and Dennis was willing to put his grievances to one side and agreed to be interviewed by me ahead of the victorious last FA Cup Final at Wembley in 2000. Dennis and Ken had a special relationship, and Dennis respected his chairman enough to put his feelings to one side. However, when I met up with Dennis at the film premier of Kerry Dixon's documentary decades later at a central London hotel, he was less than friendly and brought up the England marks in the *Mirror*. Once again I gave him an explanation in case he was too angry the first time to have absorbed the information. He was having none of it, and left early. After his ill-fated time with Newcastle he pitched up helping to run Como in Italy, and when I reached out to him with help with a commercial proposal for the club, he once again mentioned the markings, and I knew it was pointless!

Vinnie Jones

A BBC crew came to the house to film my views on the day Vinnie Jones bit the nose of my one time *Daily Mirror* colleague, Ted Graham, a bite that was fierce enough to draw blood. Ted had made the mistake of approaching a rather drunk and garish Vinnie in the breakfast room of the Dublin hotel close to the Lansdowne Road ground where England were about to play the Republic of Ireland in February 1995. The team, the media and the FA were also using the same hotel, and it had been such a late night for Vinnie and his mates that by the time they returned to the hotel everyone was there having breakfast on the morning of the game. Vinnie had insulted Gary Lineker the previous evening and Gary was on the table that Vinnie seemed determined to engage in conversation. However, our newspaper's intrepid reporter wanted a comment from him about his row with Lineker. I was having breakfast at the opposite end of the dining room, but could hear all the shouting and kerfuffle, if not a very good sight of the details. Vinnie was notorious for his off the field antics as well as being one of the game's self-proclaimed hard men, but everyone present was shocked by the ferociousness of his rather bizarre attack, biting Ted's nose. Maybe, in his defence, Vinnie would have thought that a mild bite was his way of showing some kind of affection! But due to his state, the bite was probably far harder than he intended.

Much later that day England's game had to be abandoned because of violence caused by a section of hooligans inside the stadium, so Vinnie's act of violence took on even greater significance with the back drop to a game ruined by fan violence. Vinnie was sacked by the *News of the World* as their columnist as a consequence of that attack. Given what we now know about the *News of the World* and their standards of integrity, it was clear the heat was so intense that they had no choice but to ditch their star columnist. The Editor at that time was Piers Morgan, who later became *Mirror* editor, and while fronting a TV series 'Tabloid Tales' covered the item, 'Vinnie Jones Bit My Nose' a take on the infamous headline 'Freddie Starr Ate My Hamster'.

Although Vinnie's reputation was forged as one of the leaders of Wimbledon's Crazy Gang, he later turned out for Chelsea where he often made his mark - literally. Jones was more than happy to play up to his reputation; he once served a six-month ban for 'bringing the game into disrepute' for presenting a VHS tape called *Soccer's Hard Men.* Hamming up to that hard man image led to a lucrative Hollywood career in Jones' post-playing days, from playing a mob enforcer in Guy Ritchie's *Lock, Stock & Two Smoking Barrels* to the Juggernaut in *X-Men: The Last Stand*, who possessed all the subtlety, or lack of it, you'd expect of a character with that name. Jones' immortal words from *X-Men* – "I'm the Juggernaut, bitch!" – were written into the script off the back of an online meme.

The lasting memory of his playing career, though, was the immortal image taken by the *Daily Mirror*'s legendary snapper Monty Fresco of Jones grabbing Gazza's unmentionables. Yet Vinnie is a complex character. Whilst at Leeds United, Jones strengthened race relations in the city when the National Front's influence was at its most poisonous. In recent years, he's spoken about grief and the emotional toll of his wife's death. He recently delivered a rallying talk to Chelsea players before their game against Manchester United as part of the mental health campaign #TalkMoreThanFootball as the team joined forces with group Three UK and emotional support charity Samaritans, promoting an important message. The video was screened on the jumbotron prior to the match featuring Vinnie speaking in the locker room to the likes of Cole Palmer, Nicolas Jackson, Robert Sanchez and Alfie Gilchrist. They are given a stern pep talk, now famously known as the 'hairdryer treatment', by hardman Jones, who began his talk to the Chelsea squad: "Afternoon lads. It's time we have a little chat, because we've got a problem. A problem with talking about how we're feeling. Us football fans don't talk about our emotions. We would rather talk about football day in, day out. But we forget, sometimes we need to talk about other things too. We are all team-mates on the same side, not just the 11 of us on the pitch. I'm talking about the millions of fans up and down the country. They're all your team-mates and team-mates look out for each other. They listen to each other. And that could save a life. So let's get out there and let's talk more than football."

Research undertaken by Three UK discovered that

approximately two-thirds of football fans have battled with their mental well-being. Jones said about the campaign: "I grew up in an era when mental health wasn't even a thing, yet it's something I struggled with without realising. Now I want to empower men and women to talk about it. To those of us that love football; we need to use those connections we have made to talk about more than just football. If I can do it, then you can too."

Reinvented as a Hollywood star and champion of mental health issues, in reality, as a footballer, he was a one-dimensional hatchet man, his physicality, intimidation and fearlessness were a major part of his game. His finest hour – Wimbledon's FA Cup victory over Liverpool in the 1988 FA Cup final – is best remembered for his brutal early reducer on Steve McMahon. "The boys knew I was going to smash him because I'd told them that if I could early enough, the referee wasn't going to send me off in front of in front of about 100,000 people, but I didn't get too much of a response from the lads, so it was a bit of a gamble!" Jones recalled, "so when the ball came into him, I started running. I was about 30 yards away and I kept thinking, 'just open up', and he did and thought. 'Merry Christmas'. BOOM!" The challenge would be a red card today but didn't even result in a booking and he received just three bookings during his starring role in Leeds' 1989-90 promotion-winning campaign under Howard Wilkinson.

Chelsea paid Sheffield United £575,000 to sign him in August 1991. Despite the doubters, Vinnie made an outstanding debut at home to Luton on the last day of August and set up the opening goal for Graeme Le Saux in a 4-1 victory. He quickly became a firm favourite on the terraces and before every game, home or away, he would respond to the chant of 'Vinnie, give us a song' by putting his finger to his lips for silence and then belting out the first strains of the old Chelsea favourite 'One Man Went To Mow'. His first goal, in mid-September, was a header which broke the deadlock in a 2-0 win over Aston Villa and a month later he scored in a 2-2 draw at home to Liverpool. When Kevin Hitchcock was sent off at Sheffield Wednesday with the Blues 2-0 down, Vinnie took over in goal and was beaten just the once in a 3-0 defeat. The pair of tough tacklers, Wise and Vinnie, scored to defeat Hull City as Chelsea embarked on a lengthy FA Cup run and in the fifth round, Jones faced his former side Sheffield United. He was booked after just two seconds for an awful lunge. The Blues triumphed 1-0 but Vinnie was suspended for the quarter-final against Sunderland as Chelsea stuttered to a draw. He returned for the replay at Roker Park and set up a late equaliser for Wise with a delightful pass but Sunderland scored

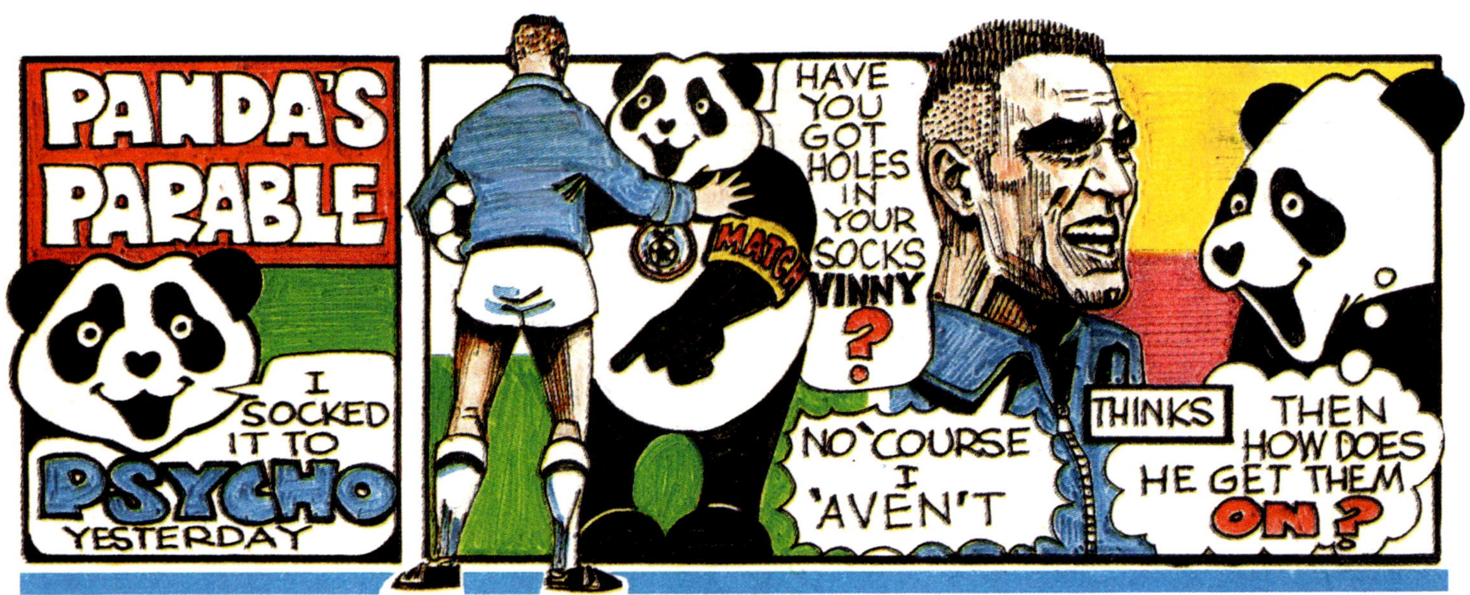

again to win 2-1.

In August 1992, three games into the new campaign, Jones scored at Hillsborough to set up a stirring Chelsea comeback from 2-0 down to draw 3-3 with Sheffield Wednesday but this was to be his last goal for the club. His final game was a 2-1 defeat at Anfield in September. He returned to Wimbledon later that month for £640,000.

To be fair, he did have his moments, perhaps more surprisingly showing some deft skills. There are few better examples of his ability than his wonder-strike against Liverpool in 1991-92, one of the greatest goals in Chelsea's pre-Abramovich history, at a time when the West London club were in the shadows of the power houses of the north and the Reds were racking up league titles in the seventies and eighties, while Chelsea were a bottom-half club when they travelled to Merseyside in February '92. "I can remember my first ever game at Liverpool when I was screaming at one of the boys and he was only eight yards away and he couldn't hear me," Jones recalled of the experience of playing at Anfield back then. "We were defending a corner in front of the Kop and when you play in front of the Kop you know it. It's like a train rushing through the net at you. It's just so loud. The buzz is so fantastic."

Without a League victory at Anfield for 55 years, prior to kick-off, Vinnie and Dennis Wise took a marker and scribbled 'We're Bothered' over the famous 'This is Anfield' sign in the players' tunnel. They then went out and scored a goal apiece. England were six months off lifting the World Cup when Chelsea had last won away at Liverpool. The last league victory at Anfield was way back in 1935. That long, long sequence ended when Jones needed just 20 minutes to open the scoring, one of six goals he scored in his one full season at Chelsea, the ball dropping to him from about 25 yards out after Liverpool failed to clear their lines with a couple of hoofs forward. Jones took a touch, setting himself up on the half-volley, before whacking it over Bruce Grobelaar and in off the crossbar. Liverpool equalised, but Chelsea regained their lead through Wise and ultimately went on to claim a win. So, Jones showed technique and genuine ability. Who said he couldn't play?

Kevin Hitchcock

A perennial back-up who played such a big part in maintaining dressing-room harmony, "Hitchy' signed for Chelsea from Mansfield Town in March 1988, as the Blues were heading towards the Second Division. He played in the play-offs for the two-legged defeat to Middlesbrough which remains the only time a club has lost their top-flight status in that manner. By the time he left for Watford in the summer of 2001 to begin a coaching career Chelsea had become regular trophy winners and welcomed a string of overseas superstars. In those 13 years between 1988 and 2001 Hitchcock made only 135 appearances and was an unused substitute 243 times, yet he was key to keeping the dressing-room together and he notably struck up a firm friendship with Gianfranco Zola through a mutual love of golf.

He was originally rejected you as a youngster by Chelsea: "I was told I was too small and I would never be big enough to be a goalkeeper. To be honest, it wasn't until I left school that I really began to grow and fill out, and I was turned down by Chelsea before that. Then I got a job as an apprentice electrician and I played non-league football for two years, which was the best thing I ever did. I learned football by playing it. That sounds very strange, so I hope you know what I mean! I had to grow up very quickly, because the lower you go, the harder it gets, especially for goalkeepers – we had to look after ourselves a lot more in those days. I had two years at Barking, near West Ham, and I was picked up by a top manager: Brian Clough. He was fantastic with me and I can remember the first reserve team game I played for Nottingham Forest, which was up at Bolton and it was quite frosty. It was 0-0 at half-time and as I was about to run out for the second half, he pulled me to one side and punched me on the arm. 'Young man, you're in this team because you're good enough. Now go out there and show me what you can do'. I felt 10 foot tall. It was brilliant."

Hitch moved on to Mansfield Town where he established himself, before joining Chelsea, but not before playing a blinder against Chelsea! "I can remember Chelsea signing Roger Freestone, who had been at Newport, and we then played against them in the League Cup. I had a good game and afterwards Ken Bates came into the dressing-room and said, 'I've signed the wrong goalkeeper!' That was when John Hollins was manager. Eddie, God bless him, got injured and they were looking for another keeper – I went on deadline day in March 1988. It was Bobby Campbell's first day as manager. The first thing he did was sign me!" Next came a quick relegation, "It was horrendous. I went into a club which was bickering. There were two groups in the camp. I'd come from Mansfield which was just a little club and everyone was together, so to join a big side like Chelsea with a big split in the middle was difficult. It took a little while to get everyone together.

"It's so hard to pick just one memory. I always seemed to do well against Manchester City and I had a couple of great games at Maine Road. I think one game that really sticks out is going away to Brugge in the Cup Winners' Cup. I played really well and in those days we used to get the same flight as the supporters; we got on the plane and they gave me a standing ovation. That was unbelievable, it's something that always sticks in my mind. We beat them in a great game back at the Bridge and then went on to play Zaragoza in the semi-final. As good as they were, we were bad. But we signed Gus Poyet a couple of years later off the back of those games."

Being a back up was obviously "frustrating" as Kevin explains, "you just want to play. I worked with Dmitri Kharine, Dave Beasant, Ed de Goey and many more, and if I wasn't playing, I'd give those other keepers every ounce of my knowledge to help them prepare for the game at the weekend. I was desperate for them to do well. I'd give my all in every session to push them on. Whenever I speak with my young goalkeepers now ahead of a small-sided game in training, I tell them, 'Make sure you're better than the guy up the other end'. I pushed Bes and Dmitri, but not so much Ed – that was towards the end of my career – and I made sure they had to be on their toes. They knew if they didn't perform that I was there. I'd like to think when I did come in and play for the club, I never let anyone down. Me and Bes were really close and it was tough when he had his problems with Ian Porterfield because I felt he was really, really hard done by. But we stuck together and I was one of the first to speak to him after that Norwich game, when the manager said he'd never play for the club again. Our friendship never wavered regardless of what happened on the pitch. I've never had an issue with another goalkeeper at Chelsea, we were always close and I was never jealous of anyone – if they played, I always wanted them to do well. Maybe that was one of my strengths. The bond seemed to spread through the camp – it was a very tight-knit group. I tell you who should get a lot of credit for that: Dennis Wise, Steve Clarke and myself. We were the senior players of the group and everyone who came in was told, 'This is how we do it here. It's our club'. And they all bought into it. We had people coming in after so much success in their career, but they all did it our way. Everybody was part of the family and that includes all of the people behind the scenes. When I go back to the club, there are still people here who were there when I started in 1988. It's a fantastic club and they'll never lose that."

Hitch ended up playing in the same teams as Ruud Gullit, Gianluca Vialli and Zola and won more trophies than he could ever have dreamed of. "I didn't expect that! No, not in a million years. I give credit to Wisey and Andy Townsend for bringing togetherness early on, but the next person who deserves so much praise is Glenn Hoddle. I've said it before and so many others have too, but he changed the club. He made it into a bigger club than what it was – and we were a sleeping giant for so many years. He signed people like Ruudy and Sparky. Then Ruudy took it on to another level – Robbie [Di Matteo], Luca, Franco. Fantastic signings. And we gelled. The foreign players we signed have to take a lot of credit for that because they took on board what we were like as a club. They accepted us straight away, we accepted them – it was a proper family club. That's why we had so much success."

Hitch played through several different managers and set ups, "I left in 2001 so I just missed the next one under Claudio Ranieri, which was when the older players started to go. But the best thing was that someone was there to carry it on: JT. He kept going with what we built, which is amazing really, and he probably took it to another level. And I love him to death."

Hitch struck up a great friendship with Gianfranco Zola after introducing him to golf, "I introduced him to golf but he's better than me now so I don't think that was the smartest thing I ever did!"

DJ Bear, Vinny and Fergie

The 1980's saw football terraces ringed with railings obstructing the fans' view of the game, in an attempt to maintain segregation between rival fans and stop hooligans invading the pitch. Watching football was now no longer FUN.

Then I had an idea and my good friend Peter Stewart, the editor of *Shoot!* magazine to which I had been a contributor for 10 years, was the first one I turned to. I suggested a campaign for the magazine to promote SPORTSMANSHIP, FAIRPLAY AND FAMILY ENTERTAINMENT with the aid of a giant panda character. Peter Stewart agreed and after much thought I arranged a meeting at Lancaster Gate with the FA's media specialist Glen Kirton but, having failed to convince him, I decided to aim much higher – the government. I managed eventually to arrange a meeting with Prime Minister Maggie Thatcher who listened to my ideas and agreed it could work and Maggie set the wheels in motion, by giving it the THUMBS UP.

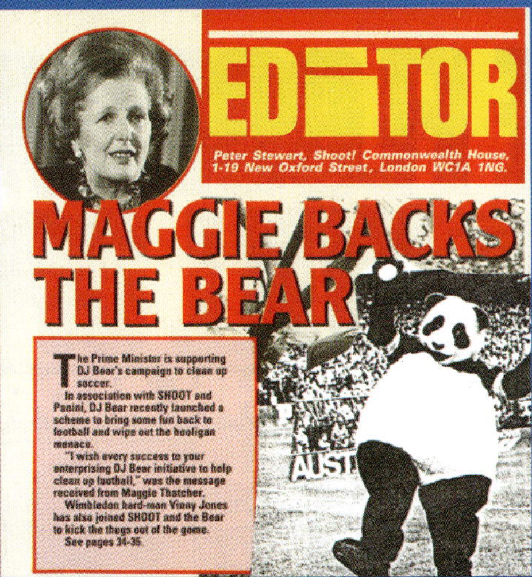

ED–TOR

Peter Stewart, Shoot! Commonwealth House, 1-19 New Oxford Street, London WC1A 1NG.

MAGGIE BACKS THE BEAR

The Prime Minister is supporting DJ Bear's campaign to clean up soccer.

In association with SHOOT and Panini, DJ Bear recently launched a scheme to bring some fun back to football and wipe out the hooligan menace.

"I wish every success to your enterprising DJ Bear initiative to help clean up football," was the message received from Maggie Thatcher.

Wimbledon hard-man Vinny Jones has also joined SHOOT and the Bear to kick the thugs out of the game.

See pages 34-35.

Peter Stewart was delighted and *Shoot!* Magazine heralded the news. But when I suggested a two-page spread for a Panda Bear club with art from the kids I could judge, with every child's birthday mentioned and a skills strip I would contribute – Peter

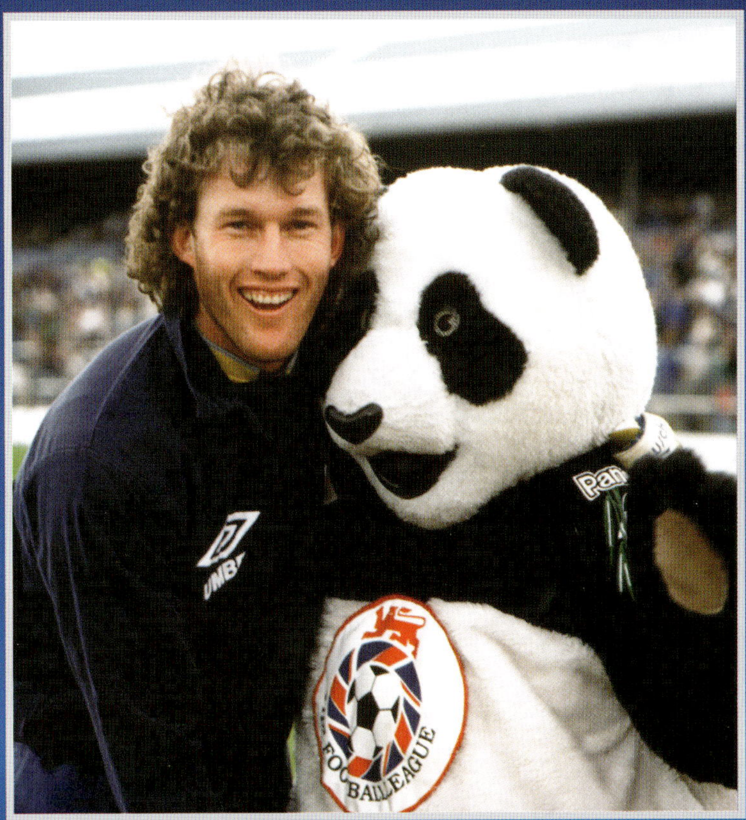

Stewart shook his head, so I turned to *Match* Magazine and they AGREED.

I decided I would be the person inside the giant panda costume and I would call him DJ BEAR – THE PANDA OF PEACE. Then, with the aid of five football mad youngsters from Dexters Football Club in Dorset, I arranged for each to have a newspaper bag slung across their shoulders with a different letter on each bag spelling out P – A – N – D – A. Each newspaper bag would be full of FREE football goodies and the five lads would hand out Panda Drinks, *Match* magazines, Panini football stickers, and DJ BEAR would kick out lightweight plastic *Match* magazine footballs into the crowd.

At every Football League club the players loved to get involved, especially Vinny Jones and Dave Beasant. Every Football League ground welcomed DJ BEAR to their club with the free football goodies for the fans. The Football League wasted no

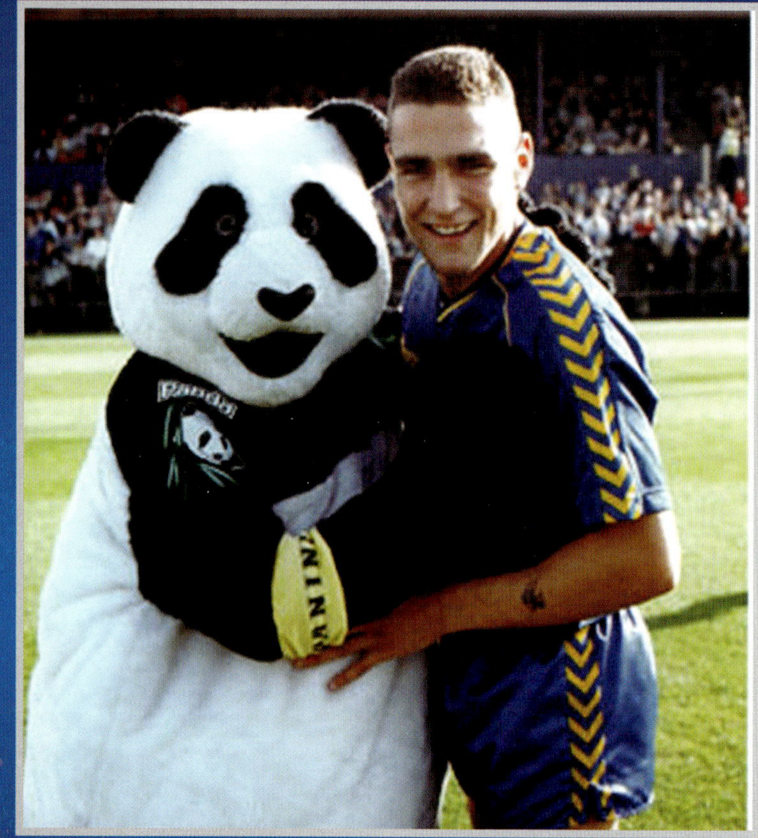

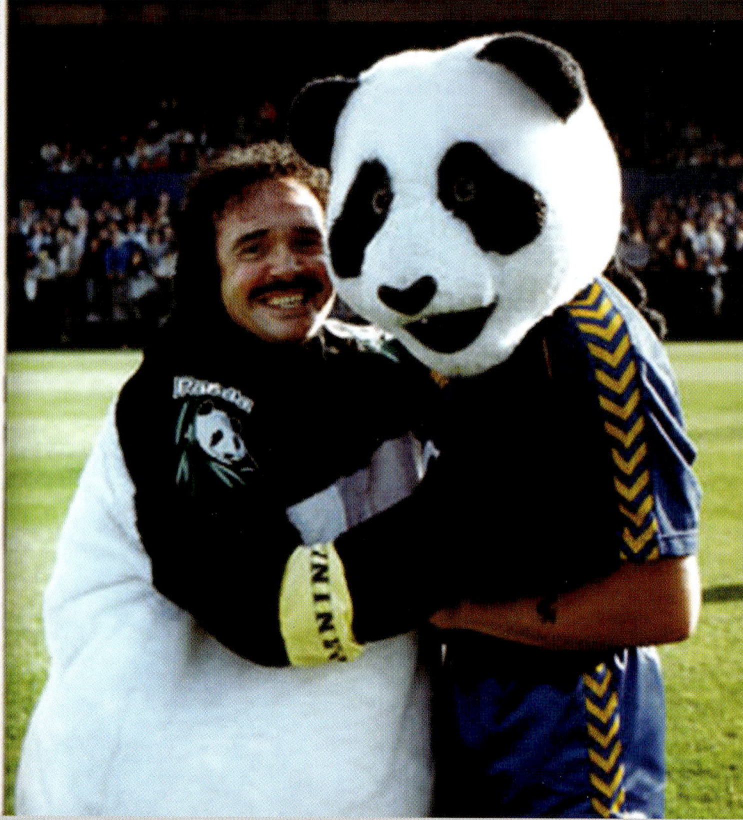

time in stepping in to join the campaign's success, by naming DJ BEAR - The Panda of Peace, the Official Football League Mascot.

Then, just when it appeared the campaign was running out of steam, Alex Ferguson stepped in and walked to the centre circle to be photographed with DJ BEAR to receive a SPORTSMANSHIP, FAIRPLAY AND FAMILY ENTERTAINMENT AWARD. Alex's gesture did the trick. The photograph made the national press and it was then onwards and upwards for the DJ BEAR Panda of Peace Campaign.

Finally, after a two year campaign THE RAILINGS CAME DOWN and I received a letter from the Football League thanking the DJ BEAR campaign. I was especially happy that the DJ BEAR mascot had encouraged every football club to have their OWN MASCOT.

PT

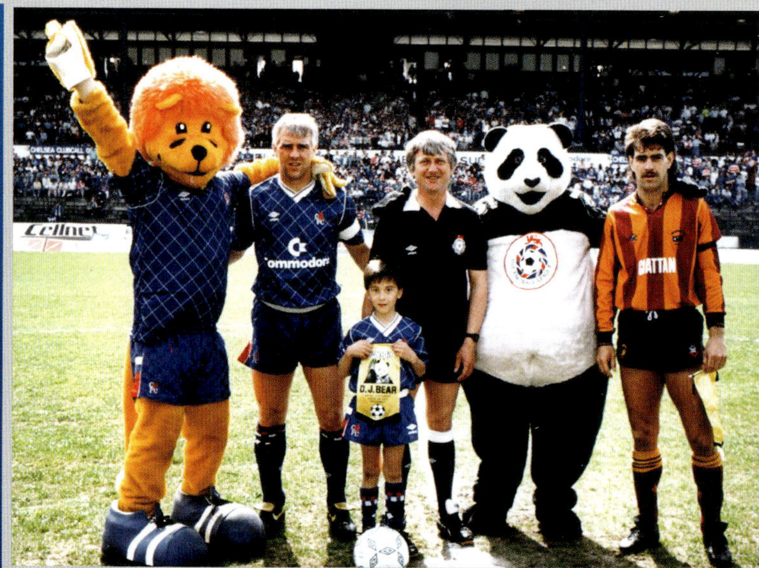

Glenn Hoddle

The Chelsea Revolution Begins

Glenn Hoddle was one of the most graceful and gifted footballers of his generation and is generally regarded as the man who inspired the Stamford Bridge revolution both on and off the pitch. He changed the playing philosophy, brought in much of the Arsene Wenger ethos which he picked up from him at Monaco, and then took on chairman Ken Bates to challenge him to bring the archaic training ground facilities up to scratch. His reputation helped to lure Ruud Gullit, Mark Hughes and Dan Petrescu to what was still an unfashionable club and within two seasons he had taken the club back towards the top of the English game.

Glenn was appointed Chelsea manager on 4 June 1993 after an impressive managerial debut with Swindon Town. At his first pre-season training session he performed an impressive keepy-uppy with both feet, knees, shoulder and head telling the assembled players, "If you don't master the ball, the ball masters you." Some wags in the press said the manager was the best footballer in training and his skill was intimidating to some of those in the squad.

Hoddle reintroduced that Chelsea touch of class, rekindling the swagger of the King's Road of the sixties and early seventies, but having had his eyes opened learning during his time with Wenger in the south of France, he also brought a new wave of professionalism: nutrition, training, preparation, and modern tactics would now be on the menu. Improvements were immediately demanded in basics such as passing and trapping, and all playing surfaces were overhauled. He broke up the cliques that had developed over the years and introduced team-building principles as well as dietary rules. More left-field innovations included a reflexologist, soon nicknamed 'Tootsie.'

There were difficulties during the first transitional season with Hoddle leading by example as a sweeper in a back three, sometimes the standout player. However gradual, the progress

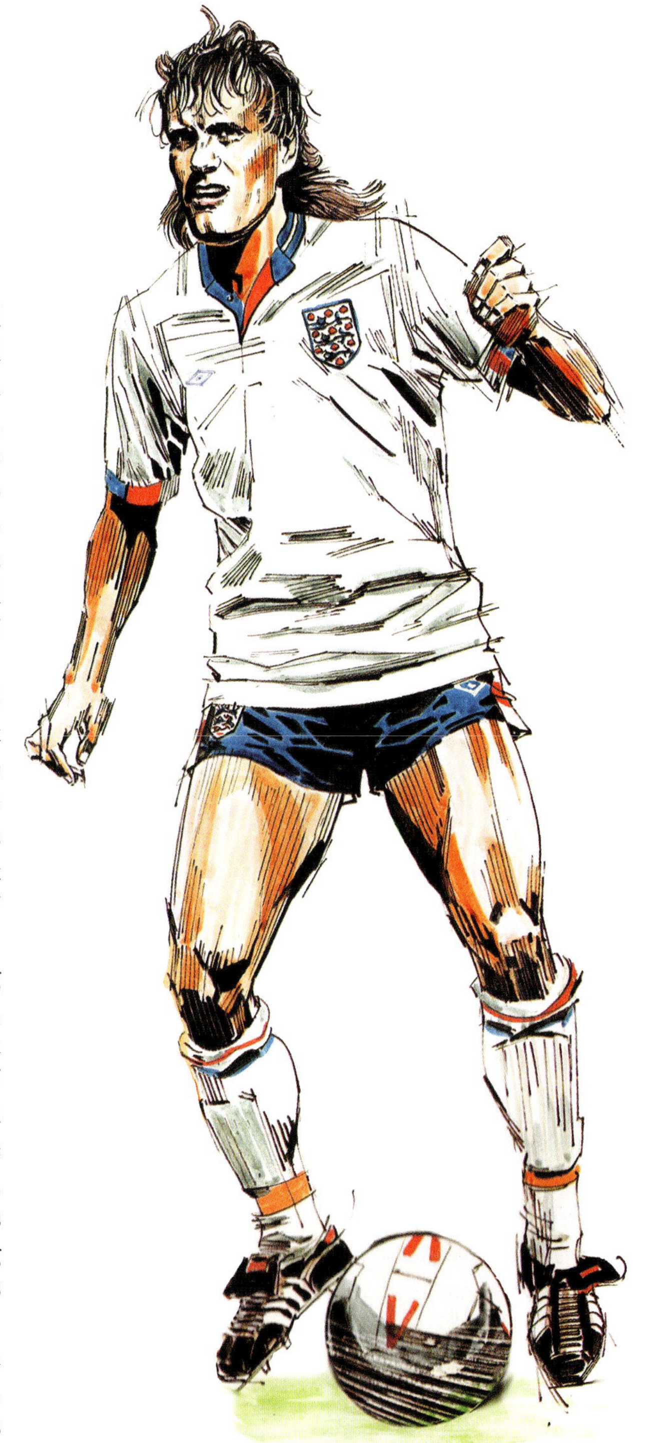

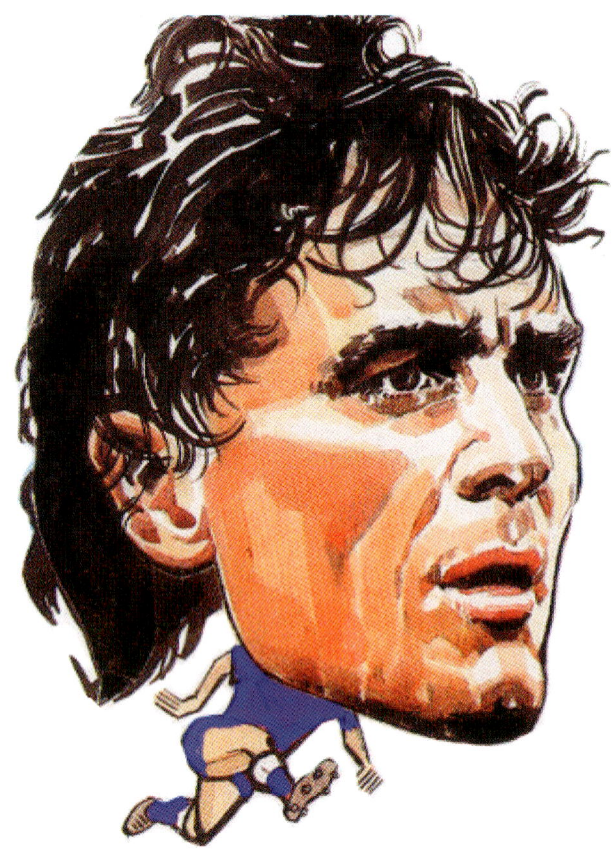

was obvious, and the manager's key signing, Gavin Peacock, earned home and away wins against Manchester United. Facing the same opponents in May 1994, Peacock hit the bar at 0-0 during Chelsea's first FA Cup final since 1970. The game ended up being lost 0-4 but the signs were hugely positive.

There followed an excellent 1994/95 Cup Winners' Cup campaign, the club's first European foray for 22 years, but while it brought back the excitement and expectations, it was fraught with difficulties for an obviously under-strength squad: UEFA's short-lived 'three foreigners' rule made aliens of non-English Brits such as Steve Clarke and John Spencer, as well as Dmitri Kharine and Erland Johnsen.

At the close of that season the board – Ken Bates, Colin Hutchinson, Matthew Harding – were confident enough in the manager and his philosophy to gamble heavily on big name signings, most stunning was the capture of Dutch icon and former World Footballer of the Year, Ruud Gullit. "Sometimes out there," noted Hoddle after Gullit's debut,"it was like watching an 18-year-old among 12-year-olds." Harding had arrived at the Bridge as a lifelong fan willing to invest a £5m loan to finance the rebuilding of a new stand, and he backed Bates with the recruitment of Hoddle as manager, who in turn brought in Gullit and Mark Hughes to change the entire dynamics of the club.

Yet Matthew wanted more, much more. He craved control of the club and Ken wasn't going to give up easily. But Harding was a fan, who in turn had the backing of the supporters, and the vast majority of the media. He was the opposite to Bates, highly approachable, happy to drink with the media in a pub across the road from the ground before the game. While Harding was The People's Choice, Bates still had a loyal following from a section of the fans who never forgot how he had worked tirelessly to save the club from the developers in the early days of his reign.

Hoddle was caught up in the cross fire, with Bates feeling his manager was siding with his board room arch enemy. In the end Harding suffered a tragic end in a helicopter crash on the way back from a Chelsea away game. Meanwhile Glenn had been at pains not to take sides and was more interested, as he told me, in getting on with his job as manager, trying as best he could to keep away from boardroom politics. Hoddle fought long and hard for football to take precedence over commercial concerns when the ChelseaVillage project was being built – the Shed End stand was reduced in size as a result of his demands for a longer pitch than originally designed. It was those principles of the glory above commercialism that Hoddle found an ally in Harding, and in turn he was perceived as disloyal by Bates in his quest to retain outright control.

In May 1996, with his contract running to a close, Harding was leading the fight to keep Hoddle at the Bridge while Bates was also keen for him to stay, but Hoddle accepted the 'once in a lifetime' offer of managing England, saying it was the only job he would have quit the Bridge for, apart from his beloved Tottenham, a role he would also eventually accept.

Glenn is rightly regarded as the man whose vision and tenacity laid the foundations for the modern Chelsea to set the revolution in the right direction as many there at the time will testify, although Bates still refuses to forgive or forget Hoddle's part in his Battle for the Bridge with Harding and, to put it politely, is not a fan!

Yet the changes inside the club were huge and came very rapidly, taking even seasoned pros by surprise, as Nigel Spackman told me: "At the outset of the Premier League in 1992 I returned to Stamford Bridge. Ian Potterfield was still the manager when I signed for the club after I'd had a great time with Glasgow Rangers. It was still the time of the three foreigner rule and there were quite a lot of top class 'foreigners' at Ibrox at that time and the manager Walter Smith had a tough task trying to keep them all happy because they all couldn't be in the team at the same time. So when Ken Bates came in for me, I felt it was the right move. I played under Ian Porterfield for a couple of games but not many because I had a bad back injury almost immediately after I signed which needed an operation and I was out for 18 months. By the time I came back Glenn Hoddle was in charge and in the process of overhauling the club; he turned it into a far more professional outfit implementing so much he learned playing under Arsene Wenger at Monaco. It was Glenn who changed the philosophy of the club and began the revolution at Stamford Bridge when he brought in players of the calibre of Ruud Gullit, Dan Petrescu and Mark Hughes.

"For a start he introduced the canteen at the training ground, where the players got fed a light breakfast before training and a meal after training, so he could oversee the nutritional aspects, but most importantly he completely changed our mentality, the way we had been used to playing for the best part of a generation in English football.The facilities at our Harlington training ground were poor; it didn't even have a gym, and we had to travel to the Bridge for gym work, but Glenn introduced the gym at training. The pitches were terrible, they were never watered as there were no sprinklers and the manager changed that, as he wanted a new style of football and it was important to him that the training pitches were up to scratch. Even the freezing cold showers were a bit warmer!

"People will find it hard to take in that this was how things were at the start of the Premier League era but Chelsea's training facilities were shocking and Glenn was the catalyst for these changes, and his reputation attracted some world class superstars such as Gullit, Hughes and Petrescu and later helped lure the likes of Gianfranco Zola to the club thanks to the changes he had made.

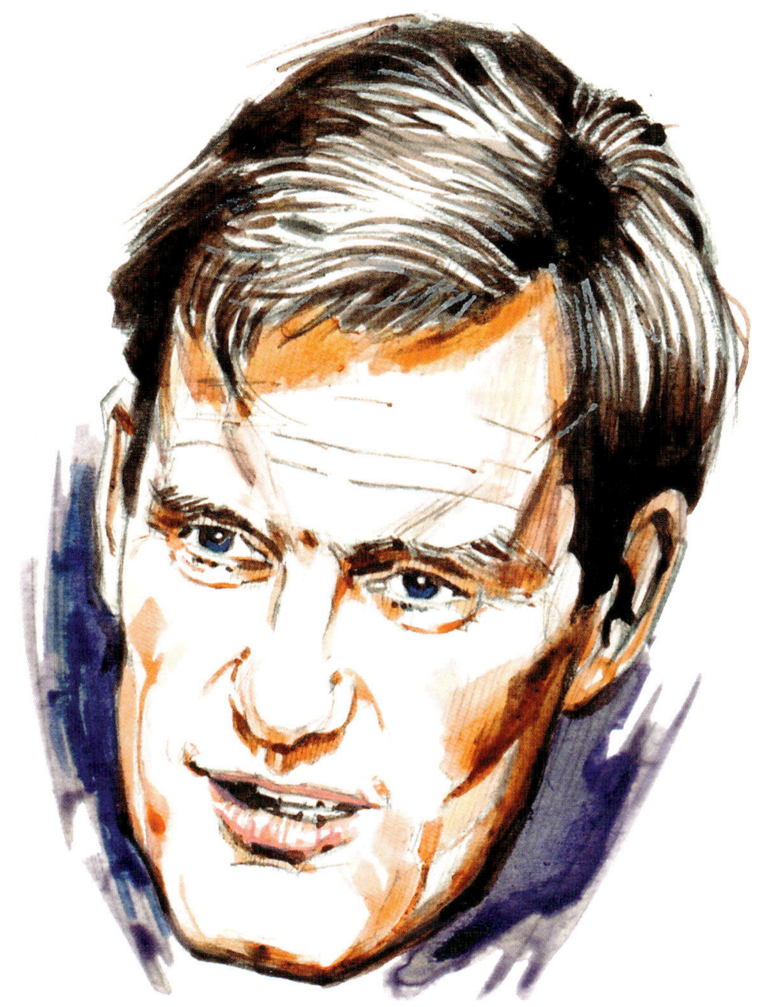

"If Glenn began the revolution at Chelsea, the club's best signing of all time was undoubtedly Roman Abramovich. Glenn as a coach was right up there with the best, tactically there were few better. He changed the age old British way of 4-4-2 and introduced 3-5-2 and the diamond formation.He rejuvenated the British game by showing there were other ways, perhaps better ways, to play the game. He had different ideas and the players responded to them. He was an exceptionally talented coach,

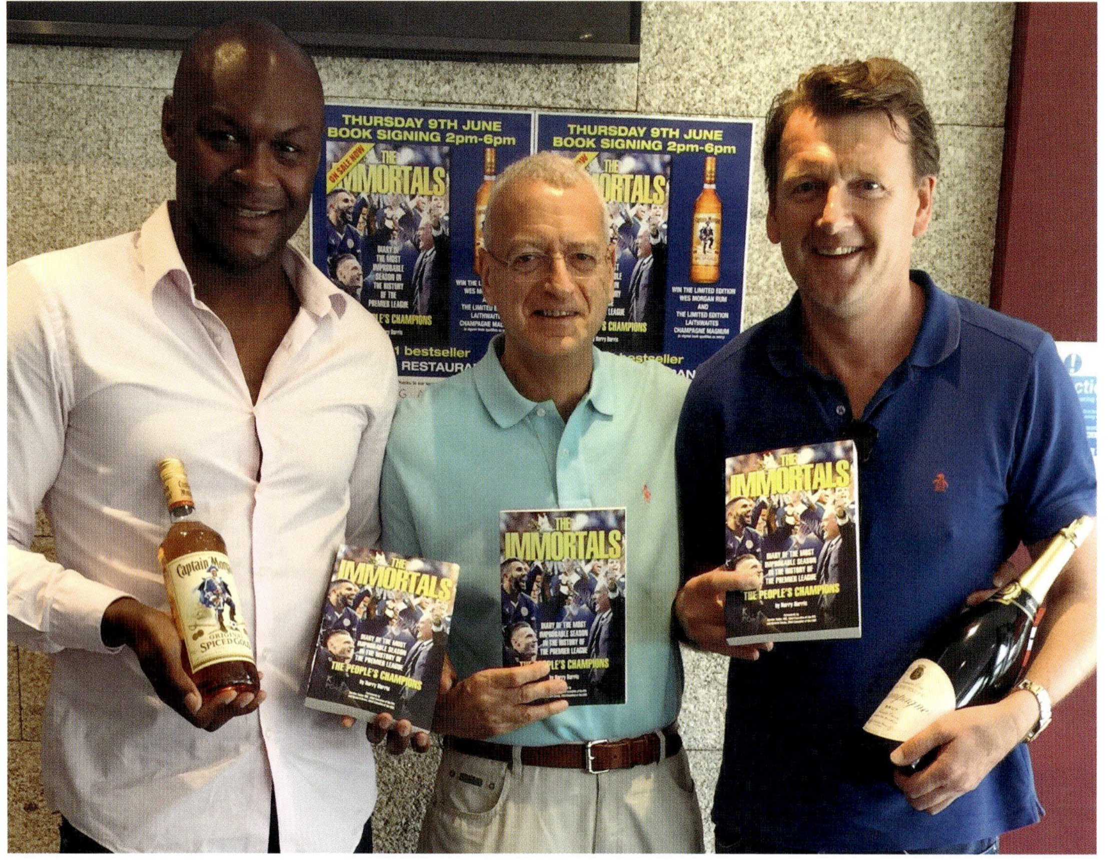

but being a manager is different; there's man-management, the business side of things. Perhaps one of his problems was that he was still fit enough to play, and in training he was still one of the best players at the club, and would sometimes pick himself, but history has proven that it is tough being a player and a manager, some of the biggest names have tried and it has not worked out for them. Perhaps also, he might have been impatient with the development of the youngsters and the level of the senior players, and tried to push them too hard to improve.They would have all improved in time but it was hardly a surprise after what he had achieved at Swindon and then at Chelsea that he would be lured away by England. You might never get that chance again, so no matter what he was building at the Bridge, the lure of the national team was far too big to turn down."

After spells as manager of Spurs, England, Southampton and Wolves, plus a spell as assistant to Harry Redknapp coaching at QPR, he starred as a pundit for BT Sport, ITV and the Premier League TV. Hoddle collapsed in the BT Sport studio on his 61st birthday. A member of the channel's production crew gave him life-saving first-aid following the incident - giving Hoddle CPR - after which he was rushed to St Bartholomew's Hospital for surgery. Fortunately Glenn made a full recovery.

Glenn and I go way back and have been friends for some time, even working together in business on a variety of footballing concepts, setting up a company called H&H Sports Media Ltd. For Glenn I tell him it is Hoddle & Harris, but to everyone else I tell them it's Harris & Hoddle! For me he was one of the greatest ever players for Spurs and indeed for England and much underated for his country when he should have won more than 100 caps, but had to settle for half that amount. He excelled in his first role as player-manager at Swindon, and again at the Bridge, and became one of the more forward-thinking England coaches of recent times, unseated by issues that were not football related. His England team at France '98 might well have won the World Cup had David Beckham not been sent off against Argentina, or indeed if Sol Campbell's late winner hadn't been ruled out.

Glenn's reign at Chelsea set them on course for the club they became, installing the blueprint of quality overseas players, big name managers and challenging for the highest honours that have epitomised the club since 1994.

Bates v. Hoddle

Ken Bates has never forgiven Glenn for quitting for England or forgotten him for siding with Matthew Harding in building a team ahead of financing his Chelsea Village development dream. Bates refuses to give Hoddle any credit for his part in kick-starting the Chelsea revolution. It's not a view I share with Bates, and told him so, but Ken insisted, "He did nothing in the history of this club, nothing. He got us to the FA Cup final, which we lost 4-0."

Despite this, Bates made every effort to keep him at the Bridge. He even threatened the then chief executive of the Football Association of breaking the FA's own rules to 'tap up' Hoddle!

"We all met up at Chelsea Harbour hotel, myself, Glenn, his agent Dennis Roach and our chief executive Colin Hutchinson," Ken told me, "we had a convivial lunch, discussed the new terms [of a Chelsea contract], shook hands on it, but by the time I got back to the Bridge I got a call from Graham Kelly at around 2.30pm. Graham asked me for permission to talk to Hoddle. I responded, 'What for?' although of course I knew full well what for! Graham continued, 'We want him as the England manager'."

So I told Kelly, "Of course you can (speak with my manager)," then asked, "Graham, can I ask you a question?"

He said, "yes, of course you can".

I went on, "I presume all the terms are agreed?"

He said, "Yes".

"Well", I told him, "You have clearly been talking to him, or his agent, behind our backs. Of course the FA have rules about illegal approaches and all that sort of thing, so you have made an illegal approach to a manager without first asking the club? So you are in breach of the FA rules."

He said, "Well, yes".

I said, "In which case, who do I report the FA to for a breach of FA rules?"

Bates was clearly toying with Kelly as he told me he knew that the FA had been courting his manager for the previous three months and he couldn't resist making Kelly aware that he knew what they had been up to. Bates tells me: "I burst out laughing and put the phone down."

I related this to Hoddle over lunch at Elaine's in Sunningdale, and Glenn couldn't help but laugh. This sort of 'sounding out' of managers was as prevalent then as it is today. As Glenn pointed out, Chelsea had made a similar approach to him when he was Swindon manager! He makes reference to this in his autobiography *Playmaker* when he was considering the Chelsea approach as he took his Swindon side to Wembley for the play-offs which would eventually see the Wiltshire club make it into the elite. He says in the book: "We had to focus. Behind the scenes, though, my head was spinning. Along with preparing for the biggest game of my short managerial career, I was also mulling over an offer to leave Swindon for Chelsea. It started when Colin Hutchinson, Chelsea's chief executive, sounded me out at the end of the league campaign. I went to see Ken Bates, Chelsea's chairman, at his house and found myself in a bind. Although I was flattered by Chelsea's interest and knew that I needed to move if I wanted to progress as a manager, my heart was telling me stay. I still had to plan our training sessions, prepare for Leicester and make sure that I was ready to play, even though I knew that my agent Dennis Roach was talking to Ken and Colin about Chelsea's offer at the same time." Rumours had begun but Hoddle said nothing to add to the speculation. He went on: "I had given my word to Chelsea and they wanted me to sign a contract immediately. Although I wanted to wait, they were worried that I would walk away, so I arranged to meet Colin at my house in Ascot to talk through the final details a couple of days before the game." Meanwhile Hoddle also got a call from Spurs, because Alan Sugar was on the look out for a new manager as he wanted Terry Venables out, and I had recommended Glenn to Alan. I even called Glenn myself, but he told me at the time that he had already given his word to Chelsea, even though he had not quite yet signed the contract. When Sugar called him at his Ascot home he told Glenn that Venables was on his way out, although he couldn't explain why at that stage.

As Hoddle recalls in his memoirs Alan said to him, "Whatever Bates is offering you, I'll give you treble." Glenn, though, had already told me he didn't think the time was right, there was so much political in-fighting at Spurs with the fans backing Venables against Sugar. As I told Glenn you never know if the chance would ever come again, but, of course, it did when the timing was right.

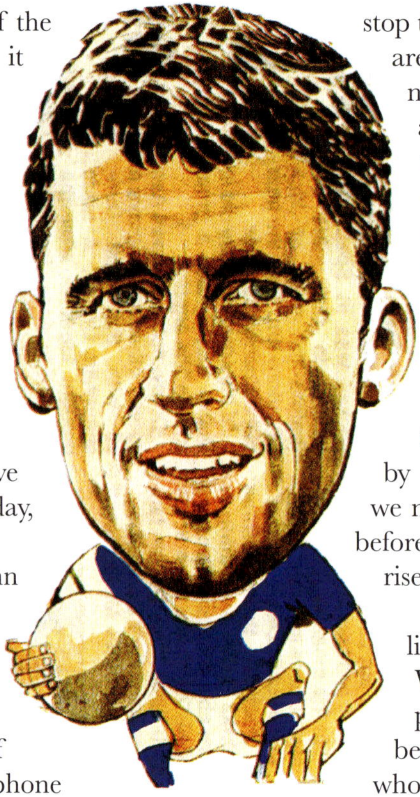

Bates only contacted Swindon after the play-off final, and I'd imagine Alan Sugar never bothered to ask Swindon permission to speak to Glenn before his approach, either.

So it was to the Bridge that Hoddle moved, and he had his first problem in pre-season when the club captain Andy Townsend wanted to move on to Aston Villa, and Hoddle had to conduct his £2.1m sale with Villa's boss Ron Atkinson. It is hard to believe, but back then transfers were all sorted out between the respective managers - why it can't still be done this way today, is beyond me.

It was during these negotiations that Glenn had his first experience of the vagaries of the club's training ground. "Keen for sone privacy, I realised that I needed to find my office at Harlington," he wrote, "I asked one of my coaches for directions and was taken to the staff changing room before being shown a BT pay phone with the bottom missing by the entrance. 'You put 50p in,' he said, 'when you hear the pips on the phone it will drop through and you'll need to put 50p in again.'

"It was ridiculous. While I was trying to complete a £2.1m deal to sell Andy to Villa, apprentices were walking through to put dirty kits in the laundry, my staff were getting changed behind me and the pips kept going on the phone when my 50p began to run out. It was embarrassing when Ron asked why he kept hearing odd noises at my end. In the end I said, 'I'll tell you what, I'm going to phone you this afternoon, I'm going to Stamford Bridge.' I was exasperated when I put the phone down. I went to the stadium later that day and didn't hold back when I met Ken Bates, 'The training ground's a disgrace,' I said, 'it's not even ours. I've tried to plan my pre-season and when I was trying to schedule in some running for Wednesday afternoon I was told that we can't do it then because Imperial College use the place for hockey!' I couldn't believe it when I found out a university hockey team had priority over a Premier League side, but it didn't stop there. I wasn't finished with Ken. 'The pitches are poor,' I said, 'There's not even a bath, there's no gym, there's nothing. No wonder the players always have 'flu.' Players were crammed inside tiny changing rooms, they walked down cold corridors and had to bring their own biscuits in because there was no food. If they went into the boot room to use the one available leg weight, they had to pause when an apprentice squeezed past them with the dirty boots. There was no sense of care, no sense of pride. We were setting ourselves up for failure and I wasn't having it. I finished by saying, 'Ken, this is Chelsea Football Club, we need to stay in better hotels when we go away before a game. The mentality of the players has to rise. We are acting like a Sunday League side.'

"Although we had good, experienced players like Nigel Spackman, Dave Beasant and Dennis Wise, they were coasting because of the club's parsimonious attitude. People didn't know any better and it was up to me to stand up to Ken, who was a tough character. 'You need to spend some money,' I said, 'you need to ask the university to put six individual baths in this area here. I need an office. The treatment room needs to be here. The gym needs to be here. Go and get the plumber!'

"Ken wasn't happy, but he accepted that we had to modernise, and it wasn't just Harlington. Anybody could see that Stamford Bridge itself fell well short of the required standard. The pitch was poor and the atmosphere was lacking during home games because a greyhound track around the pitch meant the fans were far from the action. We had to do more for the players and change the philosophy of the club. Although results were important, we had to start by opening our minds and revolutionising our approach off the pitch. It was the only way forward and I needed people to believe in my vision."

Hoddle was gratified that Bates was willing to spend on the club's infrastructure, and the first stages of 'Hoddle's Revolution' in West London was underway.

HH

Ken Bates v. Matthew Harding

Bought for £1 by Ken Bates in 1982, Chelsea were sold to Roman Abramovich for £140m in 2003 and became one of the most expensive sporting entities in the world, when Todd Boehly bought the club for £4.25 BILLION. If any club typifies the huge changes in English football it is Chelsea FC.

The Premier League was the catalyst for the explosion of such phenomenal commercial growth and Ken Bates, having saved the club, was instrumental in transforming everything about Chelsea but in turn that rapid growth brought with it a soap opera worthy of Puccini and a tragedy worthy of Shakespeare, with the club's supporters split down the middle as an incumbent and a young challenger battled for control of their football club. It made for several years of back page exclusives written by yours truly as the club fell under the prolonged glare of the media spotlight for the first time in its history.

And the fascination with the period remains. I was involved in a TV documentary, entitled *Poundland*, in 2023 that attempted to unravel the inside story behind the Battle of the Bridge; the conflict between chairman Ken Bates and City whizz-kid Matthew Harding, while also tracing the roots of the explosion of global financial investment in football in this country.

The Bates v. Harding boardroom conflict is one of the most traumatic times in the history of Chelsea with murky and unorthodox shenanigans, including phone tapping, bribery and connections to fraudsters, while Harding's arrival on the scene proved to be the catalyst for others with far deeper pockets to invest in the game in these shores with most Premier League clubs now owned by imperial wealth, multi-billionaires or US hedge funds.

Chelsea catapulted from a club associated with hooliganism; on-field thuggery, racism and even the National Front, to a cosmopolitan, global entity with a new and enlightened, corporate fanbase. Chelsea were at the forefront of that change, a revolution instigated by Hoddle, Gullit and Zola on the field, and by Hutchinson, Bates and Harding off it.

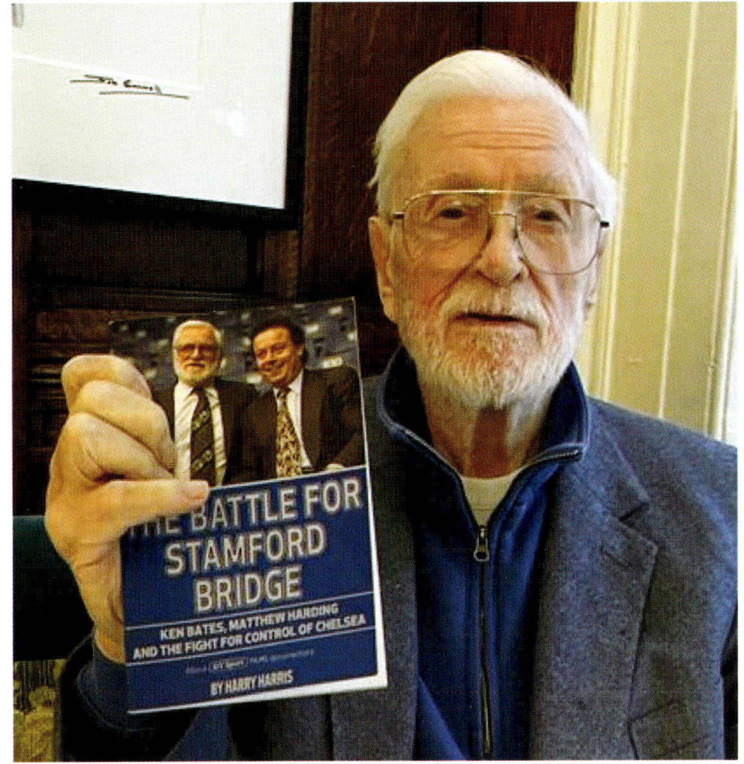

Rob Beasley, former chief football writer at the now defunct *News of the World* and a big Chelsea fan observes, "I was looking at some pictures of Stamford Bridge in the eighties, and it's a shambles. You forget how poor the stadium was! You look at the same scene in the year 2000, the whole ground had been transformed. Maybe not into an ideal new stadium because it was done so piecemeal and they maintained the old 1970s stand. So it's not like an Emirates or like the new Tottenham Stadium. They did one stand, then another, then another stand and kept the old stand. It's not perfect, but it's so much better than it was. And Chelsea suddenly went from being a yo-yo club in the eighties to being in the Champions League, and then in the 21st century actually winning it a couple of times. I never thought I'd see Chelsea win the league, let alone the Champions League!

"I love Chelsea, you know. Back when opposing fans used to sing, 'Where were you when you were not so good?'. That was always the taunt. And you go, well, Huddersfield away, Wrexham away, and that's where we were. To get promoted was fantastic, to get relegated was the abyss but you thought, well we'll be back in a couple of years. Winning the league, was just the stuff of dreams. Then suddenly you had world class footballers coming to Chelsea. Glenn Hoddle coming was massive. Glenn was playing a sweeper role then, and he was head and shoulders above everybody else on the pitch, even carrying a long standing injury and playing in an unfamiliar, deeper role. He was fabulous. Then Gullit comes, then Vialli, Zola, Hughes. When Ruud Gullit signed at the press conference, they announced Mark Hughes as well. You go, wow there's a double whammy for you; one of the greatest player in the world and Mark Hughes is one of those players that you hated when he played for Man United. He was dirty. He was tough. He was uncompromising. The minute he signs for you it's like, 'oh he's fantastic ain't he?'. Although he wasn't a prolific scorer, he scored some great goals, but he was more of a hold it up, lay it off, he was a fulcrum for the attack. He was brilliant.

"[We had] Zola and Gullit in the same team. Then Roberto di Matteo, Dan Petrescu and Frank Leboeuf. The football transformed and Chelsea were the first team to play a totally international XI - players from all around the world. But the thrill of watching it. I'm a Chelsea fan, and I wanted to see one of our own, an Alan Hudson, or Jodie Morris or John Terry; someone who has come through the ranks. Instead it was a team of Globetrotters, the Harlem Globetrotters, an all-star XI. That didn't sit right with me. But when you sat and watched them, that was beautiful football. Skill, flair, everything that you wanted for Chelsea, the team that had the King's Road swagger. They might have been international superstars from all over the planet, but that was the swagger that we associated with Chelsea."

Can it be that, in the not too distant past, Chelsea's black players were booed! Then, within a blink of an eye, those same supporters had fully embraced a cosmopolitan team of all races and nationalities. Beasley added: "I remember being in the Shed and they were singing 'ain't no black in the Union Jack, send the "bleep bleeps" home'. And a few years later there's Ruud Gullit and Marcel Desailly. I felt for Paul Canoville because he was a real role model. But there was always a section in the Shed, and around the ground, who didn't want a black player in their team. You'd be in the Shed and they say 'we're playing with ten men again are we?' because they would never accept a black player. Thankfully, that's all changed. I suppose having a winning football team can solve a multitude of problems and inadvertently, in having that international star-studded team, it dealt with it to a degree, although it's still there of course. Combat 18 was around at the time and they were all about number one is A, number eight is H. It's the initials of Adolf Hitler. So, it's not hard to understand what their philosophy was as a group. They were very dangerous, evil people who have thankfully to all intents and purposes been wiped away. That being said, Chelsea have been in the headlines in the last few seasons for anti-Semitic stuff, particularly, and for the occasional racist abuse of opposition players. So it's not completely expunged, but it's a far cry from where they were openly singing 'ain't no black in the Union Jack'."

*

Matthew Harding arrived talking about 'proper' money getting into football, and with it he bought the best players, which in turn changed perceptions. In previous eras high flyers in the City had followed the boat race or rugby at Twickenham or horse racing, but nobody would touch football. Yet, because Harding was a genuine fan, he could see where football was going before others caught on. Beasley agreed: "People in the City said he was a visionary, saw things way ahead of time with a sharp business brain. The image of football was dirty; Hillsborough, Heysel, we were banned from Europe, so who would want to invest? It was seen as a working class game played in dilapidated old stadiums, which obviously changed to a degree after Hillsborough, it was actually a catalyst for families to go. The advent of the Premier League and then, for the elite clubs, the Champions League, brought more and more money. TV rights were going up and the benefits of being on TV were a lot more lucrative. Suddenly football was going from being the great unwashed to being a sexy and interesting investment, so a different calibre of person and businessmen got involved. The days when Manchester United had been owned by the local butcher, however rich he was, it was now transformed. Nowadays there is no way a Ken Bates would be able to compete with the likes of Manchester City, with the backing of a rich oil state and limitless cash. Chelsea has just been taken over by a consortium of different billionaires in an investment company, it's staggering.

"Matthew didn't imagine it would get to the extent it is now, but he could definitely see football had re-organised and needed proper financing. His plan eventually was that he would be the chairman of Chelsea and he'd buy Bates out or they'd come to some sort of agreement, and he would then bring in some influential people from the City and beyond, people who had got an interest in Chelsea, multi-millionaires like him. Matthew saw a collection of people having the wherewithal to transform Chelsea. That was his vision for the future. Now, it is on another level beyond even that."

Ken Bates also had a vision, telling the press he wanted Chelsea to be the 'Manchester United of the South' a phrase that makes Beasley cringe: 'I hated being associated with Manchester United. Why would you want to be another Manchester United? Dear me! Oh, I can't think of anything worse. Why be a pale imitation of somebody else? We wanted to be Chelsea. Not 'Manchester United South'. I know what Ken meant, though. He wanted Chelsea to be the number one club in London, which we are now. You know, we're the only team in London to win the Champions League, not just once, but twice. So I know what he meant."

After I gave an interview for the documentary *Poundland*, in the car heading back home from the BT Sports' studio, I rang Ken Bates. It was quite late, around 10pm in Monte Carlo, and the reception wasn't good and, with the former Chelsea chairman heading toward his 91st birthday, he was ready for bed. I told him jokingly I was sending him an invoice as the only one who really knew the true story of why he fell out with Matthew Harding and would be able to tell his side of the story! In typical fashion Ken replied that he would be using my invoice as toilet paper.

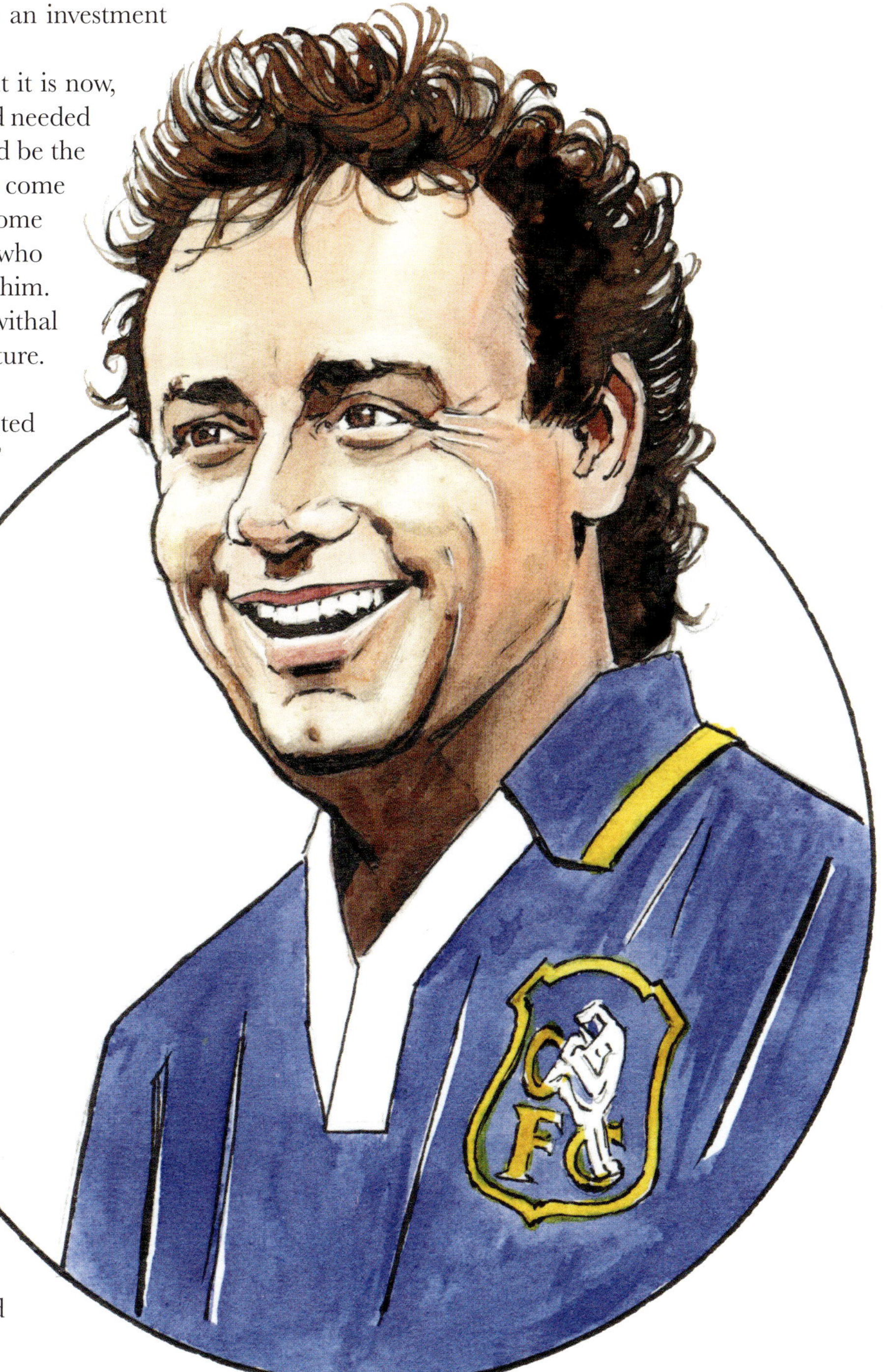

He rang me back the following morning, I missed the call, but he left this message: "Well Harry, it's 10.30 on Saturday, rang your landline, no answer, rang your mobile, on answerphone, you must be a busy boy in your old age. I'm sitting overlooking the sun-kissed Mediterranean. I've got a lovely glass of rose wine, I'm in all day. In your chauffeur driven limousine the reception was appalling. Hope you have posted your invoice. You know my number."

I rang 'Old Grey Beard' back, and for the next hour he told me why he turned down the invite to be interviewed for the documentary, and gave me the inside track on what really went on inside the board room with regards to Matthew Harding. Okay, it is a one-sided view, but it was explosive material. He even accused former FA Chairman Graham Kelly of making an illegal approach for his then manager Glenn Hoddle! More of which later. Ken began, "I was rung up by someone I don't know and asked to participate in the documentary. I asked who he would be interviewing, they were all the usual suspects and I said 'no'. I've been stung a few times in the past when giving interviews which are edited, when they pick and chose what they want and often intersperse it with other interviews, giving a certain slant to it. I have also owned three TV stations and three radio stations so I knew how these things work. Long ago I decided if I did an interview, it would have to be live, and only live, when they can't mess around with what I have to say. I recently watched a two part documentary on BBC 2 of Sir Phillip Green who lives just down the road from me, and that reinforced my view."

The Bates/Harding relationship started out as a partnership of financial convenience but soon deteriorated to a vicious board room battle. In the 1980s Bates had held out against avaricious property and land developers Cabra Estate who wanted to dispose of the prime Stamford Bridge real estate and condemn the team to a ground share with Fulham or QPR, but having won that battle he found himself unable to finance both the improvements desperately needed at the ground and keep pace with the top teams in the Premier League. When Harding arrived he gave supporters hope about the quality of football they might watch, and he set the wheels in motion for some of the richest men in the world to see the potential of English football. When a super rich fan buys his way into his beloved club, his heart rules his head. When he cohabits with a wily old businessman like Ken Bates, who only allows his head to rule his heart, there was always going to be conflict. Matthew was a life long Blues supporter, Bates supported Arsenal as a kid and only, as Ken himself put it, "a gammy leg", halted his potential career as a player with the north London club.

Bates needed investment to help fulfil his vision of Chelsea Village, and when the purse strings became too tight for comfort, he brought someone into the fold whom he thought was a lightweight compared to himself, and he would be able to control. As it proved Bates couldn't have been more wrong. Matthew Harding quickly became the fans' favourite, and although Bates was hugely popular with the supporters, he was nowhere near as charming, approachable or likeable as his new found board room ally. Despite having such a gruff exterior, and having got to know Ken intimately over many years, not just professionally, I discovered a man who wanted to be loved! Yes, loved! He wanted to be feared by his rivals, but loved by those closest to him. While he succeeded in being feared by his rivals, it was tough being loved when you were Ken Bates.

All of which made for a far more complex situation and a crash course between the pair. Bates enjoyed his love affair with Chelsea, and the affection that he got from their rank and file fan base. Yet as Harding's popularity grew, so Bates found himself displaced in their affections and he grew to dislike Harding more and more.

Matthew's time on the board in the mid-1990s was brief but headline grabbing as he captured the imagination of Blues supporters, going out of his way to portray himself as 'one of them'. His legacy, though, still stands at Stamford Bridge with the significant part he played in the growth of the club and his wish to make it even bigger than it was at the time. That was recognised by the club when his memory was honoured with a minute's applause before the club's Premier League game against Norwich City on October 21, 2021 that marked the 25th anniversary of his untimely passing.

The story starts in October 1993, after Bates had effectively saved Stamford Bridge. Harding provided £5 million to help start the stadium's much-needed regeneration, the funds going towards the North Stand that would later bear his name. The then 39-year-old also became a Chelsea director. He was introduced to the crowd at half-time in a game against Arsenal. In May 1994, with Glenn Hoddle as player-manager, the club reached the FA Cup final for the first time in a generation. Although beaten by Manchester United, it was clear that under the inspirational guidance of the country's brightest young coach, the Blues' fortunes were about to take a significant upward turn. A massive blue crowd-surfing flag was a feature of the FA Cup run, funded by Harding and his business friend Graham Bell. It was just the kind of touch that only a real fan would finance, and it served to turn Harding into an immediate cult figure with the supporters. There were also numerous stories starting to appear in the media about how he would enjoy a dozen oysters and a pint of Guinness for his pre-match meal. But he would not be in some flash Michelin star restaurant which, by all accounts, he could easily have afforded, but he would rub shoulders with the supporters in a pub across the road from the stadium where he would not just be there for a photo opportunity, but to talk with fans about the game, the players, his love for the club and his desire to take the club forward.

In June 1994 Harding started a loan fund of £5m to help purchase new players and that November the new North Stand opened and the Harding family's season tickets were relocated there from the East Stand. Yet not even the status of being one of the big wigs now would stop his pre match ritual or his desire to be with fellow supporters, so Matthew would leave the pub and his friends and change into a suit before watching games from the directors' box to comply with the dress code.

In May 1995 a game-changing board meeting took place that become known as The Marriott Accord. It was a pivotal moment in the club's history: Bates, Harding, managing director Colin Hutchinson and manager Glenn Hoddle discussed how to take the club to a new level, a vision for the future both on and off the field and committed themselves to signing Ruud Gullit and Paul Gascoigne. Gullit duly arrived, and Mark Hughes soon followed, and overnight Chelsea's ambition changed. They had acquired a former World Footballer of the Year, the captain of the great Dutch team when they won the Euros in 1988, a star of AC Milan, then Europe's biggest and best club, at a time when Italian football ruled the world with the best players paid huge salaries. Hot on his heels Welshman Mark Hughes arrived following a

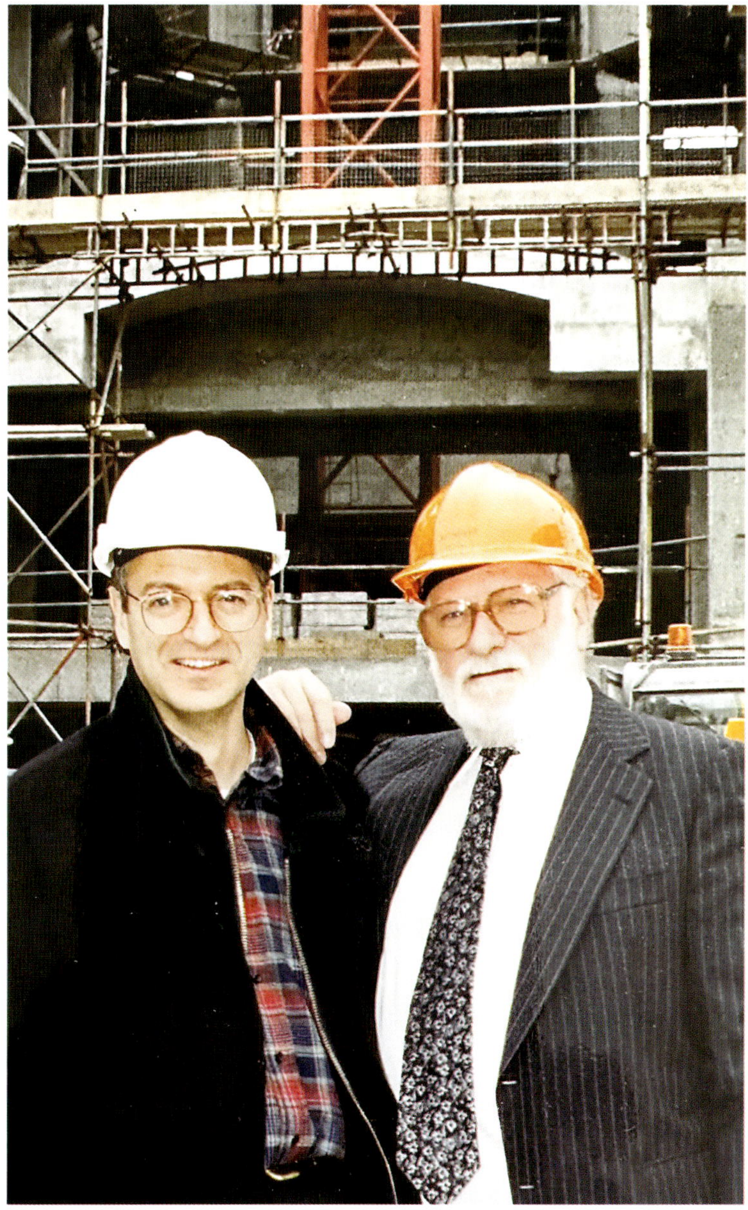

You often needed a hard hat when reading Ken's programme notes.

successful second spell at Manchester United where he had been an integral part of Alex Ferguson's transformation of the club by winning the FA Cup, European Cup Winners' Cup, League Cup and Premier League in successive seasons before completing the League and Cup double with that Wembley win over Chelsea. This was heady stuff. Harding also purchased the freehold of Stamford Bridge for £16.5m from the bank which had been in possession of it since the collapse of the property company that owned it. Bates had negotiated with the bank for the land to eventually become Chelsea's on favourable terms.

It seemed like the perfect partnership: the hard-nosed, no nonsense businessman paired with the new darling of the fans, who had so much love for the club he would pour funds into it. But it was never going to last. Bates is not the easiest to get on with. I count myself as one of his closest allies, but I fell out with him a few times, as two big profile and costly High Court libel cases can testify plus a two year ban from the Stamford Bridge press box!

By November 1995 the cracks in the Bates/Harding relationship had morphed into huge fault lines, and the simmering discord spilled over into the board room. It reached such a personal and vindictive stage that Harding was banned from the Directors' Box having resigned from the board of Chelsea Village, the parent company overseeing stadium redevelopment. Bates and Harding had disagreed violently over priorities between the Chelsea Village project, which was Bates baby, and the team, which Harding had reinvented as his domain. Of course it was tough on Bates, as in reality, he too cared about the team. He had grown to love Chelsea and dearly wanted success on the pitch, but where they differed was that Bates believed that by building a more diverse Chelsea Village, containing a hotel and mega store, the club would tap a more diverse income stream that would boost income on non-match days. In contrast Harding was obsessed with success on the pitch and cared far less for Bates' vision, certainly not as the priority for the club, and defiantly not to the detriment to the team. It was a dillemma that other clubs would face when building lavish new stadiums, such as Arsenal who had to curtail their spending on transfers while they paid off their loans on their move from Highbury to the Emirates, but such was the bitterness between Bates and Harding, they even argued about the pitch size in the new development!

Banned from the Directors' Box, Harding watched Chelsea from the North Stand instead, taking his three kids with him, and standing to applaud fans who warmly applauded him when they spotted him in the stands. Of course this only further enraged Bates as he felt that Harding had cultivated large sections of the media, welcoming them to his pre-match drinks sessions with the fans in the pub near the stadium and, for their part, the media adored Matthew as it was rare for a director to share their company in such intimate circumstances, no doubt sharing a bit of gossip that would make a headline or two. Bates was convinced that a picture of Harding and his children was stage-managed by his chums in the media, as he tipped them off where he would be, for the long lenses to capture his magic moment with the fans. Harding was a man of the people, Bates was caricatured as a grumpy, miserable old man.

Chelsea's image before Harding's arrival was of hooliganism, electric fences, a place where even the club's first black player, Paul Canoville, was racially abused... After Harding's death the club would be associated with star players such as Gullit and Zola and would take their place at the very top of the Premier League.

In March 1996 there was speculation that discussions over a new co-operation between the two would result in an end to the feud, but I knew that it would have taken a Henry Kissinger in his prime to bring these two together. While there had been discussions a contract remained unsigned and Harding's investment in Chelsea Village was put on hold. During the summer of 1996 matters moved forward and there was indeed an agreement put in place as the club paid back the loan fund Harding made available for player purchases and he invested in a large number of shares in the recently floated Chelsea Village. By agreeing the Bates deal, Harding was made vice-President of Chelsea Football Club.

Then in October 1996 the helicopter Harding was in crashed as he made his way back from a League Cup tie at Bolton. His death was confirmed a few hours later, and immediately Stamford Bridge was turned into a shrine with thousands paying tribute.

At the club's next home game, against local rivals Tottenham, an immaculate minute's silence was observed. The North Stand was renamed the Matthew Harding Stand in his honour.

These are the bare bones of a three-year saga that dominated the back pages and eventually spilled on to the front ones. Having personally lived through the board room tussle on a daily basis, to keep *Daily Mirror* readers abreast of the latest developments, it brings back memories of one of the greatest sports politics stories. Working as a chief football writer in an age prior to the internet, smart phones and social media, the public would turn to the newspapers for their news, in an age where breaking news was the most valuable commodity for a journalist. Thus it was my task to stay close to the action, and that is what I did. I was reminded of this incredible board room battle when an old friend from Radio 5 Live, with whom I had many dealings back in the day, called me to request an interview for a documentary on the Battle of the Bridge. The ethos of the documentary was to trace the explosion of English football to the Harding era, that investors could perceive the incredible returns as young coaches such as Hoddle were bringing to these shores all of the guile, fitness levels, nutrition he had gathered under Arsene Wenger at Monaco. The signs were growing that the dark ages had passed and a bright future would enable the English game to compete with the more affluent Italian and Spanish leagues. It became clear that clubs like Chelsea were credible investments, and even massive clubs such as Manchester United and Liverpool would be subject to big money takeovers.

Chelsea's image before Harding's arrival was of hooliganism, electric fences, a place where even the club's first black player, Paul Canoville, was racially abused by home supporters. After Harding's death the club would be associated with star players such as Gullit and Zola and would take their place at the very top of the Premier League and eventually become one of the biggest clubs in Europe.

In my view the revolution in English football started with Hoddle and Harding who in turn would paved the way for the arrival of Roman Abramovich, and a top flight where nearly every club is owned by individuals or consortiums with limitless wealth. Chelsea were at the vanguard of this change.

Dirty Tricks

Industrial Espionage at the Bridge?

Ken Bates claims he was "tipped off all the time", about Matthew Harding's comings and goings, claiming "I knew exactly what he was up to, I never reacted." Bates was famed for his contributions to the club programme, he penned the edgiest chairman's notes of all time: they could be biting, cruel, and vindictive. Yet you were compelled to read them to ensure you were not in them! The documentary makers asked me to read a couple of extracts from his columns from the height of his feud with Matthew Harding and every word dripped with loathing for his fellow director. Now, for the first time, Bates reveals the behind the scenes 'dirty tricks' that proved too risque even for his notorious programme notes! He didn't say he had employed a private detective, but I wouldn't have put it past him and he didn't say he hadn't!

Bates tells me the story of how he was sitting in the directors box at Anfield when he received a call from the Co-Op bank manager. "Ken, come over straight away, just leave the game and come over to see me, I'm sorry but this is something urgent but something I cannot possibly discuss over the phone."

"The bank manager booked me into a hotel in Altrincham and booked a restaurant and drove across to see me, it must have been that important. The Co-Op Bank was lending the club £3m, this was much needed finance for the redevelopment of Stamford Bridge, while I was also getting £2m from the Football Trust. I met up with the bank manager, who told me, 'Watch out for that fellow Harding, he's come up here this morning to try to persuade me not to lend you the £3m, he was very aggressive, bullying even, and told me that he would deposit £20m on a 12 month period with the Co-Op if I did what he asked and reject your £3m loan. I told Mr Harding that Chelsea Football Club were my client not anyone else.'

"I had cast iron proof that my suspicions about Harding were right, he was not to be trusted," Bates continued, "it made you

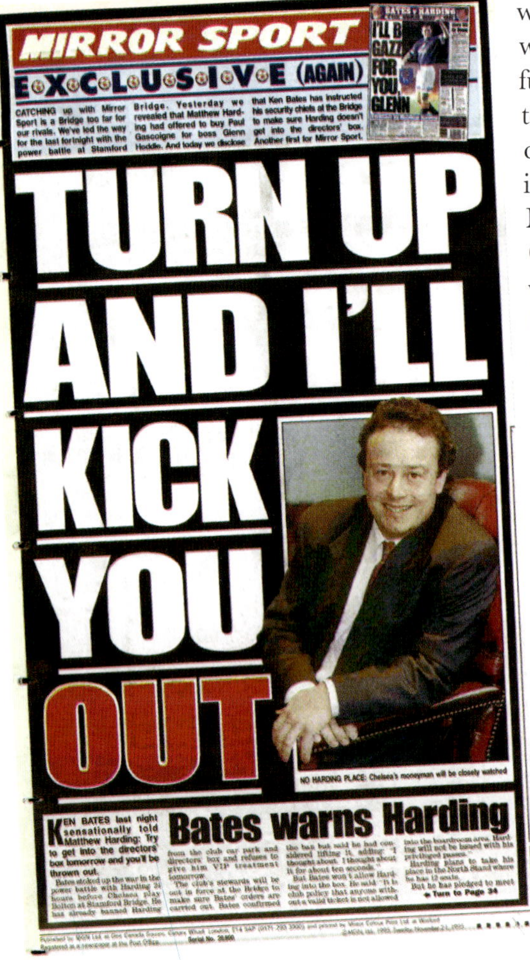

MIRROR SPORT

E·X·C·L·U·S·I·V·E (AGAIN)

CATCHING up with Mirror Sport is a Bridge too far for our rivals. We've led the way for the last fortnight with the power battle at Stamford Bridge. Yesterday we revealed that Matthew Harding had offered to buy Paul Gascoigne for boss Glenn Hoddle. And today we disclose that Ken Bates has instructed his security chiefs at the Bridge to make sure Harding doesn't get into the directors' box. Another first for Mirror Sport.

BATES v HARDING

I'LL B GAZZ FOR YOU, GLENN

TURN UP AND I'LL KICK YOU OUT

NO HARDING PLACE: Chelsea's moneyman will be closely watched

Bates warns Harding

KEN BATES last night sensationally told Matthew Harding: Try to get into the directors' box tomorrow and you'll be thrown out.

Bates stoked up the war in the power battle with Harding 24 hours before Chelsea play Bolton at Stamford Bridge. He has already banned Harding from the club car park and directors' box and refuses to give him VIP treatment tomorrow.

The club's stewards will be out in force at the Bridge to make sure Bates' orders are carried out. Bates confirmed the ban but said he had considered lifting it, adding: "I thought about. I thought about it for about ten seconds."

But Bates won't allow Harding into the box. He said: "It is club policy that anyone without a valid ticket is not allowed into the boardroom area. Harding will not be issued with his privileged passes."

Harding plans to take his place in the North Stand where he has 12 seats.

But he has pledged to meet

Turn to Page 34

wonder what else he would be doing to fulfil his ambitions to become Chelsea chairman. As it turned out Michael, the Co-Op bank manager, went ahead and lent us the £3m, an important amount, it paid for the underground car park and for all the foundations for the entire Chelsea Village project, the restaurants, the hotel, the retail shops."

Bates had dinner with the Managing Director of the Royal Bank of Scotland, Bill Samuel, at a time when the RBS was in deep trouble during the nineties banking crisis. During that dinner, Bates confirmed his suspicions that Harding was taking out a loan, and as he tells me now "transferring it into a subsidiary company Harding bought for £1" to 'invest' in Chelsea. In the media game of trying to hit the moral high ground, Harding appeared to be putting up his own money to save the club. Bates knew otherwise. He tells me: "We were flying back from an away game and one of Harding's sons had told journalists that Matthew had 'bought' the ground for £16.5m. Those journalists approached me for my comment. I told them that it was news to me that Harding had 'bought' the ground.. The truth, though, was that he had loaned money from the bank and that loan was transferred to Chelsea.

"Matthew Harding was manna from heaven for the media. They loved him and they all disliked me. Why did they dislike me so much? Perhaps it was because I was prepared to take them on if they got it wrong and didn't get their facts right… I would sue them. Here, the agenda was clear, Harding was using the media in his strategy to drive me out, but I told him I was made of sterner stuff than [Peter] Swales at Manchester City when he was driven out in similar circumstances.

"When I popped into my local newsagents, the guy there said, 'Hey, Ken you're in the headlines again'. There I was on the back page of the *News of the World* walking the plank. When I went into the office on Monday morning and saw Harding all I said was, 'how are you?' I didn't mention the *News of the World* cartoon. What was the point? If I had ranted and raved about it, and pointed the finger at Harding for providing the inside information to his pal at the *News of the World* that inspired the cartoon, he would simply deny it was him. But I knew all about it, I knew who he entertained at the *News of the World*, I knew he was behind it.

"I also heard that he let journalists take him to lunch, but he never paid or even offered to pay. But if he did buy his journalist pals a drink, it would always be in cash. Paying in cash always raises alarm bells.

"He was portrayed as a man of the people, the fan's fan, but all I can tell you is that I always invited a couple of ordinary fans to the Old East Stand as guests of the club, with lunch before the match and would place them on a long table in our executive restaurant. One day I placed Matthew down the end of that long table next to the ordinary fans as I thought that he would like it and the fans would like it too."

Not so, according to Bates. Harding felt snubbed being put down the end with the 'ordinary fans' with whom he had so closely identified. He made his feelings known to Bates, not referencing who he was placed next to, but where he was placed, put out by considering he wasn't afforded his proper status as a director. Bates loved it, telling Harding, "'Matthew, you are the man of the people they look up to you, you are the ideal person to sit with them and to get to know them'. If looks could kill! Matthew was only interested in getting pissed and didn't like it when it was pointed out to him, that that was not acceptable, it was not the protocol, in the board room. That made him reticent to come to the game and take his place in the Directors' Box, long before I banned him from the board room."

Bates knew that the media were not going to publish much of what he discovered about Harding, so he just kept quiet about it at the time, preferring to keep the information up his sleeve in case the going got so tough he would unleash it at the right time, but he didn't need to as events took a twist in his favour when Harding died tragically. It reinforced Bates' view that Harding was not a man to whom he could entrust the future of Chelsea FC, and there was another incident that also reinforced that view.

"Harding was a con man, someone who was over-taken by his own self importance, and he was overly impressed with people," Bates explains, "he came to me to let me know that he had done a deal with Richard Branson's Virgin company to sponsor his around the world hot air balloon attempt. In return he had sealed a deal for Benfield, his company, to have their name on the hot air balloon, but also on the roof of one of the Stamford Bridge stands, because so many Virgin Atlantic planes would fly over the ground and would see the Benfield name. He was overjoyed to let us all know the deal he had struck, but I told him, 'Sorry, but the answer is no - we are not doing it'.

"He was gobsmacked, but I told him, 'I'm a director of the company and we have a board of directors, this sort of contract has to be run past the board and approved by the board, not approved by you. Richard Branson tries this stunt every year, and every year it fails, with his balloon going down in the West Pacific. The only time you will see the name Benfield, is when it lands in the sea! You won't see it when it is 60,000 feet up in the skies!' Matthew Harding was running ahead of himself, and I didn't think that kind of thing would work in a football club. Yes, he put up the £5m to build the North stand, and we should be appreciative of that fact, and I am, but equally, he didn't want anyone to know that it was borrowed money. He was supposed to be the 86th richest man in the country, yet he had to borrow the money. He had a lavish salary (reputed to be £7m a year) from his company and was paid handsome dividends but his value came in the fact that he had a 30 per cent stake in an unlisted private company.

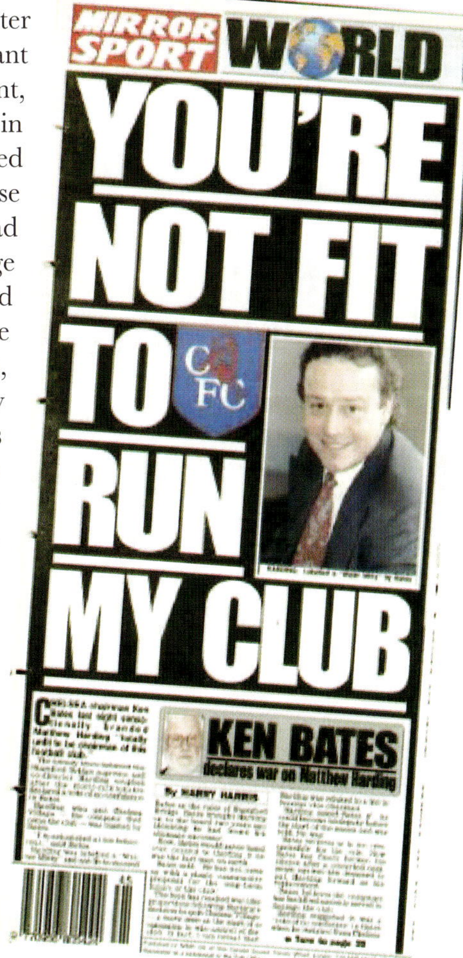

MIRROR SPORT WORLD

YOU'RE NOT FIT TO RUN MY CLUB

KEN BATES declares war on Matthew Harding

By HARRY HARRIS

"The truth of the matter was that he didn't want to do the development, he was only interested in the team, and he wanted to get rid of us because we wanted to go ahead with the Chelsea Village project which we believed would bring more finance into the club, and then, in turn, enable us to buy more players, but he was impatient to buy players first, something you hear from fans, who only are interested in the team.

"He wanted to be chairman so he could do it all his way and takeover the club, but I had put 16 years of blood, sweat and tears into Chelsea. Before I came along it was bankrupt and I feared that if Harding got his hands on the club it would end up bankrupt again."

Bates had a begrudging respect for the way Harding made his company Benfield a power house in the reinsurance field. Bates tells me, "Benfield is a broker, doesn't have assets, but has a value. Harding came up with the idea of a three-year policy for his clients which they liked because of the stability and certainty of the long term deals which he offered to them at a cheaper rate. He then went to the underwriters and took up three year guarantees, which they loved and gave him a cut price deal. He then insisted to his clients that he handle all the claims. It made Benfields a big player and the company shares valuable, but Matthew was never a millionaire. The *New York Times* launched the Rich List, and

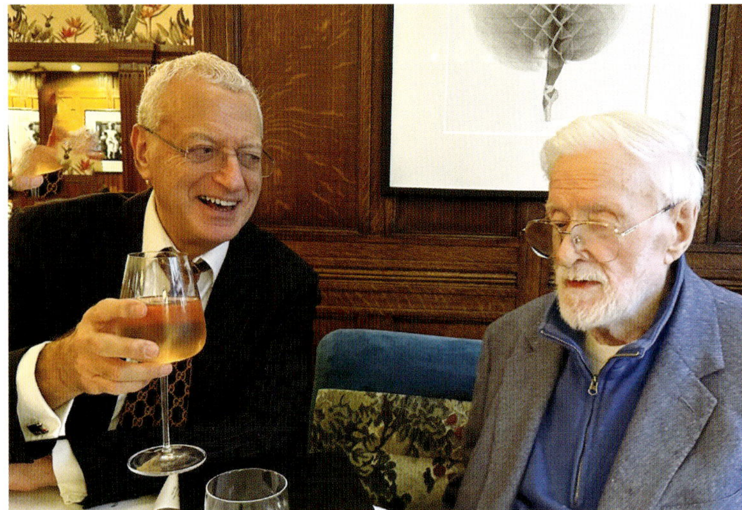

the *Sunday Times* followed suit here and valued Matthews 30 per stake in Benfield at three times profits and suddenly he was worth £100million."

Rob Beasley worked for Rupert Murdoch's notorious *News of the World*, which was later forced to shut down over phone hacking. If anyone knows about dirty tricks it would be those who used the dark arts at the 'News of the Screws' as it was known at the height of its powers with a massive five million readership. Rob was big mates with Harding, who made no secret to Beasley, whom Bates dubbed 'Yob Sleazy', that he suspected Bates was behind phone tapping of his office. Beasley knew the pair would resort to anything at the height of their boardroom battles, as he told the BT Sport documentary makers, and I obtained a full transcript of the interview in which he discussed many issues at such length that much of it would have hit the cutting room floor. "Were there dirty tricks involved? I'm pretty sure there were but I can't prove any of it. We did a story on the back page of the *News of the World* when I got called to go to Matthew's office and he said, 'look at this'. There was a secret listening device planted in his office, listening into what Matthew was talking about in the heart of his business. It could've been one of his city rivals who planted that listening device. We'll never know who put that listening device in there. But somebody clearly wanted to know what was in Matthew's mind, who he was talking to and what he was plotting and planning. What I do know is that it unsettled certain people at Chelsea in high positions who suddenly feared that maybe there was something untoward going on. The *News of the World* arranged for people to go and sweep their offices to make sure there were no listening devices in their offices. That was the reflection of the animosity at the time and the paranoia among people wondering how is this going to end? Who's doing what? All very sinister. It may have had nothing to do with Chelsea Football Club whatsoever, it might have been completely to do with the City of London and people trying to find out what Matthew's business plans were. Who knows? But when you're getting involved in that sort of thing, and I know for a fact that I was tape recorded in the Imperial Arms talking to Matthew, you wonder who did that and why they did that. But I subsequently found out about it and I was confronted about it by certain people and I just think, wow, I can't even go have a pint and a chat in a pub before a match without somebody being around with a microphone. Luckily I'm the sort of guy, Matthew was to a degree, it was water off a duck's back. You actually felt like you're in the middle of something that was important if this is going on, we must be, and this must be worth pursuing, worth delving even further into. You look back now and you think, that was a bit weird. I've never come across that before or since since and I was on Fleet Street for over 30 years. So yeah, dirty tricks. But was it Chelsea? We'll never know. But I've got my suspicions, obviously."

Did Matthew think that his own driver was reporting back to somebody, Rob was asked.

"I think he did in the end. Gotta be careful here, haven't I? Matthew had a taxi driver who picked him up one day at Chelsea, and in the glass partition of the taxi was a Chelsea sticker. Matthew asked him, 'are you a Chelsea fan? Then I want you to drive me everywhere from now on'. And he did. He was a great lad. He spent a lot of time with Matthew's kids, which is part of his job. He'd drive Matthew around and then on a Saturday afternoon, take the kids down the amusement arcade, keep them occupied while we're having a couple of pints of Guinness and some oysters in the Imperial Arms before a match. But it was such a time when you're sat trying to figure it out; because you knew people were being recorded and you're wondering why and who's responsible. You do look around and think, who could it be? Who was that

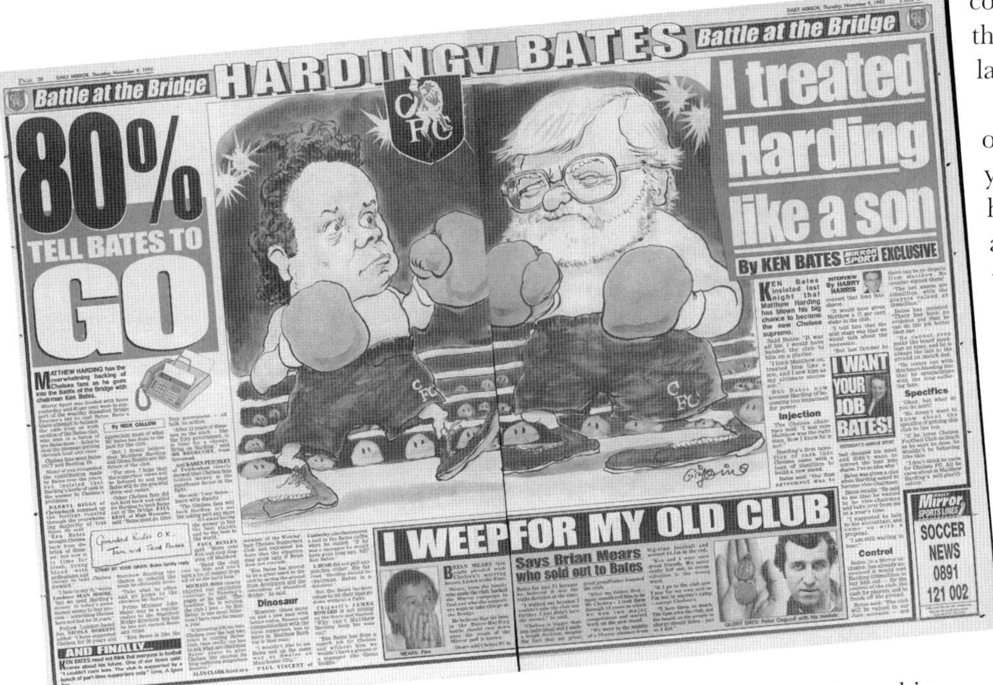
Battle at the Bridge

HARDING v BATES

Battle at the Bridge

80% TELL BATES TO GO

I treated Harding like a son

By KEN BATES MIRROR SPORT EXCLUSIVE

I WANT YOUR JOB BATES!

Injection

Specifics

Control

Dinosaur

I WEEP FOR MY OLD CLUB

Says Brian Mears who sold out to Bates

Mirror SPORTS LINES SOCCER NEWS 0891 121 002

AND FINALLY...

close? Who could record us in the pub? Who could do this? And who could do that? And there's a small number of suspects who it could be, because Matthew had quite a tight knit group of people around him. So, you know, suspicions fell on quite a few people. But Matthew did think that it might have been his driver who could have been reporting back to Bates."

Like all Chelsea fans at that time, the Chairman's programme notes was the first page you turned to as Rob said: "Ken used to write things in the Chelsea programme. And if you're a Chelsea fan, you're reading his articles, a lot of it, a lot of the time was about who he was fighting with in Fleet Street and who he'd sued and what a scumbag so-and-so was. When you were mentioned, you took it as a badge of honour because it was as if Ken Bates is calling you out, you must be doing something right. We all suffered at different times. If I had said something in the pub and it had been recorded and got back to Ken, he'd say, 'oh, that Rob Beesley'. He said this and he said that. When it appeared, I'd think did I did say that? You thought you're having a private conversation with somebody, you didn't realise that somebody was reporting back every word. I laughed about it then and I'll laugh about it now.

"Ken Bates is a piece of work. A formidable opponent," Beasley adds, "you had to be right on your business to even think about going up against him. Here's an example - it was his 70th birthday and there's a fabulous lady who works at Chelsea, worked there for years, Theresa Keneally, and she's very close to Ken and me and him had always had this sort of lively relationship, even though I was clearly much more friendly and much more on board with what Matthew was trying to do, I'd still get invited to his Christmas luncheon. And I still to this day get invited to his Christmas dos. So Theresa came to me and she said we've got a Christmas card, a birthday card for Ken, it's a folder, Gullit was in there, Roberto Di Matteo, Dennis Wise, all saying happy birthday, Mr. Chairman. Thanks for everything you did for me and all that. I thought, blimey I shouldn't really be signing this. So I thought I'm going to just put something on the page and have the final word. So, I've picked the back cover and I put at the bottom. 'Ken do me a favour, get Leeds promoted as soon as you can, I've got nobody to fight with anymore.' I signed it Rob and from then on he was like 'you're coming to the Christmas party'. He absolutely loved it because we'd had that respect for each other.

"Some of the things went beyond the pale, what he said about Matthew after his death being an evil man, absolute nonsense and completely uncalled for, completely out of order. But for the most part, we both took it as we're in a ruck here and it's nothing personal, but, you know, come on. We could see past it. We could still go out for lunch together, or we could still mix at the Christmas party and chuckle at the fact that we were sort of adversaries rather than mates. But we quite liked the idea that we were having a bit of a battle. He liked it, that's who he is. He's a fighter. He loves a fight. And if you're giving him a good fight, he probably respects you more than if you rolled over and let him tickle your tummy. So, probably there was a bit of respect in there as well. To say get Leeds promoted, let's get back to fighting again, would have tickled his fancy because, he'd love all that. I want to be back in the big time and I want to be having these battles with different people, including you, Beasley."

As Rob has indicated, Bates was a formidable foe who would stop at nothing, and when Harding bought the freehold to the Bridge, it was seen as a red flag for the chairman. Rob recalls that it didn't go down well with Bates, "I remember it vividly because inadvertently Colin Hutchinson, who was the managing director, I spoke to him on the Friday night and I got on fantastically well with Colin. Matthew called him 'Digby' for some reason. I've spoken to him and he says 'you know, Matthew's brought the freehold to Stamford Bridge'. I had no idea whatsoever. So I went 'yeah, yeah. Brilliant, ain't it? Great news.' Colin told me a little bit more information. Write this down. 'Oh fantastic. Back page lead this is: 'Matthew buys Stamford Bridge'. Oh, fantastic. I'm seeing Matthew the next day; Imperial Arms, Guinness and oysters, love it. He'll give me chapter and verse. So I get there nice and early. I'm there an hour before the allotted time. I'm sitting there waiting. I want to write this before the match. Then I can enjoy the match. Matthew comes up and I went, 'I need to talk to you, I understand, you've bought the freehold to Stamford Bridge.' He says, 'I can't say anything.' I said 'what do you mean?' He says, 'I've signed a confidentiality agreement. I can't speak about it whatsoever.' I said, 'I'm not going to let anybody…'

"'No, no, confidentiality. So, let's have a pint of Guinness.' After the first pint, 'come on mate just give me the nod'.

"'No, no.'

"Second pint. 'Come on Matt'. 'No, I'm going now. I got to get to the boardroom. I'll walk across with you.'

"So were walking across. 'Come on Matt, you know, it's just me and you now, we're just walking in the street. Nobody can hear us.'

"'No, no, no. Confidentiality. I've signed this thing. I'm not going to let you. I can't deny it. I can't confirm it. Nothing.' We get to the main entrance where he's going off to the boardroom, and I've just got to go a little bit further to get to the press box. He suddenly turned to me and grabbed me by both hands and said, 'but it's great, isn't it?' And he did this little jig. And he goes 'isn't it fantastic? Isn't it fun being me?' Then off he went. He didn't say anything about buying the freehold, but you just knew from that reaction. So, of course I wrote the story during the match. Then after the match I thought, I've got to tweak Ken's tail with this because he's been going on for years and years; 'I'm saving the Bridge, I'm saving the Bridge', but could never afford to do what Matthew had done and actually buy the freehold. So, I scribbled a note saying, 'Hi Ken. Rob Beasley, doing a story tomorrow about Matthew having bought the freehold for Stamford Bridge, just wondered if you'd like to comment.' Get in, go on, have a bit of that. He sent back this note and he said, 'Yes, I understand he's brought the freehold, but not for a lot of money'. As if that was like some put down on Matthew that he hadn't paid a lot of money. I thought well, that's even better, surely? That shows how astute he was as a businessman, that he could buy this prime real estate in south west London for 12 million quid. What a coup for Matthew, but also if it wasn't a lot of money, why didn't Ken Bates buy it? Because Ken Bates hadn't got that little bit of money to do it. I just thought, Ken you've shot yourself in the foot there. You've said not a lot of money. That's how brilliant Matthew was. Not a lot of money, but I couldn't afford to do it. I thought that was for Ken, a real faux pas."

"The way Ken would look at it is like, I've got Rob Beasley, Matthew Harding's big mate, to write an anti-Matthew Harding story in the *News of the World*."

In reality Harding's money were all loans, a lot of smoke and mirrors went into it and that was why Bates was seething. Rob was to get a shock when he discovered the truth, with a phone call from Bates, as he recalls:

"He rang me up and he said, 'I've got a story for you, Rob'.

"I said, 'okay. Go on?'

"'Your mate Matthew'

"'Oh, yeah'.

"'You know what, I'm telling you now he's not put a penny into this football club'.

"I went, 'Really?'

"He said, 'not put a penny into Chelsea'.

"I said, 'What about the £5m into the player fund?'

"'That's a loan. He's not giving us that money. That's a loan'.

"I said, 'okay, what about the £5m for the North Stand?'

"'That's a loan.'

"'What about buying the freehold?'

"'It's a mortgage. He's not actually physically put a penny into Chelsea'.

"'Well, I can see it's a bit of a fatuous argument, but I can see where you coming from. It's quite a controversial thing to say. We're the *News of the World*. We like controversy.'

"So this is in the middle of Matthew Harding versus Ken Bates saga and Bates is coming out with a line to dig at his rival. It's a bonafide story.

"He said, 'are you going to run that story'.

"So I said, 'yeah okay.'

"He rang me back later and said, 'are you doing that story?'

"I said, 'Yeah, we're doing that story.'

"'Is it going to have your name on it?'

"'Yeah'

"'Brilliant!'

"The way Ken would look at it is like, I've got Rob Beasley, Matthew Harding's big mate, to write an anti-Matthew Harding story in the *News of the World*. Yet I'm a journalist. My job is to report the news, and if the Chelsea chairman is saying something, particularly in that scenario, I'm going to report it. That's my job. All friendships and that besides.

"I rang Matthew and said, 'Just to give you the heads up, I'm doing a story that you've not put a single penny into Chelsea, and this is Ken's argument.'

'Well, you know, I have, I'm not stupid,' Matthew said, 'I don't want to give £5m to Ken Bates. I want my money to go to Chelsea and everything I give to the club will be ring-fenced to make sure that only they can spend it, not Ken Bates the individual', and that's why he'd made it in unconditional deals. There were conditions attached that could only be actioned in certain ways to protect his money and to make sure that it went into the club that he loved rather than Ken Bates spending it on Chelsea Village, putting in a

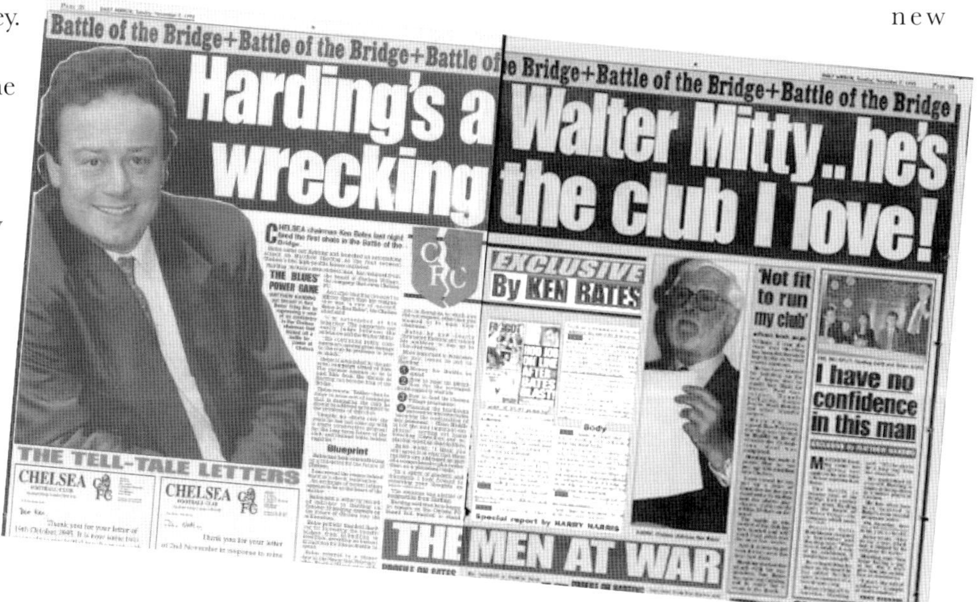

Battle of the Bridge+Battle of the Bridge+Battle of the Bridge+Battle of the Bridge+Battle of the Bridge

Harding's a Walter Mitty..he's wrecking the club I love!

EXCLUSIVE By KEN BATES

'Not fit to run my club'

I have no confidence in this man

THE TELL-TALE LETTERS

CHELSEA

THE MEN AT WAR

new

carpet in the hotel or getting a new plane for the Chelsea Travel Club or something."

Rob was unaware that Bates had been, so it was rumoured at the time, spreading gossip that Harding didn't actually, personally, have the funds. Rob was informed that I had known about this and argued, "Well, he left about £112 million didn't he? I think Matthew got a big tranche of shares, didn't he? Which related to about £24.5m that he put into Chelsea Football Club. So, the loans were then converted into shares. So, he had £24.5 million in Chelsea. And, I know when Abramovich bought the club, [his wife] Ruth kept all those shares and she got a massive payout. I think Vicki [his mistress] got some as well, but mainly Ruth. I've been to his house several times, down in Ditchlane, 220 acres. The house is fairly modest to be fair. A big house, but fairly modest. But the grounds, 220 acres and just off the South Downs. He was rich, but it's funny, the driver said he worked for all these years, he never even bought him a Christmas present. And he weren't like that. He was a generous man. But not in terms of 'oh Rob, thanks for all your help, here's a watch, it's Christmas'. He didn't see it like that. But NSPCC, the charity, dearest to his heart. Loads I mean, £1 million to the Labour Party, when they were doing that deal. He was talking with the Labour Party, and he'd said, 'I'll give you a bar', which is city slang for a million quid and it got back to Tony Blair. 'What do we want a public house for? What do we want a pub for. He's gonna give us a bar?' They didn't quite get the the city slang!"

Glenn Hoddle gave an in depth interview for the BT Sport documentary in which he was asked to recall the time he had heard about the listening devices planted in Matthew Harding's office. "Bloody hell. Well, that says it all really, doesn't it? I totally forgot about that, it was a long time ago. There was all sorts going on, I'm sure. But the main thing was 'get your head down Glenn and just concentrate on your job'. I had to deal with lots of other things when I came in. I could see that. If not, you just sit there and it all just stays the same and you probably get worse. You're very mediocre and I'd never stand for that as a player, or when I went to Swindon and I only had Swindon to fall back on and that wasn't me as a person, it was progression I wanted to see. And we got that very quickly. So it was now time to think, right where can we take this team? Where can we take this club? Chelsea was a massive club then, as it is now, but it had gone into the doldrums. We needed to repaint the house, we needed to do the house up. It was still a lovely house but it had been neglected for a long time."

Hoddle discussed his relationship with Ken Bates in graphic detail for the documentary: "Ken wasn't easy to work with, to be honest. He'd be like that now if I met him. He was always trying to be on the front foot, let's put it that way. Some would say a bit bullish, but I had a good relationship with him. He's come out and said things since about me, which I have to smile because that phone call meant a lot to me at that time, where he showed his real colours. That's when I needed a bit of a lift and a phone call like that came at the right time. So fair do's to him. But we had our battles. Ken didn't like spending money. And I was the first to go down and say, 'look, we need to spend some money', on the training ground, staying in better hotels, I knew I was making a bit of a ruffled bed for myself a little bit, but it had to be done for the club.

"Then Matthew came on board as well. I don't think Matthew would have got involved if I hadn't been manager at the time. He told me that many, many times. Matthew was totally different to Ken, they were totally different characters. You couldn't get two more different characters. I was younger, more Matthew's age, I got his sense of humour, he had an unbelievable sense of humour. He was a bit, some days, like being with Dudley Moore in *Ten*. He was that infectious, that funny and Ken thought I was sort of in his camp and I wasn't. I was between the two. They had their battles. But I think that's why Ken maybe says a few, detrimental things about me because he saw me as Matthew's guy and I was just Chelsea's guy. I was caught in the crossfire. But Matthew had this vision for Chelsea, he wanted to become chairman, and then he would have really gone for it. And I always felt there was the possibility of that happening. Ken supported me during that Christmas period when I was down, and that meant a lot. And I got on really well with Matthew, who was brilliant company to be around and just Chelsea through and through. He would even go in the pub across the road at Stamford Bridge with all his jeans and his scarf on and everything, and then come over as a director. Get in a toilet and change into his suit. He was just Chelsea through and through. He wanted to take it forward. There were other things that I wasn't privy to, financial things behind the scenes that were sort of happening and they were fighting. Politically, it was a strange time, a tough time. I tried to get my head down and get the players in that I wanted. And, you know, I knew there were constraints, financially. But I thought 'let's get on with my job'. I did a lot of groundwork, which changed a lot of the stuff. So now it was more focussing on getting to the top, this pyramid of getting more, better players. Can we play a different, a better system, that I wanted to always play..

"Colin Hutchinson and I sometimes had a little chat, we were buffers for each other because I think he felt in the middle of both of them as well. They had me as the manager, and Colin the financial man to put it all together. There was a bit of crossfire going on. Early on it was all lovely, the honeymoon period was great. You could sense there was stuff going on. I tried to keep out of the politics of it. Whether it was loans or where the money going into the club had come from, I wasn't privy to that. But it was what it was. It wasn't easy. But you know what? I was there to manage the team, I was there to get success on the pitch and I'd put the groundwork in for the first couple of seasons. So, now I'm going to concentrate on that and hopefully get the support that's needed. The crowds were coming back, Chelsea had a bit of pride about."

HH

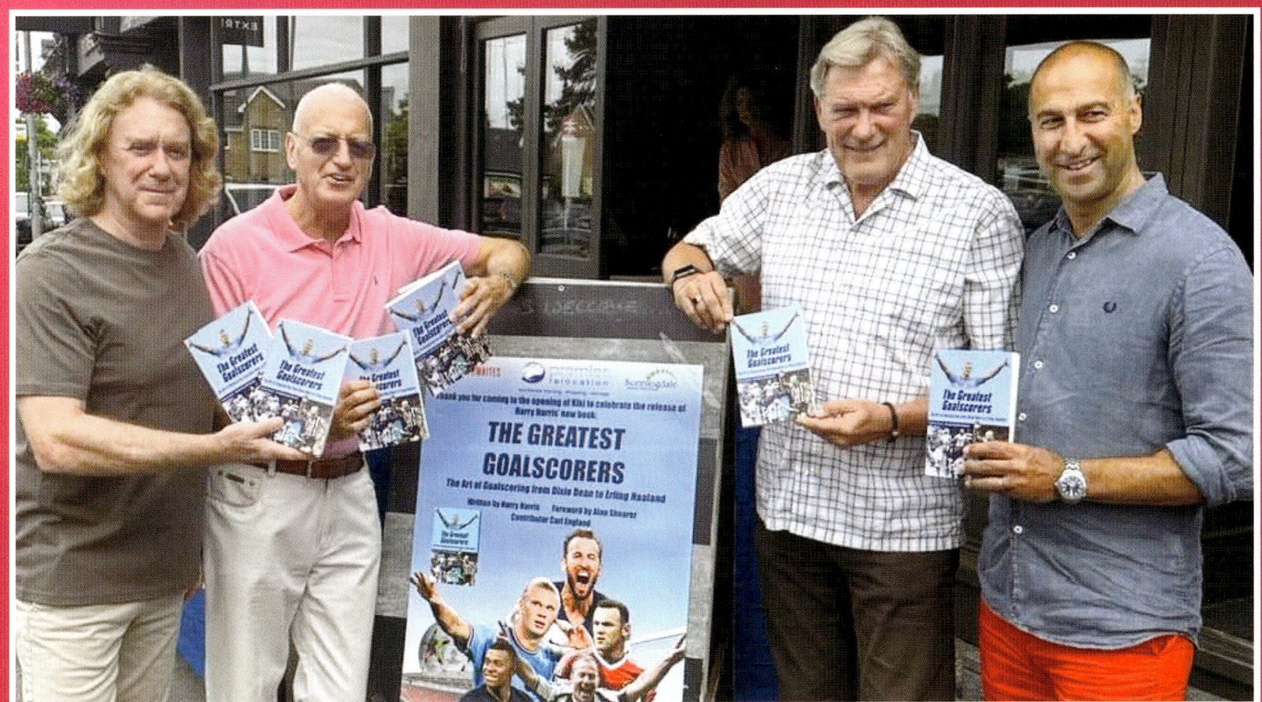

LW LAITHWAITES

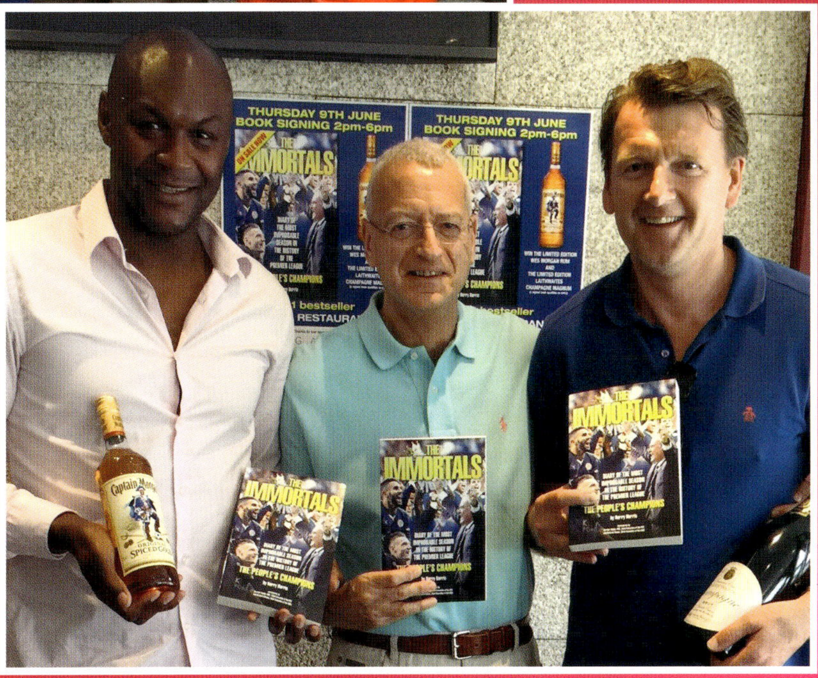

I would like to thank Laithwaites' Paul Dyer for supporting me at my recent book launches for 'The Greatest Goalscorers' at Kiki Bar in Sunningdale and 'Down Memory Lane' at their Virginia Water branch.

HARRY HARRIS

Ruud Gullit

"Sexy Football"

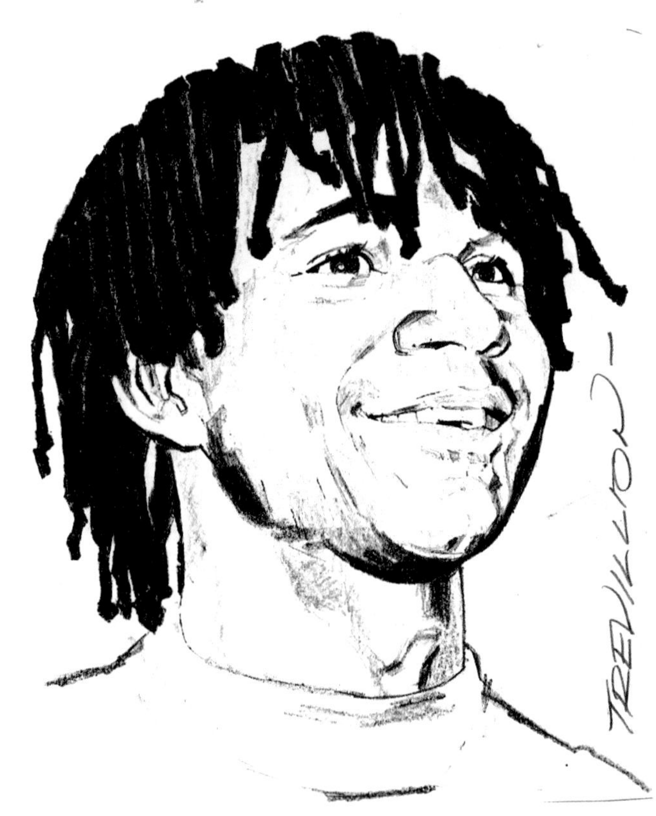

Ken Bates didn't actually want Ruud Gullit as his manager, as he was reluctant to go for another player-manager in the Glenn Hoddle mould, but fan power tipped the balance! Supporters didn't want George Graham, who was Bates' first choice, and they let the chairman know it.

Ruud's arrival in the Premier League in 1995 as one of the biggest stars to ever play in England caused a sensation, for his destination to be Chelsea was an even bigger shock. The attraction for Ruud was that Glenn Hoddle was the manager; the Dutchman loved the way Hoddle's Spurs team played the beautiful game.

Personally, it was an enormous thrill that a player of Gullit's calibre would be plying his skills in this country, albeit in the twilight of what had been an extraordinary career. As captain of a brilliant Netherlands team, he led his country to glory at Euro '88 and was twice awarded the prestigious World Footballer-of-the-Year trophy. He was the footballing genius on whom Silvio Berlusconi founded his footballing empire in Milan and the player Nelson Mandela had heard of in prison, to whom he granted a private audience. "He's as good a passer as we've had in this country for a long, long time," said Alan Hansen at the time of his arrival, "when Gullit hits a pass, it's like he's in love with the ball."

"He's a wonderful footballer," added Gary Lineker, who first saw him as a sweeper for PSV Eindhoven against Barcelona. "He was sublime. He got a standing ovation from the Nou Camp audience, 120,000. He's got tremendous presence, charisma and aura."

Such was the interest in Ruud that I decided to write the first of what turned out to be four books on him. The first was a biography and the story of his first season in English football, entitled *Portrait of a Genus*. I partnered with a long-standing friend Marcel van Der Krann who had an intimate knowledge of Ruud's rise through Dutch football. Having written books for virtually all the top publishing houses, and with my high profile as chief football writer for the *Mirror* and that of my subject I assumed that would be sufficient to guarantee a commission - but strangely not this time. The book was widely rejected by the major publishers with only Harper Collins, under their CollinsWillow imprint, willing to take it on. I dedicated the book to my wife Linda "a true Chelsea fan", and in the acknowledgements gave special praise to Editorial Director Michael Doggart, the only person I found willing to take on this project.

I asked one commissioning editor why they were reluctant to publish the story of one of football's all-time great's first season in England and his answer brought a look of incredulity to my face. He said it was because publishers generally felt that books about black people didn't particularly sell well, if at all! For someone who had campaigned on behalf of black players, earning a Race In The Media award, this was appalling, but a sign of the times when racism, notably in football, still had a vile stranglehold. He had no idea of my publishing experience, and I didn't share it with him; as it was such a disrespectful episode.

It was a joy to watch Ruud at first-hand, exhibiting the skills I had seen in many European tournaments and international competitions, but now on a week-by-week basis, within walking distance of my home in Elm Park Gardens not far from the Bridge. Ruud explained his motivation for coming to England and particularly Chelsea. "My decision to join Chelsea was mainly because of Glenn," Ruud told me, "I wanted to move away from Italy and everyone was saying I was crazy to go to Chelsea, but for me it was the right moment to do something different and go to the Premier League. It was the right time for me to come. Living in London was fantastic and I had a manager in Glenn who understood the type of football I was playing. He was trying to get that across to the team and obviously Mark Hughes came just after me as well, so it was a really fun time. I had one of the best periods of my career at Chelsea, I really enjoyed it."

Gullit's class was in evidence immediately, producing a superb individual display on his debut, a goalless home draw against Everton on the opening day of the 1995/96 campaign, which I was privileged to witness from the press box. He scored his first in his sixth game: a stunning right-footed volley in a 3-0 win over Southampton. Initially, Hoddle deployed Gullit in a sweeper role, but due to the nature of English football, he was soon pushed further forward, a position from which he scored a wonderful solo goal against Manchester City. "When I came here I understood what Glenn wanted to do, which was play the European way. I remember at the start of my Chelsea career he played me as a sweeper, and long balls kept coming over for the opposition strikers. I brought the ball down on my chest and played it to one of the other defenders, and they were saying, 'What are you doing?' That was when Glenn said to me, 'Ruud, can you do me a favour and play in midfield please?' He said he knew what I was trying to do, but you couldn't play that way over here at that time. So I said to him that was fine, I'd play in midfield."

Hoddle's ability as a player was held in the highest regard by Gullit. "Glenn was a fantastic player. We [the Dutch] were the nation who loved him while he was playing, in England he wasn't really appreciated. It must have been very frustrating for him to be the best player, and not be recognised as the best player. But when he went abroad, to Monaco, that's what happened and he was appreciated more."

Within a year Ruud had become team manager. Yet when Hoddle's departure to become England boss was confirmed before the final home match of the 1995/96 season, the newspapers suggested Bates's favoured successor was the recently departed Arsenal boss, George Graham. In response, entire stands at the Bridge chanted at length as to where the chairman might stick Graham, followed by chants for Gullit. The fans had made their point and Bates listened, promoting Gullit to player-manager on 10 May 1996.

When Matthew Harding died midway through the following season, Gullit spoke eloquently about using the tragedy as an inspiration to reach the FA Cup final and win it 'for Matthew.' He also had the vision to bring the best out of new signing Gianfranco Zola and sure enough the Blues beat Middlesbrough 2-0 at Wembley in 1997 to land the club's first major success in 26 years in Ruud's first season in management. The club also finished a creditable sixth in the Premiership. Gullit made history as the first overseas, and first black, manager to lift a trophy in English football. By this time Chelsea were fashionable for the first time since the days of the 'King's Road swingers' of Osgood, Hudson, and Cooke. Gullit did more than anyone to help dispel the image of the National Front which used to be synonymous with the club and racist elements within the fan base. Gullit said: "I get a lot of satisfaction when I hear people behind me screaming their delight for this 'sexy football'." – a term he had initially coined as a TV pundit covering Euro '96.

On the day after that Wembley triumph, Ken Bates and his wife Susannah invited Linda and I to celebrate Di Matteo's stunning goal and Ruud's historic triumph at the Town Hall where the Chelsea players and back room staff were invited to end the traditional Sunday open-top bus ride through the jammed streets of Chelsea and Fulham. Ken was never one for these type of formal occasions, especially when it was the players who, quite properly, were in the limelight. So we escaped the Town Hall hysteria through a side exit and strolled down the Fulham Road for about a quarter of a mile to Leonardo's, a long established old-fashioned Italian restaurant that had recently been refurbished and modernised; with so many of them in West London, you can see why this part of the world was a magnet for so many Italian managers and players!

However, this didn't turn out to be a quiet Sunday lunch, anything but… Ken had faced a barrage of complaints about the open-top bus route because fans had lined the Fulham Road, but the bus didn't go past there. The route had been advertised, but not everyone had spotted the diversion, and lthough the vast majority of fans were in good humour, the mood was naturally euphoric after waiting so long for silverware, so when Ken entered Leonardo's he was afforded a standing ovation. We hadn't been there long before a few of the diners came over to congratulate him and a bottle of champagne soon materialised on our table courtesy of a nearby table. It was a long and leisurely lunch until one fan spotted Ken through the window and came to the door to shout obscenities at him. Ken might have laughed them off but not when it happened in front of Susannah. He took great exception to it, and confronted the guy who poured beer over the chairman's head. Ken then set off in pursuit as the guy ran off, with little to no chance of catching him. More likely to give himself a heart attack by trying to run too fast! Then about 20 loyal fans, clearly showing their allegiance to the chairman, told Bates to leave it to them, and they set off in pursuit of the culprit. I wouldn't like to think what that mob did to him when they caught up with him. Ken might not have been very popular with large sectors of the media, but most Chelsea fans loved him for what he did for their club.

As for Ruud, the honeymoon didn't last long. Tensions soon emerged in the autumn of 1997 caused by Gullit's disdain for the usual board/manager protocols. The official line was that negotiations over a new contract to remove him from the players list to be solely "manager" had stalled. Yet I knew that behind the scenes, unknown to Gullit, Bates felt that his manager had disrespected him over a social invitation and the rift deepened. Infamously, there was a dispute over whether the salary figure was 'gross' or 'netto', as Gullit would call it, but as I was in the centre of it all, knowing Bates and Gullit so well, I would conclude this was more than about just the money, although that was a big hurdle in itself, but it was also a personal thing important to Bates in terms of 'respect'.

On 12 February 1998, with the Blues second in the league,

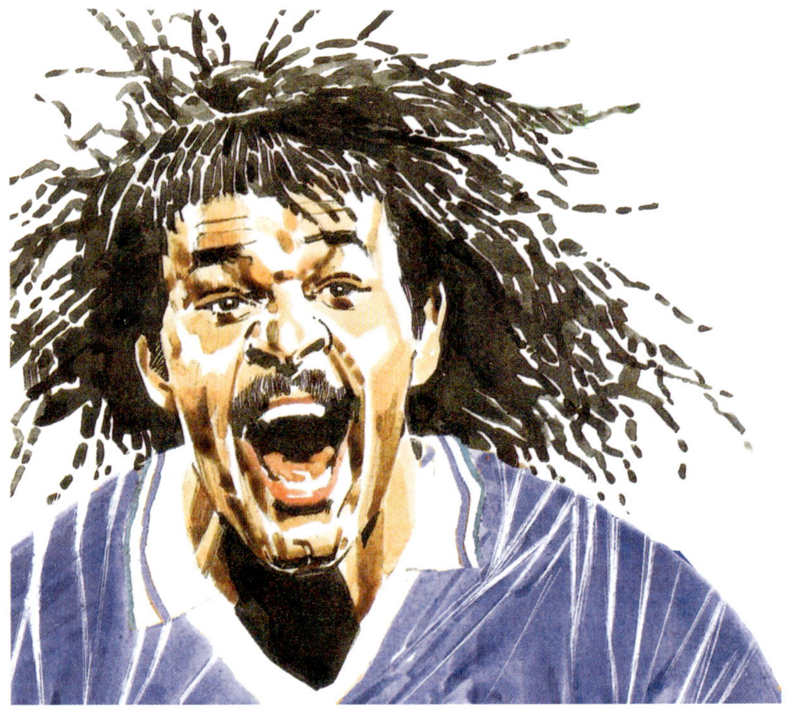

and into the quarter-finals of two cup competitions, Gullit was sacked and instantly replaced by Gianluca Vialli, whom Gullit had brought to the club from Italy as another big name surprise arrival. At a news conference in London Gullit said he'd been ready to sign a new contract and hadn't made excessive demands, and that he didn't really know the reasons for his sacking and that he was shocked that his 21-month reign as manager had come to such an abrupt end just before the second leg of a cup tie with Arsenal.

Bates disputed Gullit's explanation and said at a hastily arranged press conference at Stamford Bridge: "We were unable to match his demands." He claimed he had been locked in negotiations over a new contract with managing director, Colin Hutchinson, since October. Gullit denied that he had been involved in talks prior to a meeting just before his surprise sacking."I was astounded to find out from the media that I have been replaced as Chelsea coach by Gianluca Vialli. I had been to only one meeting in the last six months to discuss the future. This meeting took place on 5 February when Hutchinson and myself talked very amicably about a new two-year extension to my contract. At no time during my discussion was there any doubt in my mind that I would re-sign. In fact, I specifically told anyone who asked that I would sign a new deal after more talks - there were no more talks. I am committed to Chelsea, and in particular to the fans, whose dreams I have tried so hard to fulfil. It is incorrect for Colin Hutchinson to state that Chelsea Football Club tried to negotiate with me for three months - there were no negotiations."

In a statement Hutchinson said: "Uncertainty about Ruud Gullit's future at Chelsea has dragged on for several months. We have been attempting to get Ruud to commit to an extension to his contract beyond his present deal, which expires on 30 June 1998, since last October. The delay has become potentially damaging. Backroom staff with mortgages to pay couldn't be sure they would be in a job after the season ends. Because of Ruud's non-commitment we took the unusual step of guaranteeing first-team management staff a further one year employment should Ruud leave and his successor not require their services. For the good of the club and planning for next season the situation has had to be resolved.

"Ruud and I met last Thursday. During a 40-minute meeting it was established Ruud was prepared to extend by two years. For our part, we indicated that we wished the new contract could be as a manager only. We believed this would allow Ruud more time to concentrate on the team and enable him to get involved in new areas like going out to watch potential players, assess up-coming opposition and spend more time working on technique and skills with individual players after the normal training sessions. We have appreciated that Ruud has found it increasingly difficult combining playing and managing, despite us easing his workload. Unfortunately while we were prepared to give Ruud a contract which we believe would have made him the best-paid manager in the Premiership, we were not able to meet what he wanted and expected. We simply could not afford what he was asking. Naturally this was disappointing. Ruud was told at the end of the meeting that unfortunately the gap was too wide to allow further meaningful negotiations and that we would need to actively pursue lining up a replacement."

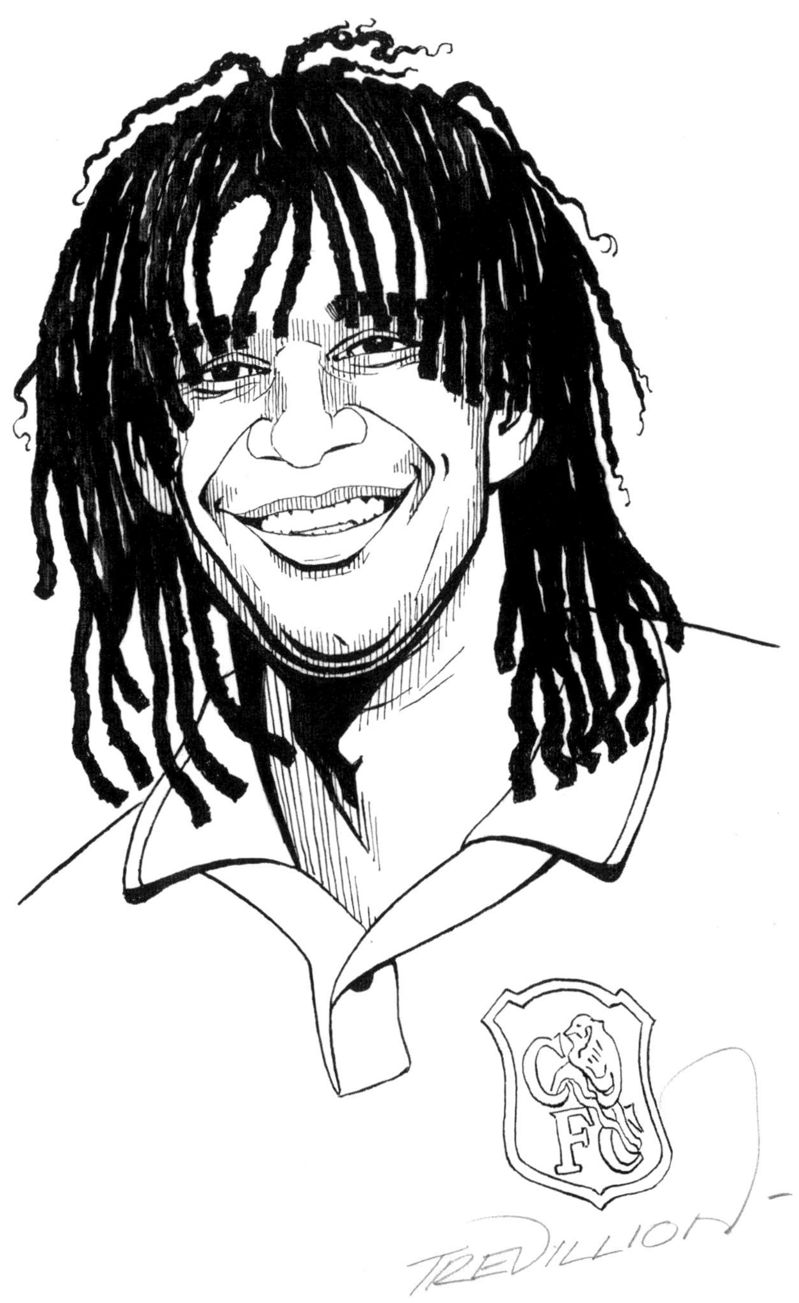

It later emerged that Gianluca Vialli had been approached on Monday and offered the job on Wednesday evening. According to Hutchison, Gullit did not hang around to hear the bad news. "I had a meeting with Ruud at lunchtime today," Hutchinson said. "But unfortunately it did not get as far as telling him that he was being replaced because he decided to call an abrupt end to the meeting."

Bates said at the time: "I'm sorry that it's come to this but we had this problem two years ago when we had another manager [Glenn Hoddle] who wouldn't make his mind up until April and as we were already planning for next season it was important to ensure a smooth continuity. There may be supporters who are sad that he is leaving and there may be others who take a contrary view, but I am delighted to pay tribute to him. He took us on to a new plane as far as football was concerned. He helped make Chelsea one of the most talked about clubs in the world and he won us the FA Cup in his first season and will always be remembered for that. I'm sad he's leaving but one has to face up to facts."

Gullit denied money was at the root of his departure, insisting at the time,"They are using that as a stick to hit me with. I want to know the real reason." Colin Hutchinson described Gullit as "crafty" by saying he wanted £2m-a-year to stay, and that what he actually wanted was £3.3m a year "netto". Hutchinson added that had Gullit been prepared to negotiate a new contract earlier he would still be their manager. Gullit admitted that he had asked for a salary of £2m-a-year, just as he had when approached he joined the club as a player, but had expected to agree a lesser figure after negotiation as had happened in 1995. However, a few hours later Hutchinson took issue with some of Gullit's claims."He has said in the press conference today, and he said to me yesterday, `You didn't make an offer.' I disagree with that and I repeated the offer to him yesterday in our meeting, just before it was aborted. I said to him, `Well Ruud, if you misunderstood, the figure was £1m per year gross. Would you have accepted that?' And he flatly said, 'No'. Ruud, who is a master of the media, very craftily said today that he asked for £2m. He did ask for £2m and I immediately responded and said, `Gross?' And he said, `No, netto. I always talk netto. £2m netto is a far bigger commitment to the club than £2m gross. For Ruud to receive £2m-a-year in his hand means that the club has got to pay tax on it. As far as we're concerned he was asking for £3,220,000 per year. But it gets worse than that because the club has to pay earnings related contributions on that. With his basic salary, and the rest, we were looking at a commitment of £3,365,000-a-year to keep Ruud and quite honestly we couldn't afford it. I explained to him that the gap was too wide for further meaningful negotiations and said that because of the time-scale we would have to start looking at alternatives."

Gullit admitted that when Hutchinson said that the club would look for a new manager he thought they were "bluffing". After Vialli's appointment was announced, Gullit sought a meeting with Bates, which was granted at 6.30pm, three hours later. After 20 minutes during which Bates, according to Gullit, passed responsibility to Hutchinson who had himself passed the buck to "the board", Bates "handed me a letter saying I am sacked". Gullit also said his relationship with Bates was restricted to match days, and that he had discovered his fate from Teletext. Instead he was told, on Thursday, that the board had decided to find another manager. Within hours he discovered that was Vialli who, he claimed, had met with Rangers' Brian Laudrup, a Chelsea transfer target, at a secret meeting on Wednesday also attended by Hutchinson and Gianfranco Zola. Laudrup, he said, had been told Gullit was too busy to attend."

At the point of his axing I had just completed writing *Ruud Gullit: My Autobiography*. We had become close in a professional capacity, I was a journalist he seemed to trust and respect, and if he read my dispatches from the Bridge, he would have known my respect and admiration for him. His life story came about when I told him how much I wanted to write his biography and that it had inspired publishers to bid due to the fact that he had become not just a hugely successful manager but also a fashion icon bringing out his own clothing brand at a lunch in central London which I attended along with my journalist partner, Linda, who wrote an article on the topic for the *Sunday People* where she was assistant editor. Gullit was big box office by this time, in huge demand for his time, despite that, he always found time for his beloved golf! Yet, he didn't seem too keen to spend his valuable time engaged in writing his life story despite fabulous offers from publishers. However I challenged Ruud saying,"You will need only four or at the most five, one-hour sessions with me and the book will be

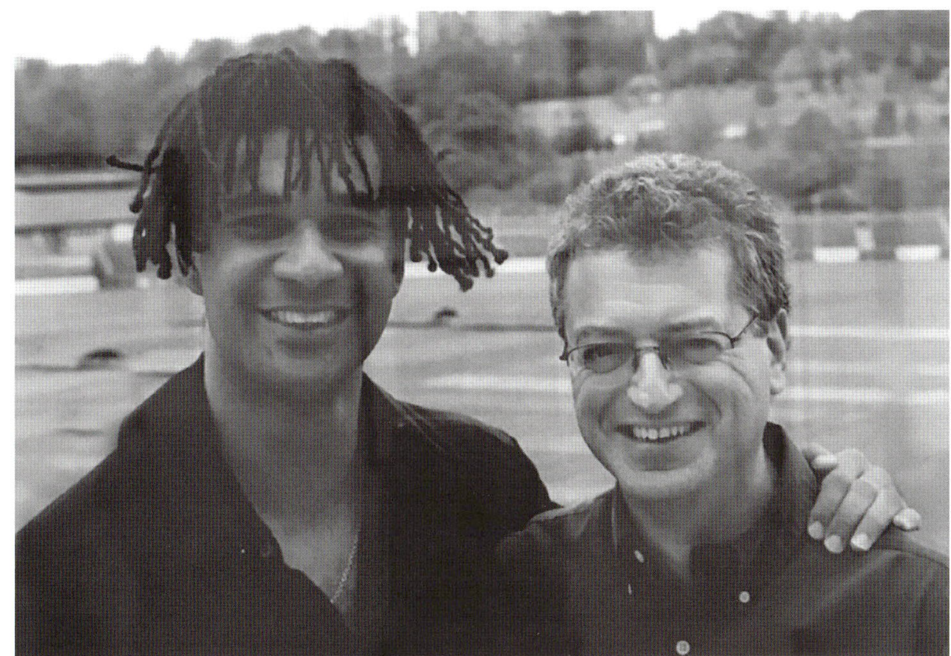

written". I'm not sure he was convinced. but reluctantly he agreed. The flat Linda and I shared just off the King's Road was the venue for Ruud's one-hour sessions. He'd leave the Bridge, and walk the short distance to Elm Park Gardens. He'd spread out his giant frame on our extra large green striped sofa and we would chat and I'd take notes, and we'd chat, and chat and chat... for hours. Way past the one hour sessions I told him it would need. But Ruud enjoyed the conversations and stayed on. In fact, we usually had to remind Ruud it was getting very late, and he might be thinking of a night cap before departing! When he made his way out of the building, we'd watch him depart from the balcony. You could tell that people who spotted him in the street would do a double take, you couldn't mistake Ruud Gullit with those dreadlocks and then see that 'No, it can't be' expression on people's faces!

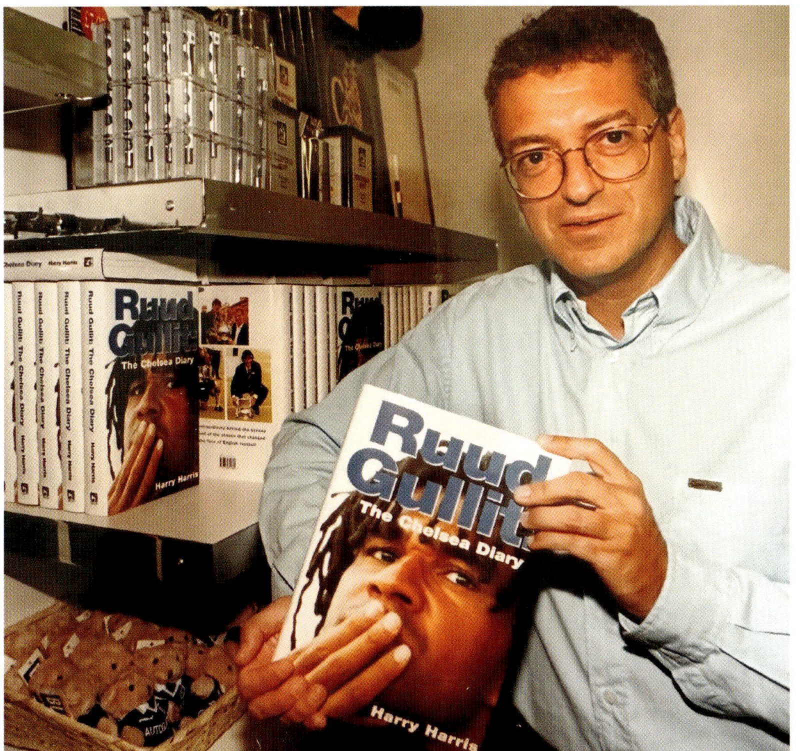

In *Gullit* he writes about the challenges of the second season that went with the high expectation and excitement. "In my first season nobody knew how far we could go and everyone was so grateful at winning the FA Cup, but I always knew the second year would be more testing, there'd be more pressure and so many people would think they knew better, because success changes a lot of people." He told me that he felt the team he'd left behind were capable of winning the title. They didn't. Would they have done had he stayed?

Gullit resumed management, albeit briefly at Newcastle, Feyenoord and LA Galaxy, before embarking on a successful TV career. While he was manager in the north-east I wrote my third book about him *Newcastle Out of Toon* when he took the team to the FA Cup Final. I travelled up to the club's training headquarters to interview him about the Final. I also broke the story in the *Mirror* how he planned to axe Alan Shearer, but of course that decision backfired, and when it came to who would go first, Shearer or Gullit, inevitably it was the manager! Today, Ruud maintains the Chelsea years were "the only time I really had fun" in football.

Ed de Goey

Norwegian Frode Grodas was brought in initially on loan to cover for an injury to Dmitri Kharine and the loss of form of Kevin Hitchcock, and ended up playing in the 1997 FA Cup Final, yet Ruud Gullit returned to his former club, Feyenoord, to sign Dutch international goalkeeper Ed De Goey for £2.25m in July 1997 making him the most expensive keeper in England at that time having won five major honours in Holland and starring in the 1994 World Cup. Crucially for the 'new' Chelsea, Ed had plenty of experience on the European club stage. He joined shortly after the conclusion of a 1996/97 season which had seen no fewer than five keepers appear at one time or another. "It was in the summer of 1997 and the national team had a game in South Africa," Ed recalls, "on the way back I spoke to Ruud Gullit, who was there with us, and he was looking for a new goalkeeper. He asked me if I was interested; my response was that I was very interested! A couple of days later I had signed my contract. And that was it. Ruud Gullit was a close friend. When I first joined Chelsea, everything was new for me so he really helped me a lot. Dennis Wise was great with me, too, but then again, he was great for everybody. Then there was Tore Andre Flo and Gus Poyet, who were living near me so it was easier to mix with them." It was the perfect time to join the club which had finally won a major trophy for the first time in 26 years, having just lifted the FA Cup. "That is correct," Ed says, "when I joined they had just won the FA Cup so it was certainly very interesting times for the club. Chelsea was a growing team with big stars joining them, trying to achieve a lot. If you see how far they are now, it has become a huge club so it was nice to be part of that in the early years."

Ed made his debut at Wembley in the Charity Shield, where the Blues lost on penalties to Manchester United, and suffered a torrid league bow at the hands of Dion Dublin as the Coventry No. 9 scored three times as the Blues lost by the odd goal in five at Highfield Road which was followed by a home debut where he gifted a goal to Southampton's Kevin Davies. Yet after this traumatic start Ed soon settled into the job and by the end of his first season he was celebrating two major cup victories. After a shaky start in which he seemed unsure of the physical nature in England, the Dutch stopper had been outstanding, making brilliant saves at crucial times in the League Cup and Cup Winners' Cup, both of which were lifted that season. His stunning save in the last minute of the semi-final against Vicenza helped Chelsea reach the final in Stockholm.

Ed won a third major trophy at Chelsea, the FA Cup, in 1999/2000, a season in which he broke the club records for most appearances (59) and clean sheets (27), although both of these achievements have since been surpassed. "That's why I signed for Chelsea – I wanted to win trophies," he says, "I knew it was a big club with huge potential and we showed that in the European run." Of his superb save against Vicenza, Ed recalls, "I remember it well! I dived to my left and flicked the ball away from two onrushing strikers. It was a vital save and because of that we were able to finish the job and go on to the final. And we all know what happened then…" The star strikers may have made the headline but Ed was a crucial obstacle in stopping them, but he could only admire Ginafranco Zola's coup de grace in the final "That's what football is all about – scoring goals and winning trophies. And, to be fair, it was something special by Gianfranco. It was my first time in a final like that and we all prepared very well for the game. They obviously did as well, because it stayed 0-0 for a long time until Franco came on…"

Unfortunately the following season injury problems saw him lose his place to Carlo Cudicini and over the next three years Ed made just 25 appearances before joining Stoke City. In all, he had kept 72 clean sheets in 179 games. Although he spent his last three years at Stamford Bridge on the periphery, he had been a reliable regular between 1997 and 2000, when the club won the FA Cup, League Cup, Cup Winners' Cup, Super Cup and Charity Shield, having won nothing at all for 26 years!

In one of the most bizarre seasons in the club's history, Chelsea, second in the league at Christmas and through to the semi-final and quarter-final of the Coca-Cola and European Cup Winners' Cups, sacked manager Gullit and replaced him with Gianluca Vialli. De Goey had kept goal for the first 25 matches of the league campaign but was suddenly replaced by Kharine for all but three of the remaining matches as Vialli rotated his keepers, preferring to use the Dutchman only in important cup ties. The Blues clinched fourth spot in the Premiership, Ed was in goal as Chelsea emerged victorious in both cup competitions. The signings of Albert Ferrer and Marcel Desailly in the summer of 1998 strengthened the defence significantly and the Londoners emerged as genuine title contenders, eventually finishing third. They were beaten just three times in the league that year, and Ed broke Peter Bonetti's record of top-flight clean sheets in one season with an impressive total of 14.

Chelsea's third place finish in 1998/99 resulted in Champions League, where De Goey performed well as the Blues reached the quarter-final losing to Barcelona. Ed played in all of Chelsea's matches, including two 3-1 victories against his old club, Feyenoord. That Champions League campaign was special for Ed. "I'd played in it with Feyenoord in the nineties, but that season with Chelsea was something special. It was a great achievement for us in the club's first year in the competition and it was a much better experience for me. The trip to the San Siro to play against AC Milan was very special and there was something very unique that happened in that game. I have never seen so many people standing up and singing for an opposition player – and that was Marcel Desailly. There was everyone in the stadium clapping for him and shouting his name. What an incredible achievement for any player and it must have felt amazing for him." That also happened to Ed when he went back to his old club, "I did, but nothing like what Marcel got from the Milan fans, to be fair! I had a great reaction from the Feyenoord fans and that was very special. The supporters know exactly what you have done for a club and it's really nice when they show you their gratitude for that."

Consolation for the devastating defeat at Barcelona came by way of two trips to Wembley, the first for an FA Cup semi-final where De Goey starred as the Blues clinched a fortunate 2-1 victory over Newcastle, the other was the final itself, a 1-0 victory over Aston Villa. The Dutchman was the club's top appearance maker, having featured in all but two of the club's

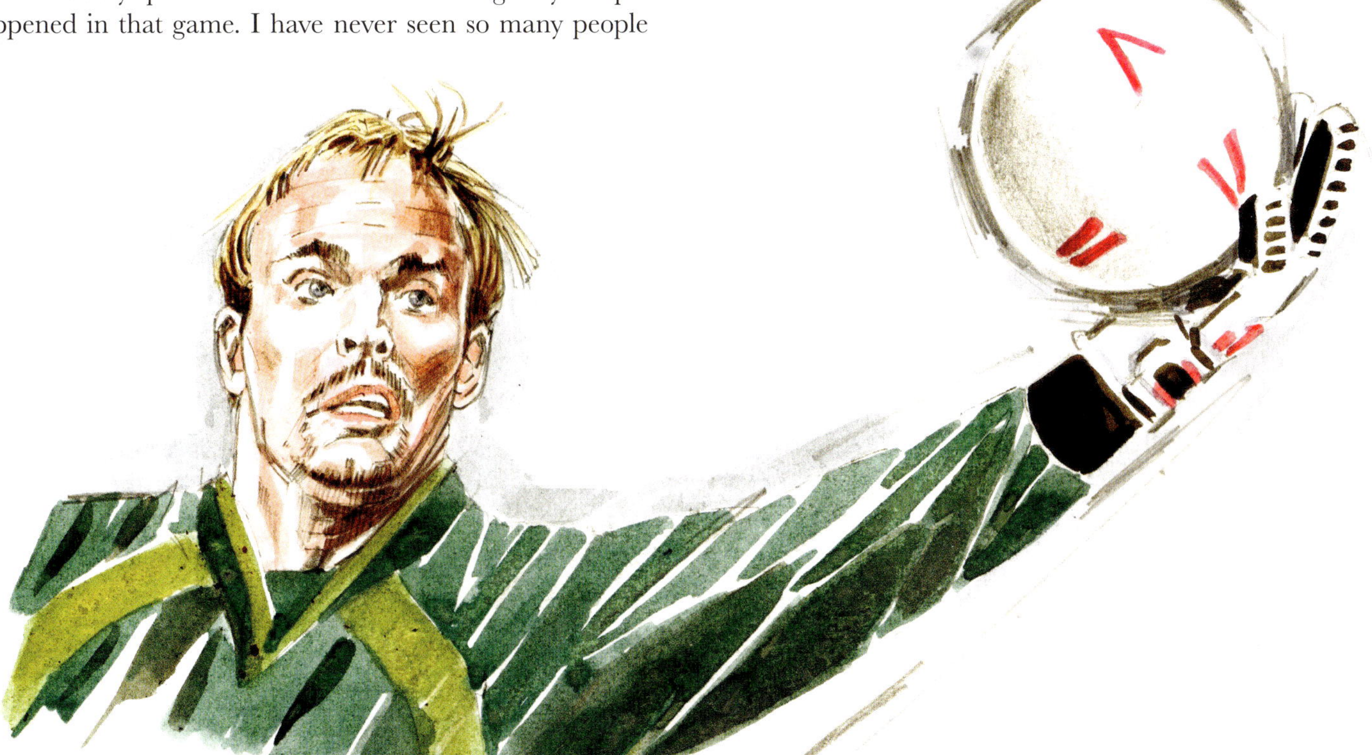

61 matches in all competitions. But Ed was dropped after just two matches of the 2000/01 season and although he returned in the autumn, he suffered a traumatic time during the Christmas period, culminating in a disastrous performance in a 2-2 draw at Ipswich on Boxing Day, his last of the season and, although he was selected for the beginning of the following campaign, an injury in October opened the way for Carlo Cudicini. De Goey was peripheral throughout 2002/03, but was given two opportunities over Christmas when Cudicini was injured and kept a clean sheet in a draw with Southampton before conceding a goal to the youngest ever Premiership scorer, James Milner, as the Blues were beaten 2-0 at Leeds.

His final appearance for the club came in controversial circumstances a week later. When Cudicini was red-carded by referee Mark Halsey during an FA Cup third-round clash with Middlesbrough after an elbow from Dean Windass, Ed came off the bench. With the crowd howling at the injustice and Cudicini's team-mates seeking revenge, De Goey performed impeccably, one save from Geremi was outstanding, as Chelsea held on for a 1-0 win. Cudicini's red card was later rescinded, had he been suspended, Ed would have been due to keep goal against Manchester United at Old Trafford. As it was, he remained on the sidelines for the remainder of the season. His contract expired in May 2003 and Ed was released and signed for Stoke City. He had no idea he wouldn't be retained, "No, I didn't know at all. The strange thing was, in a meeting with Ranieri he told me I was getting older and he wanted more young keepers. But then straight after my meeting he called the young goalkeeper [Rhys Evans], who played for England Under-21s too, and told him to leave as well! If you go for the youth, why let him go? I had mixed feelings about leaving. But I couldn't do anything about it, he was the manager and what he decided goes." Marco Ambrosio was signed as back-up keeper that summer instead. "I was at Stoke City by then," Ed added, "I'll never understand the reasons, but it's just part of football. One moment you're a great player doing well for a club and then the next minute the manager says, 'That's it, time to go' and there's nothing you can do about it. But I loved my time at Chelsea and I still follow the club as much as I can."

A clean sheet ratio of 40 per cent was far superior to any other Blues keeper who had played before him and in 1999/00 he set club records for most appearances and clean sheets in a season, although both were subsequently surpassed by Cech. He is also the joint tallest player in Chelsea history at 6ft 6in! He became a goalkeeper coach after finally hanging up his gloves. Eddie Niedzwiecki was the coach at that time. "He was not only a fantastic coach, he was a very nice person. I know how much the fans loved him for his performances at Chelsea. He was a great goalkeeper and a very warm person, so it's easy to see why he is a legend with the fans. Kevin Hitchcock was a very close friend and we spent a lot of time together. We had a smashing relationship – he helped me a lot, especially in the beginning, and we spent a lot of time together." Mostly playing golf? "Not really – he was too good! We spent some time on there, but that was mostly when we had a training camp with Chelsea and had some free time. Otherwise he was out on the course with Gianfranco, who was maybe in the same league as him. I was a couple of leagues below." Mark Bosnich and Carlo were his big rivals for the No 1 spot. "You had one who was a No.1 almost everywhere he went, while the latter was the son of one of Italy's most famous goalkeepers. With Carlo I was quite close, a bit similar to how I was with Hitchy. In the beginning I was the No.1 and then later on he was, but it didn't change anything between us; I think we just wanted to help each other as much as possible. With Mark Bosnich it was a little different. He wanted to be the best goalkeeper but it doesn't always work like that. On the pitch he was a good person to work with, but off it he was a lone guy. That's just how he was."

Ed found it tough losing his place, "That's just part of life as a footballer. I wasn't very happy with what the coaches told me as to why Carlo took my place – that's the only bit I didn't agree with, but it was the decision of Claudio Ranieri. And after that, Carlo proved he was a very talented goalkeeper." Then Carlo lost his place to Cech and no doubt learned from Ed how to take it professionally. "Although it is not easy to be No 2 and sitting on the bench, respect wise it is important that nothing changes between the players. I was always taught that if I was the second-choice keeper, my job was to make sure the No 1 was playing as well as possible – so I had to do everything in my power to make sure I was putting the right kind of pressure on him. That's what I tried to do."

Luca Vialli

Gianluca Vialli joined Chelsea as a player in 1996 on a free transfer. He had made 59 appearances for Italy, scoring 16 times, and won Serie A and the Champions League with Juventus before his spell at the Bridge brought him 40 goals in 78 games in all competitions. It was yet another major coup to snap up former world record signing Vialli on a free, and he was joined by fellow Italy internationals Gianfranco Zola and Roberto Di Matteo who arrived from Parma and Lazio respectively. The English press were quick to label it the 'Italian Invasion', whilst France international Frank Leboeuf joined from Strasbourg as Gullit was developing his dream team.

Vialli was just three games into his new life with Chelsea when he got off the mark, scoring in a 2-0 victory over Coventry alongside fellow summer signing Leboeuf. A goal in the next game followed – a thrilling 3-3 draw against Arsenal at Highbury. The pace of the Premier League was electric, but Vialli was equal to it. After a great start to the season the Blues' form tailed off, and when Matthew Harding was killed in a helicopter crash, the whole club was shaken and Chelsea went five league games without a win in November and December. Chelsea re-found their form for much of the second half of the season but, after five straight losses in March and April, could only finish sixth - Vialli, with nine goals was top scorer. However the season will be remembered for the FA Cup, with Vialli scoring a brace in a fantastic 4-2 victory over Liverpool in the fourth round at Stamford Bridge, before the Blues subsequently overcame Leicester, Portsmouth and Wimbledon to set up a final against fellow big spenders Middlesbrough. The Teesiders had already been relegated from the Premier League that season under player-manager Bryan Robson but the team had an Italian superstar of their own in Fabrizio Ravanelli and the media naturally focused on the Italian strikers. As it turned out Italian midfielder Roberto Di Matteo scored in less than a minute before Eddie Newton made it safe late on. Just like when Sampdoria won Serie A, Vialli had arrived at Stamford Bridge for the greatest moment in Chelsea's recent history.

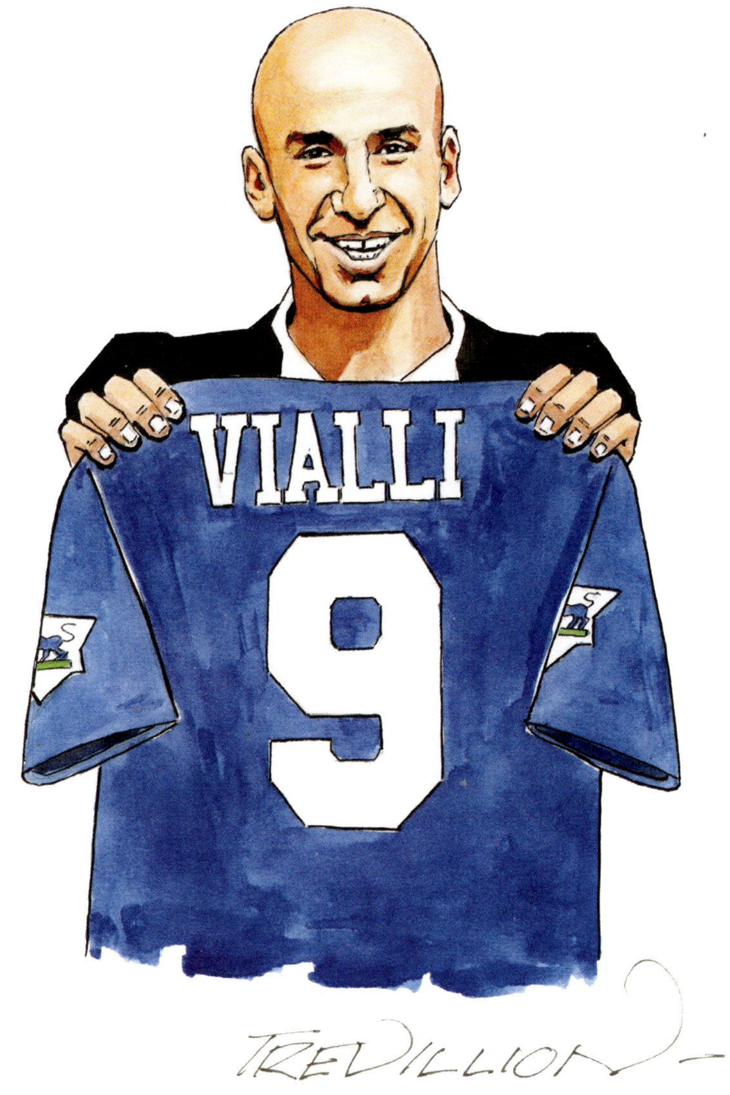

The next season, 1997/98, would change Vialli's life. After an opening day defeat to Coventry, courtesy of a hat-trick from Dion Dublin, the Premier League got to see Vialli at his absolute best in Chelsea's second game of the season when he collected four goals against Barnsley, with Chelsea winning 6-0. After a fantastic first half of the season, four consecutive league defeats in February, Gullit was fired and Vialli was appointed player-manager after only 18 months in English football. Gullit did not blame Vialli, a player he personally helped attract to the club in the first place, but there were rumblings that the Italian striker had been one of those players dissatisfied in the days prior to the Dutchman's shock departure. Vialli had frequently been sidelined under Gullit – Dennis Wise had once revealed a vest to the bench saying 'Cheer up Luca, we love you'.

When Luca took the reins at Stamford Bridge, a few days before the second leg of a League Cup semi-final at home to Arsenal, the Italian selected himself and toasted the occasion with pre-match champagne before helping his team to a 3-1 win. Ken Bates recalls how Vialli started in style, and with a record haul of trophies he continued the rapid rise of the West London club and took it onto a global scale."We'd just lost 2-1 in the first leg of the League Cup semi-final to Arsenal. Luca's first game was the second leg. He sat all the players down in the dressing-room and gave them all a glass of champagne. He made a little speech, didn't say anything derogatory about Gullit, just simply said, 'Today is the end and the start of a new era and we are all together Let's drink our glass of champagne and toast to our future' and we won the second leg 3-1. From there we won the League Cup, won the UEFA Cup Winners' Cup then came here to Monaco for the Super Cup beating Real Madrid 1-0. Last but not least we received separate letters from the President and chief executive of UEFA, offering us congratulations and saying 'welcome to the European elite.'"

After all the turmoil of Gullit's final days, Chelsea had ended the season with two trophies and nobody questioned Vialli's managerial credentials any longer. At the beginning of the following season things got even better for Chelsea... the UEFA Super Cup against Champions League winners Real Madrid, the overwhelming favourites... Vialli got it right tactically again as Chelsea came away with a clean sheet and a 1-0 win. Chelsea had their hands on another European trophy.

The new manager recalled the reasons why he decided to give his players the bubbly, because he told them, his team were "starting on a new adventure" and it was cause for celebration. "You should mark the occasion with a toast and some champagne," he said afterwards. "We wished each other all the best and said we must enjoy ourselves. Sometimes in modern football, it is hard to enjoy yourself."

Results and performances lifted with Vialli's promotion. Chelsea won six of their remaining ten games in the league, with Vialli scoring a brace against Crystal Palace and goals against Tottenham and Bolton. After winning the League Cup at the end of March, beating Middlesbrough just as they had previously to lift the FA Cup, Chelsea found themselves in the final of the Cup Winners' Cup having defeated Slovan Bratislava, Tromsø, Real Betis and Vicenza to reach the showpiece event. The Blues faced the far more difficult task of Bundesliga side VfB Stuttgart, managed by future Germany manager Joachim Löw, but Chelsea completely dominated them, with Zola's winning goal coming in the 71st minute. Vialli produced a tactical masterclass against a manager who would go on to win the World Cup. After all the turmoil of Gullit's final days, Chelsea had ended the season with two trophies and nobody questioned Vialli's managerial credentials any longer. At the beginning of the following season things got even better for Chelsea, winning the 1997/98 Cup Winners' Cup meant Chelsea were to compete for the UEFA Super Cup against Champions League winners Real Madrid in Monaco. Real, the overwhelming favourites, were managed by future Blues boss Guus Hiddink with a star-studded team that included Roberto Carlos, Raul and Clarence Seedorf. Vialli got it right tactically again as Chelsea came away with a clean sheet and a 1-0 win. Chelsea had their hands on another European trophy.

After an opening day defeat to Coventry, Chelsea only lost twice more in the entirety of the 1998/99 season, both defeats coming after the turn of the year. Remarkably, in Manchester United's treble-winning season, this near-invincibility was only good enough to see the Blues finish in third. Despite reaching the semi-finals of the Cup Winners' Cup again, their triumph of the previous season was not repeated, losing to Mallorca. By then Vialli had pretty much retired as a player, focusing his attention on management. Chelsea finished fifth the following season but

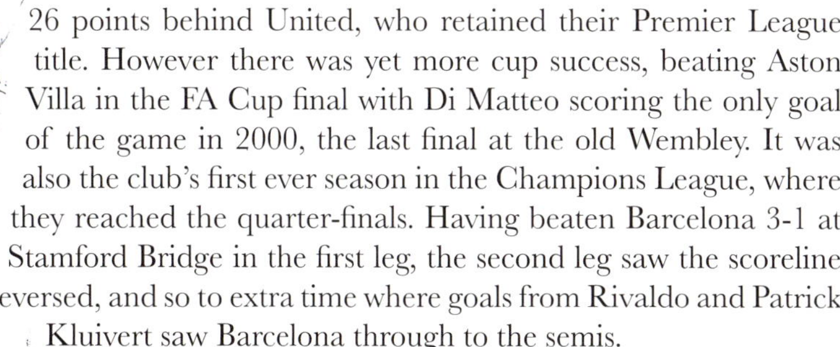

26 points behind United, who retained their Premier League title. However there was yet more cup success, beating Aston Villa in the FA Cup final with Di Matteo scoring the only goal of the game in 2000, the last final at the old Wembley. It was also the club's first ever season in the Champions League, where they reached the quarter-finals. Having beaten Barcelona 3-1 at Stamford Bridge in the first leg, the second leg saw the scoreline reversed, and so to extra time where goals from Rivaldo and Patrick Kluivert saw Barcelona through to the semis.

When Chelsea failed to win a single game from 22 August through the whole of September, Vialli was sacked and replaced by fellow Italian Claudio Ranieri. He had led Chelsea to victory in the League Cup, UEFA Cup Winners' Cup and Uefa Super Cup the same year, victory in the 2000 FA Cup final and Charity Shield and achieved the club's highest place in the Premier League (third) in the pre-Roman Abramovich era. Vialli had the happy knack of winning important matches.

Athole Still, agent of the former Sampdoria and Juventus striker, said player power had caused Vialli's departure. "The reason for Luca's sacking has nothing to do with the club's results at the start of the season. The reason was that he had lost the confidence of some of the players. The spirit in the camp was not what he or Chelsea wanted to have. Gianluca accepts that he had lost the confidence of some of the players, and therefore completely accepts the club's prerogative in choosing to dismiss him. Gianluca is extremely disappointed with the situation, but he knows that something had to be done. There is no rancour involved." Earlier, former Chelsea defender Ron 'Chopper' Harris claimed Vialli had three games to save himself from the chop. Mark Lawrenson told Five Live: "I would say the timing is all wrong, they are only five games into the season. It is very, very surprising. We have seen in the newspapers that one or two of the players have been questioning what's been going on. Vialli is one of the nicest people you could ever meet, but expectation levels are so high at Chelsea."

The Former Minister for Sport, and prominent Chelsea fan,Tony Banks MP claimed he saw Vialli's sacking coming as long ago as last spring even as the Italian and his team celebrated their success in the FA Cup final at Wembley. "Once Ken Bates makes up his mind that is it," he said, "I am very sorry for Luca as a person, because he is a bloody nice bloke. But I think this is good for Chelsea and it is good for him too." Banks cited Vialli's major problems as an inability to get his points across to his players and to keep them happy on and off the pitch. "It was his failure to communicate," claimed Banks, "there were several players I spoke to who said that he is not very good at communicating. It is not just what you do on the pitch. His treatment of Zola has also brought it to a head. You have to be able to deal with your players - but he was not able to. There was also a naivety in his coaching. I am always sad when anybody goes - but the club is bigger than anybody. It was the right decision, and I support Ken Bates in what he has done. It was always going to happen at some stage. But Ken Bates moves quickly - Ruud Gullit found that out. I am feeling quite happy about it tonight, because it clearly was not working.This was inevitable. I am a long-standing, long- suffering supporter. But even Chelsea fans lose their patience in the end - as Ken Bates has done."

While reactions to Vialli's dismissal were mixed in England, the sentiments voiced in his native Italy were of continuing admiration and sympathy. Roberto Mancini, assistant manager at Lazio, said: "I'm very disappointed for Vialli because he's a good friend and a good manager. He's done very well at Chelsea, and they've won many trophies under his management. I'm sure he'll have a good career in management, maybe not in England, but certainly in Italy."

Among those tipped as potential replacements were Vialli's assistant Graham Rix, Gianfranco Zola, George Graham, Terry Venables, Ray Wilkins, and even a return for Glenn Hoddle, but the post went to Claudio Ranieri. A club statement said that Graham Rix would be the interim manager, "for the immediate future the current staff, led by Rix, will take charge of the team." Rix was just four days in charge before the arrival of another Italian in the hot seat.

Vialli went on to have a brief spell managing Watford before beginning a job in the media but then he was struck down with pancreatic cancer in 2017 but kept it secret for a year before announcing that he was "fine now". He underwent surgery and eight months of chemotherapy and six weeks of radiotherapy, after being diagnosed. Vialli made his revelation in an interview in *Corriere della Serra*, hoping his story would inspire others battling

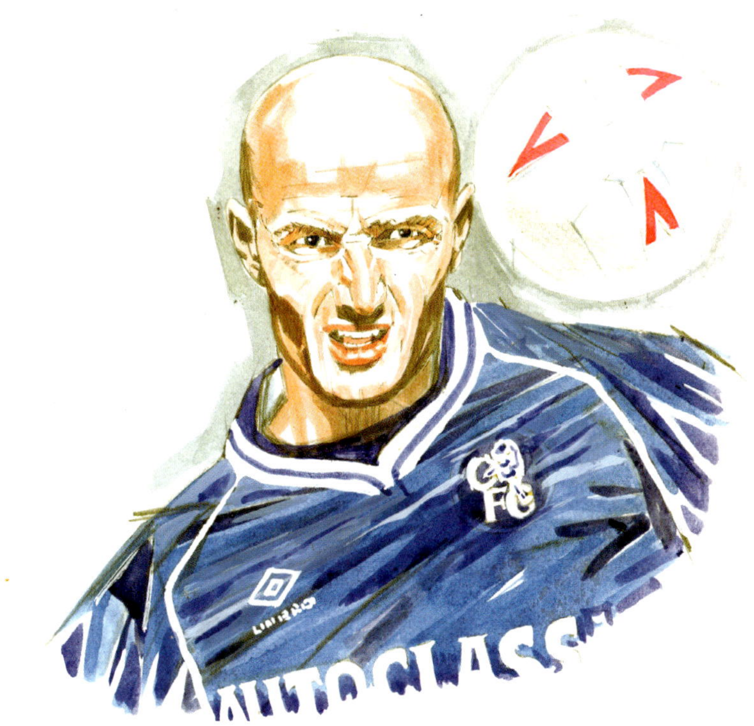

cancer. He said:"I'm fine now, very well indeed. It's been a year and I'm back to having a beastly physique, although I still have no certainty of how this match will end. I knew it was hard and it is hard to have to tell others, my family.You would never want to hurt the people who love you: my parents, my brothers and my sister, my wife Cathryn, our little girls Olivia and Sofia. And it takes you as a sense of shame, as if what happened to you was your fault."

Vialli released his autobiography soon after which detailed his incredible career as well as some dark times off the pitch. He added: "I used to wear a sweater under my shirt so no-one noticed anything. I was still the Vialli everyone knew, then I decided to tell my story and put it in the book. I hope my story can inspire people, who are at crucial intersections of their lives, and I hope mine is a book to keep on the bedside table so people can read one or two stories before falling asleep or in the morning as soon as they wake up. Life is made up of 10 per cent of what happens to us, and 90 per cent of how we handle it. I hope that my story can help others to deal with what is happening in the right way." The club tweeted:"We love this guy. Best wishes from all of us at Chelsea to Gianluca Vialli. We're all thinking of you, Luca."

Chelsea fans let the former Chelsea player and manager know he was in their thoughts during a Carabao Cup tie against Manchester United. In the build-up to the game, 'We Are The Shed', a fan group who describe themselves as 'A movement gathering #CFC supporters who sit in The Shed to create displays & improve the atmosphere' - tweeted about their intention to mark the game with a tribute to Vialli. @WeAre_TheShed tweeted: "We will display a banner in the M. Harding tonight in support of Chelsea legend Gianluca Vialli who is fighting cancer. As the players walk out & the banner is held aloft we encourage you to chant Vialli's name to let him know we are with him. Please spread the word #ForzaVialli". Fans in the Shed End unveiled two banners reading:"ForzaVialli/WeAreWithYou"before kick-off.

Luca worked as a pundit for Sky Italia TV, and during his reign at the Bridge as manager I had penned yet another of my catalogue of Chelsea books *Vialli: A Diary of his Season*. Ivor Baddiel, life long Chelsea fan, penned this review in *Total Football*: "After reading this book, you get the distinct impression that for most of the last season Gianluca Vialli had a stalker, and that stalker was the *Mirror*'s Harry Harris. Harry knows that Luca gets up at 8.40 every morning, has coffee, toast and jam, and listens to Simply Red, Morcheeba, or Cafe del Mar (not sure about Simply Red, but otherwise well hip) on his way to the training ground. He knows that on September 14, Luca dined at Scallini's. He knows that on March 12, Luca gave up using a mobile phone. Frankly, it wouldn't surprise me if he knew that on May 5 Luca had a dodgy curry and spent the night on the bog. But in this account of Chelsea and Luca's 1998/99 season, there's also the Laudrup story, the Rix incident, the Le Saux/Fowler bust-up, to name but three of last seasons's events. Okay, so there's the odd day when not much happened or Harry's telescope lens broke - November 17, double training, morning and afternoon - but, for the most part, last season is mused over, mulled over, and given pretty good going over without many stones left unturned."

Frank Sinclair

Luca Vialli took over suddenly from Ruud Gullit and it couldn't have been a tougher introduction to management. There had been quite a bit of upset in the changing rooms between some senior players, including Luca, and Ruud Gullit before he left.You could tell it wasn't quite right, there was an atmosphere as certain senior players were left out and didn't like the manager's ideas on rotation. Luca was one of a group of world class strikers at the times along with Mark Hughes, Franco Zola, and Tore Andre Flo and Ruud only picked two. It was not easy to keep them all happy, and Luca showed his frustrations when he was the one left out. Ruud and Luca were very close as team-mates, but the problem emerged when Ruud became manager, there is no doubt that it put a strain on their relationship.While some of the players were not happy as Ruud was also negotiating a new contract with Ken Bates and that came under scrutiny.Together those issues boiled over and the result was the exit of Ruud. Luca was thrown in at the deep end with his first match being the second leg of a League Cup semi-final against Arsenal, so there was an awful lot to play for still when he took over as we were also still in Europe going for the Cup Winners' Cup. Luca showed his character. He was well liked and admired by the players, and he asked the players to help him out, as he was going into something he had not prepared for. The players stuck by him and we went on to win the League Cup and the Cup Winners' Cup in his short spell as manager. He turned out to be my last of many managers at the Bridge, and I scored in the League Cup Final against Middlesbrough which turned out to be my last game for the club, but it was some way to go out as I had always dreamed as a kid of scoring at Wembley and I finally did it. I got injured in the Final, a pulled groin, but had to play on into extra time because we had used our substitutes, and that caused even more damage. It was such a bad injury I missed the semi-final and final of the Cup Winners' Cup success and while that was very disappointing, of course, it was a bitter sweet end to my Chelsea career as I fulfilled a life-long ambition to score at Wembley. After the World Cup, we come back to pre-season and Martin O'Neill made an offer to Ken Bates to take me to Leicester, and the chairman was keen to recoup some of his huge outlay on some key signings such as Albert Ferrer and Marcel Desailly that the manager wanted, and we therefore had quite a few defensive options. I'd been involved with Chelsea for 26 years so it was disappointing to have to leave, but it was a good offer and I had a few years left on my contract so I could have dug my heels in and stayed, but it would have meant not playing regularly. But after all these years, after so many managers, I couldn't face being just a squad player while Martin O'Neill told me I formed a key part of his plans. It was a no brainer for me even though it was going to a lesser club at the time, it would mean I would be in the Leicester City side week in and week out. Even if Luca wanted me to stay, it was clear the decision had been taken out of his hands.

At the training ground, Luca tried to stop me leaving when I went there to pick up my stuff. "I'm not going to let you leave," he said. I am sure it was light-hearted, although I had spoken to him at length and I knew how much he didn't want me to go, and that it had been the decision of the chairman. Having played under so many Chelsea managers, they all had their own strengths, but I would have to say Glenn Hoddle was the best. He affected my career the most. At the time he took over I wasn't a regular, but I got into his team and he improved me as an individual, improving my knowledge of the game, and improving me tactically and technically. Bobby Campbell gave me my first professional contract, and as a young kid coming through the Academy, he was an intimidating man, a remarkable presence, a steely Scouser who led with a rod of iron. He was a fearsome presence to the young players coming through. Yet, he always had time for the youngsters such as myself, Gary Stanley, Jason Cundy, Gareth Hall and encouraged a pathway to the first team. That gave me confidence I could break through. But they were tough times with him, and I can recall one scenario when I had a funky hairstyle, short at the sides then dreadlocks and plaits, same with Eddie Newton. He pulled both of us and said "If you want to get into the first team, cut your hair". I didn't cut my hair - I think he made his remark tongue in cheek! But I did make it into the first team, a debut at home to Luton, we were three down at half-time with Graeme Le Saux sent off but the 10-men came storming back in an eventful debut to say the least. I learned loads under Bobby Campbell, and I will always remember how much time he took with the youngsters encouraging them to make the big breakthrough.

Ian Porterfield took over from Bobby, he'd been a legend at Sunderland scoring that Cup Final goal, we were aware of all his achievements and he was around the place as Bobby's assistant. He wasn't the outspoken type, and when he became manager he brought in Don Howe as his assistant, an excellent coach and in many ways more of the manager, but it was good for me as he was very stern, and a disciplinarian. Don was an outstanding man, especially for defenders such as myself, improving our understanding of the game, making us grow as players. Ian Porterfield was not exactly a tactical genius, especially when you look at the guys who were soon to be coming into the club as player-managers then managers. David Webb was my next manager, a legend of the club and someone I looked up to from the age of about eleven. Again I was very aware of the exploits of the team of the seventies with Webb and co., along with Butch Wilkins and Chopper Harris coming through the Academy. Great team, great memories with what they achieved. I worshipped them from afar then here was one of them as my new manager. David Webb was very much 'old school', and I can still recall the first training session with the first team at Harlington on a soaking wet day, when he had us all doing doggy races stood 40 yards apart, with a slide tackle finish at the ball, by the end of which we were all caked in mud and soaked through. Straight away it built up a team spirit and he did a great job keeping us up which he was hired to do. I loved to speak with him about his experiences as a defender, as he played centre-half, right-back, even left-back, something similar to myself. It was special.And he taught me some naughty tricks! But you can't tackle like that in the modern game He was a great character.

Glenn Hoddle was next and he was a childhood hero of mine. Even though I was a Chelsea fan, I loved the things Glenn identified with, he was a technical genius. So when he came to the football club I was thrilled.He first arrived when Bobby Campbell invited him down to the training ground to regain his fitness after a knee problem, and even then he was happy to take time out to speak to the young players and he'd talk to them with his coaching head on. He had returned from Monaco full of new ideas, he got himself fit and went off to become player-manager at Swindon doing a fantastic job in getting them promoted to the Premier League.When he came to Chelsea as player-manager I played alongside him in a back three at times, we also had David Lee and Erland Johnsen. It was simply a pleasure to play alongside him, his technical ability was unreal even at his advancing years of his career.The things he did in training were just unbelievable, I learned so much from him.The team qualified for Europe, but it was sad when he left for the England job. I felt it wasn't quite the same when he left.

Ruud Gullit was an unbelievable signing when Glenn brought him to Stamford Bridge, he was still a world class player even though he had passed his very best from the player I'd love to watch. In fact he was still way ahead of everything you had seen in the Premier League, he was one of the top three or four players of that time. He played sweeper, then midfield, up front, on the right wing then the left wing, sometimes it was frustrating to play alongside him in back three with Steve Clarke because he would wander all over the pitch, he would do his own thing, he was a free spirit. It must have frustrated Glenn! When Glenn left for the England job, Ruud took over as manager and brought his 'sexy football' to the management side of things. But he continued to play and now as manager he did exactly what he wanted. But you had to admire his ability and to think I played alongside him. I could only imagine what he must have been like in his prime with AC Milan and the Dutch national side in those formidable teams. Ruud Gullit won the FA Cup and became the first foreign manager to win that trophy as well as Chelsea's first trophy in 26 years. All I can say is that it was such a terrific experience to play with such a world-class footballer.

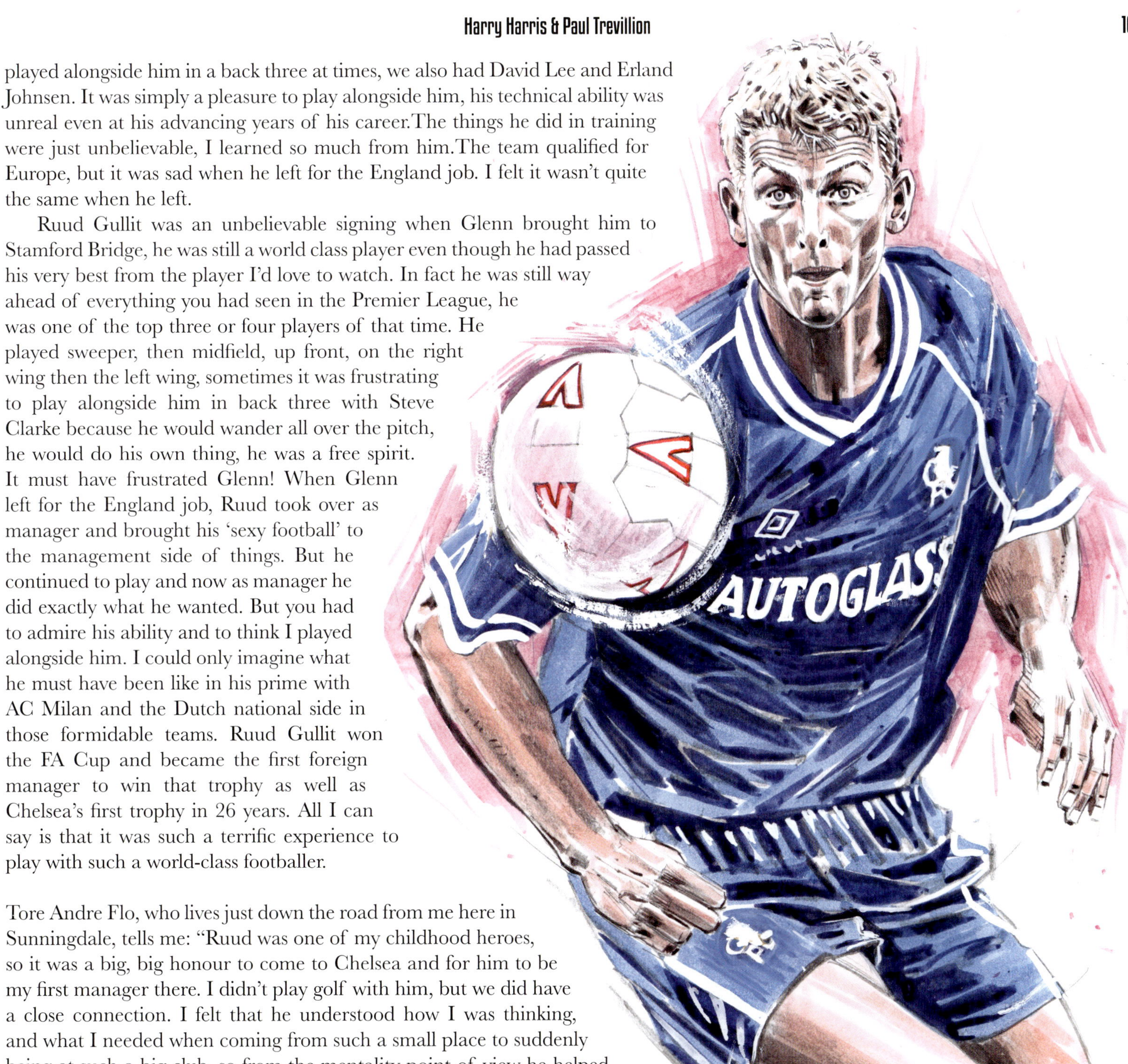

Tore Andre Flo, who lives just down the road from me here in Sunningdale, tells me: "Ruud was one of my childhood heroes, so it was a big, big honour to come to Chelsea and for him to be my first manager there. I didn't play golf with him, but we did have a close connection. I felt that he understood how I was thinking, and what I needed when coming from such a small place to suddenly being at such a big club, so from the mentality point of view he helped me enormously. Luca was my next manager, also a great guy and a very funny guy but also a hugely professional one too. He was very good at impersonations, he would do everyone, including me, but it was all harmless fun.We won a lot of things under him and it was a very happy period. In fact, all of my three managers at the club were a great experience for me, even though I wasn't at the club long, perhaps a couple of months when Claudio Ranieri was the manager but I still learned a lot from him."

The youngest of five children, Luca's self-made millionaire dad owned a construction firm and he was brought up in a castle in Cremona, Lombardy. At 16 he made his debut for local team Cremonese, then in the third tier. He always worked hard because: "I never wanted anyone to question my attitude on the football pitch." In 1984 he moved to Italian side Sampdoria, where he played alongside Graeme Souness, who broke down in tears and had to cut short his tribute while live on TV when hearing of the news of Luca's passing. Souness described his friend as a "special person" and a "gorgeous soul". Souness once got one up on renowned practical joker Vialli, who at the time was dressed in club blazer and tie, by pushing him into a lake. Vialli later responded by cutting the legs off Souness's favourite trousers, putting shaving foam in his shoes and itching powder in his pants. The Italian would later joke: "I never saw him move so quickly."

Vialli left Sampdoria for Juventus in 1992 for £12.5million — then a world record. He won the Uefa Cup and European Cup before arriving in London as a player, then player-manager, living in splendour in a luxury flat in exclusive Eaton Square, Belgravia. He said: "Here I can walk down the street with my girlfriend, I can go shopping, sit in a pub or go out to dinner and nobody asks me for an autograph.That's a dream. After 15 years of worrying, I'm finally a free man." While Luca found his new life in English football to his taste, for Chelsea it continued along a speedy path of reinventing itself and, by association, the very fabric of English football. As Bates summed it up: "Beating Real Madrid in the Super Cup was a first for this club, and yet it was only 15 years after we had nearly gone bankrupt and we were champions of Europe, and Vialli was leader in that vital year."

On match days Vialli would speed away from Stamford Bridge on a Piaggio scooter to avoid the traffic. The striker, who scored 16 goals in 59 games for the national side, soon became proficient in English but sometimes mangled turns of phrase. Once, during a press conference he remarked "when the fish are down", rather than chips. While avoiding the then heavy drinking culture in the English game, he did like a cigarette, even caught once when sitting on the substitute's bench. Despite a successful first season, a lack of minutes on the pitch — including a short run out as the clock ticked down in the 1997 FA Cup Final, soured his relationship with Gullit. Astonishingly with Chelsea second in the table in 1998, Bates sensationally sacked Gullit and replaced him as manager with Vialli, then just 33 and still a player, he was the first Italian to manage in the Premier League. Chelsea finished third in the Premier League that year — their highest finish since 1970. The practical joker sometimes found the transition to stern boss difficult, saying of his players: "They wanted me to be Luca, having a laugh all the time."

Having revealed his cancer diagnosis in November 2018, the tumour returned in March 2019, requiring nine months of chemotherapy, during which he lost the hair from his beard and eyebrows, and in 2020 he revealed he had been given the all clear from the disease after 17 months. In 2019 he was appointed as new delegation chief of Italy's team under head coach and great friend and teammate from his Sampdoria days, Roberto Mancini, winning the Euros, beating England in the Final. Before the final at Wembley, Vialli read Theodore Roosevelt's rousing "Man in the Arena" passage to the Azzurri players. The speech includes the lines that "credit belongs to the man" who "at the best knows in the end the triumph of high achievement, and who at the worst, if he fails, at least fails while daring greatly. So that his place shall never be with those cold and timid souls who neither know victory nor defeat."

He had to step away due to the aggressive return of cancer, and died soon afterwards with Chelsea making a poignant change to their social media accounts by making it black and white. Chelsea chairman Todd Boehly and co-controlling owner Behdad Eghbali then added: "This is truly an awful day for Chelsea Football Club. Gianluca's legend will live on at Stamford Bridge. His impact as a player, a coach and most importantly as a person, will be forever written across our club's history. We send our heartfelt and deepest condolences to his family and friends."

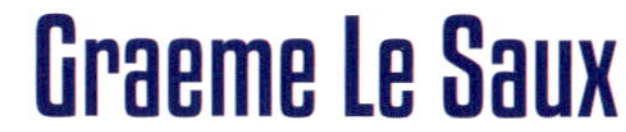

Graeme Le Saux

Recalling how he signed twice for the Blues, Graeme Le Saux tells me, "The first time, John Hollins was the manager at the time, he was in Jersey presenting a Player of the Year award and three or four people mentioned my name to him. He took the number of the secretary of St Pauls, the local amateur team I played for, and then actually had the presence of mind when he got back to London to phone and get me over for a trial. I think he just thought partly it's an unusual surname, but also because a few people had mentioned me to him he'd better follow up on it. So I had a trial for a week, and hung around like an idiot. Subsequently I was offered a contract off the back of that. I was looking at universities so I think the opportunities would have been better for me. I'd had trials from the age of 13 on and off and didn't quite make it. Once Southampton got wind that Chelsea had me on trial they got in contact and asked me to go back, so I think my definition of luck is when preparation meets opportunity. If you're working really hard at something and then an opportunity comes along, you're much more likely to take it, and that sort of defined how I got that chance. If that hadn't have happened, would I have created other opportunities for myself? Probably, but the pathway would have been different."

Le Saux's first impressions of life at Chelsea were "a mixture of excitement, shock and disappointment. Excitement about the fact I was getting to fulfil the next part of my dream which was to become a professional footballer, and writing that down when I opened my bank account was amazing. Shock in the sense that it was a real baptism of fire coming into the dressing-room culture at the time.The club wasn't doing well and we got relegated that season, which was nothing to do with me because I didn't play.There were a lot of difficulties, John got sacked and it was hard, there was a real shock that professional football was a lot different to what I'd been doing in Jersey. I was committed like a professional but the environment wasn't professional.There wasn't that competitive nature between players and that was difficult at times. I was disappointed in the attitude of some of the players and some of the things they would pick on people for. It was quite a negative culture and with hindsight, you can see some of the reasons why the team got relegated. It needed to be re-booted, in a sense, in order to improve, and I would say that didn't really happen until Glenn Hoddle arrived. So they were my first impressions but within that I was trying to develop my career and that was amazing, making my debut down at Portsmouth and playing for the reserves, playing in different positions and getting to know some of those players really well.That whole experience, and being a teenager living in London, diving into that whole environment was a magical experience. It wasn't all bad, it was just polarised.

"The second time I signed for Chelsea I was playing for Blackburn – and England - and Ruud Gullit was the manager. Ruud had identified me as a player they wanted and it was a British record for a defender, £5.5m, so it was a big deal for everyone, including myself, but more of a traditional way of signing and something which meant I then stayed at the club for another six years."

On the big managerial influences in his career Le Saux's says, "John Hollins obviously deserves a huge amount of credit but I didn't get to work with him for too long, I think he got sacked on the strength of signing me! He was fantastic as a person, I didn't really know what he was like as a coach but clearly things weren't going well. He was someone I looked up to and kept in touch with throughout my career. He was always a good pair of ears and had a lot of experience. Ruud Gullit really stood out. He brought me back to the club. Luca Vialli was also very good but they were both young managers, it was their first jobs in the game. Don Howe, who worked at the club for a spell as a coach, was tactically amazing, he was brilliant. Claudio Ranieri was my last manager at Chelsea. He was in full tinker mode then but he was a great coach. By then we were very experienced players so it was more about taking what he said and also delivering what we knew, but I'd say John and Ruud were the two."

Le Saux continued his Chelsea links. "I see different guys from my first spell, people like Graham Stuart, David Lee and Jason Cundy, Frank Sinclair and Eddie Newton. Then there are a lot of people from my second spell that I keep in touch with. The contrast between my two spells was about the culture of the dressing-room and the friendships we built, as well as the stage of my career that I was at. I didn't know a lot about myself as an adult during that first experience so I learnt a lot that probably changed me during my second spell but that's all part of growing up. I feel very fortunate to feel that I have lifelong friends that I shared those experiences with, even though we don't see each other all the time."

He looks back "fondly" at this time at the Bridge, as he says: "What would I change or do differently? With hindsight, in the first spell I wish I'd had a bit more ability to deal with some of those situations I found myself in as a young player.We weren't well-supported within the dressing-room and it was a hard, tough environment to survive in. I think if I'd been able to adapt to that environment a bit more smoothly and quicker my career would have started earlier, and if we'd had a bit more stability around the team I think I could have made an impact. But I've never been one to look back because you can't change anything. Every experience shapes you and as long as you learn something from it and don't repeat mistakes that's the way we'll all continue to learn, so would I change anything? No.The positive and negative experiences have shaped my outlook now. I definitely felt when I came back that it was an opportunity to continue that journey with the club I started at. It's 12 years of fond memories playing for such a renowned club, so it was a privilege."

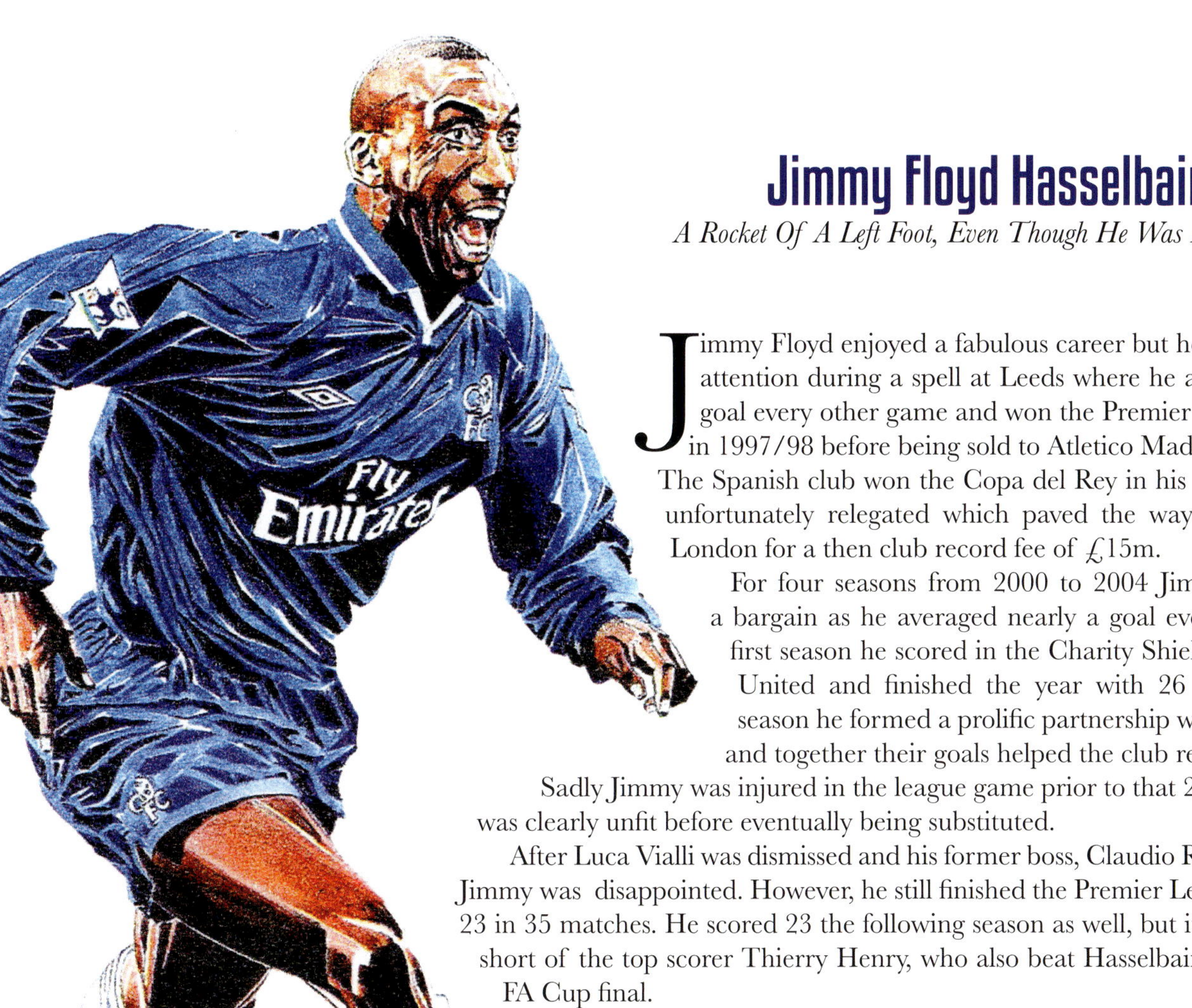

Jimmy Floyd Hasselbaink

A Rocket Of A Left Foot, Even Though He Was Right-Footed

Jimmy Floyd enjoyed a fabulous career but he first came to English attention during a spell at Leeds where he averaged better than a goal every other game and won the Premier League Golden Boot in 1997/98 before being sold to Atletico Madrid in 1999 for £10m. The Spanish club won the Copa del Rey in his season there but were unfortunately relegated which paved the way for a move to West London for a then club record fee of £15m.

For four seasons from 2000 to 2004 Jimmy turned out to be a bargain as he averaged nearly a goal every two games. In his first season he scored in the Charity Shield against Manchester United and finished the year with 26 goals. The following season he formed a prolific partnership with Eiður Guðjohnsen and together their goals helped the club reach the FA Cup final. Sadly Jimmy was injured in the league game prior to that 2002 FA Cup final and was clearly unfit before eventually being substituted.

After Luca Vialli was dismissed and his former boss, Claudio Ranieri was appointed, Jimmy was disappointed. However, he still finished the Premier League's top scorer with 23 in 35 matches. He scored 23 the following season as well, but it turned out to be one short of the top scorer Thierry Henry, who also beat Hasselbaink and Chelsea in the FA Cup final.

In the following seasons, his output was limited as Ranieri shaped the squad to get the most out of Franco Zola. Hasselbaink still managed 15, one short of Zola's record in the 02-03 season. Although the goals dried up over the next two years, he helped Chelsea qualify for the Champions League on both occasions.

In March 2004 Jimmy scored a hat-trick in a win over Wolves becoming the only player in Chelsea's history to score a hat-trick after coming on as a substitute.

He left in the summer of 2004 as the new manager looked to bring in his own players. He joined Middlesbrough and later played for Charlton and Cardiff. Ironically, his first Charlton goal was scored at Stamford Bridge and he earned an ovation from the home supporters as he refused to celebrate the goal.

Hasselbaink had a rocket of a left foot, despite being primarily right-footed. He scored a lot of spectacular goals from outside the box. Jimmy Floyd played for 10 clubs over 18 seasons, including Leeds United and Atletico Madrid, scoring 245 in the process, but it is as a Chelsea player that his career peaked.

When Burton Albion manager he insisted that José Mourinho should have kept him at Chelsea in an episode of *Kammy and Ben's Proper Football* podcast talking with Chris Kamara and Ben Shephard. Hasselbaink believed that he was unfairly sidelined when Mourinho joined in 2004. In the podcast, Jimmy revealed how tough he found it to adjust to English drinking culture when he first arrived at Leeds and how football saved him from gang life. He even revealed that his real name is actually Jerrel.

Hasselbaink joined Chelsea from Atletico Madrid in July 2000, for a fee that equalled the Premier League transfer record set by Newcastle United when they signed Alan Shearer in 1996 (£15m). He played under Gianluca Vialli and Claudio Ranieri and was at the club at the time when Roman Abramovich took over as owner in 2003. "That was where the relationship with me and Ranieri went a little bit sour," Hasselbaink says. "All of a sudden he (Ranieri) had a lot of money to spend. He called me and Eiður Guðjohnsen into his office. He said, 'I'm going to bring in two new strikers - you guys can go if you want'." Ranieri brought in Adrian Mutu and Argentine legend Hernan Crespo. Nevertheless, Hasselbaink says he told Ranieri that he wanted to stay and fight for his place. "In the end, I played anyway and I became top scorer."

Hasselbaink recalls that period in terms of the number of incoming signings. "We had Crespo coming in, Mutu, Sebastian Veron, Joe Cole, Glen Johnson, Wayne Bridge… Every day, there was someone else. What do you do? Either you be a mouse and be quiet and you're already defeated, or you stand up and have a go. You look in the mirror and see a lion, rather than a pussycat."

When a young, much-hyped Mourinho took over Hasselbaink was sent to Middlesbrough on a free transfer. He had no say and wasn't pleased. "I was absolutely gutted," Hasselbaink says. "More gutted because Mourinho never spoke to me." He believes there was outside influence on Mourinho's decision. "I bet you that Mourinho had been told that I was a difficult lad," Hasselbaink says, "hard to work with and all that kind of stuff - which was not the case at all."

Under Mourinho over the next three seasons, Chelsea became a dominant force, winning two Premier League titles, two League Cups, the FA Cup and a Community Shield. Meanwhile, Hasselbaink continued to be a high scorer for Middlesbrough over the next two seasons. He believes, though, that he was robbed of an opportunity to get silverware with Chelsea. "They got Drogba - what a signing - but surely I could have featured alongside him. I've spoken to Mourinho since and he said, 'yes, I made a mistake there.' I don't care what he said. He should have kept me and I would have had a medal." Asked whether he believes that Mourinho is 'the special one', Hasselbaink disagrees. "He's a brilliant coach, absolutely magnificent what he's done in football, but he was never the special one for me."

"I was absolutely gutted," Hasselbaink says. "More gutted because Mourinho never spoke to me." He believes there was outside influence on Mourinho's decision. "I bet you that Mourinho had been told that I was a difficult lad," Hasselbaink says, "hard to work with and all that kind of stuff - which was not the case at all."

*

In 1998, Hasselbaink was called up by Holland for the World Cup in France. The Dutch made it to the semi-finals before losing to Brazil on penalties. They had Dennis Bergkamp, Edgar Davids, Patrick Kluivert, Clarence Seedorf, Edwin van der Sar, Jaap Stam and the De Boer brothers. One of France's tournament winners that year, Marcel Desailly, told him: "Jimmy, we didn't want to play you guys. We wanted Brazil, because we felt we had a chance against Brazil." Brazil beat the Dutch on penalties in the semi-finals. "We should have won that World Cup," says Hasselbaink today, "we were the best team, but the best team doesn't always win."

Gianfranco Zola

The Crown Prince of Stamford Bridge

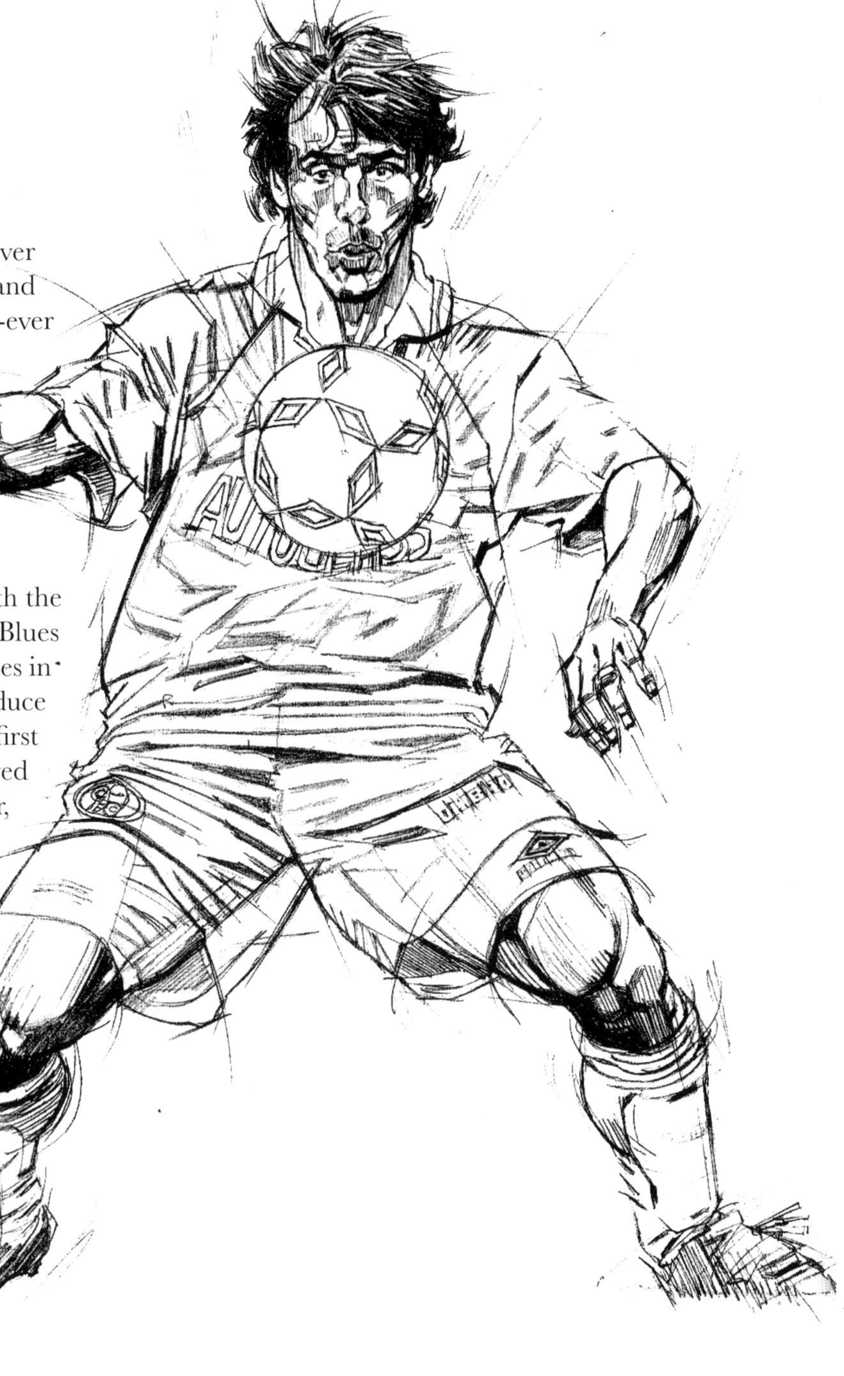

Gianfranco Zola became one of Chelsea's greatest-ever legends as he starred for the Blues between 1996 and 2003 and became one of the club's most popular-ever players. His incredible skill, ability to produce jaw-droppingly spectacular moments of brilliance, and the mutual love and respect he shared with those in the stands ensure that the diminutive Italian will be remembered as one of the Blues' all-time greats.

His greatest memory from his long and illustrious career was the incredible relationship he shared with the Blues supporters. Following the arrival of Ruud Gullit the Blues increasingly looked to Serie A for superstars to play crucial roles in the club's transformation into genuine contenders, and introduce a more modern and continental style. Gianluca Vialli was the first to join from Juventus in May and Roberto Di Matteo followed from Lazio just over a month later. Then in November, arguably the greatest talent arrived at Stamford Bridge as Zola completed a move from Parma as some of the world's biggest talents joined a club starved of success – an FA Cup final defeat in 1994 was the closest the Blues came to major silverware in 25 years.

At that time Italy was Europe's strongest league so it was a huge shock when Zola turned up at the Bridge. "I knew something about Chelsea because Robbie and Luca were talking to me about it a lot," he recalls, "plus I used to follow the other leagues, so I knew I was going into a good place. It turned out to be even better than I thought. I wanted a new experience and I was certainly looking forward to having an experience abroad. Chelsea had Di Matteo, Vialli, and Gullit. I remember when I met Luca with the national team he spoke

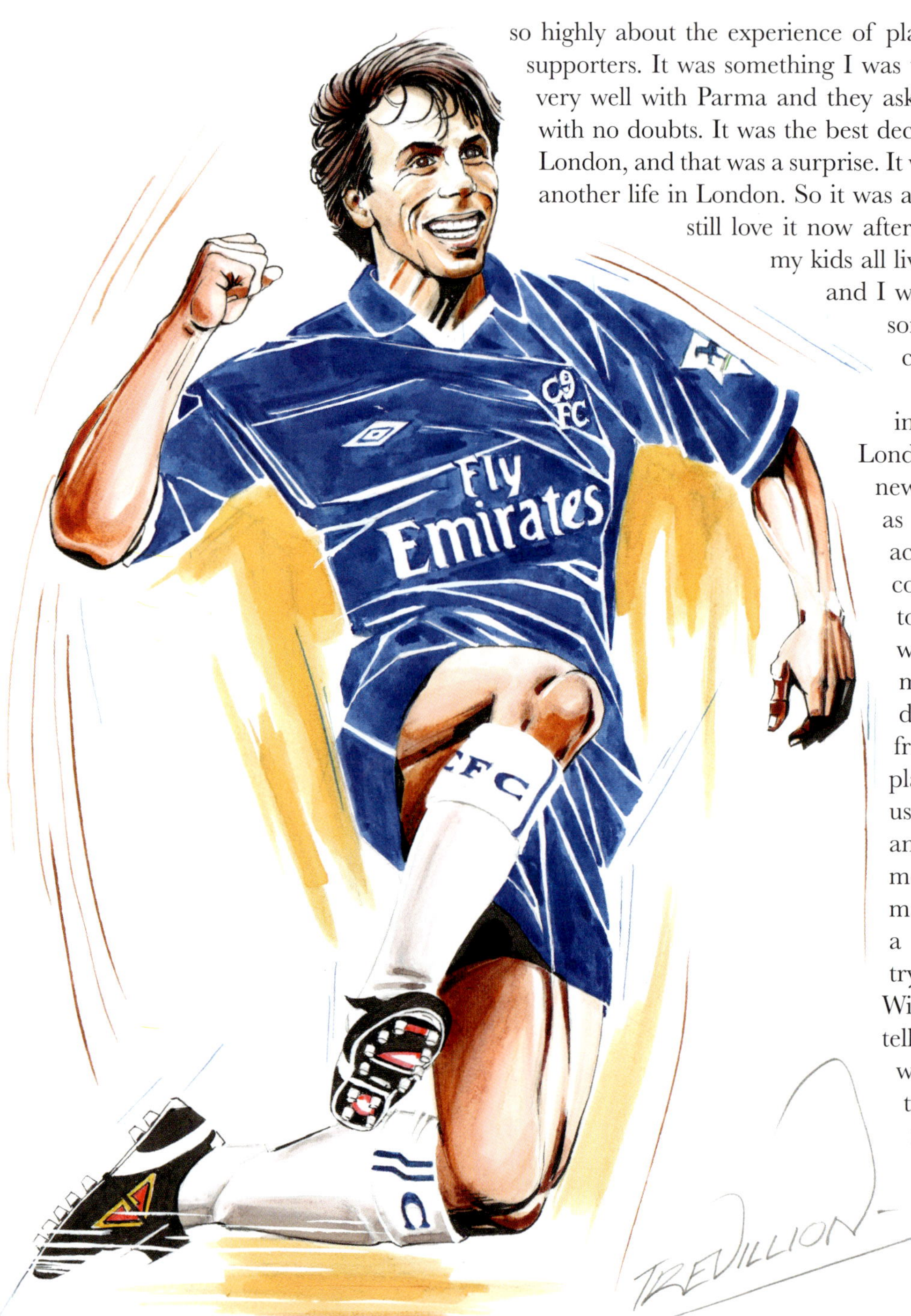

so highly about the experience of playing here, of the team, the league, and all the supporters. It was something I was thinking about and when things were not going very well with Parma and they asked me if I wanted to go to Chelsea, I said yes with no doubts. It was the best decision I ever made. I didn't know so much about London, and that was a surprise. It was not only a big city but it was another country, another life in London. So it was a discovery but I loved it from the first day and I still love it now after 30 years. One of my boys was born here and my kids all live over here. I still have a house here in London and I will always keep the house because I believe it is somewhere important to me and I want to keep my connection."

Di Matteo and Vialli played an important role in persuading the diminutive forward to come to London, they also helped him to feel at home in a new city and culture, which he admits he needed as he got to grips with the surprising variety in accents and characters among the team's British contingent, from local Londoner Dennis Wise to proud Scot Steve Clarke. "Robbie and Luca were very important because they introduced me to the environment and helped me to settle down quickly, so it was nice. They were very good friends and people. They helped me to find good places to go, restaurants and things like that. For us Italians eating good meals together with family and friends is important so it was very good. For me, it took me a while to understand all my team-mates when they were talking. I think it took me a month to understand what Steve Clarke was trying to tell me to do! Then there was Dennis Wise and his accent got me a little bit. He kept telling me about London and showing me around while saying strange phrases. I thought those two spoke completely different languages! But I really enjoyed it from day one. There were a lot of different nationalities and personalities, but we got on so well together and found that we could help each other. We brought our experience from Italy and I think it was good for the players around us, but also they taught us the English culture and the way they played football. We learned from each other and that was how we were able to play so well and be successful."

Zola became one of the most widely-respected and beloved players of the Premier League era, held in universally high-regard by Chelsea supporters and those of rivals due to his reputation as one of the sport's true gentlemen, always playing with a smile and ready with a kind and thoughtful word in victory or defeat. It is surprising to hear the legendary No.25 explain that as a veteran player at Chelsea, his performances were often fuelled by an emotion very few people would associate with him. "When I was a sub or not playing I used to get very angry about it, but I needed to be angry because I was 30 and I needed to find more energy wherever it was possible," Franco admits, "I knew I didn't want to be okay with the idea that I would become an older player who just played 30 minutes and couldn't start. I wanted always to push myself massively, and that's why I used to get so upset, but it was just looking for energy to push me in training in those situations. When I didn't play I didn't like it, but at the same time I needed that because you need to get the mental energy from somewhere when you are getting older.

"What I loved most about my time at Chelsea was the relationship that I established with the supporters. In Italy, we are used to it being either very good or very bad, and it all depends on the result. Here, it's not so much. As long as you go on the pitch and you give your best for your team, they love you and they support you all the time. That's something that I appreciate so much. It was incredible, I don't know how it happened so fast. Probably they liked my passion, they liked my style of play, and also the club started to get good results. I think all of this made the relationship start to grow very quickly and it was amazing. I remember there were Italian flags in the crowd, and also a few Sardinian flags as well, which was even better! It was great and I felt almost straight away this period was going to be an incredible experience in my life. For me, the best moment was without a doubt winning the first FA Cup. It had been a long time since the club won a trophy. It was also a surprise because in Italy the cup wasn't as important. I found out how it was here and I will always remember the day after we won it, on the bus parade, and all the people enjoying it so much. It was amazing. That relationship with the Chelsea fans is something that I still take with me. I feel very privileged to have been part of this family and, of course, it was the best thing that happened to me in football."

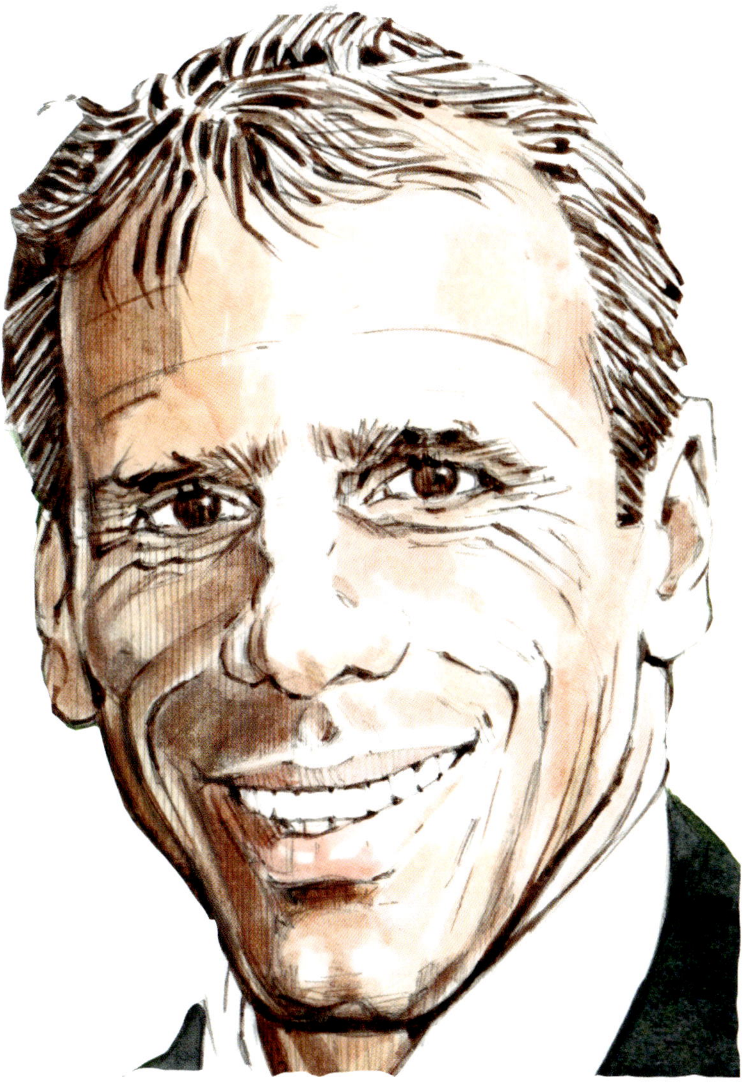

Gianfranco went on to make 229 appearances for the Blues scoring 59 goals, many of them candidates for Goal of the Month on *Match of the Day*. He was a player who people would happily pay to watch week in, week out and became emblematic of Chelsea's transformation from a footballing backwater to one of the European Elite. In Gianfranco the club had its very own Crown Prince.

Claudio Ranieri

The Tinkerman

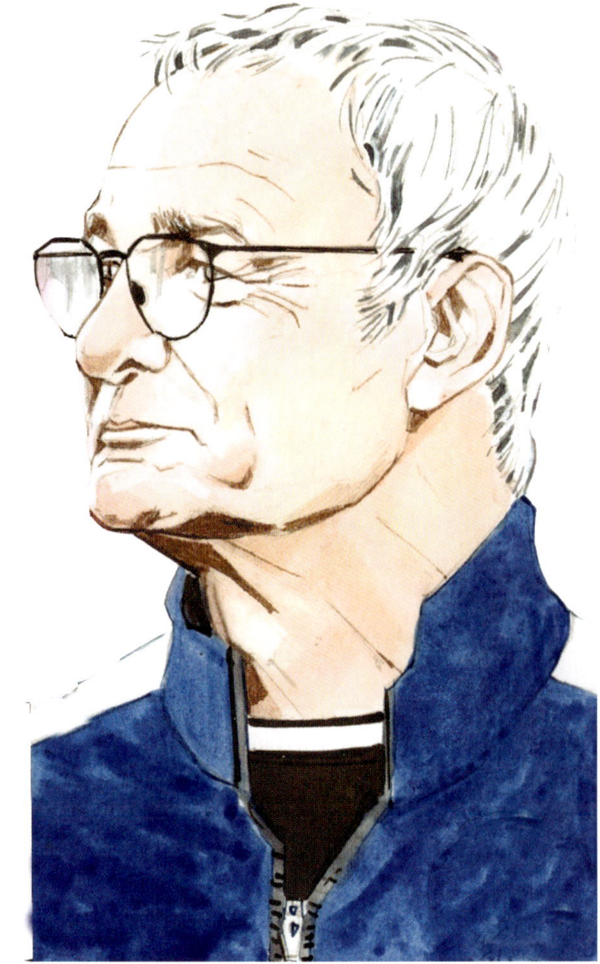

Following his dismissal in 2004, Claudio Ranieri was honoured by the Variety Club of Great Britain as Man-of-the-Year at a prestigious London awards ceremony for the dignified way he handled his controversial and untimely sacking. I was also on the roll of honour at the same awards ceremony in central London for 'Contribution to Sports Journalism' and was presented the Silver Heart by an esteemed journalist and broadcaster; I also have a picture of Claudio and myself with one of those highly-prized Silver Hearts awarded to me by the prestigious Variety Club.

The organiser was surprised that Claudio attended, and did so with great respect for the Variety Club of Great Britain and all the big name sporting stars there collecting their honours. No one would have been surprised if he had shied away from the limelight for a while after his treatment at the Bridge. Far from it, he turned up and smiled for the cameras, and was happy to talk to everyone there. This was typical of the man.

Sometimes a manager's demise comes unexpectedly, but in Ranieri's case it was a case of 'death by a thousand cuts'. For almost the entire year he had been dubbed "A Dead Man Walking", with the media speculating endlessly that he was sure to be sacked, and it was tough on the hugely popular Italian with Sven-Goran Eriksson presumed to be the next in line the moment Roman Abramovich took control of the club in June 2003.

Then, prior to the Champions League semi-final with Monaco, the Chelsea coach heard that José Mourinho had been interviewed for his job by Abramovich and Peter Kenyon. The inside track was that Ranieri's mind was affected, hardly surprising you might think, before the semi-final second leg and that might have been the reason for the bizarre second half approach to the tie in Monte Carlo when Chelsea were comfortably holding a 1-1 score in a commanding position in the overall tie having scored an away goal but went on to concede twice in the closing stages and threw away a two-goal lead to bow out. Ironically, Mourinho's Porto went on to win the tournament paving the way for José's appointment within weeks of the season ending.

Claudio was a popular figure at the Bridge. From September 2000 to June 2004 he guided the club to the Champions League semi-finals and an FA Cup Final. Prior to becoming head coach at Chelsea, he had managed Cagliari to successive promotions, reaching Serie A in 1989/90 before taking charge of Napoli the following season. Ranieri dropped back to Serie B to take charge of Fiorentina and immediately guided the Viola to the top-flight and the Florentine side picked up the Coppa Italia and Super Coppa Italia by the time he left in 1997. He then moved to Spain where he won the UEFA Intertoto Cup and Copa del Rey with Valencia in 1998/99, before briefly taking charge of Atletico Madrid, but he left before the end of the 1999/00 season.

Most Chelsea supporters hadn't heard of Claudio when he was made head coach in September 2000. In fact few in England had heard of him. He arrived as "Claudio Who?". He spoke no English and was the surprising replacement for the hugely popular Gianluca Vialli. His first task was to address dressing-room spirit, as a very successful side was ageing and he lost Roberto Di Matteo to a career-ending injury. His 'Tinkerman' nickname was introduced by himself, telling the media that this is what he was called in Italy and Spain. 'Tinkerman' became his trademark.

At home, he often deployed a 3-4-3 formation and it worked quite well, with notable big wins over Liverpool and Tottenham, but away from home results were poor. His two signings, Slavisa Jokanovic and Jesper Gronkjaer, didn't settle quickly but there were promotions for Carlo Cudicini, John Terry and Sam Dalla Bona and, after victory at Manchester City in the last game of the 2000/01 season, he earned UEFA Cup qualification. That summer the popular trio of Dennis Wise, Gustavo Poyet and Frank Leboeuf were sold and for his second season Ranieri was handed significant funds to bring in three midfielders: Frank Lampard, Emmanuel Petit and Boudewijn Zenden, plus defender William Gallas. Reconstruction of the Bridge was completed with the opening of the West Stand but for the second year running European elimination came at the hands of a minnow – this time Israeli team Hapoel Tel-Aviv - which piled pressure on Ranieri but successive wins at Elland Road and Old Trafford turned things round.

Jimmy Floyd Hasselbaink and Eiður Guðjohnsen formed a formidable strike partnership and Chelsea went on a great run, yet lost a League Cup semi-final to Tottenham, their first defeat in almost 30 games. Revenge came when Spurs were beaten 4-0 in the FA Cup and 4-0 again in the league and although the Premiership ended with them in sixth for the second season running, Chelsea reached the FA Cup final in Cardiff but lost to Arsenal despite having the better of long periods of the game.

The following summer there was no more money for investment in the team but the lack of tinkering worked. Gianfranco Zola, now aged 36, produced some of the best football of his career and Lampard and Gallas developed. Fans started chanting Ranieri's name but there was another poor exit from Europe, this time to Viking Stavanger, and the Blues needed a point on the last day of the season against Liverpool to finish fourth and pip their opponents to Champions League qualification. On a special Stamford Bridge afternoon the Blues beat the Reds to initially steady the finances but the victory also paved the way for the arrival of Roman Abramovich who was pondering the take over of several Premier League clubs.

That summer Chelsea spent over £100m on new players and by Christmas 2003 they sat second in the league behind 'Invincibles' Arsenal but they had been knocked out of the League Cup after a poor display at Aston Villa where tinkering had re-introduced the 3-4-3 formation for the first time that season. Chelsea won their group stage of the Champions League with a magnificent 4-0 win at Lazio the highlight.

Falling out of contention for the league and an FA Cup exit to Arsenal for the fourth time in Ranieri's reign brought inevitable pressure on the manager, but they memorably overcame the Gunners at Highbury in a Champions League quarter-final on the manager's most glorious night as a manager at the club and his name was now regularly chanted.

Losing the semi-final at Monaco proved to be Claudio's ultimate downfall. Despite finishing second in the Premiership they were a whopping 11 points behind 'invincibles' Arsenal. Nevertheless it represented the club's highest league finish for 49 years. However the feeling remained that Ranieri was a 'nearly man' who didn't quite have the acumen to turn the Blues into winners.

The outgoing manager could point to the form of Lampard and Terry in his final season as proof of his ability to regenerate teams. A very solid base was there for the success that followed. After his dismissal, a Chelsea statement read: "Claudio has done a first class job for the club and paved the way for future success. We would like to wish Claudio all the best for the future. We are discussing the exact terms of his departure with him and his representatives."

Ranieri had signed a contract until 2007 but had been tipped for the sack ever since Abramovich took control, even though the new owner gave him £100m to spend on new players, so he no doubt felt he gave the manager he inherited from Ken Bates, every chance, while the new kid on the block, Mourinho, was a tempting alternative. Ranieri had already said goodbye to his players after the 1-0 win over Leeds at Stamford Bridge on the final day of the season. He had urged Abramovich to make a decision on his future saying: "I would like to finish my job here. I started this job, the house isn't finished yet, only the foundations and the ground floor."

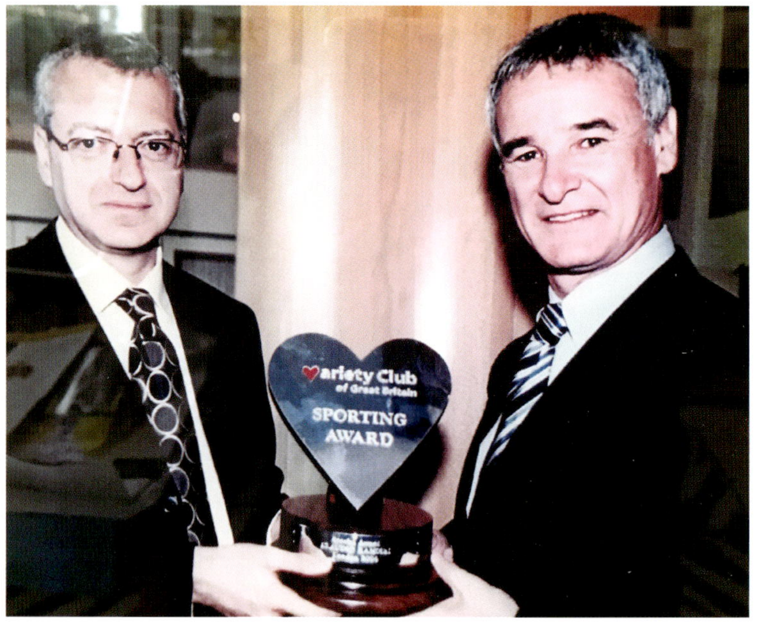

But Ranieri was replaced, as anticipated, by Mourinho and he would not win another trophy until the UEFA Super Cup in 2004 during his second stint at Valencia. Spells in Italy with Parma, Juventus, Roma and Inter Milan preceded success in France with Monaco. After winning Ligue 2 as manager of Monaco in 2012/13, Ranieri then guided the club to second in Ligue 1 in the next campaign. A short spell as Greece's national manager ended in November 2014, but it was not long before the Roma-born coach returned to management when he was announced as Leicester City manager ahead of the 2015/16 season.

Ranieri was an unexpected appointment in succession to the forthright Nigel Pearson who had kept the Foxes in the Premier League but attracted too much negative publicity for the liking of the Leicester board. By contrast the Italian was seen as a nice guy who might struggle in the widely-predicted relegation dog-fight facing the Foxes. Yet in his first season at the King Power Stadium, the likeable Italian guided the pre-season relegation candidates to their historic and incredible 5,000-1 outsiders first Premier League trophy. Ironically it was a stirring two-goal comeback by Chelsea against Spurs that clinched the title for their former manager. Leicester had started the season as no hopers to win the league and his remarkable success secured Claudio the Manager of the Season accolade. Most believed that although Pearson had laid the foundations, it took the personality of an experienced coach to mastermind the title-winning campaign.

Yet within nine months of that triumph and despite taking Leicester through to the knock-out stage of the Champions League as group winners in their first foray in the competition, he was sacked after just five Premier League victories all season left the Foxes a place and a point above the relegation zone.

Claudio returned to management ahead of the 2017/18 season with French side Nantes, but left the club at the end of that season. In November 2018, Ranieri was announced as Slavisa Jokanovic's replacement at Fulham, however his time at Craven Cottage ended on 28 February 2019 with the club 19th in the table. After another short spell with Nantes, he was named Sampdoria manager on a two-year deal in October 2019, his 20th job in football management.

Once again I turned to the articulate Italian Carlo Cudicini to put Claudio's reign into perspective. He told me: "While I was grateful to Gianluca Vialli for taking me to the club it was Claudio Ranieri who gave me the starting jersey for Chelsea and I will always be very grateful to him for that, very grateful, and for the 'story' that we spent together. The bottom line is that you reach a stage in your career that you want to play in the team. Claudio was a very Italian manager, with a lot of international experience, an Italian who also managed in Spain with Valencia, and who had now come to England. He was brought to the club by chairman Ken Bates, but was also there for the transition to Mr Abramovich, when he suddenly had quite a lot of money to spend on players. Everybody loves Claudio, starting with the supporters and then also the players, so everybody was a bit sad to see him go. I had a great relationship with Claudio, and I became part of his 'staff' as a goalkeeping coach.

"It was not a surprise that he achieved something very special with Leicester City winning the Premier League. After his experiences at Chelsea, he had all the knowledge he needed of English football, of the Premier League, the culture of the players, and with his Italian approach, it was the perfect environment to bring that Italian technical knowledge to that English team, the perfect mix and he did an unbelievable job at Leicester. Everyone was so pleased for him as he is such a nice person."

At the ripe old age of 71 Claudio was back at his spiritual home of Cagliari – his 23rd managerial job – but with no signs that his zest for coaching was in decline back in Sardinia. Two days before Christmas he was summoned with Cagliari struggling in 14th place in Serie B. "I always knew that one day I would return, I even said that in my leaving speech," he said. "The first time around (1988-91) achieving what we did convinced me that I could be a successful coach. We were as one, the fans, players and coach. This is what we need now again to push in the right direction." Claudio kept his word, guiding the club to safety following a 2-0 win at Sassuolo. He was given a standing ovation before the final game of the season, his 912th game as a manager in one of the Europe's top five leagues. Only Arsene Wenger has managed more games at that level (988).

As the first managerial casualty of the Abramovich reign, Claudio reflects: "When the chief executive (Trevor Birch) told me there is a new owner I said 'Me and you are the first who go home'." He was later deeply hurt at losing his job at Leicester after conjuring the miracle of a Premier League title for the Foxes, standing proudly alongside Andrea Bocelli as the world renowned tenor delivered 'Nessun Dorma' as part of the celebrations. He announced less than 24 hours after his parting: "Yesterday my dream died. After the euphoria of last season and being crowned Premier League champions all I dreamed of was staying with Leicester City the club I love for always."

There followed ill-fated stays at Fulham where he only won three of 17 games and Watford where he was a quick victim of their revolving door policy. Back at Cagliari, his 23rd job in football, but maybe not his last...

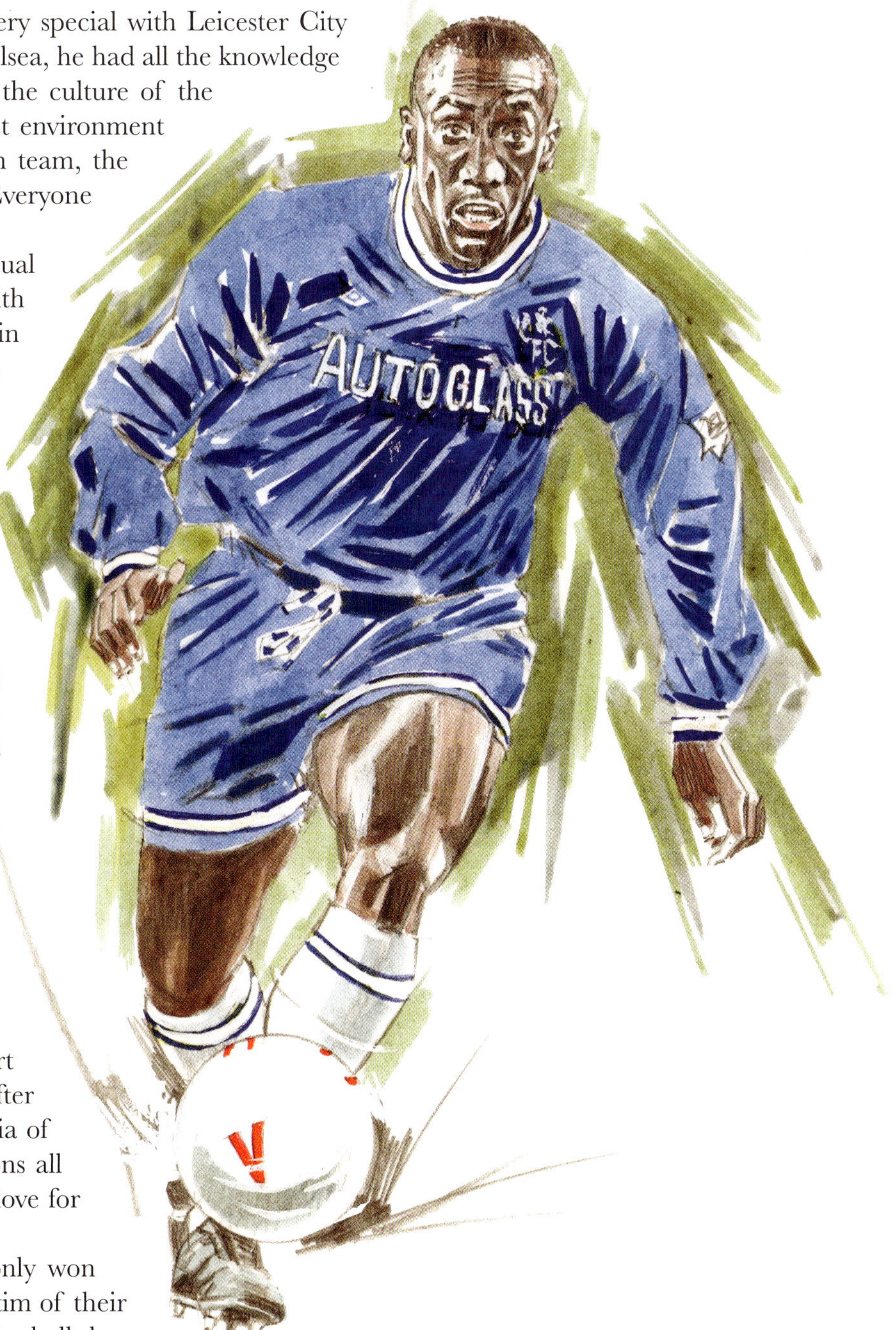

Frank Lampard

Chelsea's Greatest Goalscorer

Frank Lampard tops the list of an impressive array of goalscoring talent throughout the clubs 119-year history, which is quite a feat considering he is a midfield player unlike the other players on this list who are all centre-forwards wearing the iconic No 9. Chelsea have been blessed with legendary strikers from Bobby Tambling in the sixties, Peter Osgood in the seventies, Kerry Dixon in the eighties, through to Lampard and Didier Drogba in more recent decades. The fact that a midfield player would top this all-star list of goalscorers, illustrates Lampard's potency and ability in front of goal.

I have known Frank Lampard Snr for many, many years going back to his West Ham days when I worked on the *Evening News*, and in those days you had player's private home numbers and would call them on a regular basis for stories for the paper. I imagine that Frank Jnr answered the phone to me when he was still a boy!

Father and son turned up at a lunch in a Chelsea pub restaurant to help Alan Hudson promote his book, with Derek Dougan fronting an auction to help raise much needed funds for the former Chelsea midfield icon of the sixties who had hit hard times and was about to be thrown out of his council flat on the Worlds End estate on the King's Road.

Claudio Ranieri telephoned Frank Snr to enquire whether Frank Jnr was doing his best to shed a few pounds prior to agreeing to sign him for Chelsea. Frank Snr assured him he was working out in the less-than-glamorous location of their garage to keep in trim. While at the Hammers with his uncle, Harry Redknapp, as manager I was at a fans' meeting when one of them asked whether it was right that he should keep picking his nephew, because he was useless! Harry retorted in anger that "One day Frank would play for England he was that good." Well, Harry got it right, and proved the fan wrong. West Ham's loss was very much Chelsea's gain.

Frank Lampard junior went on to score a record 211 times in 648 appearances in all competitions between 2001 and 2014, including 147 in the Premier League. This, combined with 30 more goals for West Ham and

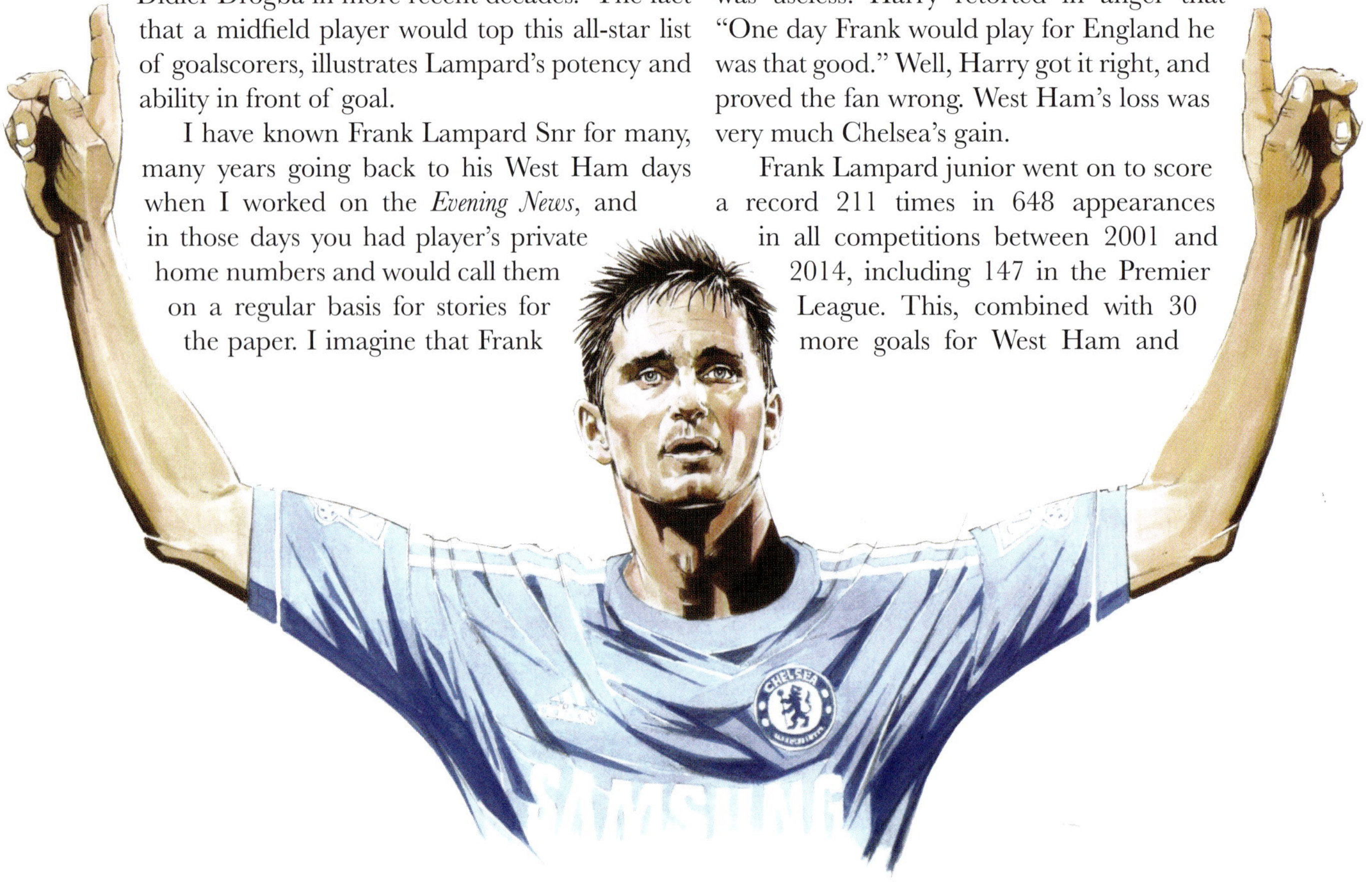

Manchester City, makes him the sixth highest scorer in the history of the competition. The next highest goalscoring midfielder in the list is Steven Gerrard who is 22nd on 121. Frank is also joint-seventh on the list of most capped England players, having made 106 appearances for his country over 15 years from 1999. During his 13 seasons as a player at Stamford Bridge he made 648 appearances and won 11 major trophies - including four Premier League titles and the 2012 Champions League.

A technically astute, box-to-box midfielder who had the knack of so often ending up the focal point for Chelsea attacks, Frank also has over 100 assists in the Premier League. Drogba and Lampard combined for 36 goals in the top flight, a record that remains unbeaten.

The West Ham Academy graduate was the stand-in captain the night when Chelsea won the Champions League as John Terry was suspended. He was also the captain one year later when Chelsea lifted the Europa League as Terry was out through injury. Lampard was later given a three year contract as manager when he replaced Maurizio Sarri at Stamford Bridge in July 2019, but only served just over half of that time. He became manager in 2020 leading them through a tough phase post-Eden Hazard's departure and the transfer ban imposed on the club. I contacted Frank to request that he write a foreword for one of my Chelsea books about the history of the club's managers. He was delighted to do so, as he said in the foreword: "I've know Harry for many years. He is well know and highly respected in the football world and I am sure that will be reflected in the quality of this book.The author has seen at first hand the difference in this game with the media, players and indeed managers and how they all went about their jobs in different ways in different eras, so I am sure we are all in for an interesting read."

Frank approved the final draft with this text….

Hi Harry,

I'm very happy with this. Let me know if you need anything else from me and of course good luck with everything.

Frank

In his personal comments he made it clear that he didn't want to tarnish his reputation as the club's greatest goalscorer by not succeeding as manager, so you see how much it would have hurt not to have achieved what he set out to do in the manager's role. His first managerial job was at Derby. In his one season in charge, they reached the Championship play-off final, where they lost to Aston Villa. Lampard became the 10th full-time manager appointed by Abramovich since the billionaire bought the club in 2003.

He said: "Since 2001 when I arrived at the Bridge from West Ham, I very quickly fell in love with the club and the area, and so I already know a fair bit about the club's history. Coming from a footballing family I'm aware of the different eras and managers through Chelsea's history, going back to some amazing players in the seventies, the King's Road set and, having spent some time in Alan Hudson's company, it was fascinating to learn even more from him about the flair players, many maverick in nature, and their relationships with their managers at the time. It is interesting to observe the comment from Ivor Baddiel, a life long Chelsea fan, whom I know through the association with my wife Christine on *The One Show*, that he discusses how football has changed through the different eras and how management has changed along with it, and the manager's relationship with their players. It is certainly a vastly different era now, there is a lot more structure to the clubs, with managers much more under the microscope than at any other time in the game's history. Of course, as I played for 13 years at this club, I played for many managers, and I had my issues from time to time, such as experiencing a tough period when Villas-Boas was the manager and he left me out of the team, so it would be true to say we had a conflict, but now I see it from the other side of the fence and see it differently than I would have done as a player.

"The job of management has also become far more intense over the last 20 years especially in the Abramovich era as there are high expectations which brings high levels of pressure, which in turn makes for some difficult decisions for managers who need a very strong squad of players with strong personalities. Having played under so many managers I have gained a great deal of experience, they have all given me food for thought on how they approach the job in different ways. I don't think a Chelsea manager 25 years ago would have needed the same qualities he would need now. I've taken many qualities from the managers I've played under, some I would disagree with, others I thought had the right approach, but all those aspects in their different ways are an aid to the way I would like to manage myself.

"It certainly would have surprised me if, when I started the Derby job, someone had told me that I would be sitting here as the Chelsea manager less than two years later. I wouldn't have dreamed it would come along after my first year at Derby. Was it the right decision to take the Chelsea job so early? Well, all the circumstances came together and it was definitely a question posed at the time of my appointment. I didn't question whether it was too early, I have the confidence in my own ability and believed I was capable of taking the job on but I understand why there were questions at the time.

"I had a wonderful playing career with Chelsea, but that has nothing to do with my new role. This is a completely new challenge. A challenge which I had no fear of taking on. My objective is simple, to be as successful a manager as it is possible to be at Chelsea. I want to be the best manager for Chelsea that I can be. If I don't, then that should not influence what I achieved in 13 years as a player but my intention is to succeed as a manager at Chelsea they way I succeeded as a player."

There was huge optimism with Lampard's arrival in the dug out, with former manager Glenn Hoddle sure that his old club would be title contenders "in two years if they recruit well" after the UEFA ban ended. "I think if he brings in the right professionals, the right experienced players, uses the right money on that level... He's got the youngsters, he knows he's got a group of young players there. In two years time, if he brings in the right pros, the good apples and good players, experience, with these kids, I think they'll be challenging for the league in two years time. That's how Chelsea owners have got to look at it, not about now. Even if he goes fifth this year and misses out on the top four, this squad and whatever manager is at Chelsea, the key is who he brings in, the experience. Those kids, they're good enough. You've got six or seven of them who are superb. And you've got a little underbelly as well, you've got a little underbelly coming through that are going to be great in two years time. But these kids now that are playing are going to have two more years experience. It is really important for Chelsea Football Club who he brings in, experienced players, to play with them. He's going to be losing Pedro and Willian, they've been great players, they're all going to be going. It's really key for how their future is and it could be exciting in two years time."

Dave Beasant was equally convinced that Lampard would be a success when he told me at the time: "Frank Lampard has done really well, especially as there were so many questions about his suitability for such a big job so early in his managerial career but just as Glenn Hoddle started out at Swindon straight from being a player and quickly made his way to Chelsea, so has Frank. Similarly Ruud Gullit and Luca Vialli took over at Chelsea straight from being a player, all of them player-managers. Frank is a student of the game, and when this big opportunity came along he was confident enough to go for it. He would take the good and the bad from his playing career having watched so many managers in his time. He would know what he would never do, and what he would take into his own managerial career. One of the big questions was how he could handle some of the big players in the team some of the strong characters, but he quickly set a precedent by selling David Luiz to Arsenal. Here was a player he had shared a dressing-room with as a player, and he was now the manager so the dynamics had changed. Whether he thought Luiz was too big a dressing-room influence or too big a personality, he made a very brave decision in selling him to one of their big rivals but that set the bench mark for his management. It was a clear message to the entire dressing-room: 'I might have been your team-mate once, but I am now your manager'."

Tore Andre Flo could observe Lampard's methods from the inside when he told me: "I'm now back at the club looking after the loan players. The club means a lot to me, and now when I go to the matches I'm jumping up in the air whenever Chelsea score. I have a strong love for the club. As for our new manager, like many other people, I like him a lot. He's very good at giving the youngsters a chance, and obviously he was a great player for the club as well. It is very nice to have him as the manager at the club now. I meet him every day, a lot of 'hi', and 'how are you?' as I don't deal with him so much in the work that I do. But he is a great guy."

Pat Nevin was another judge singing Lampard's praises: "There has been quite a turnover of Chelsea managers down the years, more so in the club's recent history, but in Frank Lampard I hope the club can recognise someone that can build a new dynasty at the Bridge. It's very difficult for me to give you a balanced view of Frank Lampard as the manager, as I am biased in favour of Frank, I like him so much, and there is much to admire. Certainly as a player he was one of the best, if not the best player in the club's history. As a manager he has certain traits that you have to admire and don't often see in modern management. He has a caring nature, and that is something special on top of all his qualities to manage the team. He has made tactical mistakes but what I admire in him is that he is prepared to say 'Yeh, yeh, I know I did something wrong and I will learn form it'. He's not too egotistical or arrogant that he cannot see where he went wrong, confess to getting it wrong, and learn from his mistakes. I talk to him virtually every other game, interviewing him for Chelsea TV, so I've got to know him, and I really like his willingness to be open with the media. In that respect he is like a throw back to the managers of my time who courted the media, which is done much less now as the modern manager finds it too much hassle to talk to people, but Frank is the opposite.

There was huge optimism with Lampard's arrival in the dug out, with former manager Glenn Hoddle sure that his old club would be title contenders "in two years if they recruit well" after the UEFA ban ended.

"More recently he has made fewer technical mistakes, bu in fact on the technical side he was outstanding in the match against José Mourinho and the way he has brought on the youngsters is just staggering, it puts him so far above the curve in his development process. He has brought the Chelsea fans together again, they are united behind the team and the manager whereas the supporters were split about the constant managerial changes. Now the fans are saying its time to stick by a manager to build something for the future, rather than like waiting for a 22 bus down the King's Road, and then suddenly five or six come along all at once, it's hard to keep track of the managers coming and going. Instead the fans want to have a manager who can build a dynasty at the club and they see that in Frank, they see that he is the guy to do it. He's been about par in the Champions League but not in the league where you would have thought it would be a mid table finish, ninth at best given all the circumstances, but to be in fourth place, even finishing fifth would be an achievement. It's hard to gauge the FA Cup but tactically he was outstanding in the Liverpool game and the way he picked Billy Gilmour was just mind-boggling. Especially against a club like Liverpool you would tend to go for the more experienced names and play it safe, but not Frank, he threw in Billy and what a game that kid had. I interviewed Billy recently and after a while I doubt whether anyone would have understood us as it transcended into pure Glaswegian! He has just turned 18, but already you can see he is a star for the future. But Frank has been brave all season bringing on the youngsters and that is exactly what the fans want to see.

"For too long there has been talent emerging from the Academy, but the players were loaned out and while the club have made a handsome profit, and the Academy has paid its way, the fans would love to see a Golden Generation emerge. Frank's attitude is to ask these kids if they are ready and he has the faith in them to put them in. Against Everton it was quite an eye-opener when Reece James, who has been outstanding all season at full-back, was brought on in midfield. After three minutes you can see why Frank did it, the boy looked even better in midfield than he has done at full-back. I know that there has been little room for patience at the club when it comes to managers, and that if you don't win anything you are out on your ear. But that won't be the case with Frank. That Golden Generation emerging from the Academy has every chance of happening while Frank is there and the club would be stupid to dispense with him if they don't win anything."

Paul Canoville was another willing to back him when he told me at the time: "I'm pleased to see Frank Lampard there now, he is Chelsea through and through and that is a perfect fit. I'm so pleased that he has given so many opportunities to the youngsters. It's about time the Academy boys had a clear pathway to the first team, as so many gifted players have come through without being given their chance. Patience is what is needed with Frank. As it is it's going to take a little time for him to get things going under all the circumstances. He has a great assistant in Jody Morris, he's such a level-headed guy who knows the youngsters having coached the under-23 team, so that's a huge advantage. Chelsea

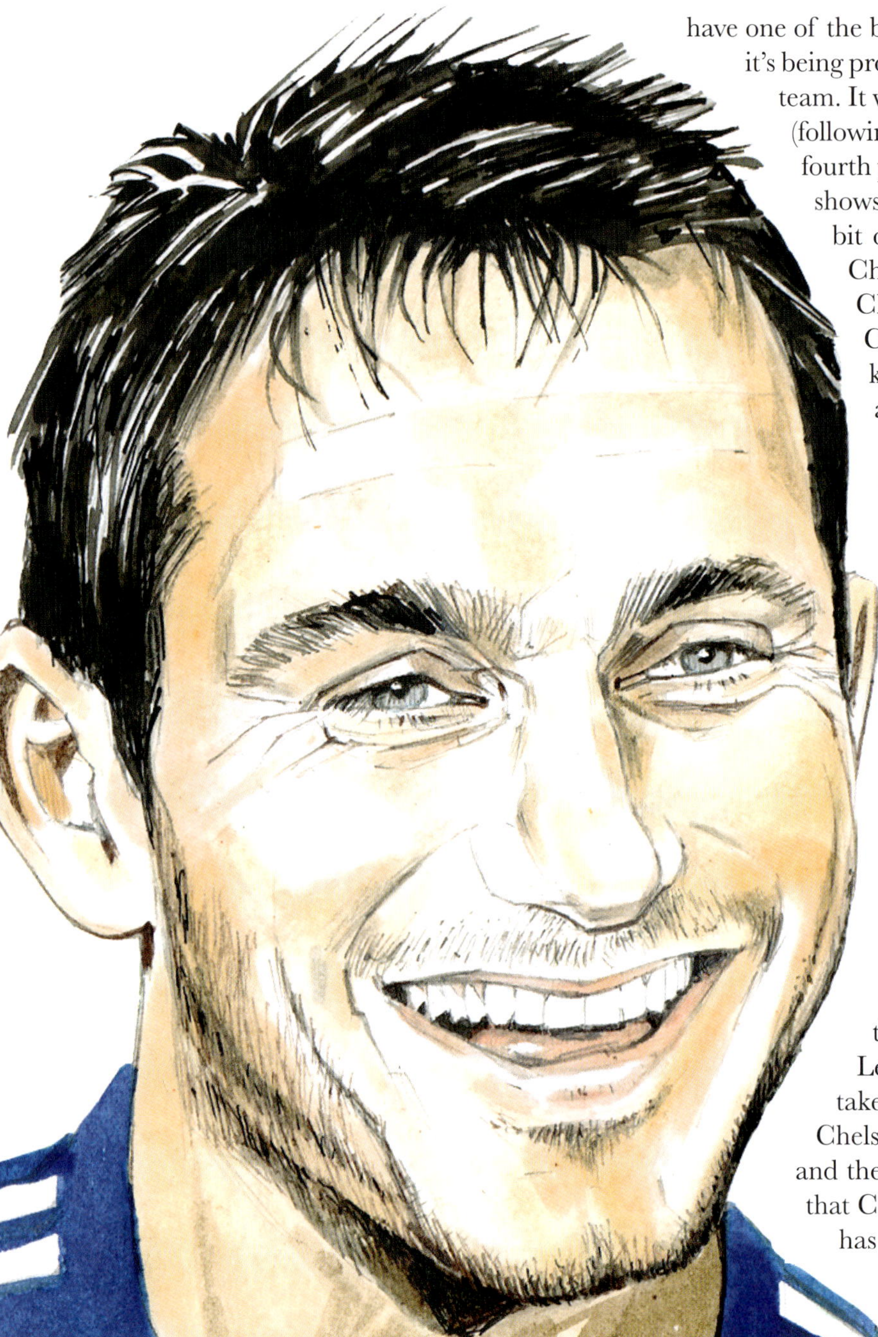

have one of the best academies in England, if not the world, and now it's being proved with as many as four or five from there in the first team. It was unfortunate to say the least the season was paused (following the Covid outbreak) as Frank was holding down fourth place as he had done for much of the season, and that shows he has done such a tremendous job. He has a little bit of experience with Derby, but it's no comparison to Chelsea. The main thing for Frank is that he knows the Chelsea family, he knows the club's history, he knows Chelsea football inside out, the fans love him, and he knows what the supporters expect, and that is his main advantage."

Nigel Spackman was another convinced when he told me: "Roman Abramovich, as I said, was the club's best ever signing, and no-one can argue with what he has brought to Chelsea, but in the past he has tended to pick the best foreign managers and coaches out there, but now has gone for Frank Lampard. It might have been a gamble but with the club's embargo on signing new players, it has left Frank to develop the youngsters and has worked out well, as Frank is doing an exceptional job under the circumstances. Frank was the right man, at the right time, in the right place. He spent a very valuable year as manager of Derby alongside Jody Morris but it's a huge step up from the Championship to the modern day Premier League and all the expectations and pressures that goes with it, especially at a club that had just won the Europa League and qualified for the Champions League. A big advantage for Frank was that he had taken his coaching badges working alongside Jody at Chelsea getting a good handle on the youth development and the best players coming through, so it all fell into place that Chelsea was the right club for him, at the time, and he has proved to be the right man for the job. It has removed some of the pressures having the transfer embargo and bringing on the kids, because this is a club where a manager is fundamentally judged on their signings and their ability to turn those signings into a winning team. That is why the club have to give Frank the chance to buy the players in the summer and to be judged on the team that he is building and how he will improve the team and improve the squad. Frank has to bring in the right players, of the right character, and I am sure Frank will do exactly that. But when the cheque book is opened up to Frank, then he will face even more severe scrutiny than he has already.

"However, at the start of this season with Frank in charge I thought that a place in the top six would be a terrific return for his first season under all the circumstances. Now it looks as though he might clinch fourth spot and a Champions League qualification and that is something no-one really could have expected. Frank's reputation as a player, as a true legend of the club, would give him time in the eyes of the Chelsea fans, but Frank won't be satisfied being a legend as a player, he wants to be a legend as a manager as well. He's a bright, intelligent, engaging guy and for me I believe he will develop into a legend as a manager as well as a player."

Unfortunately Frank Lampard was sacked after just 18 months in charge, really hardly enough time to turn things around, with former Paris St-Germain boss Thomas Tuchel replacing him. Lampard had guided them to fourth place and the FA Cup final in his first season in charge and he did not sign a single player during his first season as the club were operating under a transfer embargo, but spent more than £200m on seven major signings in the summer, including £45m on Leicester's Ben Chilwell and £71m on Kai Havertz from Bayer Leverkusen; the most Chelsea had ever spent in one summer, eclipsing the £186m they invested at the start of the 2017-18 season.

A 3-1 win against Leeds in early December put the club top of the Premier League. However the Blues suffered five defeats in the last eight league games of his reign - as many as they had in their previous 23. According to football finance journalist Kieran Maguire, Abramovich had spent £110m on sacking managers before Lampard's dismissal. Lampard's points-per-game average of 1.67 at the time was the lowest of any permanent Chelsea manager in the Premier League. During the Abramovich era, only Andre Villas-Boas (47.5%) has a worse win rate than Lampard's 52.4%, in all competitions among permanent Chelsea bosses. In contrast, José Mourinho's win rate in all competitions during his first spell in charge was 67.03%, while Sarri, Antonio Conte, Avram Grant, Carlo Ancelotti and Claudio Ranieri all had win rates over 60%.

In a statement, Chelsea said: "This has been a very difficult decision, and not one that the owner and the board have taken lightly. We are grateful to Frank for what he has achieved in his time as head coach of the club. However, recent results and performances have not met the club's expectations, leaving the club mid-table without any clear path to sustained improvement. There can never be a good time to part ways with a club legend such as Frank, but after lengthy deliberation and consideration it was decided a change is needed now to give the club time to improve performances and results this season."

Abramovich said Lampard's status as an "important icon" of the club "remains undiminished" despite his dismissal. "This was a very difficult decision for the club, not least because I have an excellent personal relationship with Frank and I have the utmost respect for him," said Abramovich. "He is a man of great integrity and has the highest of work ethics. However, under current circumstances we believe it is best to change managers."

Lampard was dismissed with the club ninth in the Premier League after defeat at Leicester City, having won once in their past five league matches. His final game was a 3-1 FA Cup fourth round win over Luton. In a statement, Lampard said he was "disappointed not to have had the time to take the club forward" and added that it had been a "huge privilege and an honour" to manage the club, adding "When I took on this role I understood the challenges that lay ahead in a difficult time for the football club. I am proud of the achievements that we made, and I am proud of the Academy players that have made their step into the first team and performed so well. They are the future of the club."

The reaction was universal among the rival managers at the time of Frank's sacking. Pep Guardiola: "People talk about projects and ideas. They don't exist. You have to win or you will be replaced. I am not judging Chelsea's decision. I respect their decision. But our world is to win as much as possible. I hope to see Frank soon and go to a restaurant with him when lockdown is finished." Tottenham boss José Mourinho: "It is the brutality of football. Anything can happen in football now, every time somebody loses their job it is sad news but he is a big boy, [with] a strong personality and strong mentality. I am pretty sure he will be

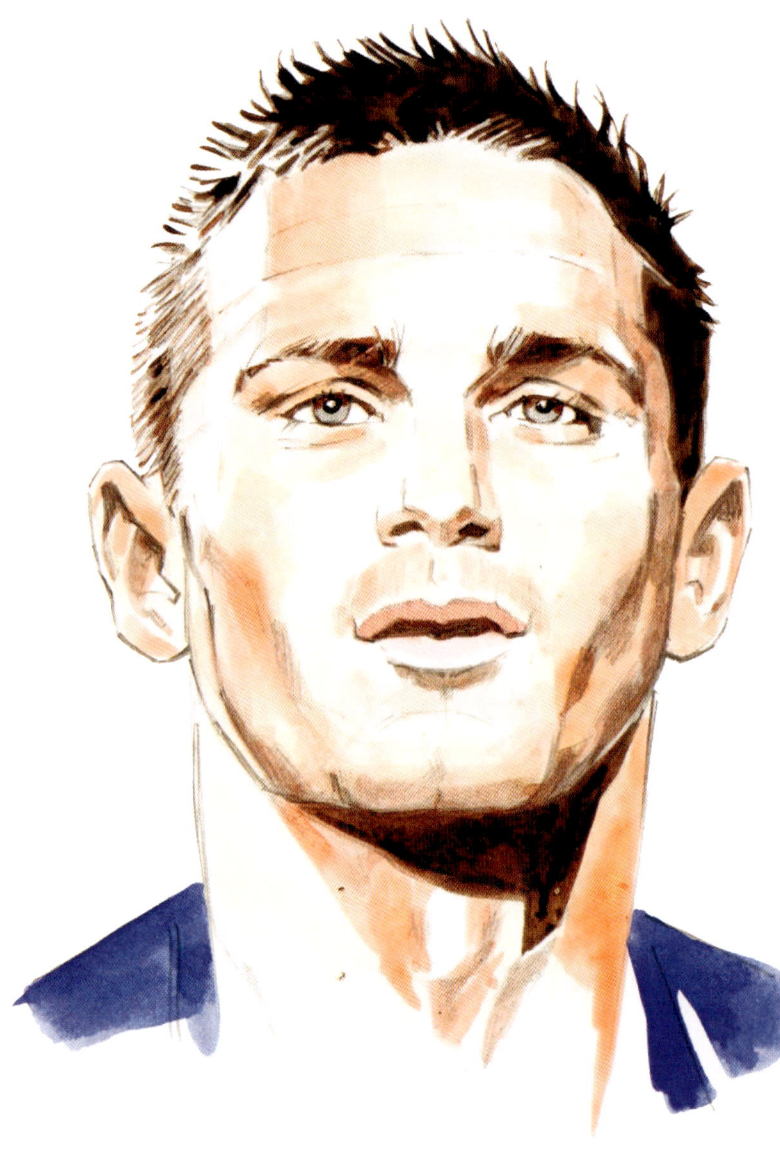

back when he wants to be back and his career will be good. I hope so." West Ham boss David Moyes: "I'm disappointed for Frank as I saw him as one of the most up and coming young English managers in the country. It's a big thing: we try to encourage our own British managers into the big leagues, if we can. I'm sure he'll come back and learn from it. He did a great job last year - he did a really good job with so many youngsters coming through the Academy. It seemed a little bit harder for him this year. I'm sure he'll take time off, come back and get better."

Leicester boss Brendan Rodgers: "Clearly I'm really sad for Frank and his staff. I know how much the club means to him. Looking at the squad and how young they are, they need time. He hasn't been given that time. I really feel for him. He did great at Derby. He had the courage to step out of an amazing career and could have taken an easier route. It was a job he couldn't turn down, even though he didn't have a lot of experience. Results haven't been what he would have wanted, but I feel it's a job that needed time." Crystal Palace manager Roy Hodgson: "It saddens me. I thought he did an excellent job last season. I was rather hoping that the idol of the fans and Chelsea legend that he is, he'd get a longer shot than 18 months. Managers who have had short stays at Chelsea have gone on to have good careers elsewhere. When you're sacked for the first time, it is a devastating blow. There's no doubt he has a pedigree to be a very good manager."

Former Chelsea striker Chris Sutton speaking on BBC 5 Live's *Monday Night Club*: "It is 52 days since Chelsea were top of the Premier League and 48 days ago that Chelsea had been on an unbeaten run of 17 games. So in the space of 48 days the owner has decided to write Frank Lampard off. How are we ever going to know if Frank Lampard is a good manager? You only every really learn about people and their characteristics and traits when they go through a little bit of adversity and Frank has gone through a little bit of adversity. Frank has basically been sacked for the owner's expectations. I feel sorry for Frank because he is a club legend. They are five points off fourth place, but the bottom line is that the owner wants to win the Premier League and that was always going to be the pressure. Chelsea should have been more loyal. We know the owner's track record - he is ruthless, he is brutal and guillotined Frank."

HH

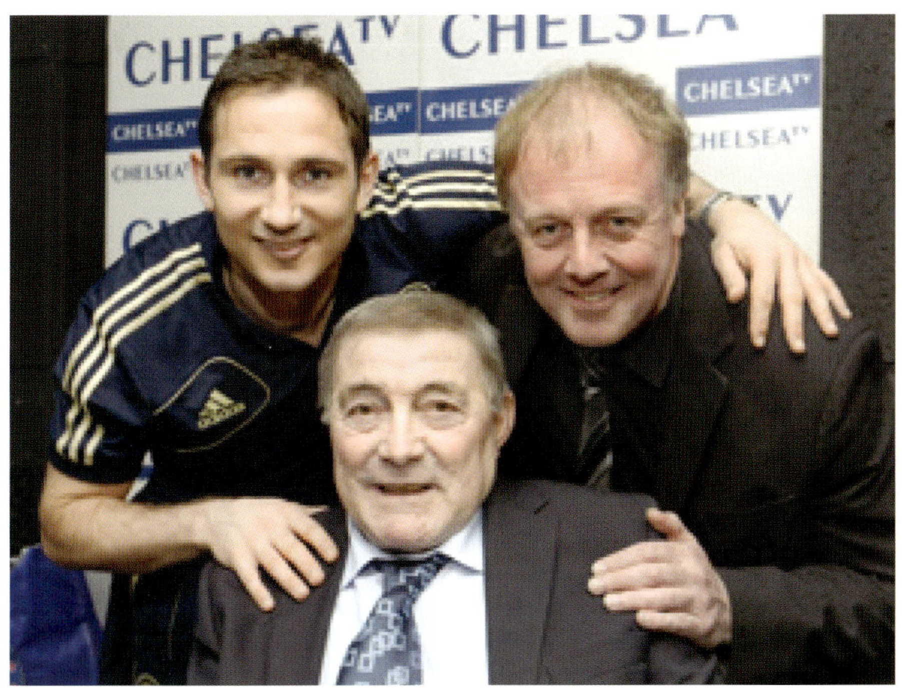

Highest Goalscorers

An historic photo of Chelsea's highest goalscorers to date; Frank Lampard overtook sixties scoring sensation Bobby Tambling on 11 May 2013 with a brace against Aston Villa.

The rest of the top ten looks like this:

4. Didier Drogba (2004-15) 381 apps, 164 goals
5. Roy Bentley (1947-57) 367 apps, 152 goals
6. Peter Osgood (1964-75) 380 apps, 150 goals
7. Jimmy Greaves (1957-61) 169 apps, 132 goals
8. George Mills (1929-43) 220 apps, 125 goals
9. Eden Hazard (2012-19) 352 apps, 110 goals
10. George Hillsdon (1906-12) 164 apps, 108 goals

FRANK LAMPARD		
Season	**Apps**	**Goals**
2001-02	53	7
2002-03	48	8
2003-04	58	15
2004-05	58	19
2005-06	50	20
2006-07	62	21
2007-08	40	20
2008-09	57	20
2009-10	51	27
2010-11	32	13
2011-12	49	16
2012-13	50	17
2013-14	40	8
TOTAL	**648**	**211**

BOBBY TAMBLING		
Season	**Apps**	**Goals**
1958-59	1	1
1959-60	4	1
1960-61	28	12
1961-62	35	22
1962-63	44	37
1963-64	38	19
1964-65	45	25
1965-66	42	23
1966-67	46	28
1967-68	30	15
1968-69	50	19
1969-70	7	0
Total	**370**	**202**

KERRY DIXON		
Season	**Apps**	**Goals**
1983-84	48	34
1984-85	53	36
1985-86	51	23
1986-87	43	12
1987-88	43	14
1988-89	44	28
1989-90	49	25
1990-91	44	15
1991-92	45	6
Total	**420**	**193**

Captain. Leader. Legend.

John Terry inducted into Premier League Hall of Fame.

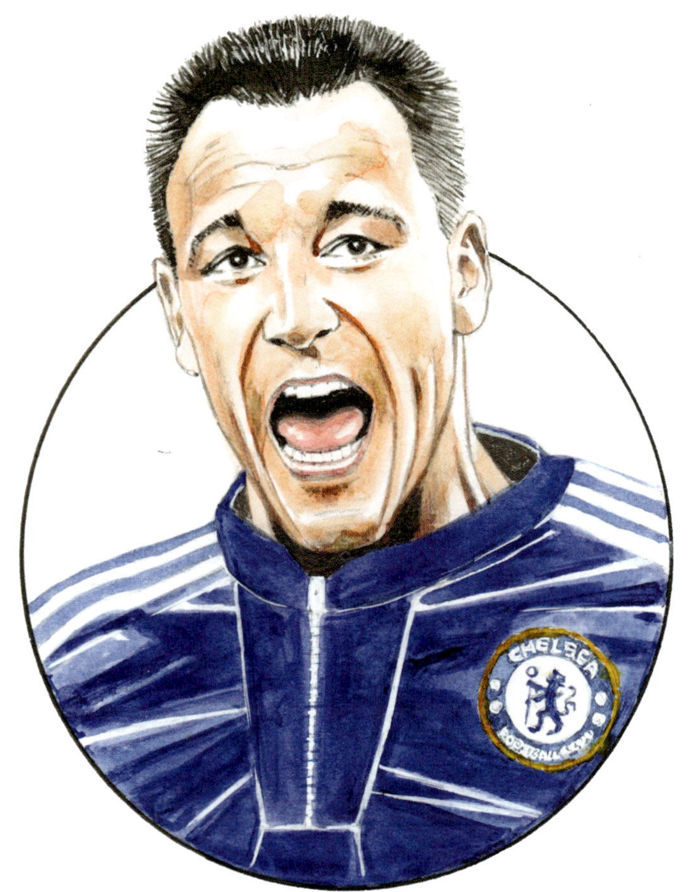

While the club might was going through a rough time on the pitch, epitomised by a 5-0 thrashing by Arsenal, one of Chelsea's biggest legends was being hailed as an all-time great when he was inducted into the Premier League Hall of Fame.

Ice cold on the pitch as one of the toughest central defenders of his generation, he was in tears as emotion took control when shown a video from José Mourinho. Of Chelsea's five Premier League titles, three of those came under the Portuguese manager who lead them to titles in 2005, 2006 and in his second spell at the Bridge in 2015. The pair also won the FA Cup in 2007, as well as the League Cup in 2005, 2007 and then again in 2015.

Who would be more suited to wishing John Terry a huge congratulations for stepping into the history books than the man who gave him the armband to go on to become the club's most successful skipper? In a video posted on the Premier League's official X page, Terry, now 43, was seen opening a black box and picking a phone up out of it. After pressing play, a clip of Mourinho appears on the screen. "Premier League Hall of Fame, John Terry?" he says before giving a little shrug. "Has to be. And now it is. I believe that for your kids, it's something really fantastic. I think, for me as one of the guys that had the privilege of working with you for about six seasons. I'm very happy, I'm very proud. You deserve [it], your career was amazing. I'm so, so happy for you and so proud of this achievement."

Kissing his hand, he finishes off by saying: "Kisses, mate."

After a brief pause, Terry looks up and smiles. "Wow," he says, as tears fill his eyes. "That's quite emotional." Terry took a moment to compose himself. "Sorry..." he says, "I think it's... I think I owe him a, you know, a huge amount for my career and the kind of direction it went in."

Terry had a joke at the end to lighten the mood. "He still frightens me to death!" he laughed. "When I see a video of him or he Facetimes me out the blue or something like that." With a smile, he added: "But I've just got so much respect for him for what he done for me and Chelsea. Chelsea means everything to me so yeah, very emotional."

The first inductees in 2021 included Roy Keane, Thierry Henry and Alan Shearer. Since then, Wayne Rooney, Ian Wright, Rio Ferdinand as well as managers Arsene Wenger and Alex Ferguson had joined them.

Days after it was announced the former skipper would be inducted, Chelsea suffered their worst defeat in a London derby

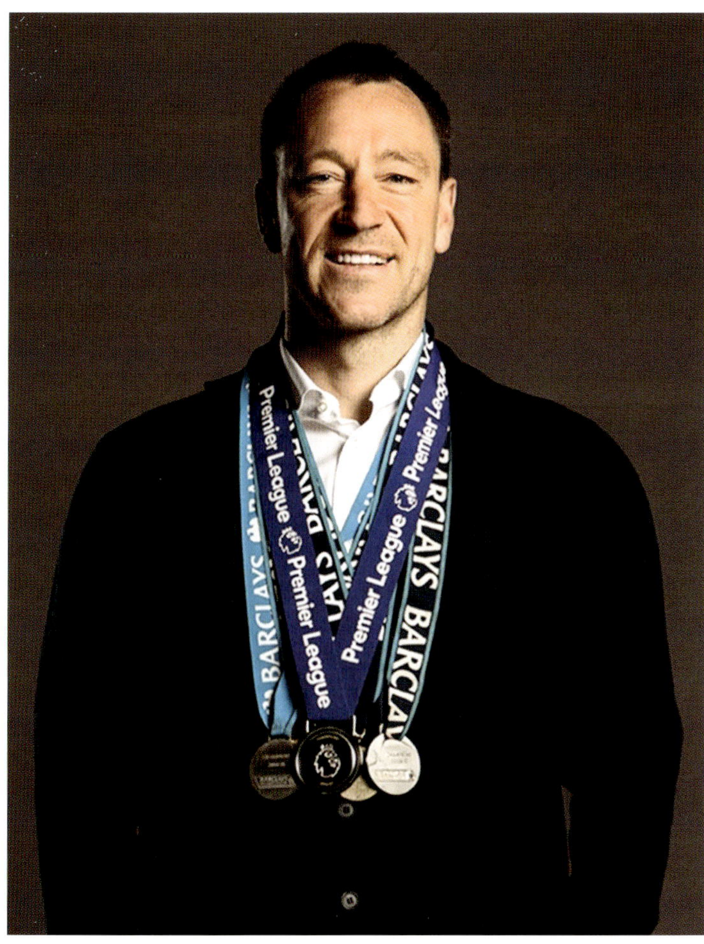

since 1986 when Arsenal beat them 5-0 and Chelsea fans now longed for the leadership of a new JT and a new hero in the shape of a Frank Lampard and Didier Drogba

It all started in October 1998 when a close-cropped teenager by the name of John Terry stepped onto the pitch for the first time as a Chelsea player. Twenty years later and five months after his final appearance, the 37-year-old announced his retirement. Terry is one of only three Blues players to have played more than 700 times for the club (Ron Harris and Peter Bonetti are the others). Terry made his full debut aged 17 and captained the first team for the first time just two days before he turned 21 - in a defeat to Charlton. He is the most successful captain in Chelsea's history and won every major honour during his time at Stamford Bridge.

An Academy graduate, an outstanding central defender for club and country, JT made his Premier League debut during the 1998/99 season and would go on to make 492 appearances in the competition with five titles along the way. The first was Chelsea's dominant 2004/05 triumph, in which they conceded just 15 goals, and kept 25 clean sheets. Both remain Premier League records. The Premier League trophy was retained the following season and lifted again in 2009/10, 2014/15 and Terry's final campaign at Stamford Bridge, 2016/17.

The legendary skipper holds the record for the most Premier League clean sheets as a defender (214) and remains the highest-scoring defender in the league's history with 41 goals. On that record of 25 clean sheets and just 15 conceded in a season he says: "I'm going to upset a couple of people here, but I think that season was as good as 'The Invincibles' season for Arsenal. They drew an awful lot of games. We only lost once, away to Man City. Paulo Ferreira gave away a penalty early on in the game and we should have come back and won. When you look at the goals we conceded that year, we conceded against sides you wouldn't expect if I'm honest and that's no disrespect to them. Looking back today, that could have maybe been nine or 10 goals conceded. I don't think it's a record that's ever going to be beaten if I'm honest. I certainly hope it's not and I'm very proud of what we did defensively. That's what we were paid to do, keep the ball out the net. It obviously helped with players around me like Petr Cech, Ashley Cole and Ricky Carvalho, so I'm very thankful for that."

Playing at the top for so long as a one-club man, he says: "You don't see it too often, one player staying at a club for so long, which enables you to achieve what I did. I first arrived at Chelsea at the age of 14 and it immediately felt like home. I've cleaned the stadium, I've cleaned the toilets, I've washed the kit, I've done pretty much everything. It was an incredible journey for me. I'm delighted we left a kind of legacy. I go back to Stamford Bridge now and bump into fans and they're very thankful for the memories that we created. Not only for them but for their parents, too. It can change and shape people's lives. You want to entertain people and, as ex-players, that's what we miss doing."

John said he loved leading out the team: "There's an awful lot of things that I learnt. I had the likes of Dennis Wise, Gianfranco Zola and all these experienced players that I learnt from along the way. When I was on the pitch, first and foremost I was me. And I wanted to be that person who trained at his very best every single day, turned up early and was never late. If I gave everything for the shirt then I could demand that from everyone around me. If you're a captain who's not doing that, they can quite easily throw it back at you when you're not doing it. That's the foundation of what you need to do.

"Away from that, there's an awful lot of stuff that goes on off the pitch for players. Understanding the group and that not everyone is the same and everyone needs to be treated differently was one of my main assets. I could be firm on the likes of Frank, Didi, Petr, and those guys but with certain other players like Joe Cole, he probably needed to be told he was brilliant and needed a cuddle at times and stuff like that.

"We had Marcel Desailly, who had just won the World Cup with France. Frank Leboeuf was part of that as well. For a 16-year-old, having those legends and people I had idolised around me was very important. There's not just one bit of advice that they gave me, it was a daily constant of little snippets: what to do, when to do it, not to dive in too early, work on your quick feet before and after training, come to the gym and stretch after training, see if it helps you. Marcel is a great friend of mine and we still often speak today and I never let him forget what he did for me as a player. When I first came into the team, Dubes (Michael Duberry) had just broken through and cemented his place in the team. Seeing him develop and grow into that position was great for me. He had so much time for me as well, shaping me as a person and a player.

"There are a few people I have to thank. First of all, Gianluca Vialli, for trusting me at a very young age to be part of the first-team group and giving me my debut at the club. The second would be Claudio Ranieri for making me captain when he did. Top of that list has to go José Mourinho. I think everyone knows how I feel about him as a manager, but as a person he was fantastic as well. I'd had my dad and my mum believing in me the whole way, but having him doing the same thing was really, really powerful for me and the whole group at the time."

It was during the nineties, under the management of Vialli, that Terry was given his first experience of senior football – and also collected his first winner's medal. "I remember those Diadora boots Luca used to wear and, as an apprentice, I used to run his baths for him. He used to like it really hot with a little bit of bubbles, so he could get in with his boots on and they would mould around his feet. He was so normal with me for someone so high profile, such a legend in the game. He was an unbelievable man and brilliant with the younger players."

When Terry made his debut in a League Cup tie against Aston Villa, the player-manager got a hat-trick. When Terry made his first start, Vialli scored both goals in a 2-0 FA Cup win over Oldham. When the defender went out on loan to Nottingham Forest to gain experience in 2000, it was a move set up by Vialli and his old Sampdoria team-mate David Platt, who was manager at the City Ground. Former England and Tottenham midfielder Jermaine Jenas recalls his time as a youth player at Forest, when he first came across a young Terry. "I always used to go and watch all the Forest games. Platty brought him in for Forest so our careers overlapped and we used to watch each other play in each other's positions. His

Terry's first two league titles under Mourinho were reasons to celebrate, but the third in the double-winning season of 2009-10 was special. The title was clinched with an 8-0 thumping of Wigan on the final day, ending the season on 103 league goals. Carlo Ancelotti's side were the first team since Tottenham in 1961 to score three figures in the top flight.

skill is the one thing that stood out then. People talk about JT and how he was a die-hard, which is spot on - he was all-round the best centre-half I have seen in the Premier League. But one of the big things I don't think he ever got enough credit for, which I was most impressed by when I watched him as a teenager playing for Forest, is how good he was with the ball at his feet."

Young players looked up to Vialli. When he arrived at Stamford Bridge, he was a superstar. It is a memory from one of Vialli's two FA Cup triumphs – shortly after Terry had returned from Nottingham – that he uses to explain why he and several other Academy graduates held the Italian in such high regard. "There were obviously a lot of experienced players around the first team at that time and I'd come back from a loan, but Luca put me, Jody Morris and Jon Harley on the bench for the final. He could have quite easily thought: 'Oh, they're young players, I'm going to go with experience'. But he pulled us in and said: 'You're the future of our football club and it's important that you're involved today'. But the key is that he said 'the future of our football club', because that's how he saw Chelsea. We went on to win, and even though I didn't get on, we felt part of that day. Just being in and around that squad was incredible, especially after the two months I'd just had at Forest. It was a really important moment in my career and Luca was a massive part of it. I'm forever in debt to him."

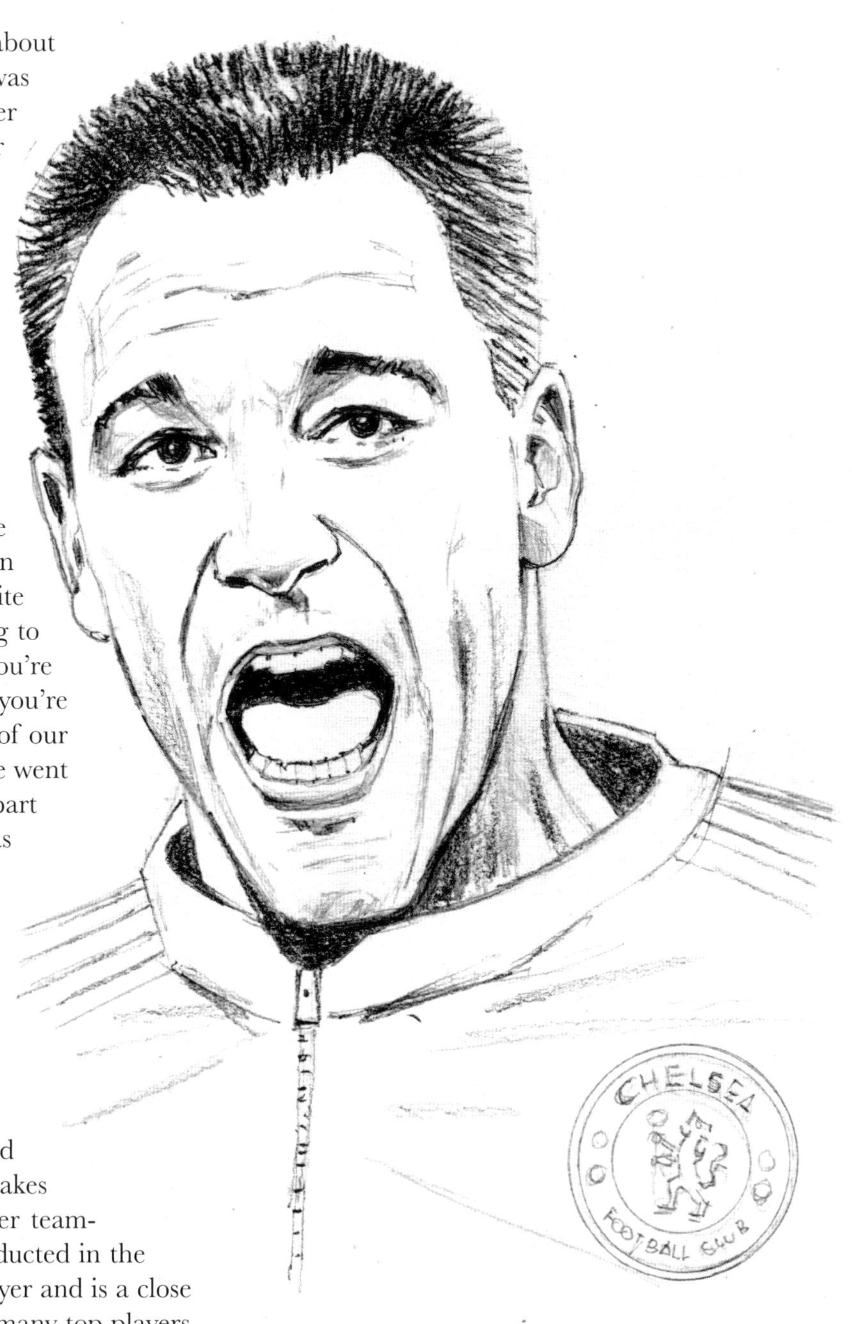

Terry joins Ashley Cole, Petr Cech, Frank Lampard and Didier Drogba in the Hall of Fame. "I'm very grateful to have been voted into the Premier League Hall of Fame," said Terry, "I'm a player that certainly gave my all whenever I stepped out on the pitch and to be recognised in this way makes me really proud. It's great to have joined my former team-mates who have already been inducted and to be inducted in the same year as Ashley Cole, who was an incredible player and is a close friend. I was lucky to share a dressing-room with so many top players.

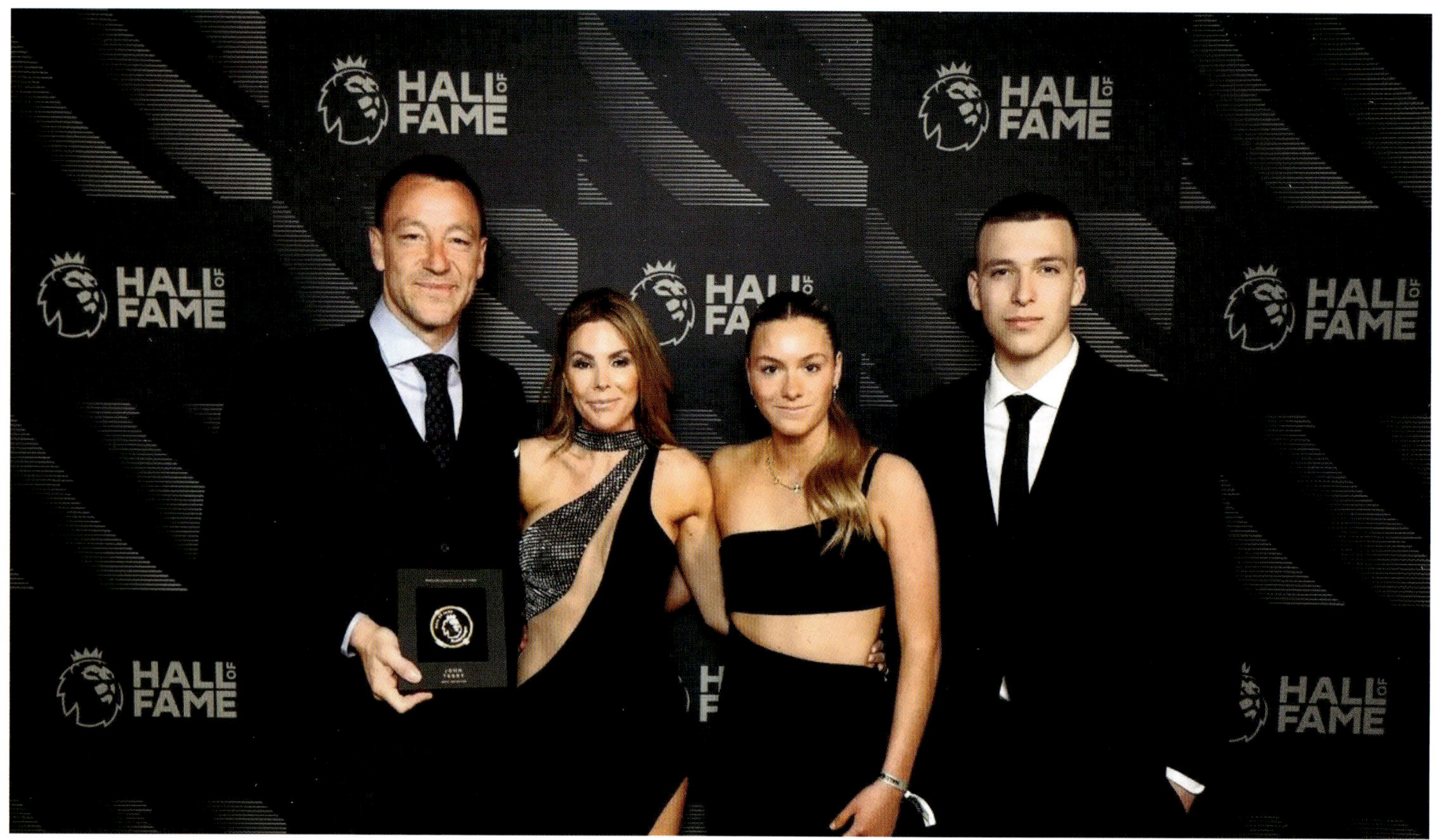

To captain a club like Chelsea and achieve what we did as a team is so special to me. The Premier League is the best league in the world, which every player hopes to play in, and I'm very proud to have won it five times.

"I fell in love with football at a young age and it's emotional to reflect on the time spent playing. It has been an incredible journey. At the time you're not thinking let's do this to become part of the Hall of Fame, you just want to work hard and try to win and to be remembered as someone who gave their all for the team and the supporters. I'd like to thank my parents, Toni, Georgie and Summer for supporting me throughout my career and understanding the sacrifices as a family we had to make."

JT enjoyed playing alongside the likes of Ashley Cole who preceded him into the Hall of Fame. "Ash was not only my team-mate, he's still a very close friend today so it's very special to share this honour with him. Ashley was an incredible player and for me the best left-back that the Premier League has ever seen. Defensively he was brilliant and an absolute joy to play with. He could give everything going forward as well with so much energy and chipped in with goals, too."

In 2005, Terry became the first defender - and the first Chelsea player - to be named the Professional Footballers' Association Player of the Year. He was recognised after helping the Blues to just their second top-flight title, while his part in Chelsea's run to the Champions League semi-finals saw him named the Uefa club defender of the year. He would go on to receive that recognition again in 2008 and 2009.

Terry's first two league titles under Mourinho were reasons to celebrate, but the third in the double-winning season of 2009-10 was special. The title was clinched with an 8-0 thumping of Wigan on the final day, ending the season on 103 league goals. Carlo Ancelotti's side were the first team since Tottenham in 1961 to score three figures in the top flight. Terry was once again integral, playing in 37 of the 38 league games and making more than 50 appearances in total. He only managed two league goals but both were vital. The first was the only goal in a 1-0 victory over Manchester United, who finished as runners-up. And the other was a late winner in a 2-1 success against Burnley. It helped Chelsea to become just the seventh club to claim the league and FA Cup double.

An integral cog in the side that won the league under Mourinho in 2014-15, he became only the second outfield player to feature in every minute of every Premier League game in a season. Also named in the PFA Team of the Year, it was quite the contrast to his perceived worth under Rafael Benitez a year earlier. The Spaniard, interim boss at Stamford Bridge from November 2012 until May 2013, said Terry could not play more than two games in a week and in that season he made just 14 league appearances. His revival during Mourinho's second spell at Chelsea played a major role in the club's 2014-15 title triumph.

Terry announced towards the end of the 2016-17 season that he would leave that summer, having rarely featured in Antonio Conte's plans as the Italian guided the club to another league title. Terry went out in typically high-profile fashion, leaving the Stamford Bridge pitch to a guard of honour after 26 minutes of his final match for the Blues, against Sunderland. Terry was synonymous with the number 26, having worn it on his shirt during his Chelsea career.

"I kind of negotiated with the manager to play 26 minutes and come off," Terry said. He would go on to join Aston Villa in the summer of 2017, helping them reach the Championship play-off final. He returned to Chelsea in a coaching consultancy role with the club's Academy, working with players and coaching staff in the youth development programme in a part-time capacity. "I'm delighted to announce that I'm coming home," he said on social media "The flexibility is key for both myself and the Academy as it allows me to continue and develop my own coaching skills and ambitions alongside other commitments."

Terry wore the Three Lions shirt with as much pride as he did the Chelsea shirt. Terry's England career brought him 78 caps and periods of heavy turbulence, including an episode that led directly to the departure of Fabio Capello. He made his debut in June 2003 against Serbia and Montenegro and started the 3-1 win against Croatia at Portman Road on 20 August that year.

Terry played for England at Euro 2004 in Portugal and the World Cup in Germany two years later, England going out to the Portuguese on penalties in the quarter-finals on both occasions. He succeeded David Beckham as England captain shortly after the 2006 World Cup. Former Fulham and England midfielder Danny Murphy played alongside Terry at international level. "He is two-footed and has always been a good footballer and a good reader of the game because that is a gift," said Murphy. "But straight away he always had that tenacity he became known for and a willingness to put his body on the line - that old-fashioned centre-half mentality. That whole combination made him an obvious candidate to become an international footballer and as the years went on he got more confident and became even better. There have been some other really good centre-halves but even if it is only marginal, he is ahead of Rio Ferdinand, Ledley King and Jamie Carragher. They were all top players but JT just had that something extra that made him the top one for me."

In January 2010, an injunction halting the media reporting on Terry's alleged relationship with Vanessa Perroncel, the former partner of his ex-Chelsea and England colleague Wayne Bridge, was lifted by the High Court, and the episode was to have major consequences for Terry's England future. He was stripped of the captaincy by Capello in February of that year, yet Terry still figured in the ill-fated World Cup in

South Africa, where England lost 4-1 to Germany in the last 16, before being reinstated as captain in March 2011 as Rio Ferdinand struggled with long-term injury. He was removed from the role by the FA in February the following year while he was waiting to stand trial over racial abuse allegations following an incident involving Anton Ferdinand at QPR during a Premier League game in October 2011. Capello challenged the FA's decision and resigned within days after talks failed to resolve the differences. An FA statement read: "The discussions focused on the FA board's decision to remove the England team captaincy from John Terry and Capello's response through an Italian broadcast interview. In a meeting for over an hour, Fabio's resignation was accepted." Terry was cleared at Westminster Magistrates' Court after a five-day trial of abusing Ferdinand in July 2012 but he retired from England duty in September 2012 saying his position had become "untenable" because the FA pursued a charge of racially abusing Ferdinand during the game at Loftus Road. He was subsequently found guilty, banned for four matches and fined £220,000 by the FA. A spokesman for Terry said he was "disappointed" the FA had reached a "different conclusion" to the "not guilty verdict of a court of law". A Twitter spat ensued between brother of Anton, Rio, and Chelsea team-mate Ashley Cole which escalated the matter even further.

Despite the controversies that dogged his career, off the pitch as much as on it, there were so many highs and positives, but inevitably regrets. Wednesday May 21, 2008 should have been a perfect moment. The Chelsea icon had the chance to score the penalty kick which would make his beloved Blues champions of Europe for the first time against their Premier League rivals Manchester United. "I walked forward to take it knowing that it was there to be won and it was all down to me. What happened next will haunt me for the rest of my life." He slipped as he made contact and his shot cannoned off the post. United went on to win the shootout 6-5 in sudden death.

The Hall of Fame celebrates individuals who have an exceptional record of success and have made significant contributions to the Premier League since its inception in 1992. JT was selected from a shortlist of 15 former players by fans worldwide through an online public vote and the Premier League Awards Panel. Each inductee receives a medallion engraved with their name and the year of their induction along with a £10,000 donation made by the Premier League to a charity of their choice.

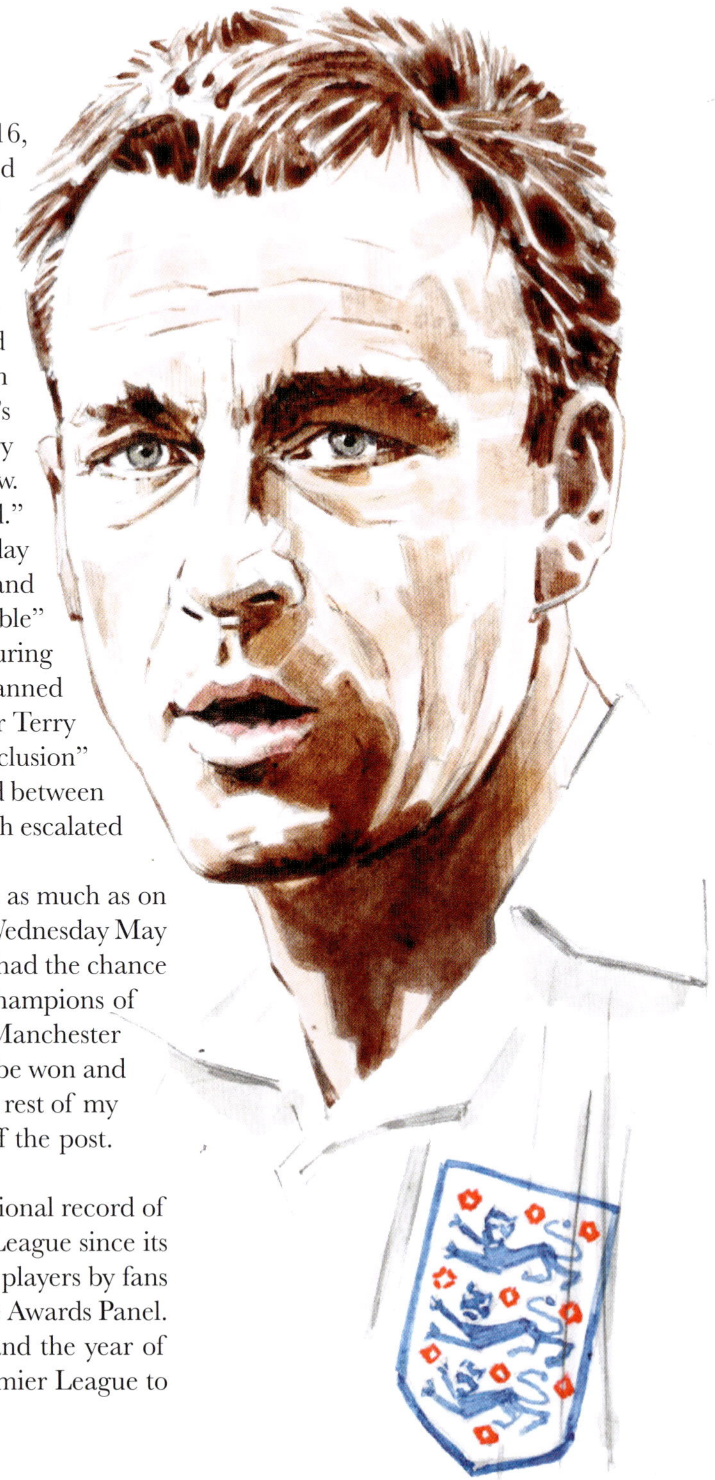

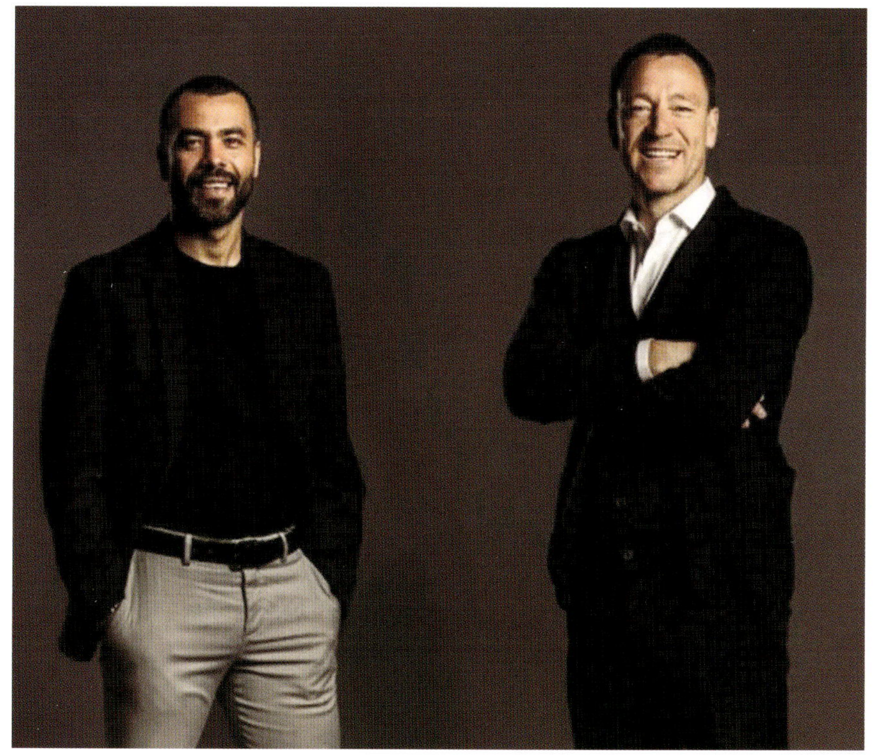

Gary Cahill helped marshal the defence alongside Terry after joining the club from Bolton in January 2012, with the two forming one of the strongest partnerships in the league. The pair were regular starters during the 2014/15 title-winning season – Terry played every game and Cahill missed only two – as José Mourinho's team finished in top spot. Both were also part of the squad that won the Premier League in 2016/17 under Antonio Conte, a season that ended with Terry claiming his fifth and final title winner's medal. Following Terry's latest accolade, Cahill gave an insight into what it felt like to play next to the club legend, citing the strengths that made him an outstanding defender. "When I first started training with him, there were two things that stood out: how tidy he was with the ball, and how well he read the game," Cahill said. "You never really see the best centre-backs getting exposed in many one-vs-one situations because they read the game so well. I felt like I just had to worry about what I was doing, knowing full well he was taking care of what he was doing. He was so established in his position, so experienced, and so good. Sometimes you've had partnerships where you're not quite sure what your team-mate is going to do or what position he's going to be in. John made life a lot easier. It was a good partnership. We were both very vocal on the pitch, both dragged each other around in terms of position and tried to drive the team but it made it a lot easier to play with somebody like him."

Once he saw Terry was nominated for induction into the Hall of Fame, he thought his inclusion was 'a formality' and that the recognition is 'thoroughly deserved'. When it came down to what separated JT from other players, Cahill pointed toward his mentality and ability to keep standards high. "He was brave and he read the game really well. He seems to sometimes get an 'old school' tag, but he was a very good and intelligent footballer. He could use his left foot and right foot equally well. One of the first things that stands out is his leadership, the way that he can take control of a group and drive players and drive standards in the club and in the team. He was destined to be a captain. He'd take control of details - down to the food, down to the treatment - and try and get the players the best outcome, which is to win trophies, which he did many times. He was fully committed to wholehearted defending. That was the way he played, the way he trained. He wanted to win everything that he did. In training, he'd want to win the small-sided game, even wanted to win head tennis. He just had that kind of drive and that winner's mentality. John Terry epitomised what Chelsea was about."

JT revealed he led a mutiny against a manager's decision to seat him in economy on a long-haul flight while the club's younger players were placed in first class. Terry related a previously untold story that Andre Villas-Boas took the controversial decision ahead of a pre-season tour of Asia that began in Malaysia which turned senior players including himself, Lampard and Drogba against him shortly after the Portuguese boss joined the club in 2011. "We get on the plane and I'm sitting in economy on a 13-hour flight. And we've got Josh McEachran, Nathaniel Chalobah, a couple of other young players all in first class. And this was part of AVB going 'no player is bigger than me, everyone's the same'. It turns out Lamps is flying out in first class and I'm flying back in first class. So if you fly out in first, you come back in economy, but basically it wasn't good enough. So, I'm going on the plane, 'No, we're not going anywhere until these young players go back in economy and the first team players, that have built this club to where we are today, go back in first'. We're on the plane, people were up and down, AVB comes up 'What's the problem?' I go, 'Well, we're not going anywhere until the young players move'. And to be fair to the young players, they're going 'This is really uncomfortable, we'll go back'. And I'm going 'No, it's not your decision, he has to own it'."

JT and the other senior stars would not have allowed the plane to take off with them on it had AVB not changed his policy, and JT admits that the new manager had "failed instantly". "This was one of his first things in front of everyone. In the end, it spun. First team players go first, younger players go economy. That's how it should be. These younger players are striving to be where we've got, and he tried to make a statement. He came in and he failed instantly, because I promise you the plane wasn't going. If it was going, it would have gone without myself, Frank and Didier." It was little surprise that Villas-Boas lasted just eight months at Stamford Bridge!

That might have been one of the unknown controversial incidents, but there were many well documented. In September 2001, Terry was one of four fined following a drinking binge in a hotel packed with American tourists grieving over the terror attacks on New York City's twin towers at the World Trade Center. The incident happened 24 hours after the attacks and the drunken behaviour took place at a hotel near Heathrow Airport, which was packed with American citizens stranded by flight cancellations. The group included Terry, Lampard, Jody Morris and Frank Sinclair. Chelsea's Uefa Cup game that night against Levski Sofia had been called off as a mark of respect to the victims of the 9/11 attacks. The then managing director, Colin Hutchinson, condemned the plauers' behaviour as "totally out of order" and said they had each been fined two weeks' wages.

Yet having hit the outside of the post in the 2008 Champions League final, Chelsea's captain finally lifted the Champions League trophy on the greatest night in the clubs history - and this is a tale of much lighter note, unless you are JT as he has been mercilessly ridiculed on social media. Terry played no part in the 2012 final - he had to watch from the stands after being sent off in the semi-final victory over Barcelona. Perhaps one of Terry's biggest regrets is his moment of madness against Barcelona, inexplicably kneeing Alexis Sanchez in the back of the thigh in an off the ball incident which saw him sent off after just 37 minutes. Somehow Chelsea managed to reach the final with 10-men, but were without their skipper, Ramires, Raul Meireles and Branislav Ivanovic for the final against Bayern Munich due to suspension. But it became one of the club's greatest ever nights when the Blues managed to scrape a 1-1 draw in normal time before winning 4-3 on penalties.

Yet JT still lifted the trophy in Munich, as he was on the bench shamelessly dressed in full kit (including shinpads) so he could lift the European Cup! He was endlessly lampooned on social media and became the victim of many a meme. "Doing a John Terry" has become a popular phrase, with Leicester's Robert Huth tweeting to say he was "Going full John Terry today!" to lift the Premier League trophy in May 2016, despite serving a three-match ban. In May 2013 Terry was at it again, picking up the Europa League trophy as Chelsea beat Benfica, despite missing the final with an ankle injury.

*

John Terry is now working part-time with the "18s, 21s and younger age groups" at the Chelsea Academy after working as assistant to Dean Smith at Aston Villa and Leicester City. "I am still waiting for a full-time job. I love my role at Chelsea. I am just waiting for the right job to come along. If that comes along, I will look into it and take it. I have done all my badges and I am ready to go. It is just about being patient and choosing the right owner, the right football club and the right people to go in with. I am very open minded about where I go. I miss it madly. It still burns a little fire in the belly. I want to manage. Fingers crossed."

Terry is keeping fit playing Padel "two or three times a week" and took part in the celebrity pro-am Padel Aid to raise money for UNICEF. Padel is one of the fastest growing sports in the world based on lawn tennis but with walls in play as in squash. "Padel Aid is very similar to Soccer Aid which is coming up in June at Stamford Bridge which I have played in for a couple of years. This was the first one and we are hoping we can grow it and make it bigger and better." Padel Aid co-founder Sarah Horrocks said: "The energy from the celebrities, GB players and pros made it such a fantastic experience. We have raised an amazing amount of money for UNICEF."

JT revealed that Sir Alex had made weekly phone calls in a bid to take him to Old Trafford at the start of his career. Terry spent 22 years at Chelsea but the iconic Scottish manager called Terry's family home every week to monitor his progress. Despite 'rolling out the red carpet' to secure his signature, the former captain insists he felt a stronger connection with Chelsea. "I was in the West Ham Academy for two or three years and one night we found out our coach had left, so I told my dad that I didn't want to go back. Then I went to Arsenal for a year and at that time I was floating between Arsenal, Manchester United and Chelsea. Arsenal and United both rolled out the red carpet for me, but Chelsea didn't do anything. I had Sir Alex Ferguson phoning my house every week to speak to me and my dad, checking that I was going to school and training correctly. Even with all that, when I walked into Chelsea I just knew it was the right club for me. I felt like it was my home, like when you walk into a house and just feel you belong there for the next 20 years."

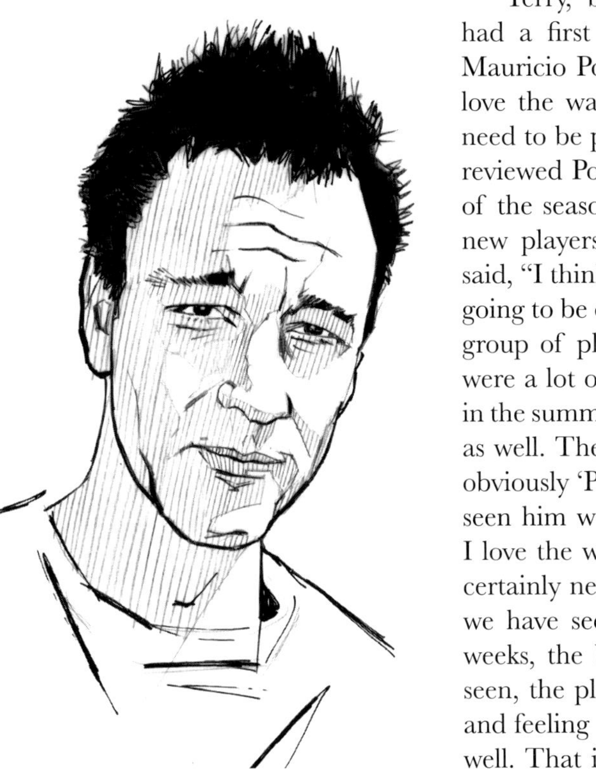

He revealed the gruelling routine he endured as a teen to ensure he made it at Stamford Bridge. "I was leaving school at 4:30pm to get to Chelsea at seven o'clock, then wouldn't get home until 11:30pm. I did that for a couple of years by myself. I absolutely loved it and I fell in love with Chelsea." Terry is a devoted admirer of José Mourinho, even considering him successful at Old Trafford, "I would look at his time at Manchester United as being a successful one, compared to where they've been. When you see the press conferences of him talking about how he won three Premier Leagues and all the other managers won two, I think he's spot on with what he said. Was he harsh on some of the United players at the time? Did they deserve it? They clearly did otherwise he wouldn't say it."

Terry, back at the club's Academy, had a first hand view of the work of Mauricio Pochettino and commented: "I love the way he is with the players. We need to be patient." New owners BlueCo reviewed Pochettino's position at the end of the season after spending a billion on new players. With results improving JT said, "I think Poch did well. It was always going to be difficult - we had a very young group of players from the outset. There were a lot of signings and a big clear-out in the summer of not only players but staff as well. There was a big turnaround and obviously 'Poch' is new in the door. I have seen him work, I love the way he works, I love the way he is with the players. He certainly needs a bit of time. And I think we have seen that in the last couple of weeks, the better performances we have seen, the players growing into their roles and feeling like they belong at Chelsea as well. That is also going to take time and I just think we need to be patient. I think every club needs stability. We have been very lucky at Chelsea. For 20 years we have had success year after year after year. We have got a young squad and we look like we have got some really good players at the moment that can grow into their roles. Hopefully next season will be better."

Despite the backing of a bona fide club legend, and after praising the "beautiful football" in the comeback at Aston Villa and two London derby wins, Chelsea co-owner Todd Boehly made the decision to fire him.

HH

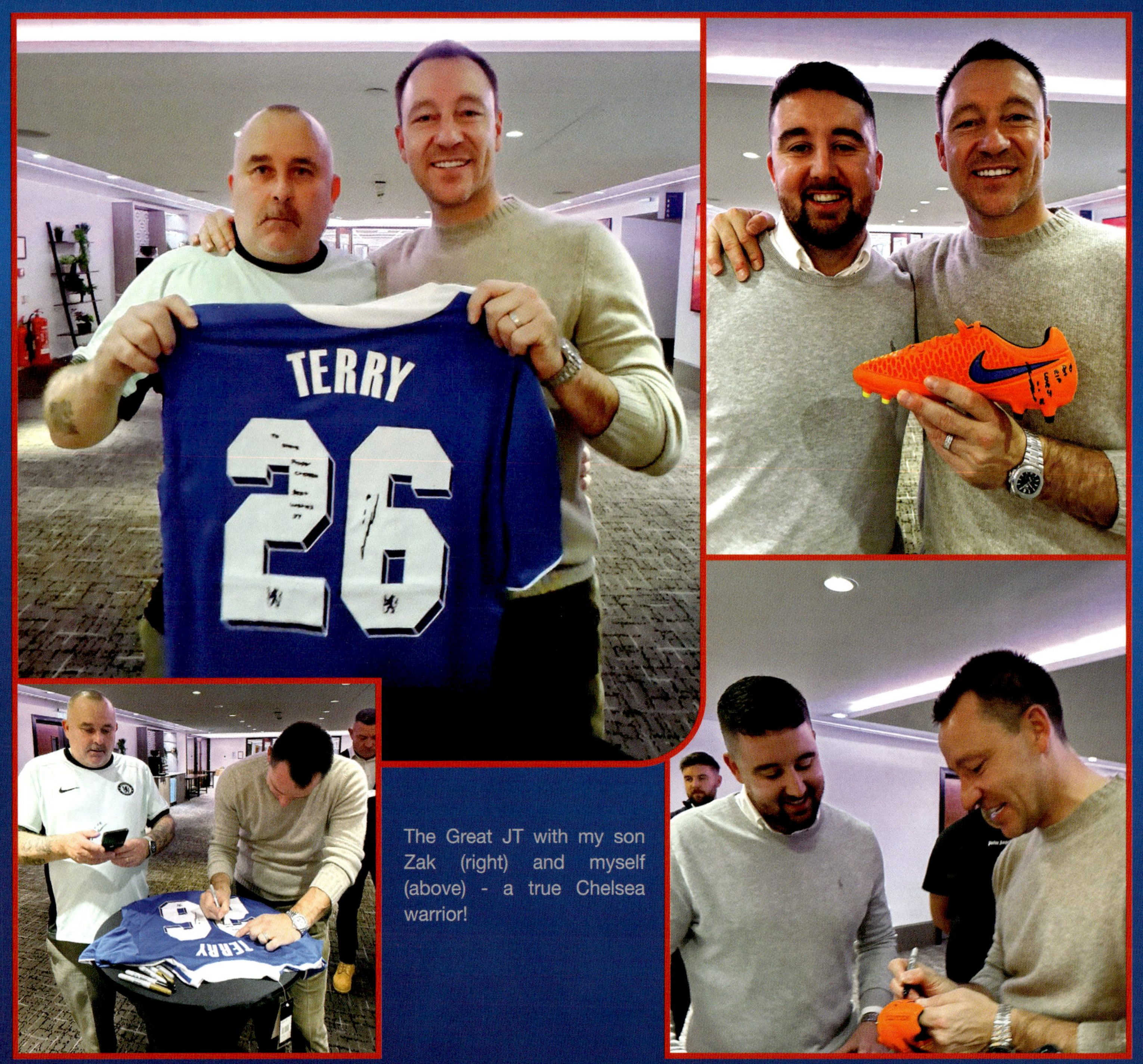

The Great JT with my son Zak (right) and myself (above) - a true Chelsea warrior!

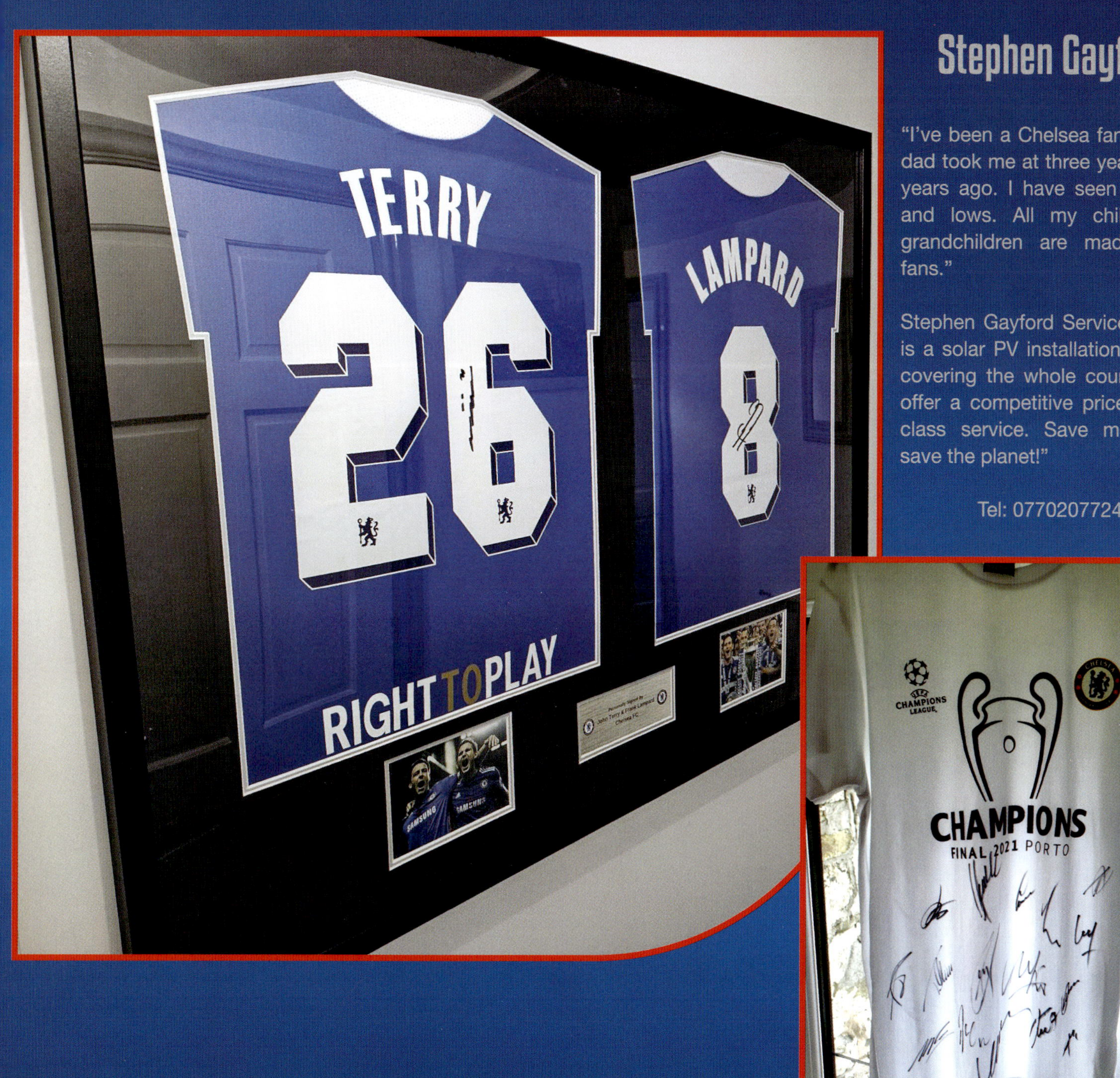

Stephen Gayford

"I've been a Chelsea fan since my dad took me at three years old, 53 years ago. I have seen the highs and lows. All my children and grandchildren are mad Chelsea fans."

Stephen Gayford Services Limited is a solar PV installation company covering the whole country. "We offer a competitive price and first class service. Save money and save the planet!"

Tel: 07702077241

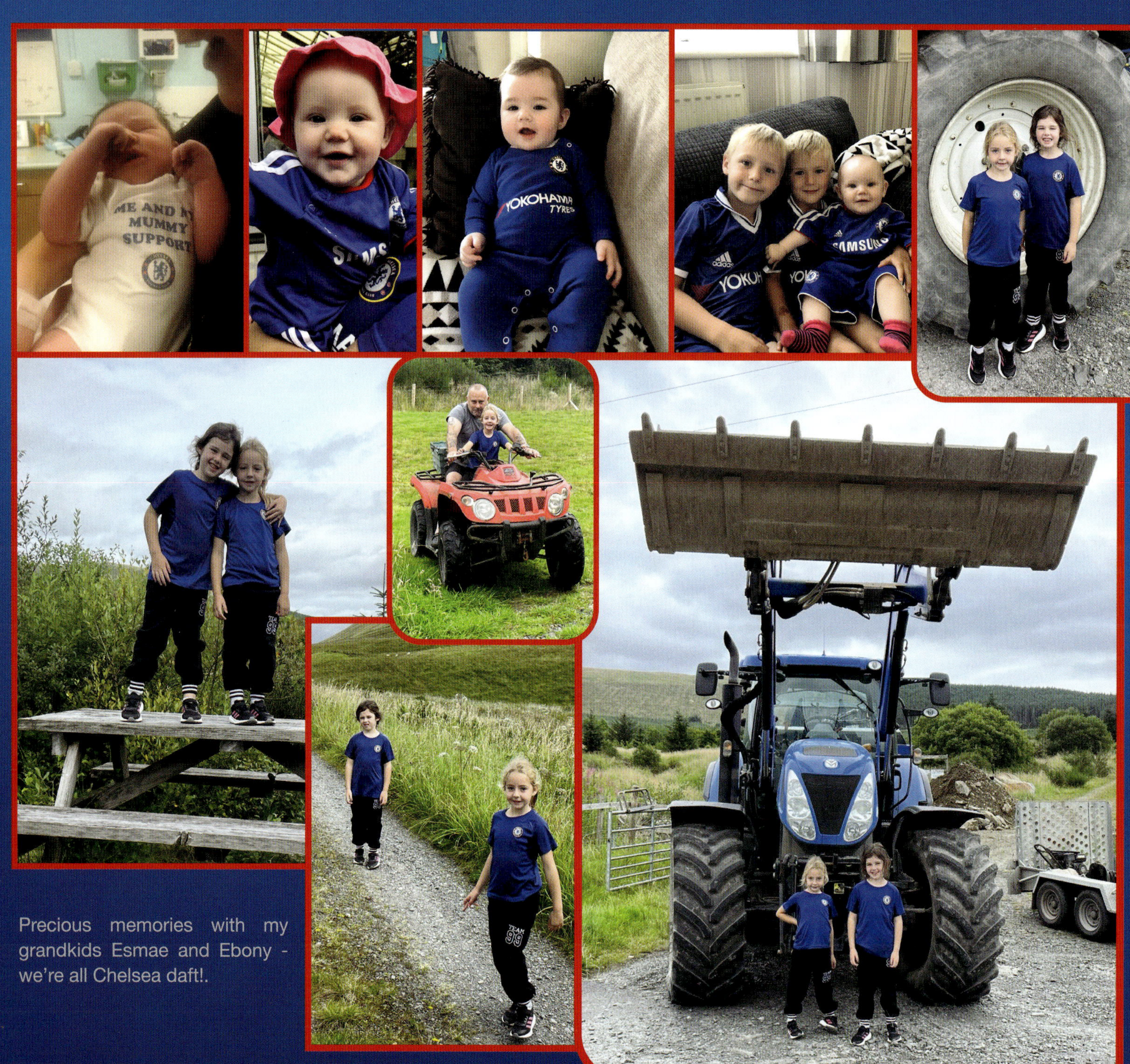

Precious memories with my grandkids Esmae and Ebony - we're all Chelsea daft!.

I had my picture taken with 'Wee Pat' in the promotion season from Division Two (1983-84) and then again 40 years later. The little wizard!

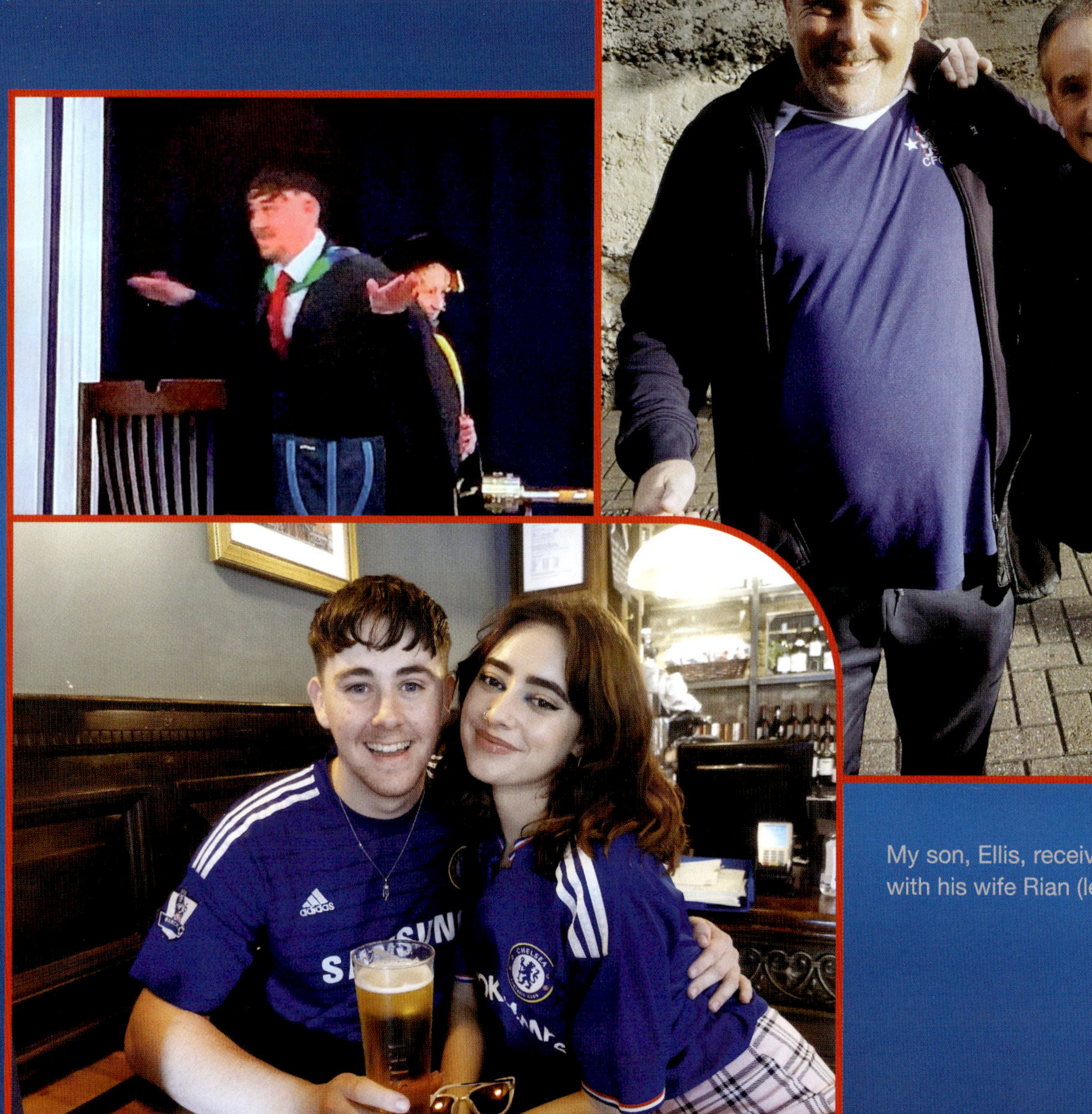

My son, Ellis, receiving his degree (above) and with his wife Rian (left).

Bad Boys

ADRIAN MUTU

One of Roman Abramovich's first signings, Mutu was bought from Italian side Parma for £15.8m in August 2003, and the one-time Romanian captain was a gifted goalscorer, until he tested positive for cocaine, which he has more recently claimed was not cocaine but a substance to enhance his sexual prowess! Mutu said: "The only reason I took what I took was because I wanted to improve my sexual performance. It may be funny but it's true. I did not take cocaine. I took something to make me feel good."

The four-time Romanian Footballer of the Year netted six from 25 Premier League appearances during his maiden term at Chelsea and ever since the club kicked him out, there has been a succession of hearings and court cases.

After a promising start at Stamford Bridge, he fell out with managers Claudio Ranieri and José Mourinho. He tested positive for cocaine in September 2004 and was sacked the following month, shortly before the FA gave him a seventh-month ban. Chelsea sought compensation from Mutu to recover a large amount of the fee they paid to sign him, with Fifa setting damages at 17.1m euros (£15.2m) in 2008, a figure that CAS and the Swiss Federal Supreme court supported. The compensation figure, based on lost earnings, was calculated on the length of time Mutu's Chelsea contract had left to run, and was the highest handed down by Fifa. Despite being banned until May 2005, Mutu joined Livorno on a free transfer in January that year before he was quickly sold to Juventus once they could offload one of their non-EU players. FIFA ruled in 2013 that Livorno and Juventus should pay some of Mutu's compensation to Chelsea but CAS overturned that decision in 2015. Mutu was also suspended for nine months in 2010 after testing positive for appetite suppressant sibutramine while playing for Fiorentina. He returned to his mercurial best at Fiorentina, netting 70 times in 143 appearances for the Viola. A brief stint at Cesena was followed by spells in France, India and his native Romania before Mutu hung up his boots aged 37 in 2016 as his country's joint-record goalscorer at international level.

Mutu lost his latest appeal against a ruling that he must pay £15.2m in compensation to Chelsea after a failed drugs test. The Court of Arbitration for Sport ordered him to pay damages to the Blues in 2009, upholding a Fifa ruling. The European Court of Human Rights rejected Mutu's appeal against the CAS decision, ruling there had been "no violation" of Mutu's right to a fair trial. After the hearing Chelsea confirmed they were still pursuing the player for the damages. "We are exercising our legal remedies to recover the amounts owed to us and we will continue to do so," a club spokesman said. Mutu alleged CAS had not been independent or impartial in its ruling because one of the arbitrators on its panel had been a partner in a law firm that represented the interests of Chelsea owner Roman Abramovich. The ECHR concluded it had "no strong reason" to overrule the Swiss Federal Supreme Court, which concluded Mutu "had not substantiated his allegations" in upholding the CAS judgement in 2010. Mutu also objected to the same arbitrator sitting on the 2009 CAS panel and a previous panel in 2005 that upheld a Premier League ruling he had breached his Chelsea contract. The ECHR said although those rulings "concerned the same facts" the legal issues to be decided were "very different" as the first was over whether Mutu had breached his contract and the second related to the amount of damages owed.

MARK BOSNICH

Bosnich's time at Chelsea was marred by injury and drugs. He failed a drug test in September 2002, leading to Chelsea tearing up his contract and the Australian being banned for nine months. The then 30-year-old failed a first test seven weeks before the results were announced, awaiting his B sample which also proved positive, when he was charged by the FA. Bosnich, whose career has stumbled since becoming one of the best keepers in the world during his time at Aston Villa, had not played for Chelsea that season as Carlo Cudicini established himself as No1, with Ed De Goey on the bench. Bosnich confessed: "The day I got caught I had what was a tenth (of a gram of cocaine), a minute amount; the forensic scientists at the hearing said I could have put my hand in it.

The worst thing I did after (the drugs test), I just started going ballistic. I thought, 'Everyone thinks I'm guilty. You know what? Stuff the world, stuff everything!' I got disillusioned. If I'd stayed clean that would have been the best way to show up people who were behind it. But that was my fault and I chose that road."

It was an acrimonious time, leading to stunning revelations about Bosnich's personal life, his life spiralled out of control while he was in a relationship with model Sophie Anderton and getting lost in the nightlife of West London. He recalls how John Terry tried to save him. Bosnich said: "Yeah, John did do that. That crowd was part of the people who sent that girl (Anderton) to me. I tried to help her, and fell in love with her. But she was sent to me for a specific reason. John had noticed similar problems with a couple of other players at that place, the Wellington. I remember saying to him, 'They're okay,' he would say, 'Baz, they're not.' And he was right. Bad crowd, bad people. The problem was I had no-one to turn to, and I had this burning desire to find out what was behind it. So I thought I'd go straight to the source, but the more you spend time with these people the more you are slipping, slipping, slipping. Until three years later people ask you, 'What have you found out?' and you say, 'Nothing yet, I'm still undercover - but I haven't got any problems, honest…'

"I'm fortunate that I got myself out of it, otherwise it wouldn't have been very pretty if you were talking to me now, if you were talking to me at all. I had given up not only on the football but on myself, which was wrong and really dangerous - I say that now whenever I go and speak to kids. I wasn't that easy to deal with. So I can understand that people probably thought, 'Just leave him; he doesn't want to listen anyway.' I was obdurate and narrow-minded. I have to take the vast majority of the blame. And the people who set me up, messing with a person's life and business just for financial gain."

Bosnich claims that he never took drugs until his career was over, insisting that his drink was spiked when he took that fated drugs test at the club. He later admitted to a $5000-a-week cocaine habit - but only took the recreational drug after he was banned. "I never touched drugs until I was 31 - but once it got hold of my life, it became a massive struggle to break free. The worst times were when I thought of doing stupid things, not so much because of the ban but because of what was going on with my girlfriend. I was slowly killing myself but I didn't care. My life was ruled by drugs and I was a mess. I was staying awake on coke for days on end. It was destroying me. I know people won't believe me but I want to come clean. I wasn't taking any drugs when I was found guilty by the FA. In 15 years of football I never touched them. But everybody believed that I was into drugs, especially because of my relationship with Sophie. So one day I thought, 'f--- it, I'm going to do it.' I went to a club, bought a wrap of coke, and brought it home to try. Basically, I cracked. I was angry and bitter and I succumbed to what everyone said I was, a coke fiend."

Bosnich said he then used the drug to try to frighten Anderton, a model with a history of drug and alcohol abuse, into going clean. "I told her that for every line of cocaine she would take, I would take two. And that's exactly what I did. I knew it would hurt her and, to be honest, I felt invincible. But I reached a stage where I was taking six grams of cocaine a day. I was staying awake on coke for days on end, just constantly playing computer games and watching TV. Once I was up for four nights in a row."

Bosnich said he was shocked into action when he almost shot his father, Mark, mistaking him for a burglar. "I was high on coke and I had my airgun in my hands. I'd been up for three or four days and was playing around in the house. I heard a noise downstairs and I thought it was a burglar, so I raced down with my pistol. As he came around the corner I grabbed him and put the gun to his head. I was so high I didn't know what I was doing. My father was shocked ... he said he wouldn't leave until I had kicked drugs. It was that moment that I realised I couldn't do this to my family and the people I loved. I had to take control of my drug problem. All I want to do is get back down to business, which for me is playing football. And I want to apologise to all the loved ones I've hurt, the people I've let down. The look in my father's eyes when I confessed to him was enough to make me want to give up cocaine. He was so disappointed in me. I have made a promise to everyone, including myself, that if I ever turn to drugs again I will immediately check myself into a rehab clinic. But I believe I'm strong enough to turn my back on drugs for good."

The former Manchester United star, at his peak, was highly

rated, regarded as one of the finest goalkeepers in the game, he won two League Cups at Aston Villa in 1994 and 1996 and Sir Alex Ferguson originally signed him as the replacement for Peter Schmeichel, the captain of the 1999 Treble winning side giving Bosnich enormous shoes to fill when he made the move. Bosnich's first appearance for the club came in his homeland, with United Down Under for a pre-season tour before jetting back across the pond to secure another Premier League title in 1999-2000 but like many players he found the pressure at Old Trafford too much to take with Sir Alex Ferguson describing Bosnich as a "terrible professional".

ASHLEY COLE

Cases of cocaine abuse are bad enough and there have been numerous unsavoury incidents dotted throughout the club's history, but arguably one of the most bizarre was the shooting of a club intern inside their own training camp by one of their biggest stars!

Ashley Cole came in for harsh criticism following the tapping up affair that hit the headlines in 2005. Chelsea chief executive Peter Kenyon, Mourinho, Cole and his agent were all spotted in the Royal Park Hotel in London's Lancaster Gate dining together in what was assumed to be a plan to engineer a move from Arsenal to Stamford Bridge. Although denied at first, the rumours intensified and eventually the truth came out, with all parties involved receiving heavy fines.

"Why not do it in the middle of the M25 and then at least everybody knows?" asked Cole's manager Arsene Wenger at the time. Ashley has since admitted that he was naive when he got angry when Arsenal offered him what he regarded as a derisory £5,000-a-week pay rise. It led to fans dubbing him "Cashley Cole" and it would be another 18 months before he eventually left Arsenal for Stamford Bridge where he won the Champions League, four FA Cups, the Premier League and League Cup, but that was nothing compared to the February 2011 incident when he shot an intern at the club's training round with an air rifle.

Quite what an air rifle was doing at the training ground remains a mystery, but Cole fired the gun, which he believed not be loaded, at a young intern from close range. The student required medical attention from the club's in-house staff and was checked over days later. The incident occurred in the wake of Chelsea's FA Cup fourth round defeat at home to Everton the day before during which Cole missed a penalty. Carlo Ancelotti's players were called in for training on Sunday to prepare for a Champions League outing. Cole arrived at Cobham holding the weapon he accidentally shot 21-year-old student Tom Cowan with by accident, claiming to be "larking about with it in the changing room". However, it has been claimed that the air rifle was in fact a gift for Cole that was sent to the training ground. A fellow Premier League footballer and close friend is said to have sent him the gun, but no-one knew what was inside the package as it was a surprise for the England left-back. One of Cole's team-mates pointed out the parcel and questioned what was inside, before taking it out and handling the weapon. Cowan, who was on a year-long placement at Chelsea as part of his degree in sport and exercise science, was stood a few yards away. The student was with Cole as he began to check out the gun himself - and that's when the accident occurred. A source said: "As Ashley held the gun he thought there was nothing (no ammunition) in it. But there was and it accidentally went off in his hand. It's not like he was going around shooting at people. Unfortunately the guy was hit, but he wasn't badly hurt. He was laughing about it. He was a nice kid. It was just an unfortunate situation."

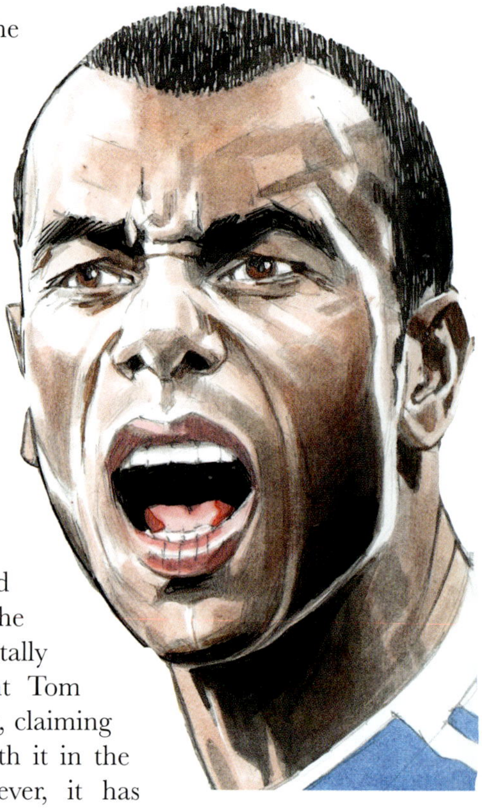

Carlo Cudicini

The Best Back-Up Keeper In The World

One of the most talented and popular keepers in Blues history, Carlo made 216 appearances between 1999 and 2009, keeping 101 clean sheets. On the periphery during his initial loan from Castel di Sangro, sitting on the bench for the 2000 FA Cup final, the Italian went on to shine after claiming the No.1 spot a short while later. Arriving at a time when Chelsea were spending significant sums on foreign superstars, Carlo cost just £160,000 from an Italian Second Division club yet made just as big an impact. In Italy he found it hard to live up to the exploits of his father Fabio, a legendary keeper for AC Milan who earned the nickname *Il Ragno Nero* – the Black Spider. Carlo had played just 51 league games by the time he moved to Chelsea at the age of 26 as back-up to Ed de Goey. "I had come to Chelsea from a Second Division team in Italy and after the first year, when I only played a few games, everything changed. Suddenly I was the first choice. I'd been lucky enough to grow up at AC Milan, which gave me an opportunity to train and play with great players. Then I was in the same situation at Chelsea, playing behind great defenders like Marcel Desailly and Frank Leboeuf. So, I was very excited." Initially on loan, Carlo had to wait patiently for a chance. When it came, in the second half of the 2000/01 season, Carlo took it brilliantly. Despite an initial challenge from Mark Bosnich, Carlo kept his place with a series of brilliant displays. Not the tallest of keepers, his speciality was the impossible-looking save. With a panache for saving penalties, Cudicini will always be affectionately remembered for standing out in a side that otherwise toiled before Abramovich's vast investment. Named Player of the Season in the 2001-02, he won the Golden Glove as the Premier League keeper of the year in 2002-03, a season in which he helped the club qualify for the Champions League. It was inevitably a struggle after Petr Cech's arrival in 2004, but he remained until 2009 as the league's best back-up keeper. Injury problems, though, surfaced in the first leg of the 2004 Champions League semi-final. "Everything started off really well for me and then I had bad injuries. Then, when they were finally behind me, my career took off again and Gianluca Vialli and Chelsea gave me the chance to join a great team. The first year enabled me to see what was going on, but then when Claudio Ranieri arrived I had a chance to perform and I deserved the spot I earned. Suddenly, everything turned around."

Only three other keepers had won Chelsea's Player of the Year, so it was a huge honour for Carlo. "It was an unbelievable moment for me. Don't forget, I'd been playing Second Division football just a few years before! The supporters were fantastic with me from day one and this award was the result of a great connection I always had with them. That day was emotional for me because you know how much your team-mates appreciate you, but to find out the supporters feel that way too is unbelievable. This award will always link me with the Chelsea supporters. I will always have a place in my heart for them." A year later, he went one better, voted the best goalkeeper in the Premier League!

"From being recognised by your own supporters to the whole of the division was another great award. It's special for me, because it's a personal one, and it was another step for me in my career. I remember being given that award on the day we qualified for the Champions League, which made it even more special. Qualifying for the Champions League was such an immense achievement in 2003, at the end of a season in which we had spent no money on new signings. There was a lot of pressure that season, but it was a great job by the manager and the team. Ranieri had the courage to put young players like John Terry into the team, and also myself because even though I wasn't young like John, I was inexperienced and unknown in England. He mixed up the team with experienced players and talented youngsters. We delivered a great season, which was finished off with a wonderful win over Liverpool on the final day to get into the Champions League."

"Me and Petr had a great relationship and we are very good friends. In his first season here, he had the opportunity to be in the team and start in goal in, and he never gave it up. Only great players have that concentration and consistency."

Carlo loved playing with fellow Italian Zola. "Gianfranco had an unbelievable career, especially at Chelsea, and everyone has said many things about him which I can only confirm. He was a great player on the field and an unbelievable person off the field – everyone loved him. He was so important in the dressing-room because everyone listened to what he was saying; not only did he have the experience, but his character meant he approached people and said things to them in the right way. It must have been nice to see the back of him at the end of that season, though, as I imagine he was a goalkeeper's nightmare in training. His free-kicks were incredible! I've heard him called a magician, and he certainly was – you never knew what he would do when you were one-on-one with him, he always had a trick.

"Gianfranco is also one of many players from that particular era at Chelsea to have become a manager. It's unbelievable to see how many of my old team-mates have gone into management. It just shows you how good that team was – there was not only one manager on the bench, but another eight or nine on the pitch. That helped the team win some big trophies for Chelsea. Goalkeepers don't tend to go into management, though, it's usually a case of coaching other keepers. Why is that? I know Ed de Goey and Kevin Hitchcock are both doing that. I think goalkeepers tend to stay in their little box! Once they quit, it's time to teach the youngsters. One thing I would say about English football is that there is a great goalkeepers' union. It's something that is part of the game – we stick together because we know how hard it is to be out there on your own. We share this pressure, this love for our position, by sticking together."

"I remember having a few problems with Luiz Felipe Scolari – then, funnily enough, a few weeks after I left, he went as well!"

When Cech signed from Rennes in 2004 Carlo reckons he became the club's greatest ever keeper. "Petr is definitely one of the best goalkeepers in the world, and he has been since he started playing for Chelsea. He is so consistent, breaking record after record. He's not looked back since joining the club. I remember the summer he joined us, he had a great Euros for the Czech Republic and was still only 22. First of all, me and Petr had a great relationship and we are very good friends. In his first season here, he had the opportunity to be in the team and start in goal in, and he never gave it up. Only great players have that concentration and consistency. I was coming from two very good seasons and was expecting to play but, in football, expectation and reality are two very different things for a player! You always have to fight for your place and suddenly I was on the bench and not very happy with that. That didn't change my approach towards Petr or anyone else – he was still a great guy – so we worked hard together and pushed each other all the way. That was my aim – to push him harder, always keep him on his toes so he could perform in every game even better than the last."

By the time Carlo left the club for Tottenham in January 2009 he had twice picked up winner's medals in the Premier League, FA Cup, League Cup and Community Shield. "There's always a start and an end to anything, and I thought it was time for me to leave and seek another fortune. I remember having a few problems with Luiz Felipe Scolari – then, funnily enough, a few weeks after I left, he went as well! But my contract was coming to an end soon and things were a bit strange, so I felt it was time for us to go our separate ways." Chelsea fans even forgave him for joining Spurs! "I have to say I was surprised in a way, because I knew how much Chelsea fans hated Tottenham! But I also knew what they were like – how they were always behind me when I was playing for their club. This is another reason why Chelsea supporters will always be in my heart. I don't know how you say it in English, the thing which connects the baby to the mum. Yeah, the umbilical cord. There's something like that – and it will be with me forever."

Carlo returned to Chelsea in 2016 to work as a club ambassador and in a variety of coaching roles under Antonio Conte as the Blues became Premier League champions and is now a loan player technical coach.

Roman Abramovich

The Man Who Transformed Chelsea into a Global Superpower

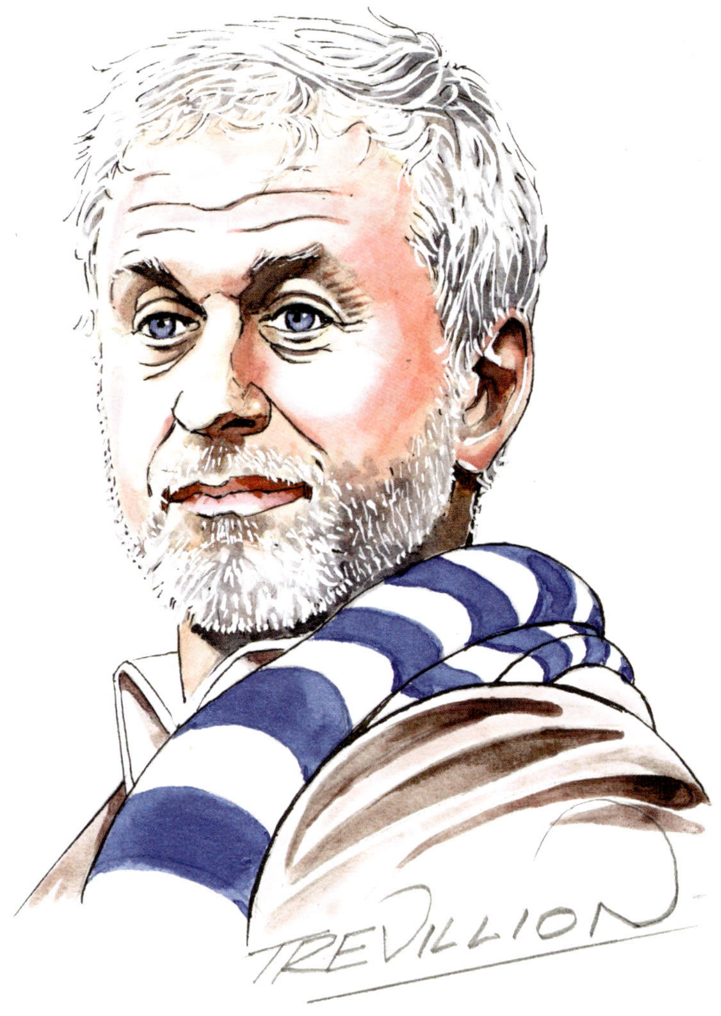

Roman Abramovich remains a hero to Chelsea fans who will never forget the enormous impact he made on their club, propelling them into the global elite. Yet he became a villain in the eyes of the British Government panicking over Putin's invasion of Ukraine and wanting to be seen to act tough with any of his real or even perceived allies by stripping them of their personal assets. As a result, the government forced the sale of a football club in an extraordinary and unique case in the history of the game.

When Abramovich bought the club from Ken Bates it was an easy target to suggest that it was his latest toy thing and he would tire of it before too long, and that his love of F1 would take him away from the Bridge and his infatuation with football wouldn't last. However, having written a few books on Roman and talking to some of those closest to him, my belief was that he never planned to sell and envisaged passing the club on to his son.

The seeds of Abramovich's ambition came at the World Cup and then in a manic Manchester one April night watching the Champions League, "I went to the quarter-finals of the Champions League at Old Trafford against Real Madrid and the whole atmosphere at the match affected me. From that moment on, I knew I had to be involved in football. On the way back to Moscow I couldn't stop thinking about it, I just told my people 'Find me a football club'."

Three months later he was installed at Stamford Bridge, a move that changed the face of English football forever, "I looked at a lot of clubs in England and one in Europe but it was Chelsea that had me most excited. It was the obvious choice for us once we'd studied all the facts surrounding it, now we have to build something special here. Champions League football was important but not decisive. It helped that Chelsea had qualified but there were four or five other factors which made up my mind. I love London and Chelsea is in the centre of London - that was important."

Shortly after buying Chelsea from Ken Bates, the reclusive Russian was persuaded to grant the financial media, and then the football journalists an interview, which turned out to be one of the few interviews he has ever given. Speaking through a trusted intermediary until he perfected his English, he said back then, "Yes, I am excited, this is the most excited I've been for a long time. I can't wait for the season to start. There is a great deal of pleasure in building something up, now we have to build something special here at Chelsea."

So, as it turned out, Abramovich didn't desert Chelsea, he was forced out kicking and screaming by an act of Government interference. It resulted in the farcical situation where fans were denied buying programmes for games as money was not allowed to go into the club while Abramovich technically still owned it!

Roman Abramovich's life story is worthy of a Hollywood movie. Orphaned at the age of three, he went on to become one of the world's richest men. But his links to Vladimir Putin stripped him of his businesses, reputation, and his assets including his football club.

"I'm sure people will focus on me for three or four days but it will pass," said the Russian multi-billionaire when he bought the club in 2003. "They'll forget who I am, and I like that." Like many before him, he greatly underestimated the media attention, the fans' thirst for information, and his only sanctuary was to reject all media requests for interviews by the sporting press, but gave a few selected comments to the financial media whom he trusted more to reflect his point of view.

Due to his ownership of a Premier League club which he turned into a force of nature with his financial muscle, intensity into his affairs only magnified relentlessly. There were years of demands for greater scrutiny of his dealings, but the gloves were off when the UK government froze his UK-held assets - including his homes, artworks and Chelsea FC - and imposed a travel ban – while accusing him of being complicit with Putin in the invasion of Ukraine. The fall from grace for a man who dominated European football was remarkable, but sharply divided sports fans in the process. His demise was cheered by Chelsea's rivals, but mourned by the fans of the West London club who recognised his role in transforming their club.

Roman Arkadyevich Abramovich was born in Saratov in south-western Russia, a few hundred miles from the border with Ukraine. His mother, Irina, died of blood poisoning when he was one year old and his father died two years later after an accident with a construction crane. Roman was raised by relatives, spending time in Komi, in north-west Russia, where money was tight and winters freezing. "To tell the truth I cannot call my childhood bad," he once told the *Guardian* in a rare interview. "In your childhood you can't compare things: one eats carrots, one eats candy, both taste good. As a child you cannot tell the difference."

He studied at the Industrial Institute in Ukhta, Komi, was drafted to military service, gained a law degree from Moscow State Law Academy in less than a year, and made his fortune from oil, aluminium, the airline Aeroflot, steel, pharmaceuticals, property, food processing and magazine publishing. Having left school at 16, he worked as a mechanic and served in the Red Army before selling plastic toys in Moscow. He moved on to perfumes and deodorants, building up his wealth as greater openness under Soviet leader Mikhail Gorbachev allowed scope for entrepreneurs.

The disintegration of the Soviet Union, and with it state command of mineral assets, provided more opportunities, and in his mid-20s he seized the oil company Sibneft from the Russian government in a so-called 'rigged auction' in 1995 for $250m (£190m). He sold it back to the government for $13bn (£9.9bn) in 2005. His lawyers have always insisted there is no basis for alleging he amassed very substantial wealth through criminality. However, in 2012, he admitted in a UK court that he had made corrupt payments to secure the Sibneft deal.

A chance meeting in 1994 with Boris Berezovsky, a tycoon with close ties to then President Boris Yeltsin, changed his fortunes. Abramovich became involved in the "aluminium wars" of the nineties, in which oligarchs - those who had accrued vast fortunes and political power after the Soviet collapse - fought for control of this vast industry. "Every three days, someone was being murdered," Abramovich said in 2011, adding that this threat to his safety had made him a reluctant participant. He proved his toughness, accruing hundreds of millions amid the chaos. He became an ally of President Boris Yeltsin, influential in Moscow's post-Soviet political structure, even having an apartment in the Kremlin for a while. When Yeltsin resigned in 1999, Abramovich was reportedly among those to back the prime minister and former KGB spy, Vladimir Putin, as his successor. As Putin established himself, he sought to assert his dominance over the oligarchs. Some went to prison, while others were exiled if they failed to pledge their allegiance to him.

When Russian media magnate Boris Berezovsky publicly clashed with Putin, he sold his stake in Russia's main TV channel to Abramovich and fled the country to escape a criminal investigation into his business dealings. In 2000, Abramovich was elected governor of the deprived region of Chukotka, in north-east Russia with a population of just 50,000. He gained popularity after investing his own money in social services but stepped down in 2008. He kept his business interests going, buying up paintings, houses, cars.

In 2005, Abramovich's political loyalty was rewarded, while other oligarchs who had built fortunes in the nineties faced legal and tax challenges or prison, in the case of Mikhail Khodorkovsky, Russia's biggest oil baron when he was arrested in 2003 after challenging Putin publicly. But Gazprom, the state-owned Russian gas giant, agreed to buy Sibneft for $13bn — providing the source of most of Abramovich's wealth. "It was a no-brainer for him," Roman Borisovich, a former Russian banker turned anti-corruption campaigner, says of the relationship Abramovich built with Putin. "He understood his days were numbered. Everyone who had been close to Yeltsin's family was being ostracised at the very least, and he was in the worst position of all. So he would do anything."

Even before the Gazprom deal, Abramovich wanted to build a new life in the west. In 2003 he purchased Chelsea, and bought at least £200m worth of UK property, including a 15-bedroom mansion in Kensington Palace Gardens, which had been the Soviet embassy. He established himself as a patron of the arts and gave half a billion dollars to Jewish causes; the President of Russia's main Jewish group said in 2018 that Abramovich deserved credit for "80 per cent" of Jewish life in the country. But despite the attempt to reinvent himself in the west, Abramovich could never fully escape claims about the route he had taken to get there.

The purchase of a Premier League football club appeared to be an unusual move for a man widely described as quiet, even shy in a deal worth £140m. But it was no surprise once you got to know how he fell in love with football watching Manchester United in a Champions League tie at Old Trafford. He had been in talks to buy Spurs, when, by chance, his helicopter flew over Stamford Bridge, and he enquired about the West London club. When he found it easier to deal with Ken Bates than Daniel Levy, hr was soon finalising a deal for Chelsea. "My whole philosophy in life is to bring in professional teams," he told the *Financial Times*, "In Chukotka I have professional teams on the ground and I will do this here too."

Abramovich famously employed a 'revolving door' approach to his managers. If they succeeded big time they stayed, however if they fell even slightly short of expectations they were out and replaced with the next big thing in management. Under the management of José Mourinho and others, Abramovich's wealth helped Chelsea towards five Premier Leagues, two Champions Leagues and five FA Cups.

Oligarch money flooded into London in the first two decades of the 21st century as the UK Government turned a blind eye to any links with Putin. The invasion of Ukraine changed all that, attitudes hardened and Chelsea indirectly suffered when Abramovich was targetted. The first thing to attract attention was his property portfolio, including a 15-bedroom mansion at Kensington Palace Gardens in West London, worth £150m, a flat in Chelsea, a ranch in Colorado and a holiday home on the French Riviera. His yachts - the *Solaris* and the *Eclipse* - are among the world's largest. Abramovich, who has been divorced three times, also owns a personal jet. Asked by the *Guardian* in 2006 about what money can do for a person, he replied: "It cannot buy you happiness. Some independence, yes." Financial media giant Bloomberg estimated his personal fortune at $13.7bn (£10.6bn), making him the world's 128th richest person.

The burning question, however, is the extent of his independence from Putin. He sued publishing house HarperCollins for libel over a book, *Putin's People* by Catherine Belton, that claimed the Russian President had ordered him to buy Chelsea. The sides settled out of court, with the publisher agreeing to make some clarifications. Abramovich's associations with Putin continued to dog him, particularly when Russian forces built up on the border with Ukraine and then invaded. When the freezing of the UK assets of Abramovich and six other oligarchs was announced, Foreign Secretary Liz Truss said: "With their close links to Putin, they are complicit in his aggression. The blood of the Ukrainian people is on their hands." In 2012, he won one of the UK's most expensive legal cases ever when a High Court judge ruled against his former ally Berezovsky, who had sued Abramovich for $6.5bn in damages over a disputed stake in Sibneft. The judge found he had been "careful and truthful" while Berezovsky had been "deliberately dishonest".

In 2018, the UK delayed his visa renewal application without explanation, prompting him to withdraw it and acquire Israeli citizenship instead. That decision was made two months after former Russian spy Sergei Skripal and his daughter Yulia were poisoned in Salisbury with the nerve agent novichok. By the time the UK moved against him, however, Abramovich was spending little time here and became a regular visitor to the US and Israel donating to elite Israeli institutions, including Yad Vashem, the national Holocaust memorial. The chair of the memorial was among those who wrote to the US ambassador seeking help to keep Abramovich off US sanctions lists. He has also taken legal action in the UK to deny claims about direct business links to Putin. He could be known for his philanthropy.

Abramovich announced the sale of Chelsea eight days before sanctions were imposed. Some fans have continued to chant his name, but many politicians called for his assets to be seized, not just frozen. "I hope that I will be able to visit Stamford Bridge one last time to say goodbye to all of you in person," Abramovich told Chelsea supporters. But a return to West London was unlikely for some time, if at all. "Please know that this has been an incredibly difficult decision to make, and it pains me to part with the club in this manner," he wrote.

Abramovich refrained from explicit criticism of Putin's war. But in the first week of the invasion, his daughter Sofia, 27, shared a post on Instagram that read: "The biggest and most successful lie of Kremlin's propaganda is that most Russians stand with Putin." On February 24, the day war began, he transferred control of Norma, an investment vehicle that manages his stakes in start-ups, and its subsidiary to David Davidovich, an Israeli business associate. Two days later, Abramovich said that he would relinquish stewardship of Chelsea to a charitable trust. He followed up days later by revealing plans to sell the club saying he would forgo £1.5bn in loans he is owed and donate the proceeds to a foundation benefiting "victims of the war in Ukraine".

In a bizarre twist, it emerged that he suffered symptoms of suspected poisoning along with senior Ukrainian negotiators at peace talks on the Ukraine-Belarus border, although it was not confirmed, nor was speculation that Abramovich offered to mediate. What is known is that as Russian tanks streamed over Ukraine's borders in the early hours of February 24, Putin summoned the country's leading oligarchs to a meeting at the Kremlin. At the time, Abramovich was staying in the south of France where he owns Château de la Croë, a large villa with 19 acres of grounds on the seafront in Antibes. He travelled to Moscow on his private plane but arrived too late for the audience, which was partly televised. Abramovich arranged to have a private meeting with Putin. He apologised to the Russian President but, according to three people with knowledge of the discussion, he also made a strong case to end the war. According to sources the Russian President heard him out and gave his personal blessing for Abramovich to act as a mediator in peace talks. The unusual intervention was risky — Putin has described elite Russians who sympathise with the west as "scum and traitors".

Abramovich criss-crossed the region, simultaneously trying to protect his fortune from sanctions, while also promoting a peace process. Abramovich was pictured listening to Turkish President Tayyip Erdogan during Russia-Ukraine talks in Istanbul. EU sanctions had forced him to put Chelsea up for sale, race two super yachts across open seas to refuge in Turkey, transfer control of at least two investment vehicles to an associate and reportedly attempt to withdraw vast sums from global asset managers. Shares in Evraz, the London-listed steelmaker and his main remaining industrial asset, were suspended after falling 85 per cent that year.

Having jetted between Moscow, Israel and Turkey helping to broker the talks and even visiting Kyiv on at least two occasions to meet Ukraine President Volodymyr Zelensky, speculation swirled around him. The attempted poisoning is said to have occurred during negotiations that caused him to completely lose his eyesight for several hours. At the latest round of talks between Russia and Ukraine, held in Istanbul, Abramovich sat with the Russian delegation and chatted with Turkish President Tayyip Erdogan — a public recognition of his formal role in the negotiations.

For two decades he played down any suggestion that he is a close confidant of Putin, sometimes using the threat of legal action in London courts to defend himself against claims about financial ties to the President. Yet Erdogan said Abramovich's presence at the talks showed that Putin "believes, trusts him". Dmitry Peskov, Putin's spokesman, said Abramovich was not an official member of the Russian delegation but was helping with "certain contacts between the Russian and Ukrainian sides".

MANAGER	GAMES	WINS	DRAWS	DEFEATS
JOSÉ MOURINHO	185	124	40	21
AVRAM GRANT	54	36	13	5
LUIZ FELIPE SCOLARI	36	20	11	5
RAY WILKINS	1	1	0	0
GUUS HIDDINK	23	17	5	1
CARLO ANCELOTTI	109	67	20	22
ANDRÉ VILLAS-BOAS	40	19	11	10
ROBERTO DI MATTEO	42	24	9	9
RAFAEL BENÍTEZ	48	28	10	10
JOSÉ MOURINHO (2)	136	80	29	27
STEVE HOLLAND	1	1	0	0
GUUS HIDDINK (2)	28	11	11	6
ANTONIO CONTE	106	69	17	20
MAURIZIO SARRI	63	39	13	11
FRANK LAMPARD	84	44	17	23
THOMAS TUCHEL	100	60	24	16

Managers appointed by Roman Abramovich

Abramovich had pushed to organise escape routes for civilians in Mariupol, where tens of thousands were trapped in a destroyed city without water, heating and electricity for weeks. But, according to Ukraine President Zelensky, these efforts failed when Russia refused to observe a ceasefire. "Everyone in Mariupol was trying, including him specifically, I know — but nothing came of it," he said.

Zelensky asked the US to hold off on imposing sanctions on Abramovich so that he could continue travelling, even if Ukraine's President said he remains sceptical about the oligarch's motives. "All these people are afraid of sanctions — I'm sure there's no great patriotism in it," he said. Nonetheless, he added, "Getting through to the Russian government was unreal. [Now] someone's getting something through." Abramovich's critics insist he used the talks to salvage his overseas assets. "I'm not sure how much his involvement in this mediation is real and effective, and how much of it is a PR tool," says Vladimir Ashurkov, executive director of the Anti-Corruption Foundation founded by the jailed Russian dissident, Alexei Navalny. "He's a creative guy, and he has creative people working for him, so it can just be a way to have a chance to ease the sanctions."

Later it emerged that Dutch side Vitesse Arnhem was given an 18-point deduction due to licensing issues which resulted in relegation from the Eredivisie. The KNVB, the governing body of Dutch football, imposed the deduction after investigators found that the club persistently fell short of meeting the requirements of licensing regulations over an extended period. According to *The Guardian*, the licensing committee concluded that there were 'indications' that Abramovich had controlled - or still controlled - Vitesse. The KNVB were aware of the 'risks' that sanctions had been violated, as they continued to investigate any ties between Vitesse and Abramovich.

Meanwhile Chelsea FC faced fresh questions over how Abramovich funded the club's success, after leaked files revealed a string of secret payments that may have breached strict football rules, including "financial fair play". Experts said the transactions, uncovered through a joint investigation by *The Guardian* and international partners, could lead to the Premier League imposing punishments. The files reveal a series of payments worth tens of millions over a decade, routed through offshore vehicles belonging to Abramovich. The transactions in question appear to have been for Chelsea's benefit, raising questions about whether they were declared in accounts submitted to football's governing bodies. Beneficiaries appeared to include the agent of Eden Hazard, an associate of the title-winning manager Antonio Conte and Chelsea officials. Other payments appear to have been connected to the purchase of the players Willian and Samuel Eto'o. The payments came to light thanks to an international investigation known as *Cyprus Confidential*, a cache of 3.6m offshore records leaked to the International Consortium of Investigative Journalists and Germany's Paper Trail Media, which shared access with *The Guardian*, the Bureau of Investigative Journalism and other media. On 18 July 2017, the files showed an Abramovich-owned company called Conibair Holdings, based in the British Virgin Islands, signed an agreement with Federico Pastorello, an Italian football agent, described in multiple reports as being close to Antonio Conte who has spoken about the manager's contract negotiations in the media. Conibair agreed to pay Pastorello £10m for a 75% stake in Excellence Investment Fund, a business based in the US state of Delaware, documents suggest. That same day, Chelsea announced that Conte, who had just guided the club to the Premier League title, had signed a new £9.6m-a-year contract. Pastorello declined to comment on whether the two deals were linked but said: "Antonio Conte is not our client."

During Conte's title-winning season, Hazard scored 16, a high point in a glittering seven-year spell that included him captaining the club and winning six domestic and European trophies. Hazard had joined in 2012 for 35m euros, a marquee signing that followed fraught negotiations with the player's agent, John Bico-Penaque, who reportedly wanted a sizeable commission worth about £6m. On 29 March 2013, documents suggest, BVI-based Leiston Holdings, owned by Abramovich, agreed to pay €7m to a Dubai-based company called Gulf Value FZE for "advisory services […] related to […] sport research and consultancy". The contract was signed on the company's behalf by Bico-Penaque. It is unclear whether the payment was declared to footballing authorities including the FA and Bico-Penaque did not return requests for comment. On another occasion, Leiston paid £1m to Association des Jeunes Espoirs de Bobo, the former club of Bertrand Traoré, via a contract signed by Traoré's brother, David. The contract is dated two months after the full-back signed for Chelsea. The files also reveal at least €7m in payments made between 2005 and 2017 to companies linked to Zoran and Vladica Lemić. The latter, a key adviser to Abramovich, was reportedly a pivotal figure in the arrival of stars such as Arjen Robben, Branislav Ivanović, Nemanja Matić and the double-winning coach Carlo Ancelotti. Separate documents show a £250,000 payment to the former Chelsea sporting director Frank Arnesen. Arnesen told *The Guardian* he would usually have expected the payment, a discretionary bonus, to have come from Chelsea rather than another company, but was unaware of any rule breaches and had declared it for tax purposes.

A company owned by Abramovich made payments that appear to have benefited the owner of a club that sold two players to Chelsea shortly afterwards. Anzhi Makhachkala, a now defunct club from Dagestan, were briefly transformed when Russian billionaire Suleiman Kerimov bought the club in 2011 and bankrolled big-money transfers. But in 2013, Kerimov slashed Anzhi's budget, plunging the club into financial turmoil and forcing a fire sale of players. That summer, Chelsea signed two stars from Anzhi in two days. The Cameroonian striker Samuel Eto'o was the first to arrive, followed by Willian. The Brazilian, who went on to win multiple trophies with Chelsea, was on the verge of signing for Spurs until Abramovich reportedly hijacked the deal via a personal phone call to Kerimov. Two months earlier the Abramovich-owned Leiston Holdings agreed to pay two companies connected to Kerimov for "services in […] relating to football, including scouting and other football-related advice". Tobeo Services Inc and Fernington Invest Corp, both based in the BVIs, were each to be paid €12m, documents dated 10 June 2013 suggest. A Chelsea spokesperson said: "These allegations pre-date the club's current ownership. They are based on documents which the club has not been shown and do not relate to any individual who is presently at the club."

The spokesperson said that during the purchase of the club by a consortium led by the US investor Todd Boehly the buyers became aware of "potentially incomplete financial reporting concerning historical transactions during the club's previous ownership". Immediately following the completion of the purchase, the club proactively self-reported these matters to all applicable football regulators. In accordance with the club's ownership group's core principles of full compliance and transparency the club has proactively assisted the applicable regulators with their investigations and will continue to do so."

Files also suggest that Abramovich secretly bankrolled efforts to overturn the FFP rules through the courts, ultimately unsuccessfully. In February 2014, Abramovich's Leiston Holdings agreed to pay £100,000 to a lawyer named Jean-Louis DuPont, who was challenging the legality and validity of FFP before the European Commission. Leiston, which is understood to have been acting on Chelsea's behalf, had a "business interest" in the outcome of the case, the contract shows.

Chelsea's finances had already been examined by the Premier League in an investigation that ran from 2012 to 2019, after the club's new ownership regime voluntarily reported that "incomplete financial information" had been submitted during Abramovich's tenure. The FA confirmed that it was also investigating Chelsea while Uefa has already fined the club £8.6m over the admission, although its powers are limited because it can only look at evidence going back three years.

Abramovich was described as a "close ally of Vladimir Putin" by football agent Saif Alrubie in court. Alrubie was questioned by the prosecution in his trial at Southwark Crown Court for allegedly sending former Chelsea director Marina Granovskaia a malicious email. During his cross-examination by prosecutor Arizuna Asante, Alrubie was repeatedly warned by judge David Tomlinson, who told him to stop being "so confrontational and unnecessary" in front of the jury. Alrubie had said it would have been a "suicide mission" to threaten Granovskaia, who he described as "the right hand of Abramovich." During his cross-examination, he again referenced Abramovich by saying: "He is a close ally of Vladimir Putin, sanctioned by the UK government." When judge Tomlinson told the jury that Abramovich and other Russian oligarchs had been sanctioned by the Government and were unable to return to the UK, Alrubie said: "By some chance, she [Granovskaia] is the only one who stayed." In his email to Granovskaia, Alrubie had said: "Feel free to go to your boss who's had his recent problems and tell him that you have a big problem with me as long as you tell him the truth about your behaviour." Alrubie pleaded not guilty to threatening Granovskaia with the intention of causing distress or anxiety. Quoting his statement given to police, Asante asked if he had been "f----- off" when sending the email to which Alrubie replied: "Excuse your French, but yeah." Asante said: "More your French than mine." Alrubie said Granovskaia was "a liar" more than once in answer to questions and said she and football agent Kia Joorabchian, "both conspired". The jury were told by Asante that Joorabchian was allegedly confronted in a restaurant by people acting for Alrubie, who took his watch and refused to return it until payment was made later when approximately 12 men turned up at his office and ordered him to pay in bundles of cash. Alrubie denied threatening Joorabchian, but confirmed in court that he had indirectly received money from him as a result of a dispute in 2009. In his email to Granovskaia, Alrubie wrote: "I'm sure you've heard the story about your other friend Kia when he owed me money for a year and how he ended up paying it. Wouldn't want you to be in the same situation just because you have a personal issue with me." Alrubie believes he is owed £300,000 in commission from the £29.1m transfer of Kurt Zouma from Chelsea to West Ham, which is what prompted his email. Alrubie told the court that he had worked on the Zouma deal with another football agent, Barry Silkman, who also appeared as a witness. On his relationship with West Ham vice-chairman Karen Brady, Silkman said: "I keep away from her to be honest." Alrubie was acquitted of sending an intimidating email after the jury deliberating for more than four hours. Granovskaia said: "Coming to court to give evidence in the Crown's case against Mr Alrubie was an extremely difficult decision. I am an intensely private person, but I was willing to do my part to ensure that no-one else – particularly no woman – was ever made to feel as I did upon receiving his email, a feeling this trial has revived."

Hi Marina, I have handled many successful investigations in my time as a journalist but never seen so much 'evidence' dressed up from hearsay, and unsubstantiated allegations, that's not so say that I disagree with the UK's current attitude and stance as they have little to no choice but to act in this way and no-one can defend the indefensible war in Ukraine, equally as I have said in a Chelsea Podcast, when Tony Blair was and is accused of war crimes does that mean anyone who contributed to Blair/Labour government at the time in terms of funding are also facing allegations of war crimes - off course they are not. Regards Harry

Hello Harry, Thank you for reaching out and for your honesty. Yes, I have seen the program, and – without going into too much detail - I have to say I share your sentiment re: fact validation in modern-day journalism.

I try very hard not to get into any political debates for all kinds of reasons, but one doesn't have to be a politician to understand that any war is wrong. However, I also agree that any war should be treated equally by governments, societies and media – because ultimately human life is equally worthy regardless of its geographical location. In any case we can only hope the two countries manage to reach a compromise soon and the world gets back to some sort of normality.

On a brighter note, Mr Abramovich got to live some wonderful triumphs and glorious moments with Chelsea FC and leaves a beautiful history of nearly 20 years which cannot be cancelled or erased, filled with trophies and unforgettable moments.

Kind regards,

Marina

As you can see I have engaged with Roman through his trusted advisor Marina. Having written three books about Abramovich I feel confident I have researched this hugely complex and controversial character as much as any other journalist.

I can safely say that Abramovich's affection, passion and commitment to Chelsea was totally genuine. He fell in love with football when he first watched Champions League football at Old Trafford, and although he first looked at Spurs, it was by chance, flying over the Bridge in his private helicopter that he asked about the West London club and eventually bought it from Ken Bates. He invested £1 billion in Chelsea to create his personal 'Roman Empire' worth £4 billion, which illustrates that he is an ultra astute businessman, but it isn't the investment potential that motivated him, it has always been his genuine love for the club and his relentless pursuit of winning the trophy most dear to his heart, the Champions League.

He brought that business acumen to his role in football with a ruthless disregard for reputations as he sought the results to drive his club to the very pinnacle of the global game, hence a revolving door philosophy for managers, hiring and firing José Mourinho twice, firing Carlo Ancelotti the season after he won the Double and even kicking out one of the club's great all time players Frank Lampard half way through his first full season to bring in Thomas Tuchel at the turn of the year with the German coach landing his second Champions League title.

Three years after his initial takeover, Abramovich gave a little more away about his insight into football. He did not see that he was inflating the transfer market, making life tougher for the less rich in English football. "I don't see the risk of that," he said. "Money plays an important role in football but it is not the dominating factor. When Chelsea play a Carling Cup game in a small city and it could result in a draw - the excitement, the spirit, the atmosphere - that's the real beauty of football in England."

One of the early accusations thrown at the Abramovich regime was that Chelsea were too aggressive in spending large sums in the transfer market and offering players larger salaries. "It's difficult to say," he said. He thought it unfair that Chelsea should be singled out, and time has proved him right with the even richer Sheikh Mansour buying Manchester City and salaries doubling the amount paid at the Bridge.

Abramovich was aware of the accusation that he would quickly tire of his 'toy' and drop football and leave Chelsea in the lurch, "People who know me said I will win one or two Premierships and will not be interested after that.The reality is that we've won two Premierships but I'm more excited about this particular season than last year or the year before. I am a fan of special nature. I'm getting excited before every single game.The trophy at the end is less important than the process itself."

Abramovich is an enigma, because he gives so little away in so few public statements or interviews, so little is really known about his personality or character. One of his closest allies, one time Chelsea chairman Bruce Buck, once described him as "shy" with his passion for Chelsea as strong as ever, as Chelsea embarked on their latest campaign to bring him the trophy he desired most, the one to which first drew him to football, the one which has become his obsession, his quest. In a book entitled *There's a Golden Sky*, Buck observed, "I would say that his passion for Chelsea has increased not decreased. His passion for football has increased, not decreased. His knowledge of football has increased exponentially. I'm not talking about what goes on at the megastore, I'm talking about football. It would be pretty hard to name a current footballer that he couldn't give you statistics for."

Abramovich attended every game in the first season following his takeover in 2003 but his attendance decreased in the wake of the financial crisis and the birth of his sixth child in 2009. "But he doesn't miss a game in the sense that wherever he is in the world he watches the Chelsea game," Buck claimed, "he calls Eugene Tenenbaum or whoever after the game and they talk about it. He is very much on top of things." Buck, at Abramovich's side since the 2003 takeover, described meeting him before the businessman had learned to speak English. "To those of us he was meeting for the first time, he was outgoing and friendly.'Have a cup of tea,' or if you were at his house, 'Have something to eat.' He wasn't cold at all; he was very warm. It wasn't like I was slapping him on the back or telling him dirty jokes, though."

After telling advisers he "wouldn't mind buying a football team", Abramovich hired investment bank UBS Warburg to write a feasibility study, which listed a number of possible options. "It said that Manchester United would be expensive and the fans would go crazy. Aston Villa was for sale but was in Birmingham and the long-term opportunities were limited. Tottenham was on the list along with Chelsea. They were in London; they were in financial trouble. Roman's advisers tried to arrange meetings with Tottenham and Chelsea but for whatever reason, they couldn't set up a meeting with Tottenham, or Tottenham didn't want to meet."A provisional deal with then-owner Ken Bates was sealed not with vodka but with Coca-Cola at the Dorchester Hotel in central London, Buck said.

Abramovich and his team had been "naïve" about the football club's place in British culture and had not anticipated the long-running media fascination with the new Russian owner. "We thought,'Yeah, it will be a decent story for a couple of weeks and then Roman will go back and have his private life.' Because he is a very private guy. He clearly didn't do things for the notoriety or publicity because that is not him." Chelsea received more intense scrutiny than the major northern teams like City, United and Liverpool because it was "a London club, a bit of an upstart".

Buck admitted that the influx of Abramovich's money had "changed football forever" and led to a new trend of high-spending foreign owners such as Manchester City's Sheikh Mansour bin Zayed al Nahyan."That's why we aren't complaining about some of the things City are doing. We started it after all but, having said that, it is a free world. Obviously what we have done has not pleased the fans of West Ham or Manchester United, but they sure have pleased the fans at Chelsea."

Buck, an American lawyer who moved to London in 1983, agreed to take on the chairman's role because of his support for Chelsea. "If [Abramovich] had taken over Tottenham, I wouldn't have wanted to do it."He jokingly described himself as "co-owner" of the club, pointing out that he owned one share in Chelsea to the Russian's 83 million. Buck said Chelsea was eager to break the cycle of short-term managers and replicate the "more stable management structure" of Wenger's tenure at Arsenal or Sir Alex's at United.

THE ROMAN CONQUEST

The whole purpose of Abramovich's purchase and obsession with Chelsea was winning the European Cup. By 2012 he had suffered many near-misses, losing to Manchester United in Moscow on penalties oin 2008 and being denied a second appearance in a final by a last minute goal by Andres Iniesta the following season and the 2011-12 season didn't look too promising. Chelsea were 3-1 down on aggregate to Napoli in the round of 16 and he was about to fire Andres Vilas Boas. What happened next is part of Chelsea folklore: the mid-season crisis brought in AVB's assistant Roberto Di Matteo as interim until the end of the season and suddenly the whole dynamic of the dressing-room changed, starting with a 4-1 home win over Napoli that took the Blues into the last eight.

Chelsea's run gathered pace with a 3-2 aggregate win over Benfica before a titanic two legs against Barcelona that saw the Blues squeeze through to face Bayern Munich in their own Allianz Arena stadium. Didier Drogba's late equaliser and winning penalty in the shoot-out produced completed Roman's quest within nine years of his purchase of Chelsea.

Abramovich was unable to watch many games in the UK due to Visa issues at the tail end of his reign, but has always done his utmost to support the team at big finals - and was first spotted during their Europa League final triumph over Arsenal in 2019 and has been visible ever since in the stands and the dressing-room. One time club captain Cesar Azpilicueta was able to get his hands on Europe's top prize having joined in 2012 - just months after the team last won the trophy, the only player common to both Champions League triumphs nine years apart.

For the second triumph, Abramovich figured that appointing a German coach he might replicate what Jurgen Klopp achieved at Anfield, and maybe immediately bring out the best in the club's hugely costly German forwards who had not got anywhere near their full potential since their arrival at the Bridge under club legend Frank Lampard. Tiago Silva had arrived on a free transfer the previous summer under Lampard, and at the age of 36 was written-off as being too old to thrive in the Premier League. It was not an auspicious start for the Brazilian recognised as one of the world's greatest defenders of the modern game after a long spell with Paris St Germain, where they always came close but not close enough to landing the Champions League. "It was special, it was my first year here," Silva added. "Tuchel changed everything, the team mentality. But it's also important to talk about Lampard. Without him, it was difficult for me to win here, thanks to him for letting me sign here."

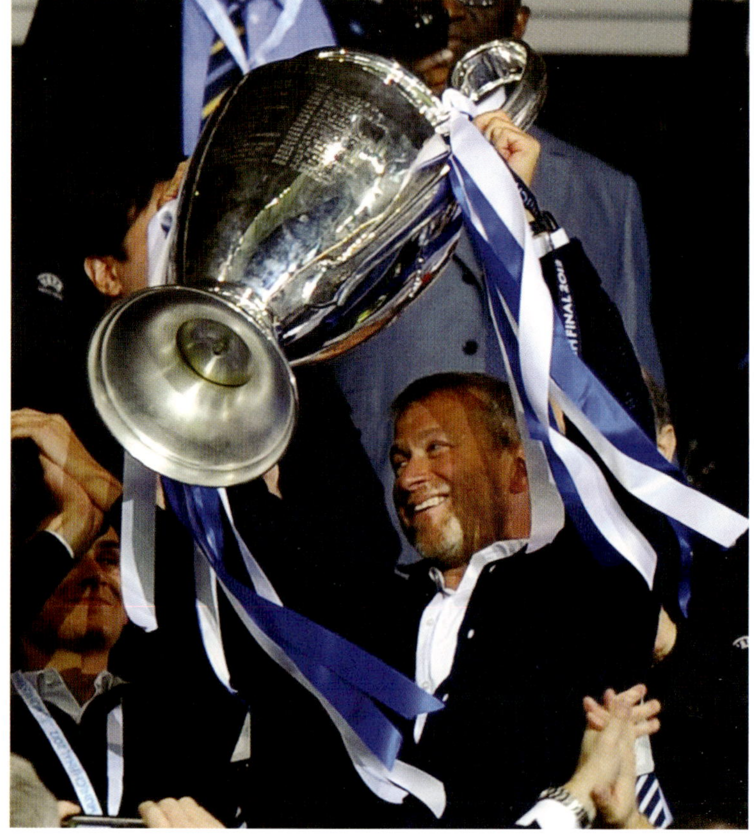

Before the final, in conversation with Jamie Redknapp in the *Daily Mail*, Frank Lampard revealed that he loved Roman Abramovich's comments following his sacking."Abramovich is the sort of owner who stays silent. He's never spoken out after sacking a manager before, but he made an exception for you" Redknapp pointed out. Indeed the Chelsea owner released a statement saying how much respect he had for Lampard and what a difficult decision it was. Lampard replied: "I loved that. I could never sit here and say I have anything but appreciation for what he did for my career. I was disappointed because I felt we could change things. I saw games coming up as opportunities to get points. Your pride takes a hit, there is no doubt about it.That's human. But with reflection, I would have been absolutely naive to think it would be any different for myself than it had been for managers in the past. History says Chelsea make changes and sometimes they have real success off the back of it. It was never for me to go against their model. I have full appreciation to Roman for the opportunity. I can only look forward."

Lampard had a host of managers – Roy Hodgson included – contacting him after he was let go in January to remind him it is a natural element of football management."All of them, first and foremost, said: 'You're not a manager until you've been sacked.' It was a hit, but then I started the reflection process. I didn't want to sit at home and throw blame elsewhere. It was more: 'What can I do better?' Roy Hodgson was amazing. I spoke to Roy a week after leaving Chelsea and he gave me some of the best calm, collected advice. I'm always willing to listen to these managers."

Lampard knew it would have been naive for him to expect to be treated differently to other Chelsea managers amid an extended run of poor form and his reputation, having won the Champions League and numerous league titles as a player, would count for nothing. He was brought in after just a season's experience as a manager with Championship Derby County at a time when Chelsea's immediate future seemed unclear: they were in the midst of a transfer ban which was complicated further by the departure of Eden Hazard to Real Madrid, forcing Lampard to look towards the club's expensive but, until that point at least, underperforming Academy. He oversaw the integration of Mason Mount – announced as Chelsea's first English Player of the Year since 2006 – Reece James, Callum Hudson-Odoi and others. Ahead of his first season when he was able to buy players, Lampard acquired highly-rated German duo Timo Werner and Kai Havertz, as well as England full-back Ben Chilwell. The experienced Thiago Silva and Edouard Mendy were added.

Tuchel was one game away from delivering a Champions League, just as Lampard did as a player and captain in Munich in 2012 when Lampard made it public that he liked what he has seen from his successor."I sent him a message the day he got the job," said Lampard."I felt it was the right thing to do. It is what it is. I remember coming into the training ground a month before and people were talking about how he had left PSG. That's football. So I sent him a message and he nicely sent me one back. People at Chelsea tell me he's a top bloke, and he's done some really positive things with the team."

Abramovich hadn't been to Stamford Bridge since 2018 following political tensions between the UK and Russia but he was in Portugal to see his latest managerial appointment mastermind a famous victory as he joined in the pitch side celebrations. Abramovich was seen embracing a group of players as they went up to collect their medals. Around 12,000 fans were in attendance for the all-English final in Porto and roughly half of that number stayed inside the stadium despite a 10:30pm curfew in the city, as supporters sought to join in with the celebratory scenes."I spoke to the owner right now on the pitch," said Tuchel as he celebrated his triumph. "It was the best moment for our first meeting, or the worst because from now on things can only get worse! We will speak tomorrow and I am looking forward to it. I can assure him I will stay hungry. I want the next title and I feel absolutely happy. I feel part of a really ambitious club and strong group that suits my belief and passion about football. We have work to do to close the gap (on City in the Premier League) and this is what I am all about. It will be nice to meet him a bit closer. We are in constant contact but not personal. He knows what is going on from me but not directly, now it is nice to meet him." Part of the discussions was a new long-term contract for the 47-year-old German who was initially offered only 18 months when he joined. Tuchel's agent had been in negotiations while he prepared for the final. "Maybe I already have a new contract, my manager said something about it. Let's check this first," he said.

After a fourth place finish in the Premier League and defeat to Leicester City in the FA Cup Final the following season, Tuchel's promised that Champions League glory would be a springboard to domestic success but the club soon became a pawn in a bigger gain which led to Abramovich being forced to sell his club.

One of my many books on Chelsea was a biography of Abramovich and, having researched it through many of his closest contacts and trusted aides, before he was really known in this country it was clear he was plotting the day he would land the Champions League having been inspired by watching a Champions League game at Old Trafford. I contacted Marina to request a lunch with Abramovich to present to him those three books and asked him to sign them. Unfortunately here was Marina's response…

Good afternoon Harry,

Thank you for your note.

We are genuinely grateful to you and your family for promoting the virtues of Chelsea FC and writing about the legends who played such important roles in the Club's history. We are sure your contribution is also appreciated by our many supporters who have been following your literary work for years.

With respect to organising lunch with Mr Abramovich, as I am sure you understand, it is extremely difficult to predict his travel plans in advance, as during his short stays in London his schedule is filled with business meetings and family commitments. Therefore, regrettably, it isn't something we can pursue at this moment in time. However, we will be more than happy to pass on your letter to him, or any of your books, if you so desire.

Thank you once again for your contribution and support.

Kind regards,

Marina

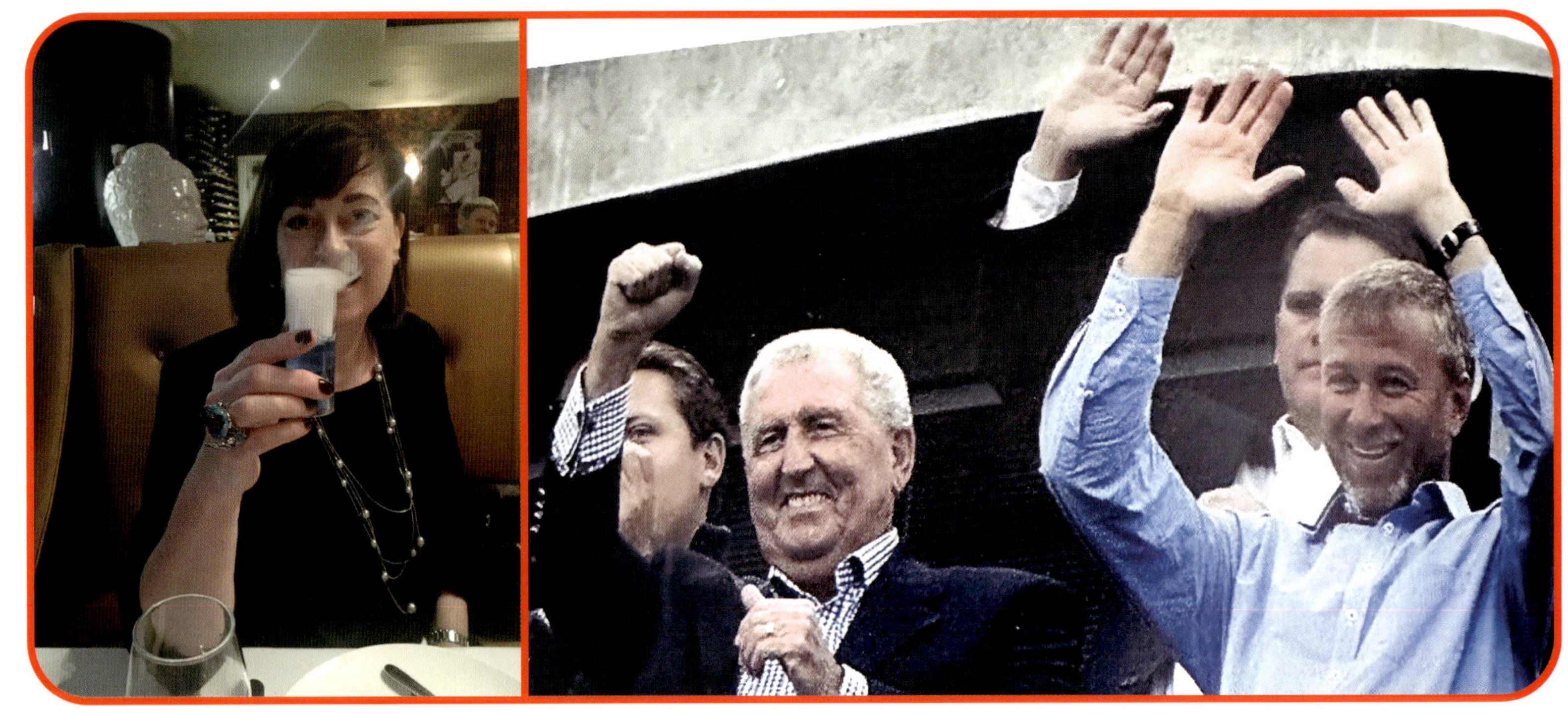

Roman, Linda and I

A Brief Glimpse of the Inner Sanctum

One afternoon, Linda and I were guests of then club sponsors, Samsung Mobile, in one of their plush £10m executive boxes at the Bridge. It turned out to be in the box next door to the one occupied by none other than Roman Abramovich, who I later found out, had been trying to re-purchase the box from the sponsors so he could extend his own private vantage point. The security checks upon arrival were intense as one would have expected once you realised the owner was next door: airport-style scanning machines, body searches and careful checking of accreditation. The boxes back then were £1m a year with a 10 year lease, so there was not much chance of any riff-raff turning up, or worse, but Abramovich wanted to make sure. Chelsea demolished Sunderland in the second half that day and everyone was in a great mood in the Samsung box with host Mark Mitchinson, the champers was flowing and no-one wanted the party to end, and in true journalistic style my wife Linda and I were the last to leave!

As we strode, or should I say lurched and stumbled, along the corridor accompanied by a couple beefed-up Abramovich minders to ensure we left the premises as instructed, they guided us past the owner's own box. But we caught sight of him, arms sternly folded, viewing us with a look of disapproval; the teetotal Abramovich was not amused at the intoxicated vision that he could see passing by. I penned a detailed account of Abramovich's first season as the owner and his aides were extremely helpful with a steady supply of information and I even sent a copy of the manuscript to them to ensure its accuracy. Special mention should go to Roman's man in Moscow, John Mann, a highly approachable and very personable young American public relations point of contact.

HH

The Special One

Nine Major Trophies Across Two Spells

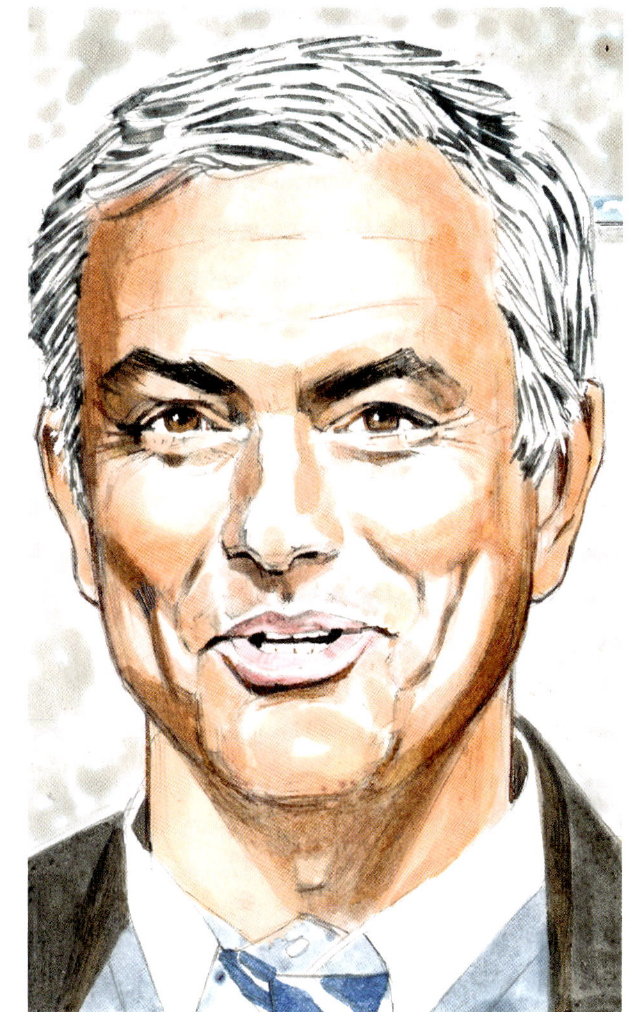

Special, Spiteful, Sensational, Sulky. Like Marmite, you either love or hate José as he has become one of the most divisive characters of his generation in the global game. Everyone has an opinion; and they are usually poles apart. But let me declare my allegiance. I am firmly of the belief that he is a genius, a great motivator, tactician, linguist, and serial winner. The reason I have written FIVE books on Mourinho is simply because he is such a charismatic character, much misunderstood, much maligned, sometimes justifiably, but overall he has been "box office" wherever he goes.

It has never been in much doubt that Mourinho can deliver on the big stage, and his impressive haul of silverware proves that point and that is the reason that so many clubs have been willing to take a chance on his unpredictability. the only predictable aspect of his personality is that he will fall out with the owner/chairman and or some players and will leave in acrimonious circumstances. He will never be a Sir Alex, Arsene Wenger or indeed a Guardiola or Klopp who have been with a top Premier League club for the long haul. Mourinho is a maverick, some call him a mercenary, but he has also left a remarkable allegiance and affection at the majority of the clubs he has served and Chelsea is no different. He has been sacked, returned, sacked again, and given a third chance I have no doubt that he would be back in the dug out at Stamford Bridge. He is adored by the fans even now, and they would welcome him back with open arms. Whether the new American owners would, is another matter.

Eventually he will be run out of different countries in which to leave his indelible mark, and maybe turn toward the national team, where his preference would be his native Portugal. He came close some time ago to becoming England manger before changing his mind. Saudi Arabia cannot be ruled out as Mourinho has consistently been the best paid manager and to regain that status the Saudis might be the last port of call for a lavish salary to match his ego.

However the Mourinho story really began at the Bridge. Of course he won the Champions League with Porto, but it was with Chelsea that he made his entrance, and his intoxicating mixture of mischief and charisma took centre stage.

Not long after he arrived in West London with his infamous "Special One" press conference, I knew there was something special about him; he had a brashness and ego that I had not encountered since the days of Brian Clough. Not even Bill Shankly or Malcolm Allison quite matched the remarkable self-confidence and self-assurance, and I was sure from the very start that this was a special career to follow.

Mourinho's arrogance was off the scale and really needed to be once he encountered Roman Abramovich. The Russian oligarch invested £1 billion in Chelsea to create a 'Roman Empire' worth £4bn by the time political issues forced him out, illustrating that he was an ultra astute businessman, but it wasn't the money that motivated him, it was a genuine love for the club and his relentless pursuit of winning the trophy most dear to his heart, the Champions League. He brought that ruthless, efficient, money-making business acumen to football with a disregard for reputations as he sought the results to drive his club to the very pinnacle of the global game, hence a revolving door philosophy for managers, hiring and firing Mourinho twice, firing Carlo Ancelotti the season after he won the Double and even kicking out one of the club's great all time players Frank Lampard half way through his first full season to bring in Thomas Tuchel.

A cartel of senior stars: John Terry, Frank Lampard, Didier Drogba and Petr Cech were Mourinho's special enforcers within the dressing-room. As Lampard himself observed: "Mourinho oozed self-confidence. Carlo Ancelotti came in with a calmer attitude, like a father figure, and I loved that side, too. Avram Grant was great for me. I'd lost my mum and he was amazing. We've seen a few people who have tried to clone a manager — they wear the scarf, they talk the same way, they use the same phrases from the coaching courses. You have to have your own ideas. There were moments when managers said things and I've walked out of his office or dressing-room and I was on my knees inside. You learn as much from that as the José Mourinho shower moment (when the Portuguese told him he was the best player in the world while Lampard was stark naked). Was it mind games? Different managers do it to on different levels and again, it's about whether it's authentic or not. You've got to be real."

For one of my many books detailing the behind the scenes Mourinho methods, I interviewed one of the not-so-big stars, but one of the most lucid, intelligent and perceptive guys I have met in the game, goalkeeper Carlo Cudicini. This is what he told me about the arrival of the self-styled 'Special One': "We already had a good team, so I guess what he brought to the club was the mentality to be champions. Arrogance, knowing the

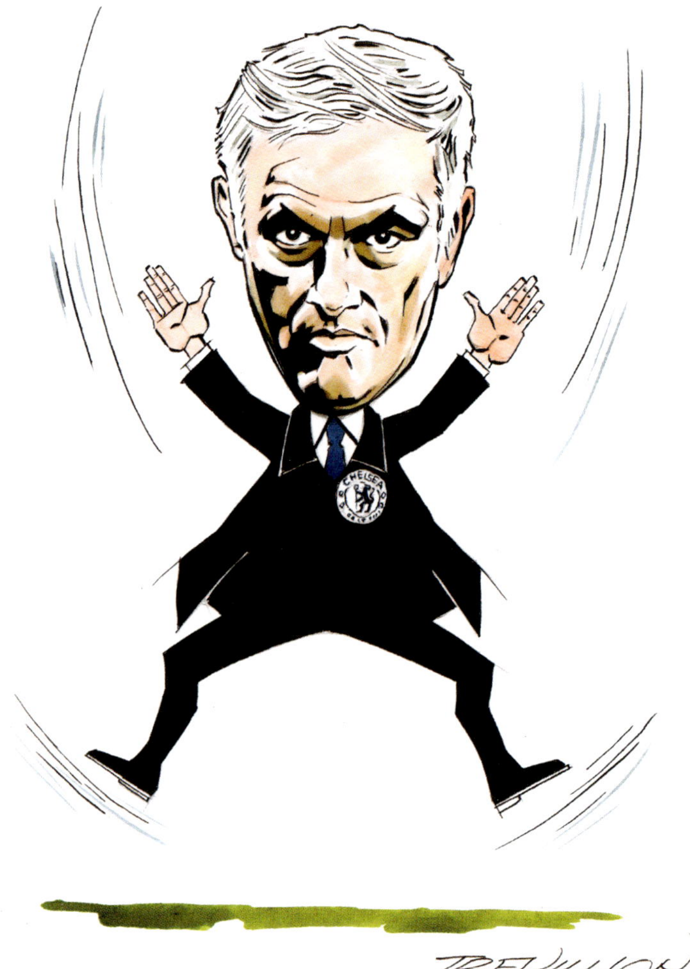

In the press conference on joining the English side, Mourinho infamously said: "Please don't call me arrogant, but I'm European champion and I think I'm a Special One," adding, "We have top players, and, sorry if I'm arrogant, but we now have a top manager."

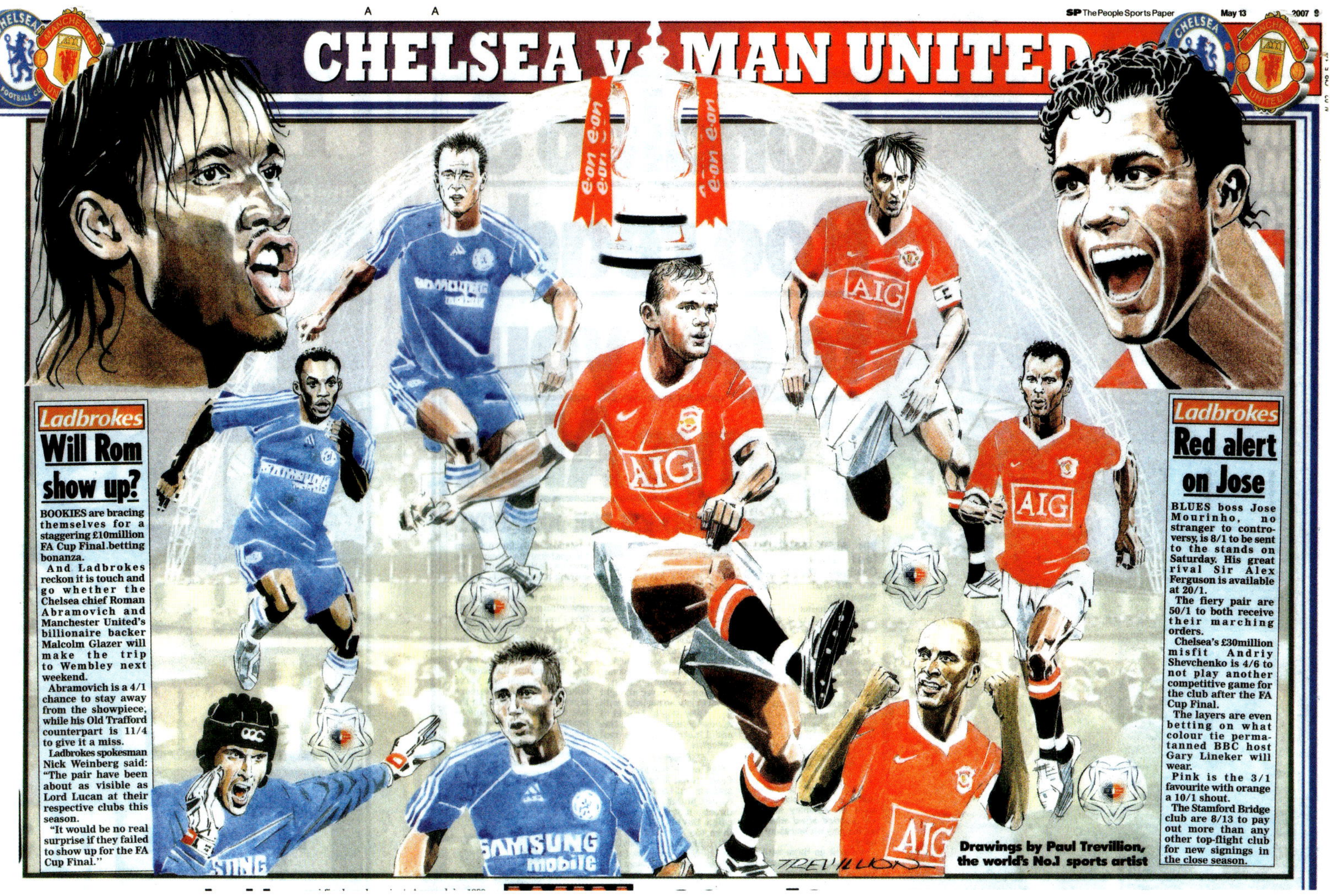

SP The People Sports Paper May 13 2007

CHELSEA v MAN UNITED

Ladbrokes

Will Rom show up?

BOOKIES are bracing themselves for a staggering £10million FA Cup Final betting bonanza.

And Ladbrokes reckon it is touch and go whether the Chelsea chief Roman Abramovich and Manchester United's billionaire backer Malcolm Glazer will make the trip to Wembley next weekend.

Abramovich is a 4/1 chance to stay away from the showpiece, while his Old Trafford counterpart is 11/4 to give it a miss.

Ladbrokes spokesman Nick Weinberg said: "The pair have been about as visible as Lord Lucan at their respective clubs this season.

"It would be no real surprise if they failed to show up for the FA Cup Final."

Ladbrokes

Red alert on Jose

BLUES boss Jose Mourinho, no stranger to controversy, is 8/1 to be sent to the stands on Saturday. His great rival Sir Alex Ferguson is available at 20/1.

The fiery pair are 50/1 to both receive their marching orders.

Chelsea's £30million misfit Andriy Shevchenko is 4/6 to not play another competitive game for the club after the FA Cup Final.

The layers are even betting on what colour tie perma-tanned BBC host Gary Lineker will wear.

Pink is the 3/1 favourite with orange a 10/1 shout.

The Stamford Bridge club are 8/13 to pay out more than any other top-flight club for new signings in the close season.

Drawings by Paul Trevillion, the world's No.1 sports artist

strength of that team, and being very good at convincing in pushing that team in the right direction, were his biggest qualities when he first came to English football and to Chelsea. Playing or not playing, happy or not happy at being in the team or not being in the team, he got everyone on the same side, especially in that first season, to all push in the same direction, and that is the reason why Chelsea won the title for the first time in 50 years. They might have already been important players but he managed to change their mentality in a way to take the entire team forward together. From a personal point of view it was something I had to deal with and the manager had to deal with because the manager picked Petr Cech in front of me. So I saw how he managed to bring his managerial abilities in convincing everyone who was happy about being in the team or unhappy about not being in the team that we were all in it together pushing for the same target, and everyone, including myself, bought into that, and that was the only way he made us champions and the reason we were champions two seasons in a row. He had a very strong personality to achieve that, and he brought a different way of training, totally different to Claudio Ranieri, he was definitely a breath of fresh air with his attitude that brought a new mentality to the team.

"I have to say that his relationship with his players was built on trust, and I trusted him, because even though he didn't start me as first choice goalkeeper, in the first couple of years I still played 13 or 14 games, which was most unusual for a reserve goalkeeper, if the first choice keeper wasn't injured."

Mourinho's first spell between 2004 and 2007 saw a meteoric rise after he finished his time in Portugal in spectacular fashion leading unfancied FC Porto to win the Champions League Final in Gelsenkirchen against Monaco, 3-0. It was the culmination of two-and-half amazing years where he won two Portuguese Leagues, the Portuguese Cup, the Super Cup and the Uefa Cup in 2003. He followed it by winning the Champions League in 2004 and Mourinho was off straight away, his move to Chelsea in June had already been negotiated as he became one of the highest paid managers in football on £4.2m-a-year, subsequently raised in 2005 to £5.2m.

When Mourinho was unveiled at Stamford Bridge on 2 June 2004, he was the most successful manager Chelsea had ever appointed and still only 41. In the press conference on joining the English side, Mourinho infamously said: "Please don't call me arrogant, but I'm European champion and I think I'm a special one," adding, "We have top players, and, sorry if I'm arrogant, but we now have a top manager."

Smart, eloquent and witty, Mourinho wowed the media with the kind of confidence that would be the hallmarks of his reign at the Bridge. His 'methodology' was based on a scientific approach to training, tactical flexibility, defensive awareness, and players allowing him inside their heads. He took the English game by storm starting with a 1-0 win in his first game at home to Manchester United.

Mourinho is usually labelled a pragmatic coach, his tactics based primarily on organisation and defence. That certainly was not the case at the start at Chelsea. With dynamic, tricky and gifted wingers Damien Duff and Arjen Robben the team hit top spot in November and never let up with a brand of fluent, fast, attacking football down the flanks and a dynamic, aggressive goalscorer in the centre. By early December, Chelsea sat top of the Premier League, reached the knock-out stages of the Champions League and Mourinho secured his first trophy by winning the League

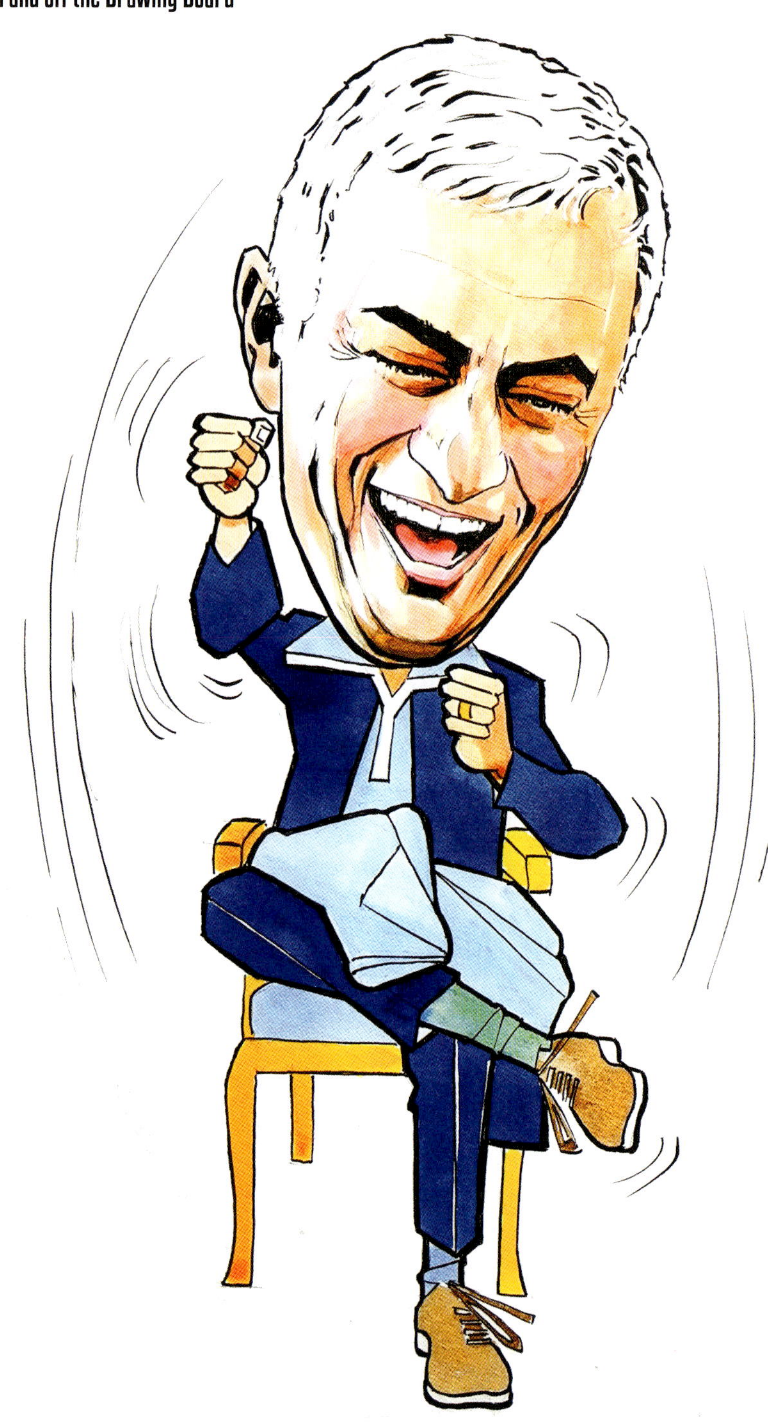

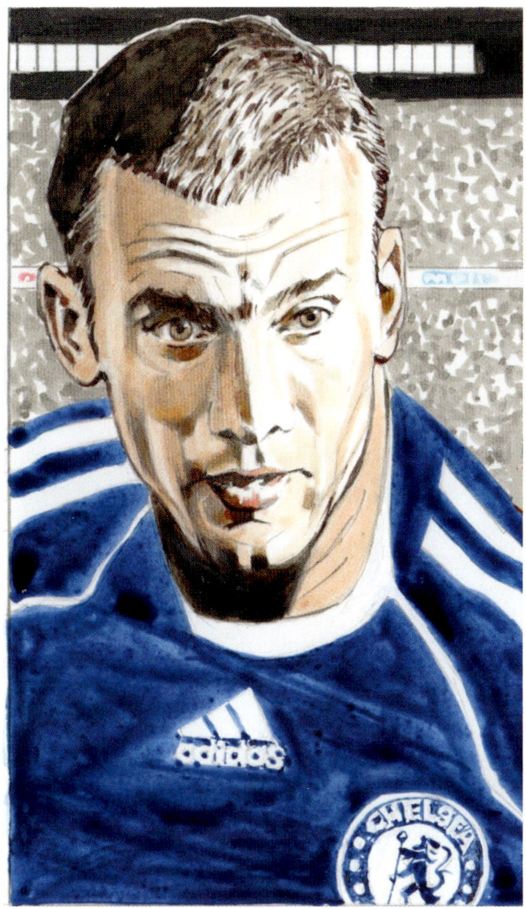

Cup against Liverpool 3–2 (AET) in Cardiff. Towards the end of the match Mourinho was escorted from the touchline after putting his finger to his mouth in the direction of Liverpool fans, as a response to taunts directed towards him whilst Liverpool were leading, before the equalising goal. It was the first, and by no means the last, nor the worst, of many touch-line antics and other devious methods. He was someone so driven he held no boundaries, including the infamously hiding in a laundry basket to circumvent a touchline ban!

Chelsea secured their first top-flight domestic title in 50 years, setting a string of records in the process, including the most points ever achieved in the Premier League (95), and the fewest goals conceded (15), securing the title with Frank Lampard's two goals at Bolton. While players and supporters celebrated at the Reebok, Mourinho calmly called his wife to tell her the score. For all his outward brashness and ego, behind the mask was a family man, and someone with a soft centre.

He failed to achieve back-to-back Champions League successes when Chelsea were knocked out of the competition by a controversial goal in the semi-finals by eventual winners Liverpool. It was at this point my first book was published. It was to be the first of five books on him. In that first season Mourinho was an intoxicating mixture of charm, innovation, and the dark arts of football management. Compelling in every sense.

Although he took a great deal of criticism from certain sections of the media for some of his unorthodox antics that he usually brought upon himself, he was the darling of the back pages. I have now written 90 books and in one entitled *Hold The Back Page*, I described Mourinho after that first season "like Brian Clough on speed". I wrote at the time: "I happen to believe someone as colourful and gifted as Mourinho can only be good for English football. It will be a sad day for me when he leaves, and a much quieter one for the game in this country."

Chelsea started the following season defeating Arsenal 2–1 to win the FA Community Shield, and topped the Premier League from the first weekend of the 2005–06 season beating rivals Manchester United 3–0 to win their second consecutive Premiership title in April 2006 to give Mourinho his fourth domestic title in a row. After the presentation of his championship medal, Mourinho threw his medal and blazer into the crowd. He was awarded a second medal within minutes which he also threw into the crowd!

Mourinho's back-to-back titles left him seemingly untouchable, but, with Robben and Duff out of form or fitness, lynchpin Claude Makelele ageing, and new signings failing to reach the same heights, the following league campaign fizzled out uncharacteristically over Christmas and New Year as a resurgent Manchester United, powered by the twin talents of Wayne Rooney and Cristiano Ronaldo, allowed Sir Alex Ferguson to regain his place at the summit of the English game. The signing of Ukrainian super star striker Andriy Shevchenko in the summer of 2006 for a club record fee became a big point of contention between Mourinho and Abramovich. Shevchenko, at the time of his signing, was one of the most highly regarded strikers in Europe during his time with Milan, where he won the Champions League, Scudetto, and Ballon d'Or in seven years. Chelsea had attempted to sign Shevchenko in the preceding two years but Milan rebuffed Abramovich's interest in him, but by the time he arrived at the Bridge, the Ukrainian captain had developed a strong personal relationship with the Russian owner. Shevchenko's first season was a major disappointment as he only managed four league goals and 14 in all competitions, while his strike partner, Didier Drogba, enjoyed the highest scoring season of his career which led to Shevchenko being dropped towards the end of the season. In the Champions League match at Anfield, Shevchenko was not even included on the bench. Abramovich's insistence on Mourinho playing the Ukrainian was a huge source of friction between the two.

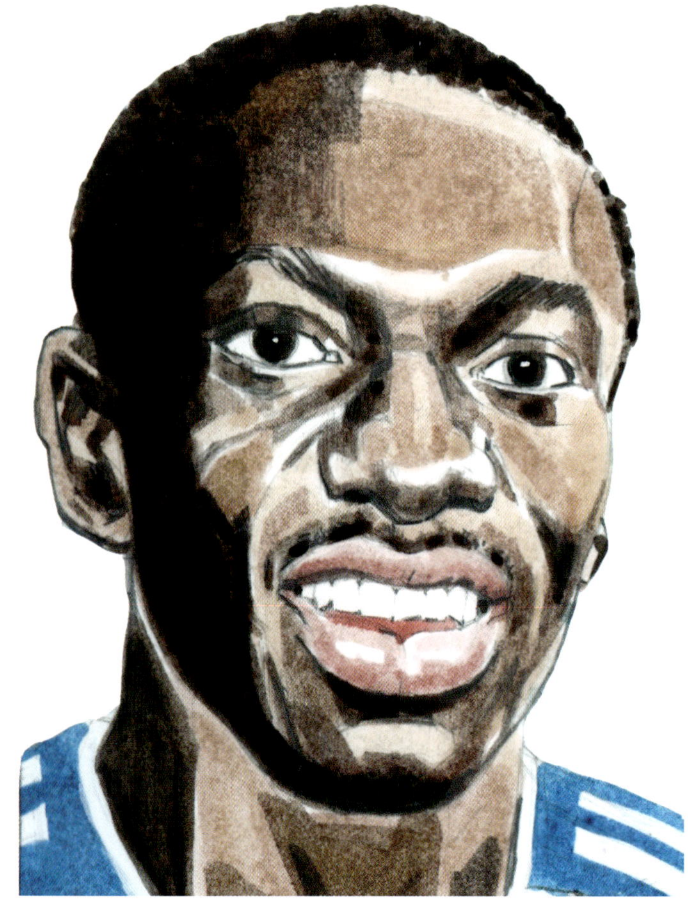

German captain Michael Ballack was signed to strengthen the midfield as a free agent from Bayern Munich, while Icelandic striker Eiður Guðjohnsen, such an important player for Chelsea under both Ranieri and Mourinho, was allowed to depart for FC Barcelona. The 2006–07 season saw growing media speculation that Mourinho would leave the club at the end of the season because of his worsening relationship with Abramovich and a power struggle with sporting director Frank Arnesen and Abramovich advisor Piet de Visser. Mourinho stated that there would only be two ways for him to leave Chelsea: if Chelsea were not to offer him a new contract in June 2010, and if the club were to sack him. He then launched an ambitious campaign aimed at becoming the first club in English football to complete "the quadruple". Despite the unrest, Chelsea won the League Cup again, defeating Arsenal in the final at the Millennium Stadium. The possibility of the quadruple was brought to an end on 1 May 2007 when Liverpool eliminated Chelsea from the Champions League on penalties at Anfield, following a 1–1 aggregate draw. Days later, Chelsea drew 1–1 with Arsenal at the Emirates Stadium on 6 May 2007 in a league match, which secured the Premier League title for Manchester United.

There was, however, to be further friction between himself and Abramovich when Avram Grant was appointed as Director of Football, despite objections from Mourinho. Grant's position was further enhanced by him being given a seat on the board. In spite of these tensions, the 2007 transfer window saw the departure of Robben to Real Madrid as French forward Florent Malouda moved to Chelsea. Shevchenko remained at the Bridge for another year. In the first match of the 2007–08 season, Chelsea beat Birmingham City 3–2 to set a new record of 64 consecutive home league matches without defeat, surpassing the record set by Liverpool between 1978 and 1981. Despite this feat, Chelsea's start to the 2007–08 season was not as successful as previous seasons. The team lost at Aston Villa, followed by a goalless draw at home to Blackburn Rovers. The opening game in the Champions League saw them only manage a 1–1 home draw against the Norwegian team Rosenborg BK in front of an almost half-empty stadium. Shevchenko scored Chelsea's only goal.

Mourinho unexpectedly left Chelsea on 20 September 2007

after a series of disagreements with Abramovich, and he was sacked after just over three seasons despite being the club's most successful manager in their history having won six trophies in three years and remained undefeated in all home league games. Grant succeeded Mourinho but failed to win any trophies in his year in charge, although he reached the final of the Champions League – something Mourinho failed to achieve at the Bridge.

After a career that took in a controversial spell as manager of Inter Milan and then Real Madrid, Mourinho returned in June 2013. Predictably his return was likened to that of the Prodigal Son and he declared he was back for the long haul and that blue blood ran through his veins. As we know, it didn't quite work out like that! Mourinho described his return as a 'great moment', conscious of the possibility he might not spark the same level of success and which could tarnish his original achievements. "When I decide to come back, there is some risk of things going wrong, but I'm not afraid," he said. "I trust myself; I think I can do it again. I'm not afraid to lose my job, and when you're not afraid, you don't feel any pressures. You are not too worried, you can express yourself in a different way. It makes you better, I think."

He wanted to give the impression he had changed, returned older and wiser, and that it would be less 'sexy football', but the motivation was there for more success. His first Chelsea experience was all silverware, even if he failed to deliver the real pot of gold – the Champions League: the trophy that at that time had still eluded Abramovich and was, ironically, delivered in Mourinho's absence. He was back, in his fifties, his hair now grey, and more than half the managers in the Premier League were younger than him. Mourinho was no longer the fashion icon, no longer the darling of the rich and famous in West London culture.

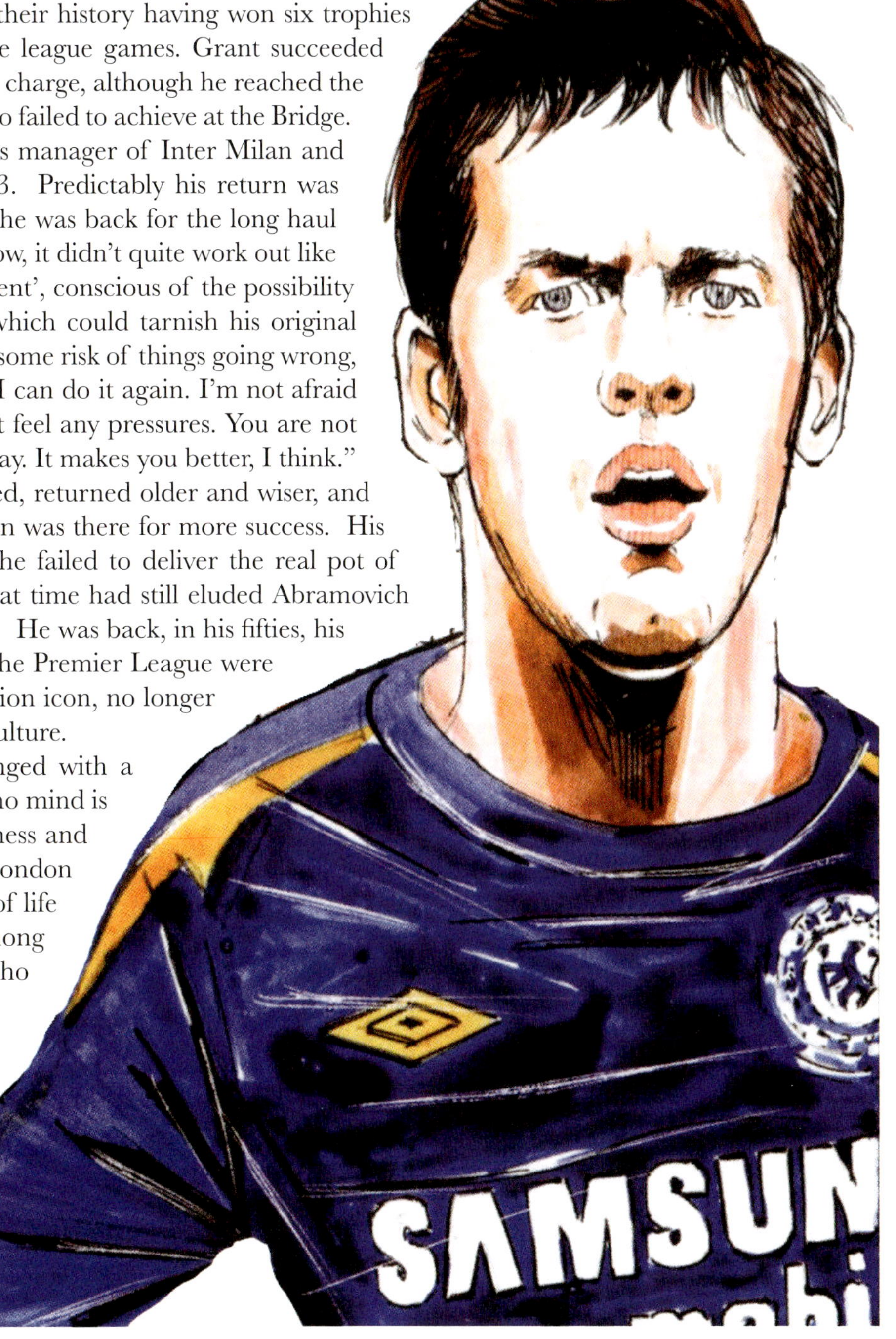

The media tagged him "The Happy One", tinged with a huge dose of scepticism; contentment in the Mourinho mind is never far away from outbursts of ego, anger, moodiness and controversy. The tranquillity he sought back in West London where he retained a family home after the turbulence of life in Madrid didn't last too long. Mourinho was back among the Chelsea faithful that adored him, the old Mourinho song soon rang out - home and away.

Apart from the Spanish Super Cup at the start of the previous season, he had endured back-to-back seasons without a major trophy: something that forced Mourinho into a passionate defence of his entire career record. Mourinho parted company with Real after three years in which he won La Liga and the Copa Del Rey and, while it seemed he might be heading to Old Trafford, he wasn't their kind of guy, with Sir

Alex recommending David Moyes instead. Moyes' six-year contract was brutally cut short when it was clear he was never going to turn around the team's fortunes and United turned to Louis van Gaal, every bit as controversial as Mourinho, and eventually did go for the manager they at first felt was too toxic to entertain.

Before Madrid, Mourinho had taken Inter Milan to Champions League glory and two Serie A titles between 2008 and 2010. He had been offered the chance to manage after he won the FA Cup in 2007, his last trophy during his first spell at Chelsea. He stayed, however, and was sacked in September.

A fondness for Inter remained but not so for Real, where antagonism and confrontation reached an unprecedented level. Yet Mourinho badly wanted Real on his impressive CV and left Inter for the opportunity. Unfortunately, though, the love affair ended in an ugly divorce. The Real hierarchy were glad to kick him out after all his antics. Mourinho split opinion – not necessarily about his ability to lead a team but because of the disparaging headlines that punctuated his time there and ruined his record.

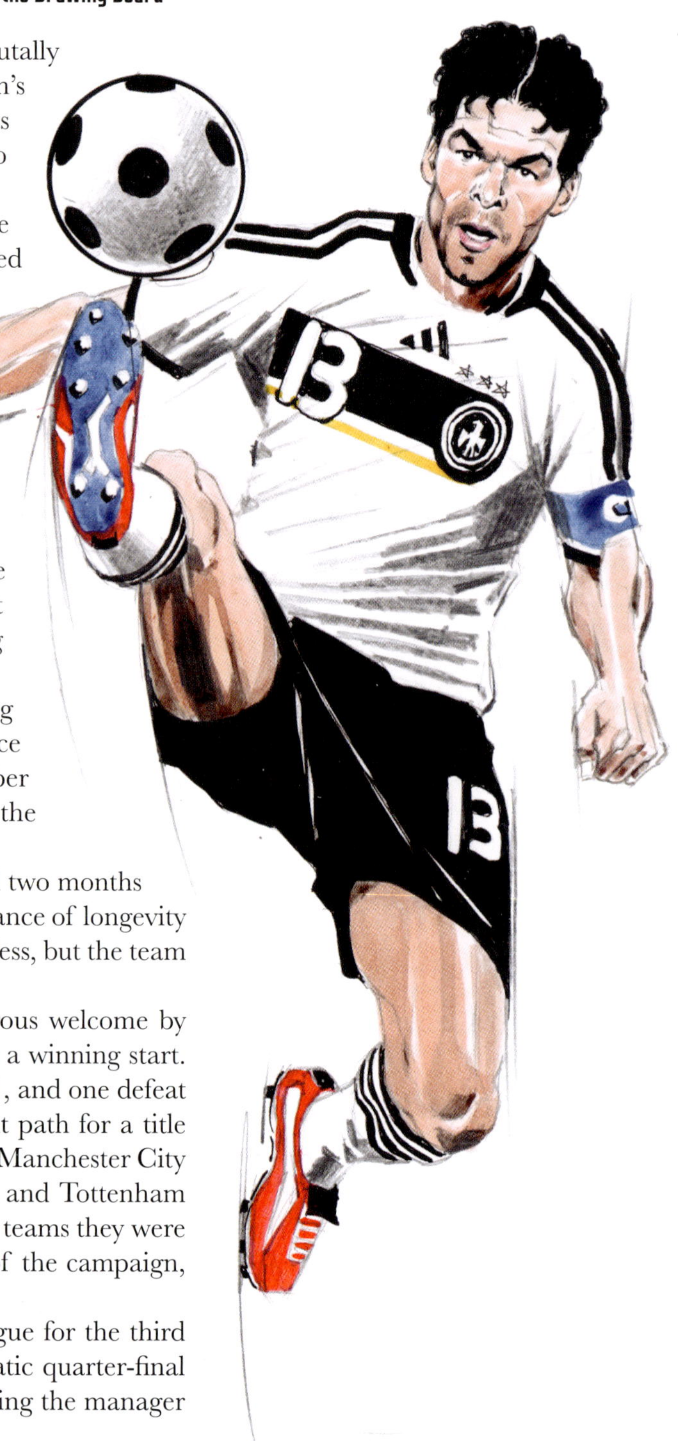

Mourinho signed a four-year contract on his Chelsea return, replacing the hugely unpopular Rafael Benitez, who had guided Chelsea to third place and won the Europa League after taking over on an interim basis in November from the hugely popular Roberto di Matteo, who had surprisingly won the Champions League that had eluded Mourinho at Chelsea.

The longest José has ever managed at any club was the three years and two months he spent at Chelsea between 2004 and 2007, so, in reality, there was little chance of longevity on his return. His first campaign back at the club, 2013/14, ended trophy-less, but the team went close both domestically and in Europe.

For his first game back, at home to Hull City, he was given a rapturous welcome by the Stamford Bridge faithful, and goals from Oscar and Lampard made it a winning start. The 4-3-3 formation, the hallmark of his first spell, made way for a 4-2-3-1, and one defeat in the opening nine Premier League matches set the team up on the right path for a title challenge. His record in the biggest games was outstanding; six points from Manchester City and Liverpool, four from Manchester United and Arsenal. The Gunners and Tottenham were beaten 6-0 and 4-0 at the Bridge, but disappointing results against the teams they were expected to beat, particularly Sunderland and Norwich towards the end of the campaign, meant a third place finish.

In Europe, Mourinho made it to the last four of the Champions League for the third time as Chelsea manager and Demba Ba scored a late winner in a dramatic quarter-final victory over Paris Saint-Germain to overturn a 3-1 first-leg deficit, prompting the manager

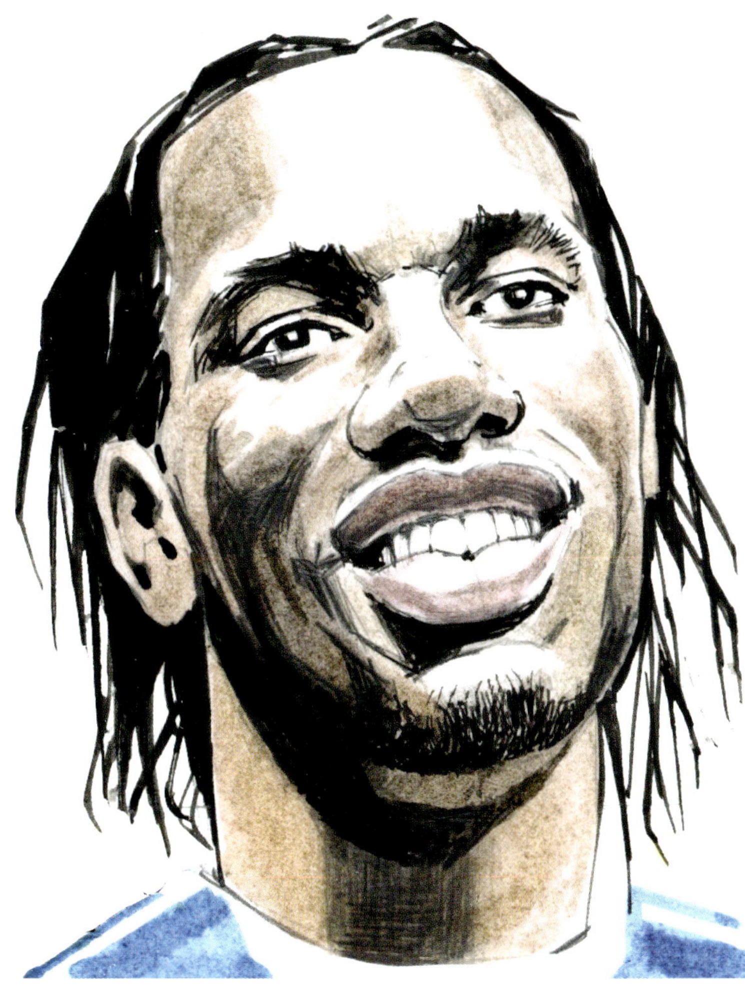

to run along the touchline in celebration, but after securing a 0-0 draw away from home against Atletico Madrid in the semi-final first leg, his team were beaten 3-1 back at the Bridge.

In 2014-15 the Blues lost just three matches over the course of the campaign, one at West Bromwich coming when Chelsea had already been crowned champions. The first part of the season will be remembered for the quality of the attacking play, with new signings Cesc Fabregas and Diego Costa flourishing. During the second half of the season they were weakened by injuries and suspensions, yet the defence was superb in securing many one-goal wins, with the victories away at QPR and at home to Manchester United outstanding, before Eden Hazard netted the only goal of the game against Crystal Palace to secure the title. Two months earlier Chelsea won the first trophy of the second Mourinho reign - the Capital One Cup – with a 2-0 victory over Tottenham at Wembley, the third time he had won the trophy, following triumphs over Liverpool and Arsenal in 2005 and 2007.

The title defence in 2015-16 began disappointingly, Chelsea losing seven of their opening 14 Premier League matches. Consecutive defeats against newly-promoted Bournemouth and Leicester City in December left the club perilously placed in 16th and Mourinho was sacked for a second time. "I stay until they want me not to stay. No club moves me from Chelsea until Chelsea wants me to move because I want to be where I am loved," Mourinho remarked in January 2014, but the mood quickly changed and, despite all the success, when Abramovich was faced with the prospect of a relegation fight he didn't hesitate to replace him after Chelsea's worst start to a top-flight season since the dark days of 1978-79.

Following the home defeat by Southampton, Mourinho insisted he would not quit and that the club would have to sack him. He suggested Chelsea would be losing the best manager they ever had if he was fired, but he also said he would walk if the players no longer backed him, and there had been rumours of a dressing-room mutiny which Mourinho addressed stating that it was not true. The club took the unusual step of issuing a statement, clearly authorised by Abramovich to 'close the media's mouth', backing Mourinho. But it turned out to be nothing more than the dreaded 'vote of confidence' and in December 2015, the love affair came to an incredible and stunning end. It was such a devastating moment in Chelsea's history, that you will always remember where you were at the time. I received a call on my mobile from LBC radio as I was leaving a matinee performance of *War Horse* at the New London Theatre in Covent Garden, asking if I could do an interview on the demise of Mourinho a little later in the evening. I'm not a Chelsea fan, but my wife Linda is and she was by my side when I broke the news to her. It came as quite a shock and she rang her family after the show, as they all support the club. My old *Daily Mirror* colleague Nick Ferrari, breakfast presenter at LBC, always likes to rustle me up when there is a major football story breaking and there had been none bigger for quite some time before Mourinho's sacking just before Christmas.

Ironically, the latest volume of my series of books on Mourinho was due to be published in late October/early November but, two months prior to the publication date, on consultation with the publishers, it was decided to put the book on hold 'pending his sacking' from Chelsea. The rationale was that, with the team doing so badly, the celebration of winning the title had already evaporated and a vastly different mood had descended on the Bridge: not a particularly good time to bring out a book to glory in Mourinho's achievements. But I reasoned that a very good time would be a couple of months later as, inevitably, he would be sacked.

I also wrote a column at that time for a football content website, of which I shared joint ownership with Glenn Hoddle, and in which I had been predicting Mourinho's sacking for some time. Then, in aftermath of the defeat at Leicester City, I had confidently predicted that he would get 'the boot' in social media postings, for a PR project I'd been working on for the launch of a new football boot.

I arrived back at the Millennium Hotel, Mayfair, where there was a clear telephone link for an uninterrupted five-minute slot to discuss the ins-and-outs of the Mourinho sacking. Having predicted for several weeks that he would be sacked, I was not unduly surprised LBC wanted to know why as there was an outpouring of emotion from Chelsea fans at the decision.

Interviewed on LBC, I commented: "Managers are judged by results; it is a results-based industry – and the results have been pathetic. So you sack the manager, irrespective of his former glories. He has taken Chelsea from champions to one point above the drop zone. If it was any other manager, you would have very little sympathy for him."

It is an irony that Chelsea's last manager, Mauricio Pochettino, is still loved by Spurs fans, while equally one of Spurs' more recent, Mourinho, is still adored by Chelsea followers, yet there is something in the make-up of the two managers that chimes with one club's concept of the game but grates with the other, and it's not all down to club rivalry.

Chelsea lost nine of sixteen Premier League matches at the start of what turned out to be a shambolic season and, while the manager was accused of 'losing the dressing-room', this, in my view, is a cop-out. Mourinho, though, did overstep the mark when he claimed he had been 'betrayed' by his players, an opinion he voiced before the game with Leicester City, for, by that point, the Chelsea board had had enough of his antics. The attitude of the players clearly defined the decision, and the fans knew it. The supporters had let some of the players know what they thought of them, booing them off at half-time or at the end, a condemnation of them more than the manager. From champions only a few months earlier, their form had been pathetically poor and Mourinho was right to feel let down.

Mourinho was proud of winning the title again with a depleted squad but delaying pre-season to give players a longer rest was a risk while his failure to sign top-class players was an even bigger one. Mourinho delivered the wish list of players he wanted for the new season but there was a lack of urgency in recruitment; a reluctance to pay over-inflated prices, and Real Madrid in particular were reluctant to sell their best players.

My book *José: Farewell to the King* gave a full insight into why it all happened; confrontational, passionate, full of chutzpah. A masterful tactician, José was surely the best Chelsea boss. There were multiple reasons but how much was the row with the first-team doctor, Eva Carneiro, at the heart of Mourinho's second sacking? The club's technical director, Michael Emenalo, let something slip when he described Mourinho's demise as a result of "palpable discord" with the players.

Mourinho went on to win trophies at Old Trafford, but not the league title he had promised, and again he was sacked as his style of football and his peculiar style of man-management, described as a scorched earth policy by supporters, grated with the fans and the board. His reluctance to move north didn't help, José spent his entire managerial reign at the plush Lowry Hotel while Pep Guardiola, who arrived at Manchester City in the same summer, quickly adapted to life in Manchester. A final straw for a lot of fans was his scruffy appearance at a Munich commemoration, with some

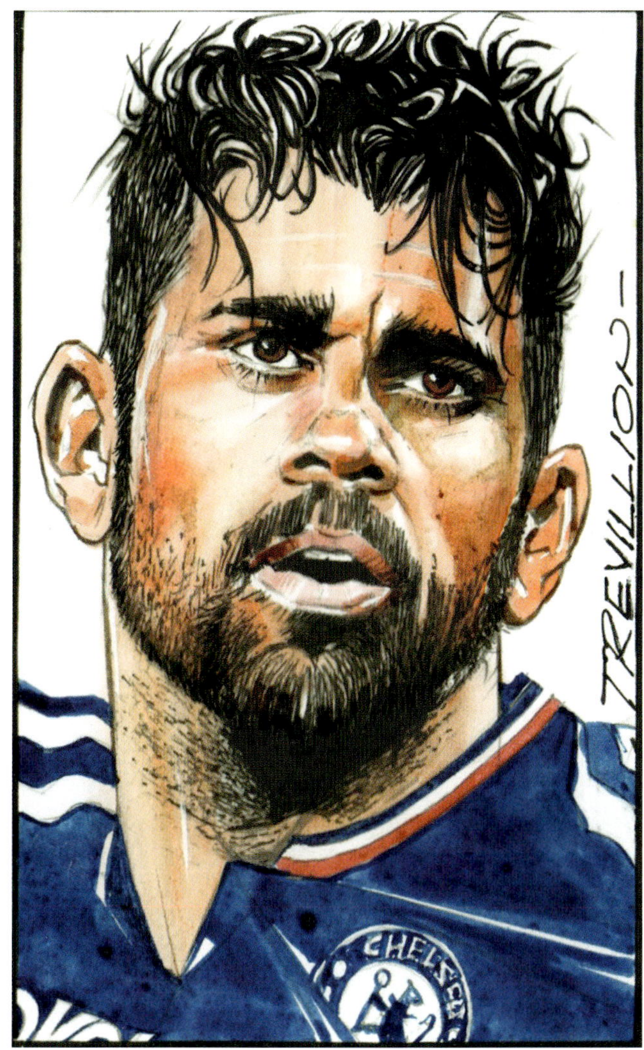

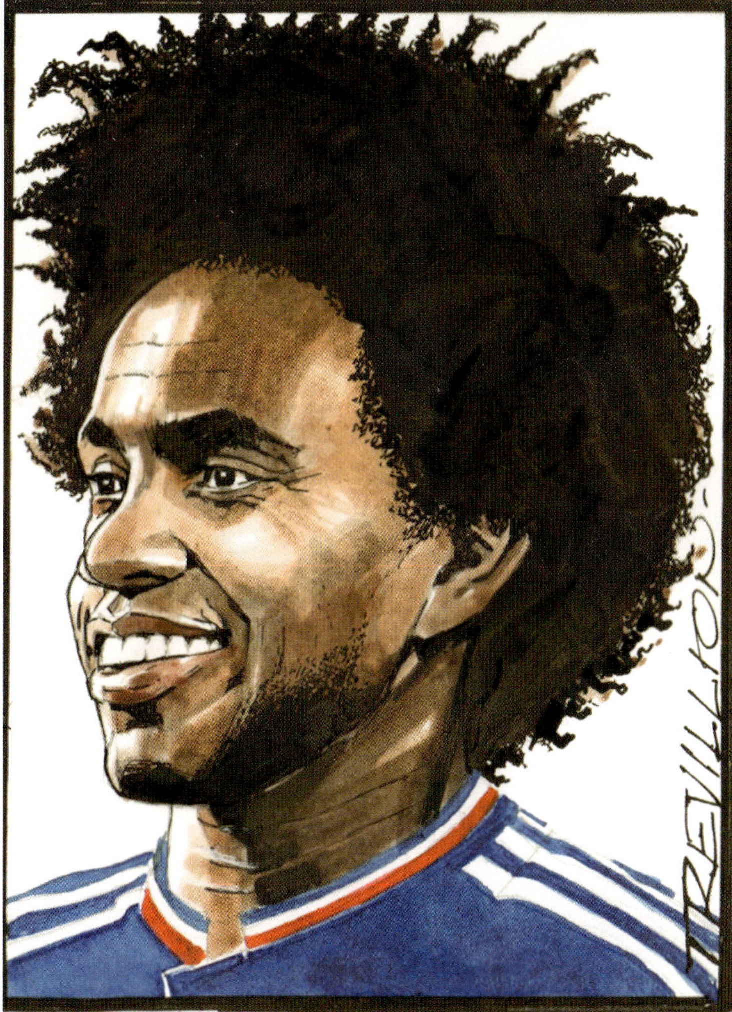

supporters claiming it showed a lack of respect. He also twice broke the transfer record to purchase Paul Pogba and Romelu Lukaku, neither of whom proved value for money. Perhaps the traditions and history of United proved too big for him, his success has mostly come at upstart clubs rather than established ones.

Despite now looking like a caricature of himself, José found one final Premier League taker at Spurs, a club desperate to win a trophy (any trophy), yet such was the animosity between board and manager that Daniel Levy sacked him just days before a League Cup final which they desperately needed to win to end a 15 year spell without one - they lost the final anyway! It is an irony that Chelsea's most recent manager, Mauricio Pochettino is still loved by Spurs fans, while equally one of Spurs more recent, Mourinho, is still adored by Chelsea followers, yet there is something in the make-up of the two managers that chimes with one club's concept of the game but grates with the other and it's not all down to club rivalry.

An unprecedented third return to the Bridge for Mourinho seems unlikely but I sense he would welcome it - as the football cliché goes "never say never."

Arjen Robben/Damien Duff

A Dynamic Duo

When José Mourinho arrived at Chelsea in the summer of 2004, he brought with him Paulo Ferreira and Ricardo Carvalho from Porto, ensuring some continuity for the manager, while attacking target Didier Drogba was also snapped up. Petr Cech's arrival from Rennes was agreed during the previous season, with Claudio Ranieri still manager, as was the recruitment of Arjen Robben from PSV Eindhoven. Mourinho, though, deserves credit for imparting a system where the Dutchman could dovetail so well with another pre-Mourinho player, Damien Duff. Robben joined Chelsea in the summer of 2004 from PSV Eindhoven for £12m and would go on to win two Premier League titles, two League Cups and an FA Cup with Chelsea during a stellar career. He later played for Real Madrid and Bayern Munich, and won 96 caps for his country, scoring 37 goals.

Signed by Claudio Ranieri before he was sacked by Chelsea in 2004, Robben played a key role as the Blues won back-to-back titles under José Mourinho in 2005 and 2006. His Chelsea start was hampered by a metatarsal injury in pre-season but after his debut in October 2004, he played a major part in the club's first successful championship challenge for 50 years, playing wide of a front three in an effective wing partnership with Duff on the opposite flank, even though further injury kept him out of action in the latter part of the campaign. Duff set up Robben for his first Chelsea goal against CSKA Moscow in the Champions League. Robben scored seven in 18 league games and was named Premiership Player of the Month for November 2004, but was pipped to the PFA Young Player of the Year by Manchester United's Wayne Rooney.

Chelsea secured the title away at Bolton to become league champions for the first time in 50 years. "The club hadn't won the title for 50 years so it was an amazing feeling, but that weekend was bittersweet. We trained at Blackburn the next day because we were playing Liverpool in the Champions League semi-final and I tweaked my hamstring. I remember breaking down in tears on the pitch, as I knew I was going to be ruled out."

Robben collected his second Premiership winners' medal for the 2005/06 season, contributing six goals in the league campaign although two red cards and more injury reduced him to 28 appearances. Mourinho's Blues conceded 37 across two seasons and used the pace and subtlety of Robben and Duff to unlock defences.

In his third and final season he made a major impact as a half-time substitute in both cup final victories, crossing for Didier Drogba's winner against Arsenal in the Carling Cup final and making a contribution at Wembley in the FA Cup final against Manchester United despite playing well short of peak condition.

Robben had nearly joined United instead of Chelsea after talking to Sir Alex, "I had a very good conversation with him over dinner in Manchester and we spoke about football and life. I also went and had a good look around the training ground and everything was good, but after I went back to PSV nothing happened. There was no real contact and the deal didn't happen. PSV were also negotiating with Chelsea at that time, so maybe they offered PSV more money? I don't really know. I spoke to Chelsea and I liked their plans. We had one meeting and everything was done pretty quickly. Had Manchester United offered me a deal straight after I met them, I would have signed there, but it didn't happen and I've got no regrets."

Having joined Chelsea at the age of 20, the Dutchman had to comply to the will of The Special One, "He was really demanding and intense, but at that age I think it was good for me and my football development. I'm a student and someone who wants to improve and work hard, so I think our personalities were a good fit. I played a lot of football under Mourinho and he was a good man-manager. He gave me a lot of confidence and I've got good memories of playing for him. When I moved to England I wanted to get better. The injury meant that I had the opportunity to focus on the physical side of my game. I had several months of intense work, so by the time I was fit again I was in fantastic condition. This gave me the confidence to show what I wanted to show in the Premier League. I never had problems with injuries as a kid or in the youth team. My injuries started at Chelsea, when I broke my foot during a pre-season game. That was just pure bad luck, but after that I had some muscular injuries too, so I had to get to know my body better. I tried to find out how to take care of it, to avoid breaking down all the time. Some players never have any injuries and others, like me, have to do more specific things to ensure they stay fit. It was really difficult. I had to work my socks off to get fit again, but by the time I made my comeback I was in fantastic physical condition and had a great start at Chelsea. In my first three matches in the starting XI, we won 1-0 and I scored two of the goals. I felt fast and strong, which I realised I needed in England, so maybe my time out did me some good."

John Terry was a big influence as well as the manager, "He's one of the greatest captains I've ever played with. The way he behaved and conducted himself on a pitch set an example to everyone."

Speculation linking Arjen with a move to Spain with Real Madrid wouldn't go away and eventually the club agreed to let him leave for £24.4m, double what Chelsea paid for him. In total he started 74 games with a further 32 sub appearances, scoring 19. "It was hard, although the system had changed a little bit at Chelsea," Robben said, "In my first two seasons we had been playing with wingers, and then José switched to a diamond with a physical midfield and two forwards. I could have played as a striker but Andriy Shevchenko and Didier Drogba were first choice at the time. Real came in for me and it was difficult to say no, as it was a forward move for my career – I had to go for it. In my first season, we won the league and beat Barcelona 4-1, which was an incredible night. In my second year, I think I played some of the best football of my career. That was when I started playing on the right wing and cutting inside, so I scored lots of goals. If you're scoring and winning trophies, the fans will always be happy with you."

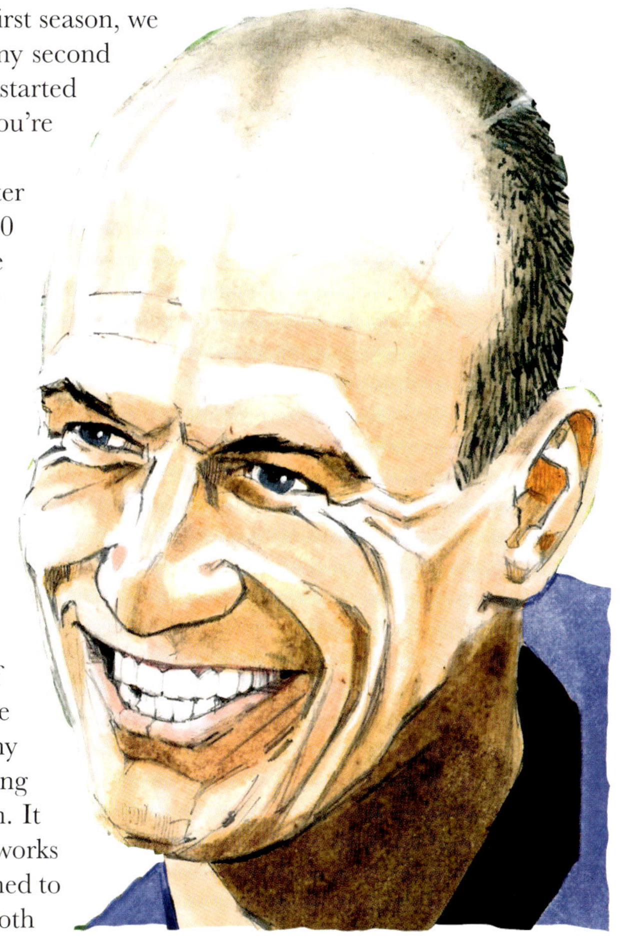

Yet it was with Bayern Munich that Arjen showed his best form after joining them in 2009 - inspiring the team to a Treble as they reached the 2010 Champions League final, losing to Inter Milan, and the 2012 final when he had a penalty saved by former team-mate Cech as Chelsea triumphed. Arjen scored the winner and was named player of the match a year later when Bayern beat Borussia Dormund at Wembley.

Having played in the 2010 World Cup final in South Africa, where the Dutch lost to Spain in the final, Robben quit international football in 2017 when the national team failed to qualify for the 2018 tournament in Russia. He retired for a second time at the age of 37. He initially hung up his boots in 2019 before reversing the decision to return to his first club Groningen. Injuries and the Covid pandemic marred his second spell. He wrote on Twitter: "I have decided to end my active football career, it was a very difficult choice. I want to thank everyone for their heart-warming support!"

The Robben-Duff combination with Drogba leading the attack was one of the most exciting forward lines, as the Irishman recalls: "It was a special time and a special team. When Ranieri pre-signed Robben, I'd just dislocated my shoulder and so things weren't going too well – I was worried he was replacing me. It took about three or four games for me to break into Mourinho's team. It was a wake-up call, it toughened me up, but if you work hard then it always works out in the end. Once I'd got into the team I stayed in it. I don't think José planned to get both of us in the same team, it just happened. We were both direct and both comfortable on either wing – we were chopping and changing. It is hard to defend."

Damien Duff has the distinction of being the first signing of the Roman Abramovich empire: "I don't really think about it like that, but I remember lying in bed in the summer, dying with a hangover, when I got the call that they wanted me. It was a bolt out of the blue. I flew over a couple of times because I wasn't quite sure, but eventually I signed and it was the right decision. Within a month they'd spent £150 million on people like Crespo and Veron. Claudio had already signed Cech and Robben before José came in. Claudio was brilliant, all the guys loved him. We may have won the league in that one season I worked with him, but nobody was catching 'The Invincibles' at Arsenal. You always had a feeling after Abramovich took over that Claudio's days were numbered, and there was definitely a shift in the mentality once Mourinho came in. There's no doubt Mourinho was the best manager I ever worked with. He squeezes every last ounce out of you and the training sessions he put on were unbelievable. He had us believing from day one that we would be champions. We ended up steamrollering everyone in that first season – even when we weren't playing well, we had a belief that we'd still win."

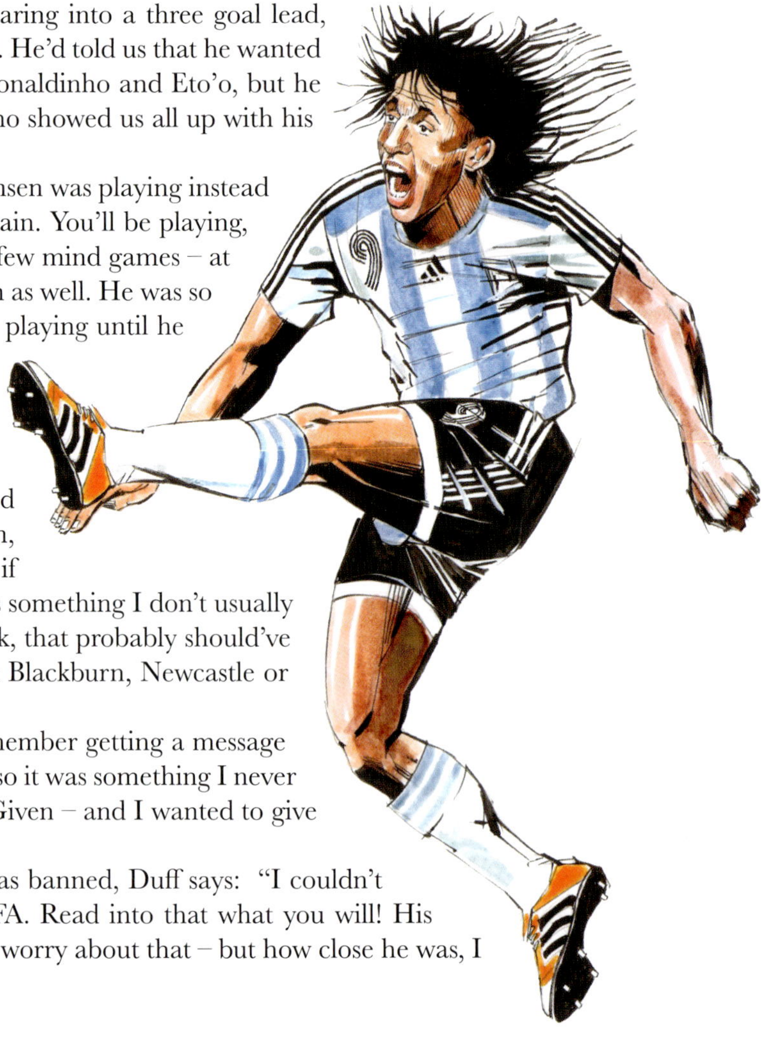

The opening spell against Barcelona in 2005 was special, roaring into a three goal lead, "We just steamrollered them – that was Mourinho being prepared. He'd told us that he wanted to draw Barcelona. We all thought that was crazy, as they had Ronaldinho and Eto'o, but he was right as usual! It was nice to score a goal, but then Ronaldinho showed us all up with his amazing performance."

Prior to the first leg Mourinho announced that Eiður Guðjohnsen was playing instead of Duff. "I was struggling with injury and José told me: 'Don't train. You'll be playing, but I'm going to announce a different team.' It was just to play a few mind games – at the press conference he named our team and he named their team as well. He was so good at doing things like that. He had me believing that I wasn't playing until he named the team the next day, so he did me a kipper as well! I started and played a role in a very important away goal."

Duff's Chelsea career to an end in 2006. "At the time I wanted to play in every game – I didn't back myself. Chelsea were signing [Michael] Ballack as well as [Andriy] Shevchenko and I was in and out of the team at the tail-end of the previous season, so I thought, 'I'm not going to play'. To be fair, José said: 'No, stay, if you play well and you're fit, you'll be in the team.' It's a regret, it's something I don't usually do. I usually stay and fight. I cried on the day I left – looking back, that probably should've told me I was making the wrong call, as I never cried when I left Blackburn, Newcastle or Fulham, or even when I retired. But it was my own decision."

Duff almost signed for Spurs when leaving the Bridge: "I remember getting a message from Martin Jol, but I was a Chelsea fan after winning titles there so it was something I never really looked at. I had friends at Newcastle – Scott Parker, Shay Given – and I wanted to give that a real go, but I went to Newcastle and had a disaster."

As for José's infamous hiding in a laundry basket when he was banned, Duff says: "I couldn't possibly mention it, there'd probably be bans coming from UEFA. Read into that what you will! His impact was massive in that tie. He still played his part – don't you worry about that – but how close he was, I couldn't tell you. Let's just say he was close by."

Petr Cech

Chelsea's Greatest 'Keeper

Petr Cech was arguably Chelsea's pivtoal signing and his arrival ensured the most successful period in the club's history. He was the best goalkeeper in the world in the mid-2000s and just as influential and effective as skipper John Terry in maintaining a superlative defensive record between 2004 and 2006, conceding 15 and 22 to win back-to-back Premier League titles. With José Mourinho installed as manager, Cech - one of nine major signings - helped transform a challenging team into champions. His sparkling 11-year playing career at Stamford Bridge saw him win every domestic and European club honour possible and surpassed Peter Bonetti's clean-sheet record to becoming the club's highest overseas appearance maker.

Of his humble origins the Czech great said, "I grew up in Plzen, a town most famous for pilsner beer and Viktoria Plzen, who were my first club when I was seven. Back then, Czechoslovakia was under a communist regime, so everything was different to what we know now, but one thing which contributed to a great generation of players – especially in the early nineties – was that sport was everything we had. If you ever wanted to be able to leave the country, sport was the tool. There was not much to do apart from training and spending time outside with your friends because there were no PlayStations, nothing on TV, no phone and no other distractions. As a child, I loved every sport. With my sisters, I played handball, basketball, tennis, hockey and of course football. But I wanted to be like the ice hockey goalie with the mask, the gloves, and the pads. I was always attracted to that. I started off playing football as a left-winger and I read the game quite well, I would just go in goal for the last 10 minutes of training sessions to allow the goalies to come out and play for fun. My coach noticed I was not afraid of the ball. Then, as a 10-year-old playing in attack, I went through on goal one-on-one with the goalie and it ended in complete disaster. I suffered a tibia fracture and ended up in a cast for months. After the injury I couldn't run for an entire game and this basically put me in goal permanently. That felt like destiny. That was the decision, and I never looked back!"

After spells with Chmel Blsany, Petr moved to Sparta Prague where he set a Czech league record for not conceding a goal for 903 consecutive minutes and he was soon snapped up by French club, Rennes in 2002. His stand-out performances soon attracted interest from Chelsea who signed in 2004 for £7m. Cech was chosen ahead of Carlo Cudicini to make his debut on the opening day of the 2004/05 campaign in a 1-0 win over Manchester United. With a defensive unit in front of him that proved almost impenetrable for long spells during that season, Chelsea romped to a first title in 50 years with Cech keeping 24 clean sheets and set a then Premier League record of 1,025 minutes without conceding a goal.

"We as a team took pride in getting clean sheets. It was not only the defenders and goalkeepers, it was everyone chipping in to make sure that if we can't win, we don't lose. If we don't concede, you only need one shot and you get three points. That's what I'm proud of. The clean sheets in that season were beautiful and something to remember, but if you finish third, then you'd think, 'OK great, I have all the records, but all I really wanted was the title.' Those clean sheets were the decisive factor in us winning the title. That's what really stands out for me – that every clean sheet not only contributed to all the records, but especially to winning the title."

The following season followed a similar pattern, with the Blues dominant and Cech producing incredible levels of consistency as the team recorded consecutive title triumphs. However he had to overcome an horrendous fractured skull following a collision with Reading's Stephen Hunt early in the 2006/07 season. By working tirelessly out on the training pitch he returned after three months and the stopper for the big occasions played a starring role in many more memorable matches. The legacy of that fractured skull was the protective headguard he has worn ever since. Of the incident that altered his career, Petr recalls, "Nobody could have known that my game would last 15 seconds, but that can be part of football. Luckily, we were close to Oxford and I could go the short distance to the hospital there for my operation. When I realised the position I was in, I thought: there are two things I can do. One is to do everything I can to recover and give myself a chance of getting back on the pitch. The second is that the injury is too big and I'm finished and I will need to do something else. I chose the first option and thought, I will show everybody that I can come back. I'll do everything. If it happens, it happens. If it doesn't happen, it doesn't happen. I came back way earlier than everybody expected because the plan was not to play again that season. As soon as I was told that my skull was solid enough with my helmet, I wanted to get back out there. The biggest advantage for me in my recovery was not remembering the incident. That first day in training, I dived at people's feet and everybody was like: 'Oh, you're crazy.' I believed I was fine and I didn't want to stop."

Petr kept a clean sheet in the first FA Cup final at the new Wembley in 2007, saved a penalty in the same fixture three years later, and made another stunning stop in the 2012 FA Cup final against Liverpool when he somehow managed to keep out an Andy Carroll header late in the game. His finest night came in Munich a few days later when an outstanding performance helped the Blues to Champions League glory. Having saved an Arjen Robben penalty during extra time, Cech got his hand to two more in the shoot-out prior to Didier Drogba's decisive kick. While not as heavily involved during his final season at the club, Petr still made a big contribution as the team lifted two trophies in 2014/15, keeping five clean sheets in six Premier League appearances on the way to being crowned champions and playing in a 2-0 League Cup final triumph over Tottenham. Cech departed the club in June 2015 having made 494 appearances, winning 13 major honours, by far the best record by any keeper to have played for Chelsea. He was a four-time winner of the Premier League's Golden Glove for the most clean sheets, and was also selected in the Professional Footballers' Association team of the year on two occasions.

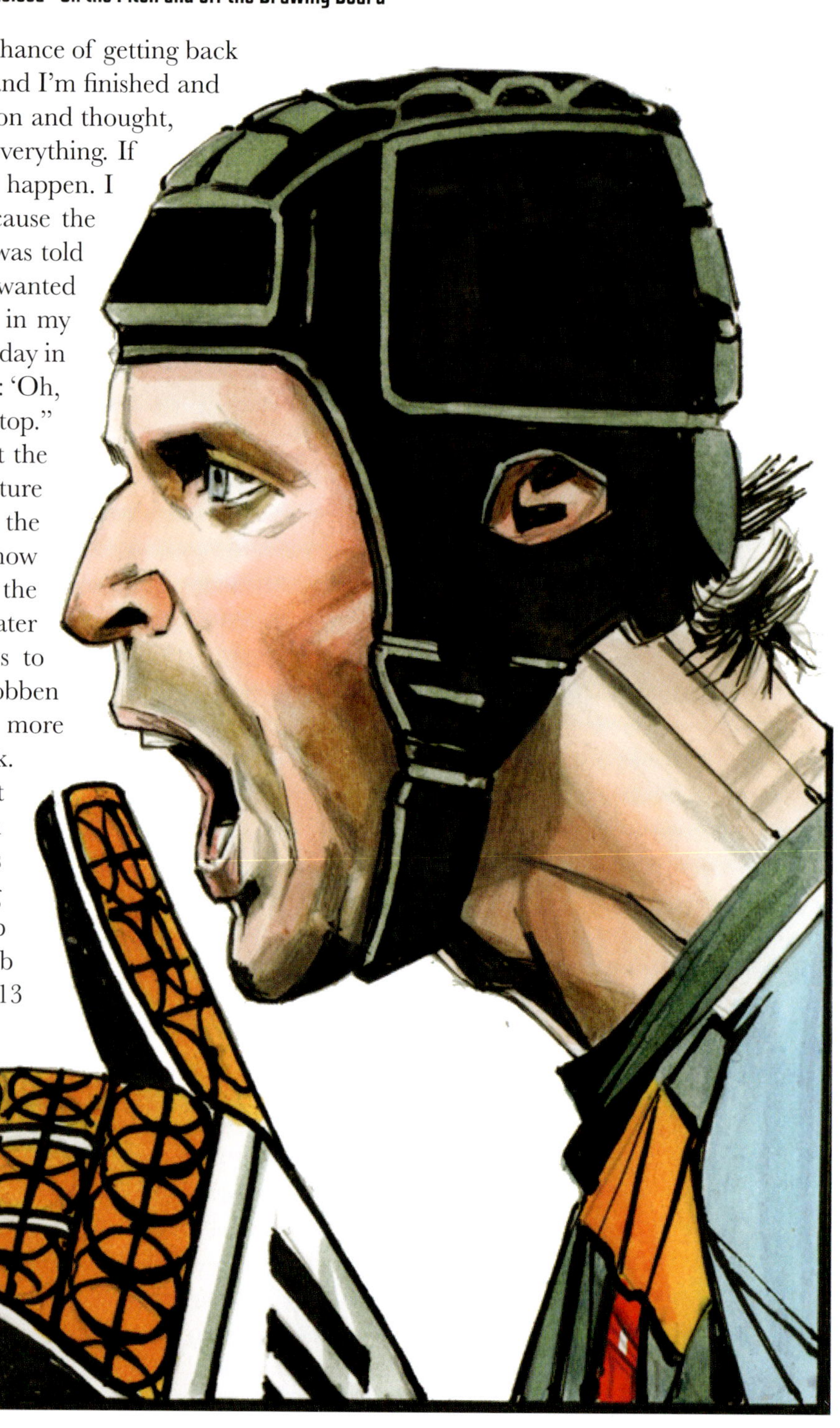

He says: "There was a lot of expectation as a lot of money that had been spent at Chelsea. There was an amazing stat that I cost more than every single goalkeeper in the history of

Chelsea Football Club. It was such a great part of my life, so it will always remain in my heart and the club is like a second family to me. I'm proud of the mark we left on the Premier League. You never really have the chance to look back on it whilst you're playing as it's so relentless, but I can look back now and know that it was a special time."

Petr moved to Arsenal before retiring, returning to Chelsea for three years in a technical and performance advisor capacity. His final game before retirement in the Europa League final against former employers Chelsea in Baku on 29 May marked the end of a trophy-laden 20-year career for the 37-year-old. At Arsenal he added an FA Cup winners medal to an already impressive collection, while registering 40 clean sheets from his 110 Premier League appearances for the Gunners. "I liked playing against Arsenal because the games were always intense. The crowd was always loud, and they were played an exciting style of football. With their history and tradition, I was so happy that I could join Arsenal. I wanted to join a club with the intention of chasing trophies and winning the league. I loved every minute of my Arsenal stay… there are obviously things which will always hurt, and that's the season where we finished second just behind Leicester City."

Until his retirement from internationals in 2016, Petr featured in several major championships for the Czech Republic, winning a record 124 caps for his country, he speaks five languages, loves ice hockey and released a charity single with Queen drummer Roger Taylor.

Petr kept a record 202 clean sheets in the Premier League. He says: "When I hit 100 clean sheets, and it was the fastest 100 as well, I thought, 'OK, that's an achievement in such a tough league.' But I am always thinking of the next milestone, 'Can you do 150?' When that happened, I thought, 'Nobody's done 200' and I thought that would be amazing. I'm proud that I managed to get more than 200 clean sheets and I saved a penalty [for Arsenal] in the Watford game to reach 200, which made it special. It's not only an achievement for a goalkeeper. You need your team-mates to come together and when defenders dive in to block shots for you, it makes it easier." Chelsea honours: four league titles, four FA Cups, three League Cups, the Europa League, and Champions League in 2012.

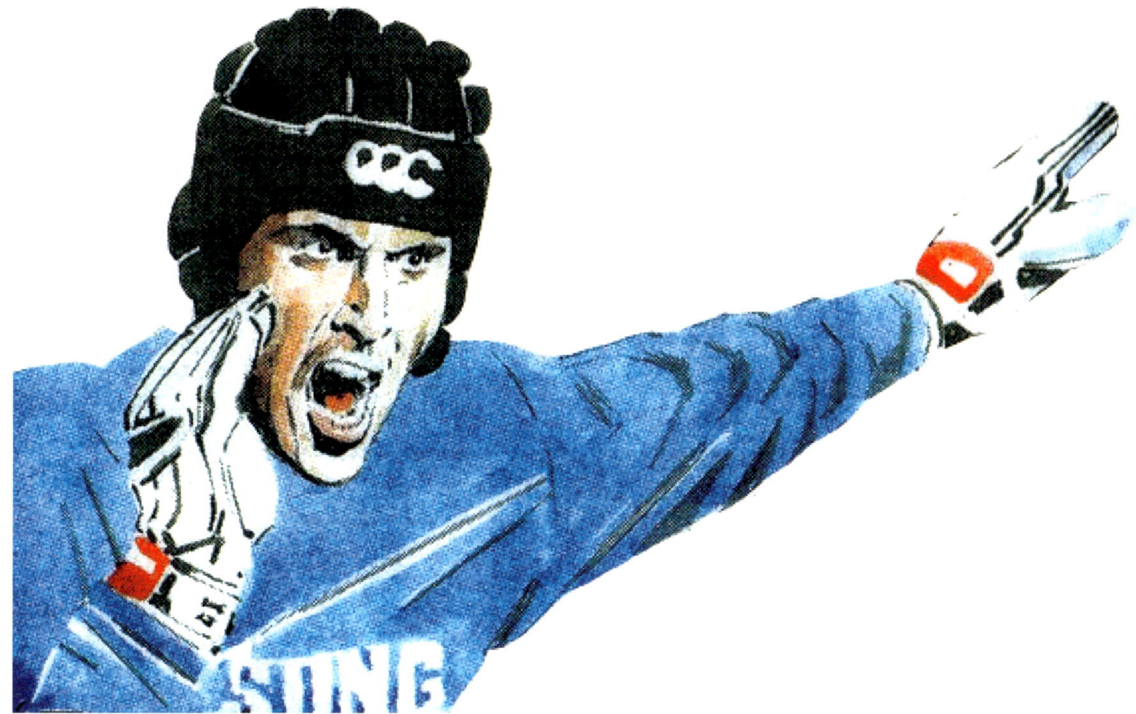

Avram Grant

One Kick Away from Immortality

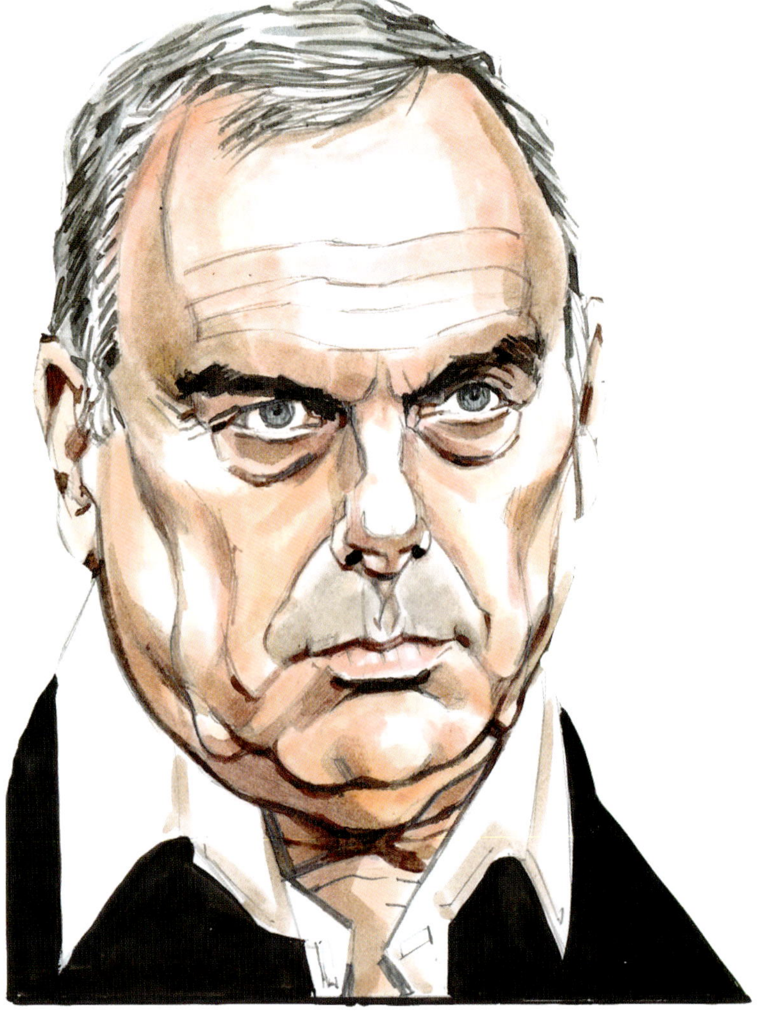

Avram Grant was manager for a year and might well have retained his role but will always be remembered as being the width of a goal post away from winning the Champions League when John Terry slipped and missed his spot kick in the 2008 final in Moscow.

The Israeli was seen as a 'personal friend' of owner Roman Abramovich from the moment he joined Chelsea as Director of Football in July 2007 due to their Jewish and Israeli connections. For that reason he was never a popular appointment among the fans who thought he had displaced José Mourinho; they were never keen on his arrival and it seemed inevitable that he would takeover at the first opportunity. Grant's arrival from Portsmouth did not please Mourinho, who was dismissed in September 2007 following a 1-1 draw with Rosenborg at Stamford Bridge in their opening Champions League game.

Grant discussed how his relationship with Chelsea's owner worked: "I enjoyed talking with José, a very intelligent guy, very nice to sit one-on-one with and I don't remember one minute of anger. When he feels attacked, he responds. I told him one time you need to count to 10 before you answer. He is very passionate and sometimes insecure. He feels the need to respond to everybody. But every minute with him as a person was enjoyable."

Avram's popularity decreased still further after he was elevated to manager when the hugely popular fans' favourite was sacked. Replacing the 'Special One' would be no easy feat for anyone, let alone someone with such close connections to the owner, and whose appointment as director of football clearly did not sit well with the man who had brought the club six trophies in three seasons.

Grant declared himself his own man, but the fans continued to believe he was Abramovich's eyes and ears inside the dressing-room. Nevertheless he had some impressive credentials, and a reasonable reputation when he went unbeaten in World Cup qualifying as manager of Israel, and enjoyed success at club level in his homeland. But he had never worked in one of Europe's top leagues, although he had been director of football at Portsmouth in 2006/07. When Grant arrived at the club, Abramovich wanted to see his team replicate the flamboyant styles of Barcelona and AC Milan; there were 'characters' in the dressing-room such as Didier Drogba, Frank Lampard and Michael Ballack, which Grant felt was essential but Abramovich wanted more. "In my time we had characters and were keen for creative players. I personally negotiated with Kaka in Milan. I did everything I could for him to come. When we were in Chelsea, we had a fantastic team. I think we played the best football Chelsea have played in that half year. If this had continued there would have been a lot of titles in Europe."

Grant's first game in charge was at Manchester United, where refereeing decisions went against him. A Champions League victory in Valencia and a 6-0 drubbing of Sven Goran Eriksson's Manchester City began to win the new manager the support of the fans as his team also re-entered a title race that had looked beyond the club early in the season and Grant was rewarded with a four-year contract in December.

An injury crisis kept Petr Cech, John Terry, Ashley Cole, Michael Ballack and Didier Drogba from action at various times, while the Africa Cup of Nations then took four of his stars to Ghana for a month. It was a huge test of Grant's managerial acumen yet he managed a run of five straight league victories after Christmas, and reached the Carling Cup final thanks to a semi-final aggregate victory over Everton before a collapse in form in February following draws with Portsmouth, Liverpool and Olympiacos and an extra-time defeat at Wembley to Juande Ramos's Spurs, which remains Tottenham's last trophy success.

"The semi-final against Liverpool was so important, but the match was on Holocaust Day. In Israel nobody works, that day is very respected. So I didn't know what to do. I asked my father... and he said 'of course, I'm so proud that you will'. Some people in my country said I didn't need to coach on that day. But he felt it very important that on that day... He was so happy when we won that game, and he came to the final. For me, winning that match on Holocaust Day, that's one of the biggest achievements in my life.

A positive reaction came at West Ham with a 4-0 victory which featured two Goal of the Season contenders from Joe Cole and Michael Ballack. The Greeks were also brushed aside at Stamford Bridge, and with a last-eight tie against Fenerbahçe, European success became a real possibility. A defence of the FA Cup looked more than possible following the early exits of Manchester United, Liverpool and Arsenal, but a 1-0 defeat at Barnsley was a huge set back after Grant had rotated his team.

Frank Lampard came to the rescue with four as Derby were hit for six, and then a win at Sunderland brought his team within three points of the Premier League summit with nine games remaining. Spurs coming back to earn a 4-4 draw before Grant's major tactical success came against Arsenal. Trailing 1-0 at Stamford Bridge he brought on Juliano Belletti and January signing Nicolas Anelka, who had struggled to make an impact, and the game turned, the Brazilian laying on one for Drogba, the Frenchman the other, as Chelsea climbed to second in the table.

The Champions League defeat in Turkey was overturned in London two weeks later, earning a semi-final date with Liverpool for the third time in four years where John Arne Riise's injury-time own-goal at Anfield meant a home victory would be enough to reach Moscow. League victory over Manchester United put Chelsea level with the champions, although behind on goal difference, before Liverpool were finally beaten after extra-time, Lampard and Drogba seeing Chelsea through to the Champions League final. Grant was pictured on his knees pointing to the heavens as the fans started to warm to a man who had taken them to the Champions League Final to face Manchester United in Moscow, but first the Red Devils were to claim a second successive league title by winning at Wigan on the final day. Grant recalled: "The semi-final against Liverpool was so important, but the match was on Holocaust Day. In Israel nobody works, that day is very respected. So I didn't know what to do. I asked my father whether I should coach, and he said 'of course, I'm so proud that you will'. Some people in my country said I didn't need to coach on that day. But he felt it very important that on that day specifically I try to bring happiness to people. He was so happy when we won that game, and he came to the final. For me, winning that match on Holocaust Day, that's one of the biggest achievements in my life. My father is my hero. He passed away almost 10 years ago, and I miss him every day. He buried his father, his mother and his sister with his own hands. And even despite all this he was so optimistic. To educate people that they have a choice. My father had the right to be bitter, or to think about revenge, but he chose to be positive. He didn't hate anybody. He didn't even hate the Nazis that killed his family. So to fight against this through education, it's very, very important. The connection between football and my father is that everybody can choose the way he can go; choose to go through hate, or go through love."

Grant delivered an address to more than 10,000 Jews at Auschwitz, and gave a speech to those he joined on Holocaust Day for the three kilometre 'March Of The Living' between Auschwitz and Birkenau. His father survived the Holocaust but only after burying just about every other member of his family. Grant paid tribute to his father when his own 14-year-old son was able to watch that Champions League semi-final from the comfort of Chelsea's VIP box, and he acknowledged that, were it not for his dad, he would not be Chelsea manager, "The fact that today I am leading one of the most glamorous football clubs into a historic Champions League confrontation, and all this 65 years exactly after the carnage, is the real victory. Not my triumph. The victory of us all. That's even more important than winning the Champions League. To coach Chelsea is a dream but it is also a very difficult adventure. The pressure being placed on me as the Chelsea coach cannot be described. The expectations are enormous.With a team like this I am not allowed to lose, not even one match. Behind me is an enormous number of fans, a demanding media and everything happens with the most crazy intensity. Every moment of this story is a personal and professional celebration and experience. I'll remember these moments, even the most difficult ones, for the rest of my life. But in the end, you remember and you understand and you know that nothing resembles what my father had to go through 65 years ago, and you get things back into proportion and distinguish between bad and good and know where you came from and where you are going back to."

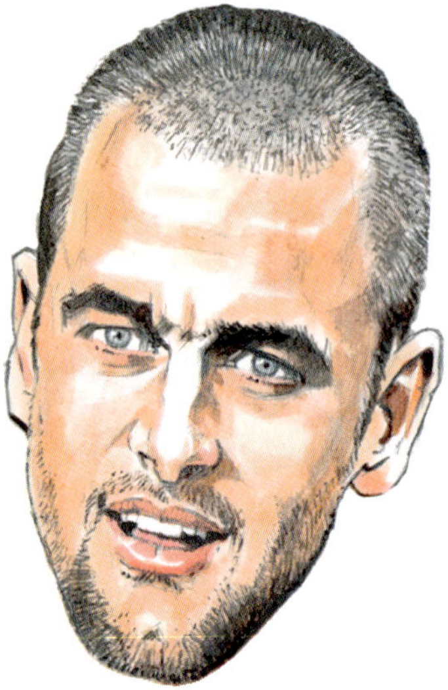

There was no hiding place in that Champions League Final, it would define Grant as a Chelsea manager. Victory would make him a hero and he'd receive the acclaim. Lose and most thought he'd get the sack. Claudio Ranieri, who lost his job after finishing second in the Premier League and losing a Champions League semi-final, knew Grant's position to be precarious. "If Grant doesn't win, I think he's finished in the job," said the then Juventus manager. "I think if Grant wins something, then okay, maybe he'll continue, but if not I don't know the mind of Roman Abramovich, it's very difficult to know what he thinks."

For Avram Grant to come within the width of a goalpost from getting his hands on the Champions League trophy and finally winning the affection of the fans must have been a bitter pill to swallow.

The final had seen favourites United put Chelsea to the sword in the first half hour and take the lead through Cristiano Ronaldo but they missed at least two gilt-edged chances to wrap up the game before Chelsea had got going. A deflected shot fell kindly for Frank Lampard just before half-time and remarkably the Londoners were level. The second half saw Chelsea in control for long periods and they themselves probably should have won it and extra time continued the trend. Yet an incident minutes from the end of extra time had a huge impact on the resulting penalty shoot-out as an altercation involving Carlos Tevez and Nemanja Vidic saw Didier Drogba dismissed. Drogba would undoubtedly have taken one of the first five penalties meaning John Terry wouldn't have had to.

As United players and fans celebrated, Grant was comforting his distraught captain and just four days later he left the club as the nearly man, who came so close to bringing that first Champions League success, but in the end departed empty-handed, as a runner-up three times after just eight months in charge. Despite losing just two Premier League games, Grant attracted criticism from fans who claimed his team lacked style. He was also criticised for losing the League Cup final against Tottenham. The decision followed two days of talks between Grant and the club's owner and chief executive Peter Kenyon. Russia coach Guus Hiddink, fellow Dutchman Frank Rijkaard and Manchester City boss Sven-Goran Eriksson were among the early favourites to replace him. Brian Laudrup and Roberto Mancini were all linked with a possible move to Chelsea with the likes of Luiz Felipe Scolari and Mark Hughes in the running.

Grant said his farewells to the players telling them it had been a 'privilege' to manage the team. Grant remains aggrieved that he didn't get the credit he deserved at the time. "We lost only one game in the league, against Arsenal, were unbeaten at home and the players deserved all the credit. We lost the Carling Cup final and it was funny because they blame me. When we win, it's other people - even the kit man.We lost only two games and they blame me only two times. I said no problem but before when we won you say it's not me and now we lose you say it's me, so I feel like I'm at home. It's like my job with my wife: to be guilty even when I'm not guilty."

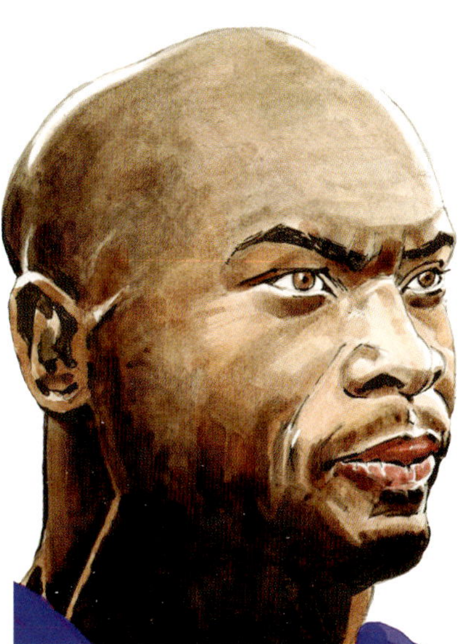

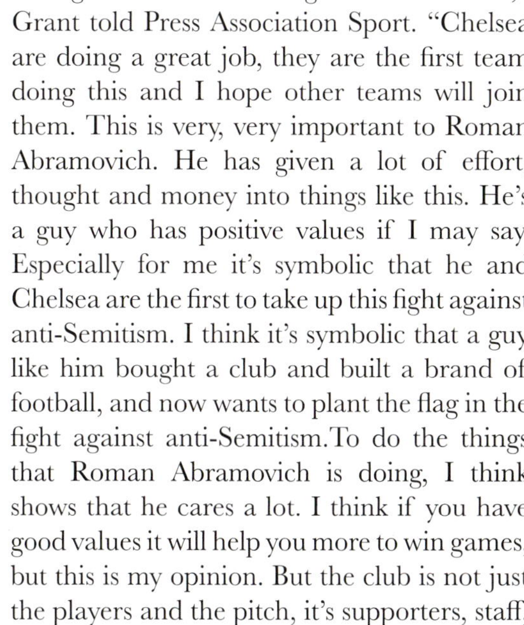

Grant re-emerged at Portsmouth to lead them to the 2010 FA Cup Final where again he would be denied at the final hurdle – this time by Chelsea! Grant has actually one of the best manager win percentages in Chelsea history but he had taken over immediately after fan favourite Mourinho and the fans never really forgave him, despite that trip to Moscow and a second place finish in the Premier League. There was even some racist abuse because of his Jewish origins, but the club took steps to protect him.

Chairman Bruce Buck attacked a minority element of the club's support for anti-Semitic abuse of their new manager, which provoked strong feeling. Buck felt some of the comment which the club had received crossed the boundaries. "We welcome all constructive points of view," Buck wrote in the match programme for the visit of Fulham."But there have been a few which could be viewed as racist and anti-Semitic and that must stop immediately. This is one thing we will not tolerate whether in written correspondence, on the chat pages, on posters or banners or through singing and chanting. And it unfairly smears the reputation of the vast majority of Chelsea fans who rightly do not want to be associated with such activity." More recently, Grant has backed Abramovich's fight against anti-Semitism, suggesting it proves his continued commitment to the club. Grant joined a host of Chelsea representatives on the annual March Of The Living, walking across Nazi death camps to mark the Holocaust when he praised the Chelsea owner for spearheading the 'Blues Say No to Anti-Semitism' campaign, urging other top clubs to follow his lead.

"I'm very proud, very proud that Chelsea and Roman Abramovich are heading this initiative to fight anti-Semitism," Grant told Press Association Sport. "Chelsea are doing a great job, they are the first team doing this and I hope other teams will join them. This is very, very important to Roman Abramovich. He has given a lot of effort, thought and money into things like this. He's a guy who has positive values if I may say. Especially for me it's symbolic that he and Chelsea are the first to take up this fight against anti-Semitism. I think it's symbolic that a guy like him bought a club and built a brand of football, and now wants to plant the flag in the fight against anti-Semitism.To do the things that Roman Abramovich is doing, I think shows that he cares a lot. I think if you have good values it will help you more to win games, but this is my opinion. But the club is not just the players and the pitch, it's supporters, staff, and a community too. It's great that Roman Abramovich wants to help people change, change through football, and it shows how much he cares."

Voice of reason Carlo Cudicini told me: "Avram took us to the Champions League Final for the first time in his one and a half seasons in charge of the team, and he was so very close to winning it for the first time for the club as well. He was a completely different manager to anything I had experienced in my entire career. A very religious guy, he was holistic in his approach, and it was very interesting in the way he brought other sports icons into the mix such as Michael Jordan, some of the world's top athletes in all sports, and applied their methods and attitudes in how they reached the top of their sports. Generally managers concentrate on their own experiences and techniques in football, but Avram took it to a different level and it was interesting to see how other top sportsmen conducted themselves and prepared for their sport, something he felt football could learn from them. He talked about them, how he had past conversations with them, what we could learn from their mental approach to their sport, he would also then show us pieces to highlight their approach, their work ethic, their professionalism, and it was refreshing to read and learn about certain aspects of other people in sport rather than only those involved in football, especially how top athletes in their respective sports mentally approached those sports.

"Avram is a kind man, someone who enjoyed having conversations with you on a one-to-one basis, he was very keen to exchange opinions and ideas not those just related to football, he was open to the world of sport not strictly the one sport in which we were all involved. In the dressing-room Avram's close relationship with the owner when he took over from José Mourinho as manager was not a question we discussed.The owner first brought him as technical director, something we were aware that José Mourinho didn't like working behind him, at least that was the rumour in the media but not something, as players, we knew was true or not. But when there is a problem with the manager, everybody naturally discusses it in the dressing-room.

"Avram was very close to winning the Champions League, just one penalty away, and it is a very good question what would have happened if John Terry's penalty had struck the inside of the post and gone in instead of hitting the outside of the post. I don't know. Would the owner have kept on the manager who had won him the club's first Champions league? No one had any idea what was in the owner's mind going into the Final, or what would have been different had we won the Champions League. It might be that there was a planned change no matter whether we had won the Final or not, we just didn't know. Maybe Avram himself had wanted to leave the job, as players we didn't know how it ended up although clearly there had been conversations between the manager and owner. Football is so unpredictable, it might even be that Avram would have left having won the Champions League, but, of course, it would have been intriguing had the final penalty gone in."

The first Chelsea manager to guide the Blues to the Champions League final regards his time at the club as one of the highlights of his career. Grant looks back fondly on his time at Stamford Bridge even though the London side were the nearly men on three fronts during a 2007/08 season in which he replaced Mourinho a month into the campaign. As well as losing out on penalties in Moscow, Chelsea finished runners-up in the Premier League and lost to Spurs in the League Cup final. "Every time you achieve something you think that it is the highlight of your career," he told UEFA.com. "Considering the public opinion, to reach the Champions League final with a team like Chelsea, after they started the season not so well, and to play the football that we played … it's the highlight."

John Obi Mikel Grant claimed Grant 'had absolutely no clue' as Chelsea manager. The ex-Nigeria international spent 11 years with the Blues under eight different managers, including Mourinho and Ancelotti. "For me, he [Avram Grant] just wasn't a manager," Mikel told ex-teammate Florent Malouda on *The Obi One* podcast. "He wasn't a manager because he [had] no clue of what he was doing. He absolutely had no clue. He [had] someone who does the training and all he does is come in and tell us stories about Michael Jordan and a fire that is burning somewhere. But it worked for him, he got us to a Champions League final."

Grant managed a win percentage of 66.67% in a season that saw Chelsea miss out on the Premier League title by two points and lose the Champions League final on penalties to Manchester United. He was sacked days after the season concluded but Malouda suggested it was a good call as he backed up Mikel's claims. "Yeah, I agree with you," Malouda replied. "I remember in training when he tried to lead the session, he realised he did not have that skill so he had to find a guy who had that skill. But, I would say when you look at the results, we reached the Champions League final. At the time, he knew [his limitations] and he knew what he needed to help him, because management is not easy - even if you are experienced, it is very, very hard. So, I think he did well, because he was not experienced but he still did the job."

Grant managed Portsmouth and West Ham in the Premier League, although he was once reportedly found asleep at his desk by players during his stint with the east London club!

Big Phil Scolari

Forced Out By Player Power

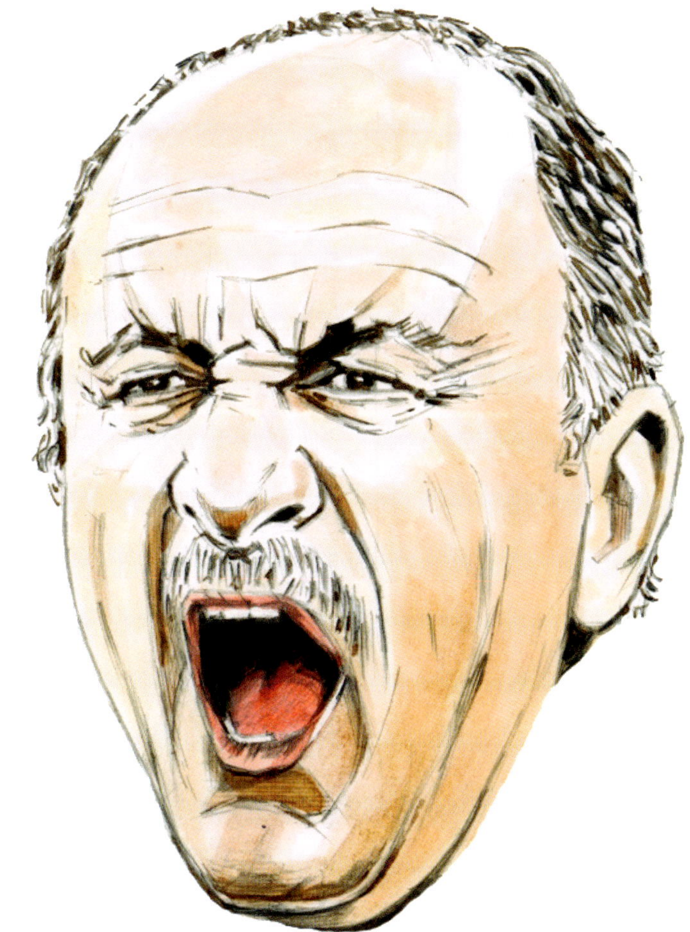

Luiz Felipe Scolari didn't only ditch England from successive major tournaments but kicked them to the kerb and ended up in West London instead of Wembley, in succession to Avram Grant. He was still in charge of the Portuguese side at Euro 2008 when the announcement was made that he had accepted the post at the Bridge once his contract with the Portuguese Football Federation expired after a six-year stint as their manager. "He is one of the world's top coaches with a record of success at country and club level," read a Chelsea statement, as the club believed 'Big Phil' was a big catch as he had won the 2002 World Cup with Brazil and led Portugal to the final of Euro 2004 and the semi-finals of the 2006 World Cup having knocked out England at the quarter-final stage on all three occasions. He had also won nine domestic trophies in Brazil.

Scolari became the fourth manager under owner Roman Abramovich's reign following Ranieri, Mourinho and Grant. A Chelsea statement at the time said, "Scolari gets the best out of a talented squad of players and his ambitions and expectations match ours. He was the outstanding choice. Out of respect for his current role and to ensure minimum disruption to this work, there will be no further comment from Chelsea nor from Felipe about his new role until his employment with us commences."

Scolari had been in charge of both Brazil and Portugal when they ended England's chances in the 2002 World Cup, Euro 2004 and the World Cup in 2006. His global reputation made him a compelling contender for the England job in 2006 but he was put off by fears of media intrusion. Yet, that's exactly what he should have expected by taking one of the highest profile jobs in world club football. Sceptics also mentioned that he had never managed a European club, although he had won the Copa Libertadores – South America's equivalent of the Champions League - with Brazilian clubs Gremio and Palmeiras. He also won a Brazilian championship with Gremio in 1996, three Brazilian cups and three South Rio Grande championships.

Speaking before the appointment, Portugal and Chelsea defender Paulo Ferreira said: "We need a good manager and Scolari is a good manager. He can do a good job and he will be good for the club" while former Chelsea player Gavin Peacock believed Scolari could make the Blues the entertaining team chief executive Peter Kenyon was looking for. "You can't argue with his record," Peacock told BBC Sport. "If you're looking for someone with charisma and presence in the dressing-room, then he is your man. His teams play with flair so it fits in with what Chelsea say they have been looking for but the everyday involvement, getting into the players' minds, will take time. I suspected he might be

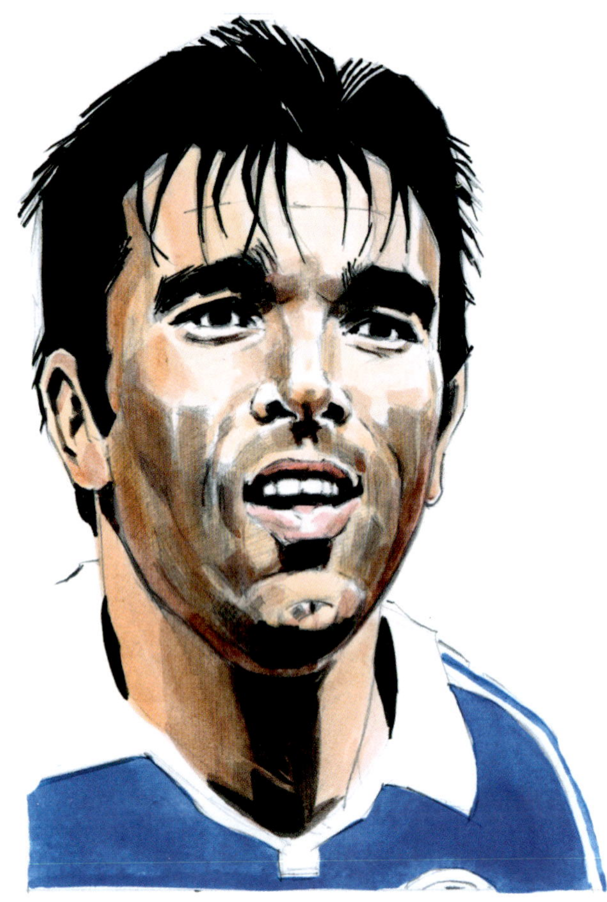

lined up when Chelsea signed José Bosingwa last month and there was talk of Deco coming to the club." However, Peacock warned that Scolari's lack of English could make things difficult for the Brazilian."My only question mark would be about his level of English. Does he speak it?" said Peacock. "For example, Mourinho, on his first trip away with the team for a pre-season friendly in the United States, sat on the plane with Joe Cole for two hours just getting to know him. Scolari will not be able to do that sort of thing." Alan Hansen added: "I think it's a very good choice. If you're going into that dressing-room you've got to have a presence - he's got that - and a great track record, and he's got that as well. He's got the right credentials and he's done fantastically well with Portugal. The big players will find you out in a minute and a half, so it's a great choice."

Scolari made an impressive start but results quickly deteriorated and of his first 36 games, only 20 were won, five lost and 11 drawn. Chelsea, who were unbeaten in the league at home for 86 matches until Liverpool's 1-0 win in October 2008, lost two home league matches and drew on five occasions, and were knocked out of the Carling Cup by Burnley on penalties. Their record against the so-called big four was poor – drawing 1-1 at home with Manchester United and losing 3-0 away, they were beaten 2-1 at home by Arsenal, and home and away by Liverpool.

A banner unfurled during Chelsea's goalless draw with Hull at Stamford Bridge called for the return of former favourites Gianfranco Zola, then in charge at West Ham, and Roberto Di Matteo, the MK Dons boss. Chelsea were booed off at the final whistle and sections of the crowd could be heard chanting "You don't know what you're doing" at Scolari.

Yet 'Big' Phil had made a blistering start as manager winning 10 of their first 13 games but just two wins in a packed December schedule saw them fall off the blistering title pace set by perennial table-toppers Manchester United and Rafa Benitez's resurgent Liverpool. By the time of that goalless draw with lowly Hull, it was clear that it was a matter of when, not if, he'd get the chop. The final straw for Abramovich was watching the fans turn on Scolari in that game at home to Hull and his overall record of a 56% percentage didn't compare favourably with predecessors Grant (66.67%) and Mourinho (67%).

With rumours of a fall out in the dressing-room, it wasn't long before he was sacked. The club's website revealed the move had been made "to maintain a challenge for the trophies we are still competing for". Chelsea were fourth in the Premier League, still harboured hopes of winning the Champions League and FA Cup, with Ray Wilkins put in charge until a successor was appointed. "The Chelsea board would like to place on record our gratitude for his time as manager. Felipe has brought many positives to the club since he joined and we all feel a sense of sadness that our relationship has ended so soon. Unfortunately the results and performances of the team appeared to be deteriorating at a key time in the season. In order to maintain a challenge for the trophies we are still competing for, we felt the only option was to make the change now. The search for a new manager has already started and we hope to have someone in place as soon as possible."

Scolari had signed a lucrative three-year deal, but barely lasted seven months and now the club faced yet another hefty compensation pay-out. Scolari's spokesman Acaz Felleger said it was Abramovich who had run out of patience. "It seems that Abramovich made the decision," Felleger told *Lance*, "Scolari was not in a comfortable situation despite having the support of the squad and Peter Kenyon." Felleger said Scolari had not been given the backing to refresh the ageing Chelsea squad. "The Chelsea squad are old. Felipe tried to rejuvenate it, but unsuccessfully. He asked (the board) to sign Deco and Robinho, but they only brought Deco."

Chelsea's accounts showed Abramovich's subsidy of Chelsea had increased from £578m in 2007 to £679.6m by June 2008. The extra £100m absorbed another annual loss of £65.7m, following the £74.8m recorded the previous year. Chelsea's wage bill was £148.5m and the loss also included £23.1m paid in compensation to the departing managers Mourinho and Grant and five members of the coaching staff. Abramovich's sacking of 'Big Phil' added a further £7.3m in compensation. Chelsea's then chief executive, Peter Kenyon, reiterated the aim of the owner for the club to be self sufficient, a target that seemed highly improbable, pointing to a 96% increase in Chelsea's annual earnings since 2003, to £213m, the fifth highest of any club in the world. Kenyon said this "aim of self- sufficiency" means that whoever is Chelsea's manager will be able to fund signings only by selling first. "Chelsea was building a strong business base in what will be challenging times," said Kenyon, "We have consistently reduced our net transfer spend over the last five years and will attempt to continue this trend."

Scolari's statement said: "I am thankful for the opportunity to have worked for Chelsea and in English football. It was a very valuable experience. I am sorry that my time with everyone could not last longer. I wish Chelsea luck in the three competitions they are participating in. I want to take the opportunity to inform that I will keep living in London. I will respond to the media soon."

Later, he revealed the depth of the behind the scenes fall out as he tried to persuade Abramovich to sell Didier Drogba because he had found it difficult to control the striker during his troubled spell at the club. He told a television station in his native Brazil that the dressing-room was driven by personality clashes and he had problems dealing with several big-name players. "I didn't leave Chelsea because of sabotage from the players but it is true that it was difficult to control the dressing-room. Drogba believed he was the star in the squad and I did have conflicts with him. He wanted to go to a hospital in Paris because of an injury but I said no. That was my first problem because Anelka did well in his absence and scored many goals. But when Drogba came back he wanted to go straight back into the team, but I refused."

Speaking to ESPN Brazil, he elaborated, "The players return, I make a meeting, and in the meeting I say: 'Look, now that the players have all returned, Drogba is back after two months, we will try to work a situation involving the two attackers playing one by the side, one in the centre, changing positions. Then Anelka, the league's top scorer, said: 'I do not play on the wing.' Well, that's when I said,'You don't play on the wing, one's going to be on the left, it's over, I'm not going to stay here arguing with you guys'. And there began a series of other things.

"I left there and our team was third in the league, three or four points behind top. Qualified for the round-of-16 or quarter finals of the Champions League. But there was this bad environment, that situation. I don't know if I had continued, what would have happened. But it was interrupted. There, I got upset. They'll say: 'Oh, because you didn't speak English perfectly'. Of course, I did not. I didn't speak English perfectly. But I understood perfectly. We understood, with my English, and the English that was spoken there, we understood perfectly."

His disagreement extended to his recommendations in the transfer market, "I wanted Robinho but it wasn't possible. I also wanted Abramovich to change Drogba for Adriano at Inter because he was easier to control than Drogba."

Scolari, in his first interview since being dismissed, told *France Football* magazine that their failure to sign Robinho - who ended up at Manchester City - from Real Madrid cost them dear. "At Chelsea we didn't have the player who can make the difference by himself by producing something magical on the pitch. In the past, Arjen Robben was at Chelsea and he could make the difference but now there is no-one. Robinho could have been this player. He is not afraid to dribble, to take a risk. As a Brazilian, I like this. The team isn't Brazilian enough. It is a 'bureaucratic' team. That's the style of the players. That's why Robinho would have

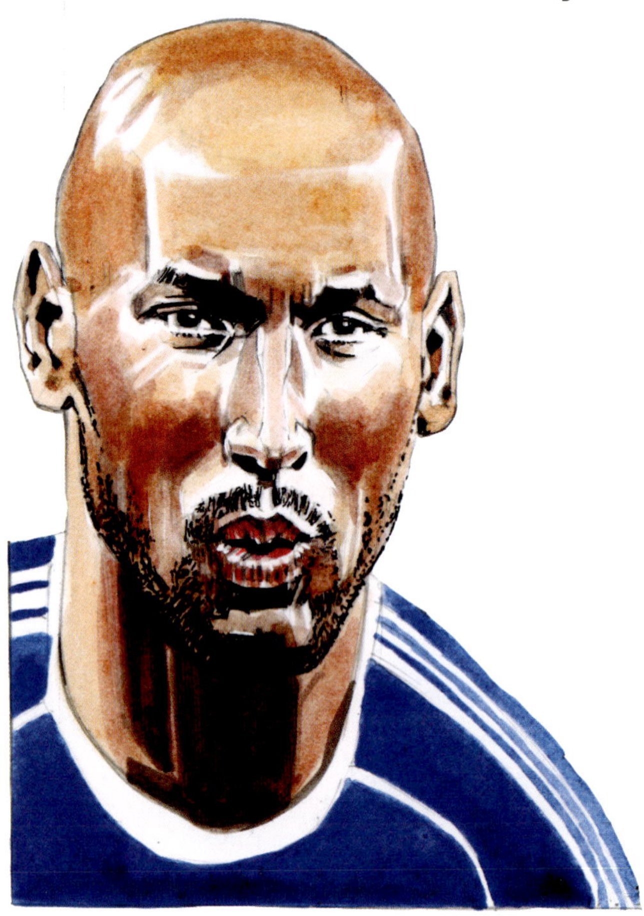

done a lot of good for the team."

But assistant Ray Wilkins responded: "Football is all about opinions, and Felipe has his own opinions on the game. My opinion is that we do have special players at this club, a number of them in fact." The interim boss was stunned by Scolari's dismissal and said he enjoyed his five-month spell under the 2002 World Cup- winning manager. "I was shocked, yes. He was a very decent man, and I enjoyed working with him immensely. But football is a tough game and a couple of results went against us and the decision was made. I was shocked, yes, and disappointed, because I enjoyed his company, he was a smashing guy."

'Big Phil' also said Michael Ballack seemed "jealous" of Deco when the Portuguese arrived at the club."I wanted Deco to work it out with Ballack but it wasn't possible. They didn't speak."

Scolari started Drogba just eight times before receiving his marching orders, he privately blamed the striker for a humiliating loss at Old Trafford and dropped him to the bench. Drogba's representative, Thierno Seydi, believed that Chelsea decided to support the forward at Scolari's expense because they considered him more valuable. Seydi added: "The fact that he was told to sit on the bench had nothing to do with sport, it was just a problem between two men that couldn't work together. One had to go and Chelsea decided to part ways with Scolari. They literally said that Didier made history at the club, that he could still bring a lot to the team, so they decided to let the coach go and to keep Didier."

Scolari elaborated on his bust-up with Drogba conflicting viewpoints within the club on how best to help him recover from surgery. He said,"Chelsea had some problems with injuries, some problems in the team. I had a form of leadership that clashed with one or two players."Asked which members of the squad in particular, he confirmed: "Anelka and Drogba. Our medical department thought that we should let Drogba go and recover in Cannes, in the middle of summer. I thought he should stay in London. I'd also like to go to Cannes in the middle of summer. I'd stay there for a month, two months, enjoying myself."

Scolari wanted to work out how he could fit both strikers into the starting line up but Anelka was reluctant. Scolari added: "When he came back, I tried to adapt so that Drogba and Anelka could play together. Anelka was the top scorer in the league. We had a meeting and Anelka said, 'I only play in one position.' So, there was a bit of a lack of friendship, of respect, of trying to play together with Drogba. They were both great, but someone had to do something different, to get back to help when we lost the ball. That was when it changed a bit. But we've met since then, me and Drogba.The last time was in Russia in 2018. We spoke openly about it. There wasn't any ill intention from him or Anelka. But it happened and I lost out on one of the great chances of my life." Carlo Ancelotti later managed to convince Anelka and Drogba to play together as Chelsea won the Double in 2010.

Although Scolari did not take over directly from Mourinho, his most influential players remained major influences. Mourinho's methods were popular with the players. Everything was done with a ball. The physical and technical work was always carried out in a footballing setting, reflecting one of the game's four moments;

having the ball, not having it, losing it and regaining it. To be sent out for a run by Scolari was seen by some of the senior players as a throwback.

United boss Sir Alex Ferguson felt sympathy for Scolari."It is a sign of the times," Ferguson told MUTV at the time. "There is absolutely no patience in the world now. There was great expectation at Chelsea that they were going to do well this year - and it is only this last month they have had a bad spell. The judgment really is only on the last month."

Former Chelsea boss John Hollins commented: "You can't knock him for what he's done internationally but club football is a different ball game. I feel he couldn't adapt to the everyday thing [of club management]. Internationally he's had time to look at a game and pick a team but [Chelsea] is instant. He had to have the players every day – some players have massive egos, it's the case all over the country. But Chelsea are a big side and he had to pick the team that could win a match. He was the man who was going to put the discipline into everything. I feel he appeared to be quite relaxed on the line, yet he shouted and screamed when he was doing his international bit. Of course the season can be saved. All the equipment is there but it's how you juggle with it and adjust it. Someone coming in has to be positive and get that winning back into the pattern again – Chelsea need that – they need to lift the supporters."

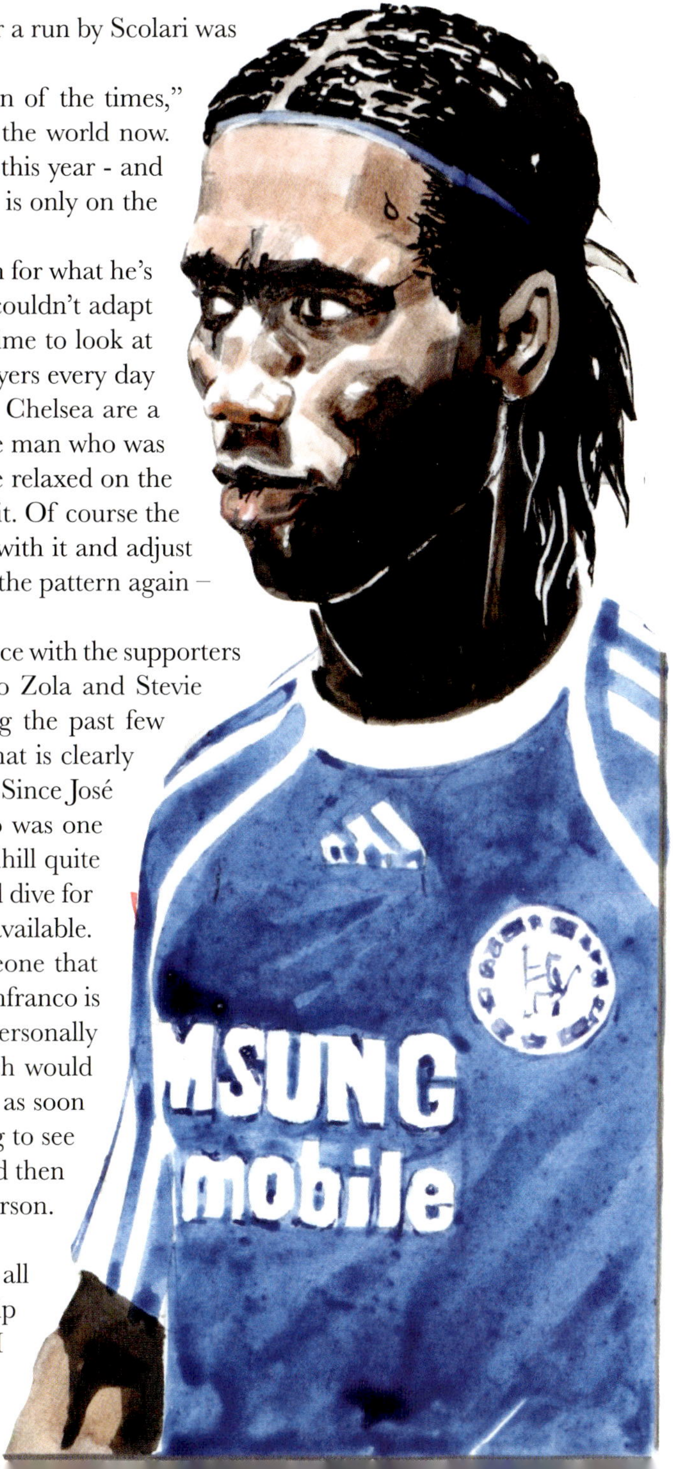

Club legend Ron 'Chopper' Harris added: "I think that if it was a choice with the supporters [for the new manager], I think that 90% would like to get Gianfranco Zola and Stevie Clarke." Pat Nevin commented: "His popularity has been plummeting the past few weeks. The question is, who is going to be able to do it with a squad that is clearly not strong enough.They've had a few changes over the past year or two. Since José Mourinho left it's not really been settled. This is a club that a year ago was one of the biggest in the world and quite clearly it seems to have gone downhill quite quickly. I hope for Chelsea's sake they don't have a knee-jerk reaction and dive for the first name that comes into their mind, the first big name that becomes available. They need to give it an awful lot of thought and maybe consider someone that isn't the biggest name in the world." Scott Minto said: "I don't think Gianfranco is quite ready for it. He has got a job so maybe at sometime in the future. I personally really like Guus Hiddink. You just wonder whether Roman Abramovich would want to take him from the Russia job. The club want to get someone in as soon as possible and there has been talk of Avram Grant. It will be interesting to see if Chelsea want to get someone from now until the end of the season and then review it or throw the cash, even if someone is in a job, to get the right person. For me, if that was the case, it would be Hiddink."

Carlo Cudicini reflected: "I had enjoyed 10 years at Chelsea, but it all came to an end when Big Phil Scolari became manager. My relationship with the Brazilian was clearly not the best. and was one of the reasons I left. It all started in pre-season when we had a few arguments over certain decisions and clearly those arguments didn't go down well with the new manager. They were technical decisions that occurred in the friendly matches, we simply disagreed on things, and I don't know the reason why the relationship was as it was, but that was the situation. After those disagreements in pre-season we didn't see eye to eye on certain things when he took decisions I didn't agree with, and he sent me to play a few games in the reserves. His decision to play me in the reserves wasn't the usual sporting decision, to keep me fit, but it was used as a punishment. But I was not the only player in the squad who had their difference with the manager! Not the only one unhappy with the situation. After six months I had the opportunity to move - and a few weeks later Scolari got the sack! Do I regret my move from Chelsea to Spurs. No, I don't, there are no regrets. The manager was not the only reason I left Chelsea. My move to Spurs was a great experience - where I met some very nice people."

Ray Wilkins took temporary control of the team and demanded the players "get the unity back" as he suggested the squad had to shoulder some responsibility for the sacking. "That's what football's all about, when you cross the white line - it's about players," said Wilkins, as he prepared to take caretaker charge for the FA Cup fifth-round tie at Watford with Guus Hiddink, the new temporary coach, watching from the stands. "All of our players realise that situation, it's about taking responsibility," he added. "It ultimately falls with the coach but those guys have to perform. The consensus is that they could have done more. They have to raise their level of performance."

Guus Hiddink, at that time boss of Russia's national team, had agreed to manage Chelsea for the rest of the season, and met with players and staff. He would work with Wilkins who conceded there was friction between Scolari and goalkeeping coach Christophe Lollichon, which indirectly affected the form of Petr Cech."It's a difficult one because it was two guys who worked together but had slightly different ideas, but I will say when you are the coach, you are the governor and that is in any walk of life, not only football."

Wilkins was asked whether he would employ a man-to-man or zonal defensive marking system at Watford after Scolari was criticised for switching between the two. Wilkins admitted it was "vitally important" not to chop and change. "We will mark in one system," he said.

Wilkins' dilemma was whether to play Drogba with Anelka. "I've just erected a boxing ring and Didier and myself are going to go hammer and tongs in a second," he said with a smile, "but I've said all along that top-quality players can play together. Intelligence and football intelligence are two totally different things. Top quality players might not speak the same language but they speak football language with their intelligence on the field. So yes, they can play together because they are both intelligent footballers." The Chelsea legend also bridled at the notion that Chelsea's short-term borrowing of Hiddink from the Russian Football Union, where he was contracted until 2010, was an embarrassing scenario."We have one of the best coaches in world football coming to work at Stamford Bridge, that's a joyous occasion not an embarrassment," he said and, while he remained unsure of his longer-term future under Hiddink, he was concerned primarily about the club. "Whether it's me in charge or whether it's Charley Farley in charge, I just want Chelsea to win."

Wilkins rested the "tired" José Bosingwa in favour of Michael Mancienne for the cup-tie and Drogba, looking far more interested, played on his own at the point of the attack with Anelka and Kalou just behind. A second-half hat-trick from Nicolas Anelka helped Chelsea progress, as expected against opponents from the bottom three of the Championship, though it took the Premier League side over an hour to make their class tell. Guus Hiddink will have observed that Anelka and Didier Drogba could play together after all and he formed a fair impression of what has been going wrong with Chelsea. It took an opening goal from the home side to force any urgency into Chelsea and while Frank Lampard was his usual industrious self Michael Ballack and Salomon Kalou once again had a game to forget. "I don't think you've seen the best of us yet," Wilkins said, "People keep saying we've had a difficult season, but we are now in the FA Cup quarter-finals and still in the hunt for the league and the Champions League. All we need is a bit more luck in front of goal."

Wilkin's air of studied indifference on the touchline changed as he punched the air in delight – so, one game, one win and a 100 per cent record for Ray Wilkins!

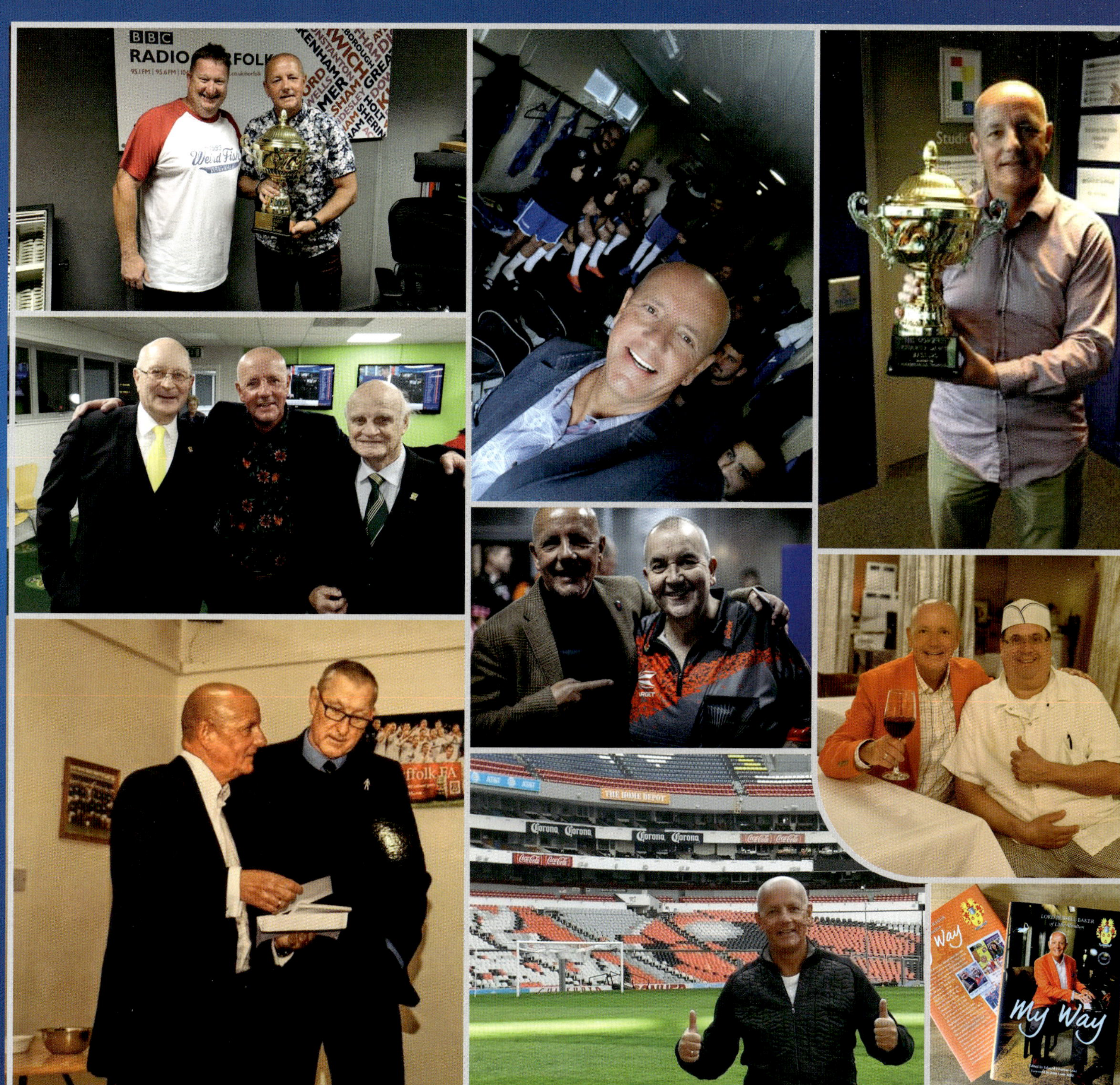

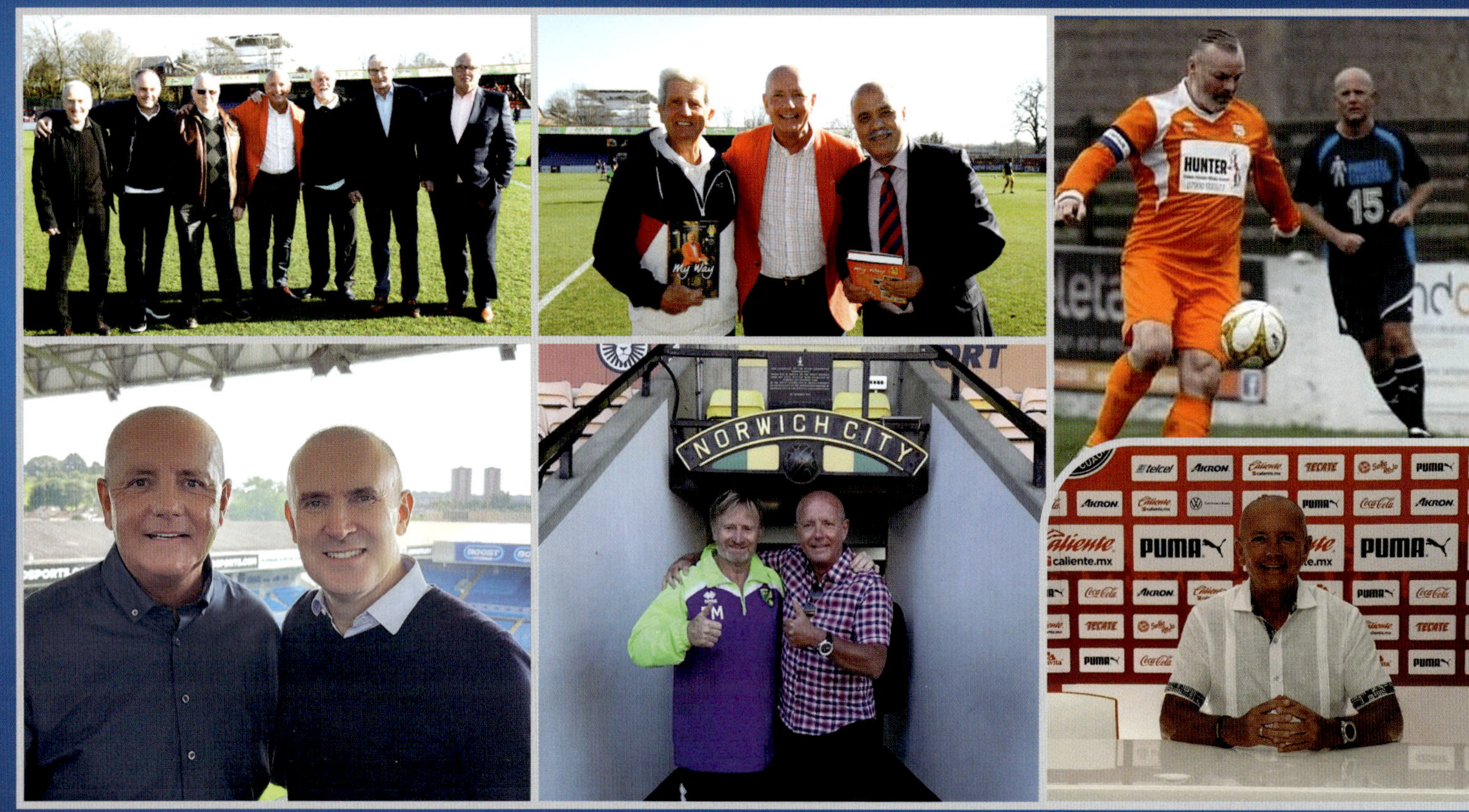

Lord Russell Baker

Lord Russell is an enormously respected figure amongst many of the leading professional sportsmen and women in such diverse sports as football, snooker and darts. Some of the famous names he has worked with include ex-Ipswich Town, Glasgow Rangers and England captain Terry Butcher, former world snooker champions Steve Davis and Ronnie O'Sullivan as well as three more former world champions in John Lowe, Eric Bristow and Keith Deller from the world of professional darts.

Yet Lord Russell does not settle at arranging events for others to take part in whilst he naturally slips into the role of host and MC for the evening. He is a very keen runner and cyclist and has taken part and completed many 10K runs and marathons for the sole purpose of raising even more funds for some of the great causes that enjoy his support.

He's now committed his life story to print! Lord Russell's first book, *My Way*, was first published in 2021. It is an honest and very frank retelling of his life so far, one which, over time, convinced him that he wanted to dedicate much of it to helping and supporting other people whilst, in the process, deriving a great deal of enjoyment from doing so.

Lord Russell's life has been, and remains, a colourful one, full of exploration and adventure. Yet, for all of the escapades that have highlighted his life so far, he remains most driven by the desire to help others enjoy it as much as he does.

He's a philanthropist first and adventurer second these days. But that doesn't mean he won't continue to have some fun combining those two passions as he tirelessly works to raise much needed money for charities throughout East Anglia.

You can find out more about him and his life and work on his website as well as discovering for yourself how you can get Lord Russell involved with your charitable organisation.

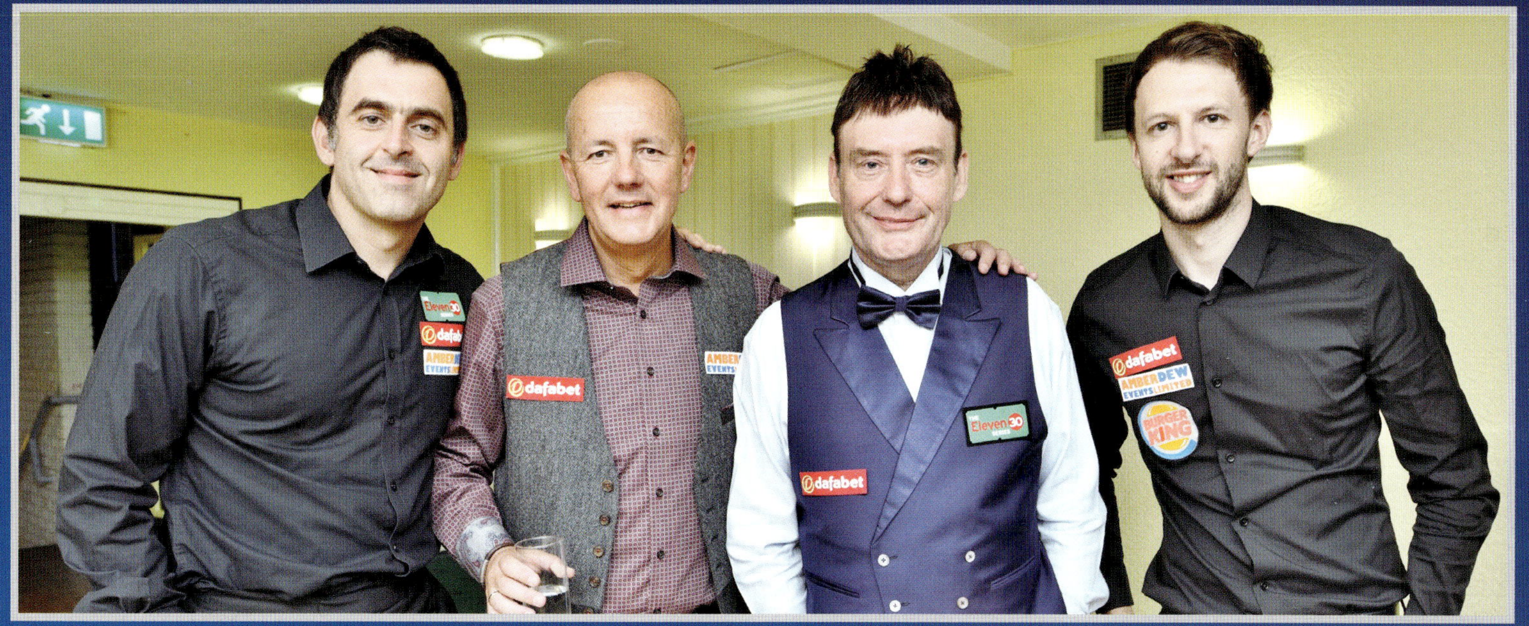

A picture with three snooker legends who need no introduction at the Cresset Theatre in Peterborough for the Eleven 30s Snooker, an event I organised and promoted in Sept 2016. I had the great honour of walking on at the end and presenting Ronnie with the trophy.

www.norfolklord.co.uk

PAGE 1 (from left to right):
Live show at BBC Radio Norfolk with the former Darts World No.1 Colin Lloyd in 2016; At Norwich City Football Club, with club icons David Sadler and Bill Punton; At The Amber Dew Events Stadium, home of Lowestoft Town,preparing for a live interview on stage with Terry Butcher: Working for BBC Radio Norfolk; Match Day Reporter for Rushall Olympics v Lowestoft Town in 2019; The World Legends Match Play Darts Championships at the EPIC TV Studio's with Phil 'The Power' Taylor in 2018; Pitchside at the iconic Estadio Azteca in Mexico City; Live show at BBC Radio Norfolk with the Norwich Charity Darts Trophy in 2015; At Patsy's Italian Restaurant, New York, in Frank Sinatra's private area, with chef Scognamillo who was Frank Sinatra's chef; *My Way*, the autobiography of Lord Russell Baker

OPPOSITE (from left to right): On the pitch at Aldershot Town Football Club, with the club legends; including ex-Chelsea FC, Jack Howarth in 2022; On the pitch at ATFC presenting signed copies of *My Way* to Shahid Azeem (Chairman) and Terry Owens (Former Chairman); Playing in a Legends Charity Football Match with Chelsea and Scotland icon Robert Fleck in 2018; With Chelsea Football Club legend Tony Dorigo at Elland Road in June 2024; At Carrow Road, with my friend Peter Mendham; In the media room at Club Deportivo Guadalajara Football Club (Chivas), of the Primera División (Liga MX), in Western Mexico in 2021.

Lord Russell Baker YouTube Channel

The Lord Russell Baker TV Channel and PodCast Talk Show. The show has guests twice a month from the world of Sport, TV, Film and Theatre. Unique and individual shows where we take you into the World of legends in life. Take a look around at the amazing shows already published, and rest assured we have many amazing guests already lined up for months to come. This is a true PodCast Talk Show and TV Channel with a difference, plus exclusive shows for all to enjoy.

https://www.youtube.com/@LordBaker

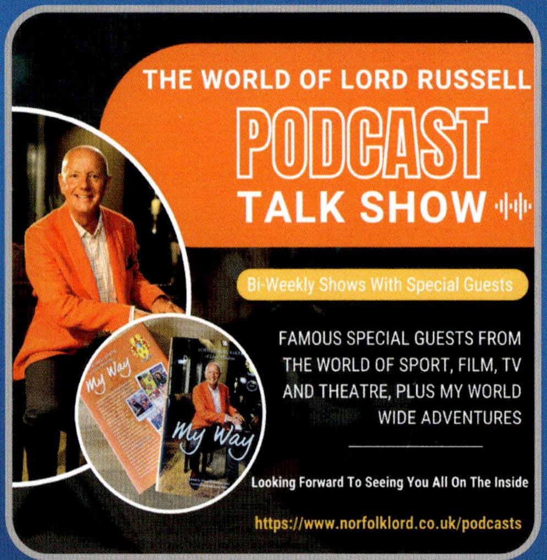

The World of Lord Russell Podcast Talk Show

The gripping adventures of Lord Russell as depicted in his autobiography *My Way*. Lord Russell's world, is a captivating world of an explorer, philanthropist, sportsman and author. The *World of Lord Russell PodCast Talk Show* focuses on Lord Russell's global adventures, explorer expeditions. Plus guests from the world of Sport, Film, TV, Theatre and Culture, by interviewing personalities, legends and icons across many diverse sports and cultures in the virtual studio; including, football, snooker, darts, cricket, rugby, boxing, Film, Theatre, the arts and many more....

A vibrant professional PodCast Show for all ages and produced in bi-weekly episodes. I'm looking forward to seeing you all on the inside.

https://theworldoflordrussell.buzzsprout.com

OPPOSITE (left to right)
Presenting Peter Wright, the forner two times World Darts Champion, with the Norwich Match Play Championships trophy; On Stage at the event with co-host Jade Slusarczyk.; And with Phil 'The Power' Taylor, Keith Deller, John Gwynne and Jade Slusarczyk; Presenting The World Legends Match Play Darts Championships Trophy to Darren Webster at the EPIC TV Studio's in 2018; At the World Legends Match Play Darts Championships at the EPIC TV Studio's with Wayne Mardle.

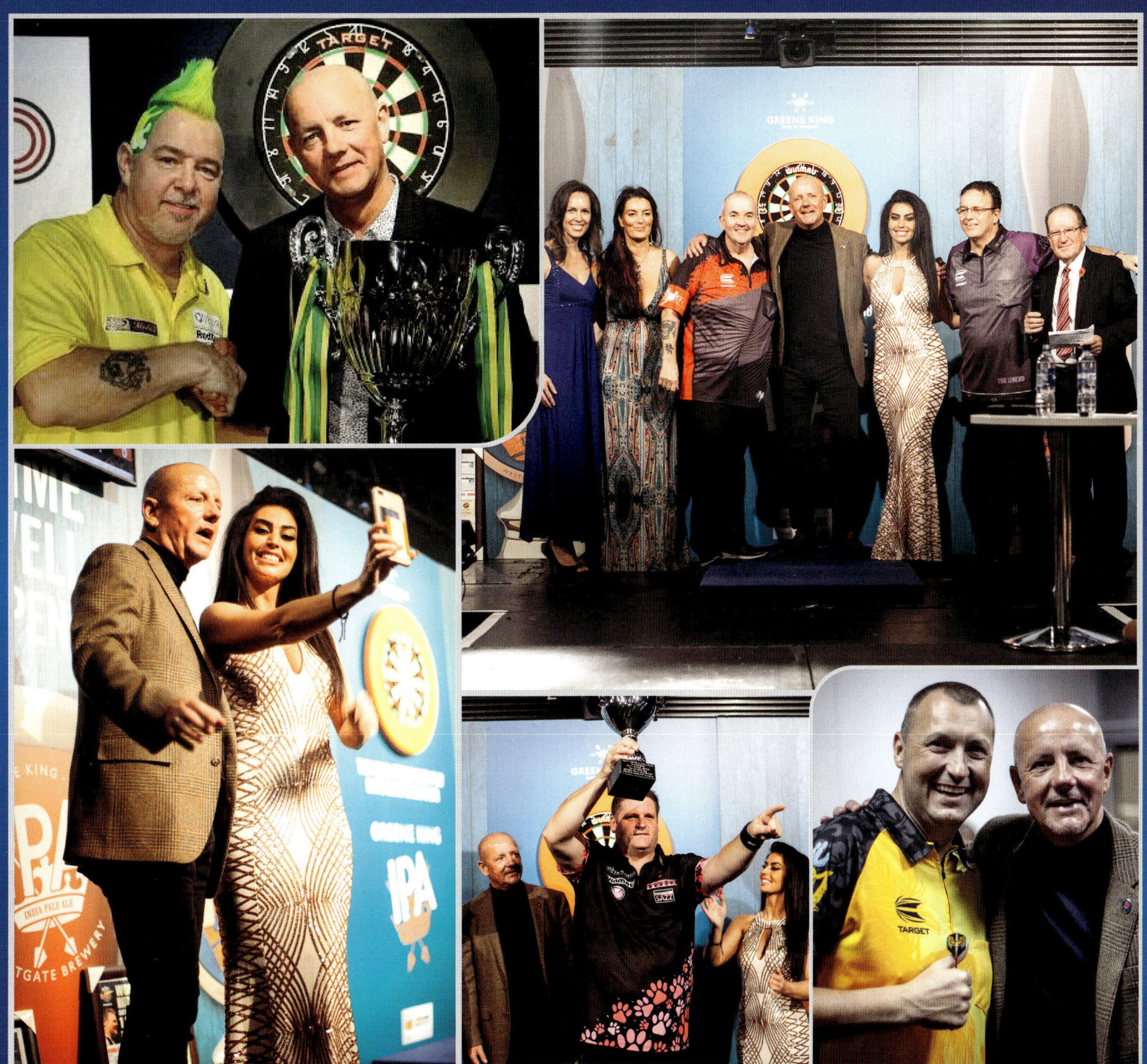
TARGET
GREENE KING
GREENE KING
IPA
INDIA PALE ALE
TARGET

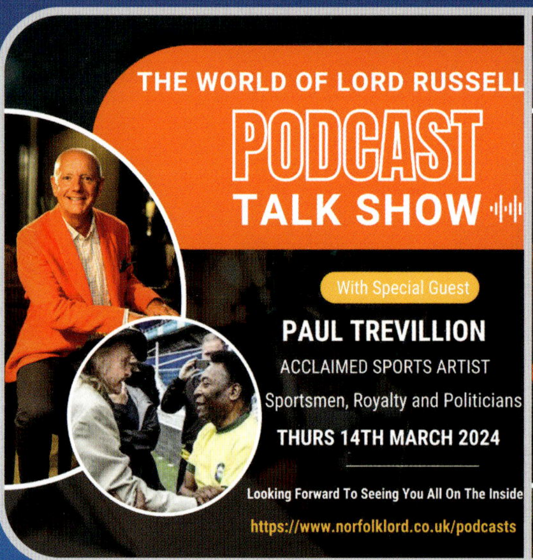

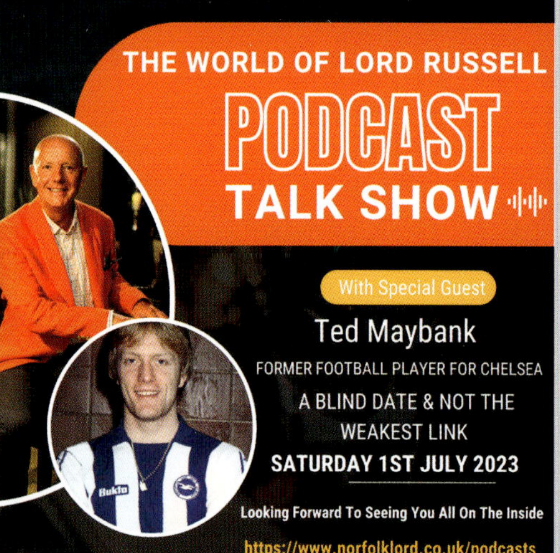

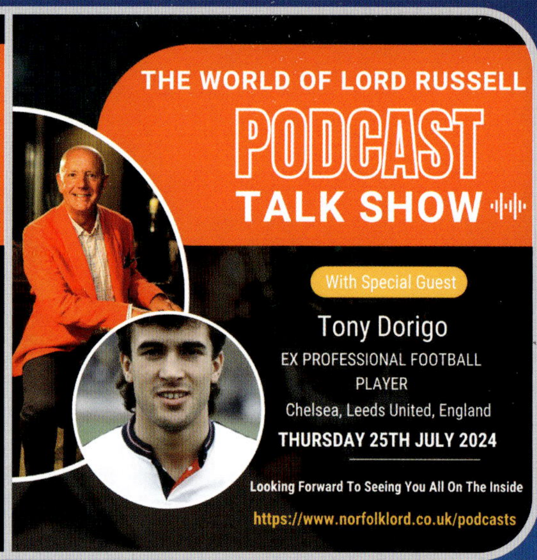

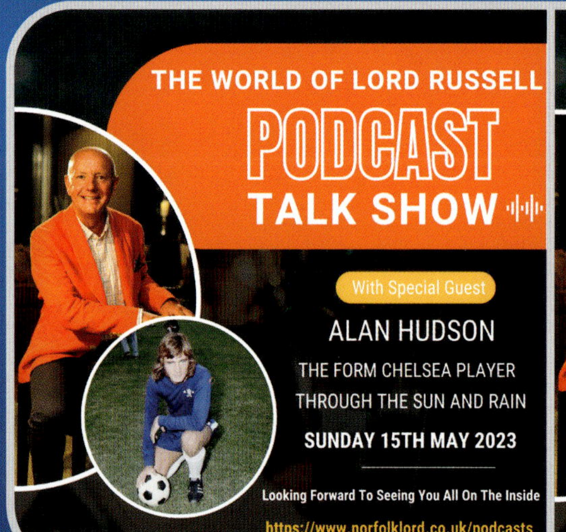

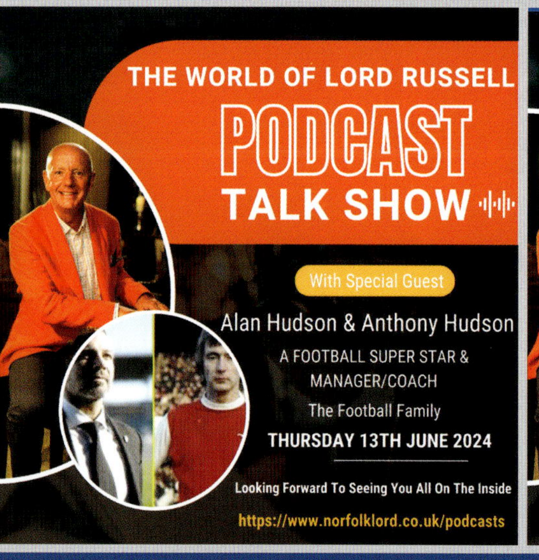

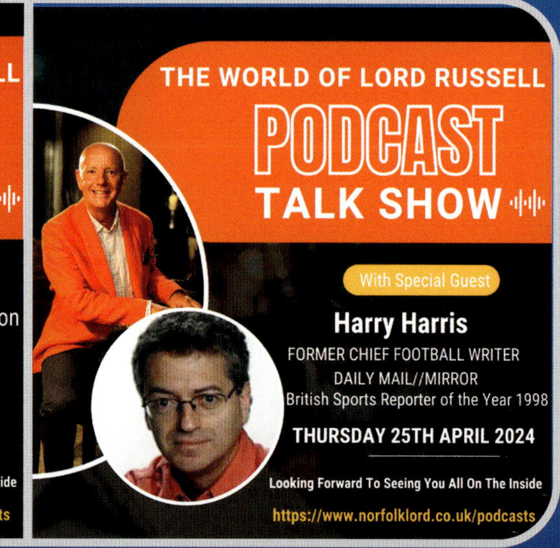

OPPOSITE
21) At the piano onboard Her Majesty's Yacht *Britannia*, the former royal yacht of the British monarch.
22) Presenting Peter Wright, the former two times World Darts Champion, the Norwich Match Play Darts Championships trophy at EPIC TV Studio's in Norwich in 2016.
23) With Bobby George, in the Gunn Club at Norwich City Football Club, for the Norwich Charity Darts Masters in 2016.
24) Front cover and editorial in the Fine City Magazine, August 2015.
25)
ABOVE
26) A few of my podcast interviews featuring Chelsea players and personalities

Guus Hiddink

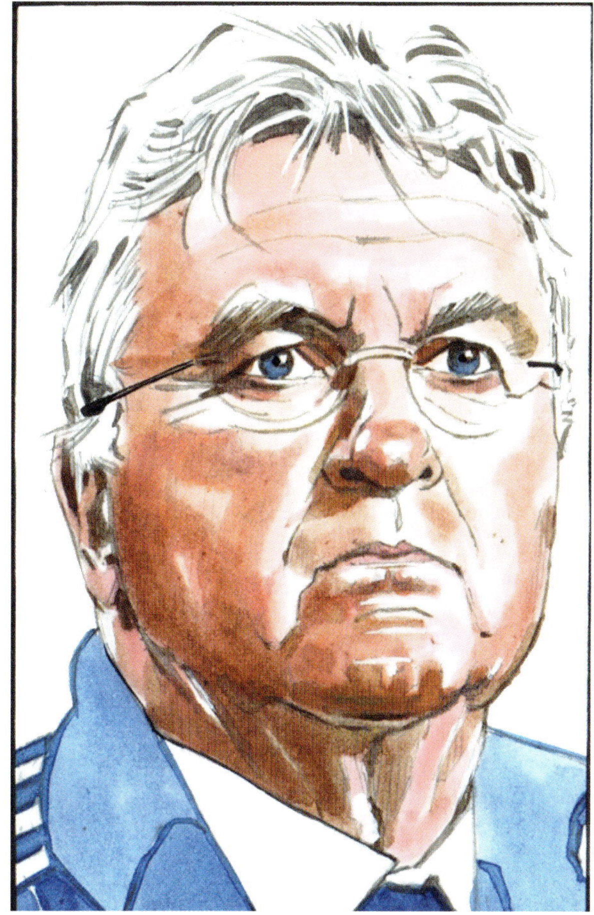

Roman Abramovich had gone from hiring an Italian in Claudio Ranieri, to a Portuguese in José Mourinho and an Israeli in Avram Grant. Now he decided it was time to go Dutch. The owner liked a cosmopolitan approach as he continued to ignore any domestic managerial options. The latest charismatic coach to take residence in the home dug-out was Guus Hiddink who still insisted Chelsea could win the league title as he took over as the club's interim manager, but he would need to draw on every element of his considerable coaching CV. Piet de Visser, Roman Abramovich's chief football adviser and the man who recommended Hiddink to the Russian FA and now Chelsea, said his Dutch compatriot is "not a coach who always demands the same system for his teams. He looks at the players, gets to know their best strengths and then decides the system."

Hiddink began coaching while captaining De Graafschap under de Visser: "Guus was my right-hand man on the field, and would talk to players, could always see the [match developing], was always talking about the passing game." That grounding came in the seventies via Holland's 'Total Football'. "I never thought 4-2-4 or 4-3-3, it was about having four defenders, three midfielders, three strikers. But you had to be compact," de Visser says. "When you have the ball, all attack together; without the ball, all defend. And Guus liked the same. Remember that Hiddink thinks more in terms of the team playing in harmony, of the players coming up and coming back together."

Hiddink won the 1988 European Cup with PSV Eindhoven in just his second season as a manager, the Dutch team famously failed to win any of their games from the quarter-finals onwards before beating Benfica in a penalty shoot-out in the final. Nevertheless the victory owed much to Hiddink's tactical nous as he deployed a 5-3-2 system in which Ronald Koeman played as a sweeper who was encouraged to step in front of the defence when PSV had possession. In attack Wim Keift was supported by Hans Gillhaus, who was also expected to defend. "If Guus has two fantastic strikers he will play with them, if he has three great strikers that will be the choice," de Visser said. The arrival of Romario in the summer of 1988 gave Hiddink a truly outstanding striker who helped PSV and Hiddink win three consecutive Dutch titles, the Brazilian operating in the middle of an attacking three. "He was short and strong, could pass and score, so he was played in front with two wingers and three midfielders," added DeVisser.

As national team manager Hiddink presided over a shocking 4-1 defeat to against Terry Venables' England but offered a lesson in man-management. Edgar Davids, the midfielder, was sent home from the tournament for declaring of Hiddink that, "the coach should not put his head in the ass of some players" and Guus was so popular that he was asked to return for the 1998 World Cup campaign. The result was a unified squad progressing to the semi-finals, only to be knocked out on penalties by tournament favourites Brazil. "Guus played Patrick Kluivert with Dennis Bergkamp a little bit behind but he could also play [right] up, so it was more a 4-4-1-1. But remember he is never thinking in lines but more in terms of the total team."

Perhaps Hiddink's greatest international achievement was transforming South Korea, co-hosts of the 2002 World Cup, by improving its record from five first round knock-outs in their previous appearances to a fourth place finish during which they defeated European giants Portugal, Spain and Italy. "He very quickly changes the attitude of a country, its team and players. When Guus went to Korea there was shyness - the younger players would not talk to the older ones," said de Visser. "Also, he had them in training for a year. I went to the camp in La Manga [Spain] once and watched. Every day he was working with them, making them fitter. He'd observed that the players were strong physically so he decided on a 3-4-3 in which the front three would always press the defenders and the midfield was [conventional] so one defended, one attacked, and there were two on the wings."

After the World Cup de Visser, who was still working as a scout for PSV, asked the club's President to bring back Guus, and he had a fantastic period of four years and three [league] titles. "This time Guus had Mateja Kezman as the main striker," he says of the Serb who moved to Chelsea in 2004."He was different to Romario but Guus allowed him to play in his style and was very good, scoring 121 goals in 140 games." Hiddink's second tenure also included a Champions League semi-final loss on away goals to Milan in 2005. Hiddink took over the Australian national team in July 2005 and combined coaching them with his duties at PSV, though he had only three competitive matches before qualification was secured for the 2006 World Cup, which was only the Socceroos second appearance. "Australia were physically very strong and good mentally, so Guus worked on their mental side. He did not use a psychologist but did this himself though he had a very good trainer." Hiddink's team included Lucas Neil, Harry Kewell, Mark Viduka and Brett Emerton and they only exited the 2006 World Cup thanks to a controversial penalty scored by Franceso Totti awarded at the end of the game.

Hiddink became Russia's first foreign head coach, his team beating England 2-1 in Moscow in October 2007 and then qualified for Euro 2008. "Russia had always played 3-5-2 but Guus changed it to a 4-3-3," de Visser said. "He had strong full-backs - Yuri Zhirkov would attack from the left and Aleksandr Anyukov did the same on the right. But Russia lost the first game at the Euros [4-1 to Spain] and he decided they were too offensive and put in an extra defender so it became a loose 4-1-3-2. Andrei Arshavin also missed the first two games [through suspension], but when he returned it was in a free role." Russia progressed to the semi-finals after Arsenal's recent signing had been the pivotal player in an extra-time demolition of Holland. It was 'Total Football' administered to the country which had invented it. "I've not experienced that very much in my career," Hiddink said immediately afterwards.

The Chelsea appointment caused a stir in Russia. "We shouldn't try to turn anyone into a God. That includes Hiddink," was the view of Gadji Gadzhiev, the former manager of FC Saturn as Hiddink would wrestle with the task of holding down two jobs 1,500 miles apart. His first league game, an awkward fixture against Aston Villa who were above Chelsea at the time, was won with an early goal and a grinding defensive performance thereafter. "It was a little bit like the old Chelsea," said Frank Lampard. "The commitment, the never-say-die attitude when Villa were throwing balls into our box. Our performances in the five months since have set a standard. It's been championship-winning form." The journey back from Birmingham was spent discussing the game "over a couple of beers". "That went down really well," said Terry. "He had a beer and walked up and down the bus speaking with the lads. When you step back, as a player, you appreciate little things like that."

Under Hiddink, the key players had all responded. "We needed to keep the ball better and move it quickly," said Lampard. "That was the main change under Hiddink." The Dutchman certainly got the top dog on board; Didier Drogba stating, "because of my knee problems and what happened with the manager, I really want to make it clear again that I'm staying here. I have worked really hard in training but the good thing is I have had the support of the players and people like Ray Wilkins."

His agent had claimed Drogba had retained his humility despite being one of the ten best paid players in the world on £200,000-a-week, which is some way ahead of team-mate Frank

Lampard's £140,000-a-week and Manchester City's Robinho £160,000-a-week. Drogba had endured a dreadful season before the arrival of Hiddink during which his attitude was questioned after he fell out with Scolari but proved to be a match-winner under a different boss.

Under Hiddink Chelsea fell short in the league despite winning 11 of 13 league games. Then there was the club's controversial exit from the European Cup on away goals to a last minute Andres Iniesta goal at Stamford Bridge following an inept refereeing performance by Norway's Tom Henning Øvrebø. However the Dutchman did succeed in leading the Blues to the FA Cup final at Wembley where they would face David Moyes' Everton after beating Coventry City in the quarter-finals and Arsenal in the semis. On the eve of the final the talk was about how Hiddink had made the place a happier camp, although it's a great truth in the industry that success brings about its own harmony. Results were generated by a happier camp. From his first week at Cobham, the temporary manager introduced strenuous work-outs and reinstalled confidence and belief. The sudden intensity lifted performances from the underachievers, most notably Drogba and Florent Malouda. "Ashley Cole and Frank Lampard have been the backbone of the side all year, the most consistent," said John Terry, "But for a few of us, myself included, our form had dipped. But he [Hiddink] raised levels again. If you make a mistake in training, or in a game, he will scream and shout at you. He gives you a kick up the backside and sometimes as a big player you need that. Certainly, since he came in we're fitter, sharper and looking a much more organised side."

Players noted with approval that his team talks rarely last more than 12 minutes."We love working with a manager who's enthusiastic, who creates that buzz about the place," added Terry. "You get it in training with him. The players ask for 'boxes' on a Monday – the routine where you go in the middle and work for the ball – but he comes back with: 'No, today we work.' Then, on a Friday, he and Ray [Wilkins] want to get involved so we do it because they want to do it. It's great to see, the enthusiasm he's still got to be involved. Ray's still got a nice left foot, actually. Guus makes a mistake on the outside and he sends you in as a punishment. No arguments, in you go.You accept it.That's the respect we have in the man. When he walks into a room everyone's on their seats. He doesn't talk long in team meetings. Mourinho was very much the same. We will always have that special connection with José, and I am sure we will have the same with Guus as well."

The League Managers' Association wrote to Hiddink to remind him that he will qualify for a pension in two years' time – "When I saw the amount I'd be receiving, I realised I had to keep working!" he joked.

"He knows how to talk to each player and get the best out of him," said Mikel John Obi at the time. "Sometimes he kicks you up the arse and wakes you up. And he brought something back that had been lacking – the fighting spirit, the need to do the dirty work."

Terry added: "He will still have a big input into Chelsea over the next few years. He has promised that to us and to Roman as well. He has seen things that need to be changed for next year and, whoever comes in, he will point them in the right direction whether it be around the training ground, the youth system, the reserves or the first team. He's worrying about the future of Chelsea. That's how much it means to him. We have all asked him to stay on but, from day one, he has said he owes it to Russia to go back. He is a man of his word and we fully respect that. He's full of fire and dignity and someone I am sure the players will forever respect. I admire his loyalty. He's a great man as well as a great manager, and now we have to make sure we give him the right send-off by winning the FA Cup."

Hiddink left the club in the way he wanted to, lifting the FA Cup with a 2-1 win over Everton ensured a problematic season ended with silverware, as it also marked the end of Hiddink's fleeting spell in charge. The Dutchman had become such a hugely popular figure that the most senior and influential players Petr Cech, Michael Ballack and John Terry led calls for him to stay.

Hiddink had already said goodbye to the home fans after Chelsea's final home game of the season against Blackburn, but insisted it was more "au revoir". Hiddink made it clear he would let his successor get on with it his way. But he would continue to monitor how the new season unfolded. Hiddink said: "I will visit every now and again as a visitor. I'm not the kind of person to put a cloud on the club or the team. I like to have contact every now and again, but just as a tourist. Unofficially. Whoever my successor is can and must work very independently. He will be a big manager, of course. You have to have a lot of confidence in what he's doing and, if he's backed up by the club, it won't be a problem. I never had a problem as a manager where previous managers have come back into the club and made a problem. It depends upon your confidence in a manager. It's not a threat. There's not intention there."

Hiddink felt that the side were capable of winning the Premier League. "It is within them to do that," he said. "It's up to the management, of course, and what they do next year. You have to renew every year on some positions, or to add players to give the squad more depth in quality. It is a well-organised club. Everyone has to perform here, but the club is well organised. I have, except with one or two losses, enjoyed it."

Naturally, he mentioned the controversial Champions League exit by Barcelona, marred by Didier Drogba's outburst at the final whistle. Hiddink described his mood in the days following as the angriest he has ever been."I didn't want anyone coming near me for two days," he said. He left the club with an enhanced reputation for playing creative football, "What I hear now, not just in England but also outside from Europe and outside Europe, that people have watched Chelsea and have appreciated the way they've promoted themselves. It's nice to know that, but on top of that it would be nice to have a bit of silverware."

Hiddink left the club in the way he wanted to, lifting the FA Cup with a 2-1 win over Everton ensured a problematic season ended with silverware, a rich reward at the end of Hiddink's fleeting spell in charge. The Dutchman had become such a hugely popular figure that the most senior and influential players such as Petr Cech, Michael Ballack and John Terry led calls for him to stay, but Hiddink had vowed to continue in his role as Russia manager. "I realised I was wasting my breath after the 20th time of asking," recalled Terry. The players showed their appreciation by presenting him with a £200,000 Rolex as a parting gift, illustrating the special bond Hiddink formed with his squad, and winning the FA Cup wasn't his only achievement as he steadied the ship after Scolari's chaotic tenure, and if it wasn't for Andres Iniesta's stoppage-time strike at Stamford Bridge he would have taken them to the Champions League final.

The Chelsea chairman at the time, Bruce Buck, confirmed the club had begun the process of finding a manager to replace Hiddink despite a number of players expressing their hope that the Dutchman will stay, most notably Terry, but Buck insisted the Dutchman returned to managing the Russian national team on a full-time basis. Chelsea were heavily linked with the Milan coach, Carlo Ancelotti, but one man who almost certainly will not take over was José Mourinho. "José was a great coach, he is a great guy but I think his time at Chelsea Football Club has passed," said chairman Bruce Buck. "It was mutual that he left the club [in September 2007]. The board and José were not seeing eye-to-eye on a number of things and it was time we parted company. We have great respect, obviously, for what he did for Chelsea Football Club, we are on great terms with him." Hiddink only lost one of his 22 games in charge, and his 73% win ratio was the best of any manager in Chelsea history.

A 'second coming' didn't just apply to José Mourinho as Guus Hiddink later succeeded him in an attempt to salvage a disastrous 2015-16 season following the dismissal of Mourinho with the club 16th in the table. Yet again Chelsea called the Dutchman as an emergency stop-gap before appointing a permanent boss. "I am excited to return," said the delighted Dutchman. "Chelsea is one of the biggest clubs in the world but is not where it should be at the moment. However, I am sure we can turn this season around."

Mourinho had been sacked with champions Chelsea 16th in the Premier League, one point above the relegation zone. Hiddink watched the visit of Sunderland from the stands, next to Abramovich and former striker Didier Drogba. Coaches Steve Holland and Eddie Newton were in charge of the team for the game against the Black Cats. "It's a fantastic appointment. I'm very happy about it. This club needs an experienced manager at the helm and Guus is clearly that," said Holland.

Since leaving the Bridge, Hiddink had endured unsuccessful spells as manager of Turkey, Russian side Anzhi Makhachkala and the Dutch national team. He stood down as Netherlands boss following a miserable Euro 2016 qualifying campaign when the

Dutch failed to reach the finals, finishing fourth in their group behind Czech Republic, Iceland and Turkey. Hiddink had succeeded Louis van Gaal after he had taken the Dutch to the semi-finals of the 2014 World Cup before signing a contract with Manchester United, but Hiddink's second spell as Netherlands manager was a disaster. While Hiddink's recent record might not have inspired confidence, the memories of his first stint at Chelsea were not forgotten. John Terry, John Obi Mikel and Branislav Ivanovic were the only Chelsea players who remained at the club from 2009, but Roman Abramovich hoped Hiddink could have the same kind of impact on and off the pitch.

He quickly steadied the ship as Chelsea cruised to the first win of Hiddink's second spell in interim charge with a 3-0 victory over Crystal Palace at Selhurst Park. He had made two changes from a goalless draw at Old Trafford, bringing back Fabregas and Costa with Nemanja Matic and Pedro dropping to the bench, but the latter was soon required as the Chelsea boss was forced into an early substitution.

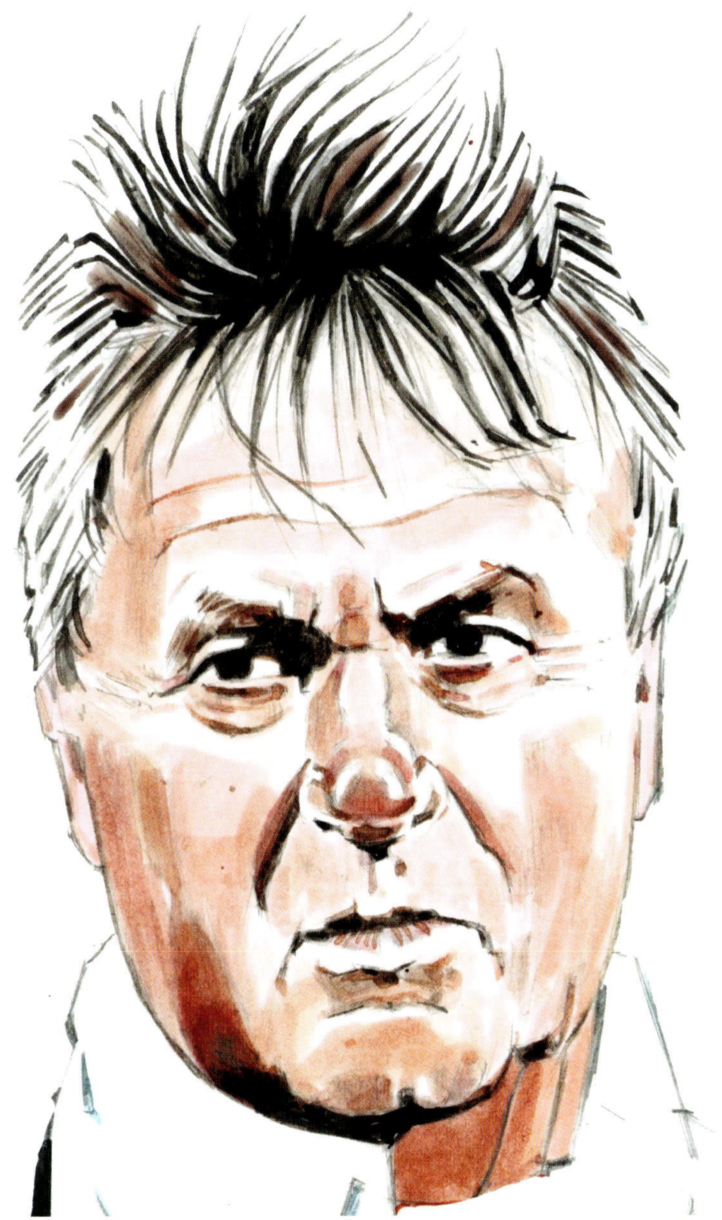

Chelsea remained unbeaten until a Champions League meeting with Paris St-Germain in February 2016. Prior to that they had won away at Arsenal and drawn home and away with Manchester United. John Mikel Obi's introduction to balance the midfield was the only change made and Diego Costa rediscovered his goal touch, as did Eden Hazard in the final games of the season. Paris St-Germain completed Chelsea's elimination from Europe and a defeat away at Everton in the FA Cup ensured there was to be no Wembley finale as there had been in 2009.

Chelsea finished in mid-table, but required a dramatic recovery to maintain their long unbeaten home record against Tottenham. John Terry observed at the time: "The way we were performing under José, we didn't do him credit, we didn't do ourselves credit, and I think this form was going to come. That's not taking away from Guus and what he's done, but it's very fair to look at it and differentiate the two because it's not fair on José because he was unbelievable what he's done at our football club, and Guus has come in and picked up the reins again and taken us in a really good direction." Hiddink indicated he would play a role behind the scenes in the future as he once again left the manager's role to a younger man, with thanks from Blues followers for coming to the clubs' aid for a second time.

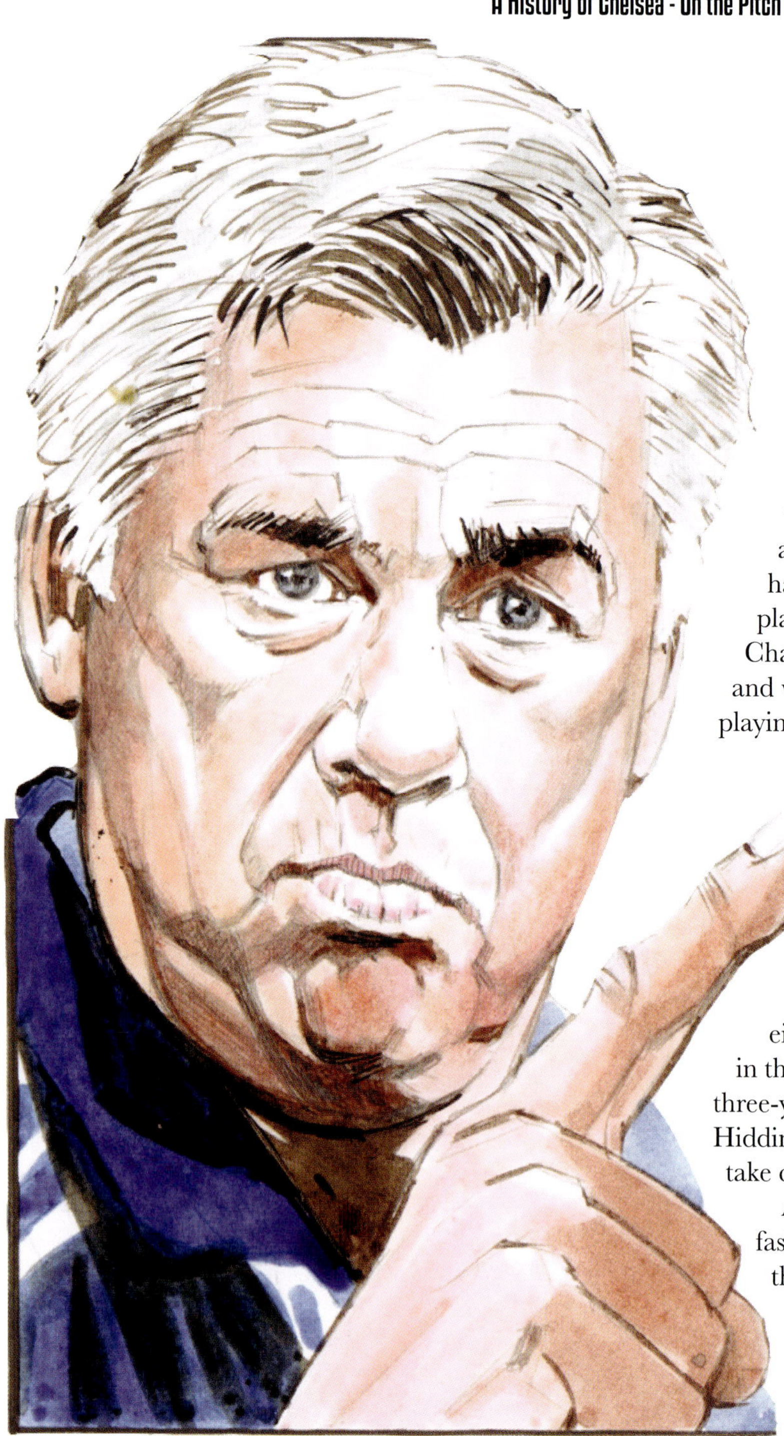

Carlo Ancelotti

The One That Got Away

Famous for that raised eyebrow, Carlo Ancelotti was one of the most decorated player and managers of his generation both before and indeed after he left Chelsea. Even before he arrived at the Bridge, he was one of the most celebrated personalities in European football having won 20 trophies during his career and was one of only three managers to win the European Cup three times, twice with AC Milan and once with Real Madrid. A versatile, creative midfielder, he had won three Serie A titles and the European Cup twice as a player with Milan. He was a key figure in Italy's 1988 European Championship campaign, where they reached the semi-finals, and was a member of the squad at the two World Cups either side, playing in Italy's 2-1 third-place play-off win over England in 1990.

Ancelotti's coaching career began as assistant to Arrigo Sacchi with Italy's 1994 World Cup finalists, before he moved into club management with Reggiana and Parma, later taking over at Juventus and then Milan. He spent seven-and-a-half years at San Siro, winning the Champions League twice and the Serie A title once before moving to Chelsea in the summer of 2009.

Ancelotti had been coveted by Abramovich after spending eight years in charge at AC Milan, due to his incredible pedigree in the Champions League both as player and manager. He signed a three-year contract in June 2009, taking over from interim boss Guus Hiddink, who had guided Chelsea to the FA Cup before returning to take charge of the Russia national team.

Ancelotti's first season in English football began in spectacular fashion, winning the Premier League and FA Cup double, sealing the title with a thumping 8-0 victory against Wigan on the final day making him the first Italian manager to win the Premier League, and he also secured Chelsea's first-ever double as the Blues beat Portsmouth in the FA Cup final.

His free-scoring side, spearheaded by Didier Drogba,

netted a then-record 103 goals as they broke Manchester United's stranglehold on the title, victory over Portsmouth in the FA Cup final shortly afterwards capped an imperious first season and secured the 60-year-old the 10th trophy of his career. But Carlo's second year proved significantly more challenging as he was twice thwarted by Manchester United domestically and in the Champions League, where Chelsea suffered a quarter-final exit to Sir Alex Ferguson's team. Ancelotti's progress was hindered when assistant manager Ray Wilkins left the club in November after they decided not to renew his contract.

Wilkins was devastated by his surprise dismissal with immediate effect. The then 54-year-old knew nothing about his sacking before being called to meet with Ron Gourlay, the chief executive, while watching Chelsea's reserves in a training-ground friendly against Bayern Munich at lunchtime. His contract had entered its final months and was up for renewal but Wilkins, who had stood alongside the manager while the second string took on the German team, did not see what was coming. Gourlay informed him that not only was his deal not going to be continued but that he would have to leave immediately.

Ray was Chelsea through and through, someone I had come to know very closely over the years, and we had discussed a possible documentary of his life. Wilkins was characteristically ruthless and clinically dismissed and it wasn't too much later that it emerged he wasn't well at the time. Chelsea stressed that there had been no major disagreements involving Wilkins and the other coaching staff or executives but the truth behind his departure was shrouded in mystery, innuendo, intrigue and Chinese whispers. Wilkins had seen areas of his responsibilities eroded. When he was hurriedly appointed by the club in the wake of the former assistant coach Steve Clarke's departure to West Ham United in September 2008, he was the man to help Luiz Felipe Scolari adapt to the demands of English football, particularly off the field. As a former Chelsea captain and coach – who had also worked under Gianluca Vialli – Wilkins was the perfect fit. Ray served under Scolari, Hiddink and Ancelotti, and sometimes addressed the media at press conferences to take the pressure off the manager, notably when things began to go wrong for Scolari.

Ancelotti brought with him his long-time confidant Bruno Demichelis when he arrived from Milan. Demichelis, a sports psychologist who speaks fluent English, had the title of assistant coach but his role was as the club's scientific co-ordinator. In his autobiography Ancelotti praised Wilkins' assistance during the double season saying, "without him, we couldn't have won a thing", and wanted to retain him.Wilkins was a well-liked member of the staff, a good coach in his own right, but there had been rumours of off the field issues.The media suggested Wilkins was sacked by Chelsea only two weeks after a bust-up with chief executive Ron Gourlay. Another reason given at the time was that the sacking was sanctioned by Abramovich after the club told Ancelotti that changes had to be made to the coaching structure. Clearly, it was not a decision made by the manager.

Chelsea announced Wilkins's departure on their website early in the afternoon, with Gourlay confirming that the decision not to renew his contract would "take effect immediately". "On behalf of everyone at the club," Gourlay said, "I would like to thank Ray for everything he has done for Chelsea Football Club.We all wish him well for the future."

The Blues had been top of the table but Wilkins shock departure coincided with a poor run of form which saw them lose 3-0 to Sunderland before a 1-0 reverse against Birmingham during a six-match winless league run. Defeats by Wolves and Liverpool followed at the start of the year before a late-season renaissance revived their title hopes. However, a 2-1 loss to Manchester United at Old Trafford on 8 May effectively sealed Sir Alex Ferguson's 12th Premier League title.

"Last year was really good, this year was not so good," Ancelotti confessed at the time and Chelsea duly sacked the Italian after he ended his second season at the club without a trophy. Carlo was ruthlessly dismissed following a 1-0 defeat at Everton, despite finishing second in the Premier League, albeit nine points behind United. Speculation had been mounting that Ancelotti would be sacked following Chelsea's first season without a trophy in three years, missing out in the Premier League as Manchester United clinched their 19th top-flight title and early exits in the Champions League, FA Cup and League Cup. Ancelotti reiterated his desire to remain at Chelsea, in what turned out to be his final press conference, when he insisted the decision was entirely down to the club's demanding hierarchy. "I am now on holiday - but I am not sure how long my holiday will be," he said in his post-match media conference shortly before he was sacked. "We haven't arranged any meeting but I think in the next week, now the season is finished, the club can address my job and they will take a decision. I have to wait and see what happens. I don't have to say anything to the club - they can judge me on my job for two years."

That evening, while still at Goodison Park, chief executive Ron Gourlay delivered the bad news just moments after Ancelotti had addressed the media. Carlo then faced the ignominy of flying home alongside his staff and now-former players. Before heading off on holiday, he said his goodbyes and took his closest aides out for a drink. The then 51-year-old had one more year left on his contract at Stamford Bridge. A club statement read: "This season's performances have fallen short of expectations and the club feels the time is right to make this change ahead of next season's preparations."

Avram Grant had suffered similar treatment when Chelsea finished second in the domestic table and lost the Champions League final in 2008 on penalties. Abramovich had bankrolled the audacious £50m purchase of Fernando Torres during the January transfer window but he failed to deliver a trophy. "Chelsea's long-term football objectives and ambitions remain unchanged and we will now be concentrating all our efforts on identifying a new manager," read the club statement.

Chelsea were seeking their seventh manager in the eight years since Abramovich took control of the club in 2003 with Porto's highly rated Andre Villas-Boas, Hiddink and former Barcelona manager Frank Rijkaard in the frame.

Hiddink, who had a close relationship with Abramovich, still had an advisory role at Stamford Bridge."Since I left two years ago I've been advising the club on things concerning the squad. Sometimes I become a sounding board. It costs me very little time and I can combine it well with my position with Turkey. There is no conflict at all."

Of his sacking by Abramovich, Ancelotti said, "I accept and I respect Chelsea's decision. I think I did a good job. Now, I think about my future. I would prefer to stay in England and in Premier League."

As for Wilkins, it later emerged that his departure might have been linked to his ever increasing drink problems. Wilkins opened up about his battle with alcoholism following what he has described as a 'very difficult period'. Wilkins, who later took up the role of assistant manager at Aston Villa, joked in an interview with talkSPORT that he would rather face former midfield rival Graeme Souness than have to deal with his drink problems."I've had some wonderful support, especially from family and friends, and it has been a very difficult period, I have to say. I'm not the only one out there, I'm sure, who's in a very similar situation. It's an awful disease that I have, and it's been a very tough period, I think more so for the family than myself. I'm the person who causes the problems, and they have to suffer the consequences to a large degree. I'm a very fortunate person to have had their support. I was fortunate, along with my family, that I was able to go into the Priory in Woking, and I was there for five weeks in a rehab centre in which I'd have to say the expertise of the therapists was quite fantastic.

"It's not easy to go into therapy; it's a very difficult place to be, but I was delighted I went in and I learnt a lot of things. I acquired a lot of tools that will hopefully help me in the years to come, and I feel so much better already. First and foremost to have got it out in the open, because there's nothing worse than having to conceal stuff, but now it's out there and I just hope we can move on and really enjoy some fabulous football and some fabulous times on talkSPORT."

Wilkins, capped 84 times by England and a former captain of his country, failed to attend a court hearing for a drink-driving charge because he was undergoing a rehabilitation programme. He eventually pleaded guilty to the offence and was banned from driving for four years after being three times over the limit behind the wheel in May 2012. Wilkins was on the road to recovery and has been clean for nearly three months. He added: "It caught up with me rapidly. It was almost unbelievable, that one minute I felt perfectly fine and then all of a sudden - bang! It was like a bit of an earthquake really. It was pretty horrendous how quickly this situation grew. I'd sooner be facing Graeme Souness any day of the week compared to what I'm going to face now. But I'm well up for the challenge of it. I've been clean now to close for three months, and I'm feeling so much better. The temptations will come, there's no two ways about it, but as they say in AA – just take one day at a time."

Ray entered the Priory Hospital in Woking for a five week rehabilitation programme. He also suffered a battle against depression and his dependency on Valium as a teenage captain of Chelsea. He endured for more than 20 years the symptoms associated with suffering from ulcerative colitis. He needed help to climb out of 'a deep, dark hole'. Wilkins spent a month away from his family confronting his problems at the Sporting Chance clinic for sportsmen who suffer with mental and addictive illnesses. "I went in there. I visited Alcoholics Anonymous. I visited Narcotics Anonymous. I needed to suss out what was going on with me."

Ray died in hospital at the age of 61 on 4th April 2018 after being treated at St. George's Hospital in London following a cardiac arrest. His family thanked "Ray's friends, colleagues and members of the public" for the many messages of goodwill. Chelsea said they were "devastated to learn of the passing of our former player, captain and assistant coach". The club added: "Rest in peace, Ray, you will be dreadfully missed."

Wilkins' family said: "It is with great sadness we announce that Raymond Colin Wilkins passed away this morning. Ray leaves behind his loving wife, Jackie, daughter Jade, son Ross, and his beautiful grandchildren, Oliver, Frankie, Ava, Freddie, Jake and Archie. We are asking for privacy at this very difficult time."

Wilkins, who had been working as a TV and radio pundit, had suffered poor health and had a double bypass heart surgery in July 2017. Before the Milan derby, former AC Milan team-mate Franco Baresi led a minute's applause in honour of Wilkins, and laid a bouquet of flowers and a 'Wilkins 8' Milan shirt in front of the famous Curva Sud stand.

The then England manager Gareth Southgate, who played alongside Wilkins at Crystal Palace, said of Ray, "When he played with us you could immediately see that his technical ability to play the ball was phenomenal. In the modern game, those attributes would have been appreciated far more than they were at that time, so he really was a top, top player. He would have been one of the earliest to go abroad and play in the Italian league. At the time, it was at a really high level so being able to transition into a club like AC Milan and be as popular as he was

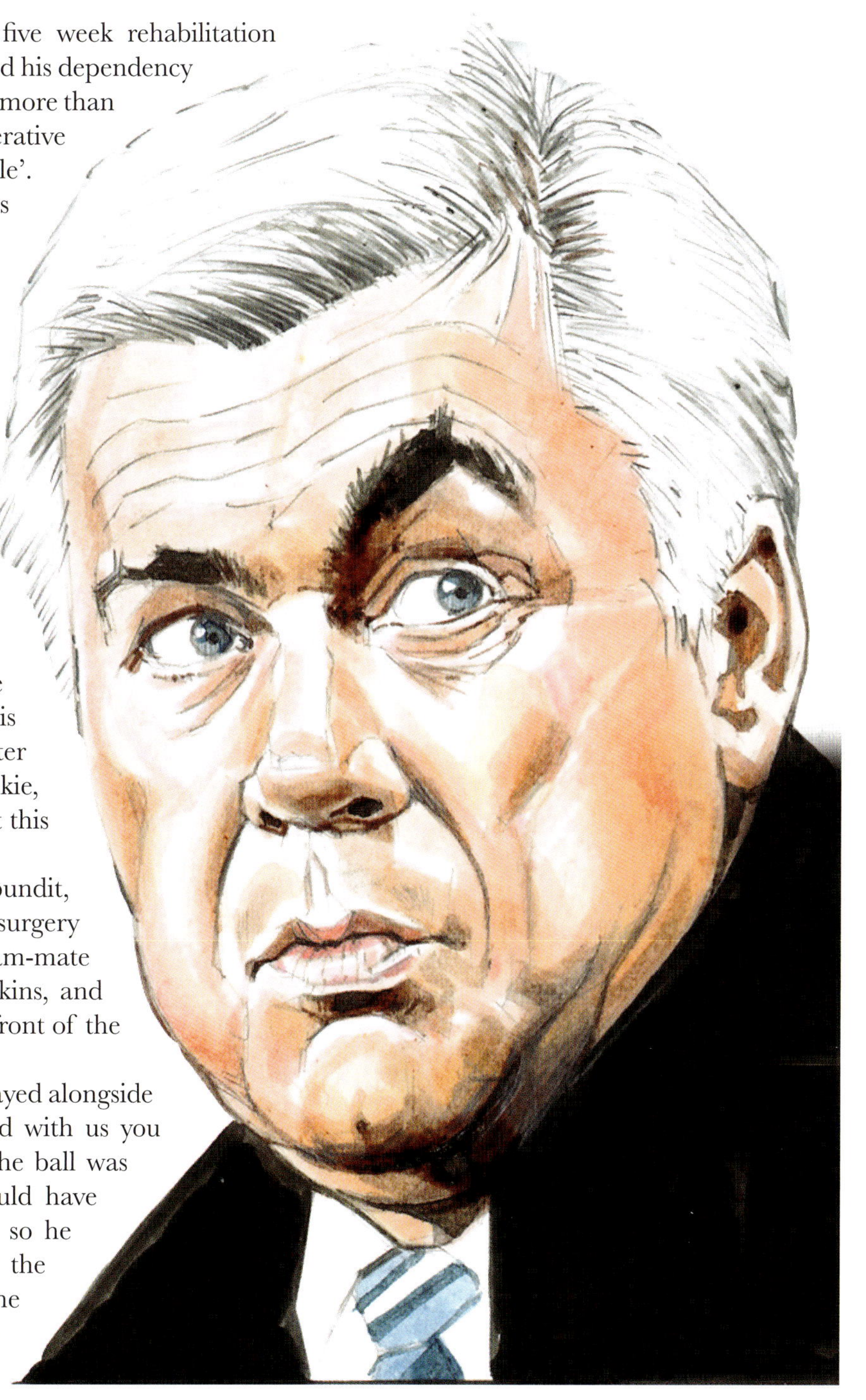

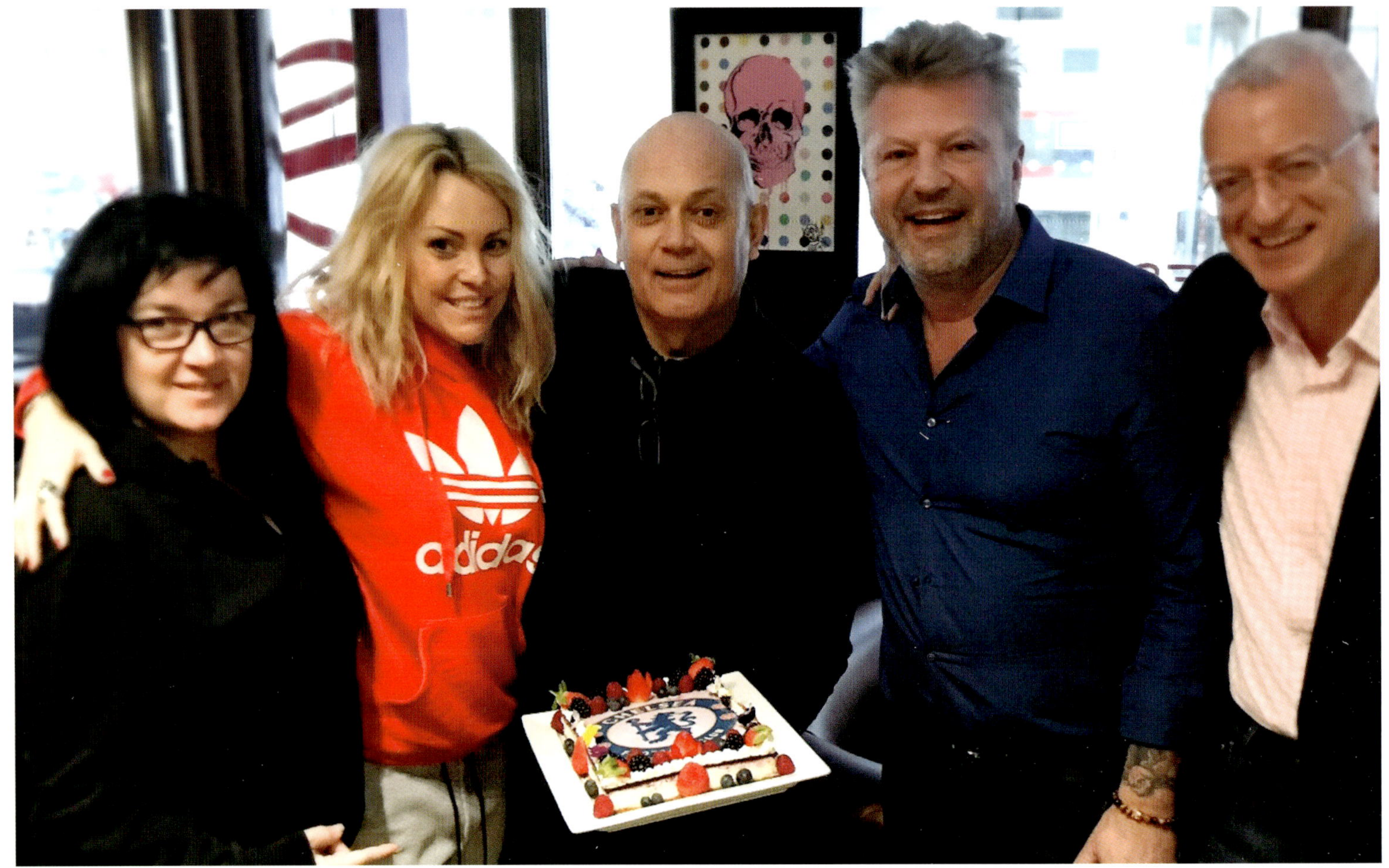

Ray Wilkins at the Sanctum hotel with owner Mark Fuller where we discussed the possibility of a documentary about his life, but after some thought he declined. Here we are all inspecting the chef's Chelsea cake for the film premiere at the hotels boutique cinema of Kerry Dixon's life story

there speaks volumes for his ability. It was really sad when I heard what happened at the weekend. It's happened so suddenly and it's tragic for Jackie and his family. Ray was a great ambassador for the game, a proud Englishman who loved playing for his country and an absolute gent - a class act."

As for Carlo Ancelotti… perhaps he was the one that got away; having failed to challenge for the Champions League at Chelsea, he ended up becoming a serial winner of club football's biggest prize, winning it five times as a manager (that's three more times than Chelsea have managed in their history) at three different clubs across four different spells. At the end of 2011 Carlo joined Paris Saint-Germain and won the Ligue 1 title in his first full season, but failed to make much impression in Europe. He moved on to take charge of Real Madrid in June 2013, lifting old big ears again, before heading off to Bayern Munich and claiming the Bundesliga crown. After a spell with Napoli, whom he guided to a runners-up spot in the league, he returned to the Premier League with Everton, where he failed to turn around something of a basket case before being lured back to the Bernabéu in 2021 and since has presided over two more successful Champions League campaigns… and counting.

Andre Villas-Boas

Sacked after 256 days

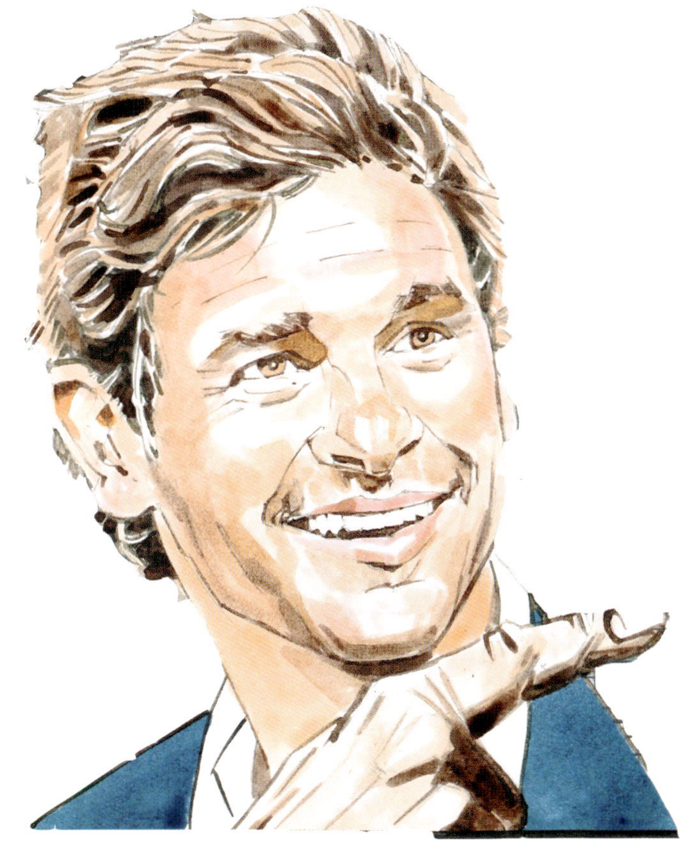

Chelsea opted for another Portuguese wonderkid as their next manager, appointing the former assistant to José Mourinho in June 2011. AVB was the youngest manager to ever win a European trophy, and was predictably hailed as the next José, yet it never quite worked out that way for a figure that came to be labelled 'Mourinho Lite'. The former Porto boss signed a three-year deal, and at the age of 33 was the same age as Frank Lampard and Didier Drogba! AVB arrived with a fabulous reputation having won the league with Porto undefeated and added their national Cup and the Europa League in his final season there. "Andre was the outstanding candidate for the job. He is one of the most talented young managers in football today," Chelsea said in a statement at the time his appointment was confirmed.

A scout for compatriot Mourinho at Porto, Chelsea and Inter Milan, he had begun his managerial career with Portuguese club Academica in October 2009. Academica were winless and bottom of the First Division at the time but finished in 11th place. They also reached a Portuguese Cup semi-final before he left to take over at Porto in June 2010. Villas-Boas, who was fluent in English, also worked with Sir Bobby Robson during the former England manager's spell in charge of Porto. The hugely upbeat Chelsea statement continued: "He has already achieved much in a relatively short space of time. His ambition, drive and determination matches that of Chelsea and we are confident Andre's leadership of the team will result in greater successes in major domestic and European competitions. Andre will bring his coaching experience back to a club he is already very familiar with, having previously worked here for three years. He has always been highly regarded at Chelsea and everyone here looks forward to welcoming him back and working with him."

Chelsea paid £13.3m compensation to release him from his Porto contract, with Villas-Boas succeeding Carlo Ancelotti. John Hollins believed Villas-Boas could prove to be a shrewd acquisition. Abramovich's dream, more an obsession at this point, was winning the Champions League, they had been beaten in the quarter-finals by Manchester United in 2011. "He could be fearless," Hollins told BBC Sport. "I think it could be a breath of fresh air, bringing in a fresh approach to this maybe tired football team. This guy is as young as some of the players are so he will be on the same wavelength with them, but is it going to be a three or four-year programme as opposed to having to win something in his first year? That is the one thing we don't know yet, but he has won three competitions in Portugal just like that, so he could be a whizz-kid. It's a gamble but I think it's a calculated gamble. I still don't know if Guus Hiddink will be coming as an adviser to the young man. If he does, that will only strengthen the position."

Pat Nevin agreed with Hollins assessment that Villas-Boas was a "calculated gamble". "There is always a risk with every managerial appointment but he is highly regarded as one of the up and coming young European coaches and has been successful in domestic and European competition. He is flavour of the month and Chelsea have seen something in him."

Under Villas-Boas Porto went unbeaten in the league, with 27 wins in 30 matches, becoming only the second Portuguese club to complete a league campaign without losing a game, after Benfica in 1972-73. Yet the high point of AVB's time at Stamford Bridge would prove to be Champions League group wins over over Bayer Leverkusen (2-0), Genk (5-0) and Valencia (3-0), yet he won only one of his last six Premier League games as Chelsea dropped out of the race for the title. He was sacked after just 256 days.

Despite winning the Portuguese domestic double and the Europa League at Porto in 2010-11, he failed to live up his billing as 'Mini Mourinho'. In 2002 he had become part of Mourinho's staff at Porto, in 2004 he followed Mourinho to Chelsea and in 2008 he moved with him to Inter Milan. After just over eight months in charge he was sacked, on March 4th, with assistant Roberto Di Matteo taking over until the end of the season, with so little time to do any tinkering with his squad, but time enough to inspire the club's first Champions League success, the trophy the owner craved the most.

Chelsea's decision to axe AVB came on the back of a 1-0 defeat by West Brom and a run of just three Premier League wins in their last 12 games. Chelsea faced two tough games in the FA Cup and Champions League over the next 10 days, a trip to Championship side Birmingham for an FA Cup fifth round replay before they attempted to overturn a 3-1 deficit against Italian side Napoli at Stamford Bridge to avoid exiting the Champions League at the last 16 stage.

Since Abramovich bought Chelsea in 2003, the club had captured three Premier League titles, three FA Cups and two League Cups but the Champions League was always the trophy the Russian coveted. After being recruited by Abramovich to implement a more attractive style, Villas-Boas suffered early defeats against Manchester United and Arsenal with questions raised about his tactical strategies. Villas-Boas endured a difficult working relationship with his senior players, several of whom were only slightly younger than him after Anelka, Alex and Lampard were left out at times.

Villas-Boas confessed that the Blues could no longer win the Premier League after they found themselves 11 points adrift on Boxing Day. After defeat at the Hawthorns he said: "It's not been good enough for some time. We're fifth and if that is the case, something's wrong. Every defeat piles more pressure on any Chelsea manager. We don't win enough and that does not make us proud."

Spurs chairman Daniel Levy saw something in AVB that they didn't see in West London, and appointed him the new head coach three weeks after Harry Redknapp was sacked. Villas-Boas was still only 34 at the time of his arrival at the Lane returning to football on a three-year contract just four months after being kicked out of the Bridge. He led Spurs to a fifth place finish and to the last 16 of the Europa League in his first season. But he came under increasing pressure as his side struggled to keep pace with the top four. Tottenham lost 6-0 to Manchester City on 24 November and, despite a draw against Manchester United and wins at Fulham and Sunderland, defeat by Liverpool proved the final straw for the Spurs hierarchy. Tottenham sacked AVB after the club's worst run at White Hart Lane in 16 years left them seventh in the table - eight points behind leaders Arsenal. In radio interviews after the loss to Liverpool, Villas-Boas looked like a broken man. He was duly sacked that night.

Some years later AVB confessed that he was out of his depth when he first moved to English football with the West London club. He had a series of bust-ups with players and accused Lampard - who was just eight months younger than him - of failing to support him as manager. He admitted: "The Chelsea experience was too much too soon. I wasn't flexible as a manager at that time. I was communicative, but I wasn't flexible in my approach. In professional football you have to live the day-to-day. The objective is the group performance, but every single individual requires a different response from a manager – you can't be the same person to each player. At Chelsea the group was more important, I stuck to my methods too much."

AVB repaired his reputation in Russia with Zenit St. Petersburg. He said: "My formative moments working with José were the best time of my life – I was able to learn many things and working with him takes you to another level. You fall in love with him and he becomes your idol. I wanted to be like him, know everything that he knew and absorb all the information he was giving. Then you fall on the wrong side of José and that's when things change and you realise that you've been blinded by someone. He has this fascinating capability of getting the best out of you, which has good or bad consequences for people. My consequences were that as a result of the argument or disagreement we had, I started my coaching career." He also had a dig at Spurs when he said:"Daniel Levy is an expert in sacking managers.There's no time for long term projects in the Premier League." He claimed the club failed to sign any of the players he had earmarked to help replace Gareth Bale after the Welshman joined Real for a world record £85.3m. "The chairman proposed a challenge to increase Tottenham's competitive level, but immediately Modric left and we didn't get any of the targets I had identified such as João Moutinho, Willian, Oscar or Leandro Damião. These were promises that were not kept. I had a group of players I had not chosen. In two years I lost van der Vaart, Modric, Bale, and all the promises made were unfulfilled.

"Tottenham set a points and victories record in my first season, missed out on the Champions League by one point and had a great run in the Europa League. In the second season, at the time I left, we had more points than in the previous campaign. I ended up leaving by mutual agreement – I wasn't sacked – because I gave full support to the football director Franco Baldini despite him having other ambitions, meaning that I ended up with players that did not fit the profile I wanted. But I don't look at my time at Tottenham as a negative experience. It was an experience I needed to have. I chose Zenit to get away from the media glare. I've had my fill of media sensationalism and false promises. I had talks with Liverpool. Returning to England is definitely not in my plans, although life takes many turns. Coaching in England was a positive experience but also many negative things happened. I was surprised and I still am by the Chelsea chairman changing his intentions.When I went there in 2011 the idea was to reformulate the team."

In truth, AVB's managerial career had already peaked by the time he joined Chelsea. Subsequent spells at Zenit, in China and at Marseille saw him last barely over a season each time. He quit football management when he was elected President of Porto in 2024.

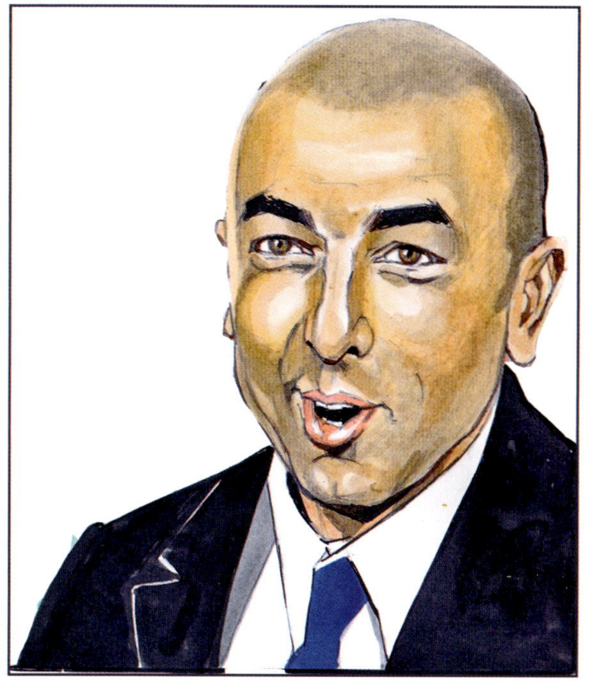

Roberto Di Matteo

Playing Legend Delivers the Holy Grail

Roberto Di Matteo was already a Chelsea icon for his exploits on the field, but no-one could believe his extraordinary feat in winning the Champions League after stepping in as a stop gap manager following the sacking of Andres Vilas-Boas, making him the first of Roman Abramovich's legion of managers to finally deliver the one trophy that the owner craved.

Roberto became a firm friend of mine when he played for Chelsea from 1996-2002 winning two FA Cups and famously scored inside 42 seconds in the 1997 final against Middlesbrough, the fastest goal in a final at the old Wembley. He was the "Italian Stallion" in Ruud Gullit's sexy midfield that finally brought a trophy to Stamford Bridge after a 26-year wait. He also won the League Cup, the Uefa Cup, the Uefa Super Cup and the Charity

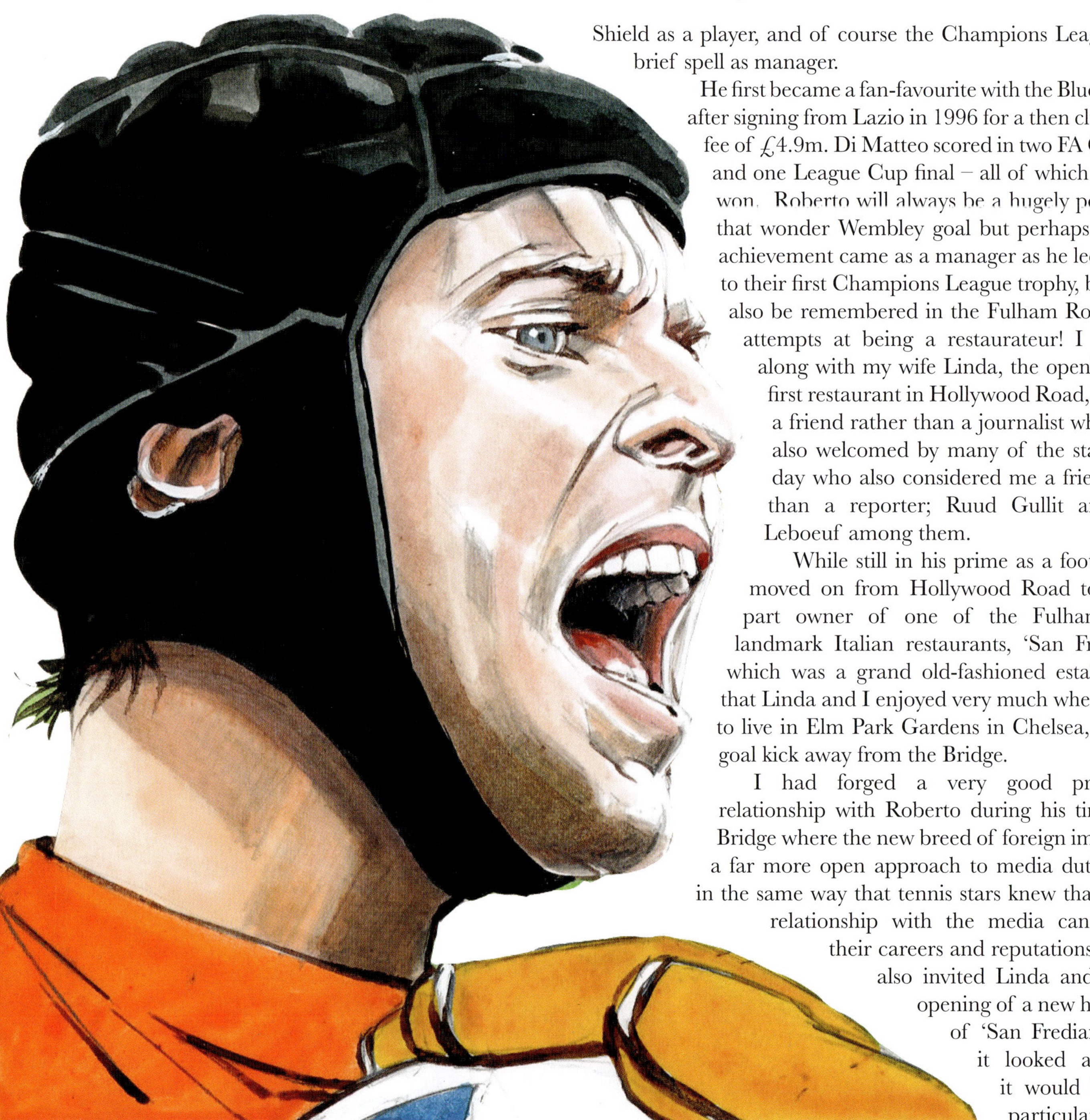

Shield as a player, and of course the Champions League in his brief spell as manager.

He first became a fan-favourite with the Blues' faithful after signing from Lazio in 1996 for a then club-record fee of £4.9m. Di Matteo scored in two FA Cup finals and one League Cup final – all of which the Blues won. Roberto will always be a hugely popular for that wonder Wembley goal but perhaps his finest achievement came as a manager as he led the club to their first Champions League trophy, but he will also be remembered in the Fulham Road for his attempts at being a restaurateur! I attended, along with my wife Linda, the opening of his first restaurant in Hollywood Road, invited as a friend rather than a journalist where I was also welcomed by many of the stars of the day who also considered me a friend rather than a reporter; Ruud Gullit and Frank Leboeuf among them.

While still in his prime as a footballer, he moved on from Hollywood Road to become part owner of one of the Fulham's Road landmark Italian restaurants, 'San Frediano's', which was a grand old-fashioned establishment that Linda and I enjoyed very much when we used to live in Elm Park Gardens in Chelsea, a clichéd goal kick away from the Bridge.

I had forged a very good professional relationship with Roberto during his time at the Bridge where the new breed of foreign imports had a far more open approach to media duties, much in the same way that tennis stars knew that a strong relationship with the media can enhance their careers and reputations. Roberto also invited Linda and I to the opening of a new hip version of 'San Frediano's', and it looked as though it would be a hit, particularly as it would inevitably be frequented by the Chelsea superstars of the day. But the dining options in that part of the city were so cosmopolitan and diverse and the competition so high that after only 18 months Roberto and his partners sold up. The far less expensive, less grand, pizzeria-style restaurant aptly named 'Friends', in Hollywood Road, just off the Fulham Road, and much nearer the Bridge was by far the better option, but nowhere near as profitable as if they could have made the up-market eatery work.

Roberto once came to me for advice on how to deal with the *News of the World*, who he told me was hounding him for a story about his private life. Roberto was convinced they planned to publish a story and had come to him for his comments and reaction. I advised him to say nothing and to suggest he consult his legal team. Often a tabloid Sunday paper would have half the facts and wouldn't be able to publish unless they could fully substantiate the claims, and one way of doing it was to coerce the target into a comment. Of course we now know the lengths to which the *News of the World* went to expose the lives of celebrities and public figures and later paid the price for their phone hacking when Rupert Murdoch was forced to sacrifice his beloved title in order to preserve the rest of his press empire. The *News of the World* even employed unscrupulous individuals on their sport desk who couldn't be trusted.

Sadly Roberto never recovered full fitness after breaking his leg badly and was forced into early retirement and returned to Rome. I can say he was badly missed by everyone, including Linda and myself. The injury happened early in the 2000-01 season when the Swiss-born Di Matteo sustained a triple leg fracture in a UEFA Cup tie against Swiss side St Gallen and did not play for the next eighteen months. He finally gave up any hope of returning from injury in February 2002 and retired at the age of 31. In his six years at Chelsea he made 175 appearances, scoring 26. He was a member of Italy's World Cup team in 1998 appearing in two of their group games, against Chile and Cameroon, the match against Cameroon in Montpellier was his last for Italy; he won 34 caps for Italy between 1994 and 1998, scoring twice.

His managerial career began at Milton Keynes Dons in 2008 where he guided the Dons to the League One play-offs in his first season, losing to Scunthorpe on penalties in the semi-finals. He moved on to West Brom securing promotion to the Premier League in his first season as the Baggies finished runners-up to Newcastle but his team were walloped 6-0 in their first match in the top flight, coincidentally at Chelsea, and he was sacked in February 2011 following a 3-0 defeat to Manchester City, the Baggies' 13th defeat in 18 games in all competitions - they had won just one in 10. Yet these failures did not prevent Roberto from a return to the Bridge as assistant to Andre Villas-Boas on 29 June 2011. What role he played in an uninspiring season is open to question but when the Portuguese manager was sacked on 4 March 2012, 'Robbie' became caretaker manager until the end of the season. Shortly after his appointment, Di Matteo brought in former Chelsea teammate Eddie Newton to work as his assistant. Di Matteo's reign began in winning form, with victories over Birmingham City, in a fifth round FA Cup match and Stoke City in a Premier League.

However his first big challenge was to overturn a 3-1 first-leg deficit against Napoli in the last 16 of the Champions League just 10 days after his appointment. In a bid to do so, he made four changes to the side beaten in Italy recalling John Terry, Ashley Cole, Frank Lampard and Michael Essien to the starting line-up. It was a move that worked wonders as Lampard and Terry both scored, along with Didier Drogba and Branislav Ivanovic, and Chelsea won a sensational game 4-1 in extra-time. "I selected a group of players with a lot of experience, who were comfortable playing with each other," explained Di Matteo at the time. "It was one of those nights that will be remembered as one of the greatest European nights at Chelsea."

While the odds were stacked against Chelsea that night,Terry later claimed that the arrival of Di Matteo had given the Blues the lift they needed at the right time."The manager changed and there was just something that happened," said the Chelsea captain."Robbie came in and he deserves an awful lot of credit for what he brought to us.There were four or five big moments from Napoli at home that led us to where we were [in Munich] and there are little things I look back on and think 'that was a great touch from him'."

Di Matteo continued to impress in the cups, even if Chelsea's league form was mediocre.The club progressed to the FA Cup final following big wins over Leicester City and Spurs while the

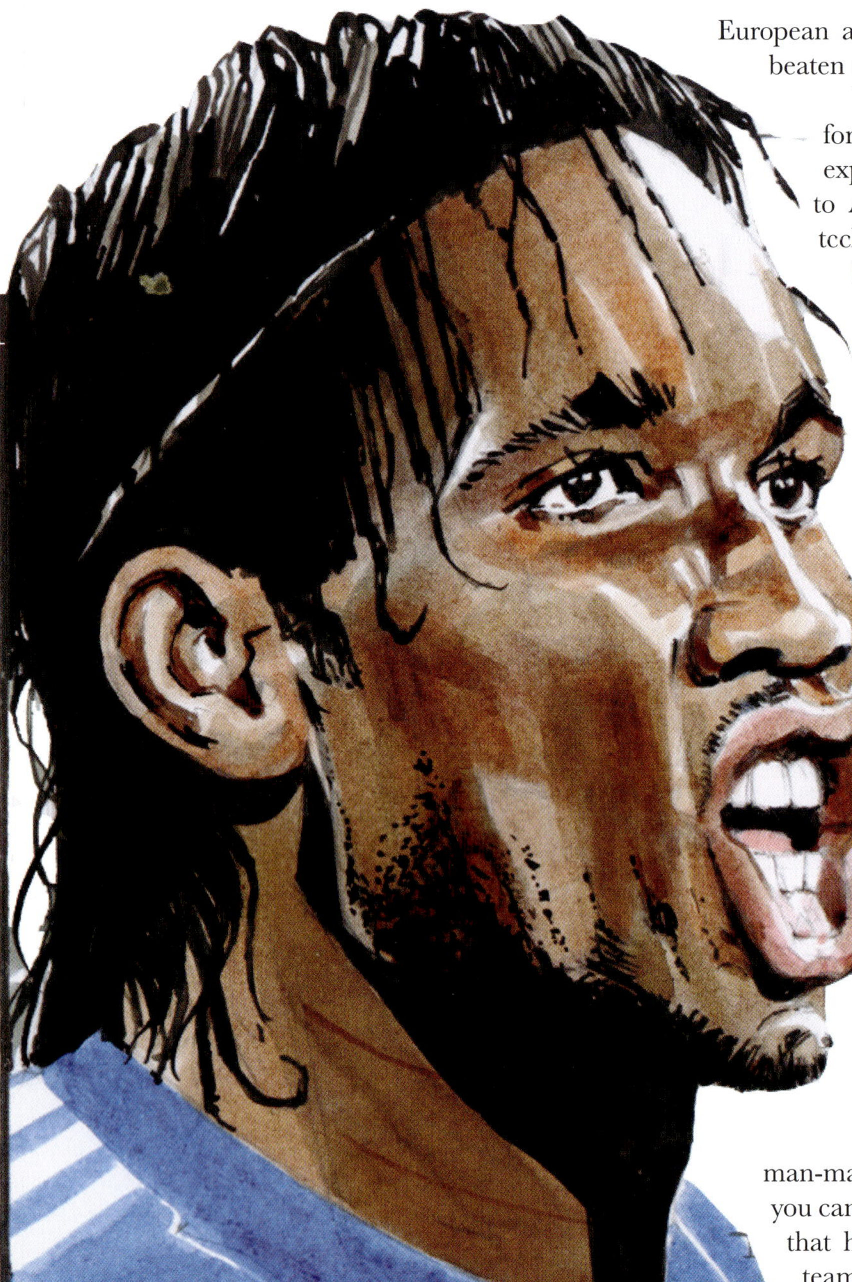

European adventure became all-consuming as first Benfica were beaten on away goals setting up a semi-final with Barcelona.

With his stock riding high, Di Matteo was interviewed for the full-time manager's job before that tie, as the club explored all their options for a permanent successor to Andre Villas-Boas. Di Matteo had already spoken to tcchnical dircctor Michacl Emcnalo about taking thc job beyond the end of the season. Barcelona manager Pep Guardiola and José Mourinho remained the top targets, but Emenalo was working to devise a Plan B for owner Roman Abramovich. Just two weeks earlier, Di Matteo had not been given any indication whether he would be considered as a long-term successor, but after being called in by Emenalo to discuss the club's future, the caretaker was told he would feature on the list of candidates. Di Matteo confirmed to Emenalo he would relish any chance of promotion and underlined his desire to stay in management rather than drop back down to become a No. 2 or first-team coach. Di Matteo was well aware Emenalo would give his recommendations to Abramovich, and that the owner's mind might already be made up, but he has impressed the hierarchy after guiding Chelsea to two cup finals while securing nine victories from his 12 games in charge.

"Roberto has to take a lot of the credit," said Lampard. "He has done brilliantly and the results speak for themselves.You can see the desire and love he has for the club, and the supporters relate to that. He has done the simple things right, and he has got individual players performing well and with real confidence.The basic skill of management involves man-management, and he has carried that out brilliantly, and you can see the whole side playing with a real confidence.When that happens, you have the chance of being a very strong team."

Along with Di Matteo, their Plan B list of candidates included Laurent Blanc, Didier Deschamps and Joachim Low along with Bert van Marwijk. Di Matteo continued his impressive start by beating Spurs in the FA Cup semi-final 5–1 at Wembley and Benfica in the Champions League quarter-finals to set up an epic semi-final with Barcelona, with memories of the controversial semi-final of 2009 on many fans' minds.

On 24 April 2012, Di Matteo led Chelsea to a 3–2 aggregate win over holders Barcelona in the Champions League semi-final, winning 1–0 in the first leg at Stamford Bridge, before a 2–2 draw in the second leg at the Camp Nou despite captain John Terry being sent off in the first half. They gained the upper hand against defending champions Barcelona thanks to that 1-0 win at the Bridge, but looked to be up against it again at the Nou Camp as talisman John Terry was sent off in the 37th minute and the Catalans scored twice to take a 2-1 aggregate lead. "Everything that you can imagine that can go wrong in one game went wrong," said Di Matteo. "All I was thinking was let's not concede one more, we still only need one to go through." Not only did Chelsea not concede again, but they pulled a goal back before the break thanks to a sublime chip from Ramires and then secured their place in the final with a late breakaway effort from Torres, after Lionel Messi had missed a 49th-minute penalty. "It's difficult to explain the emotions we went through in that game and what it meant for our players to be able to go to the final," explained Di Matteo.

On 5 May, Chelsea won 2–1 against Liverpool in the 2012 FA Cup Final at Wembley.Then came the Big One... but Chelsea had lost a Champions League final to Manchester United four years earlier, so, in a bid to try and relax the players before the game against Bayern Munich, Di Matteo arranged for their wives and children to talk and say how proud they were of their husbands and fathers.

"It was such a nice touch," said Terry, who was suspended for the final after his dismissal against Barcelona. "It was one thing that will never leave me from that year. Even the younger players in the dressing-room had their parents speaking and welcoming them and wishing them good luck."

"I needed something personal, to touch the players," explained Di Matteo. "Also, I wanted to take a bit of pressure away from them and it did exactly that."

The Champions League had become an obsession for Abramovich who poured more than £1billion into Chelsea since buying the club nine years earlier. He had come within touching distance in Moscow in 2008 and against Bayern Munich his team had to overcome the disadvantage of playing away in the German side's stadium with four players banned.

"Can we win it? Yes," Di Matteo said on the eve of the Final, handing a Champions League debut to 22-year-old Ryan Bertrand knowing this could be his final game in charge if it went pear-shaped. "My players have all the qualities you need to win this competition. I am very positive and very confident.You make your own destiny and fate. It is important the boys remember they are great football players and have been for many years."

Before the final Di Matteo confessed that he didn't "know what the future will hold," a statement that baffled Bayern's legendary boss Jupp Heynckes who couldn't believe Abramovich would contemplate sacking someone who had led the team so well to Munich. Heynckes said, "He's done a marvellous job. I can't see why whether he wins or not would have consequences. You need continuity. Atmosphere with the players and harmony between players and coach is very important. I don't think there's any argument against him continuing. From the outside, he seems a very cool person who is very much in control. Step by step, he's improved contact with the players and created harmony. He makes an excellent impression on me and, if I was Roman Abramovich, I would continue with this young man."

On 19 May 2012, Chelsea finally landed the European Cup by defeating Bayern Munich at their own Allianz Arena.This was Chelsea's first Champions League title, and qualified them for the Champions League in place of fourth placed Spurs.With this win Chelsea also became the first London club to win the Champions League and cemented Robbie's status as a club legend.

The final was tense and remained goalless for 83 minutes before Thomas Muller scored for the 'home' team but Didier Drogba's late leveller and a tense and goalless period of extra time led to the inevitable penalties.The early advantage in the shoot-out was with Bayern after Juan Mata missed but Cech denied Ivica Olic and Bastian Schweinsteiger hit the post, allowing Drogba to beat Manuel Neuer to secure victory for Chelsea."That group of players deserved that success because they had been so successful at Chelsea," said Di Matteo. "That was an immense moment of their career to finally win the Champions League."

As he climbed the stairs with his team to collect the coveted trophy he spotted the owner. They embraced. Di Matteo was heard shouting to Abramovich "I won it!" Di Matteo's reward was a two-year contract at the end of the season despite continued doubts over whether he'd get the job full-time with owner Roman Abramovich still keen to bring in ex-Barcelona coach Pep Guardiola. The appointment was a huge turnaround for Di Matteo who had been sacked from West Brom the previous season, saying , "We all achieved incredible success last season that made history for this great club. Our aim is to continue building on that and I'm already looking forward to the squad's return for pre-season."

Robbie had lost just three of his 21 matches in charge and his double success was a compelling reason to give him the job despite Abramovich's reluctance to do so. Di Matteo had to endure weeks of waiting before the contract was finally offered, making it pretty transparent that Abramovich actually wanted Pep Guardiola and was prepared to wait as long as possible in the hope of capturing him. Several senior players voiced their support of him, and Blues chief executive Ron Gourlay believed he was the man to lead the club forward.

The arrivals of Hazard, Oscar, and Moses boosted optimism, and indeed Di Matteo made a good start to the new season, as Chelsea lost just one of their opening 12 matches before a big downturn. Although Chelsea enjoyed an impressive opening to the campaign, Di Matteo faced constant questions about John Terry, who was banned for four matches and fined £220,000 by the FA for racially abusing QPR defender Anton Ferdinand the previous October. There was further controversy when the club accused referee Mark Clattenburg of using inappropriate language towards midfielder John Obi Mikel in their 3-2 home defeat by Manchester United in October.

Di Matteo would only see out a mere four months of his two-year contract as manager as he was sacked in November, in the wake of a 3-0 defeat at Juventus which left the Blues on the brink of a shock Champions League exit. Di Matteo didn't shy away from accepting full responsibility for the heavy defeat in Turin. "If anyone has to take blame, it's me. I selected a team I was convinced would win or at least draw."When asked whether he needed a vote of confidence from the club's owners he added: "No, I don't need that. The fact they put trust in me in the summer, that's enough for me" but he never had the chance to hope for salvation in the Champions League as he was shown the revolving managerial door at Stamford Bridge with Rafael Benitez lined up as an interim coach in the hope of luring Pep Guardiola in the summer.

Ideally Abramovich wanted Guardiola straight away, but the former Barcelona coach was unwilling to end his sabbatical, so the club owner had made contact with the former Liverpool manager. The writing was on the wall even before defeat by Juve. After an impressive start to the season, the Blues had won two of their previous eight games, they sat third in the Premier League table, four points behind leaders Manchester City, who they played next at Stamford Bridge.

The sacking of Di Matteo was typically ruthless, nevertheless Chelsea were in danger of becoming the first Champions League holders to exit at the group stage of the competition which was a source of deep embarrassment for the club and perhaps caused panic in the boardroom.

At 262 days in charge, Di Matteo lasted longer than Villas-Boas (256), Avram Grant (247) and Luiz Felipe Scolari (223). Ruud Gullit hit out at his former club for dismissing Di Matteo suggesting Mourinho was lined up for a return. "If you win something at Chelsea you get sacked. If you don't win you can stay for a long time. It's sad for Robbie. He hasn't even been there a year in charge. It's unbelievable, but it's part of being a coach. I already had a very good feeling when he won the Champions League maybe they had somebody else in the frame, but I don't think they took any notice of the fact that Robbie could win it. I always had the feeling Mourinho was in the frame because he signed his contract with Real Madrid just after Chelsea won the Champions League. His record says everything - a lot of people would love to see him in England." Ruud also criticised the club's board for attempting to emulate Barcelona, insisting the Catalan giants are unique in football."We thought the main thing for Chelsea was to win the Champions League, but they still sacked the manager.The board wants to play the same sort of football as Barcelona, but Barcelona is Barcelona. They want to copy something that you can't - and Barcelona have Messi. Don't put away your own identity, because sometimes you can't copy

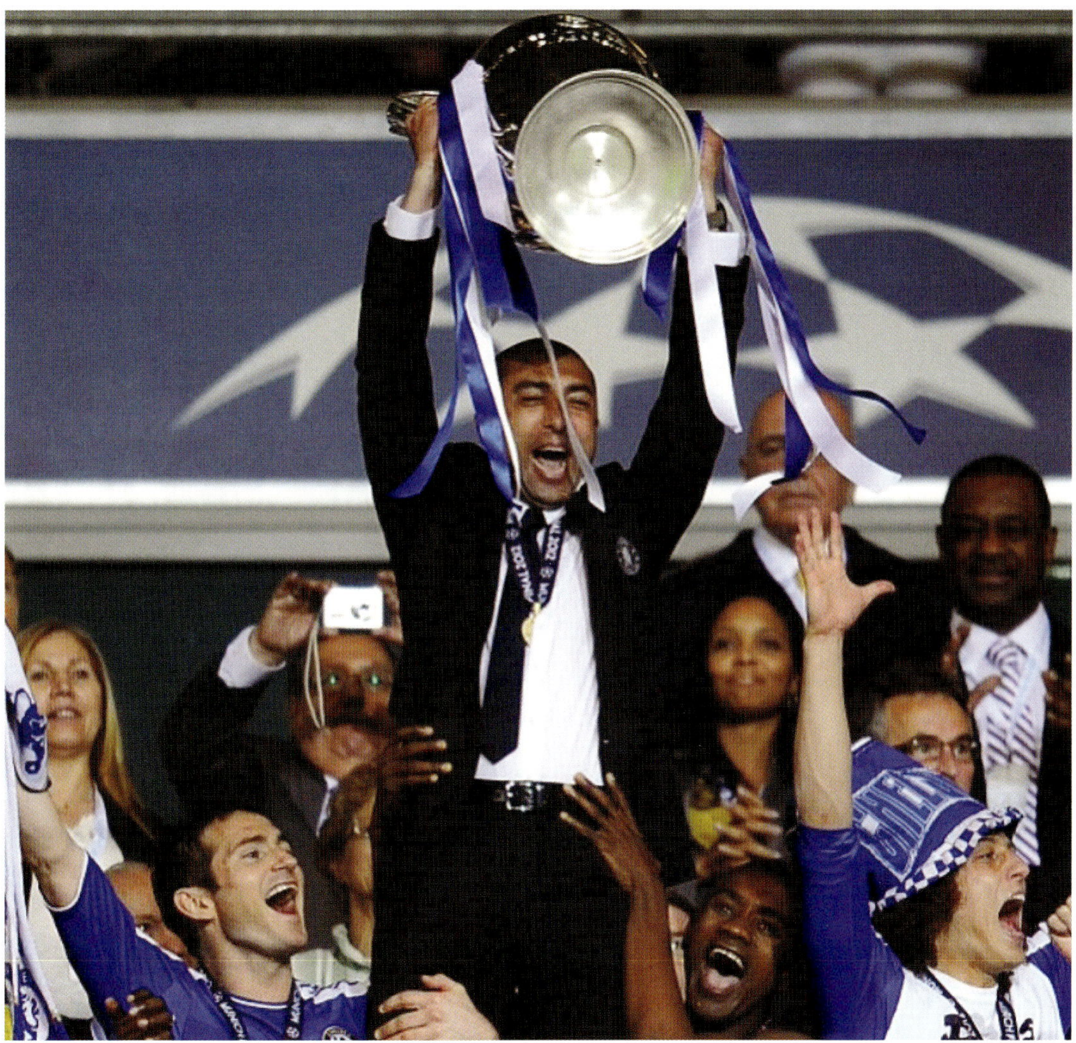

something." Gullit dismissed any potential return for himself, saying: "I'm busy with my own things. I wouldn't feel comfortable to come after Robbie because he's a very good friend of mine."

Almost a year later Di Matteo was appointed manager of struggling Schalke 04 as successor to Jens Keller. At that point, Schalke were 11th. He won his first match 2–0 against Hertha Berlin on 18 October, with goals from Klass-Jan Huntelaar and Julian Drazler. Schalke advanced from their Champions League group, with Max Meyer scoring the only goal in their final group match away to NK Maribor. On 10 March 2015, Schalke defeated Real Madrid 4–3 in Madrid. However, Schalke had lost 2–0 in the first leg and 5–4 on aggregate. He resigned on 26 May 2015 after the team qualified for the Europa League finishing sixth, following a run of just two wins in ten matches which cost them a place in the Champions League.

On 2 June 2016, Di Matteo was appointed manager of newly relegated Aston Villa working with new chairman Tony Xia. Di Matteo's former Chelsea teammate Steve Clarke was appointed as his assistant on the same day but again he only lasted until 3 October when he was sacked after a string of poor results culminating in a 2–0 defeat at Preston after just 124 days in the job - he won just one of 11 Championship games in charge. He has not been appointed as a manager since.

Nevertheless Roberto Di Matteo's Chelsea record as manager of two trophies in just eight months remains remarkable but perhaps his personality was such that he was seen as a calming influence after the rudderless Villas-Boas era, yet when it came to instilling his own coaching ideas on an experienced squad, he was found wanting. However he had written is name into the history books as both player and manager. After one billion pounds and eight managers, a penalty shoot out defeat in Moscow against Manchester United, Abramovich got his hands on the trophy he craved, the one piece of silverware all the gold of the Russian oligarch's £16 billion wealth could not buy, no matter how much he spent on players.

As Didier Drogba was handed the European Cup for the first time at the presentation ceremony, and after all the players had frantically got their own hands on the precious silverware, he handed it straight to the guy at the end wearing a suit and looking as though he had gatecrashed the party. No, this was no ordinary fan on the periphery. This was the guy whose billions helped create the Champions League winners. On the podium, man of the moment Drogba handed the European Cup to Abramovich and the picture was wired across the world.

In the dressing-room the Ivorian striker and the final's match winner talked to the trophy, it was almost like a "religious experience", he said and Abramovich gave a little thank you speech. "The message was it was all down to the boys. They did it. We've had a tough season, a bunch of highs and lows, but they grasped it and deserved all the credit."

Drogba ran Zola close as the all-time most popular player in West London folklore. Zola charmed off the field and dazzled on it, but the snarling No.9, a power house goalscoring brute of a centre-forward, was sometimes unplayable in his prime. In his twilight years, recovering from the lingering effects of malaria to regain his form and fitness, he summoned up all of his old strength to take the Champions League Final by storm. Abramovich's popularity has never been in doubt either, his rating among the rank and file supporters soared as he delivered, as he had always promised to do, the biggest prize in club football.

At 11.29 pm local time in Munich, Drogba delivered the trophy with the coolest-looking final penalty to bring home the Champions League trophy to the obvious delight of the 20,000 Chelsea fans in the North end of Bayern Munich's home ground. Drogba banished the bleakest moment of his career, when he was sent off in extra time when Manchester United won the Champions League trophy in a shoot-out when he should have been taking the penalty which ultimately became the responsibility of captain John Terry. Terry's slip on the sodden surface in Moscow resulted in his penalty hitting the outside of the post - little wonder Drogba thought it was destiny that brought him to the fifth and final penalty where he should have been four years earlier. It had got to be destiny, fate, surely. Yes, it was... a night when an English team beat a German team on penalties.

Non-playing captain John Terry, banned from the Final, gave a pitch interview saying that the club owed such a debt of gratitude to Abramovich, who had fidgeted and stressed his way through the entire 120 minutes plus the penalty shoot out as if he was kicking every ball, as he does whenever he watches the team. Prior to the Russian takeover, Ken Bates had been popular with the fans but was rapidly running out of funds to take the club to the next level. He parted with Chelsea for a knock down £59 million and Abramovich's motives were under immediate suspicion. He was regularly criticised for taking a Premier League club as a 'play thing' which he might soon tire of and dispense with. As it has proved, the opposite had been the case - he stuck with the club through the frustrating pursuit of his personal obsession, to land the Champions League. It was the same competition that had got him interested in football having watched a Champions League game at Old Trafford – from that day on he aimed at owning a club that one day would win the coveted trophy.

According to research at that time, Chelsea had the second largest fan base to Manchester United, 160 million world wide, and although they had won European trophies in the past, they had never won the biggest prize, in fact, they became the first London club to land the European Cup. Their only other historic part in the history of that elite European trophy was the fact that Chelsea declined entry to the inaugural European Cup back in 1955 after pressure from the Football League.

Rafa Benitez

The Most Unpopular Managerial Appointment in Chelsea History

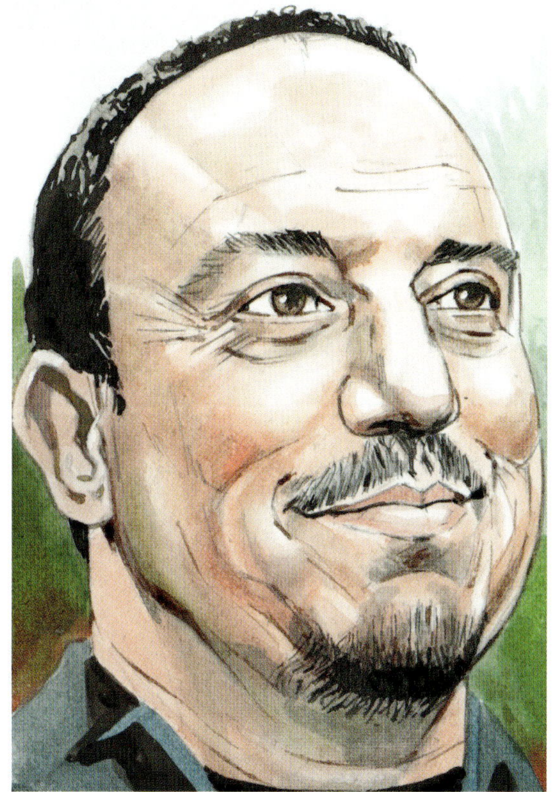

The appointment of Rafael Benitez as 'interim manager' in November 2012 has to go down as one of the most unpopular in Chelsea history, indeed one of the most unpopular in English football history. The fans were still upset about comments Benitez had made about Chelsea in his time at Anfield during which the two clubs played several epic Champions League ties creating an at times bitter rivalry. His barbed comments at press conferences were often more spectacular than the action on the pitch which was characterised by a paucity of goals.

It all started in 2005 with Luis Garcia's 'ghost goal' in front of the Kop which sent Liverpool through to that historic final in Istanbul. The teams met again in the following season's competition and played out two goalless draws in the group stages before another semi-final confrontation in 2007 which Liverpool won again, this time on penalties.The third instalment saw Chelsea finally triumph, winning 4-3 on aggregate as they progressed to the final in Moscow while the fourth meeting, in the 2009 quarter-finals, saw a veritable goal frenzy in comparison to what had gone before with the Blues running out 7-5 winners on aggregate. Benitez was Liverpool boss on each occasion and the war of words between him and a succession of Chelsea managers had angered fans, so it was always going to be hard for him to be accepted by Blues supporters.When you add in the fact he replaced a popular club legend in Roberto Di Matteo you had a recipe for disaster; there were demonstrations against him from his first game in charge.

Benitez was Chelsea's ninth manager since Abramovich became owner in 2003 but once again it was thought his short-term appointment could pave the way for Abramovich to make a summer approach for Pep Guardiola. Benitez knew he was never going to win over a sceptical fan base no matter what he achieved at the Bridge, nevertheless a Chelsea statement tried to be optimistic: "The owner and the board believe that in Benitez we have a manager with significant experience at the highest level of football, who can come in and immediately help deliver our objectives.The two-time UEFA Manager of the Year comes with outstanding pedigree."

Rafa had joined Liverpool from Valencia in 2004 where he had won two league titles in three seasons, and immediately won the Champions League in 2005, before winning the FA Cup the following year and reaching the Champions League final again in 2007, before leaving Anfield in 2010. He had been out of work since being sacked by Inter Milan in December 2010 having spent just six months in charge of the Serie A club despite winning two titles - the Club World Cup and Italian Super Cup. Before his appointment was confirmed Benitez admitted his interest in the Chelsea job to Abu Dhabi-based website 360. "I am looking for a club that can challenge for trophies and Chelsea is one of these clubs." When he was asked about the prospect of managing on a short-term basis, he added: "I am just trying to go to a team that can win. So we will find ways to have a challenge like this."

Former Chelsea midfielder Nigel Spackman suggested Benitez's appointment would be unpopular: "You won't find many Chelsea fans happy with an appointment of an ex-Liverpool manager. Benitez has got a great CV and a good record, but the only way he will win the Stamford Bridge crowd over is getting the results. Now he had to focus on trying to win the Premier League. He is the interim manager but if he does a good job maybe he will get it for longer."

David Johnstone, spokesman for Chelsea fanzine *cfcuk*, told BBC Sport that fans would be unhappy with Benitez as their new boss. "Rafa Benitez is not a Chelsea manager. Some people are born to play for or manage certain clubs and for us, Benitez isn't what we want.When he was Liverpool manager and José Mourinho was Chelsea boss there was a bit of 'beef' between them. He was very dismissive of Chelsea, very rude towards us, and my impression of him was that whenever anything went wrong it was always somebody else's fault, not his."

Former Liverpool and Germany midfielder Dietmar Hamann, a Champions League winner under Benitez at Anfield, believed his old boss would improve Chelsea."He is a very talented and outstanding manager. He's a very meticulous worker and he puts a lot of emphasis on tactical exercises."

Benitez inherited a team full of young stars in Juan Mata, Eden Hazard and Oscar amongst several established stars in Lampard, Terry and Torres and despite leading the club to a Europa League trophy, the fans were never supportive of him. There was conflict from the start between fans groups and the club when supporters wanted to bring banners into the stadium to protest over his appointment. In an exchange with the Chelsea Supporters' Group, the club responded after claims fans had been told to remove banners from the stadium. A Chelsea official wrote: "I would like to make it clear that the club does not have a policy of banning or censoring banners other than those which are threatening, offensive, discriminatory or would obstruct the view of others. Large banners can present safety concerns and are required to hold fire certificates before they will be permitted into the ground. In the past year supporters have freely displayed banners and signs expressing a range of opinions without club intervention.There has been no change to this policy."

Despite it all, Benitez insisted he had the Chelsea players support. "Fantastic," he smiled when asked to rate his relationship with players who challenged him during a team huddle before a training session.The interim manager tried to shrug off the row as a 'very brief exchange of ideas', clouded by the 'disappointment' of defeat at Manchester City.

Benitez was convinced that if he guided Chelsea to the Europa League it would be accepted he had done a good job during his short stint at the Bridge with a top-four place assured barring a mathematical miracle.As Benitez prepared to finish with a flourish by adding silverware to the campaign by facing Benfica in the Amsterdam Arena he said, "You can always make mistakes but it was not an easy situation at the beginning," he said. "We have managed it quite well. Every day, after every training session, I go home and think we are doing our best. For me it is always important to win trophies. If we win it will be easier and people will realise that to be here, at this stage of the competition, means we have done a lot of things well."

Benitez's reign as interim manager duly ended in triumph after Branislav Ivanovic's injury-time header won the Europa League with Chelsea's supporters celebrating wildly in the Amsterdam Arena as they added this trophy to the Champions League won the previous season. Fernando Torres had scored against the run of play to put Chelsea ahead on the hour but Oscar Cardozo's penalty deservedly drew Benfica level. Benitez became only the fourth manager to win the UEFA Cup/Europa League more than once. Others to have achieved that feat are: Giovanni Trapattoni 1977 (Juventus), 1991 (Inter), 1993 (Juventus); Luis Molowny: 1985 & 1986 (Real Madrid), Juande Ramos: 2006 & 2007 (Sevilla).

Petr Cech saved superbly from Cardozo and Lampard struck the woodwork in a dramatic conclusion before Ivanovic - suspended for the previous year's Champions League final - rose to meet Mata's corner deep into stoppage time to prompt a subdued clenched-fist celebration from Benitez. Chelsea rode their luck in their 68th game of the season with Hazard already out with a hamstring injury, they also had to do without captain John Terry for a second successive European final after he failed to recover from the ankle problem he sustained at Aston Villa, but he was on the pitch fully kitted out to hold the trophy for the photographers!

Benitez felt vindicated after his tumultuous seven-month spell at the club. "It was a special night for everyone involved. I'm proud for all of them. I could see everyone was happy, so I was happy too.This was a reward for how hard we've been working all season. But I think it's sad to think we are now 'a success' when we have been doing our jobs for six or seven months. It would have changed nothing if we'd won or lost this final in terms of what we have been trying to do.The job we did was hard work on the training ground, doing our jobs as professionals and, in the end, we have a trophy. We have scored 145 goals this season, a record in the history of the club, and not conceded too many. The players are growing, improving. If you have to win before people realise the job you are doing... But we did win, so hopefully people will say: 'Yes, it's not bad.' If you analyse everything, we won the Europa League with just one available striker for every single game.We managed players with yellow cards, we did the same in the league, and if you put everything together you will realise how difficult it was with a squad that was not too big.We had 18 players today, with Ake on the bench.

"This is a team in transition with young players. It was quite difficult from the beginning, but you can see the commitment of the players out there.When you have a manager who is leaving and yet you see them still fighting hard right to the end, you have to be pleased. I think we did well."

John Terry – who, along with the other Chelsea players not involved, had changed into his kit in order to comply with UEFA regulations – climbed the steps to the directors' box to accept the trophy with Lampard, just as he did in Munich the previous May. Benítez received congratulations from the board members present before joining the celebrations back on the pitch. "It's been an amazing time," Lampard said. "Talk about ups and downs. We're a group, we're a team. We were tired because of a long season but we showed a great desire. Nobody deserves it more than Ivanovic. He's been fantastic.We were fortunate but I think you make your own luck."

Benitez did not take part in the lap of honour following the trophy lift but he had at least won a few fans over as they made their appreciation known. A week later he signed a contract to take over at Napoli while Chelsea began the search for their next permanent manager.

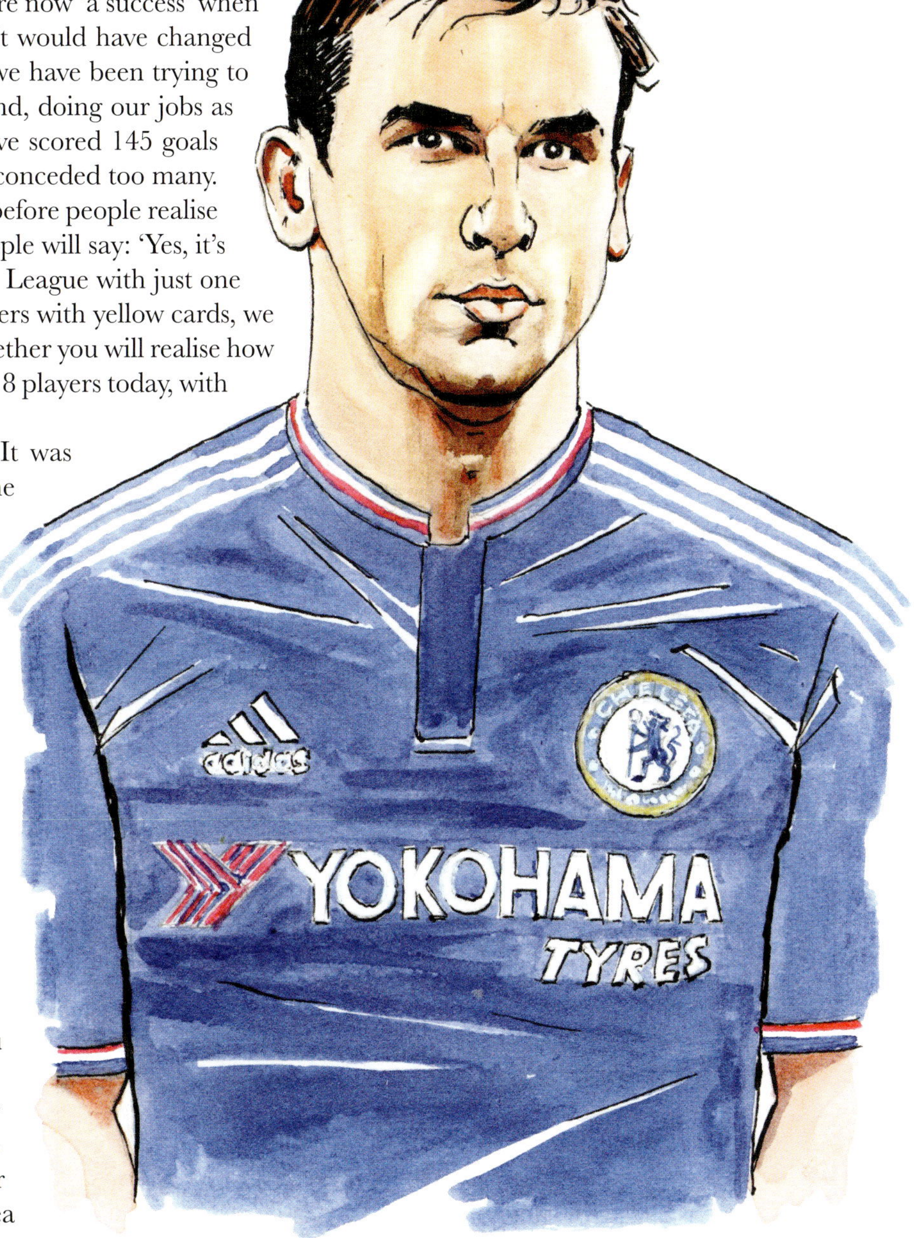

The Prodigal Son Returns

Mourinho: the man, the methods and the madness

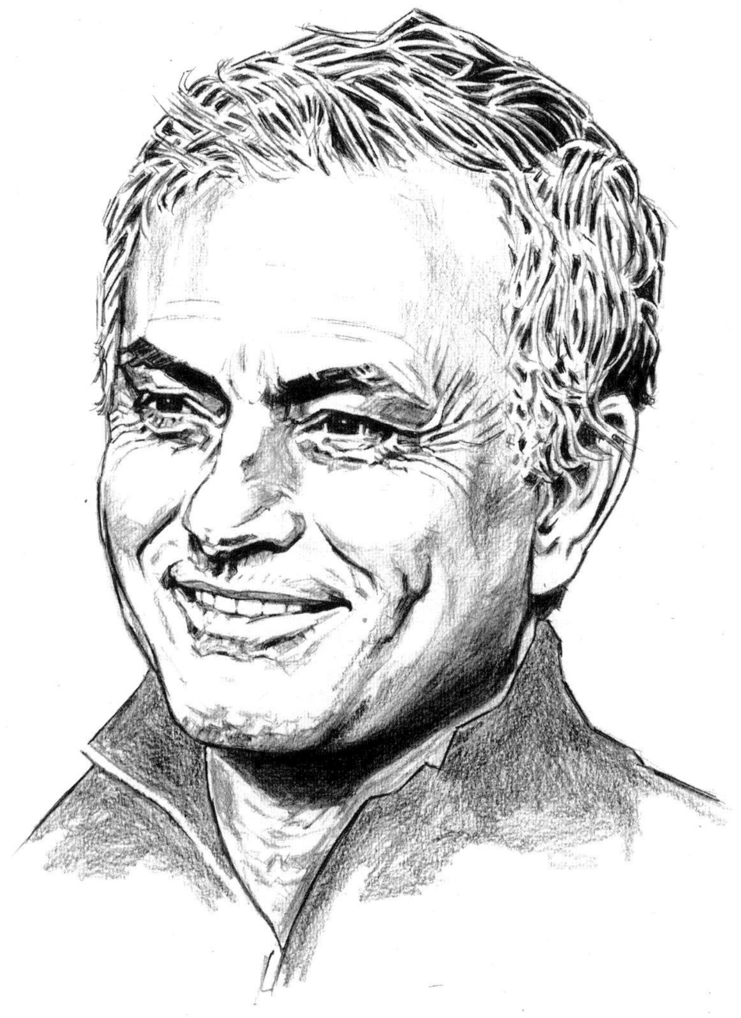

There is no doubting José Mourinho has an unbreakable bond with Chelsea, the club and its fan base. Speaking before Graham Potter was axed in April 2023, he said: "If you ask me do I have somebody that I would love to take over from 'my Chelsea' let's say that, yes, I have but I close my mouth. The club has reached such a level that it doesn't matter who it's with but Chelsea will always be Chelsea. Chelsea will always be big and my house will always be 200 metres away from the stadium so I want to keep listening to the sound of happiness and success. I'm pretty sure it's going to be like that." This wasn't the first time Mourinho had hinted at his love for Chelsea. As manager of Roma he had said, "Of course, my English connection is Chelsea, that's the way I see things, as a Chelsea man after two periods of Chelsea and six years."

That is how he still feels and it's not hard to appreciate why, as it all began when a relatively unknown Mourinho pitched up in English football for the first time. At Mourinho's unveiling the country instantly knew they were in for something special. "We have top players," he'd announced at the media conference, "and, sorry if I'm arrogant, but we now have a top manager." Smart, thorough, eloquent and witty, Mourinho wowed the media with the kind of self confidence, insight and preparation that would be hallmarks of his management. The Premier League was dominated by Arsene Wenger's Arsenal and Sir Alex's Manchester United. A brash, bold newcomer declared his intent to muscle his way into that cosy double act.

His 'methodology' was rooted in an holistic, scientific approach to training, tactical flexibility, defensive awareness, and players allowing him inside their heads; it proved sensationally successful, beginning with a 1-0 win in his first game at home to Manchester United. Chelsea's players soon came to realise that Mourinho was obsessed with winning. Mourinho tore into his players at half-time of the 2-2 draw with champions Arsenal in December 2004 after Thierry Henry had superbly scored twice. Mourinho threw Lucozade bottles and kicked tubs of Vaseline angry that his side had been on top but trailed. Eiður Guðjohnsen equalised in the first minute of the second half!

Mourinho adapted his tactics during his first season at Stamford Bridge. He intended to play a 4-4-2 diamond, with Frank Lampard behind two strikers, as Deco had done at Porto. The players struggled to create enough chances. Mourinho had the best holding player in the world in Claude Makelele - so good the position was named after him - and moved to what was called 'the open diamond which made for a flexible attack that suited Eiður Guðjohnsen or Didier Drogba and allowed the wingers to come in, perfect for Damien Duff and Arjen Robben to create havoc. It proved a shrewd tactical shift that turbo-charged the team especially elevating Duff and Robben to a force to be reckoned with.

Chelsea hit top spot in November and never let up. With Lampard's two goals at Bolton the Blues won the title for the first time in 50 years, ultimately with a remarkable Premier League record tally of 95 points and just 15 goals conceded. While players and supporters danced around the Reebok, Mourinho called his wife to tell her the score. Winning was quite normal – having already made his new team winners in the League Cup, too.

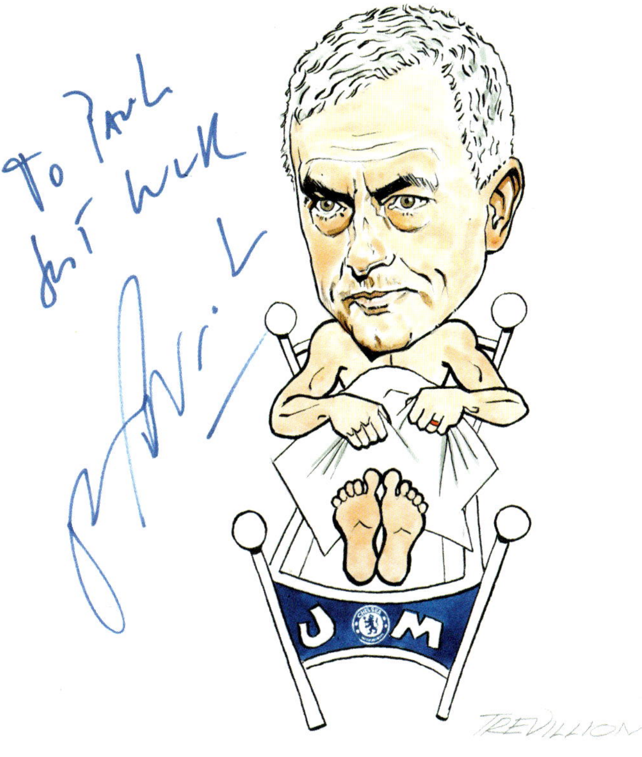

After their sole defeat at Manchester City in October, Chelsea dropped just 10 points before sealing the championship at Bolton on 30 April 2005. "You could say that our football was more attractive to watch but they are very efficient," said Wenger at the turn of 2005. "They are a bit like a matador - they wait until the bull gets weak to kill him. They have the patience to wait as they have an experienced squad. When the bull has lost enough blood and becomes a bit dizzy, they kill it off."

Mourinho told his players they would be champions, and win the league at Bolton with three games remaining. He was right as a Frank Lampard double sealed the win, but only after another half-time dressing down which saw Mourinho tell two of his players to give their shirts to him and assistant Steve Clarke. "For five minutes we will do more than you managed," he said. "And then after five more minutes, we will need oxygen and an ambulance." Lampard's goals clinched the title, with Joe Cole later leading the singing while standing on top of the mobbed team bus.

Oh the team bus! "Parking the bus" became part of the football lexicon during José's reign, but it was Mourinho who first said it about Tottenham just a month into his Premier League career. "As we say in Portugal, they brought the bus and they left the bus in front of the goal." Chelsea remained top when Wenger attempted some classic mind games by questioning whether they would stay the course. "It is a difficult psychological challenge to deal with when you're leading," he said. "When you are in front and everyone says you have already won the title you have to face up to the prospect that you can only lose it from there."

Sir Alex Ferguson suggested Chelsea's trips to Blackburn, Liverpool and Everton in January and February could be key. "It is when Chelsea come north that you will see. They have to go to Liverpool and Everton, as we do, but our record isn't bad there. It is different after the new year - there are different pressures."

Arjen Robben secured a win at a difficult Ewood Park. "Look at the blond boy in midfield, Robbie Savage, who commits 20 fouls during the game and never gets a booking," Mourinho said. "We came here to play football and it was not a football game, it was a fight and we fought and I think we fought fantastically."

Mourinho's champions set records for most wins, most away wins, most points, most clean sheets and fewest goals conceded in a Premier League season. "These are records that don't show a defensive team, they show a complete team," says Rick Glanvill, Chelsea author and official historian. "That's what made that team different. We could shut up shop and protect a lead if we needed to, squeeze the life out of a game like a boa constrictor. But that season there were a number of occasions where José would take off one of the full-backs and bring on an attacking player. His substitutions were incredible. It was such a devastating attacking team with Drogba, Gudjohnsen, Robben, Duff, Cole and Lampard. The 2005 team is definitely one of the best sides the Premier League has seen."

Chelsea won the league again in 2005-06, before Mourinho's shock departure in September 2007, but later returned and won the title again in 2014-15 during which the team displayed incredible levels of consistency, and the first part of the season will be remembered for the quality of attacking play, with new signings Cesc Fabregas and Diego Costa flourishing. During the second half of the campaign, when injuries and suspensions took their toll, he took a pragmatic approach and defended well as a unit and secured a number of wins by a one-goal margin, with the victories away at QPR and at home to Manchester United standing out, before Eden Hazard netted the only goal of the game against Crystal Palace to secure the title. Two months earlier the team won the first trophy of the second Mourinho reign - the Capital One Cup – with a 2-0 victory over London rivals Tottenham at Wembley, the third time he had won the trophy, following triumphs over Liverpool and Arsenal in 2005 and 2007.

When he returned he commented: "I'm at the club where I want to be. I'm in the country where I want to be, so I think that's a privilege because many times you prefer a club or a country but circumstances mean you do not get both. So after my experience in different countries I think I couldn't be happier."

His first campaign back at the club, 2013/14, was one which ultimately ended trophy-less, but the team went close both domestically and in Europe. For his first game back in charge, at home to Hull City, he was given a rapturous welcome by the Stamford Bridge faithful, and goals from Oscar and Lampard made it a winning start. The 4-3-3 formation which had been the hallmark of his first spell made way for a 4-2-3-1, and one defeat in the opening nine Premier League matches set the team on the right path for a title challenge. The teams' record in the biggest games was fantastic, with the Blues taking six points from both Manchester City and Liverpool, four off Manchester United and Arsenal. The Gunners and Tottenham were beaten 6-0 and 4-0 respectively on their visits to the Bridge, but disappointing results against Sunderland and Norwich towards the end of the campaign, meant third-place. In Europe, Mourinho led the team to the last four of the Champions League for the third time as Chelsea manager. Demba Ba scored a late winner in a dramatic quarter-final victory over Paris Saint-Germain, overturning a 3-1 first-leg deficit, prompting the manager to run along the touchline in celebration, but after securing a 0-0 draw away from home against Atletico Madrid in the semi-final first leg, Chelsea were beaten 3-1 back at the Bridge.

Having finished the following season as champions, the title defence in 2015-16 began disappointingly. The 2014-15 triumph had been built on Terry and Branislav Ivanovic in defence, protected in midfield by Nemanja Matic, the brilliance of Hazard and the two summer signings that transformed Chelsea from Mourinho's first season back at Stamford Bridge, Cesc Fabregas and Diego Costa. The decline in performance of that 'Big Six' played a pivotal part in the slide that led to Mourinho's departure. Terry, once described as "untouchable" by Mourinho, was left out at stages this season, while Ivanovic's form declined. Terry, embarrassed by his early substitution at Manchester City, suffered a similar humiliation in the decisive loss at Leicester when the 35-year-old was tormented by the speed and movement of Jamie Vardy and Riyad Mahrez. After losing seven of the opening 14 Premier League matches, consecutive defeats against newly-promoted Bournemouth and Leicester City in December left Chelsea 16th and the decision was made to part company with Mourinho fearing it might deteriorate into a relegation battle despite Mourinho reassuring the board and the fans that he was in control of the situation and was well placed to turn it all around.

Yet, only a few months earlier, Mourinho was about to put pen to paper on a new four-year contract. It was 7 August 2015 and all was well as favourites to retain their crown as he spoke about building a team that would give Chelsea a 10-year dynasty. Chelsea made the same mistake as Manchester City after winning the Premier League in 2012 when they failed to strengthen their squad sufficiently, bringing in low-key signings such as Brazilian veteran Maicon, Scott Sinclair, Jack Rodwell and Javi Garcia.

The title was lost to Manchester United in Sir Alex's final season. Mourinho wanted new signings, but they didn't materialise. Chelsea were linked with Juventus' Paul Pogba and Real Madrid's outstanding young defender Raphael Varane. Instead Chelsea failed in their pursuit of John Stones despite a transfer request from the 21-year-old defender. Pedro did arrive from Barcelona for £21m and left-back Baba Rahman from Augsburg for £21.7m plus £8m on Stoke City keeper Asmir Begovic to replace the departed Petr Cech. Papy Djilobodji came from Nantes for £4m and Reading's Michael Hector for the same fee. Djilobodji was barely seen and Hector went straight back to the Championship club. The loan signing of Radamel Falcao seemed to be an attempt to prove he could succeed where Manchester United and Louis van Gaal had failed. Yet the prolific Colombian also failed in West London. Chelsea did not win any of those pre-season games, including a 4-2 defeat by New York Red Bulls.

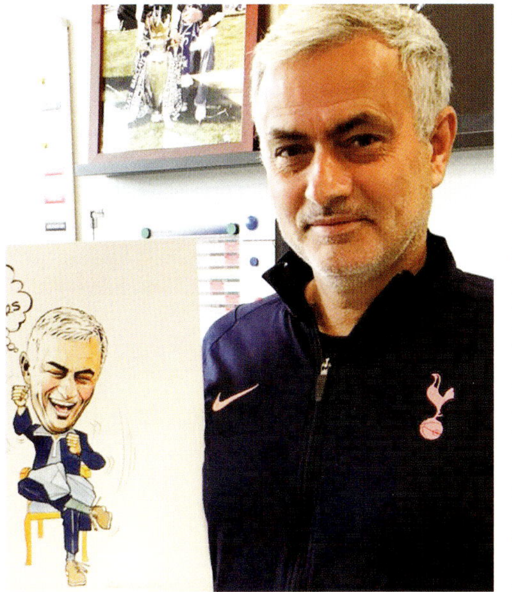

They looked off the pace against Swansea City in their opening game and momentum was never regained. Worse still, in that opener at Stamford Bridge the manager engaged in a furious row with team doctor Eva Carneiro that provided an acrimonious backdrop to the season. Chelsea were already reduced to 10 men after keeper Thibaut Courtois was sent off, Carneiro and fellow medic Jon Fearn raced on to treat Eden Hazard even though the manager felt it was not required. It was a response that led to Mourinho, angry that his side were briefly reduced to nine men, accusing the medics of being "impulsive and naive". Both had their positions downgraded but the row with Carneiro rumbled on, with Mourinho criticised by the medical profession, including the Football Medical Association, which represents medical staff in the sport. Mourinho was cleared of making discriminatory comments to Carneiro but FA chairman Greg Dyke, in a letter to FA council members, said Chelsea's manager had "made a mistake" and should apologise.

As Mourinho's struggles continued - along with brushes with authority - so did the Carneiro affair. Her lawyers sued Chelsea for constructive dismissal while Mourinho was target for legal action. His fortunes plummeted from the moment he crossed swords with the former club doctor. He was given a one-match stadium ban and a £40,000 fine for an expletive-filled rant at referee Jon Moss which led to him being sent off at half-time in the loss at West Ham in October. Mourinho had an appeal against a £50,000 FA fine and a suspended one-match ban dismissed following his claims after the 3-1 home defeat by Southampton in early October that referees were afraid of giving Chelsea penalties.

Eden Hazard's relationship with Mourinho was questioned as he struggled. Mourinho suggested the Belgian star had substituted himself at Leicester after the briefest attempt to run off an injury, meanwhile Diego Costa, overweight and struggling for goals, looked in the mood for physical confrontation with his boss, hurling a bib at his manager when it became clear he was only going to be an unused sub at Spurs in November. They later tried to laugh off the incident.

Cesc Fabregas played 18 of Chelsea's first 19 league games and created 13 goals - but in playing 16 out of the last 19 he assisted only five. In 98 home Premier League games before that season, Mourinho lost only once - to Sunderland on 19 April 2014. In the title-winning season of 2005-06, Mourinho's Chelsea won 18 games out of 19, a win percentage of 94.74%. In the first eight home league games this season Chelsea lost four times - to Crystal Palace, Southampton, Liverpool and Premier League newcomers Bournemouth. Mourinho's successes were built on that impregnability at home. That disappeared, along with poor form on their travels, the stats do not lie!

But Mourinho was not happy at suggestions he suffers third-season syndrome - he won the FA Cup and League Cup in his third full campaign at Chelsea during his first spell. Mourinho had two seasons at Inter Milan, leaving - as he did at Porto in 2004 - after winning the Champions League, as well as Serie A for the second successive season and the Italian Cup. He stayed three more seasons at Real Madrid, winning La Liga in 2011-12. On 22 May 2012, Mourinho signed a new four-year contract at Real - on 20 May 2013 it was announced he was leaving; long-term contracts do not equate to longevity for Mourinho.

Yet Chelsea fans remain loyal to Mourinho, irrespective of his faults, and chanted his name whenever it was all going wrong under new owners. They still want him back for a third time. Mourinho improved players, enhanced reputations but even at his beloved Chelsea he couldn't get everything right. He sold Mo Salah to Roma and Kevin De Bruyne to Wolfsburg. But he insists that they wanted to leave Chelsea, rather than he wanted them out and he feels it was the right decision for both of them, which is a no brainer as they ended up at Liverpool and Manchester City to become world superstars. Explaining the decision to Jon Obi Mikel on the *Obi One* podcast, Mourinho said: "To be honest, they left because they wanted to leave. They left because they didn't want to wait. History proves that their option was good because they've had the careers they have and reached a high standard, but sometimes kids make decisions like that because they can't wait, or they don't have the patience to be calm and to wait for the right moment. Sometimes their career goes in the wrong direction. When people say I let Salah go, I say exactly the opposite. I bought Salah. I was the one who said 'buy that guy'. He was going from Basel to Liverpool, and I made a fight, I made a war, to make him come to Chelsea. Then comes the part when, to be a Chelsea player, you have to perform, or you need to wait. He didn't want to wait, he wanted to go on loan. And then Chelsea, at a certain point, decided to sell. He went to Fiorentina and Roma, and that was not me deciding to sell. I was saying let him go on loan if he feels he needs to play every minute of every game.

"With Kevin, it was very similar. We went to pre-season in Asia. We went to Indonesia, Thailand, and Kevin was due to go on loan to a German side. I told the club 'no, I don't want him out on loan, I want him with me'. He stayed with me, and he began the Premier League season playing in the starting 11. After that, we played the European Super Cup in Prague against Bayern and he didn't play that game. Then, the next day, he wants to leave. We played the second Premier League game of the season against Manchester United at Old Trafford and we drew 0-0. He was on the bench and he played some minutes, but it wasn't enough for him, so he wanted to leave. When you are at Chelsea and you want to leave, go and another one comes. They were just kids who couldn't wait, and their careers say they were right, but it wasn't down to me. Probably other guys will say I pushed them out, but not them."

Romelu Lukaku was still only 22 when he was sold to Everton for £28m in the summer 2014. At one point he looked like the next Didier Drogba, but Mourinho was proven right with the Belgium striker.

Mourinho is a family man with family virtues and principles, more soft in the centre than most realise. Yet he can be so abrasive he is toxic at times, with an edge to his character. For the manager who once described Arsenal manager Arsene Wenger as a "voyeur" for his perceived interest in Chelsea and a "specialist in failure", he was certainly a one-off in whatever he said or did as Chelsea manager. When Mourinho was sent off at half-time in the loss at West Ham, he was described in referee Jon Moss's official report as follows: "At this point Mr Mourinho became very aggressive. He shouted that you [expletive] referees are weak… Wenger is right about you… you are [expletive] weak."

H

MOURINHO'S TROPHIES

1. League Cup - 2004/05

The showpiece at the Millennium Stadium in Cardiff was fiercely contested. John Arne Riise volleying Liverpool in front after just 45 seconds, before Steven Gerrard's own goal levelled. Mourinho quickly became known for his antics on the touchline and was sent off for his reaction to Chelsea's equaliser. Quickfire goals from Didier Drogba and Mateja Kezman in extra-time gave Chelsea a two-goal cushion, which Liverpool couldn't overturn despite Antonio Nunez striking to the reduce the deficit.

2. Premier League - 2004/05

In one of the most incredible title-winning campaigns, Mourinho won Chelsea their first league title for half a century during his debut season, the title was confirmed with three games to spare after Frank Lampard's double saw off Bolton Wanderers, with the Blues losing one game throughout the campaign. Chelsea's 95 points was a record at the time, 15 conceded in 38 games remains a league record. The Blues finished 11 points off London rivals Arsenal the season prior, Mourinho turned it around with the summer signings of Drogba, Cech and Ricardo Carvalho particularly significant.

3. Community Shield - 2005

Drogba was always the man for the big occasion and he was instrumental in Chelsea beating Arsene Wenger's Gunners in the Community Shield. The Ivorian striker netted twice in a 2-1 victory at the Millennium Stadium, with the Chelsea icon awarded Player of the Match.

4. Premier League - 2005/06

Chelsea romped to another Premier League title in Mourinho's second season, conceded 22 and finished on four fewer points than they had the previous campaign with 18 wins and a draw from 19 home games. Chelsea won the Premier League by beating nearest rivals Manchester United 3-0 at Stamford Bridge, William Gallas, Joe Cole and Carvalho all on the scoresheet in a famous victory. Mourinho's side lost the final two games 1-0, failing to surpass their record points tally.

5. League Cup - 2006/07

Another Chelsea final, another memorable performance from Drogba. Arsenal were once again the opponents at the Millennium Stadium, the last in South Wales. Theo Walcott gave Arsenal the lead after just 12 minutes, Drogba levelled shortly afterwards and with a header six minutes from time that would win a second League Cup crown for Mourinho and only a fourth for the Blues in total another chapter in the rivalry between Mourinho and Wenger.

6. FA Cup - 2006/07

Having lost the Premier League title to Sir Alex's resurgent United, Mourinho got his revenge. The Blues had needed extra-time to reach the last two during their semi-final against Blackburn Rovers and they would also need an extra half hour to conquer the Red Devils at the newly opened Wembley Stadium. The game between England's top two finished goalless in normal time, but Drogba hit the winning strike in the 116th minute; the one and only FA Cup that Mourinho lifted.

7. League Cup - 2014/15

Mourinho sealed his return to Stamford Bridge at the beginning of the 2013/14 season but couldn't win any silverware in his first campaign back, falling short of Manchester City and Liverpool in the Premier League. Chelsea came up against London rivals Spurs at Wembley, triumphing with a 2-0 victory. Terry and Costa scored in the final.

8. Premier League - 2014/15

Having finished third in his first season back at Stamford Bridge, it didn't take long for Mourinho to claim Premier League glory - only the second time the Blues had won the trophy since his departure. Chelsea finished the campaign on 87 points, eight ahead of runners-up Manchester City, securing the title after Hazard's strike gave the Blues a 1-0 win over Crystal Palace in West London. Despite the success of his reunion with the Blues, Mourinho would only last for half of the following season, sacked in December 2015 with Chelsea languishing in the bottom half of the table.

Thibaut Courtois

An outstanding member of Atletico Madrid's against-all-odds title win and run to the Champions League final in 2013-14, Chelsea brought him back from loan knowing it would take something special for the Belgian international to usurp the club's all-time best in Petr Cech and Courtois was so good that he was able to do just that. He started 32 games ahead of Cech as they won the Premier League title in 2014-15 and would become the undisputed No.1, adding a second league title in 2016-17, before securing a move to Real Madrid in 2018 as undoubtedly the best goalkeeper in the world. On retuning to the Bridge for the first time with Real, he recalled happy memories of representing Chelsea, despite his acrimonious departure. He won two league titles during a trophy-laden period of success at Stamford Bridge under the management of José Mourinho and Antonio Conte. Yet he was desperate to return to Spain, where he had previously cemented his reputation as one of Europe's most promising goalkeepers during his loan spell at Atletico Madrid, in order to be closer to his young family. After months of uncertainty, Chelsea finally relented and granted Courtois the opportunity to return to the Spanish capital, before spending a club record fee on Kepa Arrizabalaga. Reflecting on his departure ahead of his Chelsea reunion, Courtois commented: "It will be very nice to see a lot of familiar faces and I wish there was public at Stamford Bridge because there was a lot of happy moments I had there. Even though maybe my departure wasn't in the best way, or it was put that way, that it wasn't the best way, I only have good memories. Two Premier Leagues, a lot of other trophies – I'm really happy to play them."

At 6ft 6in Thibaut was a formidable presence despite his slender frame, and Mourinho wanted him back at the Bridge. "There was no plan set in stone when I arrived, but it was about playing in the future, and dependent upon development. The first two years at Atlético had gone well and, in 2013, Chelsea had wanted me back but I wasn't 100% sure. I knew a third year in Spain would maybe be a chance to do something special. We did that by winning La Liga and reaching the Champions League final. After that, it felt the right moment to go to Chelsea. The manager had called me just once to give his impression about the season ahead. He was talking about this campaign, saying how he saw things for all the team. He thought we'd have a strong side and wanted me to be a part of that. That was the gist: he hoped I'd come back. Working for him, it is easy to see why his sides have that fighting mentality. He motivates you. If the coach on the sidelines is not that strong, transmitting the kind of spirit he has, players won't always handle it well. Life becomes difficult. But, with Mourinho, everything is good. He knows when to be among his players, as 'one of us' making jokes as a friend, and when to be strong and distant, even severe. That's how it has to be to get the team sharp. Simeone did that, also, in his own way. He was an ex-player so he knew how we ticked."

The Argentinian, who inherited Courtois midway through that first season in Spanish football, twice masterminded victories over Chelsea with the loanee in his side; the Super Cup defeat of Roberto di Matteo's European Cup holders signalled the beginning of the end for the Champions League-winning manager. The semi-final defeat in that competition in April effectively ensured Filipe Luís, Diego Costa and Courtois would all become members of a revamped Chelsea lineup. "Not a lot of teams could have beaten us at that moment," recalled the keeper, whose smart save from a Terry header had helped progress. "We had our organisation. That was one of our biggest qualities, as well as individual class from Koke or Costa. Maybe, individually, we were not the best in Spain. If you look at us individually, this team at Chelsea is stronger than that side at Atlético last season. But what was important was to work hard for each other and to be selfless: a unit; run for one another; recover one another's mistakes; give everything you can. This side [Chelsea] is also doing that, which is maybe why we're top of the league. Not only do we have the individuals, but we also have the team ethic. That fighting mentality. At Liverpool we trailed but won and that's not easy at a place like that. Other games, when we've been struggling, we kept on playing and always came out with something."

After Courtois suffered a collision with Arsenal's Alexis Sánchez, which left him dazed and taken to hospital, Cech replaced him on the field but, even granted a potential route back into the team, the older man had other concerns. "Not long after the game had finished, and I was in hospital, Petr tried to call me twice and later he texted me," says Courtois. The injury was less serious than initially feared but Cech, who had suffered a depressed fracture to his skull eight years earlier, spent the evening advising the man who has usurped him how to use his shoulder and back to protect his head from an impact. The pair were competitors but friends. "On the day I took my original medical here, Petr came to say hello and welcome me, just like Drogba and John [Terry]. They made the effort. We train really well together now, talking a lot about things that can happen in a game. It's a nice relationship. I understand that, maybe, he's not happy he doesn't play a lot and that's normal. I would be the same. But we get on well. At Atlético, the No.2s would not always speak to me. It wasn't jealousy, more frustration, but it meant we didn't get on well. That's a pity because, normally, the goalkeepers are just alone working together. It's not like that here. I'd watch Edwin van der Sar and try and steal things with my eyes from how he played, because he wasn't all muscles and was a similar build to me. But Petr was another I'd look up to, someone I wanted to emulate."

Cech was also a member of a core of senior players whose influence at Chelsea was clear. Drogba, Terry and Lampard were elite veterans of Mourinho's first spell in charge or before. A new team developed based on the flair of Eden Hazard or Oscar, the industry of Branislav Ivanovic and, steadily, the security offered by Courtois. "At Chelsea we have JT, a great leader, as well as players like Drogba. In the dressing-room I'll leave the shouting to them."

Courtois signed a six-year deal with Real Madrid ending his seven-year spell at Chelsea. The Belgium number one, 26 at the time, completed his £34m move to the Spanish capital hours after Real midfielder Mateo Kovacic joined the Blues on loan. Real posted a clip of Courtois signing his contract alongside club President Florentino Perez. "Today I am realising a dream," said Courtois. Chelsea signed Athletic Bilbao's Kepa Arrizabalaga for £71m as a replacement. "Chelsea will always have a special place in my heart," he said in a Facebook post. "I want to thank the fans for their great support. I hope you understand that being close to my kids was considerable in my decision." Kovacic, then 24, had been at Real for three seasons since joining from Inter Milan and helped Croatia reach the final of the World Cup. Courtois was voted best keeper at the tournament in Russia, where Belgium beat England in a third-place play-off. Thibaut has gone on to star in goal during Real's period of dominance in the Champions League, first under Zinedine Zidane and later Carlo Ancelotti, winning the coveted trophy twice as well as three La Liga titles. A dispute with Belgium manager Domenico Tedesco meant he missed the 2024 Euros where Belgium exited in the Round of 16.

Eden Hazard

The fact that Eden Hazard has had to share the limelight and the fans' affections with such wing magicians as Charlie Cooke and Franco Zola only serves to highlight the profusion of mesmerising wide players in Chelsea's history. Hazard, the most coveted young player in the world, announced on Twitter he would be leaving his boyhood club Lille to sign for the Champions League winners in the summer of 2012 and eventually arrived at Stamford Bridge where he spent a mesmerising seven years delivering spell binding performances. In 352 appearances Hazard scored 110 goals and provided 92 assists, he is ninth on Chelsea's all time top-scorer lists. It was hard to imagine that any player could usurp Franco Zola in the eyes of the fans, but Hazard came pretty close.

Hazard called his seven years at Chelsea the "best memory" of his career, pinpointing his second season at the club under Mourinho as the pinnacle of his time in the game. "My best season was the second season with Mourinho when we won the Premier League and League Cup. The manager was the Special One and it's so hard to explain the feelings after games with the fans all happy." Hazard's 19-goal campaign under Mourinho led to him winning individual awards as well as team accolades.

His ability to deliver magic moments for Chelsea on countless occasions from, not just the wings but every attacking position possible means Blues will never forget him. After just six minutes of his Premier League debut the then 21-year-old served notice

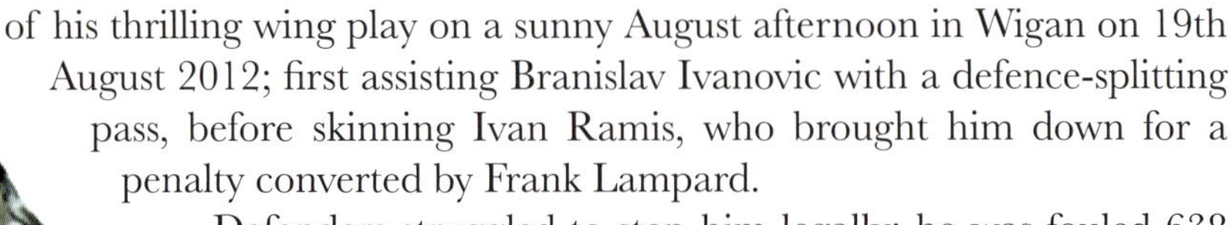

of his thrilling wing play on a sunny August afternoon in Wigan on 19th August 2012; first assisting Branislav Ivanovic with a defence-splitting pass, before skinning Ivan Ramis, who brought him down for a penalty converted by Frank Lampard.

Defenders struggled to stop him legally; he was fouled 638 times in the league, over 40 per cent more often than anyone else in the same period yet the Belgian still managed to create a league-high 595 chances for team-mates. He marked his Stamford Bridge bow against Reading by being fouled for a penalty and setting up another goal, Lampard and Ivanovic once again the beneficiaries. Three days later, with Newcastle in town, he stroked in his first Chelsea goal from the spot. Hazard scored 26 of the 31 penalties, famously heading in a rebound from a saved spot-kick against Crystal Palace in May 2015 to clinch the title. He quickly forged an irresistible relationship with Juan Mata, who had arrived a year earlier. The pair's link-up play was a key factor in the Blues' freescoring 2012/13 season. Hazard would later name Mata as the player he most relished playing alongside. His major contribution to reaching the Europa League final was a sensational display off the bench at home to Sparta Prague, capped by a magnificent injury-time thunderbolt that booked a place in the last 16. A hamstring injury sustained at Aston Villa in the penultimate league game ruled him out of the successful Amsterdam showpiece, but not before he had set up Lampard's record-breaking goals. He played a major part in the strong finish to the campaign, the longest in Chelsea history.

In Hazard's debut season he appeared 62 times, scored 13 goals and assisted 19, his performances received wide recognition as he was named in the PFA Team of the Year. He went up a gear in his second season, voted the Chelsea Player of the Year for the first time with spectacular goals against Arsenal, Liverpool, Tottenham and PSG as Chelsea went close both in the Premier League and the Champions League. He scored 17 goals in 49 games.

Hazard's imperious display in a 1-0 away win at eventual title winners Manchester City, before notching his maiden hat-trick in the game that followed against Newcastle, but his best performance in a Chelsea shirt was at the Stadium of Light on a chilly winter's evening in December 2013 in a 4-3 thriller; he conjured an assist and two solo goals. Hazard was named PFA Young Player of the Year to go with his Chelsea award, as well as being voted into the PFA Team of the Year again.

In 2014/15 it would get even better for Hazard, and Chelsea, as Eden proved to be quite simply the best player in the country, helping the Blues win the title with three games to spare and also lifting the League Cup. Starting all but five of 54 games in all competitions, Hazard's form never dipped below outstanding under José Mourinho and his link up with new arrivals Diego Costa and Cesc Fabregas, as well as Oscar and Willian, provided some of the finest attacking witnessed at Stamford Bridge. When it wasn't coming off for others, Hazard would inevitably provide the spark, as proven by his heavy involvement in four consecutive narrow away victories between February and April, the type of victories that win league titles. He scored at Villa, West Ham and Hull, and then set up Fabregas's late decider at Loftus Road. The following week Hazard netted the only goal against Manchester United at the Bridge, fittingly it was his header in the next home fixture, against Crystal Palace, that sealed the title. He finished with 19 goals and 11 assists in all competitions, was voted Chelsea Player of the Year for the second season running, was acknowledged by his peers as PFA Player of the Year and the media with the FWA Footballer of the Year, plus Premier League Player of the Season. No Chelsea player has ever won so many individual accolades in one year.

Hazard nor the team could match those levels in 2015/16. Injury and a surprising lack of confidence affected the Belgian, and he had to wait until April for his first open-play and Premier League goals. Yet he still managed to produce the campaign's most indelible moment, a stunning equaliser at home to Tottenham that was celebrated as much in the East Midlands (as it secured Leicester City the title) as it was at the Bridge, and was voted our Goal of the Season. A brilliant solo effort at Anfield followed and suggested Hazard was back to his best, and he carried that form into Euro 2016 with Belgium and the following season.

Having initially wobbled under new boss Antonio Conte, success came with a change in shape to 3-4-3 with Hazard excelling in the new formation forming a potent partnership down the left with Marcos Alonso. He scored seven during a club-record 13-game winning run to the top of the table before Christmas, a position Chelsea would never relinquish. Among them were memorable strikes against the two Manchester clubs. In the new year Hazard continued to thrive and scored one of his favourite Chelsea goals against Arsenal in February, a solo effort that began on the halfway line and ended with Arsenal defenders strewn across the turf and former team-mate Petr Cech beaten. It was voted Chelsea's Goal of the Season. Hazard was superb closing in on the title, netting twice in a 2-1 win against nearest challengers Manchester City. He fired home a sweet goal - his first at Wembley - in the 4-2 FA Cup semi-final win over Tottenham. Chelsea lost the final against Arsenal, but by then Hazard had his second Premier League winners' medal, and the day after Wembley he was named Chelsea Player of the Year for the third time. Although his self-proclaimed best season came while working with Mourinho, it was Conte who he enjoyed working under the most during his time in West London. "I think my best time at Chelsea was with Antonio Conte. All the week training. I was going out Saturday, I need to enjoy a little bit because I know the day after it's going to be back on the training ground. I have to do something, it's my only 90 minutes I can enjoy. You remember him, stopping, tactics, 'no we have to do that'. Saturday was the best day for me."

An injury on international duty over the summer delayed his return, but he was back to his best for his club. Now equally adept either in a traditional wide-left role, alongside the main striker up front, or leading the line on his own. For the FA Cup final at Wembley against Manchester United, he was paired with Olivier Giroud in attack and produced the decisive moment of a tight contest; it was vintage Hazard, an inch-perfect first touch followed by a burst of speed that took him clear. Phil Jones could only foul him as he bore down on goal, and he picked himself to tuck home the resulting penalty to collect his first FA Cup winners medal in his 300th Chelsea appearance. At the World Cup in Russia, Belgium captain Hazard was voted the second-best player at the tournament following a series of scintillating displays that helped his country reach the semi-finals, where they were only narrowly beaten by eventual winners France. Hazard played 72 times for Belgium while a Chelsea player, scoring 28.

Hazard's final year in West London was his most successful in the Premier League in terms of combined goals,16, and assists, a league-high 15, and he was a major factor in the club's third-place finish. At Watford on Boxing Day he became the 10th Chelsea player to reach 100 goals with a cool one-on-one finish. A penalty he won later in that game proved the winner. He hit a hat-trick against Cardiff, a pair of assists in a home win against hitherto-unbeaten Manchester City, two of his very best goals in a blue shirt. Her scored two hat-tricks: against Newcastle in 2014 and Cardiff in 2018

As in 2014, 2015 and 2017, Chelsea fans chose Hazard as their Player of the Year, and his fourth success was record-breaking in the prize's prestigious history. His team-mates voted for him as their Player of the Year, too, so he achieved the unique feat of winning all three club awards in the same season. His last kick at Stamford Bridge was the winning penalty in the shoot-out success over Eintracht Frankfurt, with one more majestic performance for the Europa League final that brought the curtain down on his Chelsea career. He teed up Pedro for 2-0, scored two, the first a calm penalty past Cech, the second rounding off one of the best Chelsea moves of the season. They were his sixth and seventh goals against Arsenal, who joined Bournemouth, West Brom and Newcastle as the teams to have most often suffered at his feet.

Eden announced his retirement aged just 32 in October 2023. The final few years proved to be bitterly disappointing, with injuries preventing him from making an impact at Real Madrid following his £100m switch from Chelsea four years earlier. Hazard often returned for pre-season in poor shape and overweight at Real Madrid. Hazard clocked up more injuries than goal involvements during his time in Madrid and in 2020 was voted Real's most disappointing ever signing in a poll by Marca. But he insists he does not regret the move to play under his idol Zinedine Zidane. "It was my dream. I can tell you it was my dream even if the story was not that good with injuries and this and that. When I look back, and you can see some pictures of me wearing the white Real Madrid shirt, it makes me proud."

Hazard had offers from clubs in Belgium, the United States and Saudi Arabia for one of football's last great entertainers to continue, a genius who slalomed through defences and won a Double at Lille, six major trophies at Chelsea, six at Real Madrid and earned 126 Belgium caps. "I enjoy it a lot," he says of his retirement. "I miss my football a bit, especially being with the lads in the dressing-room, but I can do what I want now. I have kids and a family. I can go to Belgium to see my family, brothers and parents. I can do a lot of things." Management does not appeal to him. He and his wife Natacha are occupied by their five boys, who he is coaching at home to follow in his footsteps. "I don't know [what's next]. I don't think I'll coach professionally, but I think I can coach for youth teams. I have kids, and I want to teach them how to play football."

Juan Mata

Mata was part of a close-knit quartet of Spaniards who formed lasting friendships at Chelsea who all contributed to the best year of his career. In 2011 Juan left his homeland to come to Chelsea with further spells at Manchester United, Galatasaray, and Vissel Kobe. His first season with Chelsea was one that has gone down in history. In 2012, Mata couldn't stop winning. He made more appearances than any other outfield Chelsea player as the trophies arrived in quick succession and he was at the heart of the team. He netted in the 5-1 thrashing of Tottenham in the FA Cup semi-final as Chelsea went on to land the trophy. He scored the crucial away goal in the Champions League round of 16 against Napoli that made the teams' famous comeback at Stamford Bridge possible. He provided the perfect assist for Didier Drogba to equalise in the final as Chelsea became the first London club to be crowned European champions.

Like Fernando Torres, Mata wasn't finished; both of Chelsea's representatives in the Spanish national team found the net to help their country beat Italy 4-0 in the 2012 European Championship final. "Fernando was in the same situation as me," Juan reflects. "The good thing is that when you win and enjoy it so much, there is a point it seems like winning is all there is. That is the problem. When you don't win any more you realise how difficult that is. But it was an incredible time and we feel so lucky in 2012 to have been able to win the FA Cup, then the Champions League, then the Euros with Spain, both of us scoring in the final. It was an incredible two or three months, probably the best summer in my life. With time you get to realise how difficult that is in a playing

LEWIS
of SUNNINGDALE

Supplying Only The Finest Cuts

Established in 1931, Lewis of Sunningdale is a third generation butcher committed to highest quality meat produce. We have gained a reputation for fabulous meat both locally and nationally. In fact we're so proud of our products, we'll personally guarantee it.

Our shop is based in Sunningdale, Berkshire and our expert staff are always on hand to give advice on anything from cuts to cooking. So feel free to drop in at any time or give us a call.

Monday - Friday: 7:30am - 5pm
Saturday: 7:30am - 4pm
Sunday: Closed

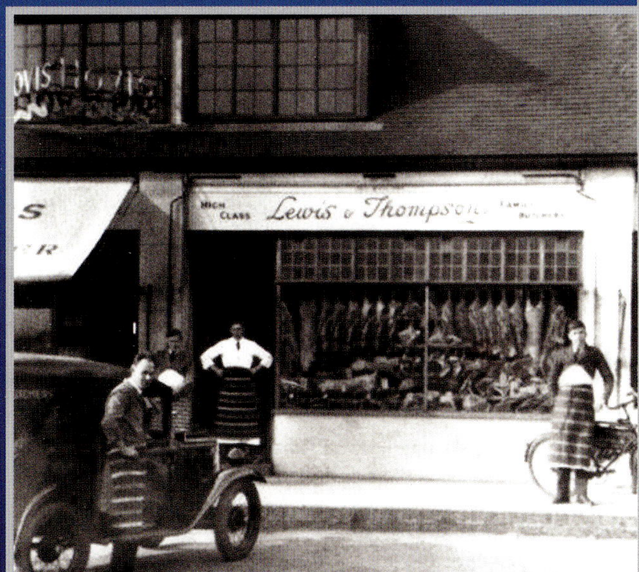

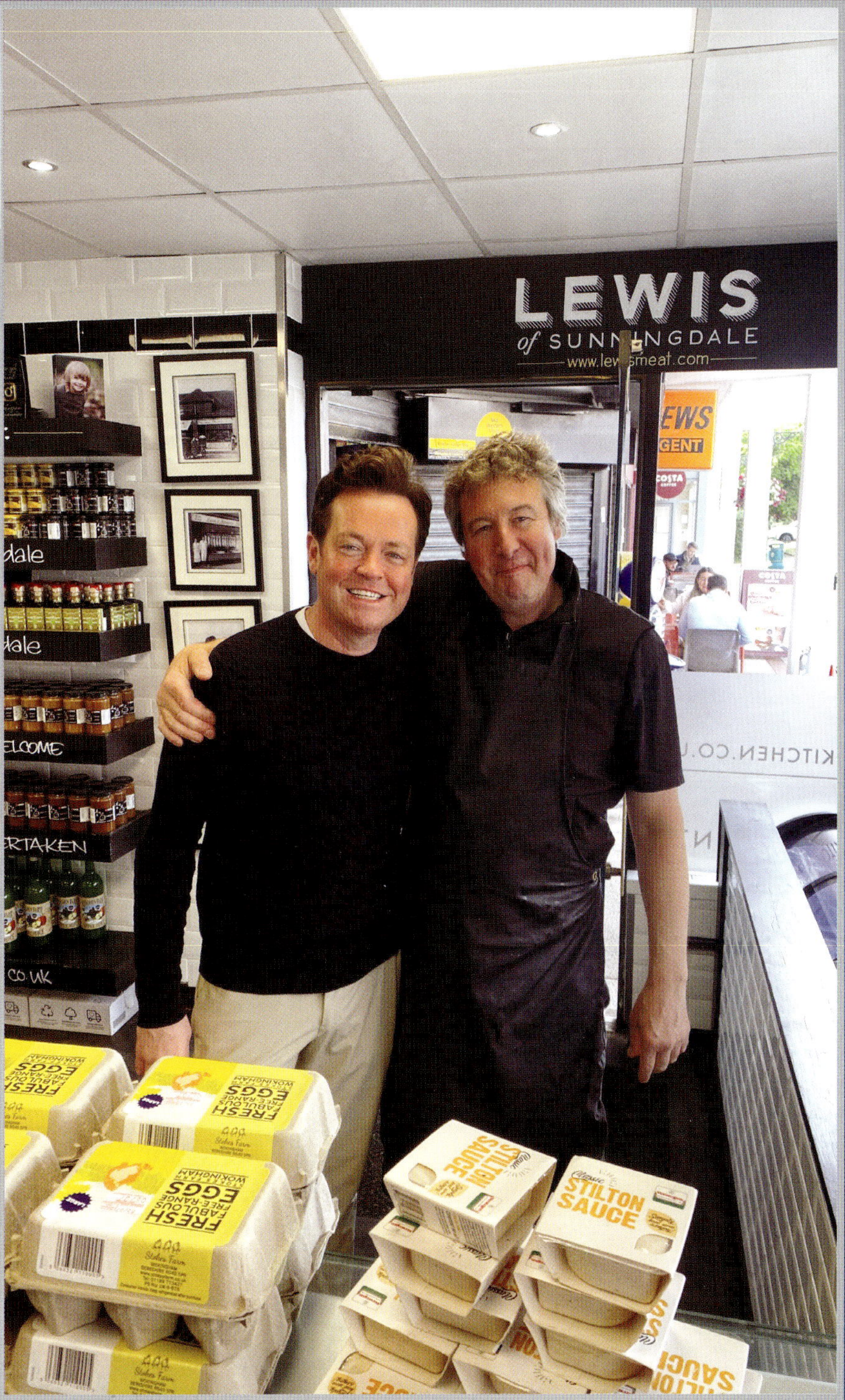

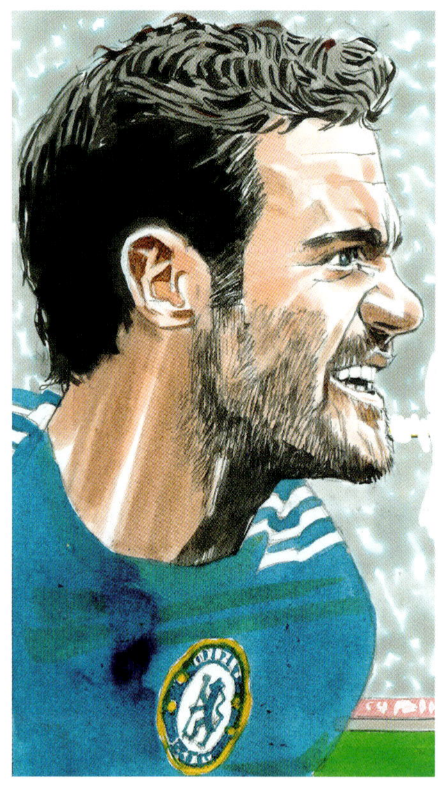

career. To win one of those trophies is a lot, but having the chance to win those trophies together, it's like a dream. We were riding a wave of positivity, of good football, and especially good results,"

Whole Juan says 'it was incredible', for the fans, he *was* incredible. They voted Mata the club's Player of the Year for 2011/12, and again the following season, when he also earned the Players' Player of the Year award.

Despite it being Mata's first time living abroad, there were no problems settling in England. When asked how he found living in a different country for the first time, Juan says, "I loved it." "As soon as I arrived in London I felt a great energy. It was positive from when I first arrived. Of course, London is a great city. I loved my life in London, getting to know a different country, different culture, different language. A city with a lot of opportunities. On the pitch it worked perfectly from the first minute; I remember scoring on my debut. So it was a big change in my life, leaving Spain, leaving Valencia where I was living for four years. But I felt it was the right time and I'm so happy that I did. My team-mates were great; we had a great dressing-room. They were very helpful in the beginning and offered their help for anything I might have needed. With their help, and also with my willingness to discover London and settle in, it was a fairly quick adaptation."

Among those team-mates they formed a close community of Spanish players. Fernando Torres had signed from Liverpool the previous January, Oriol Romeu arrived from Barcelona a few weeks before Juan in August 2011, and Cesar Azpilicueta would join the following summer. "It was super important. First to have Fernando, he was actually for me very important in the decision to go to Chelsea. He called me before when the interest was there and he told me how life was there, how the club wanted me and the coach. It made my decision easier. I had so much respect, admiration, and love for Fernando as a player and a person. He was a great help. Oriol arrived at the same time, and he is one of the best humans I've met in my whole life, not only in football. It was fantastic to be there with him, to get to know such an amazing personality. We speak a lot still. It was definitely one of my positives at Chelsea to get to know better Fernando and get to know Oriol, and Azpi who arrived later. We were more than team-mates, we were friends. Of course, my relationship with Fernando already began before with the national team, but because of our time together at Chelsea we became close friends. I consider him one of my best friends in my career. He was older and he was more experienced. He was a very important player, he was always giving me advice and the others. He was very important for all of us and I learned so much from him. I also already knew Azpi from the national team and the Under-21s and the younger generations, but again we made a strong relationship. With Oriol, we were living in the same building in Battersea, so we were going to training and back in the same car together most of the time. I got to know his amazing family, he got to know mine. We used to watch football together, on Champions League nights. We used to have dinner together. On days off we would make plans together in London. We were friends and we spent so much time together. And I can tell you, with a guy like Ori, he is someone you want to spend time with because your day will improve if you are around him! We found Spanish restaurants. The famous Cambio de Tercio on Old Brompton Road we used to go to a lot. Oriol also had friends who worked in restaurants in the east part of the city and doing Spanish guided tours. There are a lot of nationalities in London and a lot of Spanish people, plus we had a lot of visitors to watch games and things. So we were never bored!"

Mata wrote a regular blog during his time at Chelsea updating his football career and his travels exploring London. He later joined Manchester United, Galatasary and Japanese side Vissel Kobe.

THE
BARBERSHOP
SUNNINGDALE

Broomhall Chambers, London Rd,
Sunningdale SL5 0DJ
Tel: 01344 624956

Popping into the Barber Shop in Sunningdale, it is often a surprise to see who is getting their hair clipped in the seat next to you. Perhaps it might be Kevin Pietersen. The England cricketer, who was once as famous for his hairstyle as much as his flamboyant batting, lives locally and the other day I found myself sitting next Kev at the barbers,

Kevin is a big Chelsea fan, and I am sure he'll love this book when I get the chance to give him a copy!

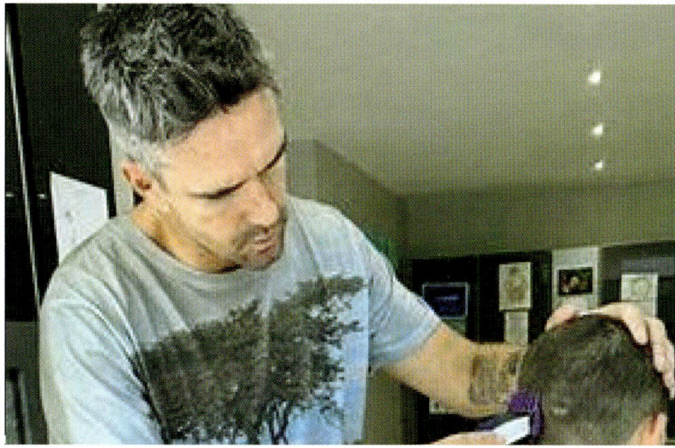

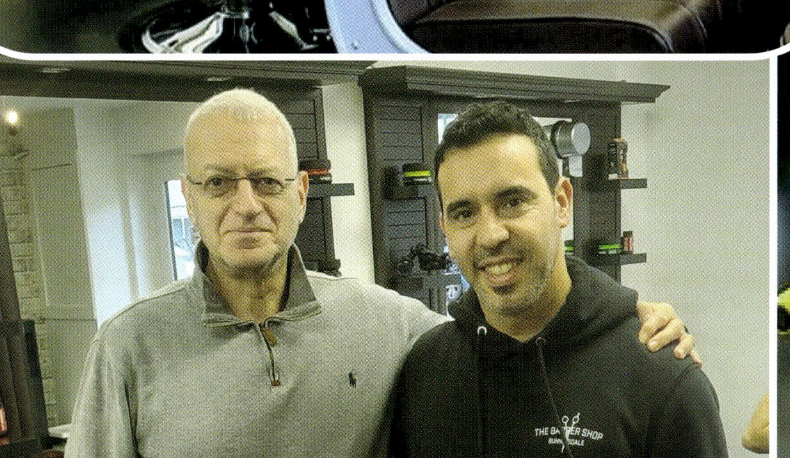

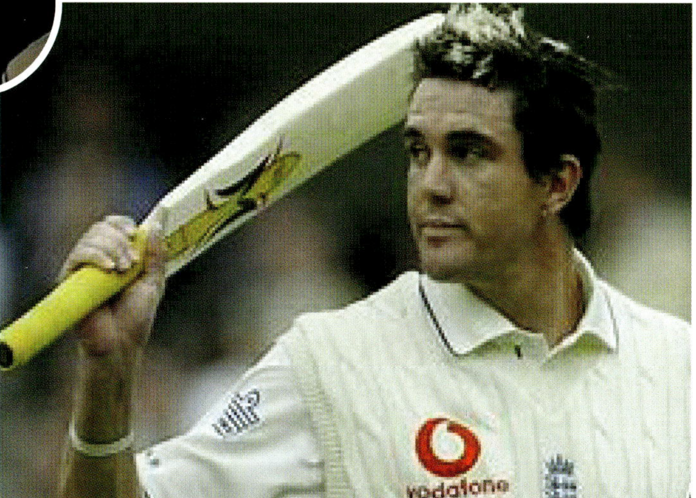

Antonio Conte

Yet More Glory and Fall Outs

The appointment of Antonio Conte, at that time manager of the Italian national side, was heralded as a major coup by Roman Abramovich. Roman Abramovich's love affair with Italian coaches continued when Antonio Conte signed a three-year contract to take effect following his country's participation in that summer's Euro 2016 tournament.

The then 46-year-old said at the time: "I am very excited about the prospect of working at Chelsea Football Club. I am proud to be the coach of the national team of my country and only a role as attractive as manager of Chelsea could follow that. I am looking forward to meeting everyone at the club and the day-to-day challenge of competing in the Premier League. Chelsea and English football are watched wherever you go, the fans are passionate and my ambition is to have more success to follow the victories I enjoyed in Italy. I am happy we have made the announcement now so everything is clear and we can end the speculation. I will continue to focus on my job with the Italian national team and will reserve speaking about Chelsea again until after the Euros."

Conte was the club's fifth Italian manager following Vialli, Ranieri, Ancelotti and Di Matteo. And just like the first three on that list, he had formerly been at Juventus, in his case as both a player and a manager.

Conte began his managerial career in the Italian lower divisions at Arezzo and Bari, winning promotion to the top flight with the latter, and was briefly employed by Atalanta before he further enhanced his reputation by guiding Siena into Serie A. Juventus hired their former player, where he won three consecutive titles, as did the Italy national team three years later when they handed him control of the Azzurri in 2014. He played 20 times for his country including a semi-final appearance in the 1994 World Cup and a quarter-final of Euro 2000. Under Conte's management, Italy qualified for the Euro 2016 finals and were undefeated in ten games in the finals but lost to Germany on penalties in the quarter-finals. Conte's coaching was characterised by tactical flexibility as he achieved the remarkable feat of an unbeaten league season at Juventus, becoming only the third Serie A team to do so. Impressively, that was in his first season in charge (2011/12) and in 2013/14 the 'Old Lady' recorded an all-time Serie A record of 102 points. In the 2012/13 campaign, Conte's side played Chelsea in the Champions League group stage, drawing 2-2 at Stamford Bridge and winning 3-0 in Turin. They went on to the quarter- finals where they lost to eventual winners Bayern Munich. In his three years as manager, Juventus lost only two home league games, contributing greatly to their new stadium being considered such a success.

As a player, Conte had been a versatile, energetic box-to-box midfielder. He was a Champions League winner as part of the Juventus side Vialli captained against Ajax in 1996. He played in two other finals of that competition and in a convincing win over Borussia Dortmund in the 1993 UEFA Cup final. He was also a five-time Serie A winner in his 13 seasons as an integral member of the Juve squad. He played for just two clubs having begun his career with his home-town team Lecce in southern Italy. Having played more than 400 games for the Italian giants, Conte's three years in charge of the team between 2011 and 2014 yielded a hugely impressive three straight Serie A titles - Juventus's first in eight years and their first three-in-a-row since the early 1930s. They had finished seventh the two seasons prior to Conte.The Bianconeri also won two Italian Super Cups with him in charge. Andrea Pirlo, Paul Pogba, Carlos Tevez and ArturoVidal were among his signings during a spell so productive he was named Serie A Coach of the Year in all three seasons there.

Former Chelsea striker Hernan Crespo wanted Conte to emulate Ancelotti. "Chelsea is still in my heart. I'm trying to work my way - because I'm a manager now – and my dream will be, in a few years, to work with Chelsea. One day [I want to manage them]. I've started to build my career to come there. I'm very happy for him [Conte], I hope he does the same [as Ancelotti, who won the double]."

Antonio did indeed almost emulate 'Don Carlo' in his first season but a runaway triumph in the title race was spoiled by Wembley defeat to Arsenal. After landing the title, Conte wanted to win the FA Cup to turn a "great season" into a "fantastic" but a late Aaron Ramsey goal won the cup for the Gunners.

Yet Chelsea cruised to their sixth title with two games to spare, securing the Premier League with Michy Batshuayi's late goal in a 1-0 win at West Brom. Chelsea had been top since November and finished the season a comfortable seven points ahead of nearest challengers Spurs. Conte had turned the season round from a poor start into a title winning one when he switched to a three-man defence in the wake of a 3-0 defeat by Arsenal in September which left them eighth, eight points behind leaders Manchester City. However the Blues embarked on a 13-match winning streak and they were 10 points clear of their nearest challengers with two games remaining."It was very frustrating for me because at the end of the Arsenal game I didn't see anything from my work or my ideas on football," said Conte. "But in this moment I found the strength to change and take responsibility and find a system for the players. It was a key moment in the season because every single player found in this system the best for him. When you arrive after a bad season and the team has arrived at 10th in the league it means there are a lot of problems. To find the right solution quickly isn't easy and for this I want to thank my players because they trusted in the new work, my philosophy, video analysis to see mistakes and they showed the right attitude and behaviour."

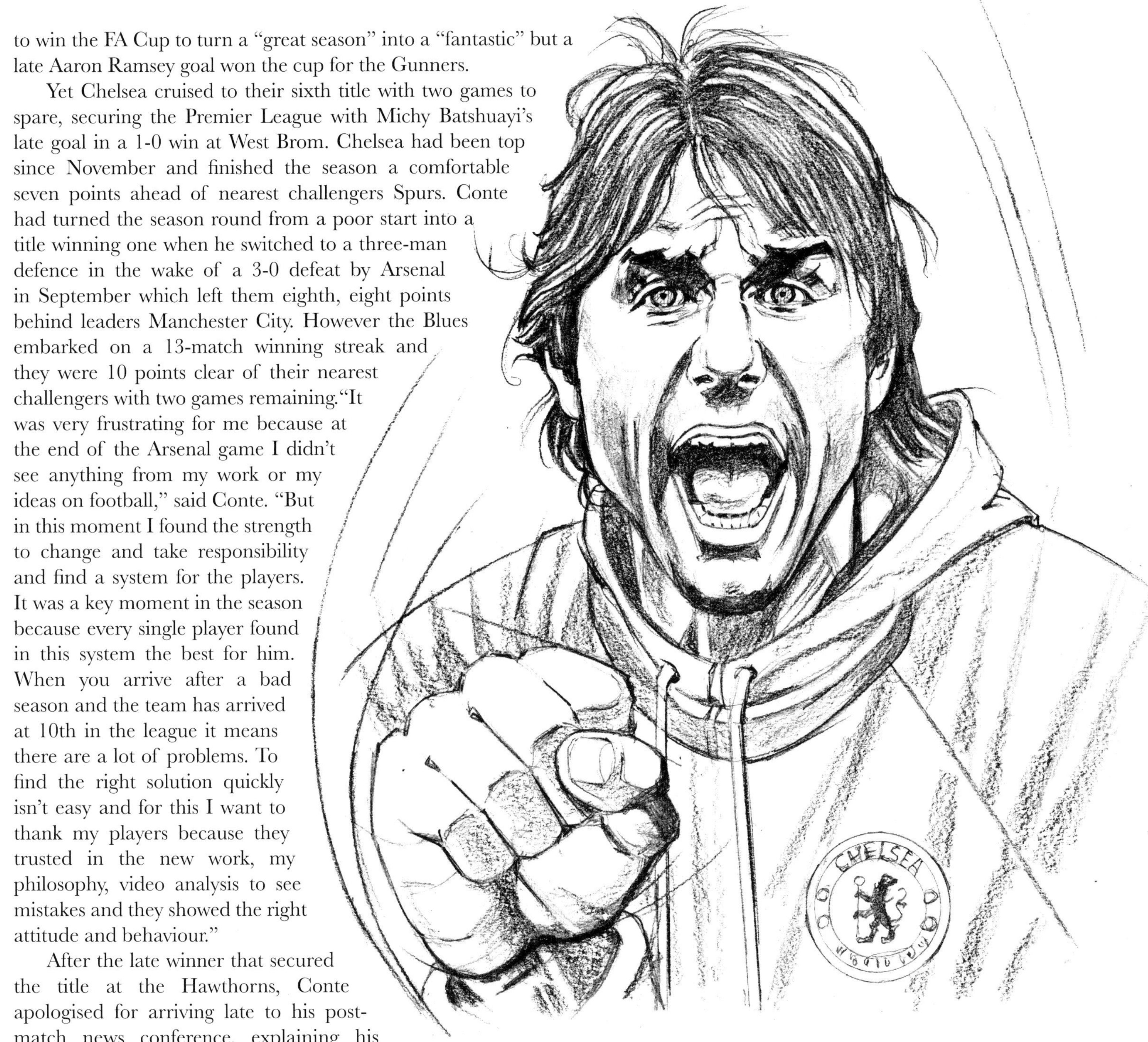

After the late winner that secured the title at the Hawthorns, Conte apologised for arriving late to his post-match news conference, explaining his players had showered him with beer and champagne and that "my suit is a disaster". He had cut his lip as he celebrated Batshuayi's winner, but it was not the first time he had been injured as a result of his joyful exuberance. "In these moments, anything can happen," he said."I hurt my lip during the Euros as well and they had to put a stitch in it after we scored against Belgium. Simone Zaza gave me a header - I don't think it was on purpose. I'm not sure if this was a header or a punch but I am ready to repeat this."

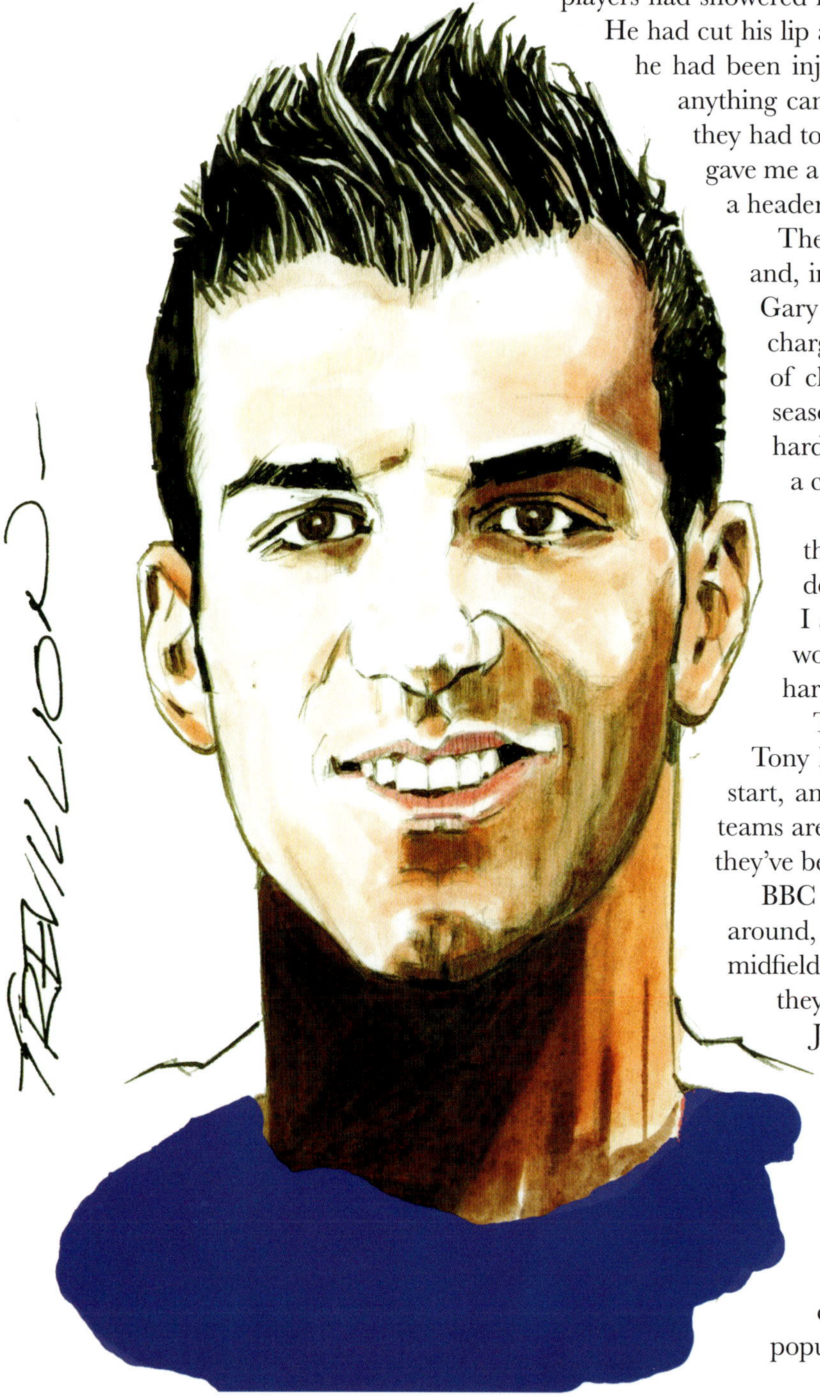

The conference came to an end when Costa, Terry and Luiz arrived and, impatient to start their celebrations, ushered him away. Captain Gary Cahill said the players always believed they could mount a title charge despite finishing 10th the previous season, 31 points adrift of champions Leicester. "We felt confident in the dressing-room all season," he said."We deserved it over the season.We worked very hard and have been the better team. It is fantastic to wrap it up with a couple of games to go. It is very difficult in this league."

David Luiz's first title was one of the reasons he returned to the club from PSG in a £34m move back in August. "When I decided to come back here I dreamed to win the Premier League. I am very happy because my dream came true," he said. "Conte works with passion every day. He deserves it because he is working hard every day."

The Chelsea boss' influence was acknowledged by West Brom's Tony Pulis. "They're worthy champions," he said. "They had a poor start, and Conte had to change things. He's made it his team. Italian teams are tactically organised and well run. He changed their shape and they've been superb from that moment onwards."

BBC analyst Jermaine Jenas gave Conte credit for turning the club around, highlighting his conversion of Victor Moses from a fringe midfielder to first-choice wing-back. "They lost their way last season, they were unrecognisable. He has come in and reinvigorated them," Jenas said, "what I like about Conte is he gave Moses a chance and trusted him. He has made him a better player and a Premier League champion."

King Conte was the title of my latest book to celebrate the managers' incredible connection with the fans and such promise after his title victory. However, the Wembley loss to Arsenal put an unexpected dampener on such a season of great promise and hope for the future. To illustrate how fickle fans can be, the cup final defeat also put a dampener on the books popularity and it didn't sell anywhere near as many copies as I would have expected.

Conte made amends by landing the FA Cup the following season but while he managed that task, his second season was filled with turmoil and disappointment, a lot of it self-inflicted. Yet he had delivered another trophy and a passionate defence of his style as supporters still loved the Italian for delivering in his first season; but it was not enough to keep his job once the dust settled after another season of uncertainty at the Bridge. Chelsea's FA Cup run put a coat of gloss on a largely disappointing season in which their title defence was so flimsy, there wasn't even a place in the top four while Champions League aspirations were ended by Barcelona at the last-16 stage.

Conte remained a hugely popular figure with fans, his name booming out as he bounded up the stairs to join his players as they prepared to lift the trophy, but as soon as celebrations were finished his departure was confirmed.

2017/18 turned out to be a fractious season with Conte outspoken about the congested festive fixture list and at times visibly agitated in news conferences when questioned about a public row with Manchester United manager José Mourinho. Then there was the sale of Nemanja Matic to Manchester United, the Serb's form helping the Old Trafford team to the runners-up spot behind runaway title winners Manchester City but these problems paled into insignificance compared to the Diego Costa saga which dogged Conte throughout the season and soured his relationship with his playing squad.

It all started when Conte sent a text to his players wishing them a good holiday at the end of the previous season, telling them to stay fit, but after Costa replied in a jokey way, the 28-year-old was told he was no longer in the manager's plans reportedly responding "Hi Diego, I hope you are well.Thanks for the season we spent together. Good luck for the next year but you are not in my plan." Costa showed the text exchange to fellow players.

Costa had scored 20 goals in 35 Premier League games to help the Blues win the title but had fallen out with Conte. "My relationship with the coach has been bad this season," admitted the Spanish striker after a 2-2 draw with Colombia: "It is a shame, I have already forwarded the message to Chelsea people to decide." The disagreement reportedly did not anger those in the boardroom, such as director Marina Granovskaia. However

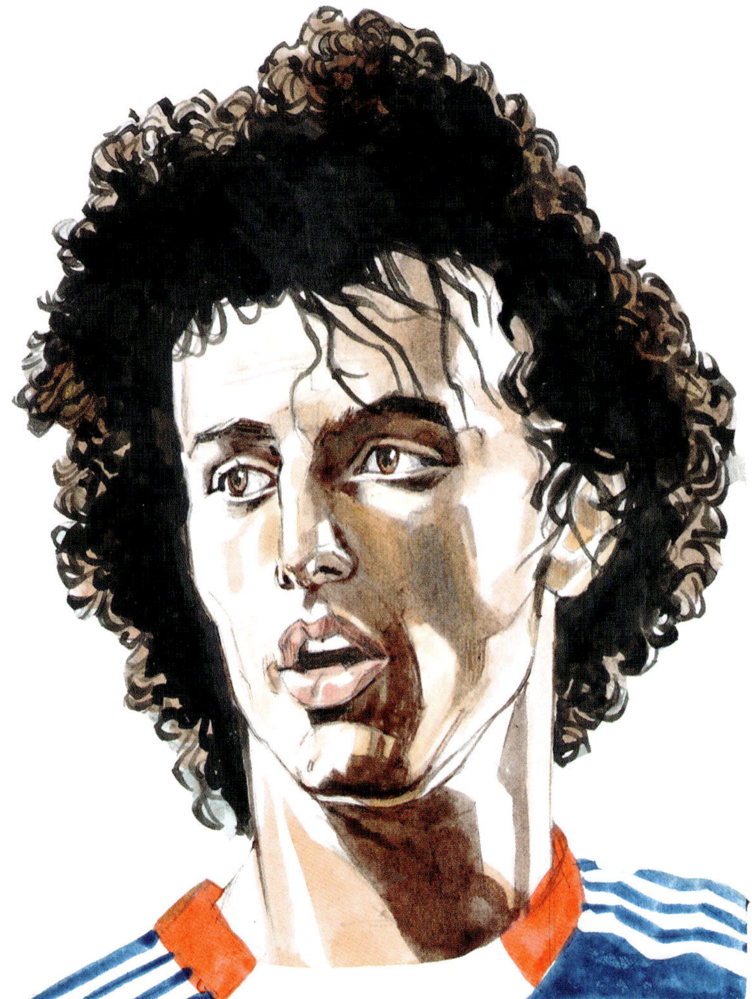

it wiped millions off Costa's asking price. Brazil-born Costa had signed for Chelsea from Atletico Madrid for £32m in 2014 and after four seasons he wanted to return, despite the La Liga club being banned from signing players until the January transfer window. "Being five months without playing? I do not know, it's complicated, but people know that I love Atletico a lot and that I love to live in Madrid," Costa said."It would be nice to go back, but it's difficult to be four or five months without playing. It's a World Cup year and there are many things to think about. I need to play, just that."

In January Costa was left out at Leicester after he had been involved in a dispute with the fitness coach, following an offer from China that would have been worth £30m a year, which Costa was eager to accept. Later in January, Tianjin Quanjian's owner said a bid to sign Costa had been scuppered by new rules over foreign players in the Chinese Super League.

But Conte's woes didn't end there, as there was inevitably bad blood with Mourinho dating from the previous season. Conte insisted he was "not mocking anyone" after appearing to antagonise Mourinho when Conte encouraged Blues fans to make more noise in the closing stages of their 4-0 hammering of United back in October 2016. Reports claimed Mourinho told the Italian at the final whistle that his actions had "humiliated" United. Conte said: "I've been a player too and I know how to behave. I always show great respect for everyone, including Manchester United." Goals from Pedro, Gary Cahill, Eden Hazard and N'Golo Kante had ensured Mourinho's first return to Chelsea since he was sacked ended in bitter disappointment. But the former Chelsea boss received a warm welcome at Stamford Bridge, however reports in the Italian media claimed Mourinho told Conte: "You don't celebrate like that at 4-0, you can do it at 1-0, otherwise it's humiliating for us."

Neither manager confirmed what was said in their post-match media conferences. "There was no incident, it was just a normal thing to do. I wasn't mocking anyone, I wouldn't do that," said Conte, "Today it was right to call our fans in a moment when I was listening to only the supporters of Manchester United at 4-0. The players, after a 4-0 win, deserved a great clap. It's very normal. If we want to cut the emotion we can go home and change our job."

Mourinho was left to lick his wounds on their heaviest Premier League defeat since the 6-1 drubbing by Manchester City in October 2011. It was the heaviest defeat for Mourinho in all competitions since Real Madrid's 5-0 defeat by Barcelona in November 2010. "To the millions of fans we have around the world they have a bad feeling and I am so sorry for that," said Mourinho. "I have to apologise as the leader of the dressing-room and the only thing I can say is I'm 100% Man Utd, not 99% for Man Utd and 1% for Chelsea. I feel deeply the situation but there is only one answer, training on Monday and keep fighting."

Yet Chelsea ultimately finished 30 points behind Premier League champions Manchester City and exited the Champions League at the last-16 stage after a 4-1 aggregate defeat by Barcelona. In mid-October the Blues were beaten by a Crystal Palace side who had gone into the match with no points from seven games, prompting Conte to dismiss rumours of unrest over his training schedule.They suffered back-to-back league defeats twice after Christmas - first by Bournemouth and Watford, and then against Manchester City and Manchester United - and a run of four straight victories late in the campaign could not secure a top-four finish.

However in contrast to previous dismissals, the process of sacking Conte seemed to drag on for most of the season - he refused to go quietly! The managerial situation dragged on into the following summer with Conte even turning up for pre-season training with one year remaining on his contract and ex-Napoli manager Maurizio Sarri expected to succeed his compatriot, and no-one expecting Conte to start the new season, even though he resumed coaching the players.

Finally Chelsea announced Conte had "parted company" with the club. A 61-word statement ended: "We wish Antonio every success in his future career." For the sixth time in eight seasons the Premier League's title-winning manager had left his job before the following summer.

Conte had a clause in his contract that guaranteed him a pay-off of £9m for the final year. He was finally sacked as Chelsea prepared to name Maurizio Sarri as their new head coach – two months after winning the FA Cup against Mourinho's United at Wembley thanks to a Hazard penalty. Conte was under contract until the summer of 2019 having only signed his new deal on July 18, 2017. Abramovich was reluctant to hand him a cheque, and hoped another job might become available which would mean an agreement could be made. It didn't and after a lengthy delay, the club bit the bullet and sacked him. Sarri became Chelsea's top target but Napoli demanded compensation, despite them having already appointed his successor in Carlo Ancelotti. Chelsea disagreed: their case was that Conte used his press conferences to accuse the board of failing to provide him with the players he wanted; Alex Sandro and Leonardo Bonucci were two targets never signed. Conte fell out with big names in the dressing-room, including David Luiz and Willian, who recently blocked him out of a picture he had posted of the team on Instagram.There were concerns that Eden Hazard might leave if Conte stayed. Chelsea claimed he was in breach of his contract. But Conte prepared a pre-season programme, just in case he kept his job. The team were due to fly to Australia a week later and he would have had a seat on the plane. Conte took training at Cobham starting the non-World Cup squad off with a double session.The players were surprised to see he was still in charge, given the rumours around the club.

Jorginho was due to follow Sarri from Napoli for £55m so Chelsea were forced to pay Conte an extra £85,000 after he won his claim for unfair dismissal. Conte won a first legal battle when an employment tribunal ordered Chelsea to pay £9m in compensation, but they argued for 10 months over the severance package since he was axed with 12 months left on the three-year deal he signed upon being appointed in 2016. Conte was so determined not to ruin his chances of a full payout that he declined an approach from Real Madrid and stayed out of work until joining Inter Milan in 2019.The club's accounts showed they had paid out £26.6m in compensation to Conte, his staff and legal proceedings associated with his dismissal, making it the most expensive sacking in football history.

An employment tribunal ruled in Conte's favour and Judge Andrew Glennie found that he was unfairly sacked saying,"The complaint of unfair dismissal is well founded. The respondent (Chelsea) shall pay to the claimant (Conte) a basic award of £1,524 and a compensatory award of £83,682, being a total of £85,206.'

Abramovich had now paid out a total of £90m on sacking managers since he took over at Stamford Bridge in 2003.

Maurizio Sarri

A Chain-Smoking Former Bank Clerk

Even by Chelsea's bizarre record of selecting managers, the next man to occupy the hot-seat was a first, Sarri was a former banker! The Italian had been a rugged, non-league centre-back mentored by the great Kurt Hamrin, the Swede who would tell his players stories about playing against Pelé in the 1958 World Cup final and all those goals he scored for Fiorentina but, unable to make a living as a footballer, Sarri worked as a foreign currency trader at the Banca Toscana attached to the international department, which involved business trips to Europe's financial centres, including the City of London. In 2001, as Italy prepared to adopt the Euro and foreign currency traders like him were no longer as useful to banks as they had been in the past, Sarri decided to take a leap of faith and leave his well-paid nine-to-five for "the only job I would do for free".

After a succession of coaching jobs in Italy's lower divisions over the next 12 years he ended up at Empoli where he won promotion to Serie A and after keeping the Tuscan team in the top flight the following season he got an offer he couldn't refuse in the shape of the top job at his boyhood club Napoli. During three years at the San Paolo Sarri did not win a major honour but guided the club to second, third and second again. Sarri was named Serie A Coach of theYear in 2016-17, and his teams were famous for an open and attacking style of play.

However any job offer from Chelsea comes with a health warning – it's fair to say that the club go through managers at a ridiculous rate, even if the post comes with a healthy remuneration package. Sarri knew he would have to deposit quite a few trophies not to have his office repossessed by Roman Abramovich's all too active bailiffs.

The new manager was joined by his star midfielder Jorginho for £50m. The Napoli play-maker was "absolutely ecstatic" to join Chelsea."It is not easy to become part of such a big team so I am very, very happy," he said. "I am excited to play in such an intense league, for a team that gives everything to play and win." The 26-year-old, born in Brazil and capped by Italy, arrived in London to complete his transfer despite Manchester City appearing favourites to sign him, but Chelsea agreed a deal with Napoli for both player and manager."We are delighted to welcome Maurizio and are looking forward to him bringing his football philosophy to Chelsea," the club director Marina Granovskaia said. "Maurizio's Napoli side played some of the most exciting football in Europe, impressing with their attacking approach and dynamism, and his coaching methods significantly improved the players at his disposal.We are delighted Jorginho has chosen to join Chelsea. He was one of the most coveted midfielders in Europe and will become an important member of the squad."

Negotiations to release Sarri from Napoli took some weeks to conclude. He was replaced there by Carlo Ancelotti but was not released from his contract, forcing Chelsea to pay a fee. Club legend Gianfranco Zola was given a role to work alongside Sarri. After earning glowing references for his tactics at Napoli, Sarri looked to have effectively introduced 'Sarri-ball' to his new players as Chelsea started their Premier League campaign with a 12-game unbeaten streak but they were soon out of title contention after losing three out of four Premier League games in January and February, including a 6-0 defeat at eventual champions Manchester City, which saw them slip to sixth in the table. Chelsea then lost 2-0 at home to Manchester United in the FA Cup and fans booed Sarri's substitutions and joined in when the visiting supporters sang "you're getting sacked in the morning".

Quite simply Sarri alienated supporters by moving N'Golo Kante, regarded as one of the best players in the world in a deep-lying midfield role, to the right of a three-man midfield to accommodate Jorginho. There was repeated speculation about Sarri's position and this increased when goalkeeper Kepa Arrizabalaga challenged his authority by refusing to be substituted in the Carabao Cup final at Wembley, shortly before Chelsea were beaten in a penalty shootout by City.

Of the 19 matches played after losing to City at Wembley, his side lost just two, as they won their first European trophy since securing the Europa League in 2012-13.They also held off the challenge ofTottenham,Arsenal and Manchester United to finish third in the league and clinch Champions League qualification.

Yet third seemed a poor return for a club that had spent a record £71m on Arrizabalaga, £50m on Jorginho and brought in former Napoli striker Gonzalo Higuain in January to replace the misfiring Alvaro Morata who went to Atletico Madrid on loan. All was not well behind the scenes as Bayern Munich made a £35m bid for Callum Hudson-Odoi, aiming to capitalise on a lack of game time for the 18-year-old, with England manager Gareth Southgate seemingly showing more faith in the youngster than the Chelsea manager. However, the winger did not leave in January and, after getting more first-team football as the campaign progressed, ruptured his Achilles tendon in April.

Given that Manchester City and Liverpool were embroiled in a ludicrous title race that saw the Anfield side lose the league having collected 97 points, being 'the best of the rest' in third might not seem so bad a return.Yet the style of the football was not quite as advertised with Premier League teams quick to figure out its weak points and Sarri slow to adapt. Added to this was the glum face of a manager who never seemed entirely happy at Chelsea or in English football while the fans never seemed overjoyed with him either, at least not until he announced he was leaving at the end of the season!

It was hardly a surprise when Sarri left Chelsea to become manager of Serie A champions Juventus on a three-year deal with compensation in excess of £5m agreed for the 60-year-old. Sarri replaced fellow Italian Massimiliano Allegri. "In talks we had following the Europa League final, Maurizio made it clear how strongly he desired to return to his native country, explaining that his reasons for wanting to return to work in Italy were significant," said Chelsea's influential director Marina Granovskaia "He also believed it important to be nearer his family, and for the well-being of his elderly parents he felt he needed to live closer to them at this point." Sarri became the ninth full-time manager to leave Chelsea under Abramovich.

The then Derby boss Frank Lampard eventually took up the reigns but Chelsea would be unable to sign players after being given a two-window transfer ban by Fifa, a decision they failed to get overturned at the Court of Arbitration for Sport.

Pat Nevin felt Sarri was capable of building on his debut season, but accepted many fans were indifferent to his departure. "I don't think they are absolutely devastated," he said. "It is one of those ones where some people wanted him to stay and some wanted him to go. I am one of the ones who would have been delighted had he stayed. However, great Chelsea managers come along like London buses every two minutes - there will be another one. He has gone. He has done a brilliant job and probably would have done even better next season. In the current situation it doesn't matter who is manager because you are not going to catch Manchester City or Liverpool at the moment."

Thomas Tuchel

Roman Abramovich's Last Appointment

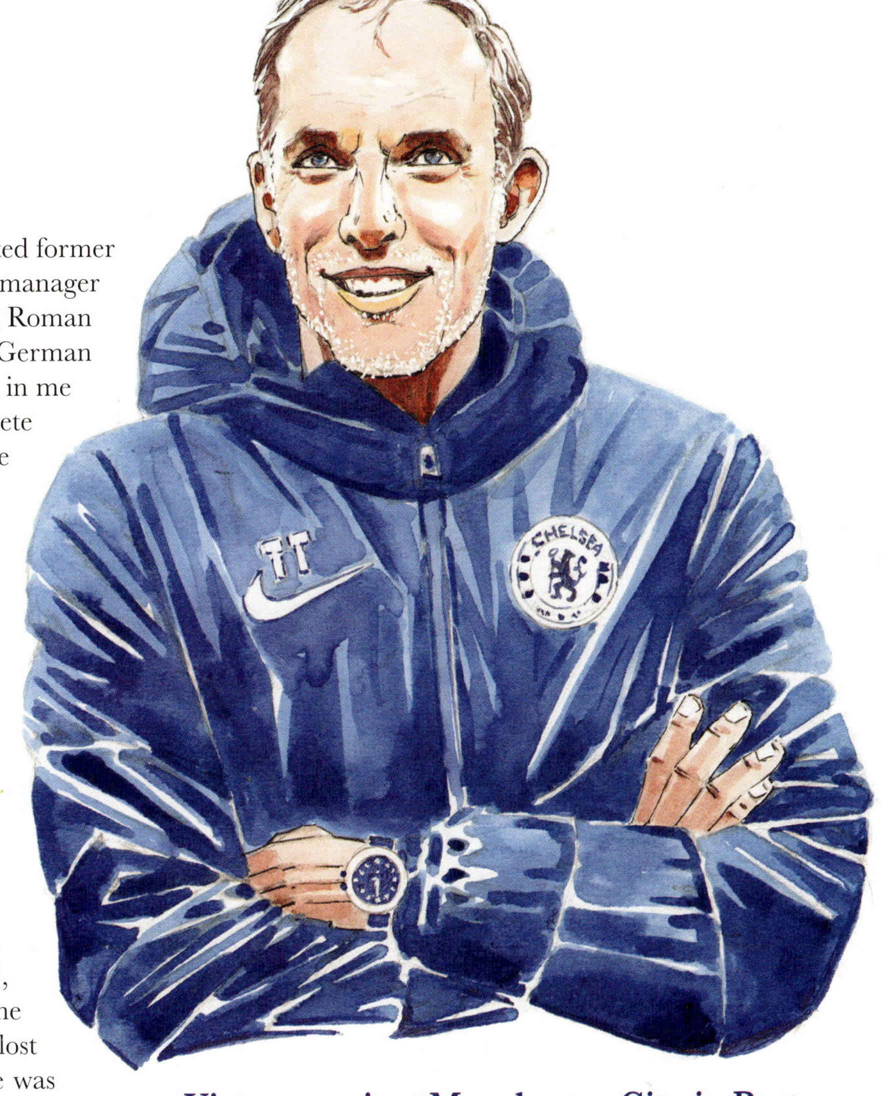

Following Frank Lampard's departure, Chelsea appointed former Paris St-Germain boss Thomas Tuchel as their new manager on an 18-month contract with an option to extend it; Roman Abramovich's eleventh permanent manager. At the time the German said, "I would like to thank Chelsea FC for their confidence in me and my staff. I cannot wait to meet my new team and compete in the most exciting league in football. I am grateful to be part of the Chelsea family. We all have the greatest respect for Frank Lampard's work and the legacy he created at Chelsea." Chelsea director Marina Granovskaia described Tuchel as "one of Europe's best coaches" adding that "there is still much to play for and much to achieve, this season and beyond".

Despite losing the 2020 Champions League Final, his CV was impressive enough; two league titles, the French Cup and the French League Cup at PSG. Previously in charge at Mainz and Borussia Dortmund - replacing Jurgen Klopp at both German clubs - Tuchel brought a reputation for being tactically astute. Tuchel had begun his career at Mainz and steered the newly-promoted team to ninth in the Bundesliga in 2009-10, he went on to win the German Cup with Borussia Dortmund in 2016-17, overseeing the development of Christian Pulisic, Ousmane Dembele and Pierre-Emerick Aubameyang. At PSG he had lost the Champions League final 1-0 to Bayern Munich and he was sacked in late December with the club third in Ligue 1, having lost four league games after months full of fights between him and sporting director Leonardo. Yet Tuchel's 75.6% win rate in Ligue 1 - over his two-and-a-half years in Paris - was the highest in the competition's history.

During his time at Dortmund, he banned head scout Sven Mislintat, who later worked for Arsenal, from the training ground because of philosophical differences and demanded certain signings from chief executive Hans-Joachim Watze and sporting director Michael Zorc.

Victory against Manchester City in Porto came via a first half Kai Havertz goal... yet it was the performance of N'Golo Kante, who seemed to be everywhere all at once, that undid favourites City. The French international put in a titanic performance keeping the Sky Blues at bay... to the clear frustration of Guardiola's men

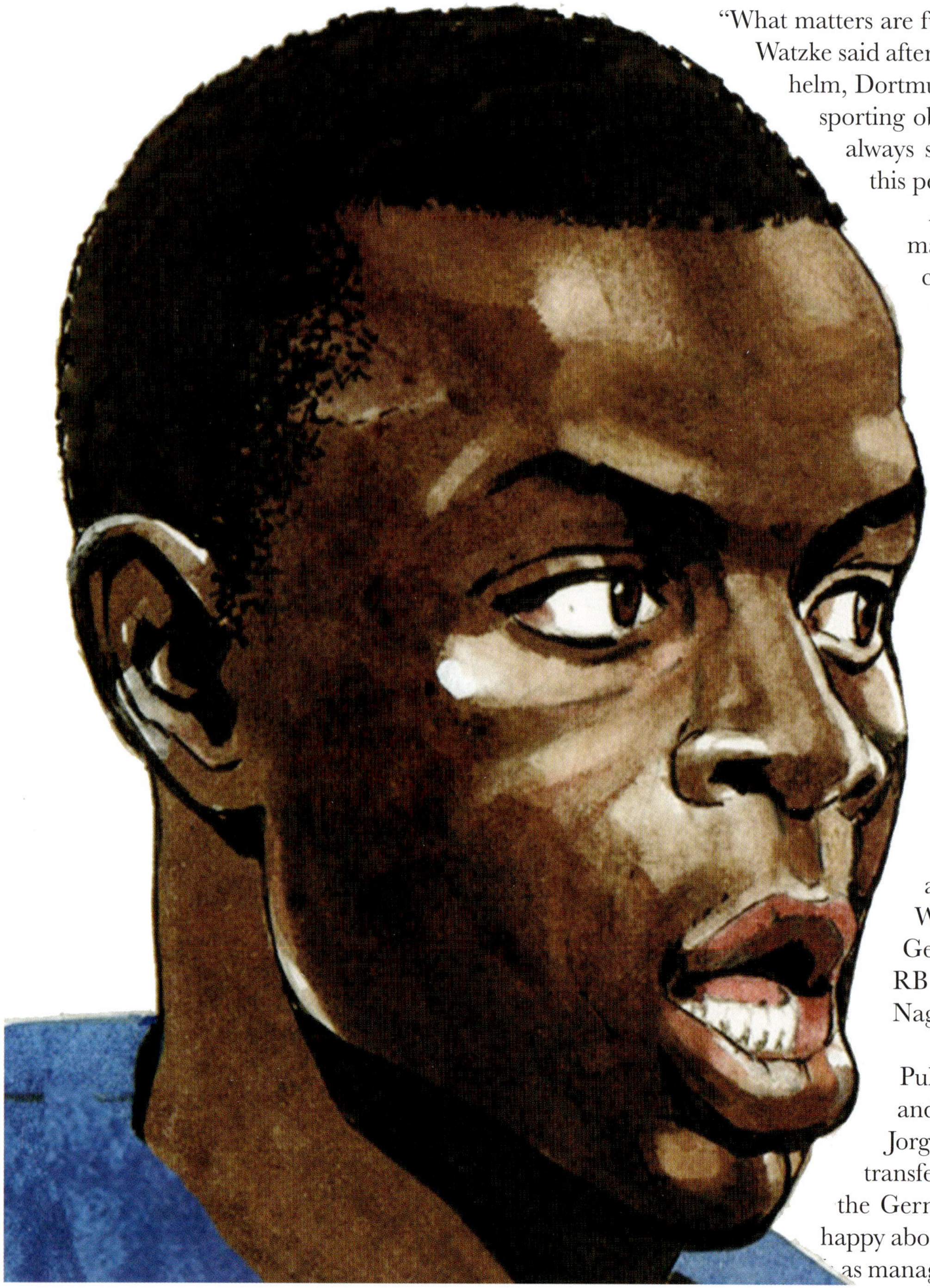

"What matters are fundamental values such as trust and respect," Watzke said after Tuchel had left. "With Thomas Tuchel at the helm, Dortmund enjoyed two successful years in which our sporting objectives were achieved. However, we did not always see eye-to-eye with the coaching staff during this period."

Although he enjoyed success at each club he managed, he always seemed to leave under a cloud and he would face a tricky situation at Chelsea as he was replacing a much loved former player and legend of the club in Frank Lampard. Chelsea had approached him shortly before Lampard's dismissal. At first, Tuchel was unsure whether he should take the job midway through the season, but he had wanted a move to the Premier League for quite some time, first engaging in talks with Chelsea in 2017 after he departed from Borussia Dortmund. He viewed the job as a chance to prove himself in England to emulate the likes of Klopp and Guardiola, who he admires.

Abramovich was convinced hiring a German coach would solve the problem of integrating, tactically, his big money forwards Werner and Havertz who were underperforming under Frank. Abramovich also sought to recreate the Klopp factor in West London. Chelsea considered several German-speaking coaches, sounding out former RB Leipzig manager Ralf Rangnick and Julian Nagelsmann's camp before settling on Tuchel.

Tuchel had worked well with Christian Pulisic at Dortmund and Thiago Silva at PSG and he asked PSG to make offers for both Jorginho and Antonio Rudiger during previous transfer windows, these players would prove key to the German's instant impact at the club. Pulisic was happy about the arrival of Tuchel. "It is a players' game. as managers only serve our players," Tuchel once said.

Rio Ferdinand was full of praise for Tuchel prior to his appointment following a meeting in Paris, saying "He is one of the most impressive managers I've met. Very insightful, a man of detail. Speaking to the players who he managed (at PSG) - Dani Alves, Gianluigi Buffon - they couldn't speak any more glowingly about him. The ambience at the club was at an all-time high. He's German and I think that's an interesting point as Kai Havertz and Timo Werner haven't caught fire yet."

Gary Neville was sure Tuchel would be sacked within two seasons if he does not perform. "Tuchel will be exposed to the exact same rules as Frank and we'll be saying the same about him in 18 months, two years. It's Chelsea... Frank has been exposed to Chelsea releasing managers every 12 to 18 months if things don't go as they want. I don't have any great deal of worry for Frank's career. Frank has had a short amount of time with a new set of players. The minute they spent the money they did, it was always going to bring more expectation and we know what happens at Chelsea when expectation comes. When you have one of the biggest budgets in the league and the biggest spend, expectation comes with it and at Chelsea their approach to managers has been consistent and Frank knew that when he got the job. Frank won't want people to feel sorry for him, he'll have an understanding that he went into a club that has always been like this with managers. The results and inconsistent form has cost him.'

Pep Guardiola called Tuchel an "exceptional manager", adding "I'm pretty sure he will have success, happy to see him here in this country. When I was at Bayern Munich I played against him at Mainz. At the last season at Dortmund he did an incredible job, the way Dortmund played was outstanding. We fought a lot as Bayern Munich to win that title. He's a friend of mine and I'm happy to see him."

Speaking two years earlier, Jurgen Klopp had praised Tuchel for his work at PSG, "A fantastic, fantastic manager. You can see really his influence, it has changed a lot their style of play, how they play, different formations and stuff like that. I know a lot of people who have worked with him, they all are full of respect for him. You cannot be in the Champions League only because of spending money, that is not how it is. You need to have on the pitch a good organisation, because all the others we are not blind. We do our job as well and you need to have the right tools in the right moments and Thomas has that."

Talking about Lampard's sacking Klopp said: "Chelsea did an incredible job in the transfer market this summer, and brought in some really good players. Things like this need time and it's real harsh to make a decision this early. Of course, Mr Abramovich gives you a chance with money but he is not the most patient person in the world. I feel for Frank because he is a young manager but he will be fine. Frank did a lot of really good stuff last year and now he can go anywhere. How many coaches have Chelsea had in the last 10 years? Quite a lot.You are either successful or you are out. For Thomas Tuchel, it is great. He is a good manager and I respect him a lot. This Chelsea squad is a present and I'm sure Thomas sees it like that."

The German was in the dugout at Stamford Bridge for the Premier League meeting with Wolves, 24 hours after arriving, just 24 hours after Lampard's exit. Tuchel was granted an exemption from Covid rules by the FA to attend matches and training upon providing a negative test before entering the UK, and then did so once again to enter a Premier League club's bubble. Outside those environments, he had to serve a quarantine period of five days.

His first task was to guide Chelsea to a top-four finish, with the club five points outside the Champions League qualification spots after Lampard's final league game in charge, a 2-0 defeat at high flying Leicester City. He drew his first match in charge to Wolves, but won his next four, eventually going unbeaten in his first 13 league games - a record for a new Chelsea manager. He secured a fourth-place finish that term, pipping Leicester to the final Champions League place on the final day despite defeat to Aston Villa. Yet it was in the Champions League that Tuchel carved his name in the club's history.

Victory against Manchester City in Porto came via a first half Kai Havertz goal assited by Mason Mount, yet it was the performance of N'Golo Kante, who seemed to be everywhere all at once, that undid favourites City. The French international put in a titanic performance keeping the Sky Blues at bay winning tackle after tackle to the clear frustration of Guardiola's men

Thomas Tuchel holds the unusual distinction of being the only permanent manager Roman Abramovich didn't fire!

Potter and Poch

Graham Potter replaced Tuchel, when the Blues were sixth, following a summer spend of £255m on transfers. New owner Todd Boehly went on another remarkable spending spree in January, shelling out £288m on Argentina midfielder Enzo Fernandez and Ukraine forward Mykhailo Mudryk were among eight mid-season signings - but the new additions struggled to click on the pitch. So out with the old, in with the new… and Potter was sacked after less than seven months in charge following a 2-0 home defeat by Aston Villa, his 11th defeat in 31 games since replacing Tuchel. Chelsea dropped to 11th in the Premier League - 12 points outside the top four - despite splashing more than £550m on new players this season alone. The club's owners said they were "disappointed" to sack Potter and added that the outgoing manager "has agreed to collaborate with the club to facilitate a smooth transition" and that Spaniard Bruno Saltor, who worked with Potter at Brighton, took charge of the team as interim head coach. In a statement, co-controlling owners Todd Boehly and Behdad Eghbali said: "We have the highest degree of respect for Graham as a coach and as a person. He has always conducted himself with professionalism and integrity and we are all disappointed in this outcome."

The decision to relieve him of his post was led by Paul Winstanley and Lawrence Stewart the co-sporting directors, with backing from chairman Boehly and co-owner Eghbali. Potter did not receive the full five years payment for his contract that he signed in 2022. He won 12 of his 31 games in charge in all competitions and managed an average of 1.27 points per game in the Premier League - the joint-lowest of any manager to take charge of 20 or more games for Chelsea in the Premier League, alongside Glenn Hoddle.

Potter's dismissal was Chelsea's 17th managerial change this century and, of the full-time incumbents of the role, his reign was by far the shortest. Only Luis Felipe Scolari (36), Andre-Villas Boas (40) and Roberto Di Matteo (42) failed to reach the 50-game mark and even interim manager Rafael Benitez (48) lasted longer than Potter. Chelsea had paid Brighton in excess of £21m in compensation to bring him to Stamford Bridge. Boehly said at the time that he fitted "our vision" and had "skills and capabilities that extend beyond the pitch which will make Chelsea a more successful club". That indicated Chelsea were looking to pursue a long-term approach in the dugout after sacking Tuchel. After a promising start of nine games unbeaten, including five successive victories and comfortable qualification for the knock-out stages of the Champions League, it all began to unravel just before the break for the World Cup. The slide began with a 4-1 humbling at his former club Brighton, followed by defeats against Arsenal and Newcastle and a Carabao Cup exit at Manchester City. Returning from the World Cup break Chelsea began with a 2-0 victory over Bournemouth, but won just three of their next 13 league matches. Potter's side were thumped 4-0 at Manchester City in the FA Cup third round in January, but overturned a first-leg deficit against Borussia Dortmund to reach the Champions League quarter-finals. In February, Potter revealed that his mental health had suffered after he and his family received anonymous abuse following the club's poor run of form.

Potter was ditched prior to Chelsea's home game against Liverpool in the Premier League and were due to face Real Madrid in the first leg of their Champions League quarter-final. While Chelsea had acquired an unwanted reputation for sacking managers, Potter was already the 13th managerial casualty in the Premier League, three more than any previous season, with Leicester sacking Brendan Rodgers. "Along with our incredible fans, we will all be getting behind Bruno and the team as we focus on the rest of the season," the Chelsea owners added. "We have 10 Premier League games remaining and a Champions League quarter-final ahead. We will put every effort and commitment into every one of those games so that we can end the season on a high."

Until his brief reign at Chelsea, Potter had enjoyed managerial success at each of the three clubs he had served. He led Swedish side Ostersunds from the fourth tier into the top flight with three promotions in five seasons and won the 2017 Swedish Cup, earning a spot in the Europa League and reaching the knock-out stages of that competition. In his one subsequent season with Swansea City in 2018-19, they finished 10th in the Championship following relegation from the top flight and reached the FA Cup quarter-finals where they led Manchester City 2-0 before losing 3-2.Potter was then recruited by Brighton and, after three seasons of steady progress, led them to their highest-ever Premier League finish of ninth, as well as collecting plenty of praise for their style of play. They sat fourth in this season's table when he left for Chelsea in September. Chelsea, though, proved a step too far, particularly as he couldn't cope with so much expensive and untried talent entering the training ground so frequently that he could hardly organise a training session or practice match without several multi-million pound new recruits hardly getting a kick!

After her Chelsea side's Women's Super League win over Aston Villa, boss Emma Hayes said: "Obviously I'm upset for Graham and the club. I know everybody wanted to make it work. If the owners feel like they have to go in another direction then of course, as always, I support the decisions and wish Graham the best. With 10 games left to play in the Premier League, I'm sure the boys will do everything to get us back on track. I'm a manager and I'm always gutted when managers lose their job."

Interim boss Frank Lampard took Chelsea to 12th in the Premier League - their lowest finish for more than 25 years. Next, Chelsea appointed former Tottenham and Paris St-Germain boss Mauricio Pochettino. The Argentine, 51, began his new role on 1 July 2023 on a two-year contract, with an option of a further year. "Mauricio is a world-class coach with an outstanding track record. We are all looking forward to having him on board," the club said. Chelsea insisted Pochettino was first choice and the only manager who was brought into the club for talks. He would work with sporting directors Paul Winstanley and Lawrence Stewart. "Mauricio's experience, standards of excellence, leadership qualities and character will serve Chelsea Football Club well as we move forward," Winstanley and Stewart said in a statement. "He is a winning coach, who has worked at the highest levels, in multiple leagues and languages. His ethos, tactical approach and commitment to development all made him the exceptional candidate." Pochettino was Chelsea's sixth permanent manager in five years following the sacking of Thomas Tuchel and Graham Potter in the previous season, which led to Lampard taking charge on a temporary basis. He was also the fourth boss of new fledgling owner Todd Boehly's reign. Since Boehly took over, Chelsea had

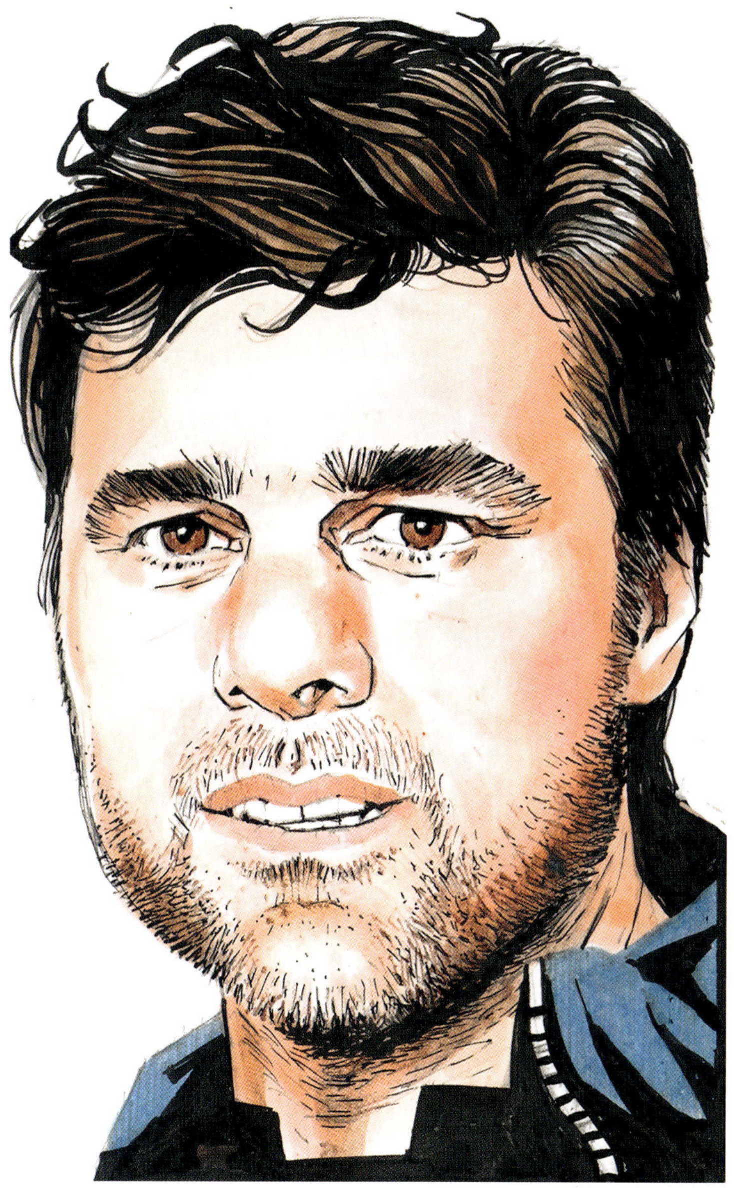

spent more than £550m on players with their Premier League record of £288m in January totalling more than all the clubs in the Bundesliga, La Liga, Serie A and Ligue 1 combined. The Blues lost to Real Madrid in the quarter-finals of the Champions League and suffered third-round exits in both the FA Cup and Carabao Cup.

Pochettino had been linked with a return to Tottenham after

they parted company with Antonio Conte in March, but he joined his former club's London rivals instead. Having started his managerial career with Espanyol before a 16-month spell at Southampton, he then managed Spurs from 2014 to 2019, guiding his side to the League Cup final in 2015 and a Premier League runners-up spot in 2016-17, with Spurs missing out on winning both to Chelsea, and the 2019 Champions League final. He oversaw an infamous London derby in May 2016 in which Spurs picked up nine yellow cards compared with three for the Blues, the result ending their title hopes for the season. Following his spell at Tottenham, Pochettino took over from Tuchel at PSG in January 2021. The French club finished second in Ligue 1 at the end of the 2020-21 season but did win the Coupe de France and the Trophee des Champions, which were the first trophies of Pochettino's managerial career. He initially turned down Boehly until he was offered more control. He needed to control the agenda as much as possible, something he could not do at PSG.

Pochettino's first season was filled with up and downs, mostly downs, with a young and inconsistent team searching to forge a team ethic. Yet ahead of his 400th game in English football, fittingly against Spurs at Stamford Bridge, he said moving to England was "one of the best decisions in my life". "Amazing. I think it is a dream come true. For me, to think and to come here to England and become a coach here, it was impossible thinking but after the decision of my wife and my friend here Jesus [Perez]," Pochettino said. "They convinced me to join Southampton. That was one of the best decisions in my life to come here to England and enjoy this great football country. Of course, I feel really comfortable. It is like home." Pochettino spent five years in charge of Tottenham before he was sacked in 2019. During that time he led them to the Champions League final in 2018-19, the League Cup final in his first full season and to second place in the Premier League in 2017. Chelsea had beaten Spurs 4-1 earlier in the season in a defining game for his old club when they had two men dismissed. "It was special when we played there because it was my first time after I left the club but now it is different," he said. "It is always emotional because we are going to meet people we worked with for a long period. Yes, I cannot hide my emotion for the club and I think it is going to be emotional."

He suggested he would need more time to make Chelsea a consistent force after a 2-0 win over Spurs, but with questions over his future dogging him for weeks, he said he realised remaining at the club is 'not my decision'. After an FA Cup semi-final defeat to Manchester City, a 5-0 thrashing by high riding Arsenal and a draw at high-flying Aston Villa - the Blues were back to winning ways courtesy of headers from Trevoh Chalobah and Nicolas Jackson to go eighth in the table. "With this team, with young guys, of course I have the responsibility," Pochettino commented afterwards, "But at the same time, we know the circumstances. I want to say, enough is enough, all the managers need time to translate their ideas and their philosophy. More when the team is [young like ours]. We need to have time. But it is not my decision." Asked if he feared the decision will be taken out of his hand, Pochettino continued: "I don't know, it is difficult to see every single week that I am [under] scrutiny and judgement, yes. But it is not my decision to be here or not to be here."

José Mourinho's availability raised the intriguing prospect of a third spell in charge at Stamford Bridge and William Gallas urged his old club to reappoint José as speculation continued to mount over the future of Poch. Gallas, who won two Premier League titles at Chelsea under Mourinho, felt that of all the options available to him a return to West London represents the best fit. "I really hope that there is an opportunity for José Mourinho to come back and manage another big club in the Premier League next season," Gallas remarked, "He has to do something because he is a special manager. I want to see him coaching again. I would love to see him back in the Premier League managing a big club. The Premier League is about to lose Jurgen Klopp. Next season, the only big, big managers in the league will be Pep Guardiola and Mikel Arteta, and Mikel hasn't won the league yet. There is room for another prestigious manager to come in and compete with those two and I think that José Mourinho could be the man to do it. We need one more big manager in the Premier League. If Mourinho came back, it would be good for the Premier League and it would be exciting. I think everyone would be excited by the prospect of seeing Mourinho pitting his wits against Pep Guardiola and Mikel Arteta – something would happen. There would be fireworks."

Asked if he saw any potential opportunities for Mourinho, he added: "That is a good question. I actually think the best club for him would be to come back to Chelsea. That would be the best possible option for Mourinho. The best thing for Mourinho would be to return to Chelsea. The question is, if he comes back to Chelsea, he will need players with a different mentality and players with more quality than Chelsea currently have. He asks a lot of his players – he demands a lot – and that can be a problem for some players that don't have the quality to give him what he needs."å

Todd Boehly

The Toddfather

In just two years, Chelsea new owners, Clearlake Capital, headed by American Todd Boehly have managed to outdo trigger-happy Roman Abramovich's 19 year reign. The Russian oversaw the hiring of 15 managers, an average of 0.78 managers a season. In just over two years, Clearlake have sacked three managers, an average of 1.5 managers a season - double the Russian's rate.

Their first sackee, Thomas Tuchel, was inherited, but the German manager came with a pedigree having previously managed Borussia Dortmund and Paris Saint-Germain, he was considered one of the contemporary game's finest tacticians. He pulled off the seemingly impossible in the 2020-21 season, rescuing a stuttering season following Frank Lampard's reign, and winning the Champions League. A Super Cup and Club World Cup win the following season bolstered his position, as he guided the club through the start of Russia's invasion of Ukraine. With Abramovich sanctioned by the UK government, Tuchel pledged to "drive a seven-seater" to Lille himself to see Chelsea feature in their Champions League tie if the club could not circumvent their mandated travel cap. He was a figure of stability and continuity during the turbulence behind the scenes. Yet, Tuchel's time at Chelsea came to a murky end, just 100 days after BlueCo's takeover. Chelsea sat sixth in the table that September, and had started their Champions League campaign with a dismal 1-0 defeat to Dinamo Zagreb in Croatia. But the cracks were more prominent away from the pitch, amid speculation that Tuchel had lost the support of a number of key voices in the dressing-room. Telling was Boehley's post-mortem, "Our vision for the club was to find a manager who really wanted to collaborate with us, a coach who really wanted to collaborate," the American chief executive said. "There are a lot of walls to break down at Chelsea. Before, the first team and Academy didn't really share data, didn't share information about where the top players were coming from. Our goal is to bring a team together; all of that needs to be a well-oiled machine. The reality of our decision was that we weren't sure that Thomas saw it the same way we saw it. No one is right or wrong, we just didn't have a shared vision for the future. It wasn't about Zagreb, it was about the shared vision for what we wanted Chelsea to look like." The club should have held on to Tuchel for the season to set up an orderly transition as none of the conditions of Tuchel's sacking primed conditions for his replacement later that month. Graham Potter was a manager far more emblematic of the new ownership's vision for the club, a progressive and creative head coach who had over-achieved with Brighton. The south coast club were a model for Chelsea's new era due to their sophisticated usage of data as Chelsea sought to replicate their formula with on-pitch talents, sporting directors, and coaches all moving north to London. For all of Potter's impressive work with the south coast club, the initial mountain to climb for the incoming coach in autumn 2022 was a raft of a transfers he hadn't requested. Some, like former Arsenal target-man Pierre-Emerick Aubameyang, had been specifically advocated for by his predecessor.

Potter had never attended a Champions League match, let alone managed a two-time winner against a seven-time champion in AC Milan, the Blues' group stage rivals. A protracted break for the 2022 World Cup in Qatar scythed through the club's budding momentum, and Potter's chances of finding harmony within his over-stuffed squad was further hampered by another dazzling transfer window spend including the arrival of World Cup winner Enzo Fernandez and Mykhailo Mudryk. A team of talented individuals could only finish 11th. In circumstances similar to his successor, Potter received his marching orders just as Chelsea seemed to be turning a corner. But too many players felt the instability with Potter's inexperience transparent when coping with stars with far bigger egos than his own modest and good-natured personality. With just two months left of the season,

Potter was out with his assistant Bruno Saltor staying on to oversee just one match - a 0-0 draw against Liverpool. "The timing is quite stunning because it coincides with me starting the job here. Now there's another coaching vacancy. That's all," Tuchel told reporters shortly after he was unveiled at Bayern Munich. "It was an intense time. But the club has changed massively. That helped me to find some distance," he added.

Next was the appointment of Lampard as interim manager in April 2023 with Boehly having done so on the advice of his close acquaintance comedian James Corden, who was friendly with the Chelsea icon after meeting him on *A League Of Their Own*, an allegation denied by Lampard himself. Earlier in the season Lampard had been fired by Everton after 11 losses in 14 games, so it came as no surprise when Lampard oversaw a miserable end to the season, Chelsea winning just one of their 11 games. Frank was brutally honest when discussing the squad's fitness levels and training conditions and departed at the end of the season.

Mauricio Pochettino's appointment represented another fresh start. The incoming manager would have a pre-season. He appeared to blend the twin values of experience with top-flight football and a 'visionary' style. Injuries were so debilitating that Pochettino barely trained during summer 2023 after signing Romeo Lavia, and the Argentine lasted just a few days short of a year at Chelsea despite an encouraging end to a turbulent campaign.

Poch took charge on 1 July signing a two-year contract with the option of a further 12 months, but was instantly under pressure after an underwhelming first half of the season before a run of five successive wins at the end of the season ensured a sixth place finish. Chelsea reached the Carabao Cup Final where they faced an injury depleted Liverpool team forced to field half of their youth team. They missed chance after chance before succumbing to a late Virgil Van Dijk header. It was a result that didn't dispel the widely held view that, as good as he was a coach, Pochettino lacked that killer instinct. Chelsea also reached semi-finals of the FA Cup but were bundled out by champions Manchester City. Despite the startling arrival of Cole Palmer to the club and some incredible wins, not least a famous come-from-behind victory over Manchester United which saw them score twice in injury time, Poch's first season was below average and only reinforced supporters doubts about him.

Nevertheless having struggled to win over the support, there were considerable complaints following his sacking. There's little doubt that Chelsea's form and style improved during the season and they emerged as dangerous opponents for clubs fighting it out at the top of the table, which hadn't been the case under Potter, a point underlined in the manager's farewell message, "Thank you to the Chelsea ownership group and sporting directors for the opportunity. The club is now well positioned to keep moving forward in the Premier League and Europe in the years to come."

Chelsea's hierarchy had seemingly made up their minds for some time and expressed interest in Ipswich manager Kieran McKenna, Sporting's Ruben Amorim and Burnley's Vincent Kompany. The return of José Mourinho or Thomas Tuchel might be the fans' choice but the Americans were looking for young talent.

Pochettino departed on amicable terms; he had even expressed some concerns himself about staying and when the time came it was inevitable that he would go, he felt leaving was the right decision following discussions with senior club officials. His mission had been to mould Chelsea into credible title contenders again after the new owners £747m expenditure on transfers during the 2022-23 campaign. He also enjoyed a significant budget, with a further £400m-plus spent on players, including Cole Palmer, Nicolas Jackson, Moises Caicedo and Christopher Nkunku. Chelsea spent more than £1bn on transfers since Todd Boehly's takeover in May 2022, and were described by Sky Sports pundit Gary Neville as "billion-pound bottle-jobs" after losing the Carabao final against a weakened Liverpool side.

In March, Pochettino addressed booing from some sections of the Stamford Bridge crowd, who chanted the name of Mourinho during a 2-2 draw with Brentford. He said: "Maybe if I was a fan, I'd be the same because we are not matching the expectation." He won back support following a 6-0 thrashing of Everton in April and a 5-0 victory against West Ham in May, although a 5-0 defeat at Arsenal in between those two results felt like another step backwards.

While some fans were surprised, Pochettino was booed on several occasions as he struggled to win over supporters, after his positive comments about Tottenham combined with mixed results had put his future on a knife edge for several months. Behind the scenes, Chairman Boehly called for patience and met "Poch" the day before the final game of the season. Co-controlling owner Behdad Eghbali is the key decision-maker, so crucial in that end-of-season review meeting. Fellow Clearlake Capital co-founder and board member José Feliciano remained in London for the review since Chelsea won the Women's Super League. Along with sporting directors Winstanley and Stewart are the main protagonists in the room despite support from the squad and senior staff for Pochettino. Signs of discontent from Pochettino were apparent at press conferences when he aired concerns about injuries and the composition of his young, inexperienced squad, exposing the decision-makers to criticism. 'Poch' remained open to continuing depending on the outcome of the post-season meeting, despite publicly expressing concerns in the final weeks of his tenure.

Chelsea spent more than £1bn on transfers since Todd Boehly's takeover in May 2022, and were described by Sky Sports pundit Gary Neville as "billion-pound bottle-jobs" after losing the Carabao final against a weakened Liverpool side.

After Poch's departure, John Terry posted on Instagram: "Gutted to see @ pochettino, @jpp_71 [Jesus Perez] @ sebpochettino Leave. I just hope we don't sign or sell any players until we get a manager in."

Pat Nevin believed issues over his "level of control" were behind the parting of the ways. "Just in the past two or three months it looked like Pochettino had actually brought them together. I don't think this is about how he's performed. I think it's about the level of control, if indeed he has any, on things like transfers. Ownership and directors of clubs are now looking for a coach, not a manager. They want to choose the players, deliver them and find someone to coach them. But most 'managers' believe they know what they need to make the team better. If they've got minimal input, they're put in the invidious position where they must decide if that's what they want or would they rather go somewhere they can have some input. In the simplest of terms, they're the ones who pay the price if it goes wrong, even if the squad are not 'their' players. As for how the fans feel, in the end it's always about results. As those improved, supporters who had been uncertain or actually quite antagonistic towards Poch had started to soften their stance. Most real football fans have some understanding of the game, especially what is going on at their own club, and I think most of them understand he was given a tough deal when he came in. The owners are very hard to second-guess, but I think they'll look for someone who is less of a big name next - someone who is willing to work to their methodology. Chelsea are not the only club who are moving towards this model but theirs seems to be the most extreme version of it. You don't know how well it will work until next season."

Pat Nevin believed the plan of the owners might be more important than the identity of his successor. "But does it really matter who the manager is? I'm not sure. That sounds like a strange thing to say, but if your only input is to go and work with the players you're given, then it depends on the quality of players that are there. There are plenty of good coaches out there they could get, but the real question is: has the signing policy worked? It's a very different, unusual, radical methodology. If you've spent a billion quid and it doesn't work next season and if you've underperformed in comparison to every other club's spending, then it's not the manager or the coach who has blown it - it's the people above who are making the decisions."

Following Poch's sacking players took to social media. Cole Palmer said: "Gaffer, thank you for everything you have done for me and making my dreams come true. All the best." The striker, who was voted the Professional Footballer's Association Premier League fans' Player Of The Year for 2023-24 with 22 goals and 11 assists was also named the club's player of the season and players' player of the season. The 22-year-old was included in Gareth Southgate's provisional England squad for Euro 2024 where he was considered their best attacking player despite only featuring as a substitute.

Pochettino had seemed to be getting the best out of him as his fantastic season proved, but how would the next manager handle him and the other talented players in Chelsea's overblown squad?

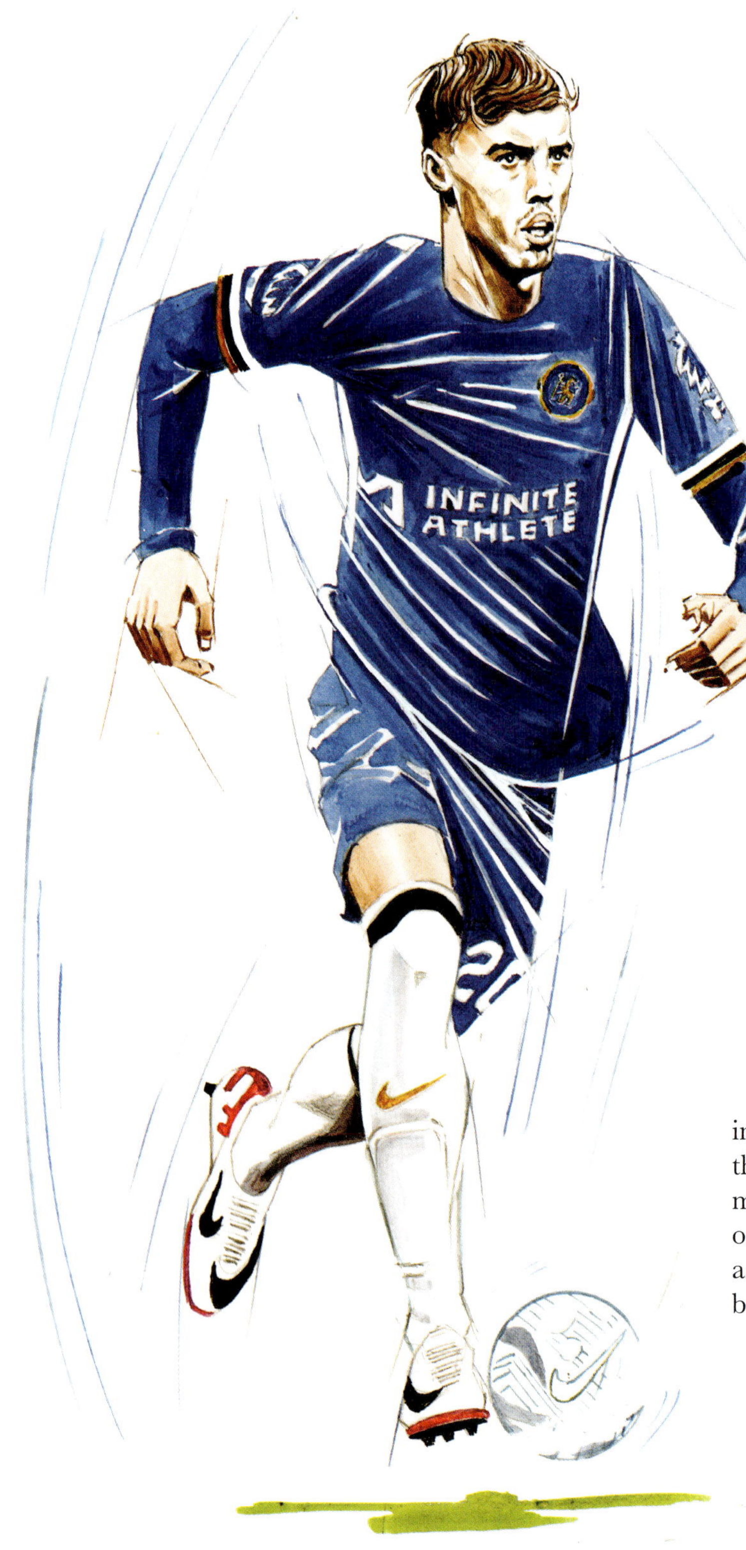

Cole Palmer

The Meteoric Rise of a Boy Wonder

Manchester United fan Cole Palmer may have been named after his boyhood club's treble-winning striker, but he emerged as Chelsea's star performer in a season that saw manager Mauricio Pochettino struggle to balance a huge squad after a rash of expensive summer signings failed to make their mark. Palmer, a surprise £40m arrival from Manchester City on transfer deadline day, quickly earned the nickname 'Cold' for his fearlessness from the spot, notably converting a last minute penalty in a 4-4 draw against his former club. The goals flowed more freely in December, leading to his nomination for the Player of the Month award, and he became the first Chelsea player aged under 21 to score ten Premier League goals and was nominated Men's Young Player of the Year at the 2024 London Football Awards in February. At the end of the season he starred at the Euros and in August he was named PFA Young Player of the Year.

Cole rose to prominence in April 2024 scoring seven goals in just four games. He opened the month by notching a memorable hat-trick, including goals in the 100th and 101st minutes, as Chelsea fought back at home in last-gasp fashion to overcome Manchester United in a seven-goal thriller. Eleven days later he notched a 'perfect' treble inside just 29 minutes and added a fourth from the penalty spot during a 6-0 mauling of Everton on April 15. The hugely influential Palmer also had an assist for Noni Madueke in the 2-2 draw at Sheffield United before being sidelined for the 5-0 demolition by title-chasing Arsenal at the Emirates Stadium.

He was the first Blues player to be awarded Player of the Month since the now-retired Eden Hazard who took the prize in September 2018. Palmer was on then nominated for both the Premier League's Player of the Season and Young Player of the

Season awards, and went on to win the Player of the Year and Players' Player of the Year at a Chelsea awards ceremony at Stamford Bridge. No Blues player has won Premier League Player of the Year honours since N'Golo Kante back in 2016-17.

Palmer finished second behind Erling Haaland in the race for the Premier League Golden Boot after scoring his 21st top-flight goal of the season in the 5-0 thrashing of London rivals West Ham, with his former City team-mate notching four against Wolves the day before to take his tally to 25.

Cole's meteoric rise didn't end there as he earned his first senior England caps and was named in Gareth Southgate's Three Lions squad for the European Championship finals in Germany where he was used sparingly but, having scored a spectacular equaliser in the final against Spain, he became just the fourth Englishman to score in a major final after Geoff Hurst, Martin Peters and Luke Shaw.

Chelsea responded to Palmer's sensational start by extending his contract by a further two years to 2033 in August. Of all the signings made by Clearlake since their arrival, Palmer is the outstanding acquisition and the club's future now seems to rest on his shoulders.

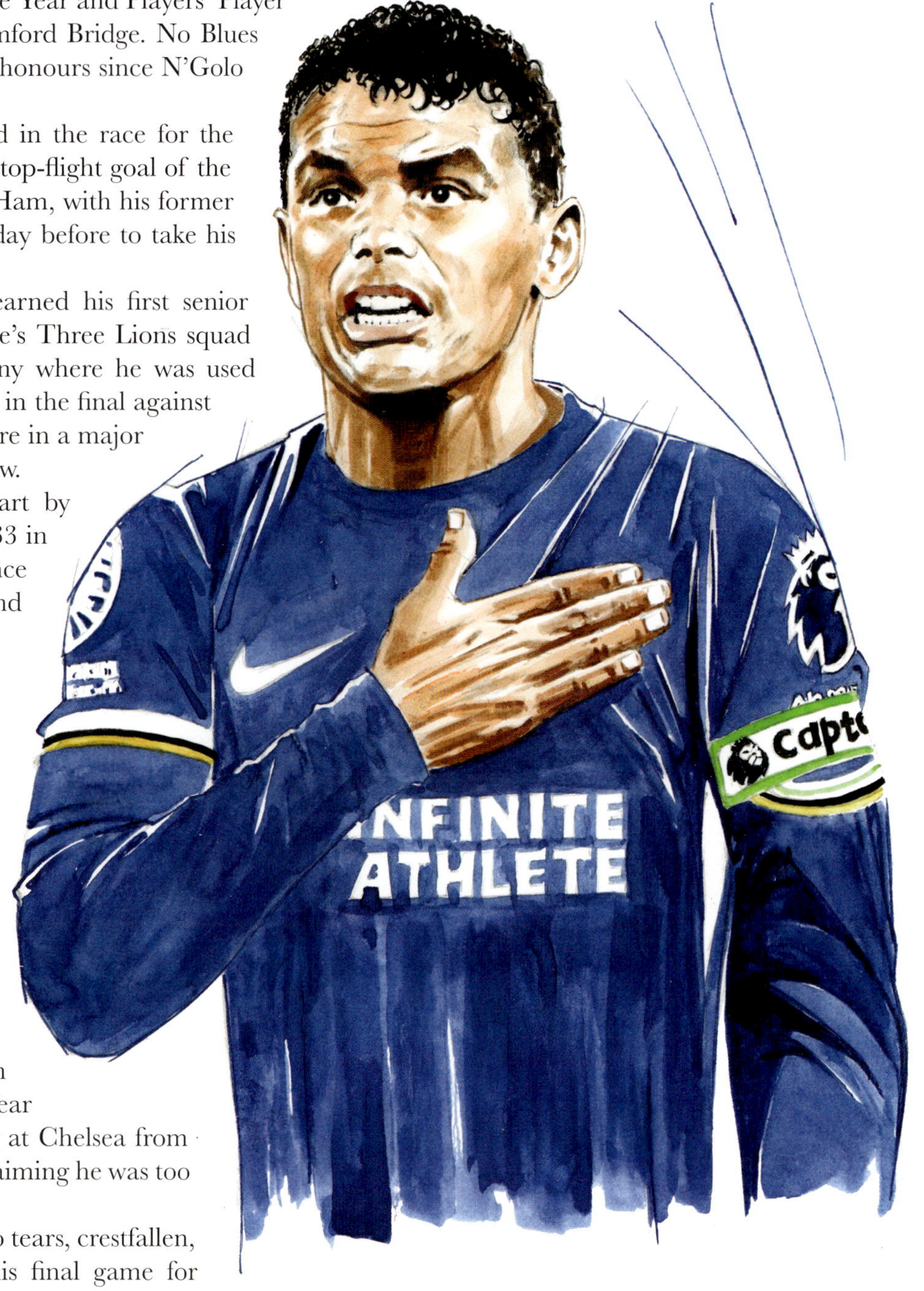

Thiago Silva

A Great Leader of Men

When Thiago Silva was allowed to leave for Fluminense on July 1 2024 the 39-year-old departed Stamford Bridge having made more than 150 appearances and lifted the Champions League, Club World Cup, and UEFA Super Cup. He forged a lasting bond with supporters and was named the club's Player of the Year at the end of the 2022/23 campaign after arriving at Chelsea from Paris St-Germain in August 2020, with the media claiming he was too old for the Premier League!

There is an iconic image of the Brazilian close to tears, crestfallen, walking past the Champions League trophy in his final game for the Paris club. Thomas Tuchel's PSG had lost the final 1-0 to Bayern Munich in front of an empty stadium in Lisbon. The then 35-year-old Silva departed as a club legend but had fallen victim to the Qatar-backed Parisians perennial European heartache, craving the greatest prize in club football with more and more chaotic results.

At his veteran stage Silva could have been forgiven for thinking that dream of ever landing that elusive prize was gone forever, but then he signed a one-year deal to join a Chelsea side on the back of a fourth-placed finish under Frank Lampard - 33 points behind champions Liverpool - having just emerged from a transfer ban. Just under five months later Lampard was sacked with the Blues ninth in the Premier League but a year on from their mutual heartbreak, Silva and Tuchel stood together again after a Champions League final - this time with winners medals around their necks.

When the Covid-19 pandemic prevented any fans from being in Stamford Bridge for the quarter-final round of 16 win over Atletico, the injured Silva's wild celebrations from the stand won the hearts of every Chelsea fan.

In the three seasons since his connection to the fans has never wavered, a connection he described in his farewell message as an "indescribable love" in a tough period where Blues fans have had few heroes. Such is his affection for Chelsea that the Brazilian stopper said he "hopes to leave the door open" for a return to the club in some capacity in the future.

His wife, Belle, who regularly shared her thoughts on her husband's career, shared snaps of Stamford Bridge on her Instagram account, with one post captioned 'end of an era' as she helped clear Silva's player's box - which ordinarily costs £91,000 per person - inside the ground. In the video, items included Silva lifting the Club World Cup with Chelsea, as she approached a door to the box before entering. Inside were three other people, with one person saying to the camera: "I know, the end of an era." The second clip was captioned: "Bye bye box 23," as Belle filmed the Stamford Bridge pitch before showing off a number of other pictures. Some showed the veteran with his wife and children, while others featured some action shots from his time at the Blues. In April, she posted three emojis representing see no evil, speak no evil and hear no evil following a 5-0 defeat by Arsenal, in which Silva played just 12 minutes. After a 4-2 loss against Wolves, meanwhile, she posted to social media: "It's time to change. If you wait any longer it will be too late," leading to fans suggesting she was calling for manager Mauricio Pochettino to be sacked. She later apologised, posting: "I'm sorry that my personal outburst as a passionate Chelsea fan has caused such an impact. I'm passionate about the team, I thrive on victories and I'm saddened by defeats. We all want the same thing, a winning team, come on Chelsea!"

Thiago's career nearly ended before it began after he contracted tuberculosis while on loan at Dynamo Moscow from Porto. After recovering he moved to Fluminese where he won the Copa do Brasil in 2007. In 2009 he moved to AC Milan where he won a Series A title which prompted PSG to buy him for a then record 42m Euros in 2012, making him the most expensive defender up until then. He won seven league titles and six cups at the Parc des Princes but the big one had always eluded him until Chelsea's win in 2021.

Thiago had been Brazil captain when they hosted the World Cup in 2014 and made 113 appearances for the Seleção.

Enzo Maresca

Enzo Maresca replaced Mauricio Pochettino on an unexpectedly long five year contract with an option for a sixth year which left Chelsea fans wondering if the Italian coach could buck the trend of trigger-happy owners and find some stability and continuity for the team.Chelsea's new owners believe the man nicknamed "Diet Peps" because of his association with Pep Guardiola (they even look alike) is a major positive. The man who once wrote a thesis entitled *Football and Chess* based on positional strategy and alignment of forces has a lot to do to convince Chelsea fans the club has made the right choice.

Maresca will need the right moves after his chess dissertation at the Coverciano, Italy's university of football in the foothills of Florence to find a solution after the under-achievement under Clearlake's ownership. Maresca said of his dissertation:

“There are a lot of similarities (between football and chess). The most important is positional play and strategy. For a coach, it’s important to have the mentality of a chess player - develop a plan, study counter-moves, choose the arrangement of the pieces.”

An acolyte of Pep, and part of Manchester City’s Treble-winning back room team, his approach is based on dominating possession and territory. Some fans christened him ‘Diet Pep’. He had a stint in charge of Manchester City’s under-23 side before returning to the club to work as Pep’s assistant in June 2022. After playing a role in City’s Treble-winning campaign in 2022-23, he moved to the King Power Stadium to bring Leicester back to the Premier League at the first time of asking. The Foxes were 12 points clear at the top of the Championship in mid-February and, despite going on a run of six defeats in 10 league games, they found form again in April to wrap up the title. Alongside their league success, Leicester also reached the last eight of the FA Cup, but lost a quarter-final to Maresca’s new club Chelsea. “To join Chelsea, one of the biggest clubs in the world, is a dream for any coach,” he said. “It is why I am so excited by this opportunity. I look forward to working with a very talented group of players and staff to develop a team that continues the club’s tradition of success and makes our fans proud.”

Maresca had won over Chelsea’s key decision makers with his willingness to work within the structure of the club as well as the style of football that helped the Foxes return to the top flight at the first time of asking.

Maresca is Chelsea’s sixth manager in five years and the fourth since American investor Todd Boehly and private equity firm Clearlake Capital bought the club in May 2022. Several candidates were on a shortlist, including former Brighton manager Roberto de Zerbi, Ipswich boss Kieran McKenna and Brentford’s Thomas Frank. Co-sporting directors Paul Winstanley and Laurence Stewart said Maresca “deeply impressed us in our discussions leading up to his appointment” and his “ambitions and work ethic align with those of the club”. He a good fit for Chelsea’s current model, a highly data-driven and sports science approach, in which the various departments at the club have input with moving away from a manager-led recruitment process, leaving the manager to focus on football, which was at times a point of friction between Pochettino and the owners. Maresca is comfortable working in this structure to focus on improving players and preparing for matches. He immediately asked the data department for profiles on every player, including Academy stars and even key club staff, as he looked to get a head start ahead of his official start date.

Maresca’s coaching staff at Leicester, including former Chelsea goalkeeper Willy Caballero, will work alongside him at Stamford Bridge. Chelsea planned to improve their record in both attacking and defensive set-pieces, as coach Bernardo Cueva joined them in a £750,000 deal from Brentford to establish a set-piece department.

A former midfielder who had spells in England, Spain, Greece and his native Italy, Maresca had a short stint at West Brom as a teenager before joining Juventus in 2000. While at Sevilla he scored twice in the club’s Uefa Cup final win against Middlesbrough in 2006. His first taste of senior management arrived in 2021 where he lasted just 180 days with Italian club Parma, winning four of his 14 games. Four wins and five draws was not enough to satisfy the American ownership at a club just relegated out of Serie A, although Maresca insists he laid solid foundations. “We signed 14 new players and it was an international environment - I was training in four different languages and it wasn’t so quick to get certain certain concepts across. The start was difficult and, from the outside, there was a tendency always to see the glass as half-empty. I was very sorry it ended so soon, but I still think we were on the right track.” At Juventus he learned the art of winning under Carlo Ancelotti and Marcelo Lippi. “I always said that with Juventus, you learn to win,” said Maresca. “When you play for Juventus, you understand how important it is.”

For Leicester it was a big loss, as they said in a statement they were “disappointed that Enzo decided at this stage he no longer wants to be part of our vision” having established “promising foundations during his single season in charge”. The club added: “However, with Enzo’s decision made and the board’s terms for his departure met, we wish him well in his future endeavours. He leaves with the appreciation of everyone at the club for his work in helping us to achieve an immediate return to the Premier League during the 2023-24 season."

Chelsea had endured a mixed 2023-24 season but won their final five games to end the campaign in sixth and qualify for the Europa Conference League. The Blues also finished runners-up in the Carabao Cup and reached the semi-finals of the FA Cup. Mauricio Pochettino claimed he was "so pleased with the level the team reached" yet was soon shown the door.

Joe Cole believes the new manager's first task is to rule London again before even thinking about the title. "Chelsea finished the season very well, now it's crucial they take back London. Tottenham and Arsenal have really made strides. It's a beautiful football city and we have some of the best teams in the world. Chelsea haven't been on top of that pile for a very long time, so that's the first thing they need to do. The new manager did a fantastic job at Leicester, he's still young in his managerial career and will need time, which is what I say with every new manager that comes in. Every manager has been hard done by, the last five appointments could and should have been given more times. That's my opinion. The owners at Chelsea will have a different view on things. They are very data driven it seems, there are two things coming out of the club, the manager needs time and the communication in terms of what and why, which is very important to supporters. Fans feel part of the club and want to see the owner and CEO of the club explaining their decision 'this is why we're doing it'. Those two things, if I was advising the board, is what I would be saying to them."

Maresca had won over Chelsea's key decision makers with his willingness to work within the structure of the club as well as the style of football he employed that helped the Foxes return to the top flight at the first time of asking. On the likelihood of Maresca instantly being able to implement the brand of football that worked so well at the King Power in the Championship, Cesc Fabregas added: "When you employ a system you need to understand what players you have. You will need to train with them. There are so many ways of doing the three plus two. You can do it with the centre backs you can do it with a No.10 dropping deep and a full-back playing as a No.10. My thought is you never know or judge any decision before he's got the time to work and prove what he's worth. It happened with Zidane, with Guardiola they started without having any type of experience. They quickly won the treble, they won three times the Champions League in a row. He will have good players, he will have a good team, he will have a good young group of players who are hungry, physically ready to go, who are very powerful. I think he will need time. His coached in Italy with Parma and at Ascoli so he's coached in different types of environments and different types of football. We'll see how it goes. Talking about strategy I can't say because you're not in the conversations behind in the background and you don't know what they're really looking for. But definitely it's a young coach who has done well. He's got a specific way of playing and hopefully they studied well and know exactly what they're going after."

His first task was to trim a squad that had grown exponentially under the new owners. At the start of the season Maresca insisted that his squad consisted of only 21 players leaving another 23 surplus to requirements, including the likes of Raheem Sterling and Trevoh Chalobah who had been integral parts of the first team the previous season. It was an early sign of the problems the Spaniard would face.

Squad Goals

Joao Felix signed from Atletico Madrid in a £46.3m seven-year deal, to become Chelsea's 10th summer signing taking spending to over £200m. Conor Gallagher moved in the opposite direction to Atletico Madrid for £36m. The ex-Benfica player joined Tosin Adarabioyo, Omari Kellyman, Marc Guiu, Kiernan Dewsbury-Hall, Renato Veiga, Caleb Wiley, Aaron Anselmino, Filip Jorgensen and Pedro Neto as Chelsea splashed £202.6m, the Premier League's top spenders in the summer transfer window, which left numerous big names out in the cold and searching for new clubs in what was described as a chaotic recrutiment plan.

The signing of Felix unlocked Gallagher's transfer to Atletico, a deal that looked to have fallen through following the collapse of Chelsea's move for Atletico striker Samu Omorodion, but the deal was revived after the Blues agreed to sign Felix. Atletico were determined to sign Gallagher, having been impressed by him during his five-day stay in Madrid and how he handled the situation when he was forced to return to West London as the two clubs tried to unlock their financial difficulties. The England international passed a medical and agreed a five-year deal while in Madrid, pictured in the Wanda Metropolitano by the club, before having to return. But the 24-year-old was finally and officially an Atletico player after signing a deal at the club until 2029. In a video message on Instagram, Gallagher said: "To everyone at Chelsea, thank you for making my dreams come true. It's been an absolute honour every time I put on the shirt, and it was a dream come true to captain the team on many occasions. I loved every moment. These memories will last forever. I appreciate all the love and support from the fans. Hearing the chant of my name at the Bridge is a special feeling, and the banner you displayed meant the world to me. Thank you for everything. I wish the club all the best for the future, and I hope to see you all soon at Stamford Bridge!"

New manager Chelsea manager Enzo Maresca said of his departing midfielder, who had played for the club since he was a teenager: "It's not only for Chelsea. Many clubs are selling players from their academies. It's very sad. In Italy we had Totti and he played with Roma for 20 years. We all loved that. But now the rules are a bit different and sometimes you need to sell your Academy players for 100 per cent profit. We need to try to respect the rules."

Gallagher's departure as the Cobham Academy graduate ended an 18-year stay at his boyhood club. Appearing in all but one of the 51 matches across the entire campaign under Mauricio Pochettino, Gallagher was captain in most of them, deputising for Reece James' in his long-term absence. Despite playing an anchor role in midfield, Gallagher chipped in with five goals and seven assists in the league as the Blues turned their year around to finish sixth, narrowly missing out on Europa League football. Under Maresca, Gallagher was informed that he would be a squad player and the shorter contract on offer reflected that. As opposed to some of his team-mates and players the club signed in the past four transfer windows, Gallagher was only presented with a two-year deal plus an option for another 12 months. Taking to Instagram, John Terry wrote: "Gutted to see you go @conorgallagher92 - good Luck mate [football, punch, and blue heart emojis]". A banner presented prior to a 2-0 win over Tottenham said, "Chelsea since birth".

Chelsea's bloated squad saw 13 players removed from first-team training, including Raheem Sterling, who demanded clarity over his situation before the opening Premier League defeat by Manchester City. Chilwell, Romelu Lukaku and Armando Broja were also left out of Maresca's matchday squad at Stamford Bridge, as the club sought a major clear out. However, ahead of Chelsea's Europa Conference League clash with Servette, Cucurella stressed that dealing with difficult situations was 'sometimes part of the job'. Asked to describe the mood in the dressing-room, Cucurella replied: "I think we are really happy. We have a good group, the main group is from the last season and this can help because you need to know other people. For sure, it's not easy because maybe you have a good relationship with one of the players and they need to leave. We know it's sometimes part of the job but if we're not happy, we need to continue speaking or chatting. But for sure, we need to be focused in our job. We know what we need to do and then the rest is not very important."

Asked if the uncertainty surrounding the squad was unsettling the players, Dewsbury-Hall observed: "No, we're in a bubble with it. You can't let that sort of thing affect you. The only thing we're doing is just going out every day and training as well as we can, getting ready for the matches. Everything that happens outside, it's not up to us. Probably when the transfer window finishes, then it can just be pure focus on the season. Of course, when it's open, you get speculations." Dewsbury-Hall said players just wanted clarity from the manager. "And he's definitely a person that gives you that. I don't think you can have any complaints on that side."

"I ask the question quite regularly: 'What is it they know that the rest of football doesn't know?' Smart clubs like Real Madrid, Bayern Munich... what do this group of owners know that the rest of football doesn't?" Gary Neville

Reports leading up to transfer deadline day suggested that Chelsea had to offload as many as 13 players who had been deemed surplus to requirements by manager Maresca. Yet far from reducing the size of the squad, Chelsea ended up signing the biggest deal on the last day of the transfer window, snapping up Jadon Sancho on loan with an obligation to buy as the minutes ticked down to the deadline. Despite Nkunku, Jackson, Neto, Mudryk, Madueke, Palmer, Felix and Guiu already in their attack, manager Enzo Maresca said he "knows" Sancho will fit his system.

"London is where I grew up and I'm happy to be back," said the England winger, "it's been a bit crazy. Obviously, it was the last day of the transfer window so it's expected to be a bit crazy, but I'm really happy it's all finally done. Chelsea is iconic. My idols growing up were Didier Drogba and Frank Lampard and now I have the opportunity to play for this club like them. It's a great feeling. I think it's the manager who really drew me to the project. I knew him from his time with Pep Guardiola in Manchester City. He spoke to me on the phone about this project and what he was building here, and for a young player like myself it's exciting and I can't wait to get started."

Sancho joined Manchester United in a £73m deal from Borussia Dortmund in July 2021 but had a difficult time at Old Trafford; highlights were few and far between during his 83 appearances in three seasons and a high-profile fall out with manager Erik ten Hag led to him training away from the first team. He re-joined Dortmund on loan in January but returned to United in the summer yet was not in the squad for their two Premier League games at the start of the new season. The last of his 23 England caps came in 2021, he was overlooked for the 2022 World Cup in Qatar and Euro 2024.

The highest profile player to walk through the exit door on deadline day was Raheem Sterling who completed a late move to Arsenal. The 29-year-old agreed a season-long loan after the England international was told he was not in Maresca's plans. Sterling made 81 appearances for Chelsea, scoring 19 times, after joining from Manchester City for £50m in July 2022. The former Liverpool star was one of the first to arrive at Stamford Bridge following the takeover by co-controlling owners Behdad Eghbali and Todd Boehly. After 43 appearances in all competitions last season, he was out of the first-team picture under Maresca after Chelsea spent more than £200m on 11 signings in the summer. When Sterling was not involved in the Premier League opener against former club Manchester City, his representatives sought clarity over his future. He had been linked with Manchester United but the possibility of the switch to Arsenal then emerged late in the window to link up again with Mikel Arteta, who was a coach at Manchester City when Sterling was there. Sterling has been capped 82 times by England and was a key part of the squad that finished runners-up at Euro 2020. He had not played for his country since December 2022 at the World Cup, when he flew home to attend a family emergency during the tournament in Qatar. Also out of the door were Armando Broja who signed for Everton on a season-long loan and academy graduate Trevoh Chalobah who went to Crystal Palace on a season-long loan.

After another "chaotic" summer at Stamford Bridge, Gary Neville and Jamie Carragher laid out the "bizarre" problems Chelsea have brought upon themselves. Neville said: "One thing we do know is they have recruited badly. There are players they bought two years ago who they are already trying to get rid of. It feels chaotic and bizarre some of the contract lengths being given.I ask the question quite regularly; 'what is it they know that the rest of football doesn't know?' Smart clubs like Real Madrid, Bayern Munich, Barcelona, Arsenal, Man City - what do this group of owners know that the rest of football doesn't?"

"Chelsea have just got to stop buying players," Carragher said bluntly, "and players have got to stop signing for Chelsea. If I was a player, I'd think 'why I would sign?' The only reason you would sign is because your agent might say, 'we're getting a seven-year deal on big money, that's guaranteed money for seven years'. You know what I would say? Back yourself, sign a four-year deal at a proper club. When you're due for renewal, your money goes up anyway. It's not a young and exciting team. They've bought Joao Felix, where's he going to play? They signed Pedro Neto a week ago, where's he going to play when you've got Cole Palmer already? You want to ask about where Joao Felix is going to play, I've got another question - where's he going to get changed at the training ground? How are all these players in one dressing-room? How are you putting on a training session?"

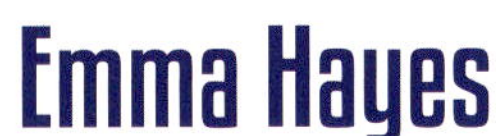

Emma Hayes

Chelsea's Most Successful and Longest Serving Manager

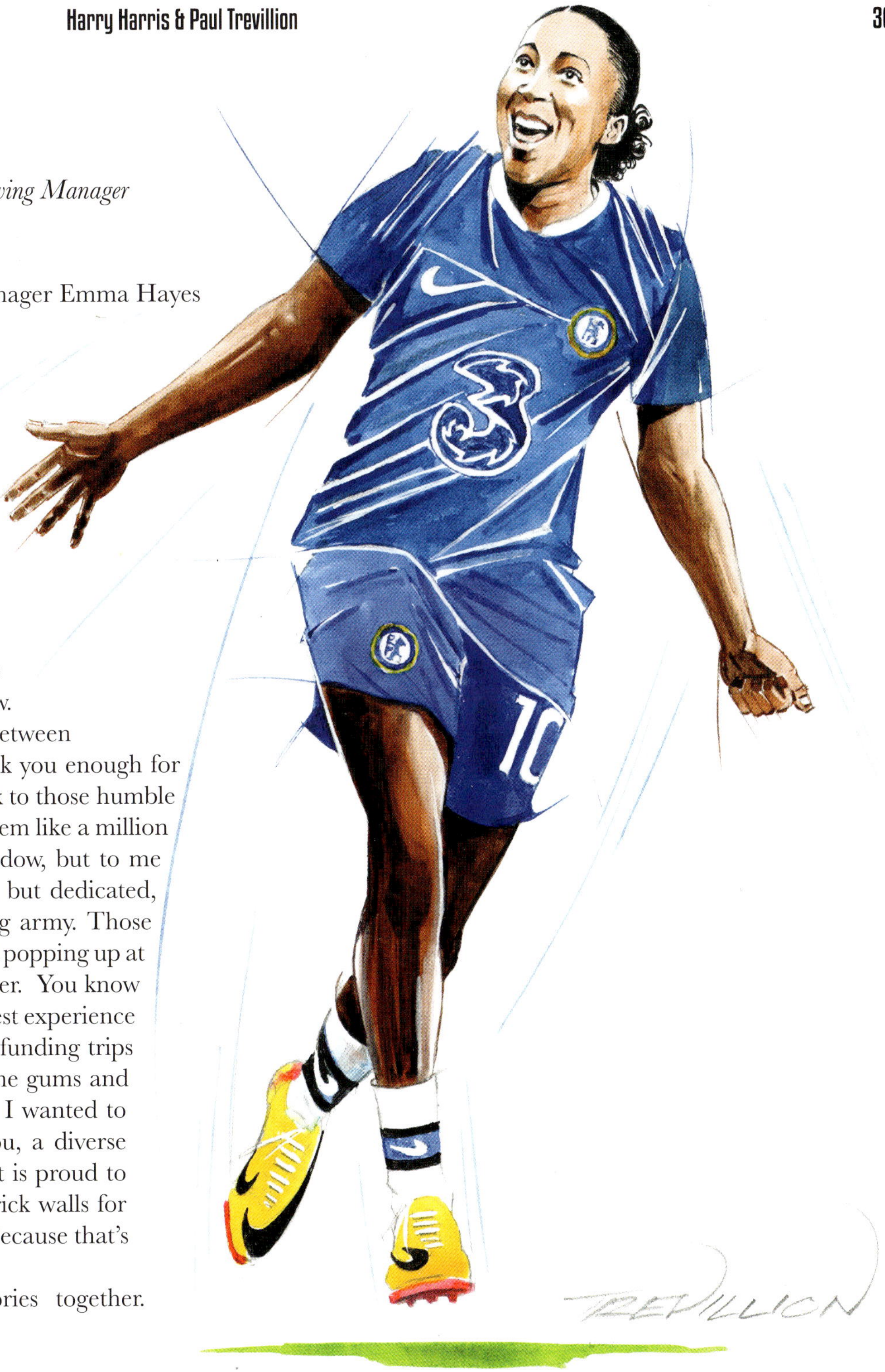

Before her last game in charge of the Blues, manager Emma Hayes wrote the following:

"As I sit down to write this letter to you all, I don't quite know where to begin, or how I feel. There's sadness, of course, that in a few short weeks this will all be coming to an end. But every time I think about you – about what we have achieved over the last 12 years, together – I can't help but smile. Because you made it. You made the experience, this journey that we have been on, far greater than you will ever know. There is nothing more special than the love between a team and its supporters, and I can't ever thank you enough for what you've given us over the years. I think back to those humble beginnings at Staines. Wheatsheaf Park might seem like a million miles away from what we've built at Kingsmeadow, but to me it was the start of something magical. A small, but dedicated, home fanbase quickly became a small travelling army. Those chants we heard at Wheatsheaf Park soon started popping up at Donny. Then Birmingham, Manchester, wherever. You know I did everything I possibly could to make it the best experience for you, pushing the club to put on buses, even funding trips myself over the years – and plying you with wine gums and mints to keep you sugared up! More than that, I wanted to provide you with a team that's reflective of you, a diverse group that we can all see ourselves in. One that is proud to represent the badge, that would run through brick walls for each other and do anything to achieve success. Because that's what you would do for us.

"We've created so many magical memories together.

From the first FA Cup win at Wembley, quickly followed by a first WSL title at Staines, to those early Champions League trips – something special was building, and it's just gone on and on from there. Honestly, there's too many highlights for me to list. When I think of the journey we've been on, I cannot imagine what it would have been like without you. We had a taste of that during Covid, and football just wasn't the same. I feel sad that you weren't able to be with us for the Champions League semi-final win over Bayern Munich, and I honestly believe it would have been a different experience if you'd been there with us in the final. But to come out of the other side of that with an FA Cup final at Wembley against Arsenal, on a cold afternoon in December, and being together again is something that will always live with me. I love that you've created a community for yourselves, starting at Wheatsheaf Park and then onto Kingsmeadow, which has become like a fortress because of you, and now Stamford Bridge. As we've grown, so have you. Wherever we go, you're there with us in huge numbers, developing your own memories from supporting the team across the country and Europe, over land and sea (and Leicester!). You've been amazing to our players throughout that time, and I know you're going to keep creating memories together long after I've gone. I want to thank you for all the songs, which kept me going so many times on the bench. I especially want to thank you in those losing moments, which fortunately there haven't been too many of. I always heard you. Always. You show your appreciation for the team no matter the scoreline or how the game has gone. That's what true fans are. You're the lifeblood of this club, the heartbeat, and I think you've been the envy of the entire league with the support you've given the team. I look forward to being one of you at some point, with Harry alongside me. From the bottom of my heart, thank you for making this the experience of a lifetime."

Emma Hayes concluded a hugely successful 12-year career with Chelsea by picking up a fifth successive title with a 6-0 thrashing of Manchester United at Old Trafford. Emma is one of Chelsea's greatest managers who helped grow the Women's Super League. Her Chelsea reign has been nothing short of sensational, having wrapped up 14 major trophies, including five successive WSL titles, the last of which was wrapped up on the final day to pip Manchester City to the title on goal difference. Widely regarded as one of the game's most influential coaches, Hayes was responsible for building a Chelsea dynasty that has seen them dominate English football for the past decade. The 47-year-old has not only transformed Chelsea, but laid foundations to ensure the club can enjoy success for years to come.

The title race in her final season was a reflection of the her 'never say die' attitude; Manchester City looked to have one hand on the trophy as they led Arsenal 1-0 in the 88th minute, but their dramatic 2-1 defeat followed swiftly by Chelsea's stunning 8-0 win over Bristol City swung the title in favour of Hayes' side with just two weeks to go - and they never looked back. When the full-time whistle blew following a 6-0 win at Old Trafford that secured the WSL title, Chelsea's substitutes jumped on Hayes before sprinting onto the pitch. Hayes left Chelsea to manage the US women's national team on a high of emotion and silverware. "I've been in Manchester City's position. If we had been in City's position, had they lost to Liverpool, we definitely would have won the next game," she said afterwards, sporting a T-shirt bearing the words 'it's never over'. "So forgive me for thinking that City should have won the title, I'm not doubting that." Pausing to take swigs from a bottle of beer as she reminisced over her time at the club, she added, "I'm so tired. I really mean it. I'm just exhausted from 12 years, not just 90 minutes of football. I don't know anyone who does it for that length of time, 12 years, but I'm always so grateful for the players and what they've done for me and the club."

The exhaustion had hit Hayes seven months before when she announced her departure, and it has been a long goodbye. At Old Trafford she seemed to take in every minute, responding to prompts from fans asking what the score was by putting up her hand to signal their 5-0 lead. She let out a roar of celebration when Johanna Rytting Kaneryd made it 2-0 within eight minutes and encouraged noise from her supporters when news of Aston Villa's equaliser against Manchester City came through. She even had time to take in the magnitude of her achievements, with this latest trophy, her 14th in an illustrious Chelsea career. "I did spend time in the second half looking at the Sir Alex Ferguson stand, the 27 years, the volume of trophies, the quotes around the stadium, the history," said Hayes. "I missed my drink with Sir Alex afterwards. He was waiting for me and I'm absolutely gutted. He rang me before I came in [for the media conference]. I'm sorry Sir Alex, I was really looking forward to that glass of red wine."

The afternoon in Manchester was one big celebration, not just for Hayes, but for the success of the club in the past decade. Legendary forward Fran Kirby came off the bench to score the final goal - a fitting end to her Chelsea career. The away fans chanted "champions of England, five times in a row, you'll never sing that" as the minutes ticked away and Hayes looked up and smiled. When the whistle eventually went and players sprinted past her to celebrate, captain Millie Bright ran the other way, jumping up and embracing her manager. Minutes later, Hayes would get pushed towards the fans by USA striker Catarina Macario, urging her to take the plaudits. Hayes, embarrassed, did so reluctantly but pointed to the badge on her shirt and waved her arms in the air. "You can tell Cat [Macario] is the American as she's not afraid of that. I'm British!" said Hayes. "If I wasn't a football manager that had to do a press conference every three days, I'm that person in a social circle that sits in the corner. I find some of this job really hard as I just want a quiet life. That's one of the things I'm most looking forward to." Hayes' fairytale ending meant she lifted the trophy with Bright before heading down the tunnel to take that phone call from Ferguson. "That's why this is the best title. We're not stupid, we know we weren't at our best," added Hayes. "I'm sorry, but I don't think you guys realise how hard it is to win and win and win.We've played significantly more games over the last five years and I think it took its toll on our senior players.I almost can't believe we've won the title, I can't believe it."

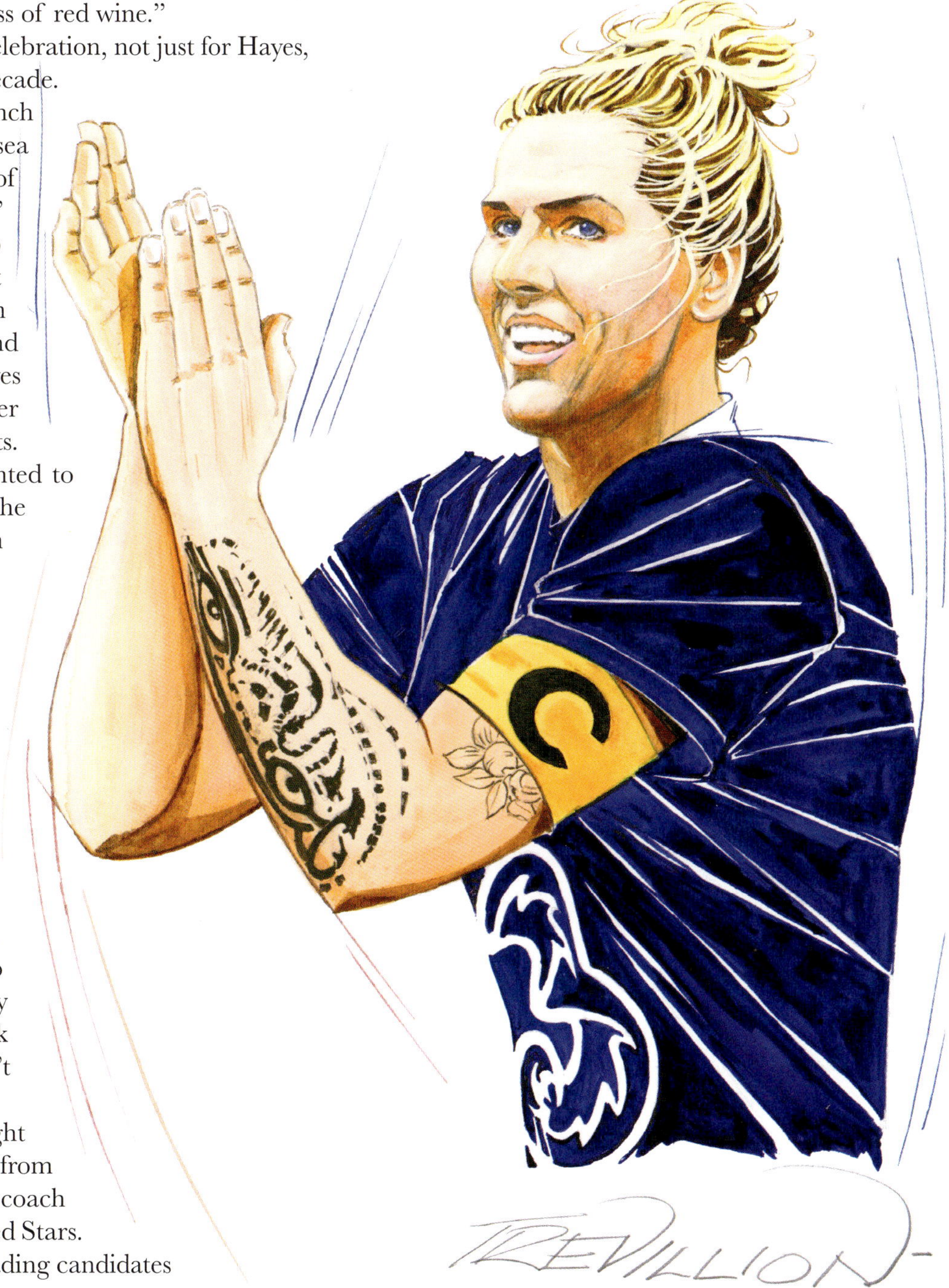

Emma arrived at the club in 2012 and brought with her the experience and education gained from her time in the United States in her roles as head coach and director of football operations at Chicago Red Stars. Now she will return to the USA as one of the leading candidates to become the new manager of the United States national team. It was in the States that Hayes saw what level women's football could reach - they were world leaders in the sport at international level - and wanted English football to find parity. As Hayes' squad delivered on the pitch, she received support off it from Chelsea. Together, the Camden-born manager and the West London club set the standard. During her WSL career, Hayes explored every possible tool in search of success; science and research were utilised to delve into areas which had not yet been looked at, constantly challenging the league, her club and her staff to improve. A spokesperson for women's health, advocating for research on menstrual cycle patterns, encouraging studies on the relationships between female footballers and anterior cruciate ligament injuries, and pushing for education in nutrition. While the women's game evolved in England on the pitch, Hayes ensured Chelsea were always ahead, creating an environment in which her players had everything they needed to perform and Hayes took away any excuse not to win. Her ruthless nature was evident in the club's 2022 DAZN documentary. In one clip she delivered a team talk in which she vowed to replace her players and "find better ones" if they did not deliver, an effective approach throughout her Chelsea career. Hayes targeted players in the transfer market she knew would thrive in a demanding environment. After being knocked out of the Women's Champions League semi-finals in 2018, Hayes pulled off one of her biggest coups to sign Aussie striker Sam Kerr, fighting off interest from six-time European winners Lyon. A year later Chelsea signed Wolfsburg's Pernille Harder for a world-record fee as Hayes pursued that elusive European crown, her side coming closer than any other English club to winning it since Arsenal's victory in 2007 - when Hayes was the Gunners' assistant manager.

Hayes leaves as Chelsea's most decorated head coach, it is the number of trophies she has won that will be celebrated most, but her biggest legacy is the impact she has had on the future of the English women's game. A role model for female coaches, a spokesperson for equal opportunities and a driver of professional standards in the WSL - Hayes' influence on the growth of the game has been immense, giving female coaches the confidence to challenge stereotypes, encouraged her players to take responsibility and grow into leaders and has set standards of success on the pitch.

Hayes made the best start possible in her new job, leading the US Olympic team to Gold in Paris with a 1-0 over Brazil in Paris. After weathering some early pressure, the Americans grew into a game which flowed from end-to-end but was decided by Mallory Swanson's composed second half finish. Brazil almost snatched an equaliser in injury time but the US held on.

Casey Stoney

A Leader On And Off The Pitch

A versatile defender capped 130 times for England, Casey was born in Basildon and signed for Chelsea's women's team in 1994, aged just 12. Having risen through the youth ranks with the Blues, the defender left the club in 1999 to join fellow London club, Arsenal. Stoney's talent at club level was immediately noticed and she made her senior debut for the England national team against France in 2000, aged just 18. Having played every single game during the 2000/2001 season, when Arsenal won the Treble, Stoney felt it was time for a new challenge. After three successful seasons with the Gunners, she signed for Charlton in the summer of 2002.

After being a non-playing squad member at UEFA Women's Euro 2005, she was an integral part of the England teams which reached the UEFA Women's Euro 2009 final and the quarter finals of the FIFA Women's World Cup in 2007 and 2011.

A captain of the England women's team, Stoney became the fifth player to make over 100 appearances for the Lionesses, making a total of 130 before retiring. Stoney played an integral part in the Lionesses's rise up the world rankings, with a third-placed finish in the 2015 FIFA Women's World Cup one of the highlights.

The defender had a successful first season at the Addicks, captaining the women's side to their first FA Women's Cup final, where they were defeated by her former club, Arsenal. Silverware did soon follow though, with Charlton winning the Premier League Cup in 2004, followed by the FA Women's Cup in 2005. In the league, the Addicks pushed for the Women's Premier League title, finishing second in 2004 and 2005 before consecutive third-placed finishes in 2006 and 2007. During this period, Stoney received her first start for the Lionesses against Norway in 2002 and scored her first international goal against Portugal in 2005. Stoney became a key member of the squad that qualified for the 2007 FIFA Women's World Cup – England's first appearance on the world stage for 12 years. The Lionesses finished in second place in the group stage, before being defeated in a difficult last-16 tie against the United States. Stoney was one of four players to feature in every minute in the tournament.

Following Charlton's relegation from the Premier League in 2007, the women's team was disbanded as part of a series of cutbacks. This resulted in Stoney re-signing for her childhood club, Chelsea, along with fellow England internationals Eniola Aluko and Siobhan Chamberlain. They were joined by American World Cup winner, Lorrie Fair. While the Blues had the talent, the trophies did not arrive and after a fifth-placed finish in 2008 and a title challenge failing to materialise in 2009, manager Steve Jones departed, Stoney took over as player/manager for the rest of the campaign which ended with a third-placed finish behind Everton and champions Arsenal. Whilst at Chelsea, Stoney also won the FA International Player of the Year award in 2008. England again qualified for the 2009 European Championships, where Stoney played at left-back. Despite a suspension in the group stage, she returned and helped the Lionesses reach the Final, where they earned a silver medal.

With the formation of the Women's Super League in 2011, Stoney decided to leave Chelsea and joined Lincoln City due to the opportunity of training full-time. In her three seasons with the Imps, the defender made 38 league appearances in which she scored one goal and was a WSL Cup runner-up in 2013, where Lincoln lost 2-0 to Arsenal.

Stoney captained the Lionesses to the 2011 FIFA Women's World Cup quarter-finals in Germany. Now in central defence, she featured in every match, as England beat the eventual world champions, Japan, before a penalty-shootout defeat to France.

With the 2012 Olympic Games being held in London, an 18-player women's team and Stoney was awarded the captaincy. The defender led Team GB to the quarter-finals of the competition,

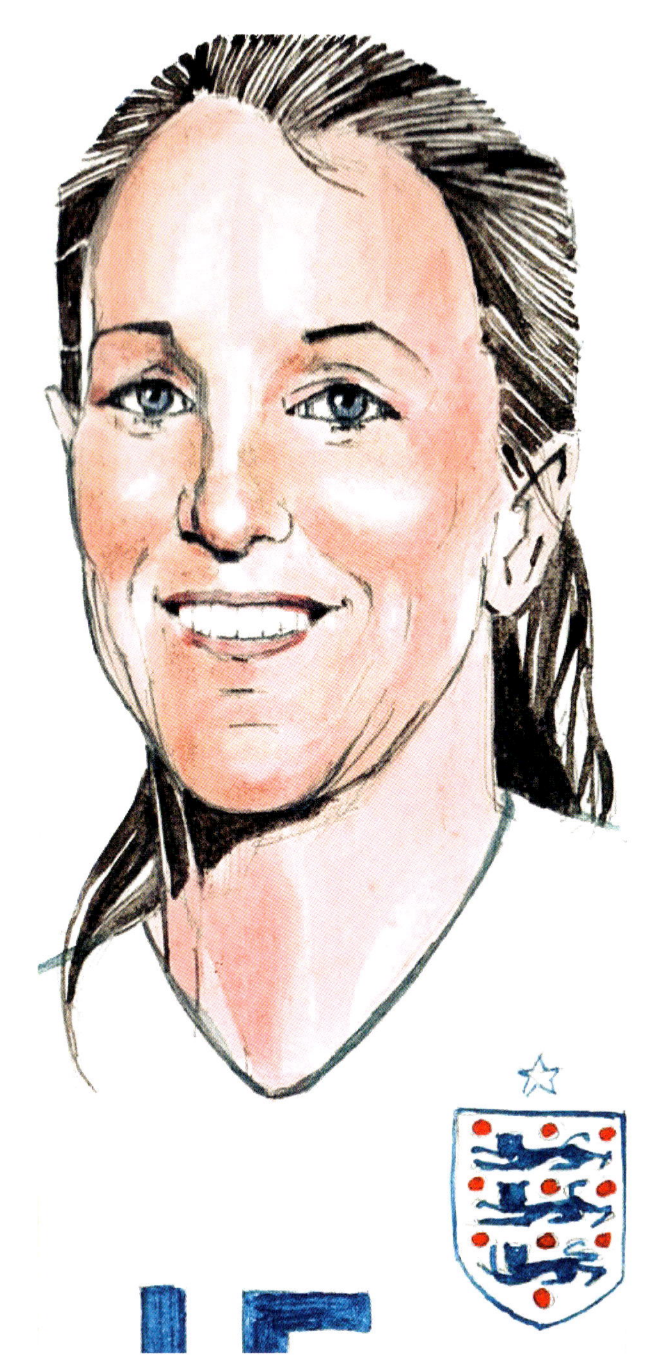

scoring in the second group stage match against Cameroon and featured in a memorable 1-0 victory against Brazil in front of over 72,000 fans at Wembley Stadium.

Twelve years after she originally left Arsenal, Stoney left Lincoln City and re-signed for the Gunners in 2014, citing her desire to win trophies. This was duly delivered with Arsenal winning the FA Women's Cup in 2014 and 2016, with a 2015 WSL Cup victory sandwiched in-between. During Stoney's time at Arsenal, the Lionesses reached the semi-finals of the 2015 FIFA Women's World Cup in Canada. Despite coming close to the final, England won their third-placed play-off against Germany. Stoney was also part of England's squad that reached the semi-finals of the European Championships in 2017.

While Stoney was with the England squad in Canada in 2015 she received an MBE for services to football, highlighting how far the women's game has progressed in England.

Casey spoke publicly about being gay for the first time in 2014 deciding to come out after the positive reaction to Tom Daley and because of the "loving relationship" she was in. "I was living a lie," Stoney said. "I've never hidden it within football circles because it is accepted. But to the outside world, I've never spoken about my sexuality." The then Arsenal Ladies and England captain added: "I feel it's really important for me to speak out as a gay player because there are so many people struggling who are gay, and you hear about people taking their own lives because they are homosexual. That should never happen. How can I expect other people to speak about themselves if I'm not willing to do that myself?" The decision had taken "a long while to get to" but that "a huge weight" had been lifted from her shoulders. "For the last 10 years I've always cared too much what other people think. I was frightened of the stereotypes, frightened of being judged, frightened of what other people might say, especially the abuse you can get through social media. But I think I'm in a place where I feel so comfortable in my own skin, I feel so loved by the person I'm with, that I feel I can face anything.

"I looked at the response that Tom Daley got. It was incredibly positive, and I thought 'wow the world is changing and it's time for me to stand up and tell my side of the story'."

Casey went to great lengths to keep her private life a secret and spoke openly about why other women football players have not come out as gay. She also said it was "incredible" that World Cups were awarded to Russia and Qatar given their attitudes towards homosexuals. She wanted to help others who might also feel trapped by their identity. "In the past, I made up lies about having a boyfriend or acted a certain way because I felt like that's how I had to act and be accepted by the modern world. But I wasn't happy doing that, because I was always lying, and lying to myself as well." She hopes her experiences would inspire others. "I could look at it two ways. Is it because people don't feel like they need to come out and talk about it because it's never been an issue? Or is it because, like I have been for the last 10 years, people are frightened? Even in this day and age, frightened of being judged, frightened of what people might think of them, or what they might say? It doesn't change you as a person. Can you really be happy, can you really be yourself? If you are not comfortable in yourself and you are not comfortable in social settings or your surroundings, how can you go into a team environment and be yourself and train hard and feel relaxed with your team-mates if you don't know who you are? It's taken me many years, and help. I've worked with a sports psychologist on certain issues and it's been a struggle, but I've got here now."

Stoney represented Arsenal, Charlton, Chelsea, Lincoln Ladies and Liverpool in a club career that spanned 20 years. After two WSL seasons with Liverpool, Stoney announced her retirement from football and began coaching in February 2018. Stoney worked at the David Beckham Academy for two years and coached at a number of WSL clubs including Chelsea Ladies' U18 Academy, Lincoln City U17s and Arsenal Centre of Excellence U12s. She also served as the Academy assistant coach at Charlton Athletic. She joined Phil Neville's coaching setup with England as the Lionesses attempt to qualify for the 2019 FIFA Women's World Cup. The 41-year-old, who enjoyed a stint at Manchester United before heading to the USA, has been tipped to manage England one day.

Stoney was considered one of the leading candidates to take over from Emma Hayes, who left Stamford Bridge to take charge of the USA women's national team but said she wished to remain at NWSL side San Diego Wave where she led the club to their first NWSL Shield in 2023.

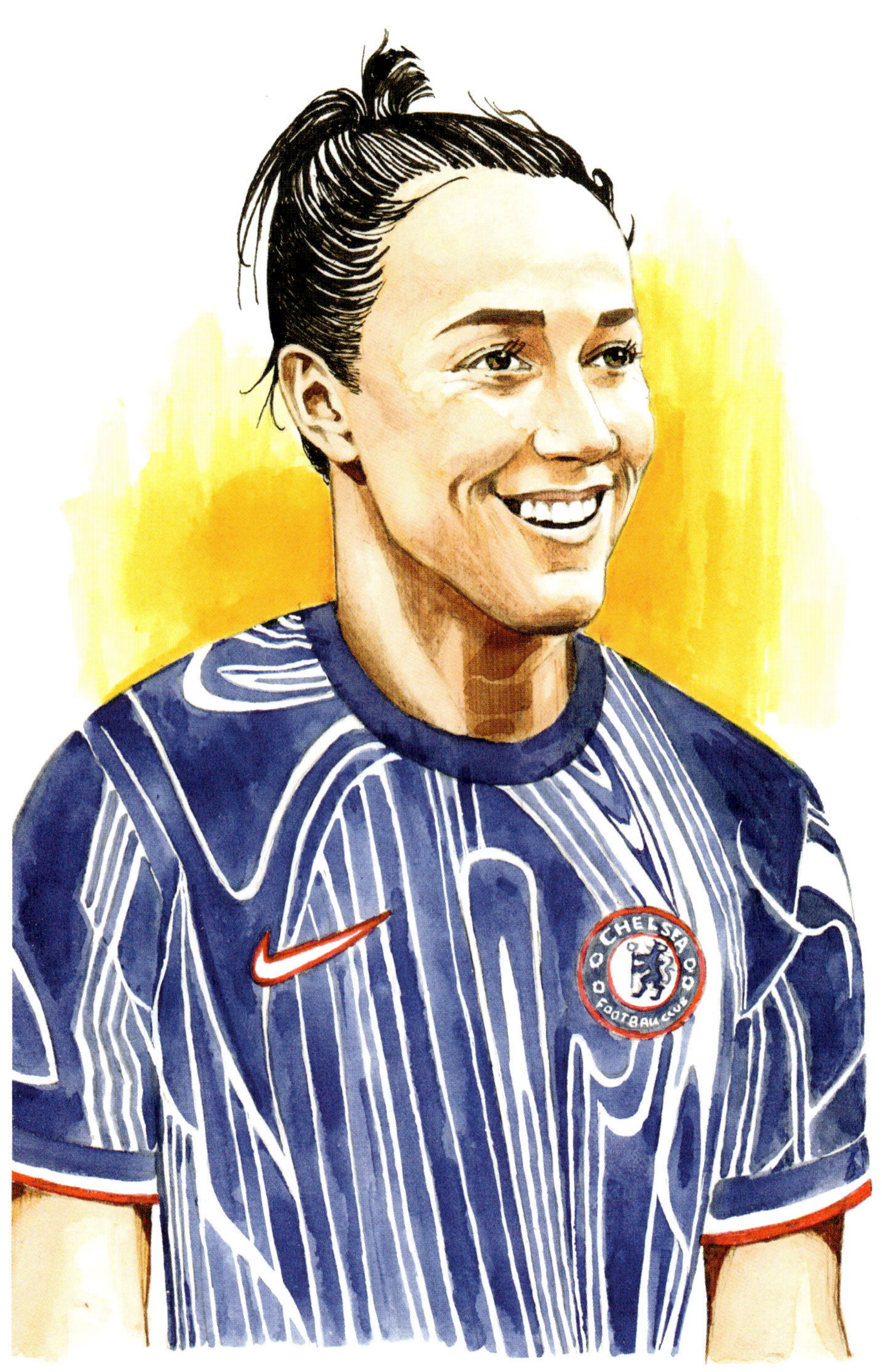

Lucy Bronze

England defender Lucy Bronze joined Women's Super League champions Chelsea on a free transfer. The 32-year-old signed a two-year contract after leaving Barcelona once her contract expired. "To know I'm a Chelsea player still feels a little bit surreal," said Bronze. "I'm really excited to be back in England. My family are so excited as well to get to more of my games. I'm excited to be in London, to see what the capital holds and to be at a club that is renowned for winning so many trophies."

Bronze won 23 club trophies, including five Champions League titles and eight domestic league titles, and was part of the England team that won Euro 2022. She became Chelsea's fourth signing of the summer after the arrivals of Julia Bartel, Sandy Baltimore and Oriane Jean-Francois, and the most high-profile player to join since Sonia Bompastor succeeded Emma Hayes as manager. "Lucy will bring leadership to the group. She is a serial winner and a versatile defender," said Chelsea general manager Paul Green. "She has lots of experience and a winning mentality which we feel will fit well into the squad."

Bronze won three successive Champions League titles with Lyon and two with Barcelona, the most recent as part of the domestic treble last season. Chelsea assistant manager Camille Abily was part of the coaching staff when she played at Lyon. She was offered a contract extension at Barcelona but was not guaranteed a starting role amid competition from Spain defender Ona Batlle. Bronze, who has played for Sunderland, Liverpool, Everton and Manchester City, was named Fifa Best Women's Player of the Year in 2020. She was key in the Euro 2022 triumph and helped England reach the World Cup final last year.

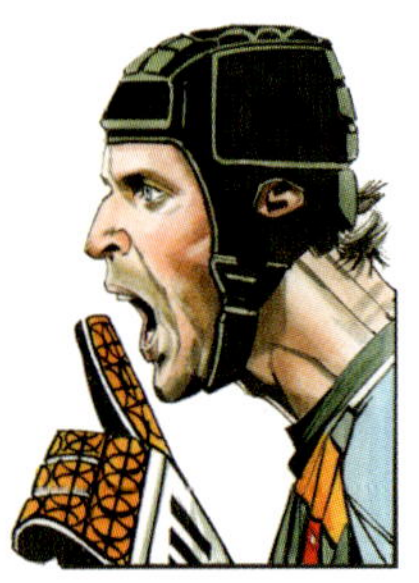

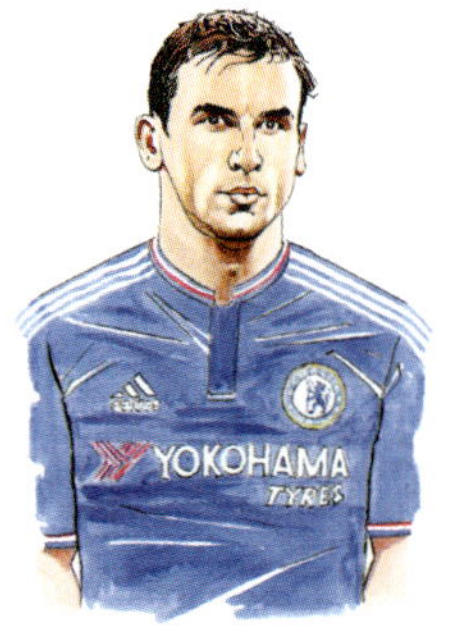
YOKOHAMA
TYRES

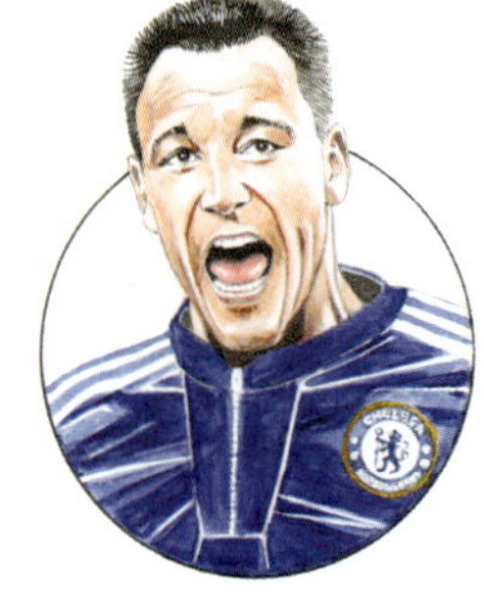

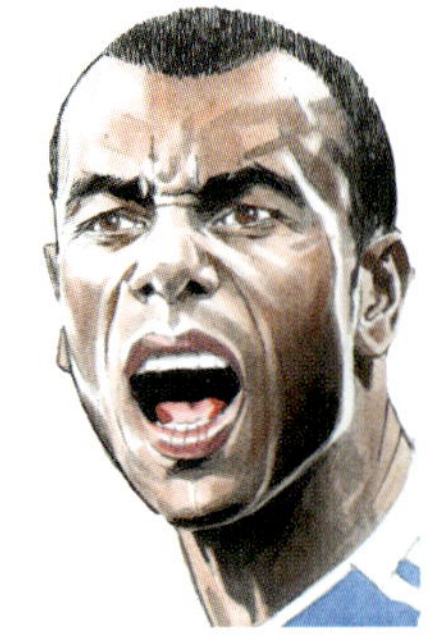

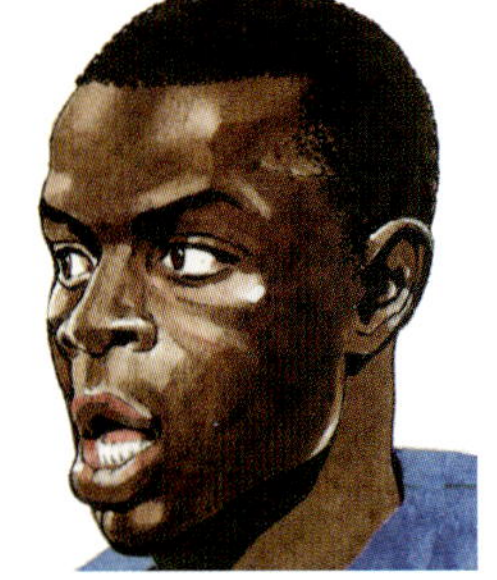

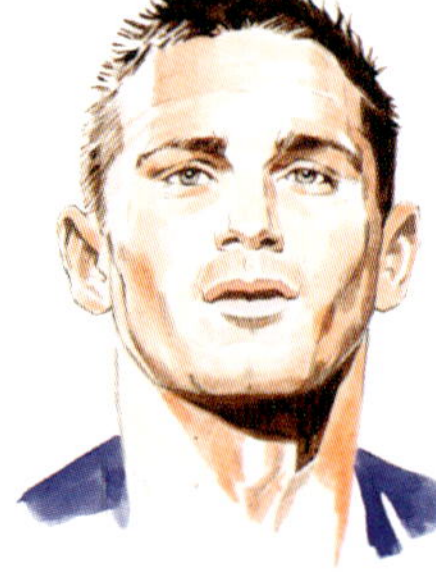

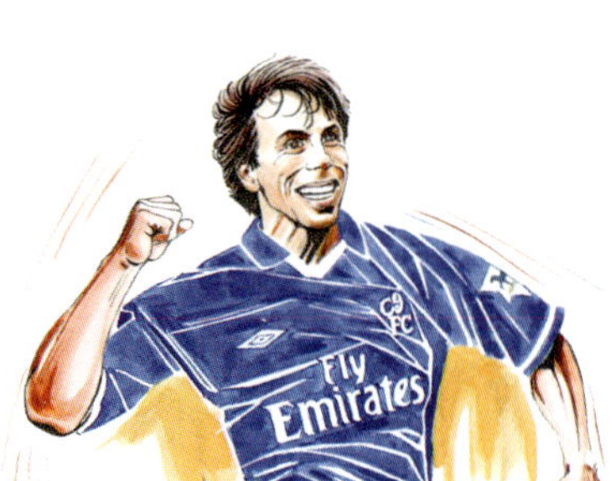
Fly
Emirates

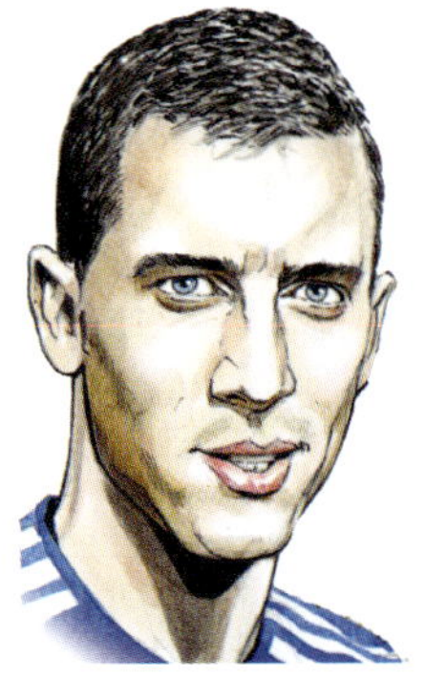

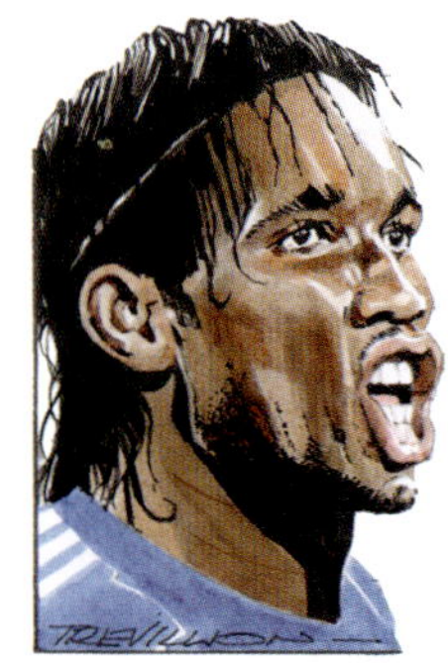

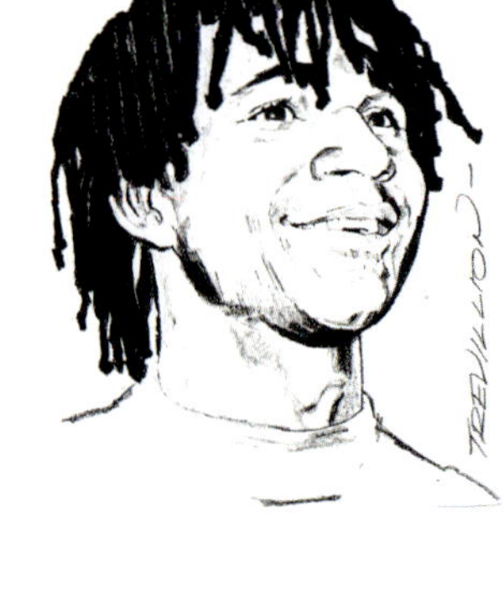

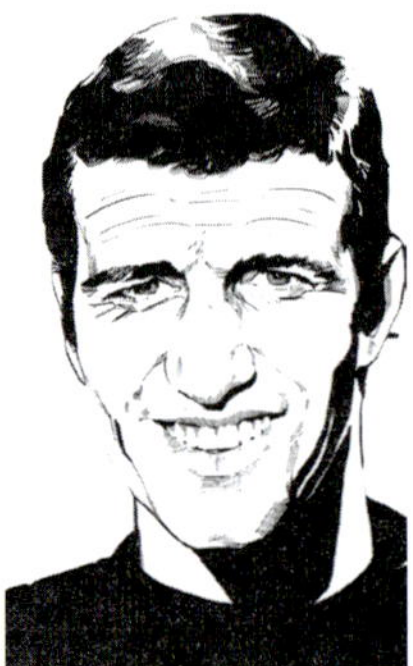

Chelsea's Greatest

The Vote

GREATEST ALL-TIME PLAYER: FRANK LAMPARD

GREATEST EVER TEAM:

CECH; COLE, TERRY, IVANOVIC; KANTE, LAMPARD, GULLIT, ZOLA, HAZARD, DROGBA, OSGOOD.

With so many super talented performers and World Footballers of the Year, it is a formidable task to select Chelsea's greatest ever team, and even harder to select their greatest ever player - so who better to nominate The Greatest than the clubs legends who played with or saw from close range some of the Blues' best ever players.

Yet, the choice was so tough for so many that 32 players earned at least one vote or more for a place in the starting line up, let alone many more named as possible subs! Peter Osgood earned a stating place as the main striker edging out Jimmy Greaves by just one vote.

As for the Greatest Ever player, it was very close between Franco Zola and Frank Lampard with Lampard winning out by just one vote.

Chelsea won their first English League Championship in 1955 when Roy Bentley was the club's own Roy of the Rovers, he was both captain and top scorer with 150 in 367 appearances for the Blues and went to the 1950 World Cup. But few will have seen Roy play, probably few would even remember him, which makes a Greatest Player selection and best ever team selection so subjective. Bentley stayed as the club's record scorer until Bobby Tambling overtook him with 202 goals between 1958 and 1970 when Chelsea become England's glamour club synonymous with Swinging London and showbiz stars such as Raquel Welch invited to games by celebrity fan and director Dickie Attenborough. This was the era when Ossie was crowned The King of Stamford Bridge as Chelsea won the FA Cup and European Cup-Winners' Cup in successive seasons. Peter scored in every round including the final and the subsequent replay against Real Madrid. Tall and elegant, Osgood made his debut at 17 and team-mate Terry Venables quipped: 'Where have you been all this time?' Charlie Cooke and Alan Hudson were other skilful mavericks who fitted into the team's King's Road image. By contrast Ron 'Chopper" Harris made a record 795 appearances for Chelsea and now says: 'With VAR, I'd be lucky to see out the warm-up.' David Webb was also a tough nut who scored a rare goal to win the 1970 FA Cup against Leeds in a notorious match that modern ref Michael Oliver said he'd have issued 11 red cards.

Following a huge decline in the late 1970s, the club was bought for just a quid by Ken Bates who began to turn things round, yet it was a late winner at Bolton in 1983 from Clive Walker (who voted for himself in this poll) which might be the most important goal ever scored for the club as it saved them from relegation to Division Three.

In the 1980s Kerry Dixon was a terrace favourite during a nine year stay at the club, twice firing the club to promotion and winning the First Division Golden Boot. Along with mercurial winger Pat Nevin he revived the idea of Chelsea as a cool place to watch football. However with their departures Chelsea slumped again before the glamour and stardust returned to West London with the arrival of Glenn Hoddle and Ruud Gullit, who became the first black manager to win a trophy in English football as Chelsea ended a quarter of century wait for a trophy when he lifted the FA cup. Gianfranco Zola joined Chelsea from Serie A in 1996 and was a formative figure in the Premier League becoming a global attraction. Before Zola, it was questioned whether smaller players from overseas could cope with the physicality of English football. Their new No25 ended that theory and capped a glorious spell by scoring the winner in the 1998 European Cup-Winners' Cup final.

After Gullit, Luca Vialli brought more glory to the club and the arrival of Roman Abramovich in 2003 and his appointment of José Mourinho a year later saw the Blues take off as they ended a 50-year wait for a championship and established themselves among England's elite clubs. John Terry was club captain for all five Premier League titles though he was suspended when they finally lifted the Champions League in 2012. Terry gets into many all-time Premier League dream teams and is generally regarded as the best skipper of the last 30 years alongside Manchester United's Roy Keane. JT's vice-captain Frank Lampard scored a club record 211 goals from midfield and later returned to Stamford Bridge as manager. 'Super Frank' was twice on target at Bolton in 2005 that clinched Chelsea's all-important first championship.

Big-match goalscorer Didier Drogba twice scored winning goals for Chelsea in FA Cup finals and most importantly headed their equaliser against Bayern Munich in the 2012 Champions League final that the Blues went on to win on penalties. He took the winning kick in the shoot-out as Chelsea upset the Germans in their own back yard. He also won the Premier League Golden Boot with 29 goals in 2009/10 when Chelsea won their only League and FA Cup Double.

Chelsea won titles in 2015 and 2017, largely due to the influence of Eden Hazard voted the Footballer Writers' and PFA Player of the Year in 2015. He scored twice and set up another in the 2019 Europa League final against Arsenal – his final Chelsea game before an ill-fated move to Real Madrid.

Chelsea's second Champions League crown arrived under Thomas Tuchel in 2021, when N'Golo Kante was the main man as a holding midfielder that earned him Footballer of the Year four years after helping Chelsea win the Premier League in his first season.

Cech, Cole, JT, Lampard, Zola and Drogba are certs for the all-time greatest team, as were Hazard and Jimmy Greaves.

Giving a mark for each player selected by the panel of the best experts possible, we formulated the Greatest Team and The Greatest Ever player.

Harry Harris

For Greatest Player, four candidates stood out; Jimmy Greaves, Gianfranco Zola, Frank Lampard, and John Terry. The final vote came down to a split between Lampard and Zola, not just two of the most gifted and effective stars but also the most popular.

As for the team there was quite a few worthy of selection, so it was a close run race who would actually make the final selection. 'Chopper' Harris attracted votes as did Kante, Carvalho, Desailly, Osgood and Greaves.

As for my personal choice, having watched the team in the sixties and seventies and more closely from the press box in the eighties, nineties and to this present day, my 1-11 would be three at the back, but the strength of those three would be a barrier to any attack. In midfield the industry of John Hollins has the edge over my old friend Ray Wilkins, while Lampard, Hazard and Zola are no brainers, they were a must for any team when they were at the peak of their powers. Up front I've gone for those who recall his goalscoring prowess I've selected Bobby Tambling, who cannot be left out, while Didier Drogba is a battering ram. Jimmy Greaves is by far the club's greatest ever goalscorer, even though he wasn't there long enough to set a mark that would never have been beaten had he stayed a one club man. In fact Greaves edges my vote over Zola as the club's greatest ever player.

Cech; Desailly, Gullit, Terry; Zola, Hollins, Lampard, Hazard;
Greaves, Drogba, Tambling.

HH

Paul Trevillion

Cech; Harris, Cole, Terry, Silva; Lampard, Cooke, Hazard;
Osgood, Greaves, Gullit
Subs: Bonetti. Drogba, Hutchinson, Nevin, Webb
Greatest Ever Player: Frank Lampard

Players

Paul Canoville

"My choices are made on balance. The strikers are all very clever and mobile, Drogba will bully any defence into submission, Jimmy Greaves will score from anywhere, the best striker ever in my opinion, and Zola is such a clever player who would link up everything with the added danger from set pieces. The midfield is based on a ball winner and a very good distributor in Kante, Gullit can play anywhere on the field except for goal, Lampard will score loads, and Hazard can keep hold of the ball.

The defenders are all solid, and the best anywhere in the world, Terry would be captain. Tell me - who can do better than this team…"

Čech; Thiago Silva, Cole, Gullit, Terry.; Desailly, Kanté, Lampard; Greaves, Zola, Drogba.
Subs:.Osgood; Hudson; Bonetti; Hazard

He added: "Greatest Player? Tough one. But I would go for Jimmy Greaves."

Scott Minto

"Eden Hazard is the most talented but it's between Frank and JT for greatest player. On the toss of a coin think I'll give it to JT, an inspirational leader".

Cech: Ivanovic, Carvalho, Terry, Cole: Lampard, Makelele, Essien; Hazard, Zola, Drogba.
Subs: Bonetti, Desailly, Harris, Lebouef, Bridge, Newton, Ballack, Di Matteo, Kante Cooke, J Cole, Robben, Costa, Osgood

Clive Walker

Bonetti; Locke, Chilwell, Pates, Terry; Lampard, Cooke, Wilkins; Dixon, Hazard, Walker; sub: Palmer

So why did Clive vote for himself? Clive tells me: "I'm proud of the number of goals scored and playing so many games. I loved the crowd and the passion they showed for the club. I finished playing at 42 with Cheltenham. We won the Conference in '99 and I then retired."

Ken Monkou

Cech; Ivanovic, Terry, Carvalho, Cole; Essien, Kante, Lampard, Hazard; Drogba, Zola.
Subs: Cudicini, Ramierez, Williams, Costa, Crespo.

Danny Granville

Cech, Azpilicueta, Terry, Carvalho, Cole, Hazard, Poyet, Lampard, Robben, Zola, Drogba.
Subs: Wise, Dixon, Rüdiger, Joe Cole, DiMatteo.

"Greatest ever player is tough but will say John Terry."

Tony Dorigo

"Not easy, but here goes…"

Cech, Harris, Terry, Desailly, Cole, Makele, Lampard, Zola, Hazard, Drogba, Osgood
Bench: Bonetti, Azpilicueta, Essien, Cooke, Mata, Dixon

Greatest ever: Lampard

Fans

Chris Hollins

Bonetti: The cat. Not the biggest but so athletic and a key member of the great team of the sixties and seventies.
Azpilicueta: Mr consistent at right-back/centre-half and even left-back. Won so many trophies
Terry: great centre-half and a better leader during the most successful period of the club
Desailly: truly world class. Moved to centre-half at Chelsea. Key player in the transformation of the club
Ashley Cole: one of the best left backs in world football. Brilliant going forward and so underrated in defence.
Hollins: a product of the Chelsea youth system and became a key member of the Chelsea teams which won the FA, League and Cup winners cups for the first time.
Kante: the complete midfielder and so consistent. Turned up when it really counted.
Lampard: what can I say? So many goals, so many match winning perfumes and so many trophies. A Chelsea legend.
Houseman: so underrated and often overlooked when people talking about the Cup winning teams in the 70's. Scored very important goals
Osgood: what a player and what an entertainer. There's a reason he's got a statute at the Bridge. The shed loved him
Zola: I thought he might struggle in English football but how wrong could I be! An artist with ball, a creator, provider and a brilliant finisher!

Subs: Hazard, Greaves, Cooke, Ivanovic, Tambling, Harris - I can't believe these guys are on the bench!

As for the best player I have to go with my heart. It's got be Dad. I was not old enough to watch him in his prime. But thankfully so many supporters tell me how good he was! Player of the year twice 70/71. That's not too bad!

Alec Stewart

Former England test captain and Surrey Director of Cricket

"I've picked this team on the players I've actually seen live playing for Chelsea and therefore not included players like Greaves, Tambling etc."

Cech, Harris, Cole, Desailly, Terry, Makelele, Lampard, Zola, Hazard, Drogba, Osgood

Subs: Bonetti, Petrescu, Ivanovic, Carvalho, Hollins, Hudson, Cook, Dixon.

Ivor Baddiel

Comedy script writer/author

(Pictured opposite)

"My favourite player is Pat Nevin because, at a time when Chelsea were shit, and when I was young and going to the Bridge, he was a shining light in the darkness, but for me the greatest ever player would have to be Gianfranco Zola"

Cech, Cole, Terry, Desailly, Ivanovic, Lampard, Zola, Nevin, Hazard, Greaves, Drogba.

Subs: Bonetti, Thiago Silva, Rudiger, Osgood, Robben, Gullit, Fabregas, Gallas, Harris, Hughes, Mata, Torre Andre Flo

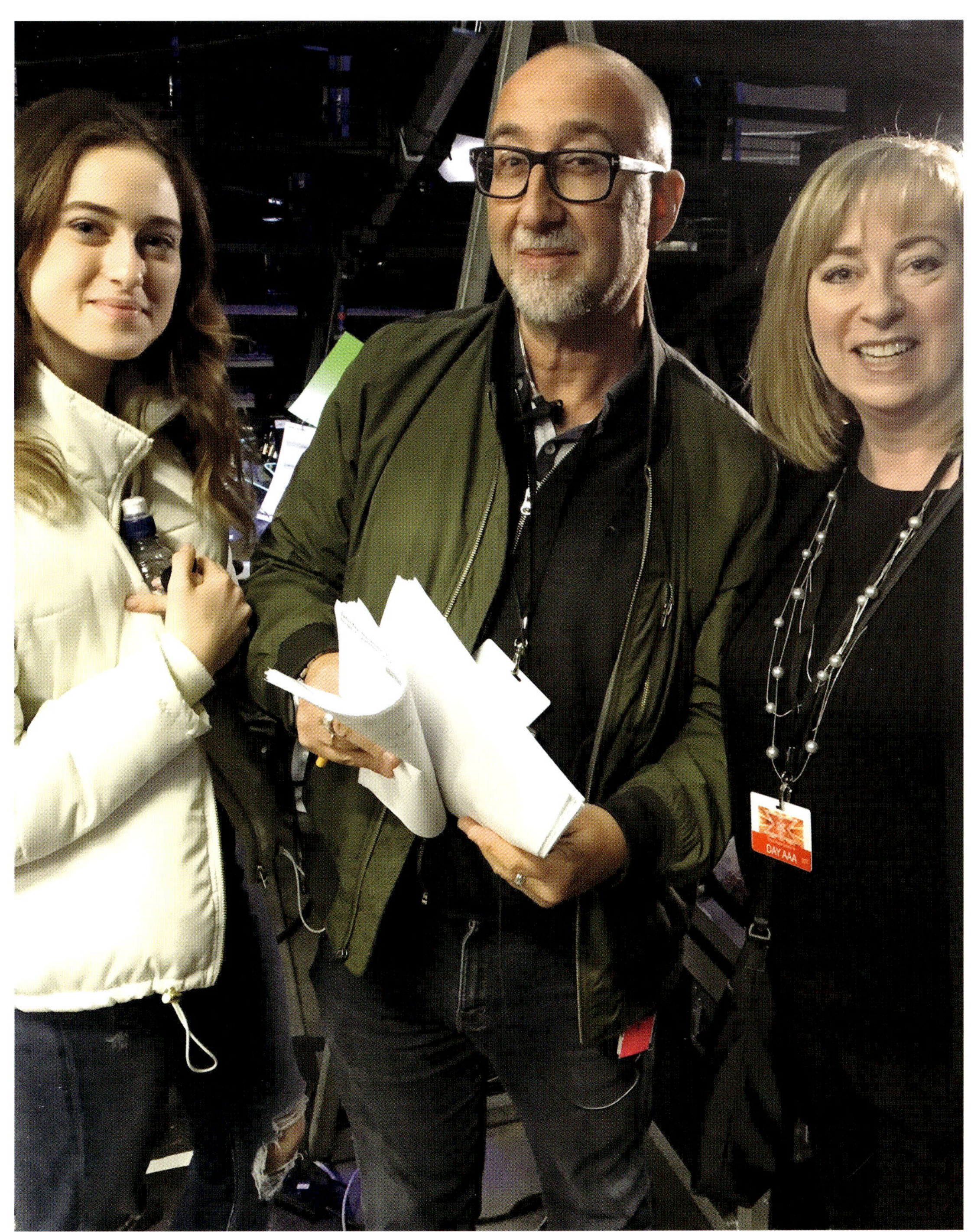

Script writer Ivor Baddiel with Harry's wife Linda and daughter, Poppy.

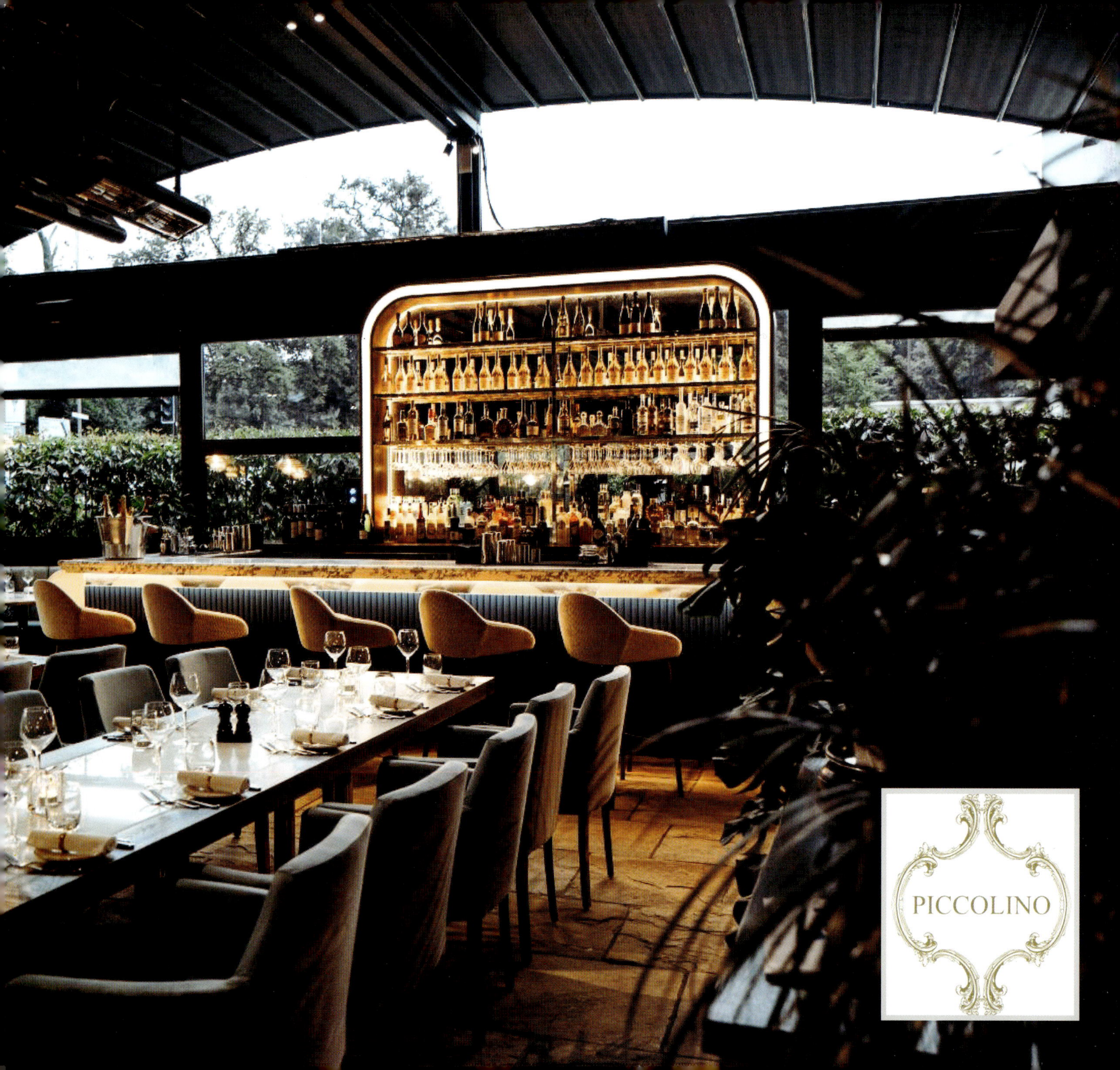
PICCOLINO

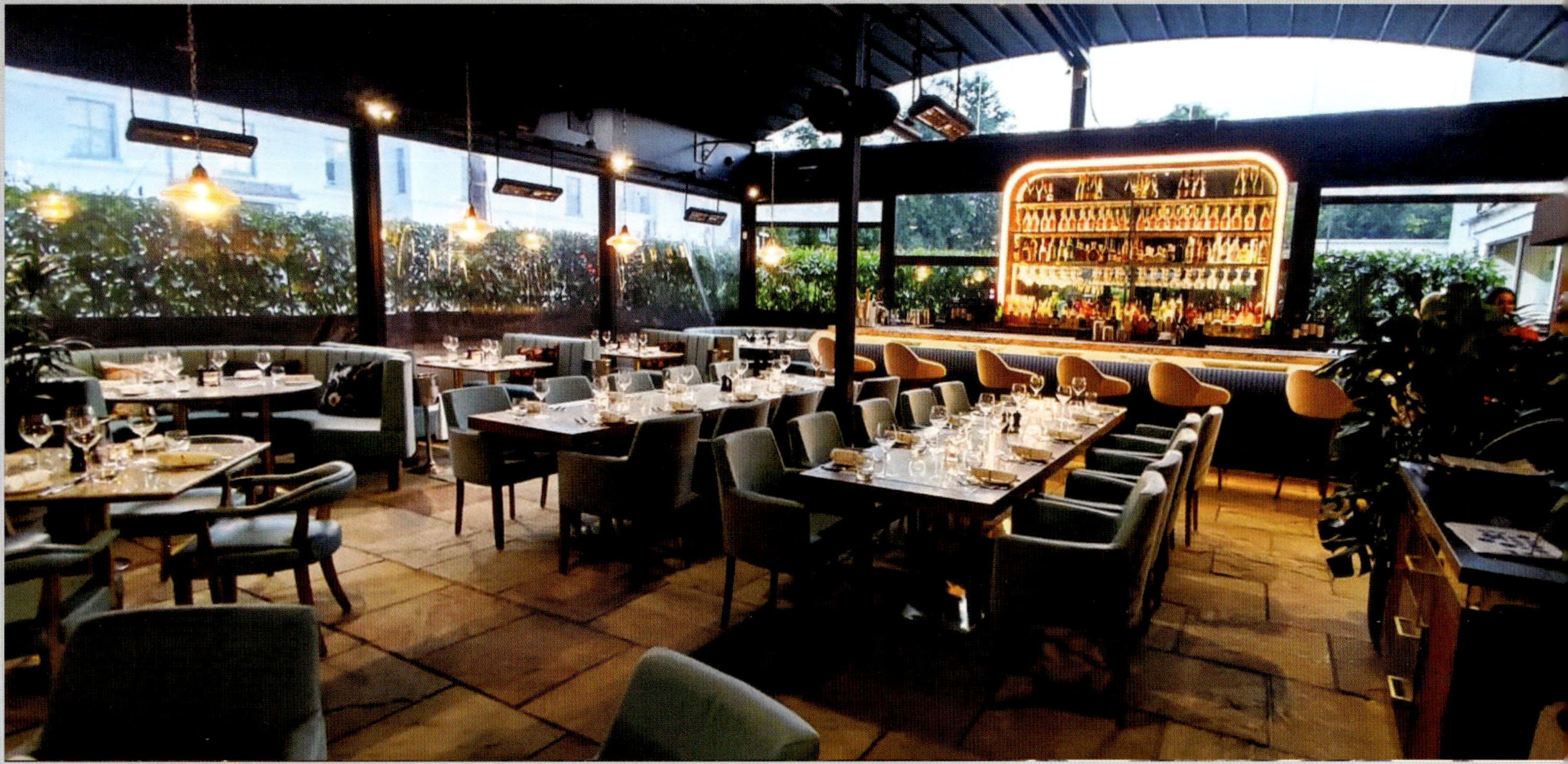

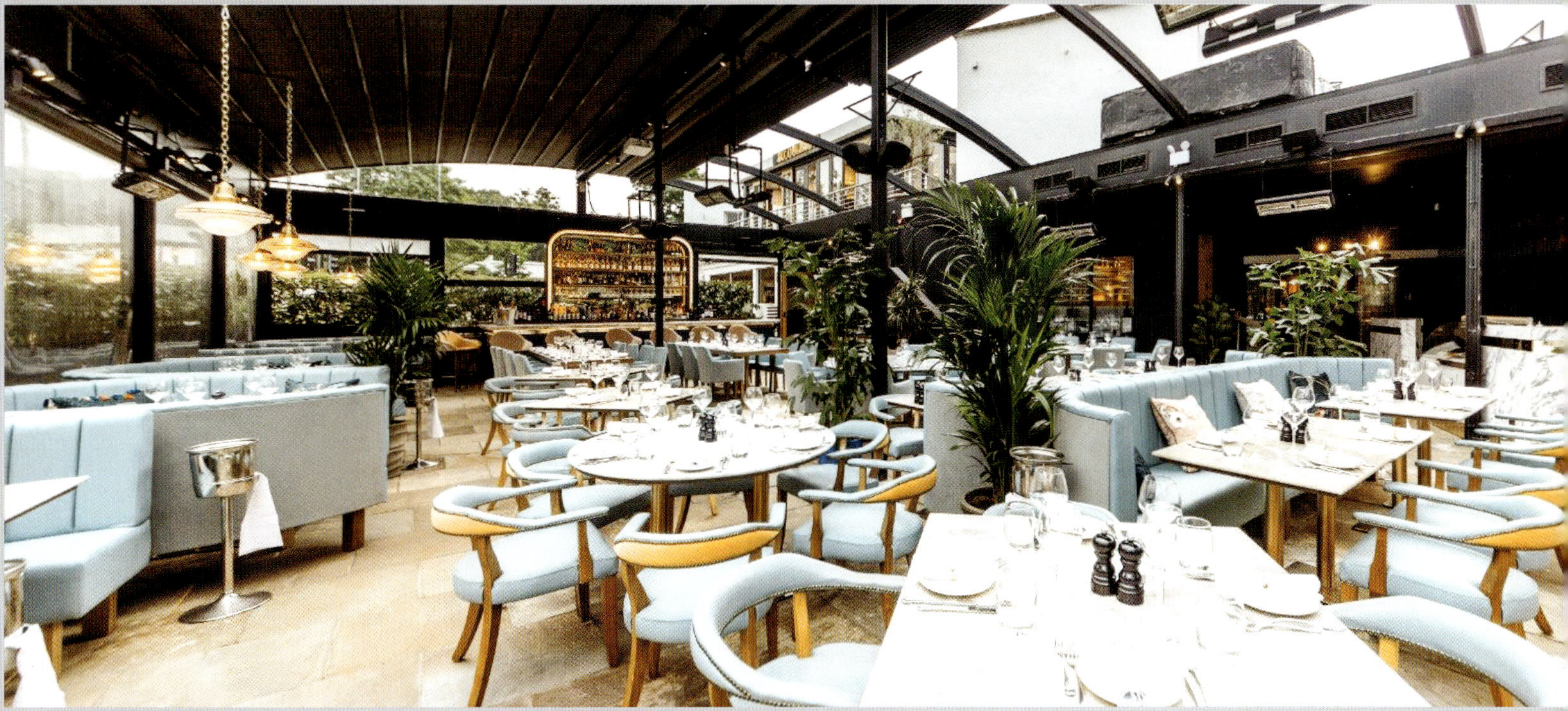

Myself and my son Alexandro Hameti love to go to the matches. Alex was 3 years old when we first started going and he is a huge fan of Chelsea.

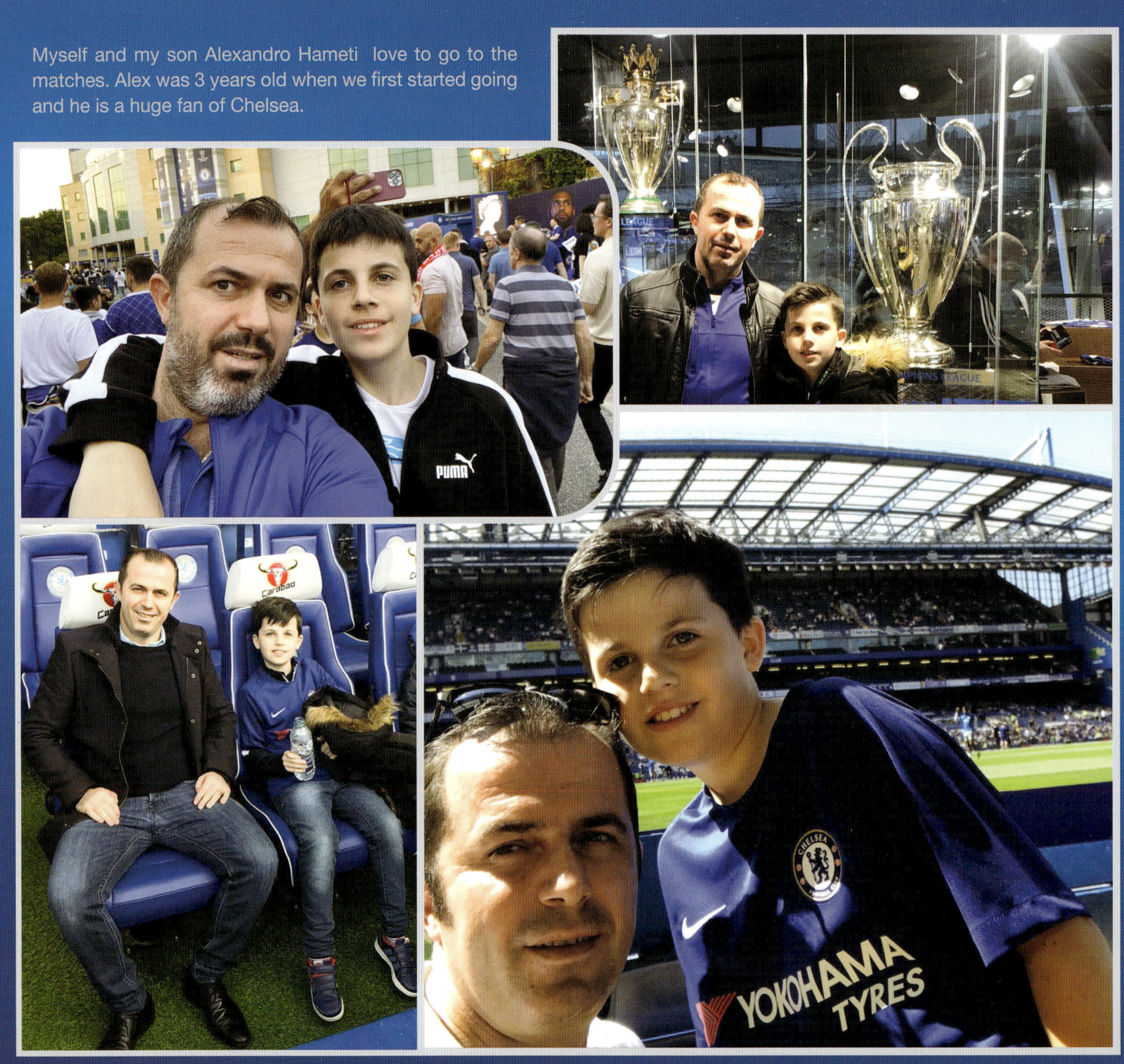

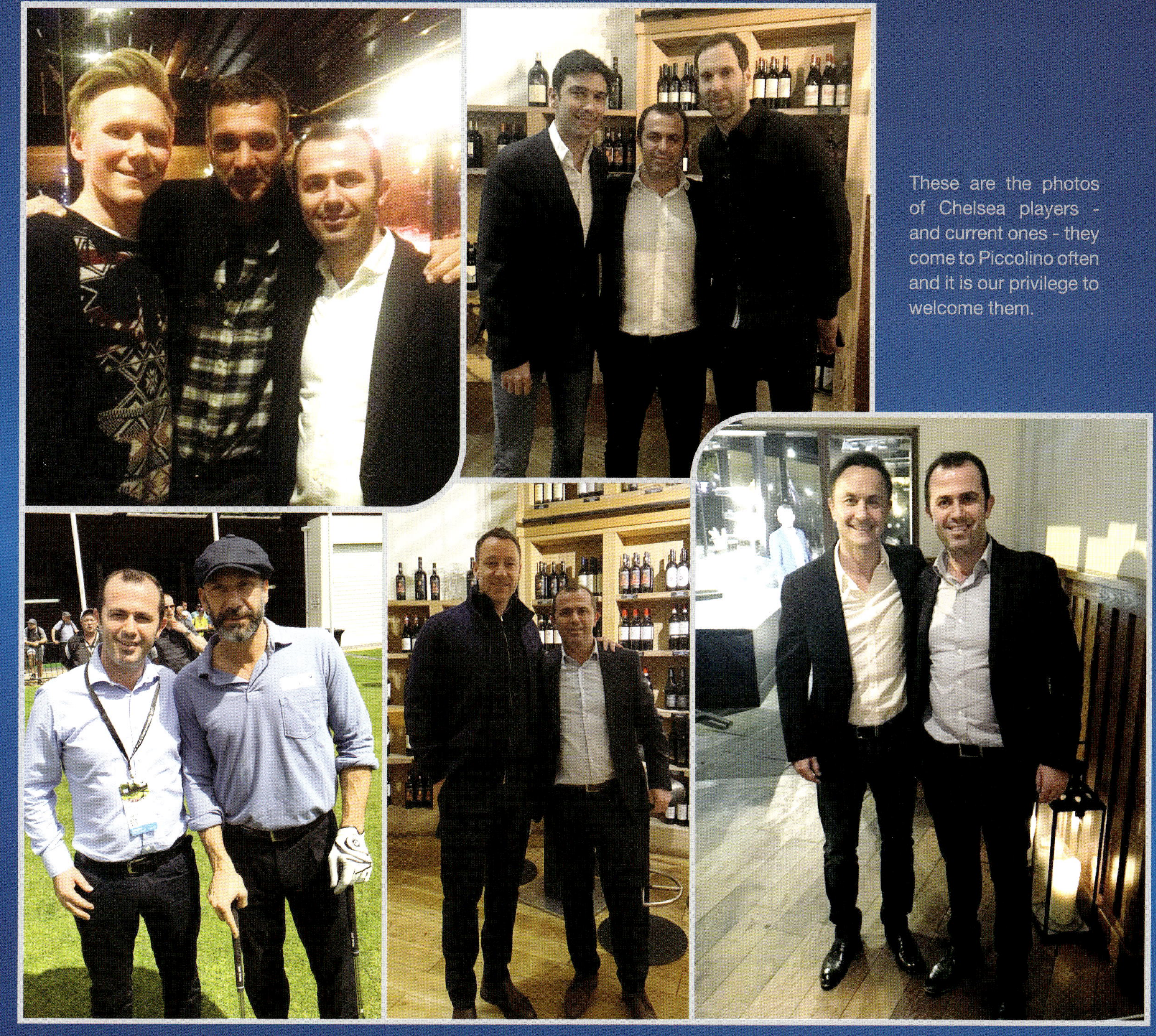

These are the photos of Chelsea players - and current ones - they come to Piccolino often and it is our privilege to welcome them.

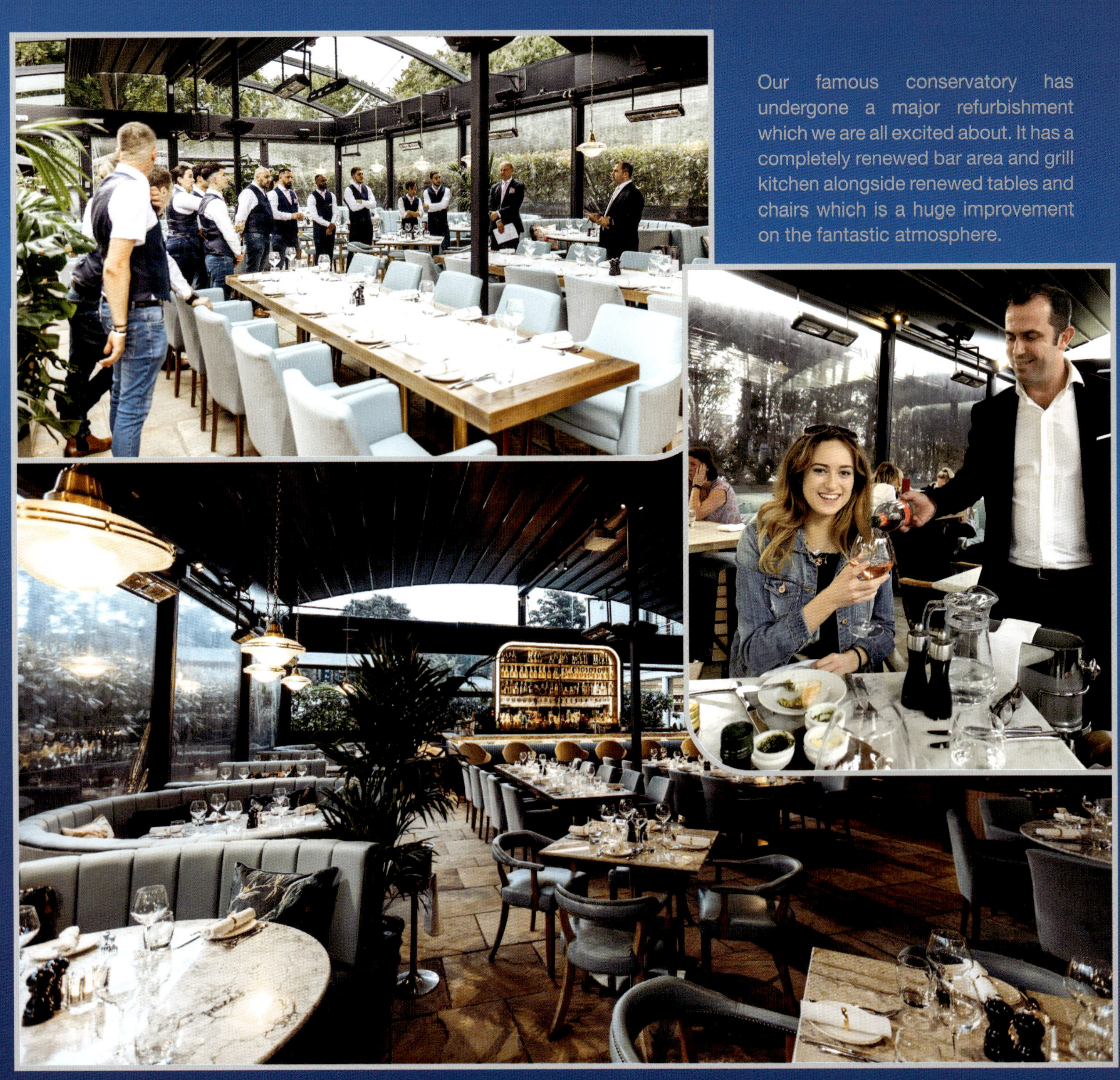

Our famous conservatory has undergone a major refurbishment which we are all excited about. It has a completely renewed bar area and grill kitchen alongside renewed tables and chairs which is a huge improvement on the fantastic atmosphere.

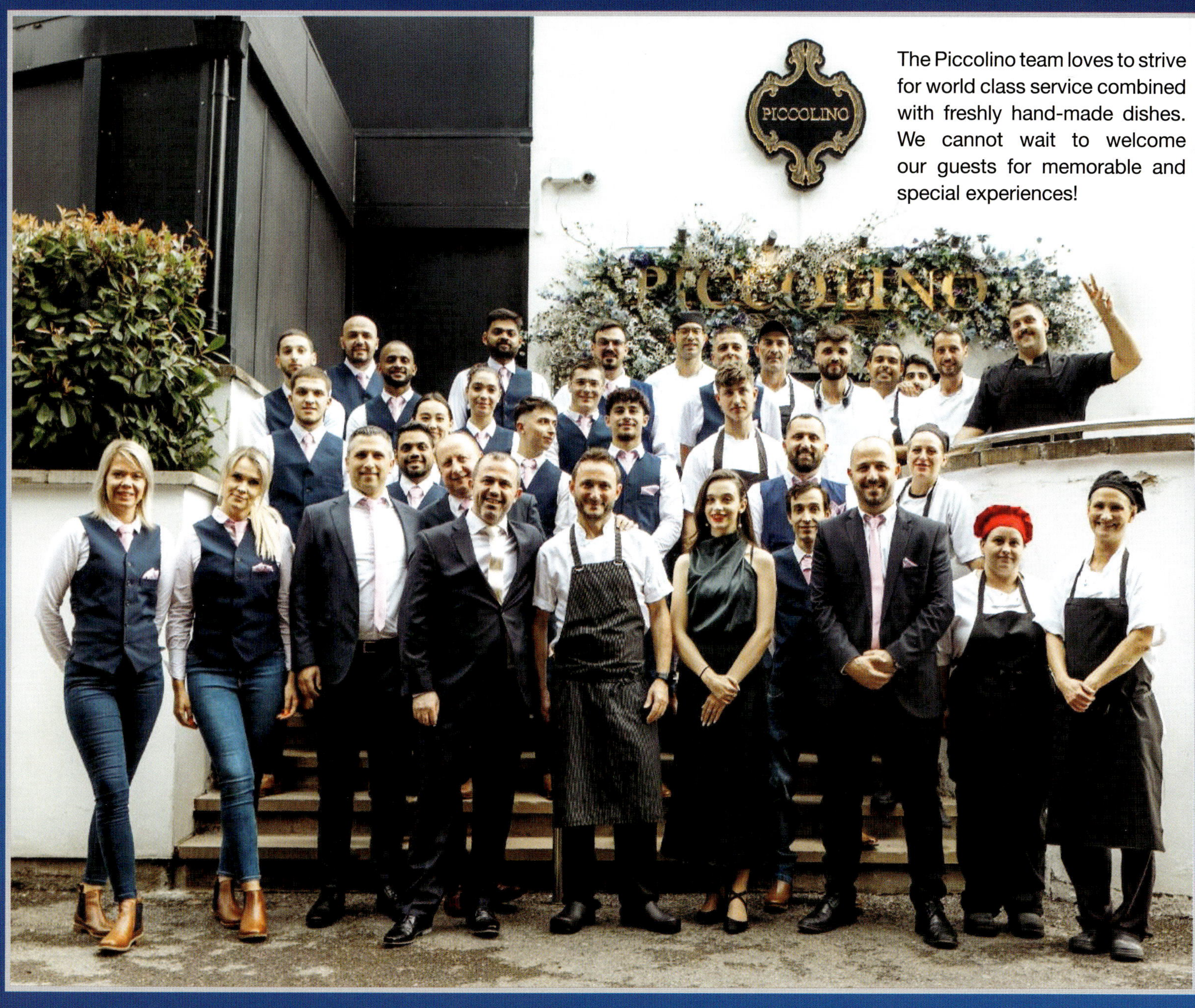

The Piccolino team loves to strive for world class service combined with freshly hand-made dishes. We cannot wait to welcome our guests for memorable and special experiences!

By the Same Authors

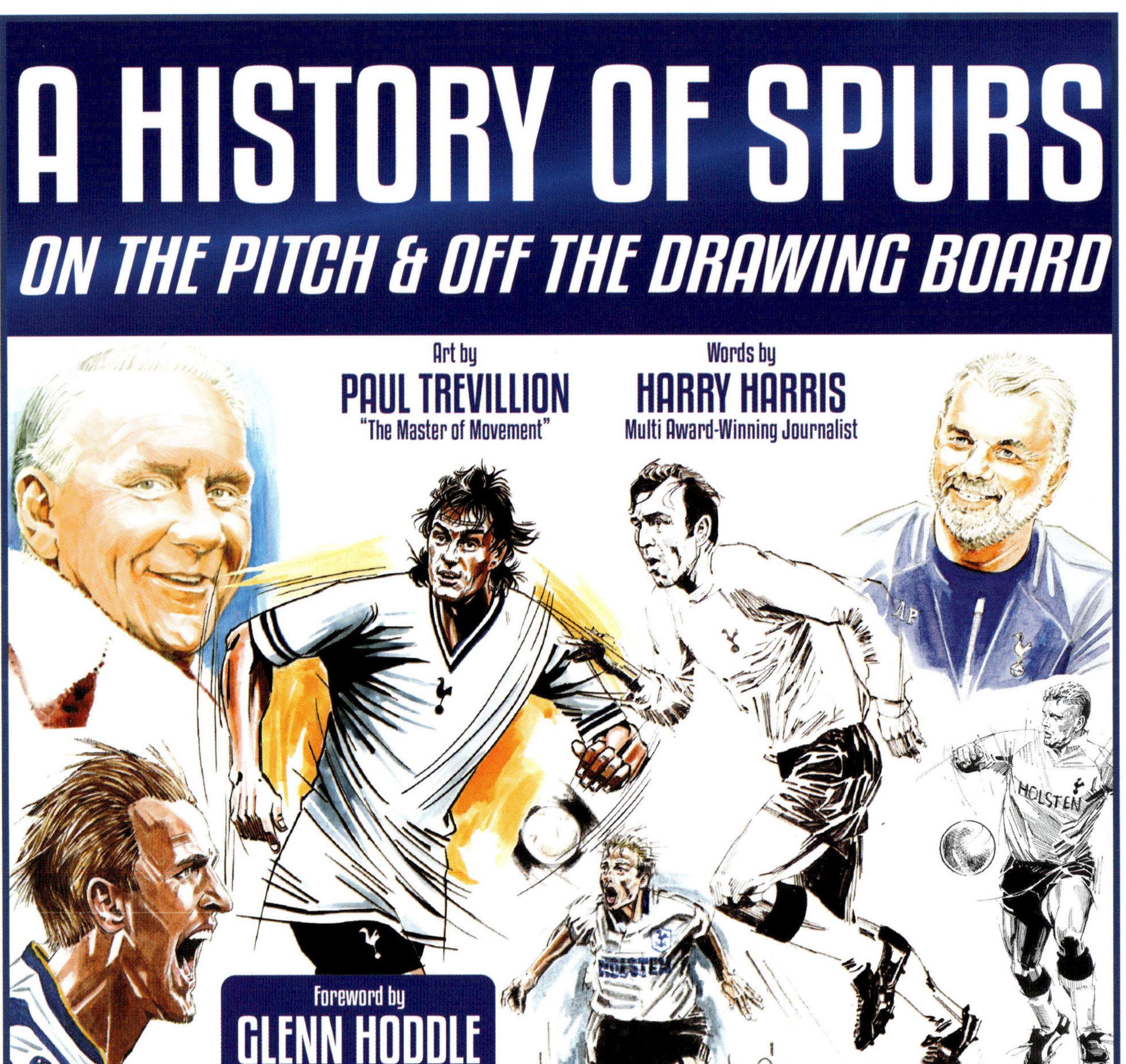